TWELVE LECTURES ADDRESSED TO THE ANGLICAN PARTY OF 1833

THE WORKS OF

JOHN HENRY NEWMAN

BIRMINGHAM ORATORY

MILLENNIUM EDITION

VOLUME XV

SERIES EDITOR

JAMES TOLHURST DD

ASSOCIATE EDITOR

ANDREW NASH MA PhD

CERTAIN DIFFICULTIES

FELT BY ANGLICANS

IN CATHOLIC TEACHING

CONSIDERED:

*I. In Twelve Lectures addressed to the Party of the
Religious Movement of 1833*

BY

JOHN HENRY CARDINAL NEWMAN

VOL. I

With an Introduction and Notes by

EDWARD SHORT

and Textual Appendix by

ANDREW NASH

GRACEWING

First published 1850
Revised editions 1872, 1876

Published in the Birmingham Oratory Millennium Edition
in 2021
by
Gracewing
2 Southern Avenue
Leominster
Herefordshire HR6 0QF

www.gracewing.co.uk

Typography by Andrew Nash

ISBN 978 0 85244 412 2

CONTENTS

TWELVE LECTURES ADDRESSED IN 1850 TO THE PARTY OF THE RELIGIOUS MOVEMENT OF 1833

PART I

COMMUNION WITH THE ROMAN SEE THE LEGITIMATE ISSUE OF THE RELIGIOUS MOVEMENT OF 1833

On the Relation of the National Church to the Nation

Contents

PART II

DIFFICULTIES IN ACCEPTING THE COMMUNION OF ROME AS ONE, HOLY, CATHOLIC, AND APOSTOLIC

Contents

ACKNOWLEDGMENTS

Jonathan Swift once said, "The world is divided into two sects: those that hope for the best, and those that fear the worst." Father James Tolhurst, the General Editor of the Millennium Edition, showed his allegiance to the first when, he tapped me to edit the splendid lectures that you hold in your hands. Another optimist who placed his hope in me was Mr. Tom Longford, the most clubbable of gentleman publishers, for whose stalwart support I am always thankful. As soon as the Chinese virus passes from both our lands, I look forward to celebrating the publication of the book with him, if he can pull himself away from his blue remembered hills. My warm thanks also go out to Father Ian Ker, the finest of Newman scholars, who, in looking over the annotations for the lectures, as well as the introduction, was full of encouragement and astute good counsel. In addition, I am thankful to two other critical readers, Professor J.J. Scarisbrick and Father Carleton Jones, O.P., both of whom generously read my typescript and made helpful suggestions. My grateful thanks also to Dr. Andrew Nash for all his work compiling the Textual Appendix.

It is a pleasure to express my abounding gratitude to John Greenacombe, the crack Handel and architecture scholar, who helped me to secure the rights to the image I chose for the book's cover from the Survey of London series, to which he has been so distinguished a General Editor.

Another good friend who helped knock my typescript into presentable shape was Mrs. Nora Malone whose copyediting skills are matched only by her eye for overlooked howlers.

Acknowledgments

There are others to whom I am grateful for their support while I made my way to the completion of my labors, and they include Miss Anne Marie Mullin, Mr. and Mrs. Heinz Becker, Miss Margaret Fernandez, Mrs. Constance Short, Mrs. Francis Phillips, Mr. and Mrs. Eugene Sylva, Mr. Robert Crotty, Mr. Allen Roth, Mr. Neil Merkl, Mr. Jeremy Paff, Mr. James Grant, Professor Richard Greene, Father Richard Smith and Mr. and Mrs. Maxime Nogier and their newborn son, Master Dominic Robert Marie, on whose glorious birthday I downed tools.

Lastly, I am thankful to my children, Sophia and Sebastian, and my wife, Karina, whose love and sympathy not only sustained me in my burrowings but kept me faithful to Swift's jollier sect.

Edward Short
Astoria, New York
22 August 2020
Queenship of the Blessed Virgin Mary

ABBREVIATIONS AND REFERENCES

The abbreviations used for Newman's works are those listed in Joseph Rickaby, S.J., *Index to the Works of John Henry Cardinal Newman* (London, 1914), together with those in Charles Stephen Dessain, ed., *The Letters and Diaries of John Henry Newman* (1961–2008).

References to works included by Newman in his uniform edition are always, unless otherwise stated, to that edition, which was begun in 1868 with *Parochial and Plain Sermons* and concluded in 1881 with *Select Treatises of St. Athanasius*. From 1886, until the stock was destroyed in the Second World War, all the volumes were published by Longmans, Green and Company.

All references to the *Apologia pro Vita Sua*, *Fifteen Sermons Preached before the University of Oxford*, *The Idea of a University*, and *An Essay in Aid of a Grammar of Assent* are to the editions published by the Clarendon Press, Oxford.

In the present edition, references to individual sermons include volume number, sermon number, and page number, together with the date on which the sermon was first preached.

All biblical references are to the Authorized (King James) Version.

Since I have plundered many reference books for the annotations (mostly from Oxford University Press, whose reference books, on balance, are reliable, allowing for blind spots and biases), I have not abbreviated their titles, with the exception of those well-known reference books listed below, which I cite frequently.

Abbreviations

Apo.	*Apologia pro Vita Sua*, ed. Martin J. Svaglic (Oxford, 1967)
Ari.	*The Arians of the Fourth Century*
AW	*John Henry Newman: Autobiographical Writings*, ed. Henry Tristram (London, 1956)
Call.	*Callista: A Tale of the Third Century*
D.A.	*Discussions and Arguments on Various Subjects*
Dev.	*An Essay on the Development of Christian Doctrine*
Diff., i, ii	*Certain Difficulties felt by Anglicans in Catholic Teaching*, 2 vols.
Ess., i, ii	*Essays Critical and Historical*, 2 vols.
GA	*An Essay in Aid of a Grammar of Assent*, ed. I.T. Ker (Oxford, 1985)
H.S., i–iii	*Historical Sketches*, 3 vols.
Idea	*The Idea of a University*, ed. I.T. Ker (Oxford, 1976)
Jfc.	*Lectures on the Doctrine of Justification*
LD	*The Letters and Diaries of John Henry Newman* ed. Charles Stephen Dessain et al., vols. i–ix (Oxford, 1978–2006), xi–xxii (London, 1961–72), xxiii–xxxii (Oxford, 1973–2008),
LG	*Loss and Gain: The Story of a Convert*
MD	*Meditations and Devotions of the Late Cardinal Newman* (London, 1893)
Mix.	*Discourses Addressed to Mixed Congregations*

Abbreviations

Moz., i, ii	*Letters and Correspondence of John Henry Newman during His Life in the English Church*, ed. Anne Mozley, 2 vols. (London, 1891)
OS	*Sermons Preached on Various Occasions*
PS, i–viii	*Parochial and Plain Sermons*, 8 vols.
Prepos.	*Present Position of Catholics*
SD	*Sermons Bearing on Subjects of the Day*
US	*Fifteen Sermons Preached before the University of Oxford between A.D. 1826 and 1843*, ed. James David Earnest and Gerard Tracey (Oxford, 2006)
VM, i, ii	*The Via Media*, 2 vols.

CBH	*Companion to British History*, ed. Charles Arnold-Baker
DNB	*Dictionary of National Biography*
OCBH	*Oxford Companion to British History*
ODNB	*Oxford Dictionary of National Biography*
ODCC	*Oxford Dictionary of the Christian Church*
OED	*Oxford English Dictionary* (1st edition, 1933)

A NOTE ON THE TEXT

The text used for this Gracewing volume is that of the Longmans, Green and Co. uniform edition of Newman's works. The page layout and headings have been designed to match that edition, with the exception of the addition of the Editor's footnotes. Other works by Newman, except the *Letters and Diaries*, are also cited in the uniform Longmans editions.

Newman's own footnotes are followed by [N] to distinguish them from the Editor's Notes. Some of Newman's notes need further explanation, so the [N] is sometimes followed by an Editor's Note. All other footnotes are by the Editor.

It is the practice of Newman scholars to cite his works using the uniform Longmans editions. To facilitate this in the present volume the page numbers of the Longmans edition are placed in square brackets at the appropriate places in the margins of the text. All references in the Editor's Introduction are to these page numbers.

"I venture to ask you whether you will allow me to put your Lordship's name at the head of... a series of discussions, which consist of a perpetual skirmish."

John Henry Newman to Bishop Ullathorne (1850)

EDITOR'S INTRODUCTION

I: Overview: "A Perpetual Skirmish"

It is one of the commonplaces of the genius of Saint John Henry Cardinal Newman that while he might have written for set occasions, he always found ways to transcend them.[1] Examples of this abound. We can point to the letters he wrote to the editor of the *Times* in 1841 under the pseudonym *Catholicus* to protest the launching of the Tamworth Reading Room, which might have taken issue with Lord Brougham and Sir Robert Peel for launching a library to promote the march of mind, but which nevertheless made a permanent contribution to our understanding of the radical limits of merely secular knowledge.[2] We can point to the *Lectures on*

---

[1] "I never can write well, without a definite *call*.... I almost think it is part of the English character, though in this day there seems a change.... Grote, Thirlwall, Milman, Cornwall Lewis, Mill, have written great works for their own sake. So did Gibbon last century, but he was half a Frenchman. Our Great authors have generally written on an occasion—controversially as Burke, or Milton, officially, as Blackstone—for money as Dryden, Johnson, Scott etc or on sibyl's leaves as Addison and the Essayists." Newman to J. Walker Scarborough (5 August 1864), *LD*, xxi, 185.

[2] Cf. "I have been reading with great pleasure in the Newman selections," the former Master of Eton George William Lyttelton (1883–1962) wrote to the publisher Rupert Hart-Davis in January 1957. "So far my favourite is his masterly trouncing of Sr. R. Peel and Brougham in *The Tamworth Reading Room*. It is superb in its ease and force—which come out particularly well when one reads it aloud, as I do when all have gone to bed." The same is true of the superb declamatory prose of *Anglican Difficulties*. Lyttelton quoted in *The Lyttelton Hart-Davis Letters*, vols. 1 and 2 (1955–7), ed. R. Hart-Davis (London: John Murray, 1985), 232. Lyttelton's overall estimation of Newman is also worth quoting: "Newman's writing is continuing to give me the deepest of all satisfactions —great thoughts, beautifully expressed, and springing from a manifestly great mind and character." Ibid., 241.

the Present Position of Catholics in England (1851), which Newman might have undertaken to respond to the No Popery hysteria that greeted Pius IX's reconstitution of the hierarchy in England during the period known as "papal aggression," but which brilliantly undermined the Whig interpretation of the English Reformation more than a hundred years before the revisionist histories of J.J. Scarisbrick and Christopher Haigh. Similarly, Newman began the writing of the *Apologia pro Vita Sua* (1864) to answer Charles Kingsley's aspersions but ended by giving his readers a work of autobiography of incomparable depth, richness, beauty, and charm. The *Letter to the Duke of Norfolk* (1875) is yet another example: Newman might have written it to repulse Prime Minister William Gladstone's "rambling and slovenly" attacks against the probity of English Catholics after the First Vatican Council,[3] but when he put down his pen, he had produced a book on the nature of conscience that entirely transcended any debate that his contemporaries might have wished to have on the advisability of the Church's calling a council to define papal infallibility.[4] These are just a few examples of how

---

[3] "You must be very impatient to hear from me. You may be sure, however, I should have written, had I any thing to say. For 5 or 6 weeks I have been hard at it for perhaps 5 or 6 hours a day, and have produced nothing. I have written quires, but not pleased myself and begun again. Gladstone is so rambling and slovenly it is so difficult to follow him with any logical exactness. I can't get a plan." Newman to Lord Emly (23 November 1874), *LD*, xxvii, 159.

[4] One brief extract will serve to show how far Newman transcended the occasion of the *Letter to the Duke of Norfolk* when he took up the theme of conscience. "The Supreme Being is of a certain character, which, expressed in human language, we call ethical. He has the attributes of justice, truth, wisdom, sanctity, benevolence and mercy, as eternal characteristics in His nature, the very Law of His being, identical with Himself; and next, when He became Creator, He implanted this Law, which is Himself, in the intelligence of all His rational creatures. The Divine Law, then, is the rule of ethical truth, the standard of right and wrong, a sovereign, irreversible, absolute authority in the presence of men and Angels. 'The eternal law,' says St. Augustine, 'is the Divine Reason or Will of God, commanding the observance, forbidding the disturbance, of the natural order of things.' 'The natural law,' says St. Thomas, 'is an impression of the Divine Light in us, a participation of the eternal law in the rational creature.' This law, as

Newman's ebullient mind outsoared the confines of the occasional. Yet one work of his continues to be misjudged by being wrongly relegated to such confines, and that is his *Lectures on Certain Difficulties Felt by Anglicans in Submitting to the Catholic Church* (1850; final edition 1876), which he addressed to his erstwhile friends in the Tractarian Movement, or what he styled the "Movement of 1833." It is true that the lectures largely seek to dissuade the Anglo-Catholic party from remaining within the National Church of England, but it is very much more than that. First and foremost, it is a far-ranging meditation on one of Newman's most abiding and insistent themes, the Church and the World, a theme which he would take up not only in his sermons but in *Arians of the Fourth Century* (1832), *An Essay on the Development of Christian Doctrine* (1845), *Loss and Gain* (1847), *Callista* (1850), and *The Idea of a University* (1875).[5] It is a reaffirmation of the unity of the Church. It is an inquiry into the varieties of Erastianism, which, as Newman shows, presents a continual threat to the integrity of the Church's unique mission in the world. It is a meditation on the nature of history, proof that the best historians are not always those who call themselves historians.[6] "History is at this day undergoing a process of revolution; the science of criticism, the disinterment of antiquities, the unrolling of manuscripts,

---

apprehended in the minds of individual men, is called 'conscience;' and though it may suffer refraction in passing into the intellectual medium of each, it is not therefore so affected as to lose its character of being the Divine Law, but still has, as such, the prerogative of commanding obedience. 'The Divine Law,' says Cardinal Gousset, 'is the supreme rule of actions; our thoughts, desires, words, acts, all that man is, is subject to the domain of the law of God; and this law is the rule of our conduct by means of our conscience." *Diff*, ii, 246-7. See also Matthew McCusker's altogether outstanding "The Teaching of Bl. John Henry Newman on Conscience and Obedience," *Voice of the Family* (19 May 2018).

[5] See Andrew Nash, "The Church and the World," in *John Henry Newman: Doctor of the Church*, ed. Philippe Lefebvre and Colin Mason (Oxford: Family Publications, 2007), 130–44.

[6] See Andrew Meszaros, *The Prophetic Church: History and Doctrinal Development in John Henry Newman and Yves Congar* (Oxford University Press, 2016).

the interpretation of inscriptions, have thrown us into a new world of thought," Newman wrote in Lecture V, "characters and events come forth transformed in the process; romance, prejudice, local tradition, party bias, are no longer accepted as guarantees of truth; the order and mutual relation of events are readjusted; the springs and the scope of action are reversed" (156). In revisiting the "romance," "prejudice," "local tradition," and "party bias" of the National Church, Newman fired off a wonderful salvo in that "revolution," though it remains a salvo that some quarters have understandably preferred to leave unanswered. Since the theme that Newman eventually settled upon required him to speak of his own contributions to the Movement of 1833, the book includes elements of autobiography, which, *pace* his detractors, show how averse he was to anything smacking of self-vindication. On the contrary, no one comes in for more pointed criticism in the lectures than Newman himself. In this sense, it is a dress rehearsal for the *Apologia pro Vita Sua* (1864). Elaborating on the *Essay on Development* and foreshadowing certain aspects of the *Grammar of Assent* and the *Letter to the Duke of Norfolk*, it irradiates the unity of Newman's work. Lastly, as many who attended the lectures saw, they are a dazzling exhibition of Newman's considerable literary gifts[7] —which can hardly be appreciated or enjoyed if the lectures are discounted in advance as little more than volleys in superannuated controversy.

Newman delivered the lectures at what was then the London Oratory, formerly the Lowther Dancing Rooms,[8] near Charing Cross in King William Street, the thoroughfare linking Lombard Street—where his father had worked as a private banker in the firm of Ramsbottom, Newman and

---

[7] For an amusing essay on Newman's literary qualities, see Ian Ker, "John Henry Newman," in *The Oxford Handbook of English Literature and Theology*, ed. Andrew Hass, David Jasper, and Elisabeth Jay (Oxford: Oxford University Press, 2009), 627–37.

[8] After the Oratorians decamped to Brompton, the Lowther Arcade became the site of the most beloved of Victorian toy shops.

Company—to London Bridge.[9] The twelve *Lectures on Certain Difficulties Felt by Anglicans* were presented twice a week, on Thursdays and Fridays, beginning on 9 May 1850 and ending on 5 July, but omitting 23–24 May, 20–21 and 27–28 June. The *Daily News*[10] described the object of the lectures as being "to remove the difficulties which [Newman's] former followers (the 'Anglicans' as he now calls them) have in following the example of his perversion." The paper described the Oratory as a:

> large, square room, without any architectural embellishment, and badly lighted from the roof; at one end is a profusely but gaudily decorated altar, at the other a larger gallery in which there is an organ; in a recess formed at one side of the apartment there is another chapel and an altar less decorated. On the walls in the greater room are scriptural pieces of little or no artistic merit; whilst on those of the recess are wooden figures the size of life, representing the Crucifixion, the Virgin, and some of the Saints. The room is fitted up with benches and chairs closely packed, and will hold a few hundred people. The Oratory is itself in the back part of the premises; the other portions being used as a

---

[9] Cf. "Faber took a lease on the Lowther Rooms off the Strand. It was a seedy place, in fact, as he wrote excitedly to Newman, 'It is a gin shop.' The Lowther Rooms, built in about 1830 in King William Street, were the epitome of the stucco-fronted late-Georgian style that Pugin most detested. The Oratorians' move to London was a page of *Contrasts* [Pugin's manifesto against such style] in reverse. They had left a handsome Gothic church and chosen instead to fit up a meeting-room behind a commercial façade. Faber was having a lovely time getting it all ready ('calls—walks —bustle—hardly time to say Office') and found a thrill in slumming. It was rather fun, he reported to Newman, 'to borrow a few chairs from a policeman.' Pugin could, just about, see the funny side." Rosemary Hill, *God's Architect: Pugin and the Building of Romantic Britain* (New Haven: Yale University Press, 2007), 417.

[10] Founded in 1846, the London *Daily News* provided a Liberal alternative to the morning Conservative newspapers, most notably the *Times*. The opening editorial of the first issue announced that the paper would advance the "Principles of Progress and Improvement; of Education, Civil and Religious Liberty, and Equal Legislation." The founding editor was Charles Dickens, though he held the post of editor for only a few weeks.

place of residence for the priests or brethren of the Order of St. Philip Neri.[11]

The paper's description of Newman himself is amusingly vivid: "The father is a tall, thin, lifeless, unintellectual looking person, with a lack lustre eye and a face of inordinate length. The tribune [the lectern] scarcely reaches to his waist, and this gives increased length to his tall figure. The lecture (or full notes) is contained in a manuscript book, and from it the father reads in a rapid, unmodulated, and not very distinct tone, holding the book close to his face, and thereby adding to the difficulty of hearing and following the discourse." The Anglican newspaper the *Guardian* describe him thus: "In front of a profusely decorated altar was seated Father Newman, in ecclesiastical costume; and the walls, on either side were hung with pictures of the virgin and saints. As Father Newman read his lecture seated in his chair, he literally addressed his audience *ex cathedrâ*; he spoke in a low, measured, plaintive, but rather monotonous tone, varied, however, occasionally by sarcastic emphasis given to particular sentences."[12]

The rather heterogenous audience that the lectures attracted did not go unnoticed by the newspapers. As the *Daily News* reported:

A considerable part of the room is set apart for ladies, who probably constitute one-third of the audience. Gradually, as the hour of five approaches, the room fills—now a party of elegantly and fashionably dressed women enter in all the confidence of rank and position; then a twopenny postman and a hard working mechanic sheepishly follow; now three or four young templars, then as many hard faced Irishmen, bowing reverentially to the altar as they pass; priests and neophytes of the Romish persuasion glide gently and noiselessly in from a side door and take seats in the first rows: concurrently clergymen of the 'Anglican' church enter hastily, with curious

---

[11] St. Philip Neri (1515–95), Florentine priest and founder of the Congregation of the Oratory. See fuller note in annotated text.
[12] *The Guardian* (11 May 1850).

looks and uneasy steps, and seek places as much out of sight as possible, if obtainable under the gallery. On the whole, however (the ladies, of course, in their gay dresses and piquant bonnets, excepted), the auditory is not a distinguished and scarcely a pleasant or agreeable one; there are in it few accomplished or thoughtful looking gentlemen; but in their stead not a little of dirty looking youthful enthusiasm; sinister eyed priests, and priggish 'Anglicans.' To all appearances there is a preponderance in the audience who pay no obeisance to the altar.[13]

The *Guardian* correspondent was equally struck by the audience. "I went to the oratory," Newman's old Tractarian friend Frederic Rogers wrote in the paper, "and found it filled with an audience evidently of a mixed character. One could scarcely mistake the varied physiognomical expression. There were devout Roman Catholics, anxious Anglicans, antagonistic Protestants, and critical free inquirers, of whom some received implicitly what was spoken, others hesitated, but were apparently shaken, while others again, by smiles, mingled with occasional looks, that had a resisting or even contemptuous expression, manifested strong Protestant opinions or predilections. The audience in the oratory seemed to me a miniature of that 'world' at present agitated by religious questions."[14]

In April of 1850, Newman wrote the ardent convert whom he had put in charge of the London Oratory, Father Frederick Faber, "Tell me what length my lectures should be? if they last an hour, they must be as much as 30 pages octavo letter press, or something like 40 duodecimo, which seems enormous—Let me know; I will conform whatever it is." He was also concerned about giving such lectures in the Oratory. "I am perplexed—either some of them will be most impressively dull—or they will be too much on the other tack; and I am frightened at the chance of being satirical etc before the Blessed Sacrament. Would a curtain be possible?

---

[13] *The Daily News* (19 June 1850).
[14] *The Guardian* (11 May 1850).

The Litany etc I think are to be in the *Lady Chapel.*"[15] Faber assured him that the Blessed Sacrament would not be in the Lady Chapel.

Settling on the right theme for the lectures did not come easy to Newman. Faber had suggested he consider writing on "Persecution" or on "Influence of opinions in producing character," but neither subject suited Newman.[16] Preoccupied with putting the London Oratory on a sound footing and tending to the Irish poor in Birmingham, many of whom had been driven to the city's noisome rookeries by the Famine, Newman could not have undertaken the planning of the lectures at a more inauspicious time. He was also concerned, as he would be twenty-five years later, when he was preparing to respond to Gladstone over the Vatican Decrees, that if he did not acquit himself effectively, he would only undermine the case for Catholicism.[17] "Tell me if any subject strikes you which I could take up for Lectures in Lent," he wrote Faber in October of 1848, "—for, *unless I get a good subject*, I had better not come. Depend upon it, we cannot have a *little* war. To give lectures is to open the whole subject of Catholicism —there will be replies, and, before I know where I am, I may be defending the 4th Lateran and Paul iii's bull"[18]—that is to say, the Fourth Council of the Lateran (1215), which defined transubstantiation and required Catholics to make an annual confession, and the bull that inaugurated the Council of Trent (1545–63). To the founder of the Catholic review, *The Rambler*, J.M. Capes (1816–88), who had converted to the Catholic Church in June of 1845 after spending time at Littlemore, Newman wrote a letter in November of 1849 that offers a fascinating glimpse into what an arduous ordeal even

---

[15] Newman to F.W. Faber (28 April 1850), *LD*, xiii, 468.

[16] *LD*, xiii, 367, n. 1.

[17] "Unless I really succeed, I shall do the Catholic cause harm. A failure would be really deplorable—Protestants would say, Now we know all that can be said—and we see how little that is." Newman to Lady Georgiana Fullerton (10 November 1874), *LD*, xxvii, 156. See also Edward Short, "Newman and Gladstone," in *Newman and His Contemporaries* (London: T&T Clark, 2011), 235.

[18] Newman to F.W. Faber (28 October 1849), *LD*, xiii, 276.

laying the groundwork for composition could be for him: "As to myself," he wrote, "... my thoughts are at present indefinitely fidgetted by the prospect of having to preach in Lent in the London Oratory. When one has got one's subject, one's thoughts are simply *occupied*; but before, while searching for one, I at least, whatever be the case with others, am troubled as by a bad dream, seeking I know not what, with a load of responsibility which I cannot fulfil, and the fear of something to come. And the worst is, this seems the necessary process to my finding a subject—for, did I put the matter away and determine to take my chance, I should simply get idle and sluggish, and should never come across what I am seeking for."[19] Later, in December of the same year, he wrote: "As to the subject on which you would have me write [Capes had wished him to write on "eternal punishment" for his paper], it is a noble one—but one can no more *command* a set of lectures on it than raise spirits from the vasty deep."[20]

Taking up the cudgels of controversy always brought out the critical humility in Newman. "I feel more and more," he confessed to Capes, "and have for years, how little one's mind is in one's own power. Difficulties of years are sometimes overcome in a moment—yet one cannot foresee the time. It is very mysterious, and brings before one the great Christian truth, that man *in puris naturalibus* is a most imperfect being and depends on principles and powers external to him for the power of thinking and acting." Rather than exhorting his auditors to heed the counsels of holy fear, however sensible those counsels might be, Newman wished to do something different. "What I *want* to do and can't ... is to construct a *positive* argument for Catholicism. The negative is most powerful — 'Since there must be one true religion, it can *be none other* than this —' but the fault of this is that it involves what many people call scepticism—a cutting away everything else but Catholicism — showing the difficulties of such portions of truth as Protestantism contains etc.... Now as to *positive* proof, I can only rest the argument on antecedent

---

[19] Newman to J.M. Capes (28 November 1849), *LD*, xiii, 312.
[20] Newman to J.M. Capes (2 December 1849), *LD*, xiii, 319.

probabilities or verisimilia—which are to my mind most powerful, (and practically sufficient, for they are in fact the Notes of The Church,) but they seem argumentatively imperfect; and I would give much to be able to strike out something — but I feel myself quite helpless."[21]

One of the ironies surrounding *Anglican Difficulties* is that the convert Capes, with whom Newman confided so much of his initial struggles with the lectures, eventually left the Catholic Church. "With the one great exception of Dr. Newman," the liberal editor complained, "not one of the converts of the last twenty-five years has been a man of much historical knowledge, or distinguished for Biblical criticism of a high order. Their tendencies have been generally Ultramontane in a marked degree." Still, Capes did appreciate that "the actual inner life of Catholicism is, indeed, a thing very little understood by Protestants, however candid, charitable, and well informed. Its vitality as a spiritual system is, I think, largely underrated."[22]

---

[21] Newman to J.M. Capes (2 December 1849), *LD*, xiii, 319; *Dev*, 169-200.

[22] J.M. Capes, *Reasons for Returning to the Church of England* (London: Strahan & Co, 1871), 117, 121. See also the exchanges between Newman and Capes after Capes left the Church in 1858 over the issue of "certainty" in religious belief. *LD*, xviii, 437–8; 461; 471–2. It is ironic that Newman should have broached his interest in writing of "perplexity of intellect" with Capes in 1849 because it was precisely on this ground, what Newman called "the great philosophical difficulty in Catholicism," that the convert came to grief. Newman to J.M. Capes (1 October 1858), *LD*, xviii, 471. However, despite Newman's solicitude for the perplexed editor, which is clear from these and other exchanges—a solicitude recalling his care for his old Anglo-Catholic friends in his King William Street lectures—Capes accused Newman in the *Guardian* (11 September 1872) of acceding to the doctrine of papal infallibility out of irrational obeisance to Rome. Newman replied in a letter to the editor of the *Guardian*: "I underwent then no change of mind as regards the truth of the doctrine of the Pope's Infallibility in consequence of the Council. It is true I was deeply, though not personally, pained both by the fact and by the circumstances of the definition; and, when it was in contemplation, I wrote a most confidential letter, which was surreptitiously gained and published, but of which I have not a word to retract. The feelings of surprise and concern expressed in that letter have nothing to do with a screwing one's conscience to profess what one does not believe, which is Mr. Capes' pleasant account of me. He ought

Later in the same month, Newman wrote to the London Oratorian Richard Stanton (1820-1901), "As to Lent, my great difficulty is first to get a subject for my Lectures and secondly time to write them. Recollect oratory is not my forte; I must have *matter* in what I deliver, if it is to be worth any thing."[23] This, in its way, was another proof of Newman's humility, for when he eventually gave the lectures, he would show that he did have an orator in him, as the editor of the *Spectator*, Richard Holt Hutton, could attest. "I shall never forget the impression which his voice and manner, which opened upon me for the first time in these lectures, made on me," Hutton recalled. "Never did a voice seem better adapted to persuade without irritating. Singularly sweet, perfectly free from any dictatorial note, and yet rich in all the cadences proper to the expression of pathos, of wonder, and of ridicule, there was still nothing in it that anyone could properly describe as insinuating, for its simplicity, and frankness, and freedom from the half-smothered notes which express indirect purpose, was as remarkable as its sweetness, its freshness, and its gentle distinctiveness."[24] Charlotte Brontë, who also attended the lectures, confirmed Hutton's characterization, referring to them as having been delivered in "a very concise, quiet, graphic way."[25] That Newman often finished the lectures minutes before he was to deliver them—after sleepless nights of headache and toothache—only made the suavity of their presentation the more impressive.[26]

However, in December of 1849, Newman was so undecided about how to proceed with his lectures that he contemplated shelving them. "My present wish would be to put off coming up to London," he told Capes, "if I could do it without disappointing them in King William Street." As late

---

to know better." See *LD*, xxvi, 166–7. In old age, perhaps mercifully, Capes went blind.

[23] Newman to R. Stanton (30 December 1849), *LD*, xiii, 352.

[24] R.H. Hutton, *Cardinal Newman* (London: Methuen, 1891), 207–8.

[25] Brontë quoted in Winifred Gérin, *Charlotte Brontë: The Evolution of Genius* (Oxford: The Clarendon Press, 1967), 597.

[26] *LD*, xiii, 473, 474.

as April of 1850, this undecidedness had only worsened. In a letter to Faber, he admitted: "As to a course of Sermons, what I said to F Antony was, that I really had the heart and wish to do them—but could not—that I spent for a long time every moment of my leisure time on the thought, and had done nothing—that everything crumbled away under me. I got one or two subjects, but could make nothing of them, and what I have to read is frightful." Still, in this same letter, a possible solution presented itself. "It struck me whether there was any way in which I could turn the present Anglican crisis to account—for I fear interfering in a quarrel—it might do more harm than good. I am extremely desirous of doing something in London, but if I ought, St Philip would enable me."[27] As it happened, Saint Philip did come to Newman's aid: by the end of April 1850, he had finally decided on his topic. As Wilfrid Ward (1856-1916) points out in his biography of Newman:

> On March 8, 1850, came the celebrated decision of the Privy Council in what was known as the 'Gorham case'—overruling the refusal of the Bishop of Exeter (confirmed by the Court of Arches) [Bishop Henry Phillpotts] to institute Mr. G. C. Gorham to the vicarage of Brampford Speke on the ground that he denied the doctrine of baptismal regeneration. Here was a glaring case of the civil power asserting its supremacy over the spiritual as to what was the orthodox doctrine in an English clergyman, and making its decision on behalf of latitudinarian doctrine. Many Tractarians who had hitherto held back from Rome, including such influential men as Hope-Scott, Manning, and T. W. Allies, felt keenly this challenge to their position. Their following in Newman's footsteps appeared to be imminent. A strongly signed protest was at once drawn up at the house of Mr. Hope-Scott in Curzon Street against the action of the Privy Council. The matter caused great excitement in the press and among Anglicans generally, and seemed to call for some public comment from Newman.[28]

---

[27] Newman to F.W. Faber (7 April 1840), *LD*, xiii, 460.

[28] Wilfrid Ward, *Life of Cardinal Newman* (London, 1912), i, 231. James Hope-Scott (1812–73) was a parliamentary attorney and good friend of Newman. In 1843, he took his degree of D.C.L. at Oxford. "In 1844, at the

Editor's Introduction

The decision to go with the Gorham case as his subject for
the Lenten lectures, despite St. Philip's nudging, might appear
to have been an about-face. In March, Newman had written to
Faber: "Thanks for Phillpotts' pamphlet.[29] I agree with you
that our wisdom is not to spoil a pretty fight. In my own
judgment, the Puseyites have justice, except legal, out and
out, or rather simply—the sentence is an atrocious one. Why
the judges did not confine themselves to the *fact*, founded on
precedents, that Evangelicals might hold preferment, I can't
think — but they have gone on to dabble in theology and the
history of doctrine—and have burned their fingers, or at least
their reputation. However, as the English Church has brewed,
so must it drink, the cup of indignation and wrath. And we

---

suggestion of the Bishop of London (Dr. Blomfield), he was accepted by
the Lord Chancellor as one of the persons to consider the chapter on
offences against religion and the Church in the proposed Code of Criminal
Law. In a short time, however, his practice seems to have merged in the
department with which his name is principally connected, that of railway
pleading. This branch of the profession, though affording little or no scope
for those powers of oratory which his first speech before the Lords showed
that he possessed, nor yet opening those avenues to power and fame which
usually tempt minds of his class, was undoubtedly highly lucrative..."
[*Memoirs of James Robert Hope-Scott*, ed. Ornsby, ii, 104-5]. Converting
in 1851 after the Gorham case, he became a trusted counsellor of Newman,
who preached the eulogy at his requiem Mass, noting, in particular, the
munificence with which he supported Catholic causes over his lifetime.
Henry Edward Manning (1808–92) also converted in 1851 and founded the
Oblates of St. Charles Borromeo in London. He was made archbishop of
Westminster in 1865. Although they had their personal differences,
Manning and Newman always saw eye to eye on the dogmatic faith. See the
brilliant revisionist work on Manning by Professor Christian Washburn of
the University of St. Thomas, especially his "The First Vatican Council,
Archbishop Henry Manning and Papal Infallibility," *Catholic Historical
Review* 102 (2016): 712–45. Thomas William Allies (1813–1903) was a
Catholic convert and writer who came into the Church in 1850. Newman
made him Lecturer in History at the Catholic University of Ireland in 1855.
He was a frequent correspondent of Newman.
[29] *A Letter to the Archbishop of Canterbury from the Bishop of Exeter*
(London, 1850). This was the letter, dated 20 March, that went through
twenty-one editions, protesting against the decision of the Judicial
Committee of the Privy Council in the Gorham case, even though the
decision had been approved by the archbishop of Canterbury.

have nothing to do with it."[30] Although this shows that Newman was opposed to interjecting himself directly into the controversy that followed the case, it does not rule out the possibility—which I should judge a probability—that he eventually saw the case as a springboard for addressing the larger theme, as I have noted, of the Church and the World, with all of its attendant ramifications. Apropos this theme, Newman might almost have provided a *précis* of his *Anglican Difficulties* in *The Idea of the University*, where he confirms that "the world is a rough antagonist of spiritual truth: sometimes with mailed hand, sometimes with pertinacious logic, sometimes with a storm of irresistible facts, it presses on against you. What it says is true perhaps as far as it goes, but it is not the whole truth, or the most important truth. These more important truths, which the natural heart admits in their substance, though it cannot maintain,—the being of a God, the certainty of future retribution, the claims of the moral law, the reality of sin, the hope of supernatural help,— of these the Church is in matter of fact the undaunted and the only defender."[31]

The theme he chose also offered him the chance of addressing his Anglo-Catholic friends candidly about what he regarded as the untenability of their remaining within a National Church that could not gratify their true aspirations or principles. Tribal defensiveness has always played a part in obscuring the fact, but a good deal of Newman's motivation for taking his Tractarian friends to task was what the psychologists call "tough love"—a genuine solicitude for their spiritual well-being. He wrote to them as a Dutch uncle. Like all good Christian satirists, from Swift to Evelyn Waugh, he used the barb of satire to laugh them out of their folly. Those who doubt or work to controvert the solicitude at the

---

[30] Newman to Faber (31 March 1850), *LD*, xiii, 453. "The same shall drink of the wine of the wrath of God, which is poured out without mixture into the cup of his indignation; and he shall be tormented with fire and brimstone in the presence of the holy angels, and in the presence of the Lamb" (Revelation 14:10).
[31] *Idea*, 516.

heart of his satire do not understand Newman. It is plain as day in the letter he wrote to Pusey's biographer Henry Parry Liddon when the canon of Christ Church lay dying:

The Oratory March 31. 1878

My dear Dr Liddon

Your letter, so kindly sent me, has of course troubled me much. I fear Pusey cannot last long, and I am troubled, first on that account, and next as to my own duty under that anticipation.

I know you will give me credit for honesty and simplicity of purpose, as I do you.

If his state admits of it, I should so very much wish to say to my dearest Pusey, whom I have loved and admired for above fifty years, that the Catholic Roman Church solemnly lays claim to him as her child, and to ask him in God's sight, whether he does not acknowledge her right to do so.

Were I now writing to an ordinary Anglican, I should expect you to answer, 'If I do ask him for you, he will be sure to make a strong declaration of his fidelity to the Church of England, and so you would be balked, as you ought to be.' This would be the answer of a controversialist, but you will understand me quite otherwise. Should he make a simple avowal of his confidence in the Anglican Church, as part of the Church Catholic, at least I should gain this comfort from it, that he died in simple good faith.

I cannot let him die, if such is God's will, with the grave responsibility lying upon me of such an appeal to him as I suggest; and, since I cannot make it myself, I must throw that responsibility on some one else who is close to him as you are; and this I do.

Oh what a world is this, and how piercing are its sorrows. This requires no answer.

Yours most sincerely John H Newman[32]

---

[32] Newman to H.P. Liddon (31 March 1878), *LD*, xxviii, 337–38. The tragic chasm between Newman and his Anglo-Catholic friends was never more starkly displayed than in Liddon's reply to Newman on the first of April, 1878: "When the Athanasian Creed was attacked four years ago, [Pusey] had made up his mind, if it was withdrawn from her, to resign his preferments; but he had no thought, so far as I know, of secession. He always of late spoke as if the Definition of the Immaculate Conception and the Vatican Council had made that step impossible." *Life and Letters of*

Even after choosing his subject, Newman still suffered terrible anxieties about what he referred to as his "troublesome London Lectures."[33] On 3 May, Father Faber turned the screws tighter when he told his fellow Oratorian that Wiseman "says men quote you as an authority for waiting after conviction—that in a letter to him you once said you did not stop an hour after conviction,"[34] to which Newman replied, with understandable asperity: "I am writing then intellectually against the grain more than I ever recollect doing any thing—and now you bother me by putting an additional fetter on."[35]

Much has been made of Newman's use of the phrase "against the grain." What did he mean by it? Newman's Anglo-Irish friend, the poet Aubrey de Vere suspected the composition of the lectures was uncongenial to the Oratorian because "he anticipates an unprecedented outburst of infidelity all over the world"—an "outburst" he thought it was his "especial vocation" to "withstand"—and he was "quite annoyed at having to spend time on Anglicanism."[36] Certainly, Newman's letters at this time show him preoccupied with Catholic matters, especially his letters to Capes. "I heartily wish I could promise you a series like the Church of the Fathers,"[37] he writes in one letter; in another he speaks of the need for proofs of Christianity that do not "speak of the argument for Catholicism as a demonstration," proofs, in other words, that allow for the "force in objections" and the "perplexity of intellect" in those unpersuaded by the faith.[38] Yet it does not follow that such Catholic concerns made the Anglican issues broached in the lectures "annoying" to Newman—or "against the grain." After all, in one of his

---

Henry Parry Liddon, ed. John Octavius Johnston (London: Longmans, Green & Co., 1904), 246.

[33] Newman to J.M. Capes (2 December 184), *LD*, xiii, 318.

[34] Faber to Newman (2 May 1850), *LD*, xiii, 470.

[35] Newman to Faber (2 May 1850), *LD*, xiii, 470.

[36] De Vere quoted in Wilfrid Ward, *Memoir of Aubrey de Vere* (London: Macmillan, 1904), 182.

[37] Newman to J.M. Capes (28 February 1849), *LD*, xiii, 69.

[38] Newman to J.M. Capes (8 December 1849), *LD*, xiii, 334.

letters to Capes, Newman takes issue with what he regarded as the limitations of Rome's theologians precisely because "they have not a dream what England is, and what is the power of fascination which the Anglican Church ... exerts in the case of many minds."[39] Taking up the writing of the lectures might have gone "against the grain" for Newman at the outset because prose composition was always an ordeal for him. When Hutton praised his verses, Newman replied: "I should give myself up to verse making; it is nearly the only kind of composition which is not a trouble to me, but I have never had time. As to my prose volumes, I have scarcely written any one without an external stimulus; their composition has been to me, in point of pain, a mental child-bearing and I have been accustomed to say to myself, 'In sorrow shalt thou bring forth children.'"[40] *Anglican Difficulties* was no exception. In addition, as he told his Anglo-Catholic friends in his final lecture, he was unsure about the theme he had settled upon because, as he said:

> I could not address you on the subjects which I proposed, without introducing myself into the discussion; I could not refer to the past without alluding to matters in which I had a part; I could not show that interest in your state of mind and course of thought which I really feel, without showing that I therefore understood it, because I had before now experienced it myself; and I anticipated, what I fear has been the case, that in putting before you the events of former years, and the motives of past

---

[39] See also a letter that Newman wrote to G. Talbot in August of 1850 after the lectures had been delivered: "As to my Lectures, I very much doubt if they will do to translate. They are addressed solely to Puseyites, about whom the good Monsignori and Padri of Rome are about as ignorant as Protestants are of them. They are based upon principles and arguments, of which *they* never heard—and will not feel interest in—or may misunderstand." *LD*, xiv, 35. However, Talbot subsequently wrote of *Anglican Difficulties*: "I find they have made a sensation all over Europe.... They are very well calculated to give an idea to the Italian Divines of what Puseyism really was and is." *LD*, xiv, 35, n. 1. The French Catholic writer and statesman Charles-Forbes Forbes-René de Montalembert (1810–70), for example, admired the book. *LD*, xiv, 94.

[40] Newman to R.H. Hutton (3 March 1864), *LD*, xxi, 69.

transactions, and the operation of common principles, and the complexion of old habits and opinions, I should be in no slight degree constructing, what I have ever avoided, a defence of myself. (396–7)

That the autobiographical bits of the lectures are some of the best in the series—being at once deeply personal and ruthlessly self-critical—only makes this admission more understandable. It also refutes Owen Chadwick's claim that the lectures were "against the grain" because they somehow constrained Newman "to shout louder than his inward judgement truly approved." First of all, there is no "shouting" in *Anglican Difficulties*: the writing, as so many critics have pointed out, even unsympathetic critics, is of a sustained urbanity, even when Newman is most critical of his subjects; and, secondly, there is no evidence that his "inward judgement" disapproved of the charges he levelled against the Establishment and the Anglo-Catholics. If that had been the case, he would not have chosen to include the lectures in the collected edition of his works twenty-five years after he had written them. It is true, as the textual appendix shows, that he made changes to the text for the final edition; but these are always stylistic rather than thematic changes; Newman never had any hesitation whatever when it came to following Q's advice and killing his darlings. To be fair to Chadwick, he does acknowledge that "in these most hostile of lectures [Newman] never lost that characteristic sense of continuity evident in the *Essay on Development* five years earlier and the *Apologia* fourteen years later." Chadwick is right: the continuity of the lectures exhibits the unity of Newman's thought profoundly. However, Chadwick mischaracterizes the upshot of that continuity when he says that Newman "was not contending that the Oxford Movement had been 'uncatholic,' but that, though Catholic and because Catholic, the Movement was always strange in the Church of England."[41] Of course, this is grossly false. In the lectures, Newman shows that the

---

[41] Owen Chadwick, *The Victorian Church* (Oxford: Oxford University Press, 1966) i, 289.

Oxford Movement might have had Catholic impulses, it might have had Catholic aspirations, it might even have pretended to Catholic principles, but they were thwarted so long as the Anglo-Catholics remained within the unreal Protestant Anglican Church.

Another reason why Newman was anxious about the lectures is that he feared that they might enmesh him in the sort of otiose Anglican controversy that he had left for good when he left the National Church, though he addressed this fear by attending to the Gorham case simply as a point of departure for the discussion of many other matters. If Ward was right to rely on de Vere in asserting that "the controversy with the Church of England did not go to the root of the deepest difficulties of the day," he could hardly justify the praise he showered on the lectures, calling them, as he did, "brilliantly witty."[42] Again, the occasion of the lectures might have been the Gorham case, but the lectures succeed precisely because they transcend that occasion: they do not limit themselves to Anglican controversy. Moreover, the Erastianism that Newman deplored in the lectures not only in the Anglican Church but the Roman Church had everything to do with the "unprecedented outburst of infidelity" to which de Vere referred. It was at the heart of the unreality that made Protestant Christianity so increasingly unattractive to Newman's contemporaries. T.S. Eliot might not have had Newman's lectures in mind when he wrote "The Wasteland" (1922), but some of its more memorable lines echo the lectures' preoccupation with unreality.

> Unreal City,
> Under the brown fog of a winter dawn,
> A crowd flowed over London Bridge, so many,
> I had not thought death had undone so many.
> Sighs, short and infrequent, were exhaled,
> And each man fixed his eyes before his feet.
> Flowed up the hill and down King William Street,
> To where Saint Mary Woolnoth kept the hours

---

[42] Ward, *Life*, i, 231.

With a dead sound on the final stroke of nine.[43]

If Eliot drew upon Dante in order to describe his "Unreal City," Newman drew upon both Anglican and Roman Catholic church history, the Bible, and the Fathers to describe an unreal National Church. "The want of congeniality which now exists between the sentiments and ways, the moral life of the Anglican communion, and the principles, doctrines, traditions of Catholicism," he told his Anglo-Catholic friends in the lectures, "... show that that movement of 1833 was from its very beginning engaged in propagating an unreality."[44] This is why Newman was impelled to urge his erstwhile companions to reconsider their attachment to the Erastian National Church, though it is also why he reminds his Catholic readers to be wary of allowing their Catholic faith to be corrupted by similarly worldly travesties. Our skirmish with the world, in other words, is perpetual.

---

[43] One might say that to cite Eliot in this context hardly makes my point: after all, he was himself an Anglo-Catholic. Nevertheless, despite his own example—an example inseparable from his desire to remain in the good graces of the Establishment—he also knew that, for the discriminating, there could be no accepting counterfeits. Apropos Arnold's contention, for instance, that "the best poetry supersedes both religion and philosophy," Eliot was adamant: "Nothing in this world... is a substitute for anything else; and if you find that you must do without something, such as religious faith or philosophic belief, then you must just do without it." T. S. Eliot, "Matthew Arnold" (1933), in *The Use of Poetry and the Use of Criticism* (London: Faber, 1933), 113. That Eliot could not see that this same principle obtained in his attempt to substitute Anglo-Catholicism for Roman Catholicism is a puzzle, but there we are. Perhaps it was precisely his own failed conjuror's trick in this line that made him so appreciative of the illusory. In all events, in 1938, he admitted: "I think the term [Anglo-Catholicism] is a dying one, and I personally shall not be sorry to see it disappear... the Church of England is one of the most difficult institutions of the country to explain to anyone outside, and one really has to live in England in order to understand how the English mind works in theological matters!" Eliot to Henri Fluchère (18 February 1938), *The Letters of T.S. Eliot: Volume Eight: 1936-1938* ed. Valerie Eliot and John Haffenden (London: Faber & Faber, 2019), 815.

[44] *Diff*, i, 48.

II: Publication

The first edition of the book was brought out on August 7, 1850, by the London Catholic publisher James Burns, under the imprint of Lambert and Burns.[45] A second edition by the same publisher followed the same year. In 1851, an American edition was published by the Office of the *New York Freeman's Journal*.[46] In 1857, the Irish publisher James Duffy[47] released a "new and revised" edition. The fourth edition, with minor corrections, was brought out by Longmans, Green & Co. in 1872, together with Newman's *Letter to Dr. Pusey* in a two-volume edition entitled *Difficulties of Anglicans*. Newman saw to the publication of the definitive edition in 1876 by Longmans, Green and Company, with additional emendations, which constitutes the present text. In July of 1872, Newman wrote to William Longman that he wished to have the two titles published

---

[45] James Burns (1808–71), Scottish founder of the leading Catholic publishing house Burns and Oates, of which Burns and Lambert was an offshoot, began his career as a printer of Anglican books but converted in 1847 as a result of Newman's influence. Newman's relationship with the publisher, however, was not inveterately sunny. In 1857, when Burns took it upon himself to criticize a translation of Ambrose St. John as "crabbed," Newman wrote his Oratorian friend: "I think Burns's letter an impudent one. He cannot have written it without consulting *some one*—and I cannot help the suspicion that Brompton is at the bottom of it.... If I were you, I should write a civil letter to Burns, thanking him, and saying you would thank him *to return your MS at once*—" Newman to St. John (16 January 1857), *LD*, xxvii, 498–9.

[46] The *Freeman's Journal* was Ireland's oldest nationalist newspaper, founded in Dublin in 1763 by Charles Lucas (the "Irish Wilkes") to tout the great eighteenth-century Anglo-Irish parliamentarians Henry Grattan and Henry Flood.

[47] James Duffy (1809–71) was an Irish Catholic publisher of Bibles, missals, Irish nationalist books and magazines. Born in County Monaghan, he was educated at a hedge school and began his publishing business as a purveyor of Bibles. In 1830 he founded his own company, James Duffy and Sons, and issued *Boney's Oraculum*, or *Napoleon's Book of Fate*, which had a huge sale. The character Captain Boyle in Seán O'Casey's 1924 play *Juno and the Paycock* refers to the book.

together "in consequence of my aiming at making a uniform edition of all that I have written."[48]

III: Lectures

The two-part scheme that Newman set himself for the ordering of the lectures was straightforward. The first seven lectures constituted the first part and were given over to arguing why the Anglo-Catholic party should leave the Established National Church for the Roman Catholic Church; and the remaining five lectures forming the second part explained why the perceived failings and disadvantages of Catholics and their Church should not impede Anglo-Catholics from making their exit from an Establishment with which all of their principles were at variance and joining the Catholic Church.

Dedication Page
Apropos the book's dedication, Newman wrote to Bishop Ullathorne:

Alcester Street July 19. 1850

My dear Lord,

I called yesterday, and should have called today if possible, to find your Lordship's feelings on a request I wished to urge, which I hardly could do, as I should wish, in conversation, and still less by letter.

I am quite aware how very occasional and incomplete a work the Lectures will make which I have lately been delivering, and you may think it quite thoughtless in me to wish to connect them, in any way, with your Lordship. And yet I venture to ask you whether you will allow me to put your Lordship's name at the head of them.

Pray let not this bold request be any embarrassment to you — and should you think it would be better that a series of discussions, which consist of a perpetual skirmish rather than a grave and regular engagement, should not be dedicated to any one in authority, I shall acquiesce, I was going to say, concur in your Lordship's decision. Only be so good as to take the offer as

---

[48] Newman to William Longman (6 July 1872), *LD*, xxvi, 132.

the sincere wish on my part to show that I am, My dear Lord,
Your Lordship's faithful & grateful Servt.

John H Newman Congr. Orat.[49]

Thirty-six years later, Bishop Ullathorne returned the
compliment by dedicating *Christian Patience* (1886) to
Newman, writing: "Deeply sensible of the incalculable
services which you have rendered to the Church at large by
your writings, and to this Diocese of our residence in
particular, by the high and complete character of your virtues,
by your zeal for souls, and by the influence of your presence
in the midst of us, I wish to convey to you the expression of
my affection, veneration and gratitude."[50] No unjaundiced
reader can pick up *Anglican Difficulties* without seeing the
author's "zeal for souls" on nearly every page. It was what
made him such a holy exile in the world. In the *Apologia,*
Newman summed up his high regard for Ullathorne with a
compliment that he knew would please the foursquare
Yorkshireman: "Did I wish to point out a straightforward
Englishman, I should instance the Bishop."[51] Since
straightforwardness epitomizes the lectures of *Anglican
Difficulties*, it is fitting that Newman should have dedicated
them to Ullathorne, who would have seen the instructive fun
of Samuel Johnson's characterization of the great apologist of
English Erastianism, William Warburton (1698–1779). "'The
table is always full, Sir,' Johnson said of the learned Bishop.
'He brings things from the north, and from the south, and
from every quarter.... He carries you round and round,
without carrying you forward to the point; but then you have
no wish to be carried forward.' "[52]

---

[49] Newman to Bishop Ullathorne (19 July 1850), *LD*, xiv, 15.
[50] Ullathorne quoted in Henry Tristram, *Newman and His Friends* (London:
The Bodley Head, 1933), 143.
[51] *Apo.*, 271.
[52] *Boswell's Life of Johnson*, ed. Hill and Powell (Oxford: The Clarendon
Press, 1934), iv, 48–9.

Preface

In the preface, Newman forestalled criticism of the exclusion of any "direct proof of Catholicism" in the lectures by arguing that such proof would be superfluous. After all, the world itself did not deny the "divine origin of the Church," and in elaborating on this fundamental truth, Newman gave his readers a foretaste of the literary fireworks that lay in store for them. "She bears her unearthly character on her brow, as her enemies confess, by imputing her miracles to Beelzebub," he wrote, with his accustomed concinnity.

> There is an instinctive feeling of curiosity, interest, anxiety, and awe, mingled together in various proportions, according to the tempers and opinions of individuals, when she makes her appearance in any neighbourhood, rich or poor, in the person of her missioners or her religious communities. Do what they will, denounce her as they may, her enemies cannot quench this emotion in the breasts of others, or in their own. It is their involuntary homage to the Notes of the Church; it is their spontaneous recognition of her royal descent and her imperial claim; it is a specific feeling, which no other religion tends to excite. Judaism, Mahometanism, Anglicanism, Methodism old religions and young, romantic and commonplace, have not this spell. The presence of the Church creates a discomposure and restlessness, or a thrill of exultation, wherever she comes. Meetings are held, denunciations launched, calumnies spread abroad, and hearts beat secretly the while. The babe leaps in Elizabeth's womb, at the voice of her in whom is enshrined and lives the Incarnate Word. Her priests appeal freely to the consciences of all who encounter them, to say whether they have not a superhuman gift, and that multitude by silence gives consent. They look like other men; they may have the failings of other men; they may have as little worldly advantages as the preachers of dissent; they may lack the popular talents, the oratorical power, the imposing presence, which are found elsewhere; but they inspire confidence, or at least reverence, by their very word. Those who come to jeer and scoff, remain to pray. (vii-viii)

Before settling down to work on the lectures, Newman had admitted to Faber, "There are too many eagerly on the look out to prove that Catholicism hampers me."[53] It is clear that he was careful to compose the preface in such a way as to dispel any invidious comparisons between the "Anglican" and the "Catholic" Newman, though, of course, the very positing of such suppositious entities is dubious: there is only one Newman. Still, the rigor and the finish with which he heralded his theme showed his readers that in prosecuting it, there would be no falling off.

Newman also took advantage of the preface to share with his readers what he would and what he would not cover in the lectures. "The first duty of Catholics is to house those in who are near their doors," he wrote (ix), sounding rather like Kent in the mad scene of *King Lear*. The good faith of *Anglican Difficulties* inheres in Newman's confidence that the Anglo-Catholics were near those doors. Of course, such confidence might prove delusive, but Newman, in his prophetic way, made allowance for that, even before many within the party showed the extent to which they were prepared to hunker down. For Newman, what might seem the futility of trying to win over his old friends to the One True Fold of the Redeemer never militated against its necessity. Nor could he ever rule out the possibility that his Anglo-Catholic friends' difficulties might be overcome.

> Every one is obliged, by the law of his nature, to act by reason; yet no one likes to make a great sacrifice unnecessarily; such difficulties, then, just avail to turn the scale, and to detain men in Protestantism, who are open to the influence of tenderness towards friends, reliance on superiors, regard for their position, dread of present inconvenience, indolence, love of independence, fear of the future, regard to reputation, desire of consistency, attachment to cherished notions, pride of reason, or reluctance to go to school again.... Yet those very same persons who would willingly hide the truth from their eyes by objections and difficulties, nevertheless, if actually forced to look it in the face, and brought under the direct power of the Catholic arguments, would often have strength and courage enough to

---

[53] Newman to Faber (11 January 1850), *LD*, xiii, 382.

> take the dreaded step, and would find themselves, almost before they knew what they had done, in the haven of peace. (xii)

What he would not cover in the lectures demonstrates how rich a theme he had chosen to essay, considering all of its ramifications. He would not speak of "the tests of certainty," "the relation of faith and reason," "the matter of Catholic evidence," or Protestant objections to such Catholic doctrines as Purgatory or the Intercession of the Saints, though all of these might very well have fallen within his remit (xiii). Instead, forgoing such germane but involved themes allowed him focus on the call of charity, which demanded that he enter into his friends' difficulties, whatever the result.

The fact that English Protestants, of all varieties, tended to deplore the Anglo-Catholics as "Romanizers" showed that they were at least moving in the right direction. It was Newman's task, as he saw it, to encourage them to move still further in the same direction.

> Those surely who are advancing towards the Church would not have advanced so far as they have, had they not had sufficient arguments to bring them still further. What retards their progress is not any weakness in those arguments, but the force of opposite considerations, speculative or practical, which are urged, sometimes against the Church, sometimes against their own submitting to her authority. They would have no doubt about their duty, but for the charges brought against her, or the remonstrances addressed to themselves; charges and remonstrances which, whatever their logical cogency, are abundantly sufficient for their purpose, in a case where there are so many inducements, whether from wrong feeling, or infirmity, or even error of conscience, to listen to them. Such persons, then, have a claim on us to be fortified in their right perceptions and their good resolutions, against the calumnies, prejudices, mistakes, and ignorance of their friends and of the world, against the undue influence exerted on their minds by the real difficulties which unavoidably surround a religion so deep and manifold in philosophy, and occupying so vast a place in the history of nations. (x)

In other words, for Newman, the difficulties preventing Anglicans from even considering the Roman Catholic Church were not only real but formidable. As he would say so memorably in his final lecture, "It is no work of a day to convince the intellect of an Englishman that Catholicism is true" (399). Accordingly, if one of his primary charges against the Anglican Church was its refusal to face facts, especially with respect to the Erastian expediency on which it had been founded, he was careful to show his readers that he harboured no illusions about the appeal of the Roman Church for English Protestants, even Anglo-Catholic Protestants.

> It would be wonderful, indeed, if a teaching which embraces all spiritual and moral truth, from the highest to the least important, should present no mysteries or apparent inconsistencies; wonderful if, in the lapse of eighteen hundred years, and in the range of three-fourths of the globe, and in the profession of thousands of millions of souls, it had not afforded innumerable points of plausible attack; wonderful, if it could assail the pride and sensuality which are common to our whole race, without rousing the hatred, malice, jealousy, and obstinate opposition, of the natural man; wonderful, if it could be the object of the jealous and unwearied scrutiny of ten thousand adversaries, of the coalition of wit and wisdom, of minds acute, far-seeing, comprehensive, original, and possessed of the deepest and most varied knowledge, yet without some sort of case being made out against it; and wonderful, moreover, if the vast multitude of objections, great and small, resulting from its exposure to circumstances such as these, acting on the timidity, scrupulousness, inexperience, intellectual fastidiousness, love of the world, or self-dependence of individuals, had not been sufficient to keep many a one from the Church, who had, in spite of them, good and satisfactory reasons for joining her communion. Here is the plain reason why so many are brought near to the Church, and then go back, or are so slow in submitting to her. (x)

In reading the preface, one can see why Newman undertook his lectures with such foreboding. He had set himself an arduous task. He might remind his readers that "conversion is a simple work of divine grace;" that "faith depends on the will, not really on any process of reasoning"; and that all he was resolved on doing in the lectures was "to clear away from the path of an inquirer objections to Catholic truth." But he also knew that "'where the desire of truth is languid, and the religious purpose weak,'" the difficulties he described "will suffice to prevent conviction, and faith will not be created in the mind, though there are abundant reasons for its creation." This was his challenge, and he marshalled his lectures to meet it (xi-xii).

Lecture I: On the Relation of the National Church to the Nation

Newman opened his first lecture with a question that must have been on many of his auditors' minds, both Anglican and Catholic. Why should he attack an Anglican Church that, for all of its "shortcomings or errors," still upheld "what is right and holy"? Was not that, in effect, to "co-operate with a levelling party, who are the enemies of God, and truth, and virtue?" After all, the Anglicans over the centuries had done the Catholic Church homage by "attempting a mimic Catholicism." Indeed, from time to time, some Anglicans had even suffered for such mimicry—Pusey, most notably. In all events, the Anglicans had preserved the Catholic Church's "forms," "rites," "customs," her "old churches," even "in a measure, her Creed." Indeed, many Anglicans "looked wistfully" at the Catholic Church "in their forlorn struggle with their enemies ... for sympathy and encouragement." Over three centuries, they had "repressed the extravagance and diluted the virulence of Protestantism." They had produced faithful theologians. Taking all of this into account, surely Catholics should give their "countenance" to the Anglican Church over all of the other English sects and "compassionate her in her hour of peril" (2–3).

Newman's response to these considerations was to admit that he "did not know what natural inducement there [was] to urge [him] to be harsh with [the Anglican Church] in this her hour." He was "come to a time of life, when men desire to be quiet and at peace." Moreover, his own faith urged him "to forget the external world, and look forward more steadily to the future." His only reasons for stirring himself were, as he said, "my intimate sense that the Catholic Church is the one ark of salvation, and my love for your souls" (3–4). One can only imagine the bristling that this must have set off in the avowed Protestants in the audience. It certainly still annoys detractors of Newman who disapprove of what they style his "dogmatism," a slur, which, in and of itself, epitomizes their misunderstanding of the crucial place dogma holds within the Roman Church and, indeed, within Newman's lifelong defense of the dogmatic principle. For Newman, as he pointed out in his sermon, "The Theory of Developments in Religious Doctrine" (1843), dogmas are vital because they are "propositions expressive of the judgements which the mind forms... of Revealed Truth."[54] Yet Newman had another motive to divulge for writing his lectures.

It is this keen feeling that my life is wearing away, which overcomes the lassitude which possesses me, and scatters the excuses which I might plausibly urge to myself for not meddling with what I have left for ever, which subdues the recollection of past times, and which makes me do my best, with whatever success, to bring you to land from off your wreck, who have thrown yourselves from it upon the waves, or are clinging to its rigging, or are sitting in heaviness and despair upon its side. For this is the truth: the Establishment, whatever it be in the eyes of men, whatever its temporal greatness and its secular prospects, in the eyes of faith is a mere wreck. We must not indulge our imagination, we must not dream: we must look at things as they are; we must not confound the past with the present, or what is substantive with what is the accident of a period. Ridding our minds of these illusions, we shall see that the Established Church has no claims whatever on us, whether in memory or in hope; that they only have claims upon our commiseration and our charity whom she holds in bondage, separated from that faith and that Church in which alone is salvation. If I can do aught towards breaking their chains, and bringing them into the

---

[54] *US*, 320

Truth, it will be an act of love towards their souls, and of piety towards God. (4–5)

It is a shame that Newman's life has never been put on the stage in any proper way, for it had moments of great drama, and this was one of them. Here, we have to imagine the lean and unimposing Newman, seated in his simple black cassock, with his lovely, gentle, unearthly voice, telling the Establishment to its face that it was a fraud and, what is more, telling his King William Street audience that he fell for the fraud himself. Indeed, the great advocate of the *Via Media* all but admitted that he had played his own inglorious part in fostering the imposture. How could this have been?

> If, indeed, we dress it up in an ideal form, as if it were something real, with an independent and a continuous existence, and a proper history, as if it were in deed and not only in name a Church, then indeed we may feel interest in it, and reverence towards it, and affection for it, as men have fallen in love with pictures, or knights in romance do battle for high dames whom they have never seen. Thus it is that students of the Fathers, antiquaries, and poets, begin by assuming that the body to which they belong is that of which they read in times past, and then proceed to decorate it with that majesty and beauty of which history tells, or which their genius creates. Nor is it by an easy process or a light effort that their minds are disabused of this error. (5)

The litotes of that last line could not have been packed with more personal pathos. It must have been moving to hear Newman utter it himself. If this first lecture is trained on the unreality of the *Via Media*, it also takes a hard look at the disillusionment caused by the unmasking of that unreality—and not just anyone's disillusionment, but Newman's own, which he describes with unsparing starkness. The "error" that attaches Anglicans to their Anglican Church "is an error for many reasons too dear to be readily relinquished," he told his listeners.

But at length, either the force of circumstances or some unexpected accident dissipates it; and, as in fairy tales, the magic castle vanishes when the spell is broken, and nothing is seen but the wild heath, the barren rock, and the forlorn sheep-walk, so is it with us as regards the Church of England, when we look in amazement on that we thought so unearthly, and find so commonplace or worthless. Then we perceive, that aforetime we have not been guided by reason, but biassed by education and swayed by affection. We see in the English Church, I will not merely say no descent from the first ages, and no relationship to the Church in other lands, but we see no body politic of any kind; we see nothing more or less than an Establishment, a department of Government, or a function or operation of the State—without a substance—a mere collection of officials, depending on and living in the supreme civil power. Its unity and personality are gone, and with them its power of exciting feelings of any kind. It is easier to love or hate an abstraction, than so commonplace a framework or mechanism. We regard it neither with anger, nor with aversion, nor with contempt, any more than with respect or interest. It is but one aspect of the State, or mode of civil governance; it is responsible for nothing; it can appropriate neither praise nor blame. (6)

Like George Lyttelton, one has to read such passages aloud to savour their full declamatory beauty, though Newman assures his readers that he "said all this ... not in declamation but to bring out clearly to you, why I cannot feel interest of any kind in the National Church, nor put any trust in its past history, as if it were ... a guardian of orthodoxy. It is as little bound by what it said or did formerly, as this morning's newspaper by its former numbers, except as it is bound by the Law; and while it is upheld by the Law, it will not be weakened by the subtraction of individuals, nor fortified by their continuance. Its life is an Act of Parliament" (8).

Newman goes on to make the ancillary point that, as a national church, the Church of England is answerable to the Nation, in all of its exuberant incoherence,[55] and this is yet

---

[55] Cf. "If the Ark of Peter won't hoist the Union Jack, John Bull must have an Ark to himself, with patriotic clergy of his own manufacture tugging at

another reason why any claim it might make to apostolicity is so vexed.[56] Moreover, he implicates himself in the charge because he was one of the Anglo-Catholics who might have protested but still acquiesced in this unholy union.

> Now Protestantism is, as it has been for centuries, the Religion of England; and since the semi-patristical Church, which was set up for the nation at the Reformation, is the organ of that religion, it must live for the nation; it must hide its Catholic aspirations in folios, or in college cloisters; it must call itself Protestant, when it gets into the pulpit; it must abjure Antiquity; for woe to it, if it attempt to thrust the wording of its own documents in its master's path, if it rely on a passage in its Visitation for the Sick, or on an Article of the Creed, or on the tone of its Collects, or on a catena of its divines, when the age has determined on a theology more in keeping with the progress of knowledge! The antiquary, the reader of history, the theologian, the philosopher, the Biblical student may make his protest; he may quote St. Austin, or appeal to the canons, or argue from the nature of the case; but *la Reine le veut*; the English people is sufficient for itself; it wills to be Protestant and progressive; and Fathers, Councils, Schoolmen, Scriptures, Saints, Angels, and what is above them, must give way. (21)

In the appendix in the *Apologia* on the Anglican Church, Newman would reiterate what he had said here in his King William Street lectures, remarking how, though it might be true that the "National Church has hitherto been a serviceable breakwater against doctrinal errors more fundamental than its own," it was also true that "the Nation drags down its Church

---

the oar, and with nothing foreign in the hold save some sound old port." Augustine Birrell, "Cardinal Newman," *Res Judicatae* (London, 1892), 177.
[56] Newman might never have been uncritical of the English, but, by the same token, he was never dismissive of them either, as he made clear in his *Apologia*: "I consider … Englishmen the most suspicious and touchy of mankind; I think them unreasonable, and unjust in their seasons of excitement; but I had rather be an Englishman (as in fact I am) than belong to any other race under heaven. They are as generous, as they are hasty and burly; and their repentance for their injustice is greater than their sin." *Apo.*, 8.

to its own level."[57] Newman was aggrieved to have to admit as much; he knew he would "pain dear friends by saying so;" he knew he opened himself up to Kingsley's charge that he had "turned round on Mother-Church with contumely and slander." But, "in this sense, if in no other sense," he had to "plead guilty" and "without a word in extenuation." The National Church could not "take the rank, contest the teaching, and stop the path of the Church of St. Peter."[58]

In 1966, the founding editor of Newman's *Letters and Diaries*, Charles Stephen Dessain, asserted that "Newman showed powerfully the extent to which the Anglican Church depended on the State, but the lesson of history has been that he exaggerated, or rather that, thanks to Tractarianism, it later won greater independence."[59] Of course, the "lesson of history" has shown that Dessain was wrong: Tractarianism did nothing to disenthrall the Anglican Church from its captivity to the State. If anything, since Dessain wrote, that captivity has only become ghastlier. At the same time, since the extent of the Anglican Church's subjugation to the State, and the Nation that flows from the State, has complicated its confessional pretensions, Newman's strictures against it might seem *passé*, but they still constitute a useful cautionary tale for Roman Catholic Church authorities today who subordinate her interests to those of secular states. They also remind all Christians that there is a consequential gravity to our religious professions. *"We can believe what we choose,"* Newman wrote to his good friend Mrs. William Froude two years before delivering his lectures. "We are answerable for what we choose to believe."[60]

---

[57] *Apo.*, 298.
[58] *Apo.*, 297.
[59] Charles Stephen Dessain, *John Henry Newman* (London: Nelson, 1966), 97–8.
[60] Newman to Mrs. William Froude (27 June 1848), *LD*, xii, 228.

Lecture II: The Movement of 1833 Foreign to the National Church

In the second lecture, Newman takes pains to remind his Anglo-Catholic friends of how opposed they and their ostensible principles were to the Anglican Establishment. And here he quotes from the writings of his friend Hurrell Froude (1803–36), the "ecclesiastical agitator,"[61] as he wished to be known, who, as the true founder of the "Movement of 1833," delighted in exposing the illegitimacy of the National Church.

> For instance, one, who, if any, is the author of the movement altogether, and whose writings were published after his death, says in one of his letters, "It seems agreed among the wise, that we must begin by laying a foundation." Again he writes to a friend, "I am getting more and more to feel, what you tell me, about the impracticability of making sensible people," that is, the High Church party of the day, "enter into our ecclesiastical views; and, what is most discouraging, I hardly see how to set about leading them to us." Elsewhere he asks, "How is it we are so much in advance of our generation?" And again, "The age is out of joint." And again, "I shall write nothing on the subject of Church grievances, till I have a tide to work with." Further he calls the Establishment "an incubus upon the country," and, "a upas tree:" and, lastly, within three or four months of his death, his theological views still expanding and diverging from the existing state of things, he exclaims, "How mistaken we may ourselves be on many points, that are only gradually opening on us!" (36–37)

By quoting his friend, Newman not only vindicates the prophetic good judgment of someone who had come in for a good deal of predictable criticism but confirms his own good judgment in taking Froude's lead. Conversely, Newman quotes the Broad Church Julius Hare[62] to give his readers a

---

[61] *LD*, iii, 97.

[62][62] Julius Charles Hare (1795-1855) Anglican clergyman, born in Valdagno Italy, where his distressed parents sought sanctuary for their ardent republicanism. On the family's return to England, Hare's bluestocking mother tutored him for five years before enrolling him in Tonbridge School. In 1802, the boy returned with his family to the continent where his parents

sense of the comical fatuousness that often animated those who wrote in defense of the Establishment. Here, also, is a good example of how Newman helped himself to the writings of others to give his satirical purposes an added éclat.

> "Surely, my dear friend," says this accomplished writer, "with a reference to the present controversy, "it requires an inordinate faith in one's own logical dreams, an idolising worship of one's own opinions, to believe that the Church of England, blest as she has been by God for so many generations, raised as she has been by Him to be the mother of so many Churches, with such a promise shining upon her, and brightening every year, that ... she, who has been chosen by God to be the instrument of so many blessings, and the presence of the Lord and His Spirit with whom was never more manifest than at this day, should forfeit her office and authority, as a witness of the truth, should be cut off from the body of Christ's Church, and should no longer be able to dispense the grace of the sacraments, because her highest law court has not condemned a proposition asserted by one of her ministers, concerning a very obscure and perplexing question of dogmatical theology. Surely this would be an extraordinary delusion; ... for, whatever the dogmatical value of the opinion" in question "may be, the error is not one which indicates any want of personal faith and holiness, or any decay of Christian life in the Church." (45)

For any Anglican, even a Broad Church Anglican, to refer to baptismal regeneration, the doctrine that set off the Gorham case, as "a very obscure and perplexing question of dogmatical theology" was fairly ludicrous. Nevertheless, for Anglicans reading this, who might be inclined to cry foul—

---

settled in Weimar and befriended Goethe, Schiller and the cosmopolitan diarist Henry Crabb Robinson. This continental upbringing left Hare with an eccentricity that he would never shake. At Trinity College, Cambridge, he befriended Connop Thirlwall, William Whewell, J.F.D. Maurice and John Sterling. Although subsequently a friend of Manning (before he converted), Hare was always contemptuous of Newman, to whose occasional strictures against Luther he took vehement exception. Although a frequent literary and theological controversialist, Hare is now remembered mostly for touting German literature and attempting to make mad changes to English spelling. *ODNB*.

the eccentric Hare being hardly representative of the Broad Church, even allowing for its renowned elasticity—Newman was careful to temper his satire with a passage from the Anglo-Catholic party—in this case, something he had written himself. "We require a recognised theology," he insists, "and, if the present work, instead of being what it is meant to be, a first approximation to the required solution, in one department of a complicated problem, contains, after all, but a series of illustrations demonstrating our need, and supplying hints for its removal; such a result, it is evident, will be quite a sufficient return for whatever anxiety it has cost the writer to have employed his own judgment on so serious a subject" (39).

This is not free of fatuousness itself. Yet Newman's gloss on his own Anglo-Catholic musings shows that when it came to making fun of the unreality of Anglicanism, he could be just as hard on himself as he was on others. "I must add, in justice to this writer," he says dryly of himself, "and it is not much to say for him, that he did not entertain the presumptuous thought of creating, at this time of day, a new theology himself; he considered that a theology true in itself, and necessary for the position of the Anglican Church, was to be found in the writings of Andrewes, Laud, Bramhall, Stillingfleet, Butler, and other of its divines, but had never been put together" (39). The elusiveness of Anglican theology notwithstanding, Newman returned to glossing Hare's response to those who protested the Privy Council's ruling with a show of still more comical even-handedness.[63] Eyewitness accounts of the lectures attest that their delivery was interrupted by a good deal of laughter. This passage shows why:

> The eloquent writer just quoted, in ridicule of the protest made by twelve very distinguished men against the Queen's recent decision concerning the sacrament of baptism, contrasts "logical

---

[63] For a sympathetic account of Anglican theology, see the best of the Anglo-Catholic historians, Mark D. Chapman, *Anglican Theology* (London: Bloomsbury, 2012).

dreams" and "obscure and perplexing questions of dogmatic theology" with "the promise" in the Establishment of a large family "of daughters, spread round the earth, shining and brightening every year." Now, I grant that it has a narrow and technical appearance to decide the Catholicity of a religious body by particular words, or deeds, or measures, resulting from the temper of a particular age, accidentally elicited, and accomplished in minutes or in days. I allow it and feel it; that a particular vote of parliament, endured or tacitly accepted by bishops and clergy, or by the Metropolitans, or a particular appointment, or a particular omission, or a particular statement of doctrine, should at once change the spiritual character of the body, and *ipso facto* cut it off from the centre of unity and the source of grace, is almost incredible. In spite of such acts, surely the Anglican Church might be to-day what it was yesterday, with an internal power and a supernatural virtue, provided it had not already forfeited them, and would go about its work as of old time. It would be to-day pretty much what it was yesterday, though in the course of the night it had allowed an Anglo-Prussian See to be set up in Jerusalem,[64] and had disavowed the Athanasian Creed. (49)[65]

---

[64] The Jerusalem Bishopric, as I indicate in a note in the text, was the joint bishopric set up between the Lutheran and Anglican churches, which made mincemeat of any claim to catholicity that the Anglican episcopate might make. Newman's response to the joint bishopric was memorably acerbic: "It really does seem to me as if the Bishops were doing their best to uncatholicize us—and whether they will succeed before a rescue comes, who can say? The Bishop of Jerusalem is to be consecrated forthwith—perhaps in a few days—Mr Bunsen is at the bottom of the whole business, who, I think I am right in saying, considers the Nicene Council the first step in the corruption of the Church." Newman to Keble (5 October 1841), *LD*, viii, 286. In 1841, Baron Christian Karl Josias von Bunsen (1791–1860), Prussian diplomat, theologian and scholar, was sent to London to set up the joint Anglo-Prussian Jerusalem Bishopric and subsequently appointed ambassador at the English court. For an excellent piece on Newman's response to the bishopric in the context of his larger response to the issues of authority and infallibility, see James Tolhurst, "'My Own Bishop Was My Pope …': John Henry Newman on Magisterium," *Faith Magazine* (July–August 2010).

[65] The common yearning on the part of Anglicans, including Newman when he was one of their number, that the Anglican Church "would go about its work as of the old time" was nicely captured by John Mason Neale (1818–66) in his hymn "Oh, Give Us Back the Days of Old" (1839). See Geoffrey

Hare had responded to the opponents of the Gorham ruling by claiming that the decision could not nullify the "life" and "faith" of the Anglican Church. Newman, recognizing the seriousness of such a fallacy, cast aside his satirical playfulness and took up a more sombre tone, urging his audience to reconsider what such vague claims as "life" and "faith" might mean in this context.

> If then "life" means strength, activity, energy, and well-being of any kind whatever, in that case doubtless the national religion is alive. It is a great power in the midst of us; it wields an enormous influence; it represses a hundred foes; it conducts a hundred undertakings. It attracts men to it, uses them, rewards them; it has thousands of beautiful homes up and down the country, where quiet men may do its work and benefit its people; it collects vast sums in the shape of voluntary offerings, and with them it builds churches, prints and distributes innumerable Bibles, books, and tracts and sustains missionaries in all parts of the earth. In all parts of the earth it opposes the Catholic Church, denounces her as antichristian, bribes the world against her, obstructs her influence, apes her authority, and confuses her evidence. In all parts of the world it is the religion of gentlemen, of scholars, of men of substance, and men of no personal faith at all. If this be life, if it be life to impart a tone to the court and houses of parliament, to ministers of state, to law and literature, to universities and schools, and to society,—if it be life to be a principle of order in the population, and an organ of benevolence and almsgiving towards the poor,—if it be life to make men decent, respectable, and sensible, to embellish and refine the family circle, to deprive vice of its grossness, and to shed a gloss over avarice and ambition,—if indeed it is the life of religion to be the first jewel in the Queen's crown, and the highest step of her throne, then doubtless the National Church is replete, it overflows with life; but the question has still to be answered, Life of what kind? Heresy has its life, worldliness has its life. Is the Establishment's life merely national life, or is it something more? Is it Catholic life as well? Is it a supernatural life? Is it

---

Rowell, *Hell and the Victorians* (Oxford: Oxford University Press, 1974). Rowell was the first to transcribe the words to the hymn, which begins: "Oh, give us back the days of old! Give me back an hour/ To make us feel that Holy Church o'er death hath might and power."

congenial with, does it proceed from, does it belong to, the principles of Apostles, Martyrs, Evangelists, and Doctors, the principles which the movement of 1833 thought to impose or to graft upon it, or does it revolt from them? (47)

Here, one might say, was the nub of the question, and Newman paid the Anglo-Catholics the compliment of reminding them that it had been they who had first posed it. The problem was that so few of them acted on it once it became evident that the Establishment would not accept "the principles of Apostles, Martyrs, Evangelists, and Doctors"— the principles, that is to say, to which the "Movement of 1833" itself subscribed.

Newman was doubly intent on treating this fallacious reasoning seriously because it had also been advanced by John Mason Neale,[66] who had argued in *A Few Words of Hope* (1847), his response to the Gorham case, that the life of

---

[66] John Mason Neale (1818-66), High Churchman and hymnologist, best known for his hymns, "Jerusalem and Golden" and "O happy band of pilgrims." In 1860, when a correspondent sent Newman a book of Neale's on the Immaculate Conception, entitled *Voices from the East, Documents on the Present State and Working of the Oriental Church* (London, 1859), and asked for his response, the Oratorian replied: "In this then lies the difference of view, taken by Catholics and Protestants respectively, of the doctrine of the Immaculate Conception; that Catholics do not view it as a substantive and independent doctrine, so much as one of a family of doctrines which are intimately united together, whereas Protestants consider it as separate from every other, and as requiring a proof of its own as fully as if it were the only thing that we knew of the Blessed Virgin." Newman to Arthur Osborne Alleyne (16 June 1860), *LD*, xix, 362. In responding specifically to Neale's text, Newman supplied his readers with a nice assessment of his opponent's critical powers by singling out this passage for comment: "p 146. 'Since *the earliest ages of Christianity*, the orthodox Church has glorified the Blessed Virgin, naming her more precious than the Cherubim, and infinitely (!) more glorious than the Seraphim, supplicating her as the most powerful Mediatress with the Lord, and the mightiest Advocate of the Christian world.' I cannot help thinking, that, whatever be the differences of opinion between Catholics and Protestants, they will here, for once in a way, be in agreement: viz in judging, that a writer, who holds all this, yet is shocked and indignant at the doctrine that our Lady was without any taint of sin and ever full of grace, is straining out a gnat and swallowing a camel." Ibid, 370.

the Anglican Church was "not that of a machine ... where one serious injury will disturb all regularity, and finally put a stop to action. It is that of a living body, whose motions will be irregular, incapable of being exactly arranged and foretold, and where it is nearly impossible to say how much health may co-exist with how much disease." And he speaks of the line of reasoning that he is opposing, as being "too logical to be real." For Neale, "men, do not, in the practical affairs of life, act on such clear, sharp, definite theories. Such reasoning can never be the cause of any one leaving the Church of England. But it looks well on paper, and therefore may, perhaps, be put forward as a theoretical argument by those who, from some other feeling, or fancy, or prejudice, or honest conviction, think fit to leave us."[67]

Newman's response to such evasive reasoning was withering:

> No; the question before us is nothing narrow or technical; it has no cut-and-dried premises, and peremptory conclusions; it is not whether this or that statute or canon at the time of the Reformation, this or that "further and further encroachment" of the State, this or that "Act of William IV," constituted the Establishment's formal separation from the Church; not whether the Queen's recent decision binds it to heresy; but, whether these acts, and abundant others, are not one and all evidences, in one out of a hundred heads of evidence, that, whatever were the acts which constituted, or the moment which completed the schism, or rather the utter disorganisation of the National Church, cut off and disorganised it is. No sober man I suppose, dreams of denying, that, if that Church be un-apostolical and impure now, it has had no claim to be called "pure and apostolical" last year, or twenty years back, or for any part of the period since the Reformation. (51–2)

In October of 1845, days after Newman's secession, Neale had written a letter that captured the essence of his sentimental approach not only to the news of Newman's

---

[67] John Mason Neale, *A Few Words of Hope on the Present Crisis of the English Church* (London: Joseph Masters, 1847), 11–12.

secession but to the whole question of the tenability of Anglo-Catholics' remaining within the Establishment, in which he wrote:

> As you do not see *The English Churchman*, you have probably not read Dr. Pusey's letter on Newman's secession.... I think Dr. Pusey's letter goes too much on the hypothesis that God cannot raise up some one of Newman's talents in our Church, or do His own work without them. As to me, this event can have no influence, excepting that naturally, when one's mother is betrayed, however weakly or wickedly she may have acted (which yet in this case I do not see that our Church *as* a Church has done) one is more desirous than ever of working for her and serving her.[68]

Newman would never countenance the notion, advocated here by Neale, that one should stay in or defend the Anglican Church simply because one had been born into it. In 1885, thirty-five years after delivering his King William Street lectures, Newman had Father Neville respond to a correspondent who had speculated that the convert might have

---

[68] Neale quoted in *Letters of John Mason Neale, D.D., Selected and Edited by His Daughter* (London: Longmans, Green & Co., 1910), 85. Cf. "If Keble responded to the crisis of Tractarianism with agonizing indecisiveness, Pusey responded as though there really had been no crisis. Newman went over to Rome, Pusey claimed, out of pique. 'It is an exceeding mystery that such confidence as he had once in our Church should have gone,' Pusey wrote in a long letter to the *English Churchman* after Newman's secession. 'Even amidst our present sorrows it goes to the heart to look at that former self, and think how devotedly he worked for our Church; how he strove to build her up. It looks as if some good purpose for our Church had failed; that an instrument raised up for her had not been employed as God willed and so is withdrawn. There is a jar somewhere. One cannot trust oneself to think, whether his keen sensitiveness to ill was not fitted for these troubled times. What, to such dulled minds as my own, seemed as a matter of course, as something of necessity to be gone through and endured, was to his ... 'like the piercing of a sword.'" Newman, from his standpoint, confessed that he and Pusey were at cross purposes well before 1845. "I had from the first," he wrote in the *Apologia*, "a great difficulty in making Dr. Pusey understand such differences of opinion as existed between himself and me." Edward Short, *Newman and His Contemporaries* (London: Continuum, 2011), 107–8.

wished to return to the Anglican fold: "Cardinal Newman wishes his fingers allowed him to write a longer letter than this. The statement is simply untrue that he ever for a moment has wished to return to the English Church. The Catholic Roman Church is the only oracle of Truth and Ark of Salvation, no other Communion has the promises, no other has the Grace of the Redeemer. St Paul did not tell Jews to remain Jews because they had [been] reared members of the Jewish Church; nor is it any reason why Protestants should remain Protestants because they were born Protestants."[69]

In November of 1845, after Newman had published his *Essay on the Development of Christian Doctrine* (1845), Neale wrote: "As to Newman's book, I am so thoroughly and morally persuaded of the defensibility of our position, that if I were to feel shaken by its beginning, I would shut up the book. I cannot express to you the firmness of my conviction. It seems to grow on me the more others waver."[70] Here was the sort of blind faith in which dispirited Anglo-Catholics could rejoice; indeed, they call on his blind faith still. In his *précis* of Neale's response to *Anglican Difficulties*, James Pereiro shows how little the hymn writer's thinking had changed by the time Newman delivered his lectures.

In 1851 John Mason Neale, a Cambridge graduate of Tractarian sympathies, would dispute the converts' facts and conclusions. The Oxford Movement, he said, had been an intervention of the Holy Spirit in order to restore Catholic doctrine and practice within the Anglican Church, and to revitalize also its missionary zeal. Its providential character was shown, among other things, by the gradual rediscovery and adoption of Catholic doctrine and principles. Their sudden introduction would have generated a rejection in some, while others might have been led to Rome to seek there what they could not find in the Church of England. The converts were blamed for having set back the progress of Catholic ideas, now contaminated in the public mind by the desertion of many of their supporters. Those who remained in the Church of England had been left with an uphill struggle.

[69] Newman to John Waugh (24 March 1885), *LD*, xxxi, 49.
[70] *Letters of John Mason Neale*, 83.

They worked under suspicion and, at times, suffered open persecution. What required greater heroism, to leave the Church of England for that of Rome or to remain fighting against the odds for the recovery of the Catholic inheritance of Anglicanism?[71]

In concluding his second lecture, Newman honored the good faith of his Anglo-Catholic friends by refusing to regard the evasive Neale as representative of their band. Instead, he addressed them as though open to breaking free of the heterodox Establishment.

> If, my brethren, your reason, your faith, your affections, are indissolubly bound up with the holy principles which you have been taught, if you know they are true, if you know their life and their power, if you know that nothing else is true; surely you have no portion or sympathy with systems which reject them. Seek those principles in their true home. If your Church rejects your principles, it rejects you;—nor dream of indoctrinating it with them by remaining; everything has its own nature, and in that nature is its identity. You cannot change your Establishment into a Church without a miracle. It is what it is. (65)

Lecture III: The Life of the Movement of 1833 Not Derived from the National Church
In his third lecture, Newman returns to the question of whether "inward evidences of grace" legitimate a party within the Establishment otherwise illegitimate on external grounds. "I have no intention at all of evading their position," he says of the Anglo-Catholics' position, "I mean to attack it" (74). And so he does by quoting long passages from his sermon "Grounds for Steadfastness in Our Religious Profession" (1841) in which he had strenuously sought to commend such evidences, only to conclude: "No one can read the series of arguments from which I have quoted, without being struck by

---

[71] James Pereiro, "The Oxford Movement and Anglo-Catholicism," *The Oxford History of Anglicanism: Volume III, Partisan Anglicanism and Its Global Expansion 1829–c. 1914*, ed. Rowan Strong (Oxford: Oxford University Press, 2017), 198–9.

the author's clear avowal of *doubt*, in spite of his own reasonings.... He longed to have faith in the National Church, and he could not" (79).

Unlike many of his contemporaries, Newman was always insistent about the need for objectivity in making such judgments. "It is quite impossible for us to conclude with any fairness of argument," he says with aphoristic dispatch, "that a certain opinion is true, or a religious position is safe, simply on account of the confidence or apparent excellence of those who adopt it" (94). For Newman, the criterion for right judgment in such matters was never one of ecumenical sentimentality. Indeed, he would have scoffed at any rationale for staying put within the Establishment, according to which, to borrow Pereiro's paraphrase of Neale's reasoning, it "required greater heroism ... to remain fighting against the odds for the recovery of the Catholic inheritance of Anglicanism" than to convert to the One True Fold of the Redeemer. No, for Newman, the question was whether the Catholic Church was the Ark of Salvation. If one had the means of seeing that it was, there could be no twaddling of "heroism" or "fighting against the odds." One was duty bound to submit to Christ's Church—period.[72] And Newman expresses this reality with becoming simplicity: "The highest gifts and graces are compatible with ultimate reprobation" (84).

This is not a sentence that one sees often cited by commentators on the lectures, but it is at their very heart.[73]

---

[72] "I wish you would consider whether you have a right notion how to gain faith. It is, we know, the Gift of God, but I am speaking of it as a human process and attained by human means. Faith then is not a conclusion from premises, but the result of an act of the *will*, following upon a *conviction* that to believe is a *duty*. The simple question you have to ask yourself is, 'Have I a *conviction* that I *ought* to accept the (Roman) Catholic Faith as God's word?' if not, at least, 'do I *tend* to such a conviction?' or 'am I *near* upon it?' For directly you have a conviction that you *ought* to believe, reason has done its part, and what is wanted for faith, is, not proof, but *will*." Newman to Mrs. Froude (27 June 1848), *LD*, xii, 228.

[73] A lively exception was Gerard Manley Hopkins, who wrote to an Anglo-Catholic priest who contemplated leaving the Anglican for the Catholic Church but thought better of it. "I know that living a moral life, with the

Reprobation means "rejection by God; the state of being so rejected or cast off and thus ordained to eternal misery" (*OED*). For Newman, Catholicism was not "a philosophy, or literature" but "a sacred deposit" (218) replete with consequence for the salvation of one's soul. Choosing not to submit to the Church because one preferred to preoccupy oneself with "the Catholic inheritance of Anglicanism" put the salvation of one's soul in peril.

This was truth telling of an uncompromising stripe. Yet Newman was not finished, impatient as he was with the Anglo-Catholics' claim that their allegiance to the Establishment was justifiable because their Anglo-Catholicism somehow bestowed on them special "gifts and graces."[74] "As regards ... the evidence of sanctity in members

---

ordinances of religion and yourself a minister of them, with work to do and the interest of a catholicwards movement to support you," Hopkins wrote, "it is most natural to say all things continue as they were and most hard to realise the silence and the severity of God, as Dr. Newman most eloquently and persuasively has said in a passage of the Anglican Difficulties; but this plea or way of thinking—all things continuing as they were—is the very character of infidelity. The difference between a state of grace and a state of reprobation, that difference to [which] all other differences of humanity are as the splitting of straws, makes no change in the outer world; faces, streets, and sunlight look just the same: it is therefore the more dangerous and terrible." G.M. Hopkins to Edward William Urquhart (13 June 1868), *The Collected Works of Gerard Manley Hopkins: Volume I: Correspondence 1851–1881*, ed. R.K.R. Thornton and Catherine Phillips (Oxford: Oxford University Press, 2013), 180–1.

[74] Here, one can contrast the entrenchment of Neale and other Anglo-Catholics with G.K. Chesterton's need to follow Newman in repudiating Anglo-Catholicism, which; he described thus in *The Well and the Shallows* (1935): "Men need an image, single, coloured and clear in outline, an image to be called up instantly in the imagination, when what is Catholic is to be distinguished from what claims to be Christian or even what in one sense is Christian. Now I can scarcely remember a time when the image of Our Lady did not stand up in my mind quite definitely, at the mention or the thought of all these things. I was quite distant from these things, and then doubtful about these things; and then disputing with the world for them, and with myself against them; for that is the condition before conversion. But whether the figure was distant, or was dark and mysterious, or was a scandal to my contemporaries, or was a challenge to myself—I never doubted that this figure was the figure of the Faith; that she embodied, as a

of the National Establishment, on which you insist, Catholics are not called on to deny them," Newman wrote.

> We think such instances are few, nor so eminent as you are accustomed to fancy; but we do not wish to deny, nor have any difficulty in admitting such facts as you have to adduce, whatever they be. We do not think it necessary to carp at every instance of supernatural excellence among Protestants when it comes before us, or to explain it away; all we know is, that the grace given them is intended ultimately to bring them into the Church, and if it is not tending to do so, it will not ultimately profit them; but we as little deny its presence in their souls as they do themselves; and as the fact is no perplexity to us, it is no triumph to them. (84–5)

Newman might have left matters there, calling such claims of sanctity into reasonable question, without going any further.

---

complete human being still only human, all that … [God] had to say to humanity. The instant I remembered the Catholic Church, I remembered her; when I tried to forget the Catholic Church, I tried to forget her; when I finally saw what was nobler than my fate, the freest and hardest of all my acts of freedom, it was in front of a gilded and very gaudy little image of her in the port of Brindisi, that I promised … [God] that I would do, if I returned to my own land." *The Collected Works of G.K. Chesterton, Volume III: The Catholic Church and Conversion, Where All Roads Lead, The Well and the Shallows*, ed. James J. Thompson (San Francisco: Ignatius Press, 1990), 463. The editor's gloss on the passage is worth quoting: "To trace the path that he traversed from the free-thinking Victorian ethos of his youth to his entry into the Church in 1922 would be to compose Chesterton's spiritual biography, a book that has yet to be written. But the story can at least be adumbrated. By the early twentieth century he had found refuge in the Anglican Church, specifically in an Anglo-Catholicism that prides itself on preserving the true Catholic faith in opposition to the perversions of Rome. Chesterton did not rest comfortably for long in this way-station; a decade or more before his embrace of Roman Catholicism he discerned the inadequacy of the Anglo-Catholic compromise. Why it took him so long to make the final step to Rome remains something of a mystery, although various writers attribute the delay to his reluctance to open a spiritual chasm between himself and his wife, who remained at this time staunchly committed to the Anglican Church." Ibid., 16. For a discussion of GKC's uneasiness with Anglo-Catholicism as it related to his wife, see Ian Ker, *G.K. Chesterton: A Biography* (Oxford: Oxford University Press, 2011), 428–430.

But he could not resist giving his reeling friends one more wallop, which he dealt, not in mean-spiritedness or malice but with true pastoral *caritas*. If the Anglo-Catholics were to fulfill the obligations of their special destiny, they would need to be shaken out of their complacency.

> Really I am obliged in candour to allow, whatever part the evil spirit had in the work, whatever gross admixture of earth polluted it, whatever extravagance there was to excite ridicule or disgust, whether it was Christian virtue or the excellence of unaided man, whatever was the spiritual state of the subjects of it, whatever their end and their final account, yet there were higher and nobler vestiges or semblances of grace and truth in Methodism than there have been among you. I give you credit for what you are, grave, serious, earnest, modest, steady, self-denying, consistent; you have the praise of such virtues; and you have a clear perception of many of the truths, or of portions of the truths, of Revelation. In these points you surpass the Wesleyans; but if I wished to find what was striking, extraordinary, suggestive of Catholic heroism—of St. Martin, St. Francis, or St. Ignatius—I should betake myself far sooner to them than to you. (89)

Over the years, we have heard a good deal from the former Yale professor Frank Turner and his followers about Newman's unfairness to the Evangelical party.[75] Here, in *Anglican Difficulties*, we can see that he was prepared to pay that party very handsome compliments indeed, even if at the expense of the Anglo-Catholic party.

---

[75] For confirmation of my point, see the bits about Newman and the Evangelicals in what is undoubtedly the worst collection of essays ever put together on Newman, *The Oxford Handbook of John Henry Newman*, ed. Frederick D. Aquino and Benjamin J. King (Oxford: Oxford University Press, 2018). It says nothing of any substance about *Anglican Difficulties*, though, to be fair, Stephen Prickett has one good moment when he refers to the Erastian Church of the Anglo-Catholics as "a kind of glove puppet manipulated by the Parliament on whose statutes it depends for its every motion... a zombie, the living dead." (583). The rest of the contributors, insofar as they mention the book at all, treat it (to use one of the editor's strictures) as though it were not "fully rehabilitated." For Newman's detractors, the controversialist in Newman is a scarcely corrigible criminal.

Lecture IV: The Providential Course of the Movement of 1833 not in the Direction of the National Church

In the *Grammar of Assent*, Newman had occasion to argue that the religion of England consisted "not in rites or creeds, but mainly in having the Bible read in Church, in the family, and in private." Many good things came of this. "At least in England, it has to a certain point made up for great and grievous losses in its Christianity. The reiteration again and again, in fixed course in the public service, of the words of inspired teachers under both Covenants, and that in grave majestic English, has in matter of fact been to our people a vast benefit. It has attuned their minds to religious thoughts; it has given them a high moral standard; and it has served them in associating religion with compositions which, even humanly considered, are among the most sublime and beautiful ever written." However, the shortcomings of this *sola scriptura* Christianity were no less numerous. "It has been comparatively careless of creed and catechism; and has in consequence shown little sense of the need of consistency in the matter of its teaching. Its doctrines are not so much facts, as stereotyped aspects of facts; and it is afraid, so to say, of walking round them. It induces its followers to be content with this meagre view of revealed truth; or, rather, it is suspicious and protests, or is frightened, as if it saw a figure in a picture move out of its frame, when our Lord, the Blessed Virgin, or the Holy Apostles, are spoken of as real beings, and really such as Scripture implies them to be." Still, for Newman, "what Scripture especially illustrates from its first page to its last, is God's Providence; and that is nearly the only doctrine held with a real assent by the mass of religious Englishmen."[76]

In this category, Newman clearly meant to include the country's Anglo-Catholics, for in his fourth lecture, he speaks of his old friends as at a Providential crossroads, largely as the result of the relative success of the Movement of 1833. After all, it was a party that had made itself known not only in

---

[76] *GA*, 56–7.

England but "to the police of Italy" and "the backwoodsmen of America." It caused genuine excitement. It was "getting stronger and stronger every year." But its very success presented a problem. The party had "come into collision with the Nation, and the Church of the Nation, which it began by professing especially to serve; and now its upholders and disciples [have] to look about, and ask themselves where they are, and which way they are to go, and wither they are bound" (97–98). For Newman, the moral of this moment of truth was unmistakable: "Providence does nothing in vain, so much earnestness, zeal, toil, thought, religiousness, success, as has a place in the history of that movement, must surely have a place also in His scheme, and in His dealings towards His Church in this country, if we could discern what that place was" (98). The question, then, became, what would become of the Anglo-Catholic party? "Is it to melt away as if it had not been? Is it merely to subserve the purposes of Liberalism, in breaking up establishments by weakening them, and in making dogma ridiculous by multiplying sects? or is it of too positive a character, both in its principles and its members, to anticipate for it so disappointing an issue?" Newman was generous to the party in holding that while the application of its principles might be "vague," the principles themselves were definite, stemming as they did from its "first principle," what Newman nicely styled "ecclesiastical liberty." As such, from its very outset, the party was opposed to "the heresy of Erastus"[77] (101) and, more particularly, the Royal Supremacy, which had made the assassin and apostate King Henry VIII Supreme Head of the Church of England. That the party and the Establishment should eventually collide was inevitable.

> Every breath, every sigh, every aspiration, every effort of the movement was an affront or an offence to the Establishment. In its very first tract, it could wish nothing better for the Bishops of the Establishment than martyrdom; and, as the very easiest escape, it augured for them the loss of their temporal

---

[77] Thomas Erastus (1524–83), Swiss-German theologian, who held that the Church should be subordinated to the State.

> possessions. It was easy to foresee what response the Establishment would make to its officious defenders, as soon as it could recover from its surprise; but experience was necessary to teach this to men who knew more of St. Athanasius than of the Privy Council or the Court of Arches. (106)

Here was another reference to Newman himself, for, in his innocence, he, too, "knew more of St. Athanasius than of the Privy Council or the Court of Arches." He certainly never anticipated the fury that Tract 90 would unleash in an episcopate contemptuous of what they regarded as his "'Romanizing ways." In fact, such innocence coloured a good deal of Newman's Anglican ministry. Indeed, it was his unworldly desire to purify the episcopate that ultimately led the bishops not only to recoil from but to denounce him. The servant of Truth in Newman had no idea how inexpedient Truth was to the servants of Lambeth Palace. On this score, the penny only gradually dropped. Thus, when Newman gave his readers a litany of the abuse hurled at the Movement of 1833—"how they were called ... 'superstitious,' 'zealots,' 'mystical,' 'malignants,' 'Oxford heretics,' 'Jesuits in disguise,' 'tamperers with Popish idolatry,' ... 'agents of Satan' ... 'snakes in the grass,' " (112)—he was chronicling his own disillusionment with an Establishment that he had once been avid to serve.

Many passages from the lectures constitute a kind of draft history of the Oxford Movement, and this is one of them. The autobiographical contributions Newman made to the understanding of that history are important, especially for the light they shed on how one of its architects viewed its inherent contradictions. Newman's detractors hold that Newman's testimony regarding his own part in that Movement, or, indeed, any aspect of his life, is, by definition, not only suspect but inadmissible. Newman's part in the Oxford Movement, in other words, needs to be sorted out by consulting not what Newman himself made of the matter but

what commentators contemptuous of Newman make of it.[78]
Caveat lector.

After listing the slurs levelled at the Anglo-Catholics, Newman wrote: "Is it not then abundantly plain, that, whatever be of the National Church, there is no tendency in it towards a coalition with the Establishment? It cannot strengthen it, it cannot serve it, it cannot obey it. The party may be dissolved, the movement may die—that is another matter; but it and its idea cannot live, cannot energize, in the National Church" (112–13). This was not "abundantly plain" to some of his former Tractarian allies. In November 1850, only months after Newman's lectures were delivered, Newman's friend Frederic Rogers, later Lord Blachford, who refused to speak to Newman for twenty years after his conversion, would write to his sister, "Manning, Dodsworth, and Aubrey de Vere are going together to Palestine. I suppose they will join Rome out there, at least I don't suppose any one would join Manning and Dodsworth who did not intend to follow them. I hear cases of disquiet every here and there. However, I don't see any shaking in our clique; Keble is as firm as a rock and stouter in acquiescing in aggression against Rome than I ever thought to see him. There is a degree both of attack and of liberalism in my articles which I feared he

---

[78] One of the more egregious offenders in this line is Prof. Cyril O'Regan, who, following Turner, describes the *Apologia* as an exercise in "magisterial self-exoneration," though the professor is never altogether clear as to what the charge is from which Newman sought to exonerate himself. "Chastity, asceticism, living in community with other men, for the historian of the Victorian period and the actual Victorian Kingsley, bespeak sickliness and lack of manliness," O'Regan writes, in his typically insinuating way, but this hardly constitutes a coherent charge. He also follows Simon Skinner in accusing the Newman biographers Wilfrid Ward, Meriol Trevor and Ian Ker of being uncritical 'hagiographers,' in the vulgar, pejorative sense of the word. Vilifying Newman's biographers may not be as bad as vilifying Newman himself, but it still exhibits something of the professor's contempt for his subject. C. O'Regan, "Reception of Newman the Saint: An Analysis and Critique" in *Receptions of Newman* ed. Frederick D. Aquino and Benjamin King (Oxford: Oxford University Press, 2015), 220.

would not approve. But he does wholly."[79] (The articles to which Rogers refers appeared in the *Guardian* between 24 July and 6 November 1850.) For all of their Anglo-Catholic convictions, Rogers and Keble were Establishment men to their fingertips. Neither the Jerusalem Bishopric nor the Gorham case budged them one iota from their allegiance to the National Church. As Rogers would say in another context, "Pound a monkey in a mortar and his monkeyism will not depart from him."[80]

Newman had no illusions about the "stay put" proclivities of Anglo-Catholics. Indeed, the barrister in him set out a justification for their remaining where they were that was better than his friends could ever have set out for themselves. If the party were not to break with the Establishment, he writes, it could choose to "remain just what it is at present, not in power or authority, but as a sort of principle or view of religion, found here and there with greater or less distinctness, with more or fewer followers, scattered about or concentrated, up and down the Establishment; with no exact agreement between man and man in matters of detail or in theoretical basis, but as an influence, sleeping or rousing, victorious or defeated, from time to time, as the case may be." Of course, Newman was needling his friends, but there were grounds for the needling. "If you cannot do any positive good to the nation," he advised, "yet at least … you may prevent evil." As Newman saw it, "to be a drag upon the career of unbelief, if you are nothing else, is a mission not to be despised; moreover, if it be not a heroic course of action, or look well in history, still so much the more does such an office become those who are born in a fallen time, and who wish to be humble" (113–14). If this was the course of action that the party chose, however, it would come with a price.

> A policy, then, resting on such a temper of mind as I have been describing,—viz., a determination to act as if the course of

[79] Frederic Rogers to Miss Rogers (23 November 1850), *Letters of Frederic Lord Blachford*, ed. G.E. Marindin (London: John Murray, 1896), 141.
[80] Ibid., 142.

events itself would, in some way or other, work for Apostolical truth, sooner or later, more or less; to let things alone, to do nothing, to make light of every triumph of the enemy from within or without, to waive the question of ecclesiastical liberty, to remain where you are, and go about your work in your own place, either contented to retard the course of events, or sanguine about an imaginary future,—this is simply to abandon the cause of the movement altogether. It is simply to say that there is no providential destiny or object connected with it at all. (124)

This was cutting rather close to the bone. As it happened, the question of "ecclesiastical liberty" was one that the Anglo-Catholic party would never put to rest: it haunts them still. To aid them at their Providential crossroads, Newman ended his lecture with something like a prayer, a reminder of God's most deep decree.

It is true, my dear brethren, you *may* knowingly abandon altogether what you have once held, or you may profess to hold truths without being faithful to them. Well, then, you are of those who think that the movement has come to an end; if in your conscience you think so—that it was a mere phantom, or deceit, or unreality, or dream, which has taken you in, and from which you have awakened,—I have not a word to say. If, however, as I trust is the case, God has not in vain unrolled the pages of antiquity before your eyes, but has stamped them upon your hearts; if He has put into your minds the perception of the truth which, once given, can scarcely be lost, once possessed, will ever be recognized; if you have by His grace been favoured in any measure with the supernatural gift of faith, then, my brethren, I think too well of you, I hope too much of you, to fancy that you can be untrue to convictions so special and so commanding. No; you are under a destiny, the destiny of truth —truth is your master, not you the master of truth—you must go whither it leads. (124)

Lecture V: The Providential Course of the Movement of 1833 not in the Direction of a Party in the National Church
The fifth lecture begins with another moving autobiographical passage, proof that Newman was not preaching anything to his Anglo-Catholic friends that he had not practiced himself.

It is not an easy thing to prove to men that their duty lies just in the reverse direction to that in which they have hitherto placed it; that all they have hitherto learned and taught, that all their past labours, hopes, and successes, that their boyhood, youth, and manhood, that their position, their connections, and their influence, are, in a certain sense, to go for nothing; and that life is to begin with them anew. It is not an easy thing to attain to the conviction, that, with the Apostle, their greatest gain must be counted loss; and that their glory and their peace must be found in what will make them for a while the wonder and the scorn of the world. (126)

No one but a convert who had suffered the sacrifices that Newman had suffered as a result of his conversion could speak of such things with such ungainsayable authority.

Newman then proceeds to argue that if the Anglo-Catholic party looked to the Prayer Book as the justification of their position, they were implicitly acknowledging the argument of authority over private judgment. The Prayer Book may not be "perfect," but "it had a sort of practical Perfection, and though it was not unerring, it was a sure and sufficient safeguard against error" (134). For Newman,

the Prayer Book, then, according to the first agents in the movement, was the arbiter, and limit, and working rule of the ten thousand varying private judgments of which the community was made up, which could not all be satisfied, which could not all be right, which were, every one of them, less likely to be right than it. It was the immediate instrument by means of which they professed to make their way, the fulcrum by which they were to hoist up the Establishment, and set it down securely on the basis of Apostolical Truth. And thus it was accepted by the party, not only as essentially and substantially true, but also as eminently expedient and necessary for the time. (135)

And to show how he was not unaware of the threat of this capitulation to expedience, even when he was an Anglo-Catholic himself, Newman quoted from one of his own Tractarian writings, "How to Accomplish It" (1836), a dialogue between an Anglo-Catholic content to work within the Establishment and one who is "Romanizing." "Hildebrand found the Church provided with certain existing means of power; he vindicated them, and was rewarded with the success which attends, not on truth as such, but on this prudence and tact in conduct," the advocate of the Anglo-Catholics remaining within the Establishment argues. "St. Paul observed the same rule, whether in preaching at Athens or persuading his countrymen. It was the gracious condescension of our Lord Himself, not to substitute Christianity for Judaism by any violent revolution, but to develop Judaism into Christianity, as the Jews might bear it" (136–7). Newman's response to this specious thinking is that it is all very well "if expedience was the end," but it "required some intellectual basis," and this was what threw the Anglo-Catholics on the writings of the divines of the Anglican Church, the only problem being that the Anglo-Catholics had no rule to determine which divines were authoritative and which were not. Again, private judgment ruled where authority was absent.

But here, Newman cast the issue of private judgment in an autobiographical light—one that was hardly flattering to himself. When he was an Anglo-Catholic, he recalled, he could not help being struck by the unanimity with which the Anglican divines spoke against the Church of Rome.[81] And his response to this bias is revelatory. The autobiographical passage in which this appears is long, but it bears quoting because it shows that if Newman was critical of his Anglo-Catholic friends, he was never uncritical of himself when he was one of their band. Indeed, it is precisely his transparency

[81] That the essential doctrine of Anglicanism, set forth by the Caroline divines, was "repudiation of the Catholic Church" was clearly recognized by Hilaire Belloc, who had occasion to observe that: "If it be true that Anglicanism is the expression of English patriotism in religion, Oxford is, as I have called it, the very quintessence of Anglicanism: not of doctrines, for there are no doctrines, save repudiation of the Catholic Church. A man may deny the Resurrection, the Incarnation or what he will, so that he remain national and deny the Universal Church. Oxford means the very heart of this national thing, the Church of England." Belloc quoted in Edward Short, *Newman and His Family* (London: Bloomsbury, 2013), 270.

about his own culpability that gives his criticism of theirs its cogency, especially as this relates to the crucial issue of private judgment.

In a Retractation, then, which he [Newman] published in the year 1843, of some strong statements which he had made against the Catholic Church, these words occur: - "If you ask me how an individual could venture, *not simply to hold but to publish* such views of a communion so ancient, so wide-spreading, so fruitful in Saints, I answer, that I said to myself, *I am not speaking my own words*, I am but following almost a *consensus* of the divines of my Church. They have ever used the strongest language against Rome, even the most able and learned of them. I wish to throw myself into their system. While I say what they say, I am safe. Such views, too, are necessary for our position." Now, this passage has been taken to mean, that the writer spoke from expediency what he did not believe; but this is false in fact, and inaccurate in criticism. He spoke what he felt, what he thought, what at the time he held, and nothing but what he held with an internal assent; but still, though he internally thought it, he would not have dared to say it—he would have shrunk, as well he might, from standing up, *on his own private judgment*, an accuser against the great Roman communion, and unless in doing so he felt he had been doing simply what his own Church *required* of him, and what was *necessary* for his Church's cause, and what all his Church's divines had ever done before him. This being the case, he "could venture, not simply to *hold* but to *publish*;" he was not "speaking his own *words*," though he *was* expressing his own *thoughts*; and, as using those words, he was "throwing himself into," he was sheltering himself behind "a system" received by his Church, as well as by himself. He felt "safe," because he spoke after, and according to its teaching and its teachers. It had, indeed, been one sin that he had thought ill of the Catholic Church; it had been another and greater, that he had uttered what he thought; and there was just this alleviation of his second sin, that he had not said it wantonly, and that he had said what others had said before him. There is nothing difficult or unnatural, surely, in this state of mind; but it is not wonderful that to the mass of Protestants it was incomprehensible that any one should shrink from the display of that private judgment in which they themselves so luxuriated, that any one should think of clearing himself from what in their eyes was simply a virtue, or should be shocked at having the credit given him of making use of a special privilege. (141–2)

Having shared with his readers the character of his own peculiar reliance on the authority of the Anglican divines, Newman then asks on what Anglo-Catholics based their trust in this authority, and, of course, he answers that they based this authority on the authority of the Church Fathers, though, naturally, as Newman dryly remarks, they were "not very solicitous (if I dare speak for others) how far the Fathers seemed to tell for the Church of Rome." Such delicious irony did not sit well with Aubrey de Vere. "The only part of [Newman's] mind which I do not like," the poet confessed, "is that which comes out of his vein of irony."[82] If Newman's "vein of irony" were removed from the lectures, or, indeed, his work as a whole, a good deal of its rhetorical zest, not to mention its wisdom, would be removed. Newman's use of irony is always exquisite, but it is especially masterly in *Anglican Difficulties*. At times, laugh-aloud funny and, at others, unanswerably biting, it is always inseparable from the *caritas* that animates his appeals to his old friends. Again, the point of Newman's irony is always to laugh his friends out of their false positions, to make them see the absurdity of such falsity. His little disquisition on the Anglo-Catholic view of the Fathers is a case in point. "On the whole," Newman says, the Anglo-Catholics took it into their heads to believe that the Fathers "did not tell materially" for the Church of Rome.

---

[82] Ward, *Memoir of Aubrey de Vere*, 182. In his essay on the Non-Jurors, the essayist Augustine Birrell observed: "To anyone blessed with an ironical humour the troublesome history of the Church of England since the Reformation cannot fail to be an endless source of delight." A. Birrell, "The Non-Jurors," *In the Name of the Bodleian* (New York: Charles Scribner's Sons, 1905), 97. In his entry on Birrell in the *Dictionary of National Biography*, the historian R.C.K. Ensor notes that "during his Liverpool years [Birrell] absorbed a vast quantity of sixteenth- and seventeenth-century literature, including the *arcana* of long-forgotten divinity and social history."

But it was no matter … [that the Fathers] partially seemed to do so; for their great and deadly foe, their scorn, and their laughing-stock, was that imbecile, inconsistent thing called Protestantism; and there could not be a more thorough refutation of its foundation and superstructure than was to be found in the volumes of the Fathers. There was no mistaking that the principles professed, and doctrines taught by those holy men, were utterly anti-Protestant; and, being satisfied of this, which was their principal consideration, it did not occur to them accurately to determine the range and bounds of the teaching of the early Church, or to reflect that, perhaps, they had as yet a clearer view of what it did not sanction, than, of what it did. (145)

And this, of course, had interesting consequences for the exercise of private judgment, precisely the thing of which the Anglo-Catholics most disapproved.

They saw, then, that there simply was no opportunity at all for private judgment, if one wished to exercise it ever so much, as regards the question of the anti- Protestantism of the Fathers; it was a patent fact, open to all, written on the face of their works, that they were anti-Protestant; you might defer to them, you might reject them, but you could as little deny that they were essentially anti-Protestant, as you could deny that "the Romanists" were anti-Protestants. It was a matter of fact, a matter of sense, which Protestants themselves admitted or rather maintained; and here, in this public and undeniable fact, we have arrived at what the movement considered the ultimate resolution of its faith. (145–46)

Consequently, for Newman, "the Oxford Movement claimed to represent the theological and ecclesiastical teaching of the Fathers; and the Fathers, when interrogated, did but pronounce them to be the offspring of eclecticism, and the exponent of a State Church." (426) Newman's use of the word "eclecticism" here reminds one of a telltale passage from *Lectures on the Prophetical Office* (1837), in which, even as an Anglo-Catholic, he could not conceal his uneasiness with an Anglo-Catholicism that abounded in altogether unavoidable eclecticism.

When men choose or reject from religious systems what they please, they furnish melancholy evidence of their want of earnestness; and when they put themselves above existing systems, as if these were suited only to the multitude or to bigoted partisans, they are supercilious and proud; and when they think they may create what they are to worship, their devotion cannot possess any high degree of reverence and godly fear. Surely, then, it may be said, such theorizing on religious subjects is nothing else than an indulgence in that undue use of reason, which was so pointedly condemned in the commencement of these remarks.

I would not willingly under-value the force of this representation. It might be said, however, in reply, that at the worst the evil specified would cease in proportion as we were able to bring into practical shape that system which is wanting. But after all the true answer to the objection is simply this, that though Anglo-Catholicism is not practically reduced to system in its fulness, it does exist, in all its parts, in the writings of our divines, and in good measure is in actual operation, though with varying degrees of consistency and completeness in different places. There is no room for eclecticism in any elementary matter. No member of the English Church allows himself to build on any doctrine different from that found in our book of Common Prayer. That formulary contains the elements of our theology; and herein lies the practical exercise of our faith, which all true religion exacts. We surrender ourselves in obedience to it: we act upon it: we obey it even in points of detail where there is room for diversity of opinion. The Thirty-nine Articles furnish a second trial of our humility and self-restraint. Again, we never forget that, reserving our fidelity to the Creed, we are bound to defer to Episcopal authority.[83]

This rather let the cat out of the bag, especially when the bishops, as in the case of the Gorham ruling, could not be bothered with upholding the Creed.

In the fifth lecture, having established the self-evident unsoundness of the Tractarian citadel, Newman proceeds to address his friends with the blunt, stinging directness that was one of the hallmarks of his English style.

---

[83] *VM*, i, 22–3.

My brethren, when it was at length plain that primitive Christianity ignored the National Church, and that the National Church cared little for primitive Christianity, or for those who appealed to it as her foundation; when Bishops spoke against them, and Bishops' courts sentenced them, and Universities degraded them, and the people rose against them, from that day their "occupation was gone." Their initial principle, their basis, external authority, was cut from under them; they had "set their fortunes on a cast;" they had lost; henceforward they had nothing left for them but to shut up their school, and retire into the country. Nothing else was left for them, unless, indeed, they took up some other theory, unless they changed their ground, unless they ceased to be what they were, and became what they were not; unless they belied their own principles, and strangely forgot their own luminous and most keen convictions; unless they vindicated the right of private judgment, took up some fancy-religion, retailed the Fathers, and jobbed theology. They had but a choice between doing nothing at all, and looking out for truth and peace elsewhere. (152–3)

Apropos Newman's celebrated style, Gerard Manley Hopkins once remarked in one of his letters:

The beauty, the eloquence, of good prose cannot come wholly from the thought. With Burke it does and varies with the thought; when therefore the thought is sublime so does the style appear to be. But in fact Burke had no style properly so called: his style was colourlessly to transmit his thought. Still he was an orator in form and followed the common oratorical tradition, so that his writing has the strain of address I speak of above. But Newman does not follow the common tradition—of writing. His tradition is that of cultured, the most highly educated, conversation; it is the flower of the best Oxford life. Perhaps this gives it a charm of unaffected and personal sincerity that nothing else could. Still he shirks the technic of written prose and shuns the tradition of written English. He seems to be thinking "Gibbon is the last great master of traditional English prose; he is its perfection: I do not propose to emulate him; I begin all over again from the language of conversation, of common life."[84]

This is not entirely true. Newman's prose is great because his thought was great: the magnificence of his thought required that his prose be equally magnificent to do it justice. Newman also wrote a good deal in the formal tradition of Johnson and Gibbon. In fact, as a young man, he set himself to school to both.[85] Conversely, Johnson, in *The Lives of the Poets* (1783) and Gibbon in his *Autobiography* (1796) could deviate from this tradition themselves to write a more relaxed, less studied, more unbuttoned English. But Hopkins is right that Newman tuned the "language of conversation, of common life" to an entirely new rhetorical force, shot through with "unaffected and personal sincerity," and the foregoing passage exemplifies this.

Newman's more colloquial prose also accounts for the witty incisiveness of the lectures. Admitting that if he were still an Anglo-Catholic, he, too, might be prone to "take a line of my own," he nevertheless makes a point of saying that he would not broadcast it. Why? "I never could get myself to say, 'Listen to me, for I have something great to tell you, which no one else knows, but of which there is no manner of doubt.' I should be kept from such extravagance from an intense sense of the intellectual absurdity ... such a claim would involve.... I should feel I was simply making a fool of myself" (154–5). One might be inclined to say that Newman here was simply mocking his friends for the sake of mockery. But there is an important point to the mockery. Gibbon had chosen to base his history of the early Church on the assumption that history could treat only the externals of the rise of Christianity; and, therefore, he treated Christianity, in effect, as a man-made phenomenon. All of the nineteenth-century rationalists with whose work Newman took issue

---

[84] Hopkins quoted in *The Collected Works of Gerard Manley Hopkins, Volume II: Correspondence 1882–1889*, ed. R. K. R. Thornton and Catherine Phillips (Oxford: Oxford University Press, 2013), 898–9.
[85] *LD*, i, 85.

followed suit. For them, to treat of Christianity in terms of its supernatural faith would be to credit credulity and fanaticism.[86] Newman is careful to show his Anglo-Catholic friends that their refusal to meet the obligations of "ecclesiastical liberty" and to base their faith on genuine authority rather than on expedient private judgment put them in a like Socinian bind. "I can quite enter into the sentiment with which members of the liberal and infidel school investigate the history and the documents of the early Church," he writes.

> They profess a view of Christianity, truer than the world has ever had; nor, on the assumption of their principles, is there anything shocking to good sense in this profession. They look upon the Christian Religion as something simply human; and there is no reason at all why a phenomenon of that kind should not be better understood, in its origin and nature, as years proceed. It is, indeed, an intolerable paradox to assert, that a revelation, given from God to man, should lie unknown or mistaken for eighteen centuries, and now at length should be suddenly deciphered by individuals; but it is quite intelligible to assert, and plausible to argue, that a human fact should be more philosophically explained than it was eighteen hundred years ago, and more exactly ascertained than it was a thousand. (155–6)

For Newman, were the Anglo-Catholics to continue to make their profession along these Socinian lines, and reject the warrant of authority, they would have no alternative but to reconcile themselves to the consequences not only of their inconsistency but of their incoherence. And, here, again, Newman's more colloquial style serves him well.

> In some points you prefer Rome, in others Greece, in others England, in others Scotland; and of that preference your own private judgment is the ultimate sanction. What am I to say in answer to conduct so preposterous? Say you go by any authority

---

[86] See "Newman, Gibbon and God's Particular Providence," in Edward Short, *Newman and History* (Leominster: Gracewing, 2017), 3–80.

whatever, and I shall know where to find you, and I shall respect you. Swear by any school of Religion, old or modern, by Ronge's Church, or the Evangelical Alliance, nay, by yourselves, and I shall know what you mean, and will listen to you. But do not come to me with the latest fashion of opinion which the world has seen, and protest to me that it is the oldest. Do not come to me at this time of day with views palpably new, isolated, original, *sui generis*, warranted old neither by Christian nor unbeliever, and challenge me to answer what I really have not the patience to read. Life is not long enough for such trifles. Go elsewhere, not to me, if you wish to make a proselyte. (160–1)

Lecture VI: The Providential Course of the Movement of 1833 not in the Direction of a Branch Church

In opening up his sixth lecture, Newman continues in the ironic vein that he had pursued in the previous lecture. "There are persons who may think that the line of thought which I pursued in my last two Lectures had somewhat of a secular and political cast, and was deficient in that simplicity which becomes an inquiry after religious truth," he writes. "We are inquiring, you may say, whether the National Church is in possession of the Sacraments, whether we can obtain the grace of Christ, necessary for our salvation.... On this great question depends our leaving its communion or not" (164). Of course, this is a great question, and Newman endeavors to treat it with suitable gravity. "Now, to persons in this cruel strife of thought, I offer the consideration on which I have been dwelling, as a sort of diversion to their harassed minds," he assures his audience. "You wish to know whether the Establishment is what you began by assuming it to be—the grace-giving Church of God. If it be, you and your principles will surely find your position there and your home. When you proclaim it to be Apostolical, it will smile on you; when you kneel down and ask its blessing, it will stretch its hands over you; when you would strike at heresy, it will arm you for the fight.... When you proclaim its relationship to Rome and Greece, it will ... embrace you as its own dear children; you will sink happily into its arms, you will repose upon its breast, you will recognise your mother, and be at peace" (166). The unsettlement that characterized so much Anglicanism throughout the Victorian period being what it was, Newman was certainly right: it would be a boon to the Anglo-Catholics if they could be assured that the Establishment was, indeed, "Apostolical." But what if

> the more those great principles which you have imbibed from St. Athanasius and St. Augustine, and which have become the life and the form of your moral and intellectual being, vegetate and expand within you, the more awkward and unnatural you find your position in the Establishment, and the more difficult its explanation; if there is no lying, or standing, or sitting, or kneeling, or stooping there, in any possible attitude; if, as in the tyrant's cage, when you would rest your head, your legs are forced out between the Articles, and when you would relieve your back, your head strikes against the Prayer Book; when, place yourselves as you will, on the right side or the left, and try to keep as still as you can, your flesh is ever being punctured and probed by the stings of Bishops, laity, and nine-tenths of the Clergy huzzing about you; is it not as plain as day that the Establishment is not your place, since it is no place for your principles? (166–7)

This is of a piece with Newman's description of the grief Anglo-Catholics suffered when set upon by Establishment bishops for their "mild misdemeanours."

> Soon the living rulers of the Establishment began to move.... They fearlessly handselled their Apostolic weapons upon the Apostolical party. One after another, in long succession, they took up their song and their parable against it. It was a solemn war-dance, which they executed round victims, who by their very principles were bound hand and foot, and could only eye with disgust and perplexity this most unaccountable movement, on the part of their "holy Fathers, the representatives of the Apostles, and the Angels of the Churches." It was the beginning of the end. (151–2)

In tackling the theme of the so-called branch theory of the Church, beloved of Anglo-Catholics in his own time and in ours, Newman is at once witty and remorseless. "While you are looking about for a new Communion, have nothing to do with a 'Branch Church,'" he writes with tongue-in-cheek sententiousness. "You have had enough experience of branch churches already, and you know very well what they are. Depend upon it, such as is one, such is another. They may differ in accidents certainly; but, after all, a branch is a branch, and no branch is a tree" (169). Then, again, he tells his auditors: "a Branch Church ... you will see at once ... is virtually synonymous with a National; for though it may be in fact and at present but one out of many communions in a nation, it is intended, by its very mission ... to spread through the nation; nor has it done its duty till it has so spread, for it must be supposed to have the promise of success.... On the other hand, it cannot extravagate beyond the nation, for the very principle of demarcation between Branch and Branch is the distinction of Nation or State; to the Nation, then, or State it is limited, and beyond the Nation's boundaries it cannot properly pass" (171). Lest his auditors have somehow not taken his point, Newman drives it home anew: "Recollect, then, that a Branch Church is a National Church, and the reason why I warn you against getting your orders from such a Church, or joining such a Church, as, for instance, the Greek, the Russian, or some Monophysite Church, is that you are in a National Church already, and that a National Church ever will be and must be what you have found your own to be, an Erastian body" (172).

For Newman to expend so much time on such self-evident truths might seem surprising or even tedious, especially to the properly catechized; but there was a point to his reiterations. Newman wished to begin to draw a very fundamental line between the Catholic Church and the World, and the "branch theory" was the perfect place for him to start. "You are going to start afresh," he told his Anglo-Catholic friends. "Well, then, I assert, that if you do not get beyond the idea of Nationalism in this your new beginning, you are just where you were. Erastianism, the fruitful mother of all heresies, will be your first and your last. You will have left Erastianism to take Erastianism up again,—that heresy which is the very badge of Anglicanism, and the abomination of that theological movement from which you spring."

This was perhaps unwarrantably blunt. Telling anyone that his religion is bogus is hardly endearing. Yet Newman was a servant of Truth, and he did not scruple to speak the Truth simply because some might find it bad form. He also recognized that, for Anglicans, acknowledging that their Anglicanism was bogus was the difficulty of difficulties. After all, it had been extremely difficult for Newman himself. He spent six long torturous years coming to grips with the inescapable untenability of his own Anglicanism. For Newman, however, the problem was not merely an Anglican problem. Erastianism had been with the Catholic Church from her very inception. In fact, Christ and His Church introduced the problem into the world, as the historian in Newman saw so clearly:

> It can scarcely be said to have existed before; for, if not altogether in Judaism, yet certainly in the heathen polities, the care of public worship, of morals, of education, was mainly committed, as well as secular matters, to the civil magistrate. There was once no independent jurisdiction in religion; but, when our Lord came, it was with the express object of introducing a new kingdom, distinct and different from the kingdoms of the world, and He was sought after by Herod, and condemned by Pilate, on the very apprehension that His claims to royalty were inconsistent with their prerogatives. Such was the Church when first introduced into the world, and her subsequent history has been after the pattern of her commencement; the State has ever been jealous of her, and has persecuted her from without and bribed her from within. (174–5)

This battle between Christ's Church and the World had been raging for "the whole eighteen centuries of Christian history," and Newman supplies a plethora of examples to substantiate its embattled course, all of which are identified in the notes:

For even in the ante-Nicene period, the heretic Patriarch of Antioch was protected by the local sovereign against the Catholics, and was dispossessed by the authority and influence with the Imperial Government of the See of Rome. And since that time, again and again would the civil power, humanly speaking, have taken captive and corrupted each portion of Christendom in turn, but for its union with the rest, and the noble championship of the Supreme Pontiff. Our ears ring with the oft-told tale, how the temporal sovereign persecuted, or attempted, or gained, the local Episcopate, and how the many or the few faithful fell back on Rome. So was it with the Arians in the East and St. Athanasius; so with the Byzantine Empress and St. Chrysostom; so with the Vandal Hunneric and the Africans; so with the 130 Monophysite Bishops at Ephesus and St. Flavian; so was it in the instance of the 500 Bishops, who, by the influence of Basilicus, signed a declaration against the Tome of St. Leo; so in the instance of the Henoticon of Zeno; and so in the controversies both of the Monothelites and of the Iconoclasts. (185)

Newman concludes the sixth lecture by quoting from the writings of the bishop of Gloucester, William Warburton. In thus drawing on the work of the most celebrated defender of Erastianism—work written with no satirical intent at all—Newman advances his own satirical purposes to splendid effect. In one passage, he has the bishop declaring the first of all truths of Erastian Christianity, namely: "God so disposed things, that the means of attaining the happiness of one state [of existence] should not cross or obstruct the means of attaining the happiness of the other. From whence we must conclude, that where the supposed means of each—viz., opinions and civil peace do clash, there one of them is not the true means of happiness. But the means of attaining the happiness peculiar to that state in which the man at present exists, being perfectly and infallibly known by man, and the means of the happiness of his future existence, as far as relates to the discovery of truth, but very imperfectly known by him, it necessarily follows that, wherever opinions clash with civil peace, those opinions are no means of future happiness, or, in other words, are either no truths, or truths of no importance" (192–3). Of course, that many Anglo-Catholics and their defenders fail to see the unintended satire inherent in such admissions only makes it funnier. Newman's gloss on the passage epitomizes the lectures' salutary mockery: "Behold the principle of the reasonings of the Committee of Privy Council, and the philosophy of the Premier's satisfaction thereupon! Baptismal regeneration is determined to be true or not true, not by the text of Scripture, the testimony of the Fathers, the tradition of the Church, nay, not by Prayer Book, Articles, Jewell, Usher, Carleton, or Bullinger, but by its tendency to minister to the peace and repose of the community, to the convenience and comfort of Downing Street, Lambeth, and Exeter Hall" (193).

Lecture VII: The Providential Course of the Movement of 1833 not in the Direction of a Sect
Returning to the theme of Erastianism in Lecture VII, Newman asks a simple question: "For what conceivable reason should two societies be set up to do the work of one?" (202). Here, again, the appeal he makes is to common sense, not to the problematizing of dons. Bishop Warburton had defended an Erastian alliance in which Church and State do "one and the same thing: the Church preaches truth, the State pursues expediency; but Christian truth is identical with political expediency" (203). In this comical logic, Newman saw another more fundamental logic: "Either no Church has been set up in the world, or it is not set up for no thing; it must have a mission and a message of its own. Everything is defined, or made specific by its object: if the duties of the Church, its functions, its teaching, its working, be not specially distinct from those of the State, why, it will be impossible to resist the conclusion, that it was meant to be amalgamated with the State, to join on to it, to be a part of it, to be subordinate to it. We do not form two guilds for the same trade. Either assign to the Church its own craft, or do not ask that it should be chartered. Its object is its claim" (202).

He then proceeds to quote from his old Oriel colleague Richard Whately, whose textbook on logic was read by generations of Oxford undergraduates. In an anonymous tract, Whately took to task what he saw as the Erastianism of the Anglican Church: "It was Satan who first proposed an alliance between the Christian Church and the State by offering temporal advantages in exchange for [the State's] giving up some of the 'things that be God's'—and which we ought 'render unto God—for not 'serving Him only,' whom only we ought to serve" (209). Newman was fine with this, as far as it went; but he was adamant that it did not go far enough.

> If the Church be a kingdom, or government, not of this world, I do trust you have provided for her a message, a function, not of this world, something distinct, something special, something which the world cannot do, which "eye hath not seen, nor ear heard, nor heart of man conceived." It is not enough to give her morality to preach about; why a heaven-appointed Society for that? With the Bible in his hands, if that be all, I do not see why one man, if properly educated, should not preach morality as well as another, without any disturbance of the rights of the magistrate or the order of civil society. (209)

Again, Newman insists, if the Church is not simply to be a department of the State, she must have a mission separate from the State — something that she, and she alone, can do.

With that distinct mission in mind, Newman says: "It is sometimes said in bitterness that the Church's work is priestcraft. I have already accepted the word; it is a craft, a craft in the same sense that goldsmiths' work, or architecture, or legal science is a craft; it must have its teaching, its intellectual and moral habits, its long experience, its precedents, its traditions; nay, it must have all these in a much higher sense than crafts of this world, if it is to claim to come from above." But this sense of the Church's possessing a higher, heavenly "craft" is precisely what is absent from Whately's anti-Erastianism, and this leads Newman to wonder whether Church and State in England might be better off simply doing the State's work alone. It is true that some of the English might wish the Church to have some separate work to do.

> But in proportion as this author fails in this just anticipation, and disappoints the common sense of mankind, if he has nothing better to tell us than that one man's opinion is as good as another's; that Fathers and Schoolmen, and the greater number of Anglican divines, are puzzled-headed or dishonest; that heretics have at least this good about them, that they are in earnest, and do not take doctrines for granted; that religion is simple, and theologians have made it hard; that controversy is on the whole a logomachy; that we must worship in spirit and in truth; that we ought to love truth; that few people love truth for its own sake; that we ought to be candid and dispassionate, to avoid extremes, to eschew party spirit, to take a rational satisfaction in contemplating the works of nature, and not to speculate about "secret things;" that our Lord came to teach us all this, and to gain us immortality by His death, and the promise of spiritual assistance, and that this is pretty nearly the whole of theology; and that at least all is in the Bible, where every one may read it for himself—(and I see no evidence whatever of his going much beyond this round of teaching)—then, I say, if the work and mission of Christianity be so level in its exercise to the capacities of the State, surely its ministry also is within the State's jurisdiction. (211–12)

If this was payback for Whately's taking against Newman while they were at Oriel together, it was witty payback. Its satirizing of the platitudinous is reminiscent of one of Johnson's *Idler* essays, with which Newman was doubtless familiar: "He only can please long," Johnson wrote, "who by tempering the acid of satire with the sugar of civility, and allaying the heat of wit with the frigidity of humble chat, can make the true punch of conversation: and as that punch can be drank in the greatest quantity which has the largest proportion of water, so that companion will be oftenest welcome, whose talk flows out with inoffensive copiousness and unenvied insipidity."[87]

Newman's attack on the unreality of Whately's anti-Erastianism recalls the theme of self-deception that often preoccupied Newman in his sermons.[88] Whately parades what he imagines his criticism of the Establishment's Erastianism in a show of independence and fearlessness; whereas, in fact, the future archbishop of Dublin was only proving the inescapability of Erastianism in a society that had lost any sense of genuine Christianity. The Church is a craft in "the same sense that goldsmiths' work, or architecture, or legal science is a craft," because of her dogma and sacraments, because of the Mass.

> Herein is the strength of the Church; herein she differs from all Protestant mockeries of her. She professes to be built upon facts, not opinions; on objective truths, not on variable sentiments; on immemorial testimony, not on private judgment; on convictions or perceptions, not on conclusions. None else but she can make this profession. She makes high claims against the temporal power, but she has that within her which justifies her. She merely acts out what she says she is. She does no more than she reasonably should do. If God has given her a specific work, no wonder she is not under the superintendence of the civil magistrate in doing it. If her Clergy be Priests, if they can forgive sins, and bring the Son of God upon her altars, it is obvious they cannot, considered as such, hold of the State. If they were not Priests, the sooner they were put under a minister of public instruction, and the Episcopate abolished, the better. But she has not disturbed the world for nothing. (216–17)

---

[87] Samuel Johnson, "*The Idler*: No. 34. Saturday, 9 December 1758," in *The Yale Edition of the Works of Samuel Johnson, Volume II, The Idler and The Adventurer*, ed. W.J. Bate, John M. Bullitt, and L.F. Powell (New Haven: Yale University Press, 1963), 108.

[88] For an excellent essay on how the homilist in Newman saw the "allure of religion" bamboozling its devotees, see Eric Griffith, "Newman: The Foolishness of Preaching," in *Newman after a Hundred Years*, ed. Alan Hill and Ian Ker (Oxford: Oxford University Press, 1990), 64.

Here, Newman is not simply contrasting the Church—the real Church—with the temporal power, but the real Church with the would-be Church, the "'mimic Catholicism" of the Anglo-Catholics, and the polemicist in him gives no quarter. Some will always find such taunting rhetoric distasteful, but it is of the essence of the charge Newman set himself in the lectures. For Newman, the real Church commands the allegiance of his Anglo-Catholic friends precisely because she is real.

> Her precision and peremptoriness, all that is laid to her charge as intolerance and exclusiveness … her claim to reveal the unknown and to communicate the invisible, is, in the eye of reason (so far from being an objection to her coming from above) the very tenure of her high mission.... She cannot be conceived without her message and her gifts. She is the organ and oracle, and nothing else, of a supernatural doctrine, which is independent of individuals, given to her once for all, coming down from the first ages, and so deeply and intimately embossomed in her, that it cannot be clean torn out of her, even if you should try; which gradually and majestically comes forth into dogmatic shape, as time goes on, and need requires, still by no private judgment, but at the will of its Giver, and by the infallible elaboration of the whole body;—and which is simply necessary for the salvation of every one of us. It is not a philosophy, or literature, cognisable and attainable at once by those who cast their eyes that way; but it is a sacred deposit and tradition, a mystery or secret, as Scripture calls it, sufficient to arrest and occupy the whole intellect, and unlike anything else. (217–18)

In reading this resplendent prose from their erstwhile leader, the Anglo-Catholics might have felt as Newman described himself feeling when he found himself at the mercy of the Anglican bishops' "war-dance" during the Tract 90 hysteria—"bound hand and foot" and looking on at his tormentors "with disgust and perplexity"—but, for all of his derision and pitilessness, Newman genuinely loved his old friends. After all, he was entering into their predicament. He had chosen to regard their predicament with the utmost seriousness. He was showing them that he cared for their spiritual, not merely their mundane, well-being. "The *onus probandi* will be on your side then," he insisted. "Now you are content to be negative and fragmentary in doctrine; you aim at nothing higher than smart articles in newspapers and magazines, at clever hits, spirited attacks, raillery, satire, skirmishing on posts of your own selecting; fastening on weak points, or what you think so, in Dissenters or Catholics; inventing ingenious retorts, evading dangerous questions; parading this or that isolated doctrine as essential, and praising this or that Catholic practice or Catholic saint, to make up for abuse, and to show your impartiality; and taking all along a high, eclectic, patronising, indifferent tone; this has been for some time past your line, and it will not suffice; it excites no respect, it creates no confidence, it inspires no hope" (226–7).

Lecture VIII: The Social State of Catholic Countries no Prejudice to the Sanctity of the Church
If Newman spent the first seven lectures parrying the objections Anglo-Catholics had to leaving the Anglican Church, he spends the final five parrying those they had to joining the Catholic Church, and one of the first objections he takes up is to the perceived degeneracy of Catholic countries, a common complaint of the Victorian English, who, preening themselves on what they fancied their Protestant enterprise and uprightness, looked down their noses at poor Catholic Ireland, France, Belgium, Spain, and Italy. Catholics in the eyes of the Victorians were the world's "deplorables," and Newman nicely described how they were perceived by his Podsnappian countrymen.

> Those countries, you say, which have retained Catholicism, are notoriously behind the age; they have not kept up with the march of civilization; they are ignorant, and, in a measure, barbarous; they have the faults of barbarians; they have no self-command; they can not be trusted. They must be treated as slaves, or they rebel; they emerge out of their superstitions in order to turn infidels. They cannot combine and coalesce in social

institutions; they want the very faculty of citizenship. The sword, not the law, is their ruler. They are spectacles of idleness, slovenliness, want of spirit, disorder, dirt, and dishonesty. There must, then, be something in their religion to account for this; it keeps them children, and then, being children, they keep to it. No man in his senses, certainly no English gentleman, would abandon the high station which his country both occupies and bestows on him in the eyes of man, to make himself the co-religionist of such slaves, and the creature of such a Creed. (230)

In response, Newman got at the heart of the true nature of this radical bias, which cast the suppositious "gifts and graces" they claimed to have received from their Anglo-Catholic faith in an interesting light:

I propose to make a suggestion in answer to this objection; and, in making it, I shall consider you, my brethren, not as unbelievers, who are careless whether this objection strikes at Christianity or no; nor as Protestants proper, who have no concern about so expressing themselves, as to compromise the first centuries of the Church; but as those who feel that the Catholic Church was in the beginning founded by our Lord and His Apostles; again, that the Establishment is not the Catholic Church; that nothing but the Church of Rome can be; that, if the Church of Rome is not, then the Catholic Church is not to be found in this age, or in this part of the world; for this is what I have been proving in my preceding Lectures. What, then, you are saying comes, in fact, to this: We would rather deny our initial principles, than accept such a development of them as the communion of Rome, viewed as it is; we would rather believe Erastianism, and all its train of consequences, to be from God, than the religion of such countries as France and Belgium Spain and Italy. This is what you must mean to say, and nothing short of it. (230–1)

This was part of the response that Newman wished to make to his Anglo-Catholic friends. But he also wished to speak to them of what the Roman Catholic Church really was, and, here, again, he was obliged to contrast her with the world.

The world believes in the world's ends as the greatest of goods; it wishes society to be governed simply and entirely for the sake of this world. Provided it could gain one little islet in the ocean, one foot upon the coast, if it could cheapen tea by sixpence a pound, or make its flag respected among the Esquimaux or Otaheitans, at the cost of a hundred lives and a hundred souls, it would think it a very good bargain. What does it know of hell? it disbelieves it; it spits upon, it abominates, it curses its very name and notion. Next, as to the devil, it does not believe in him either. We next come to the flesh, and it is "free to confess" that it does not think there is any great harm in following the instincts of that nature which, perhaps it goes on to say, God has given. How could it be otherwise? who ever heard of the world fighting against the flesh and the devil? Well, then, what is its notion of evil? Evil, says the world, is whatever is an offence to me, whatever obscures my majesty, whatever disturbs my peace. Order, tranquility, popular contentment, plenty, prosperity, advance in arts and sciences, literature, refinement, splendour, this is my millennium, or rather my elysium, my swerga; I acknowledge no whole, no individuality, but my own; the units which compose me are but parts of me; they have no perfection in themselves; no end but in me; in my glory is their bliss, and in the hidings of my countenance they come to nought. (235–6)

No one could attest to these truths better than a refugee of Erastianism like Newman. The historian in him also knew that the State has always sought to dragoon the Church into serving not her own but the State's "majesty:" it is in the nature of her rivalrous, insatiate, fanatical power lust. But the Roman Catholic Church cannot be co-opted by any State: "it moves in a simply opposite direction" (236). Here, Newman was speaking not of any passing Anglican controversy but of the abiding condition of the Church Militant.[89] "The Church,

[89] Cf. "Catholicism makes itself manifest, and is recognized. Outward circumstances or conditions of its presence may change or not; the Pope may be a subject one day, a sovereign another, Primus inter pares in early times, the episcopus episcoporum now; there might be no devotions to the Blessed Virgin formerly, they may be superabundant of late; the Holy Eucharist might be a bare commemoration in the first century, and is a sacrifice in the 19th ... but I say, even supposing there have been changes in doctrine and polity, still the *ethos* of the Catholic Church is what it was

you know," he told his friends, "is in warfare" (233). "It has
… a foe in view; nay, it has a battle-field, to which the world
is blind; its proper battlefield is the heart of the individual,
and its true foe is Satan" (236). In his *Arians of the Fourth
Century*, he was even more explicit: "Since there is a popular
misconception, that Christians, and especially the Clergy, as
such, have no concern in temporal affairs, it is expedient to
take every opportunity of formally denying the position, and
demanding proof of it. In truth, the Church was framed for the
express purpose of interfering, or (as irreligious men will say)
meddling with the world. It is the plain duty of its members,
not only to associate internally, but also to develop that
internal union in an external warfare with the spirit of evil,
whether in Kings' courts or among the mixed multitude; and,
if they can do nothing else, at least they can suffer for the

---

of old time, and whatever and whoever quarrels with Catholicism now,
quarrels virtually, and would have quarrelled, if alive, 1800 years ago, with
the Christianity of Apostles and Evangelists.… When we go on to inquire
what is the ethical character, whether in Catholicity now or in Christianity
in its first age, the first point to observe is that it is on all hands
acknowledged to be of a character in utter variance with the ethical
character of human society at large as we find it at all times. This fact is
recognized, I say, by both sides, by the world and by the Church. As to the
former of the two, its recognition of this antagonism is distinct and
universal. As regards *Catholicism*, it is the great fact of this very day, as
seen in England, France, Germany, Italy, and Spain. On the other hand, we
know that in the *Apostolic* age Christians were called the '*hostes humani
generis*' (as the Quarterly called *Catholics* within this two years), and
warred against them accordingly. This antagonism is quite as decidedly
acknowledged on the side of the Church, which calls society in reprobation
'the world', and places 'the world' in the number of its three enemies, with
the flesh and the devil, and this in her elementary catechisms. In the first
centuries her badge and boast was martyrdom; in the fourth, as soon as she
was established, her war-cry was, 'Athanasius contra mundum': at a later
time her protests took the shape of the Papal theocracy and the dictatus
Hildebrandi. In the recent centuries her opposition to the world is
symbolized in the history of the Jesuits. Speaking then according to that
aspect of history which is presented to the eyes of Europeans, I say the
Catholic Church is emphatically and singularly, in her relation to human
philosophy and statesmanship, as was the Apostolic Church, 'the Church
militant here on earth.'" Newman to John Rickards Mozley (3 December
1875), *LD*, xxvii, 387.

truth, and remind men of it, by inflicting on them the task of persecution"—hardly something in which Erastian clergymen or their chums in the Establishment could take any practical interest.[90] For Newman, these were realities that could not be sidestepped. He was not saying such things to win debating points.

> My dear brethren, do not think I am declaiming in the air or translating the pages of some old worm-eaten homily; as I have already said, I bear my own testimony to what has been brought home to me most closely and vividly as a matter of fact since I have been a Catholic; viz., that that mighty world-wide Church, like her Divine Author, regards, consults for, labours for the individual soul; she looks at the souls for whom Christ died, and who are made over to her; and her one object, for which everything is sacrificed—appearances, reputation, worldly triumph—is to acquit herself well of this most awful responsibility. Her one duty is to bring forward the elect to salvation, and to make them as many as she can to take offences out of their path, to warn them of sin, to rescue them from evil, to convert them, to teach them, to feed them, to protect them, and to perfect them. Oh, most tender loving Mother, ill-judged by the world, which thinks she is, like itself, always minding the main chance; on the contrary, it is her keen view of things spiritual, and her love for the soul, which hampers her in her negotiations and her measures, on this hard cold earth, which is her place of sojourning. (236–7)

It is in the context of this moving testimony to the Church's mission that readers should see the characterization of her mission, to which Charles Kingsley took such indignant exception in his controversy with Newman, especially since it was this that triggered the writing of the *Apologia*. "This, then, is the point I insist upon, in answer to the objection which you have to-day urged against me," Newman wrote.

---

[90] *Ari.*, 257–8.

The Church aims, not at making a show, but at doing a work. She regards this world, and all that is in it, as a mere shadow, as dust and ashes, compared with the value of one single soul. She holds that, unless she can, in her own way, do good to souls, it is no use her doing anything; she holds that it were better for sun and moon to drop from heaven, for the earth to fail, and for all the many millions who are upon it to die of starvation in extremest agony, so far as temporal affliction goes, than that one soul, I will not say, should be lost, but should commit one single venial sin, should tell one wilful untruth, though it harmed no one, or steal one poor farthing without excuse. She considers the action of this world and the action of the soul simply incommensurate, viewed in their respective spheres; she would rather save the soul of one single wild bandit of Calabria, or whining beggar of Palermo, than draw a hundred lines of railroad through the length and breadth of Italy, or carry out a sanitary reform, in its fullest details, in every city of Sicily, except so far as these great national works tended to some spiritual good beyond them. (240)

This was provocative enough, but then, to make sure his readers truly appreciated the contrast he meant to make between the Church and the World, he threw out an even more arresting hypothetical. "Take a mere beggar-woman," he urged his readers, "lazy, ragged, and filthy, and not over-scrupulous of truth — (I do not say she had arrived at perfection) — but if she is chaste, and sober, and cheerful, and goes to her religious duties ... she will, in the eyes of the Church, have a prospect of heaven, which is quite closed and refused to the State's pattern-man, the just, the upright, the generous, the honourable, the conscientious, if he be all this, not from a supernatural power — (I do not determine whether this is likely to be the fact, but I am contrasting views and principles) — not from a supernatural power, but from mere natural virtue. Polished, delicate-minded ladies, with little of temptation around them, and no self-denial to practise, in spite of their refinement and taste, if they be nothing more, are objects of less interest to her, than many a poor outcast who sins, repents, and is with difficulty kept just within the territory of grace" (249–50).

Here, Newman was exemplifying what Flannery O'Connor had in mind when she told her readers that "The novelist with Christian concerns will find in modern life distortions which are repugnant to him, and his problem will be to make these appear as distortions to an audience which is used to seeing them as natural; and he may well be forced to take ever more violent means to get his vision across to this hostile audience. When you can assume that your audience holds the same beliefs you do, you can relax a little and use more normal ways of talking to it; when you have to assume that it does not, then you have to make your vision apparent by shock—to the hard of hearing you shout, and for the almost blind you draw large and startling figures."[91] In Charles Kingsley's response to Newman's "large and startling figures," one can hear the incomprehension of an entire Protestant civilization:

> Indeed, the whole teaching of this lecture and the one following it concerning such matters is, I confess, so utterly beyond my comprehension, that I must ask, in blank astonishment, What does Dr. Newman mean? He assures us so earnestly and indignantly that he is an honest man, believing what he says, that we in return are bound, in honour and humanity, to believe him; but still—What does he mean? ... I must ask again, What does Dr. Newman mean by this astounding passage? What I thought that he meant, when I first read it, some twelve years ago, may be guessed easily enough. I said, This man has no real care for truth. Truth for its own sake is no virtue in his eyes, and he teaches that it need not be. I do not say that now: but this I say, that Dr. Newman, for the sake of exalting the magical powers of his Church, has committed himself unconsciously to a statement which strikes at the root of all morality. If he answer, that such is the doctrine of his Church concerning "natural virtues", as distinguished from "good works performed by God's grace", I can only answer, So much the worse for his Church. The sooner it is civilized off the face of the earth, if this be its teaching, the better for mankind. For as for his theory that it may be a "natural

[91] Flannery O'Connor, "The Fiction Writer and His Country" (1957), in *Mystery and Manners: Occasional Prose*, ed. Sally and Robert Fitzgerald (New York: Farrar, Straus & Giroux, 1969), 33–4.

virtue", I value it as little as I trust every honest Englishman will do. I hold it to be utterly antiscriptural; to border very closely (in theological language) on the Pelagian heresy.[92]

This is comical stuff, but it is emblematic of precisely the sort of ignorance that predictably resulted from England's counterfeit Erastian Church. "The Church aims at realities, the world at decencies," Newman reminded his audience (252). That Kingsley could not fathom the distinction proves how necessary it was. (Only a very oddly catechized Anglican clergyman could have construed Newman's passage as "Pelagian.") Yet here again, Newman's audience was never limited to King William Street; it was never limited to the Anglo-Catholics who had difficulty seeing the appeal of the Catholic Church; it was not limited to Anglicans or Catholics. Everyone everywhere can benefit from Newman's testimony to the Church's saving mission, expressed, as he expresses it, with such moving urgency. "Provided she can do for the soul what is necessary," he wrote of the Church that meant so much to him, "if she can but pull the brands out of the burning, if she can but extract the poisonous root which is the death of the soul, and expel the disease, she is content, though she leaves in it lesser maladies, little as she sympathises with them" (252).[93]

---

[92] *Apo.*, 373.

[93] Cf. "But, in truth, a Catholic theologian has objects in view which men in general little compass; he is not thinking of himself, but of a multitude of souls, sick souls, sinful souls, carried away by sin, full of evil, and he is trying with all his might to rescue them from their miserable state; and, in order to save them from more heinous sins, he tries, to the full extent that his conscience will allow him to go, to shut his eyes to such sins, as are, though sins, yet lighter in character or degree. He knows perfectly well that, if he is as strict as he would wish to be, he shall be able to do nothing at all with the run of men; so he is as indulgent with them as ever he can be. Let it not be for an instant supposed, that I allow of the maxim of doing evil that good may come; but, keeping clear of this, there is a way of winning men from greater sins by winking for the time at the less, or at mere improprieties or faults; and this is the key to the difficulty which Catholic books of moral theology so often cause to the Protestant. They are intended for the Confessor, and Protestants view them as intended for the Preacher." *Apo.*, 248.

The "maladies" left unattended by the Church can be made to seem rather monstrous by a World always interested in wrongfooting the Church. The susceptible young are now enjoined to see the contrast between the Church and the World in terms of what the World calls "social justice." In addition to gratifying the moral vanity of those who wish to appear dedicated to "justice," it is also commended as a means of looking after one's neighbor, though it deprecates alms and only reinforces the power of the irresponsible, bureaucratic, grasping State. Newman, of course, lived long before the phrase "social justice" became popular, but he certainly knew the clamor for the thing itself, and his animadversions on it are worth quoting: "Now, were it to my present purpose to attack the principles and proceedings of the world, of course it would be obvious for me to retort upon the cold, cruel, selfish system, which this supreme worship of comfort, decency, and social order necessarily introduces; to show you how the many are sacrificed to the few, the poor to the wealthy, how an oligarchical monopoly of enjoyment is established far and wide, and the claims of want, and pain, and sorrow, and affliction, and guilt, and misery, are practically forgotten." Here one can see what a model Gladstonian Liberal Newman might have made, if he had only put his mind to it. "But I will not have recourse to the commonplaces of controversy when I am on the defensive," he tells his audience. "All I would say to the world is,— Keep your theories to yourselves, do not inflict them upon the sons of Adam everywhere; do not measure heaven and earth by views which are in a great degree insular, and can never be philosophical and catholic." Instead, Newman, many of whose friends were good, charitable Catholic women,[94] who did the work of charity without any assistance from the State, speaks of a kind of sanctity of which the world can never be too full. "You do your work, perhaps, in a more business-like way, compared with ourselves, but we are immeasurably more tender, and gentle, and angelic than you. We come to

---

[94] See "Newman and the Female Faithful," in Short, *Newman and His Contemporaries*, 177–212.

poor human nature as the Angels of God, and you as policemen.... Shallow philosophers! is this mode of going on so winning and persuasive that we should imitate it?" (252–3).

At the end of the lecture, apropos the Church's often unseen sanctity, Newman suspects that he has left his audience unpersuaded, though he remains adamant that his is the better argument. "You tell me, that the political and civil state of Catholic countries is below that of Protestant: I answer, that, even though you prove the fact, you have to prove something besides, if it is to be an argument for your purpose, viz., that the standard of civil prosperity and political aggrandisement is the truest test of grace and the largest measure of salvation" (259–60). Newman's description of how the World regards public men shows how difficult an argument that would be to make: "The world ... praises public men, if they are useful to itself, but simply ridicules inquiry into their motives ... All public men it considers to be pretty much the same at bottom; but what matter is that ... if they do its work? It offers high pay, and it expects faithful service; but, as to its agents, overseers, men of business, operatives, journeymen, figure-servants, and labourers, what they are personally, what are their principles and aims, what their creed, what their conversation; where they live, how they spend their leisure time, whither they are going, how they die—I am stating a simple matter of fact, I am not here praising or blaming, I am but contrasting,—I say, all questions implying the existence of the soul, are as much beyond the circuit of the world's imagination, as they are intimately and primarily present to the apprehension of the Church." (247-8)

The understanding of the World that informs this and, indeed, all of the lectures of *Anglican Difficulties* is the understanding of it that we encounter in one of Newman's most harrowing sermons, "Mental Sufferings of Our Lord in His Passion," which he included in *Discourses Addressed to Mixed Congregations* (1849), written only a year before the King William Street lectures; and, to put it mildly, Newman's understanding of the World is not the same as the World has of itself. Writing of the suffering of Christ on the Cross in contemplating the World that put him on the Cross, Newman depicts something that neither humanitarians nor Erastian prelates ever stop to consider:

> It is the long history of a world, and God alone can bear the load of it. Hopes blighted, vows broken, lights quenched, warnings scorned, opportunities lost; the innocent betrayed, the young hardened, the penitent relapsing, the just overcome, the aged failing; the sophistry of misbelief, the wilfulness of passion, the obduracy of pride, the tyranny of habit, the canker of remorse, the wasting fever of care, the anguish of shame, the pining of disappointment, the sickness of despair; such cruel, such pitiable spectacles, such heartrending, revolting, detestable, maddening scenes; nay, the haggard faces, the convulsed lips, the flushed cheek, the dark brow of the willing slaves of evil, they are all before Him now; they are upon Him and in Him. They are with Him instead of that ineffable peace which has inhabited His soul since the moment of His conception. They are upon Him, they are all but His own; He cries to His Father as if He were the criminal, not the victim; His agony takes the form of guilt and compunction. He is doing penance, He is making confession, He is exercising contrition, with a reality and a virtue infinitely greater than that of all saints and penitents together; for He is the One Victim for us all, the sole Satisfaction, the real Penitent, all but the real sinner.[95]

Here, we can see an understanding of the World that puts the travesties of Erastianism in their true light, and this understanding not only informs Newman's lectures but gives them an applicability far beyond the Gorham case.

Lecture IX: The Religious State of Catholic Countries no Prejudice to the Sanctity of the Church
In the ninth lecture, Newman addresses yet another objection to the Church: that she has not the sanctity herself that she has been instituted to impart to the world and that she therefore

---

[95] *Mix.*, 338–9.

does not merit converts, an objection which prompts Newman to draw more revelatory distinctions between the Church and the World.

> The Church, though she embraces all conceivable virtues in her teaching, and every kind of good, temporal as well as spiritual, in her exertions, does not survey them from the same point of view, or classify them in the same order as the world. She makes secondary what the world considers indispensable; she places first what the world does not even recognise, or undervalues, or dislikes, or thinks impossible; and not being able, taking mankind as it is found, to do everything, she is often obliged to give up altogether what she thinks of great indeed, but of only secondary moment, in a particular age or a particular country, instead of effecting at all risks that extirpation of social evils, which, in the world's eyes, is so necessary, that it thinks nothing really is done till it is secured. Her base of operations, from the difficulties of the season or the period, is sometimes not broad enough to enable her to advance against crime as well as against sin, and to destroy barbarism as well as irreligion. The world, in consequence, thinks, that because she has not done the world's work, she has not fulfilled her Master's purpose; and imputes to her the enormity of having put eternity before time. (261)

Like many Victorian Englishmen, Newman enjoyed following the progress of the British empire, though he was no jingoist and had none of the racialist prejudices that addled some of the imperialists. Yes, he was favorably disposed to Unionists, but he could also be sympathetic to the Irish in their nationalist aspirations.[96] He could certainly poke fun at

---

[96] For example, Newman commended a letter to Henry Wilberforce that appeared in the *Times* (21 July 1856) from a man described as "of Irish blood, intellect, and sympathies, who has been watching the Irish Parliamentary efforts of the last five years with constant interest and from a peculiar point of view." The letter began: "Rebellion in earnest is a good thing. Submission in earnest is the next best thing; and submission in earnest ought now to set in. I do not understand how pride or honour can forbid the rebel of 1848 to declare now for the Queen.... The English submitted to the House of Hanover; the Scotch submitted to the House of Hanover; why not the Irish?... Ireland may enter frankly without reserve, without reticence, into the British Empire, and yet in no way became

the peculiar moral pretensions of the empire builders. Contrasting the Church with the Empire, he wrote:

> And next, let it be observed that she has undertaken the more difficult work; it is difficult, certainly, to enlighten the savage, to make him peaceable, orderly, and self-denying; to persuade him to dress like a European, to make him prefer a feather-bed to the heather or the cave, and to appreciate the comforts of the fireside and the tea-table: but it is indefinitely more difficult, even with the supernatural powers given to the Church, to make the most refined, accomplished, amiable of men, chaste or humble; to bring, not only his outward actions, but his thoughts, imaginations, and aims, into conformity to a law which is naturally distasteful to him. It is not wonderful, then, if the Church does not do so much in the Church's way, as the world does in the world's way. The world has nature as an ally, and the Church, on the whole, and as things are, has nature as an enemy. (263–34)

Besides being amusing, this is rather profound. As Newman says, it *is* difficult to bring man's "thoughts, imaginations and aims into conformity to a law … naturally distasteful to him." And this is precisely why so much of Newman's work as a

---

degraded into an English province. Canada is British, Australia is British, Scotland is British. What Englishman would dare to assert that these are English?" The letter's conclusion was solidly Unionist, though with a twist: "It will be a great day when the members for Ireland cease to be Irish members and become members of the House of Commons; and when they discontinue the function of local delegates, and enter upon the privileges of Imperial legislators. It is to that liberal party in England, which is not English but British ... which has given self-government to the colonies, which is waiting for universal suffrage for England, that Ireland must look; and it is in the ranks of that party that the Irish popular members should explicitly enter. Against what have the Irish contended from the first? Against the Norman aristocracy which conquered the English. It is against that governing class that the English are also contending. In England a nation is rising up, that will destroy a caste. Let us ally ourselves with that nation." See *LD*, xvii, 330. This was a far cry from the view of James Anthony Froude, who dubbed the Irish "the spendthrift sister of the Aryan race." See Froude quoted in Shane Leslie, *The Celt and the World: A Study of the Relation of Celt and Teuton* (New York, Scribner & Sons, 1917), 188.

convert was devoted to education; to making the English see the appeal of a Church that they had been brought up to abominate; to making English Catholics see what a treasure trove their Church was. This is also why Newman would never measure the success of the English Church by the number of her converts. The work of the Church was too incalculably subtle for any such number to be indicative of her real efficacy. As he said himself: "Her best fruit is necessarily secret: she fights with the heart of man; her perpetual conflict is against the pride, the impurity, the covetousness, the envy, the cruelty, which never gets so far as to come to light; which she succeeds in strangling in its birth." Then again, for Newman, "from the nature of the case, she ever will do more in repressing evil than in creating good; moreover, virtue and sanctity, even when realised, are also in great measure secret gifts, known only to God and good Angels; for these, then, and other reasons, the powers and the triumphs of the Church must be hid from the world, unless the doors of the Confessional could be flung open, and its whispers carried abroad on the voices of the winds" (264). For an English audience denied for centuries the encouraging consolations of the Confessional, this passage must have been fascinating. For Catholics, it must have been a reassuring reminder of their "perpetual skirmish."

As we have seen, Newman's modish detractors like to take issue with what they characterize as his "dogmatism" and in this they follow a long line of critics not only of Newman but of the Roman Church. Newman's response to the charge is too funny and too apt not to quote. In his dramatic way, he puts the objection into the mouth of one of his censorious Anglo-Catholics, who says, apropos Roman Catholics, "There is a bold, shallow, hard, indelicate way among them of speaking of even points of faith, which is, to use studiously mild language, utterly out of taste, and indescribably offensive to any person of ordinary refinement" (266). To which Newman replies: "I admit both your fact and your account of the fact … but I would add to it, and turn a particular fact into a philosophical truth. I say, then, that such a hard, irreverent, extravagant tone in religion, as you consider it, is the very phenomenon which must necessarily result from a revelation of divine truth falling upon the human mind in its existing state of ignorance and moral feebleness" (268).

What is winning about Newman's handling of the issue of the Church's sanctity—or lack of it—is its realism. He never glosses over the villainy of man, though he never forgets that it is this villainy that makes the Church's solicitude for his redemption unceasing. It is also this villainy that makes her sacraments so attractive. Again, for an English audience that had been denied the sacraments for generations, such passages must have been riveting. But they also show how vital education was to Newman's apostolate. Here, the educator in Newman can be seen at his finest—lucid, revelatory, encouraging.[97]

> A soul which has received the grace of baptism receives with it the germ or faculty of all supernatural virtues whatever,—faith, hope, charity, meekness, patience, sobriety, and every other that can be named; and if it commits mortal sin, it falls out of grace, and forfeits these supernatural powers. It is no longer what it was, and is, so far, in the feeble and frightful condition of those who were never baptized. But there are certain remarkable limitations and alleviations in its punishment, and one is this: that the faculty or power of faith remains to it. Of course the soul may go on to resist and destroy this supernatural faculty also; it may, by an act of the will, rid itself of its faith, as it has stripped itself of grace and love; or it may gradually decay in its faith till it becomes simply infidel; but this is not the common state of a Catholic people. What commonly happens is this, that they fall under the temptations to vice or covetousness, which naturally and urgently beset them, but that faith is left to them. Thus the many are in a condition which is absolutely novel and strange in the ideas of a Protestant; they have a vivid perception, like

---

[97] For an excellent study of the educator in Newman and a useful refutation of the manifold errors of Colin Barr's account of Newman and the Catholic University of Ireland, see Paul Shrimpton, *The 'Making of Men': The Idea and Reality of Newman's University in Oxford and Dublin* (Leominster: Gracewing, 2014).

sense, of things unseen, yet have no desire at all, or affection, towards them; they have knowledge without love. Such is the state of the many; the Church at the same time is ever labouring with all her might to bring them back again to their Maker; and in fact is ever bringing back vast multitudes one by one, though one by one they are ever relapsing from her. The necessity of yearly confession, the Easter communion, the stated seasons of indulgence, the high festivals, Lent, days of obligation, with their Masses and preaching,—these ordinary and routine observances and the extraordinary methods of retreats, missions, jubilees, and the like, are the means by which the powers of the world unseen are ever acting upon the corrupt mass, of which a nation is composed, and breaking up and reversing the dreadful phenomenon which fact and Scripture conspire to place before us. (273–4)

Lecture X: Differences among Catholics no Prejudice to the Unity of the Church

Newman's tenth is the most learned lecture of the lot, necessarily, since it seeks to demonstrate the unity of the Church, despite the manifest disunity that threatened her over the centuries. Newman's explanation for this apparent paradox is that while the Church was divided, her divisions reinforced her unity. Nowhere does the teacher in Newman shine more brightly than in this involved, rewarding lecture. Here are a few examples of the lecture's brilliant insights. On how divisions within the Church affect the Church's teaching, he writes:

No one can pretend that the quarrels in the Catholic Church are questions of faith, or have tended in any way to obscure or impair what she declares to be such, and what is acknowledged to be such by the very parties in those quarrels. That Dominicans and Franciscans have been zealous respectively for certain doctrinal views, which they declare at the same time to be beyond and in advance of the promulgated faith of the Church, throws no doubt upon that faith itself; how does it follow that they differ in questions of faith, because they differ in questions not of faith? Rather, I would say, if a number of parties distinct from each other give the same testimony on certain points, their differences on other points do but strengthen the evidence for the truth of those matters in which they all are agreed; and the greater the difference, the more remarkable is the unanimity. (311)

On how the divisions of the Roman Church differ from those of the Anglican Church, he is unsparing to his Anglo-Catholic friends, fond as they are of their Caroline divines:

> In truth, she not only teaches in spite of those differences, but she has ever taught by means of them. Those very differences of Catholics on further points have themselves implied and brought out their absolute faith in the doctrines which are previous to them. The doctrines of faith are the common basis of the combatants, the ground on which they contend, their ultimate authority, and their arbitrating rule. They are assumed, and introduced, and commented on, and enforced, in every stage of the alternate disputation; and I will venture to say, that, if you wish to get a good view of the unity, consistency, solidity, and reality of Catholic teaching, your best way is to get up the controversy on grace, or on the Immaculate Conception. No one can do so without acquiring a mass of theological knowledge, and sinking in his intellect a foundation of dogmatic truth, which is simply antecedent and common to the rival schools, and which they do but exhibit and elucidate. To suppose that they perplex an inquirer or a convert, is to fancy that litigation destroys the principles and the science of law, or that spelling out words of five syllables makes a child forget his alphabet. On the other hand, place your unfortunate inquirer between Luther and Calvin, if the Holy Eucharist is his subject; or, if he is determining the rule of faith, between Bramhall and Chillingworth, Bull and Hoadley, and what residuum will be left, when you have eliminated their contrarieties? (312–13)

Far from conceding that critics of the Church have a point when they question the integrity of Catholic teaching by questioning the Church's unity, Newman argues that it is precisely because Catholic teaching has been assailed by so many heresies over the centuries that its infallibility has forged unity from division. He also chooses to cite an interesting source for this criticism. "It is imprudent in opponents of the Catholic Religion to choose for their attack the very point in which it is strong,' he argues.

> As truth is tried by error, virtue by temptation, courage by opposition, so is individuality and life tried by disturbance and disorder; and its trial is its evidence. The long history of Catholicism is but a coordinate proof of its essential unity. I suppose, then, that Protestants must be considered as turning to bay upon their pursuers, when they would retort upon us the argument available against themselves from their religious variations. "The Romanist must admit," it has been urged, "that the state, whether of the Church Catholic or of the Roman Church, at periods before or during the Middle Ages, was such as to bear a very strong resemblance to the picture he draws of our own. I do not speak of corruptions in life and morals merely, or of errors of individuals, however highly exalted, but of the general disorganized and schismatical state of the Church, her practical abandonment of her spiritual pretensions, the tyranny exercised over her by the civil power, and the intimate adherence of the worst passions and of circumstantial irregularities to those acts which are vital portions of her system." Such is the imputation; but yet, to tell the truth, I do not know any passages in her history which supply so awful an evidence of her unity and self-dependence, or so luminous a contrast to Anglicanism or other Protestantism, as these very anomalies in the rule and tenor of her course. (313–14)

The "imprudent" quote is taken from Newman himself—from his *Lectures on the Prophetical Office* (1837). So much for self-vindication.

Newman's response to the threat of heretical division within the Church is animated not only by his wonderfully practical grasp of history but by his faith. This may not deflect him from calling attention to what he sees as the heretical character of the National Church, but it does encourage him to urge his Anglo-Catholic friends to ask themselves whether what Cranmer and Parker wrought will be spared the fate that befell Arius and Nestorius, Eutyches and the Iconoclasts, the Manichees and the Lollards. Owen Chadwick chose to regard

Newman's lectures as those of an overzealous convert.[98] Readers can judge for themselves whether the historical context in which Newman places his contentions bears that interpretation out. Here is Newman at his most prophetic:

> *Noli æmulari* Is it not written in the book of truth, that the ungodly shall spread abroad like a green bay tree, and then shall wither? that the adversary reaches out his hand towards his prey, in order that he may be more emphatically smitten? "Yet a little while, and the wicked shall not be: I passed by, and lo! he was not; I sought him, and his place was not found. Better is a little to the just than the great riches of the wicked; for the arms of the wicked shall be broken, but the Lord strengtheneth the just." So was it with the great Arian heresy, which the civil power would fain have forced upon the Church; but it fell to pieces, and the Church remained One. So was it with Nestorius, with Eutyches, with the Image-breakers, with Manichees, with Lollards, with Protestants, into whom the State would put life, but who, one and all, refuse to live. So is it with the communion of Cranmer and Parker, which is kept together only by the heavy hand of the State, and cannot aspire to be free without ceasing to be one. One power alone on earth has the gift and destiny of ever being one. It has been so of old time; surely so will it be now. Man's necessity is God's opportunity. *Noli æmulari*, "Be not jealous of the evil-doers." (325–6)

Lastly, the tenth lecture exhibits the unity of Newman's thought by foreshadowing a well-known passage in the *Apologia* where the convert speaks of how the infallible Church brings unity out of division by dint of her Authority. Of course, Newman is not unaware that "it will at first sight be said that the restless intellect of our common humanity is utterly weighed down, to the repression of all independent effort and action whatever, so that, if this is to be the mode of bringing it into order, it is brought into order only to be destroyed." Yet, at the same time, in this brilliant passage, he recognizes that

---

[98] Newman, according to Chadwick, "was suffering from the disease of being a new convert." O. Chadwick, *The Victorian Church* (Oxford: Oxford University Press, 1966), i, 289.

this is far from the result, far from what I conceive to be the intention of that high Providence who has provided a great remedy for a great evil,—far from borne out by the history of the conflict between Infallibility and Reason in the past, and the prospect of it in the future. The energy of the human intellect "does from opposition grow"; it thrives and is joyous, with a tough elastic strength, under the terrible blows of the divinely-fashioned weapon, and is never so much itself as when it has lately been overthrown. It is the custom with Protestant writers to consider that, whereas there are two great principles in action in the history of religion, Authority and Private Judgment, they have all the Private Judgment to themselves, and we have the full inheritance and the superincumbent oppression of Authority. But this is not so; it is the vast Catholic body itself, and it only, which affords an arena for both combatants in that awful, never-dying duel. It is necessary for the very life of religion, viewed in its large operations and its history, that the warfare should be incessantly carried on. Every exercise of Infallibility is brought out into act by an intense and varied operation of the Reason, both as its ally and as its opponent, and provokes again, when it has done its work, a re-action of Reason against it; and, as in a civil polity the State exists and endures by means of the rivalry and collision, the encroachments and defeats of its constituent parts, so in like manner Catholic Christendom is no simple exhibition of religious absolutism, but presents a continuous picture of Authority and Private Judgment alternately advancing and retreating as the ebb and flow of the tide;—it is a vast assemblage of human beings with wilful intellects and wild passions, brought together into one by the beauty and the Majesty of a Superhuman Power,—into what may be called a large reformatory or training-school, not as if into a hospital or into a prison, not in order to be sent to bed, not to be buried alive, but (if I may change my metaphor) brought together as if into some moral factory, for the melting, refining, and moulding, by an incessant, noisy process, of the raw material of human nature, so excellent, so dangerous, so capable of divine purposes.[99]

The history that Newman encapsulates in the tenth lecture not only corroborates the unifying "Majesty" of this

---

[99] *Apo.*, 225–6.

"Superhuman Power" but shows how the National Church has never exercised anything like the same authority. To see the force of Newman's comparison, readers should attend to the lives of the Anglican churchmen at the end of the following passage, all of whom figure in the annotations. The tough-minded polemicist in Newman did not cite these figures carelessly. "It is impossible, I am sure," Newman contends,

for any one patiently to read the history of this series of controversies, whatever may be his personal opinions, without being intimately convinced of the oneness or identity of the mind, which lived in the Catholic Church through that long period which baffled the artifices and sophistries of the subtlest intellects, was proof against human infirmity and secular expedience, and succeeded in establishing irrevocably and for ever those points of faith with which she started in the contest. "Any one false step would have thrown the whole theory of the doctrine into irretrievable confusion; but it was as if some individual and perspicacious intellect, to speak humanly, ruled the theological discussion from first to last. That in the long course of centuries, and in spite of the failure, in points of detail, of the most gifted fathers and saints, the Church thus wrought out the one and only consistent theory which can be formed on the great doctrine in dispute, proves how clear, simple, and exact her vision of that doctrine was."[100]

Now I leave the retrospect of this long struggle with two remarks—first, that it was never doubtful to the world for any long time what was the decision of authority on each successive question as each came into consideration; next, that the series of doctrinal errors which was evolved tended from the first to an utter overthrow of the heresy, each decision of authority being a new and further victory over it, which was never undone. It was all along in visible course of expulsion from the Catholic fold. Contrast this with the denial of baptismal grace, viewed as a heresy within the Anglican Church; has the sentiment of authority against it always been unquestionable? Has there been a series of victories over it? Is it in visible course of expulsion? Is it ever tending to be expelled? Are the influence and prospects of the heresy less formidable now than in the age of Wesley, or

---

[100] *Dev.*, 438.

of Calamy, or of Baxter, or of Abbot, or of Cartwright, or of the Reformers? (319–21)

Needless to say, there is no corresponding "oneness" in the testimony of Wesley, Calamy, Baxter, Abbot, Cartwright, or the Reformers. All they can attest to is the acrimony of sectarians at variance.

Lecture XI: Heretical and Schismatical Bodies no Prejudice to the Catholicity of the Church

The objection Newman sets himself to address in the eleventh lecture is one that will always beguile those in pluralist societies who imagine that pluralism has something to do with truth. "There is no objection made at this time to the claims of the Catholic Church more imposing to the imagination," he writes, "yet less tenable in the judgment of reason, than that which is grounded on there being at present so many nations and races, which have kept the name of Christian, yet given up Catholicism."

Newman responds to the objection in several ways. First, he argues that "truth is opposed not only by direct contradictions, which are unequivocal, but also by such pretenses as are of a character to deceive men at first sight, and to confuse the evidence of what alone is divine and trustworthy" (337); hence the various sects of Christianity, all disputing the catholicity of the Catholic Church, without which their own pretentions to that catholicity would be impossible. Secondly, he argues that objections to the catholicity of the Church have been with the Church from time immemorial because such objections are woven into the very fabric of the unbiddable, proud, unshriven intellect. For Newman, such objections lie in "the very constitution of the human mind; corruptions of the Gospel being as necessary and ordinary a phenomenon, taking men as they are, as its rejection." If Anglo-Catholics wish to argue that the Catholic Church is somehow not Catholic because there are Protestant sectaries and Mohammedans going the roads, they might as well point to the "unreclaimed populations of paganism" as well, or "the political power of the British Colonial Empire" to justify their staying put (348). But Newman asks a more fundamental question, at a time of great civil, moral, and religious unrest throughout Europe. After all, Newman was delivering his lectures only two years after the revolutions of 1848, which called into question most of the authority that had made Europe's recovery from the Jacobin French Revolution possible under the tutelage of Metternich. Accordingly, Newman places the challenges to the Church's authority in the context of the challenges to political authority taking place throughout Europe at the time. "Is misbelief a greater marvel than unbelief," he asks,

> or do not the same intellectual and moral principles, which lead men to accept nothing, lead them also to accept half of revealed truth? Both effects are simple manifestations of private judgment in the bad sense of the phrase, that is, of the use of one's own reason against the authority of God. If He has made it a duty to submit to the supreme authority of the Holy See (and of this I am all along assuming there is fair proof), and if there is a constant rising of the human mind against authority, as such, however legitimate, the necessary consequence will be the very state of things we see before our eyes,—not merely individuals casting off the Roman Supremacy (for individuals, as being of less account, have less temptation, or even opportunity, to rebel, than collections of men), but, much more, the powerful and the great, the wealthy and the flourishing, kings and states, cities and races, falling back upon their own resources and their own connections, making their home their castle, and refusing any longer to be dependent on a distant centre, or to regulate their internal affairs by a foreign tribunal. Assuming then that there is a supreme See, divinely appointed, in the midst of Christendom, to which all ought to submit and be united, such phenomena, as the Greek Church presents at this day, and the Nestorian in the middle ages, are its infallible correlatives, as human nature is constituted; it would require a miracle to make it otherwise. (348–9)

Thirdly, Newman addresses the objection by arguing that most non-Catholic Christians are not non-Catholic by any theological design: they are non-Catholic because they suffer from what the Church regards as "invincible ignorance," or ignorance over which they have no control and for which they cannot be deemed culpable. And, of course, in these instances, the abounding grace of the Church protects them from their ignorance, for "it is consolatory to reflect how the schism or heresy, which the self-will of a monarch or of a generation has caused, does not suffice altogether to destroy the work for which in some distant age Evangelists have left their homes, and Martyrs have shed their blood." Moreover, for Newman, those "in invincible ignorance on those particular points of religion on which their Communion is wrong, may still have the divine and unclouded illumination of faith on those numerous points on which it is right." (353-4)

For Newman, however, these allowances cannot be extended to the Anglo-Catholics. Why? They cannot claim invincible ignorance. The very inadequacies of the Anglican Church accentuate the catholicity of the Catholic Church, and, for Newman, the Anglo-Catholics have no excuse for not acting in accordance with that inescapable realization.

> You, by means of that very system in which you find your selves, have been led to doubt that system. If the Mosaic law, given from above, was a schoolmaster to lead souls to Christ, much more is it true that an heretical creed, when properly understood, warns us against itself, and frightens us from it, and is forced against its will to open for us with its own hands its prison gates, and to show us the way to a better country. So has it been with you. You set out in simplicity and earnestness intending to serve it, and your very serving taught you to serve another. You began to use its prayers and act upon its rules, and they did but witness against it, and made you love it, not more but less, and carried off your affections to one whom you had not loved. The more you gazed upon your own communion the more unlike it you grew; the more you tried to be good Anglicans, the more you found your selves drawn in heart and spirit to the Catholic Church. (359)

Here, it is clear that Newman drew more on his own appreciation of this discrepancy than on that of any of his old Tractarian friends. Needless to say, it is difficult to imagine the unbudgeable Pusey or Keble characterizing his experience of such inadequacies in anything remotely like the fashion Newman describes, though this was obviously not the case with Manning, James Hope-Scott, Edward Badeley,[101] Robert Wilberforce,[102] William Maskell,[103] William Dodsworth,[104]

---

[101] Edward Lowth Badeley (1803–68), ecclesiastical lawyer. Educated at Brasenose College, he became close friends with Newman in 1837. Called to the Bar as a Member of the Inner Temple in 1841, he was one of the Tractarians' leading lawyers. He was also counsel for the bishop of Exeter in the Gorham case in 1850, as well as one of the signatories protesting the Privy Council's ruling. He became a Catholic in 1852 and assisted Newman during the Achilli trial. Since it was on Badeley's advice that Newman chose not to accept Kingsley's inadequate recantation of the charge of mendacity that he had levelled against the Oratorian, we have Badeley to thank, in part, for Newman's *Apologia. ODNB*.

[102] Robert Isaac Wilberforce (1802–57), Roman Catholic convert. The most brilliant of the Liberator's sons, Wilberforce took first-class honors at Oriel, where he befriended Newman, Keble, and Hurrell Froude. After converting to the Church in the wake of the Gorham case, he planned to join his friend Manning's Oblates of St. Charles Borromeo to minister to the London poor. But first he entered the Accademia Ecclesiastica in Rome on the pope's nomination, and while in minor orders he was taken ill with gastric fever and died in Albano on 3 February 1857. He was buried in Rome in the St. Raymond's Chapel of the Church of Santa Maria sopra Minerva. "Manning, who had been at his friend's bedside until the end, reported to Henry Wilberforce: 'In Rome the one thing remarked in him … was his childlike humility. He had in truth entered the kingdom of God as a little child' (Newsome, *Parting of Friends*, 409)." *ODNB*. John Henry Overton echoes what most of his contemporaries thought of Wilberforce: "Of all of the four celebrated brothers Wilberforce, none was so learned, so saintly, so eminently lovable in every respect as Robert Isaac." J.H. Overton, *The Anglican Revival* (London: Blackie & Son, 1897), 183.

[103] William Maskell (1814–90), "liturgist and medievalist, matriculated at University College, Oxford, in 1832, was greatly influenced by the Tractarians. He took Orders in 1837, and was Rector of Corscombe, Dorset, from 1842 until 1847, when he succeeded George Coleridge as Vicar of St Mary Church, Torquay. He was also appointed examining chaplain to Bishop Phillpotts of Exeter, and took part in the latter's interminable examination of G.C. Gorham. Maskell, who had written in 1848 on Baptism, held Catholic views as to the Sacraments, and so took a prominent part in the Gorham Controversy. After two pamphlets *On the Present*

and T. W. Allies. In any case, the autobiographical character of Newman's testimony is striking. It is almost as though the lecturer in him had left off lecturing and chose instead to share with his auditors the most personal counsel that he had given himself in the crisis of his own conversion. "Oh, look well to your footing that you slip not; be very much afraid lest the world should detain you; dare not in anything to fall short of God's grace, or to lag behind when that grace goes forward," he urges his auditors.

> Walk with it, co-operate with it.... You are not the first persons who have trodden that path; yet a little time, and, please God, the bitter shall be sweet, and the sweet bitter, and you will have undergone the agony, and will be lodged safely in the true home of your souls and the valley of peace. Yet but a little while, and you will look out from your resting place upon the wanderers outside; and will wonder why they do not see that way which is

Position of the High Church Party, and correspondence with his Bishop and the Archbishop of Canterbury, he was received on 22 June 1850 at Spanish Place. Maskell was an inopportunist, and had a public controversy with Manning after the definition of papal infallibility. He was a widower at the time of his conversion and later married a second time, living most of his life in Cornwall, where he became deputy lieutenant of the county. He was an authority on medieval service books and ivories." *LD*, xxv, 487. "A conscientious and profound liturgical scholar, Maskell was also a keen theological controversialist. Particularly adept at legalistic and historical argument, he would castigate his opponents with firm belief in his superior logic and in the complete righteousness of his cause." *ODNB*.

[104] William Dodsworth (1798–1861), Tractarian clergyman and Roman Catholic apologist. An Evangelical in his youth, he adopted Tractarian views after befriending Newman in the late 1830s. As an Anglican minister, he was a popular preacher at Margaret Street Chapel, Cavendish Square, London, He married Elizabeth (1799–1856), youngest daughter of Sir Francis Yarde Buller, second baronet, and sister of the first Baron Churston, in 1830. They had seven children, the youngest of whom, Cyril Dodsworth (1844–1907), became a Redemptorist priest in America. After the Gorham judgment, Dodsworth joined the Roman Catholic Church on 1 January 1851. Being married, he was barred from taking orders in the Catholic Church, though he published a number of Roman Catholic apologetic works, including "Popular Delusions concerning the Faith and Practice of Catholics" (1857) and "Popular Objections to Catholic Faith and Practice Considered" (1858). *ODNB*.

now so plain to you, and will be impatient with them that they
do not come on faster. And, whereas you now are so perplexed
in mind that you seem to yourselves to believe nothing, then you
will be so full of faith, that you will almost see invisible
mysteries, and will touch the threshold of eternity. (360–1)

Addressing his old friends about a move that he knows
most of them will find too painful even to contemplate, while
sharing with them his own experiences of the very same move
required a good deal of rhetorical finesse. But Newman did
something else besides. In recalling his own painful
conversion, he showed his friends that it was of them, not
himself, that he was thinking. Bungling commentators
unappreciative of the core *caritas* of Newman's work rate him
for self-absorption, but here we can see that even when
dwelling on his own innermost life, he could still be intent on
ennobling the lives of others.

And you will be so full of joy that you will wish all around you
to be partakers of it, as if for your own relief; and you will
suddenly be filled with yearnings deep and passionate, for the
salvation of those dear friends whom you have outstripped; and
you will not mind their coolness, or stiffness, or distance, or
constrained gravity, for the love you bear to their souls. And,
though they will not hear you, you will address yourselves to
those who will; I mean, you will weary heaven with your
novenas for them, and you will be ever getting Masses for their
conversion, and you will go to communion for them, and you
will not rest till the bright morning comes, and they are yours
once again. Oh, is it possible that there is a resurrection even
upon earth! O wonderful grace, that there should be a joyful
meeting, after parting, before we get to heaven! (361–2)

As this shows, *Anglican Difficulties* is suffused with the life
of prayer. Yes, it has polemical elements; Newman could not
always resist hurling the odd mud pie; but the essence of the
lectures is that, taken together, they are a prayer because they
are a cry of love. They also constitute a moving coda to the
Oxford Movement, as this passage attests:

It was a weary time, that long suspense, when with aching hearts we stood on the brink of a change, and it was like death both to witness and to undergo, when first one and then another disappeared from the eyes of their fellows. And then friends stood on different sides of a gulf, and for years knew nothing of each other or of their welfare. And then they fancied of each other what was not, and there were misunderstandings and jealousies; and each saw the other, as if his ghost, only in imagination and in memory; and all was sickness and anxiety, and hope delayed, and ill-requited care. But now it is all over; the morning is come; the severed shall unite. I see them as if in sight of me. Look at us, my brethren, from our glorious land; look on us radiant with the light cast upon us by the Saints and Angels who stand over us; gaze on us as you approach, and kindle as you gaze. We died, you thought us dead: we live; we cannot return to you, you must come to us,—and you are coming. Do not your hearts beat as you approach us? Do you not long for the hour which makes us one? Do not tears come into your eyes at the thought of the superabundant mercy of your God? (361–2)

Lecture XII: Ecclesiastical History no Prejudice to the Apostolicity of the Church

In his twelfth and final lecture, Newman takes up one of the most abiding and yet least tenable of Protestant objections to Roman Catholicism, and that is that the Church was somehow not Apostolical because it was a corruption of the Primitive Church, despite the fact that, as he says, "the world at large has no such view of any contrariety between the Catholic Church of today and the Catholic Church of fifteen hundred years ago" (364). Although the rigorous historian in Newman nicely disposed of this objection in his *Essay on the Development of Christian Doctrine* (1845), his including it in *Anglican Difficulties* testifies to its strange continuing appeal even for fairly sophisticated, Oxbridge-educated Anglo-Catholics. After all, the Anglo-Catholic conception of the nature of the Christian deposit of faith has always been one of peculiar stasis, limiting itself to the first five hundred years of the Primitive Church and regarding Providence as somehow missing in action for the following thirteen hundred years.

Although he did not put himself to school to St. Thomas and the Scholastics with any thoroughness, Newman knew that the Primitive Church could be understood only in the light of the doctrinal developments of the Middle Ages meticulously delineated by St. Thomas and his friends. These developments were not superstitious accretions, the work of pious fraud or episcopal chicane, but authentic unfoldings of the Truth of the living Church.

While the priest in Newman might have seen the survival of this objection as an example of obdurate error, the psychologist in him saw it as a shrewd piece of table turning. "Since attack is much easier and pleasanter than defence," he writes, "it has been the way with certain disputants, especially with the Anglican school, instead of accounting for their own serious departure in so many respects from the primitive doctrine and ritual, to call upon us to show why we differ at all from our first Fathers, though partially and intelligibly, in matters of discipline and in the tone of our opinions" (365).

The issue of the Fathers prompts Newman to share with his auditors his own personal testimony to show that, far from the Fathers' dissuading him from entering into the appeal of the Catholic Church, they were instrumental in his conversion:

> I say, then, that the writings of the Fathers, so far from prejudicing at least one man against the modern Catholic Church, have been simply and solely the one intellectual cause of his having renounced the religion in which he was born and submitted himself to her. What other causes there may be, not intellectual, unknown, unsuspected by himself, though freely imputed on mere conjecture by those who would invalidate his testimony, it would be unbecoming and impertinent to discuss; for himself, if he is asked why he became a Catholic, he can only give that answer which experience and consciousness bring home to him as the true one, viz., that he joined the Catholic Church simply because he believed it, and it only, to be the Church of the Fathers. (367)

If it took Newman some time to realize this, it was only because when he first read the Fathers, he was reading them with Protestant eyes, which blinded him to their Catholic purposes (372). He makes the same criticism of Gibbon. The Enlightenment historian's account of the rise of Christianity is unreliable precisely because he, too, looked on his subject with Protestant eyes; he had no "due formation" in the Faith, nor did he ever consider acquiring one necessary, for all of his undeniable learning.[105]

Before leaving his audience, Newman makes one additional clarification, and that is to redefine the *Via Media*[106]—a parting shot that could not have amused his Anglo-Catholic auditors. Doubtless, there was a kind of

---

[105] "It is very remarkable that it should not have occurred to a man of Gibbon's sagacity to inquire, what account the Christians themselves gave of the matter. Would it not have been worthwhile for him to have let conjecture alone, and to have looked for facts instead? Why did he not try the hypothesis of faith, hope, and charity? Did he never hear of repentance towards God, and faith in Christ? Did he not recollect the many words of Apostles, Bishops, Apologists, Martyrs, all forming one testimony? No; such thoughts are close upon him, and close upon the truth; but he cannot sympathize with them, he cannot believe in them, he cannot even enter into them, because he needs the due formation for such an exercise of mind." *GA*, 462–3. Elsewhere in the *Grammar of Assent* Newman says: "We need the interposition of a Power, greater than human teaching and human argument, to make our beliefs true and our minds one." (*GA*, 375). See also Edward Short, *Newman and History* (Leominster: Gracewing, 2017), 27.

[106] The rationalist Benn had a different take on the *Via Media* from either the Anglo-Catholics or Newman: "The dread of Rome and the dread of rationalism were just strong enough to hold each other in check. As was natural in the home of compromise, truth passed for being a mean between two extremes; and several distinct directions disputed among themselves the honour of being the genuine *Via Media*. But none of them could show a fixed point of departure nor a goal where all might meet. Unable alike to advance or to recede, and occupied with the pettiest personalities, Church parties were dying of intellectual inanition, as the people were dying of hunger in their factories and fields. Yet they were still strong enough to prevent other guides from undertaking a task which they had proved powerless to perform; for while the clergy were sinking ever lower in popular estimation, they retained nearly the whole education of the country in their hands." A.W. Benn, *The History of Rationalism in Nineteenth-Century England* (London: Longmans Greene & Co, 1906), i, 366.

mercilessness about this, especially in light of his friends' pitiable vulnerabilities, but, of course, it could not be avoided. The *Via Media*, he says, "is an interposition or arbitration between the extreme doctrines of Protestantism on the one hand, and the faith of Rome which Protestantism contradicts on the other. At the same time, though it may be unwilling to allow it, it is, from the nature of the case, but a particular form of Protestantism. I do not say that in secondary principles it may not agree with the Catholic Church; but, its essential idea being that she has gone into error, whereas the essential idea of Catholicism is the Church's infallibility, the *Via Media* is really nothing else than Protestant" (377). He is even more unsparing of his former Anglo-Catholic friends when he speaks of the Eusebians or semi-Arians, as they were sometimes called, who clearly bore a remarkable resemblance to the party of Keble and Pusey in their attempts to straddle the stools without making any inconvenient commitments.[107]

---

[107] The Anglican historian John Henry Overton shows how Keble and Pusey's response to the Gorham case epitomized their Anglo-Catholic straddling of the stools: "Immediate steps were taken (1) to vindicate the church from complicity in the Gorham judgment, and (2) to encourage friends and prevent them from seceding to Rome. Church unions were formed in all parts of the country, and monster meetings were held in London, at one of which, held in the Freemasons' Hall in July, 1850, both Keble and Pusey uttered some weighty words. Keble, sounding his characteristic note of 'patience', made a telling point by reminding the meeting that 'the early church had been content to wait fifty-six years'— that is, from the Council of Nice in 325 a.d. to the Council of Constantinople in 381—'for rest from troubles on a chief point of doctrine', while 'we', he adds, 'are now in 1850, and some eager ones think it much too long to wait for 1851 or 1852 for settlement of our present trouble'. Then rising to an unwonted strain of eloquence, 'The whole air', he said, 'of England seems to me to ring with voices from the dead and from the living, especially from the holy dead, all to this effect: *Stay here; think not of departing; do here your work.* Pusey recommended a bold front: 'We stand where two roads part—the way of the world and the way of the church; the way of man and the way of God.... If the state will not, as Magna Charta pledges it, allow that the church should have her liberties inviolate, we must ask that the state will set us free from itself, and go forth, as Abraham, not knowing whither he went, poor as to this world's goods, but rich with the blessing of that seed in whom all nations of the earth shall be blessed.' At the same time he was far too well-read a man to agree with

Take, for instance, the history of Arianism. Arius stood almost by himself; bold, keen, stern, and violent, he took his stand on two or three axiomatic statements, as he considered them, appealed to Scripture, despised authority and tradition, and carried out his heretical doctrine to its furthest limits. He absolutely maintained, without any reserve, that our Lord was a creature, and had a beginning. Next, he was one of a number of able and distinguished men, scattered over the East, united together by the bond of a common master and a common school, who might have been expected to stand by him on his appealing to them; but who left him to his fate, or at least but circuitously and indirectly served his cause. High in station, ecclesiastical and civil, they found it more consistent with their duties towards themselves to fall back upon a more cautious phraseology than his, and upon less assailable principles, to evade inquiry, to explain away tests, and to profess a submission to the voice of their forefathers and of the Catholic world; and they developed their formidable party in that form of heresy which is commonly called Semi-Arianism or Eusebianism. They preached peace, professed to agree with neither St. Athanasius nor Arius, excited the jealousies of the Eastern world against the West, were strong enough to insult the Pope, and dexterous enough to gain the favour of Constantine and the devoted attachment of his son Constantius. (379–80)

Having dealt this final blow, Newman made one last appeal to his auditors, an appeal that could only have made the theological parting of friends more excruciating still:

If I have been excessive here, if I have confused what is defective with what is hollow, or have mistaken aspiration for pretence, or have been severe upon infirmities of which self-knowledge would have made me tender, I wish it otherwise. Still, whatever my faults in this matter, I have ever been trustful

---

the extravagant theories which, in the recoil from the judgment of a lay court, some put forth on the church's entire independence of the state." Throughout *Anglican Difficulties*, Newman was careful to show how the testimonies of the Anglo-Catholics themselves exposed the quicksand on which they staked their ground. Here is just another example of that, compliments of one of the Anglican Church's most sympathetic historians. Overton, *The Anglican Revival*, 184–5.

in that true Catholic spirit which has lived in the movement of which you are partakers. I have been steady in my confidence in that supernatural influence among you, which made me what I am, which, in its good time, shall make you what you shall be. You are born to be Catholics; refuse not the unmerited grace of your bountiful God; throw off for good and all the illusions of your intellect, the bondage of your affections, and stand upright in that freedom which is your true inheritance. (398)

Yet, having said this, Newman also recognized that, in the "perpetual skirmish" between the Church and the World, he might not have entirely succeeded in his King William Street campaign, and he admitted to that likely failure with becoming humility.

The Eternal God deals with us one by one, each in his own way; and by standers may pity and compassionate the long throes of our travail, but they cannot aid us except by their prayers. If, then, I have erred in entering upon the subjects I have brought before you, pardon me; pardon me if I have rudely taken on myself to thrust you forward, and to anticipate by artificial means a divine growth. If it be so, I will only hope that, though I may have done you no good, yet my attempt may be blessed in some other way. (399)

Here, in this undertaking, as in so many others throughout his long life, he recognized that "it is the rule of God's Providence that we should succeed by failure."[108]

In conclusion, we might consider the case of another English Catholic truth teller, over a hundred years after Newman delivered his lectures, which shows the ineludible

---

[108] Newman to Lord Braye (29 October 1882), *LD*, xxx, 142. Readers should also remember in this context what Newman wrote in 1862 to the Anglo-Catholic Daniel Radford, with whom he had a lively correspondence: "I feel extremely the kindness with which you speak of me and my writings;—after a life which to myself appears to be a history of failures, (except that personally I have gained what is the compensation for all,) it is a pleasure to be told that in points of view in which I seem to have done nothing I may after all have something to show for my labour." Radford had told Newman that "a great portion of my intellectual life has been lived in your writings." *LD*, xx, 330.

persistence of the questions Newman raises in *Anglican Difficulties*. In *Our Age: English Intellectuals between the World Wars* (1990), Lord Noel Annan (1916–2000), the spokesman of the English Establishment for much of the second half of the twentieth century, heaped praise on his generation for liberating John Bull from what he regarded as the prison house of Victorian values, but he also singled out one contemporary for sustained abuse: "Evelyn Waugh was the real deviant of my generation," Annan wrote. "He went against the grain of decent opinion; he deviated from the values we esteemed." Not only a "snob," a "reactionary," a "disillusioned romantic," a "malignant tease," and a "*deraciné* from the twenties," Waugh was what Annan called an "Augustinian Catholic." For the donnish humanitarian, Waugh was a deviant because, like St. Augustine, he believed in original sin; he believed in the reality of evil; he believed that sinful man was reliant on God's grace to help him contend not only with the evil in the world but the evil in himself; he believed that the Catholic Church was the means through which man attained this grace. In response, Annan countered that his contemporaries had "no difficulty in finding explanations why the world [was] so full of evil." Politics and social science supplied all of the requisite explanations. His contemporaries might be "less ready" to find reasons why they themselves were "so prone to rage," to "conceit," to envy, to causing "others unhappiness in order to give [themselves] pleasure," but still they managed to find reasons, and "when things [got] bad the analyst [was] at hand."[109] Waugh abominated psychiatry. As he told the Anglo-Catholic poet John Betjeman in 1946: "People are going mad & talking balls to psychiatrists, not because of accidents to the chamber-pot in the nursery, but because there is no logical structure to their beliefs." He also spoke bluntly to Betjeman about his faith. "Your ecclesiastical position is entirely without reason," he told the poet, whose wife, Penelope, would convert to Rome two years later, in 1948,

---

[109] Noel Annan, *Our Age: English Intellectuals between the World Wars: A Group Portrait* (New York: Random House, 1990), 158–9.

largely as the result of Waugh's assiduous proselytising. "You must not suppose that there is anything more than the most superficial resemblance between Catholics and Anglo-Catholics.... The true Church is unique & indivisible & nothing is remotely like it. This may not be apparent from the outside. But I think more violence is done to the Mystical Body by those who imitate it than those who frankly hate it."[110] Betjeman's clipped reply did not dispute Waugh's point: "All I can do now is to read, pray and study the life of Our Lord. That I am doing."[111] But the epistolary evangelist in Waugh would not relent. "One deep root of error is that you regard religion as the source of pleasurable emotions & sensations and ask the question, 'Am I not getting just as much out of the Church of England as I should from Catholicism?' The question should be 'What am I doing for God?' Nothing less than complete abandonment is any good. His will is plain as a pikestaff that there shall be one fold & one shepherd and you spend all of your time perpetuating a sixteenth-century rift & influencing others to perpetuate it. I wouldn't give a thrush's egg for your chances of salvation at the moment."[112] Needless to say, this was not the sort of proselytizing in which most of Waugh's Catholic contemporaries—or ours—would engage, even those

---

[110] Waugh to John Betjeman (22 December 1946), in *The Letters of Evelyn Waugh*, ed. M. Amory (New York: Ticknor & Fields, 1990) 242–3.

[111] Betjeman to Waugh (23 January 1847), in *The Letters of Evelyn Waugh*, 247.

[112] Waugh to Betjeman (May 1947), in *The Letters of Evelyn Waugh*, 250. At the time of this exchange, Waugh was writing *Helena* (1950), which he dedicated to Betjeman's wife Penelope. The critical editor of *Helena* points out: "Helena is Waugh's simplest and most straightforward Catholic ambassador, a saint who demonstrated in her actions a clear-headed path to faith... Helena in Waugh's fictional form offers a very different persuasive tactic from his own bullish approach to conversion, as revealed in letters... to Betjeman." "Introduction to Evelyn Waugh, *Helena* ed. Sara Haslam (Oxford: Oxford University Press, 2020), lix. As for Waugh's 'bullish approach' to the Truth, one should keep in mind something that Father D'Arcy said about his unusual catechumen: "I have never myself met a convert who so strongly based his assents on truth." *Evelyn Waugh and his World*. ed. David Pryce Jones (London, 1973), 64.

favorably disposed to that great French spiritual classic *L'Abandon à la divine providence*, but it exemplifies the uncompromising force of Waugh's faith. (Apparently, Betjeman was so upset by it that he had to take to his bed for three days.) Yet Waugh's tack was not altogether dissimilar from the tack that John Henry Newman had taken with Anglo-Catholics in his *Anglican Difficulties* lectures. For Newman, as for Waugh, conversion in the case of those familiar with the creeds was not merely an option: it was an imperative for the salvation of their souls.[113] When Newman's sister Jemima baulked at her brother's converting, convinced that it would lessen his influence in Protestant England, Newman replied in words that Waugh would have keenly understood: "What a doom would have been mine, if I had kept the Truth a secret in my own bosom, and when I knew which the One Church was, and which was not part of the One Church, I had suffered friends and strangers to die in an ignorance from which I might have relieved them! Impossible."[114]

Since it was Newman's rule of life to serve the Truth, regardless of the pressures put on him to sidestep or attenuate it, we can see how it was this quality—the one that Kingsley would seek so crudely to deny him fourteen years after the King William Street lectures—that most animated not only his conversion and his account of his conversion but his solicitude for his unconverted Anglo-Catholic friends.

IV: Critical Reception

One proof of the unjust neglect that *Anglican Difficulties* has suffered since its publication is its absence from lists of classic works published in England and America in 1850—a year that saw the release of Dickens' *David Copperfield*, Carlyle's *Latter-Day Pamphlets*, Tennyson's "In Memoriam,"

---

[113] In Lecture X, Newman could not be more categorical: "Let it be considered that the primary question, with every serious inquirer, is the question of salvation." (310)

[114] Newman to Mrs. John Mozley (14 October 1845), *LD*, xi, 16.

Hawthorne's *The Scarlet Letter*, Kingsley's *Alton Locke*, Thackeray's *Pendennis*, and Wordsworth's *The Prelude* (posthumous). In R.W. Chapman's *Annals of English Literature 1475–1950*, a classic in its own right, all of these are listed; indeed, even Frank Newman's *Phases of Faith*, which the rationalist A.W. Benn called "'the most formidable direct attack ever made against Christianity in England,'" is listed.[115] *Anglican Difficulties* is not.

Contemporary Newspapers

The contemporary response to the lectures and their subsequent publication was decidedly mixed, though fairly predictable given each paper's party line. The Liberal *Daily News* took a dim view of the lectures.

> In language and in style of thought the lectures possess the general characteristics of Father Newman's other writings; sentences of inordinate length worked out with a wondrous lucidity; facility over words quite extraordinary; subtlety of distinctions and differences founded very much on that facility of the rarest order; constant references to the fathers, little notice of the scriptures, the largest demands on the belief of the auditory, and the most comprehensive denial of Christianity to all who differ from him. It is difficult to suppose that lectures so characterised can achieve their object; nor do they appear to have much effect on the auditory. They are as devoid of all eloquence or rhetoric as they are eminently defective in logical cogency. They are, in fact, a favorable specimen of what may be termed *Christian Platonism*. They are strictly limited to an hour; and on their conclusion, the organ raises its tone and plays the auditory to the doors, where stand a string of handsome carriages and neat broughams.[116]

---

[115] Benn quoted in Gordon N. Ray, *Thackeray: The Age of Wisdom 1847–1863* (New York: McGraw Hill, 1958), 122. Alfred William Benn (1833–1902) was a British botanist, publisher, and rationalist, whose two-volume *History of Rationalism in Nineteenth-Century England* (1906) is full of abuse of Cardinal Newman and his work.
[116] *Daily News* (19 June 1850).

This appeared in the paper in June of 1850; in October of 1851 there was another, even more contemptuous notice of the lectures, in which the correspondent described how "in the course of the lectures [Newman] delivered some eighteen months ago to a queer admixture of female fashion and Irish filth, assembled in rooms once devoted to lewd revels, but now the abode of the Fathers of the Oratory, [Newman] avowed his belief in the liquefaction of St. Januarius' blood, in the motion of the eyes of the picture of the Madonna, in so-called saints having raised the dead, crossed seas without vessels, multiplied grain, cured incurable diseases ... and having avowed this credulity in the incredible, he proceeded to place his belief in them on a level with the universal acceptation which all Christians give to the holiest of revealed mysteries; thus practically elevating his own credulity to the standard of inspiration."

The Tory *Morning Post* acknowledged the justness of Newman's criticisms of the Erastianism of the Established Church without entertaining the possibility that Catholicism might be its antidote; the paper gave Newman credit for sounding the tocsin, though they disputed the nature of the alarm and what should be the response to it. "Establishment-men must have secret fears at the perception, too late, of their own folly," the paper's reviewer argued, "in tampering with the spiritual nature of the Church at such a time as this, treating the sacred Church of England as if it were a human creation, with no divine claims—no life or conscience of her own. Dissenters must be very blind if (with such an example before them) they acknowledge not (what their best forefathers owned) that the destruction, or even serious weakening, of the Church of England could only issue in the triumph of Infidelity and Popery." The reviewer then contrasts Newman's lectures with his brother's *Phases of Faith*:

> They both began life as Evangelicals, and the elder brother has ended (if it be the end) as an Ultramontane Romanist, the other as a German Eclectic. The two brothers have worked out their conclusions, apparently, in two opposite directions. Mr.

Editor's Introduction

Newman the elder has laboured to destroy all ground of credit for every Church except the Roman, which he accepts as a refuge from total unbelief of all Christianity. Mr. Newman the younger has performed, to his own satisfaction, the same work of demolition on the Holy Scriptures; prophets, evangelists, and apostles being discovered by him to be, without exception, unworthy of our faith. The difference between the two is perhaps, however, less than they suppose. Mr. Newman, the priest, announces that the evidence of the truth of Christianity is, in itself, unsatisfactory; the Scriptures, according to him, cannot be verified by the common rules of human criticism; the miracles of Christ and the apostles cannot be distinguished from those of the Middle Ages; and if he is to acquiesce in Christianity at all, it must be in that form of it which ignores all difficulties, dispenses with all evidence, and forbids all criticism. Mr. Newman, the laic, in his "Phases," reveals exactly the same unbelief as his brother. He agrees with him in the defective and unsatisfactory state of the Christian evidences, only he does not see why he any longer should go through all the ceremony of acknowledging the gospel at all.

Having ventured this comparison, the reviewer turns his attention to the book under review and finds it "replete with learning, pathos, wit, humour and paradox," though its object "is to remove the few remaining 'difficulties' out of the way of certain 'Anglicans' ... in order that they may plunge with him into that same gulf of disbelief which he misnames 'Catholicity.' " And the reviewer defends this interpretation of matters by arguing that whereas "to accept Roman Catholic theology because it would bear examination—because it had those marks of truth of which the mind and conscience of man takes cognizance, would be an intelligible course ... to accept it because you can believe nothing on its own merits, or its independent evidence, is such a repudiation of both reason and conscience as amounts to total infidelity." In fine, for the reviewer, "to join the Church of Rome is not to have a faith, but a substitute for faith." The reviewer then contrasts the Catholic with the Anglican Newman:

Had such a volume as the present been produced by some unknown writer, in whose antecedents the world had no interests, it would have been very sad, because it betrays such versatility of genius—such perceptions of the true and good—such capacities for the highest and most glorious ends. But when we think of it as the production of the author of the "Parochial Sermons," which have left so deep an impression on the religious heart of England, it is simply confounding.

For the reviewer, the "mystery" was:

> how such gifts should have been permitted to be combined in one so placed among us, and wielding such influence; so much moral insight with such disheartening subtlety; a pathos of tone so attractive with a nature so alien and cold; such mastery of the intellect and heart with such isolation from actual sympathy; the genius of Voltaire and the sweetness of Massillon; more than the erudition and sarcasm of Gibbon with more than the elegance and scepticism of Hume.

Putting the contention aside, that Newman squanders his talents in the lectures in defense of an indefensible Church, he does concede that:

> we must acknowledge that all the force of his arguments against the Church of England is derived from the actual state of things brought about by the Government of the day. What is now unhappily known as the "Gorham Case" is but the latest of a series of attempts on the part of the State to convert the Church into a merely human institution, the creature of legislators ... the events of recent years have made some of her most sanguine sons despond, and her weaker children have but too easily believed that everything sacred was departed from her.... This is (let us be very sure) the secret strength, the *only* strength of Popery among us. It is the strength which Mr. Newman wields against us with such power in his first four lectures.... Only let the earnest and religious people of this country be shown that the Church of England is a human invention—with no power, no means of acting for God in holy things—and one by one,

family by family, neighborhood after neighborhood will *drop off*.[117]

The *Guardian* reporter characterized the lectures as "an exposition of the 'difficulties' which must be felt by all conscientious Anglicans in remaining within a church distracted by disputes, which has no competent authority to declare what is the truth, which is the mere creature of the legislature, and rests on the shifting sands of popular opinion, that may unmake as it has made. There was considerable skill in the arrangement of the topics of the lecture, although I fancied that a popish casuistry was too transparent; but, on the whole, I should fancy that Father Newman is qualified to win over doubting Anglicans, whom Tractarianism has carried halfway to the church of Rome, and who are distressed by what they consider to be the 'uncertain sound' uttering by the Church of England, on the subject of baptismal regeneration." The correspondent also noted the "striking contrast" between Newman's lectures and Francis Newman's *Phases of Faith*. The brothers were educated at Oxford, he said, and are "remarkable examples of the fact that the Oxford 'movement' has propelled some minds into the extremest ascetism of Roman Catholicism, while others have gone into the opposite extreme of speculative free inquiry.... But if 'popery' has been the natural termination of the Oxford career of Father Newman, we may retort on his younger brother, that scepticism is the natural result of unrestricted free enquiry. As both the Newmans are men of superior mark their characters and careers may be fairly taken as illustrations of modern mental phenomena, and as indicating the conflicting currents that disturb the opinions of the age."[118]
    In his novel, *Pendennis* (1848–50), Thackeray (1811–63) would ponder the same contrast between the brothers.

"The truth, friend!" Arthur said, imperturbably; "where is the truth? Show it me. That is the question between us. I see it on

---

[117] *Morning Post* (14 September 1850).
[118] *Guardian* (11 May 1850); see *ODNB* for FW Newman.

both sides. I see it on the Conservative side of the house, and amongst the Radicals, and even on the ministerial benches. I see it in this man, who worships by Act of Parliament, and is rewarded with a silk apron and five thousand a year; in that man, who, driven fatally by the remorseless logic of his creed, gives up everything, friends, fame, dearest ties, closest vanities, the respect of an army of churchmen, the recognised position of a leader, and passes over, truth-impelled, to the enemy, in whose ranks he will serve henceforth as a nameless private soldier:—I see the truth in that man, as I do in his brother, whose logic drives him to quite a different conclusion, and who, after having passed a life in vain endeavours to reconcile an irreconcilable book, flings it at last down in despair, and declares, with tearful eyes, and hands up to heaven, his revolt and recantation. If the truth is with all these, why should I take side with any one of them?"[119]

William Makepeace Thackeray

When Thackeray attended Newman's lectures in King William Street, he must have listened to Newman's passage about the pious beggar woman with particular interest because it echoed something from his own work. In *The Irish Sketchbook* (1843), Thackeray had also spoken of the piety of a beggar woman, which he actually encountered outside Carlow Cathedral. "There is a convent by the side of the cathedral," he recalled, "and, of course, a parcel of beggars all about ... profuse in their prayers and invocations of the Lord, and whining flatteries of the persons whom they address. One wretched, old, tottering hag began whining the Lord's prayer as a proof of her sincerity, and blundered in the very midst of it, and left us thoroughly disgusted after the very first sentence."[120] This was hardly sympathetic to the devotions of an old and doubtless confused woman, but still it was responsive to experience. Thackeray's response to Newman's

---

[119] W.M. Thackeray, *Pendennis*, ed. J. Sutherland (Oxford: Oxford University Press, 1994), 801–2.
[120] W.M. Thackeray, *The Irish Sketchbook* (London: Smith Elder, 1843), 16.

passage about his beggar woman had no basis in experience and relied instead on stock No Popery caricature.

> A man who admits that a lousy lying beggarwoman who goes to confess and says her prayers is more likely of salvation than a good wise honest humble conscientious man earnestly trying to fulfill his duty: a man who glories in asserting that every scoundrel who has been executed at Rome goes straightway and secure with the sacerdotal passport to Heaven, while his denouncer very likely goes to the Devil, ought to be let go on. The more he preaches in this way, the better for the Truth: the more he shows what the figure is under those fine copes and embroideries and behind all that chandlery and artificial flower-show, the better for the people who are now attracted by the splendour and the ceremonial and the sweet-chanted litanies and the charms of the orator's rhetoric. Put out the lights and lock up the incense pots. Stop the organ and take off the priest's fine clothes—and when we come to Mr. Newman's naked beau ideal, it seems to me we get a creature so hideous degraded and despicable, that the public scorn will scout him out of the world again.[121]

Thackeray's letter is as revealing for what it says as to whom it was written. Robert Montgomery (1807–55), his correspondent, was in many respects a rather Thackerayan character. Born in Bath, the illegitimate son of the resident clown at the Bath Theatre, who also appeared on the stage of the Haymarket and the English Opera at the Lyceum, Montgomery realized, from an early age, that he should have to make his way in the world by his wits. In this, he was rather similar to Becky Sharp, the irrepressibly enterprising heroine of *Vanity Fair* (1847–8). After meeting with early success with a book of poems entitled *Poetical Trifles* (1825), he wrote three more full-length books of verse, all of which were extravagantly praised by Southey and Crabbe. Once he became famous, he highlighted what many saw as his

---

[121] *The Letters and Private Papers of William Makepeace Thackeray*, ed. Gordon N. Ray (Harvard: Harvard University Press, 1946), ii, 675–6. Hereinafter, *Thackeray's Letters & Private Papers*.

physical resemblance to Lord Byron. Montgomery also produced numerous works of sermons and theology. In the pulpit, he could be memorably droll, once likening dead humanity to a "decayed Stilton cheese," which would be restored to its proper ripeness only by trumpeting angels at the Last Day.[122] In his own lifetime, Montgomery commanded a huge audience. *The Omnipresence of the Deity* (1828) alone went into twenty-eight editions. At a time when Christian belief was being eroded by an industrializing culture antagonistic to Christianity, Montgomery's poems offered consolation amidst growing apostasy.

That the author of *Vanity Fair* went out of his way to concur with this versifying preacher is revealing. In sending off his letter, Thackeray was defending something of the undogmatical faith that his mother had taught him when he was a child, a faith to which he resorted, fleetingly, after his wife lost her mind and, then again, when he was gravely ill with gastric fever in 1849; indeed, his mother might have been one of the readers that sent Montgomery's verses into so many popular editions. Thackeray was also showing support for the Broad Church, though that heterogeneous communion might have welcomed seeing the newly converted Newman taking the Tractarians to task for unreality and imposture. Nonetheless, to another correspondent, Thackeray described his sense of kinship in terms that were almost tribal. "Newman," Thackeray complained, "is obliged to condemn the best and purest of all of us, his own mother, friends, brethren,—everybody.—Will we subscribe to that? Will we let that Lie go unquestioned among us?"[123] Here was the nationalist defense of Anglicanism—Anglicanism as inseparable from the English Nation, from family, from friends, from home—which Gladstone, Keble, Pusey, and so many other Anglicans mounted to parry what they considered Newman's foreign Romanizing. It is also one of the main criticisms that Newman mounts against the National Church —that it cannot claim any apostolicity because it is at the

---

[122] See *ODNB*.

[123] *Thackeray's Letters & Private Papers*, ii, 705.

mercy of the Nation, of the Nation's *amour propre*, fickleness, ignorance, impulsiveness, and unbelief. In his sermons, Newman warned against making the sentiments of men the measure of faith, insisting that:

> such is the religion of the natural man in every age and place;—often very beautiful on the surface, but worthless in God's sight; good, as far as it goes, but worthless and hopeless, because it does not go further, because it is based on self-sufficiency, and results in self-satisfaction. I grant, it may be beautiful to look at, as in the instance of the young ruler whom our Lord looked at and loved, yet sent away sad; it may have all the delicacy, the amiableness, the tenderness, the religious sentiment, the kindness, which is actually seen in many a father of a family, many a mother, many a daughter, in the length and breadth of these kingdoms, in a refined and polished age like this; but still it is rejected by the heart-searching God, because all such persons walk by their own light, not by the True Light of men, because self is their supreme teacher, and because they pace round and round in the small circle of their own thoughts and of their own judgments, careless to know what God says to them, and fearless of being condemned by Him, if only they stand approved in their own sight. And thus they incur the force of those terrible words, spoken not to a Jewish Ruler, nor to a heathen philosopher, but to a fallen Christian community, to the Christian Pharisees of Laodicea,—'Because thou sayest I am rich, and made wealthy, and have need of nothing; and knowest not that thou art wretched, and miserable, and poor, and blind, and naked; I counsel thee to buy of Me gold fire-tried, that thou mayest be made rich, and be clothed in white garments, that thy shame may not appear, and anoint thine eyes with eye-salve, that thou mayest see. Such as I love, I rebuke and chastise; be zealous, therefore, and do penance.'[124]

Months after writing to Montgomery about the King William Street lectures, Thackeray gave proof of the ambivalence that always characterized his response to Catholicism. "After making a great noise myself," Thackeray

---

[124] John Henry Newman, "The Religion of the Pharisee, the Religion of Mankind" (1856), in *OS*, 26.

wrote to the diarist Allingham, "I begin to wonder why we have made so much to-do about the Cardinal [Cardinal Wiseman, whose reconstitution of the English hierarchy instigated the period known as Papal Aggression]. Why shouldn't he come and set up a winking Virgin in the Strand? The claims of the Bishop of Oxford ... are not much less preposterous: and Dr. Pusey says 'quite right, it's not Popery the parsons have to fear but universal Protestantism.'—Is it coming?—it must, to get rid of these Papists—the old sixteenth century Protestantism can fight them: they've the best of that battle."[125] By the same token, Thackeray was a conventional enough Englishman to abominate monasticism. Speaking of *The Imitation of Christ* of Thomas à Kempis, he observed: "The scheme of that book carried out would make the world the most wretched useless dreary doting place of sojourn—there would be no manhood no love no tender ties of mother & child no use of intellect no trade or science—a set of selfish beings crawling about avoiding one another, and howling a perpetual miserere."[126] Then again, two years after attending the King William Street lectures, Thackeray read Newman's Anglican letters and wrote to his friend Mary Holmes, the Jane Eyre–like governess who was one of Newman's regular correspondents as well, "I am sure Newman's is a great honest heart.... [His] letters read very honest—better than that poor Bulwer[127] with his bosh. It is very difficult for literary men to keep their honesty. We are actors more or less all of us."[128]

Newman would have agreed, though in the more consequential sense that authors are responsible for what they write because their writings are "actions." He would certainly have agreed with the novelist that literary men are often public figures whether they choose to be or not. Newman may

---

[125] *Thackeray's Letters & Private Papers*, ii, 711–12. Cf. Lecture IX, 283–4.

[126] *Thackeray's Letters & Private Papers*, ii, 616.

[127] Edward George Earle Lytton Bulwer-Lytton, first Baron Lytton (1803–73), English playwright, politician, and novelist.

[128] *Thackeray's Letters & Private Papers*, iii, 13.

not have been as reluctant a saint as some have claimed—his sanctity, after all, was eminently practical, even humdrum—but he was always a reluctant public man. However ambivalent about the world, which he both courted and scorned, Thackeray never imagined himself free of its follies. To the journalist Robert Bell, who had taken exception to what he thought the satirical severity of *Vanity Fair*, Thackeray explained that his object in the book was "to indicate, in cheerful terms, that we are for the most part an abominably foolish and selfish people 'desperately wicked' and all eager for vanities.... Good God don't I see (in that may-be cracked and warped looking glass in which I am always looking) my own weaknesses lusts follies shortcomings?... We must lift up our voices about these and howl to a congregation of fools.... You have all of you taken my misanthropy to task—I wish I could myself: but take the world by a certain standard ... and who dares talk of having any virtue at all."[129] This readiness to include himself in his satire also recalls Newman's readiness to include himself in the satirical forays of *Anglican Difficulties*. Chesterton certainly saw the utility of such moral introspection. "The one supreme and even sacred quality in Thackeray's work is that he felt the weakness of all flesh," Chesterton wrote. "Wherever he sneers it is at his own potential self. When he rebukes, it is selfrebuke; when he indulges, he knows it is self-indulgence.... Here then was his special contribution to that chaos of morality which the nineteenth century muddled through: he stood for the remains of Christian humility, as Dickens stood for the remains of Christian charity."[130] However, No Popery prejudices, together with disgust for his mother's rabid Bible religion always prevented Thackeray from embracing any definite Christianity. Apropos Newman's

---

[129] *Thackeray's Letters & Private Papers*, ii, 423–34.
[130] G.K. Chesterton, introduction to *The Book of Snobs* (London: Blackie & Son, 1911), ix. See also Gordon N. Ray, *Thackeray: The Use of Adversity* (Oxford: Oxford University Press, 1955), 377.

friend John Hungerford Pollen,[131] with whom Thackeray became friendly as well, the novelist wrote to one correspondent: "I try and understand from him what can be the secret of the religion for which he has given up rank chances and all good things of this life." But Thackeray had to confess that he was still "so far off believing it," that he feared that when "poor Pollen ... finds that I am only looking at it artistically as at Paganism Mahometanism or any other ism [he] will withdraw from me in sorrow, and ... our pleasant acquaintance won't come to much."[132] Here Thackeray's faith stalled, and although there were times when he wished to advance beyond his unsatisfactory skepticism, he never managed it. Consequently, his settled view of Newman's lectures—and of the Roman Catholicism they recommended —was the view he had first articulated on coming away from them: "It is either Rome or Babylon, and for me it is Babylon," which was not so much a rejection of the Catholic polemicist in Newman as it was an acceptance of the natural man in Thackeray.[133] And yet that Babylon *was* Rome according to traditional No Popery gives Thackeray's statement an unintended ambiguity, which is somehow fitting for this most ambivalent of would-be believers.

John Mason Neale

In his *Lectures on Church Difficulties* (1852), John Mason Neale responded to Newman's lectures without making any specific references to the lectures themselves or their publication or even by mentioning Newman by name. However, in his discussion of Erastianism, it is clear that he is responding to Newman's criticisms of how Erastianism

---

[131] John Hungerford Pollen (1820–1903), convert, decorative artist, architect, and professor of fine arts for Newman's Catholic University in Dublin, for which he designed the Byzantine University Church. For an unusually good account of the creative work of Pollen and Newman, see Guy Nicholls, *Unearthly Beauty: The Aesthetics of John Henry Newman* (Leominster: Gracewing, 2019).

[132] *Thackeray's Letters & Private Papers*, iii, 341.

[133] Thackeray quoted in Ray, *Thackeray: The Age of Wisdom: 1847–1863*, 121.

undermined any claim that the National Church might make to apostolicity. The "fearful Erastianism that tainted the greatest divines of the Laudian school … [can] be detected even in Andrewes," Neale writes; it "blazes forth in Overall, and Montague, and Cosin"; and this accounts for "the hatred with which Church principles were received by the democratic party, as inseparably connected with monarchical ideas, in their strictest, and highest, and (to them) most offensive form." He then defends Erastianism as an unfortunate, though inescapable component of the "all things to all men" Broad Church — an odd rebuttal to Newman's castigations.

Hence, again, in 1688, the disruption of the English Church: those who remained in her, with their divine right principles surrendered also their Church doctrines; those who went out of her were guilty of a schism, because they could not separate the two ideas. Even granting that the nonjuring bishops were right in refusing the oaths—though such would not have been the conduct of the Primitive or the Mediaeval Church—the perpetuation of the succession showed the bitter fruits of the admixture of the politics of this world with the Catholic faith. And the tradition lived even to our own times, nay, and to a certain extent does survive still. Even now we meet with persons who cannot imagine any but one political view to be that of Churchmen. But those who see more deeply have occasion to bless GOD that the case is far otherwise; that the Church is, even in this sense, made all things to all men; that from the highest pitch of Toryism to the lowest descent of Radicalism, all sentiments find a place among her most devoted sons, and that each and all of these, in their own ways, and among their own partisans, are working for her good. How should we exist if the case were otherwise? What way could the Church make among Chartists, if she came among them, clothed in the aristocratical garb of Caroline times? What chance, humanly speaking, would she have among her aristocratical children, if she appeared to them with the democratic politics of her Belgian sister? How would she be received by Manchester operatives, if she were a Protectionist body? or by Lincolnshire farmers, if she were identified with Free Trade doctrines. Here, we may depend upon it, is the strength and the wisdom of the Clergy, to keep as much aloof as lies in their power from all politics: or, if they must take them up, to let it be seen that, whatever their views may be, those views have no connection with the Church, and may be opposed by others who are equally her devoted sons. If there is much in which we may take example from Laud, and Ken, and Sancroft, let us in this take warning. To hear some clerical politicians of the present day, one might imagine them desirous of renewing the exhortation of the Venetian General, when about to engage the Papal forces, "Soldiers, remember that you were Venetians before you were Christians!"[134]

J.M. Capes

In the wake of Newman's lectures, J.M. Capes (1816–89) wrote a long three-part piece entitled "The Rise, Progress and Results of Puseyism" in his paper, *The Rambler*, which touched on the lectures only here and there but nonetheless cast an interesting light on the context in which the lectures were written. That Capes was both a convert to Catholicism and a revert to Anglicanism (if one can use such a droll phrase) makes his analysis doubly interesting. In early 1850, "the [Gorham] judgment was given," Capes wrote.

All the world knows what it was, and we should but weary our readers with more details. It was, in brief, the common-sense reply to the special pleadings of Puseyism. Whatever is written in the baptismal service and the Catechism, said the judges, as a matter of fact the Anglican Church has always tolerated Mr. Gorham's views in her ministers. The Queen was therefore advised to send word to Sir Herbert Jenner Fust that his decision was reversed, and that he must desire Dr. Phillpotts to induct Mr. Gorham. Dr. Phillpotts, having written a bulky pamphlet, in which he protested that he would never yield, and that he "renounced communion" with the Archbishop of Canterbury and all Mr. Gorham's supporters, continued the sham fight through a few formalities more. The Court of Arches installed Mr. Gorham; and the Bishop turned the whole affair into a farce, by telling the parishioners of Brampford-Speke that they ought to attend the ministrations of their heretical vicar, but that if he

---

[134] John M. Neale, *Lectures on Church Difficulties* (London: J.T. Hayes, 1871 edition), 199–201.

preached heresy, they were to inform their diocesan. Thus were the pretensions of Anglo-Catholicism, as a principle of the Anglican Church, legally extinguished. They who believed that the majority of the Puseyites were sincere expected many conversions. We, who believed them to be sincere *only up to a certain point*, anticipated what immediately followed. There was an outburst of words, which cost nothing, and a storm of pamphlets, which cost just the amount of the printers' bills; but the conversions were very few, and of these probably the greater part would have taken place if Mr. Gorham had lived and died a Puseyite.

Still, the Gorham decision was a fatal blow, though its *direct* consequences were small. It consummated the destruction of the Anglo-Catholic theory, and scattered the dust which obscured the vision of many awakened minds.

Three courageous Anglicans, Archdeacon Manning, Dr. Mill, and Mr. Robert Wilberforce, issued a declaration of their interpretation of the royal supremacy, which had inflicted this judgment upon the Establishment, and sent it round to the whole body of the established clergy. Their memorial was, in fact, a denial of the Queen's supremacy. In a victorious party it could not have been tolerated; in a vanquished minority it might be treated with contempt. Of the 15,000 established clergy, about 1700 signed this declaration of independence; but few did any thing more; they signed it one day, the next they signed receipts for tithes, or repeated their signatures to the Thirty-nine Articles. Ere the ink of the 1700 subscriptions was dry, Archdeacon Manning resigned his archdeaconry and his living.

Then, while the echoes of the "protesting" Puseyites—faithful to the one principle of Protestantism—yet lingered in the air, a wild shout arose, beneath which their sullen whispers were overwhelmed. From the whole of that class of Englishmen upon which Puseyism flattered itself that it had wrought an impression, a cry went forth and rent the air with imprecations against its most distant approach, sufficient to convince the most infatuated that "Anglo-Catholicism" was an abhorred thing in the eyes of the whole nation. That it had won the slightest hold upon the feelings of the poor, or upon the lowest of the middle classes, not even the Puseyite periodicals, habituated as they are to manufacture history according to their wishes, had ever ventured to say. Yet it was thought that among commercial, professional, and aristocratic Englishmen—in other words, among those who constitute the sole *bona fide* adherents of the Establishment,—a deep practical attachment to the principles of Church authority, Church independence, and the whole system of dogmatic and ceremonial Anglicanism, had taken firm root. A few days sufficed to dispel the illusion. No sooner was it known that the Pope had created Catholic dioceses throughout England than the whole Anglican body, with scarcely an exception, rose up and proclaimed itself ultra-Protestant to the heart's core.

And herein lay the peculiar force with which the agitation, while it struck one blow at the Pope, struck two against the Puseyites. The "Papal aggression" was denounced far less on account of the obnoxious nature of separate Catholic doctrines, than because it was a denial of the Queen's spiritual supremacy. Granting the stupidity which permitted the remonstrants to confound the Pope's denial of the Queen's ecclesiastical powers with a denial of her temporal rights, the *fact* was this, that the clergy and people of the Anglican communion *identified* the spiritual with the temporal power. So intensely Erastian is the entire body, that it could not separate the two supremacies even in idea. No sooner was the denial of the doctrinal basis of Puseyism consummated by the induction of Mr. Gorham, than the basis of its ecclesiastical claims was scattered to the winds. Who could be now so simple as to imagine the possibility of "Catholicising," in the Puseyite sense, such a nation as this? The Church of England *could* not regard itself as other than a function of the Government. Two things only it abhorred and cast out; and neither of these two was the great body of Catholic doctrine and worship as found existing in the Church of Rome. It abhorred the Papal supremacy, *because it is a denial of the Queen's supremacy*; or ... because it is a denial of the supremacy of each individual Englishman, the Queen being at once the sovereign and the servant of the nation; and it abhorred the Puseyite doctrines and ceremonies, not as being false and antichristian, but as being in *Protestants* mere mummeries, and as symptoms of a traitorous disaffection to the nationality of an Englishman's religion.

To the literal extinction of Puseyism nothing more is needed. It is but a few months since the course of Lectures whose title we have prefixed to the present sketch was delivered by Father Newman in London. If there was any point in these Lectures which was driven home into the innermost heart of Anglo-

Catholicism, it was this, that the Anglican Establishment is a function of the state. And now, while the Anglo-Catholic readers of the Lectures were still writhing beneath the point of the preacher's spear, a new confirmation of the bitter truth springs up when least anticipated, and the Anglo-Catholic theory is razed to its foundations. The demonstration of the ineradicable Erastianism of the Establishment afforded by the recent agitation [the "papal aggression" disturbances] is far more complete than could have been supplied by parliamentary acts or judicial decrees. Its spontaneousness and its stupidity are the best proofs of its genuineness. The English Church cannot recognise a spiritual supremacy anywhere but in the head of the government. It is not that she will not, she has not the power to do otherwise; you cannot force into her mind the notion that the two supremacies are possibly separable. She sees two religions in the world, and two opposing spiritual chiefs: the one national, non-dogmatic, convenient, useful, and *her own*; the other anti-national, dogmatic, intolerant, unmanageable, and *foreign*.[135] Each of these she views as a reality. She upholds the first, because she likes it; she resists the second, because she detests it. But as [for Anglo-Catholicism], a bastard Popery, a religion of shams and imitations, she scorns it, she kicks it, she tramples on it, and yet all the while she so despises it that she would not stoop to strike it, but that she fears it will let in the true Catholicism, before which she is already trembling.

What, then, has the movement of 1833 done for the interests of the Catholic Church in this country? Has it conduced in any degree to the preparation of England for the reception of the Catholic faith? That it should have given many converts to the Church, now amounting to many hundreds, is so far a good deed; but the conversion of even thousands, as individuals, is quite different from the effecting a permanent change in the temper of the nation, or of the most influential classes in the nation. That the movement has wrought this latter result, for ourselves, we think undeniable. It has wrought it in two ways: partly by familiarising the minds of the upper and middle classes with the *idea* of Catholicism, and by bringing the existence,

---

[135] This echoes Duff Cooper's *bon mot*: "For the English, there are only two religions: Roman Catholicism, which is wrong, and all the rest, which do not matter." Duff Cooper, *Old Men Forget* (London: Rupert Hart-Davis,1953), 128.

doctrines, and claims of the Church of Rome prominently before the national eye; and partly by attracting to itself the first outbursts of popular fury against the ideas thus brought forward. From the moment that the Oxford Tracts commenced, the Catholic Church assumed a position in the country which she had never before attained since the schism of the sixteenth century. With what a depth of indescribable horror of Catholicism the whole *mind* of England was formerly saturated, few can comprehend who have not personally experienced it. There are hundreds of persons now Catholics who can remember the time when they felt an aversion towards the very name of Rome, in comparison of which the recent displays of passion are gentle remonstrances. The sons and daughters of Anglicanism were brought up to regard the Catholic Church as the devil's masterpiece. The least bigoted and intolerant among them could not help feeling towards a living Catholic in much the same way as we should feel on finding ourselves side by side with a person who had the plague. The intensity and peculiar virulence of this hate was not brought into constant action, simply because the nation regarded the Catholic body as an utterly insignificant sect of ignorant simpletons or powerless knaves. When an occasional writer or speaker palliated the enormities of Rome, he was regarded as a charitable speculator, who could not see things in their real colours, but as no more likely to turn Protestants into Catholics than to turn Englishmen into Italians. No one read Catholic books; no one entered Catholic churches; no one ever saw Catholic priests; few people even knew that there were any Catholic Bishops resident in England. Except in connexion with Ireland, the Catholic Church was forgotten.

See now the change which has come over the English people as a nation. Violently Protestant still, its attitude to the Catholic Church is extraordinarily changed. It dislikes her, but it no longer despises her. It is filled with misconceptions, and the dupe of an endless tissue of anticatholic nonsense; yet it will, in some circumstances, hear a Catholic in his own justification. It mocks at Catholic miracles, and accounts transubstantiation to be folly; but it no longer thinks it impossible for a pious man, a learned man, or an acute man, to submit to the Church of Rome with his whole heart and soul. Frantic against the "mummeries" of Puseyism, it half admits that in a Catholic these same ceremonies are mummeries no longer. Wildly crying for a penal law against the new hierarchy, it cannot find in its heart to ask for any thing peculiarly ferocious or bloody. Crowds attend the services of Catholic and of Puseyite churches; but while in the latter there is hissing and groaning, in the former a stillness. The most profound pays strange homage to the elevation of the most Holy Sacrament. None but fools and fanatics deny *some* merits to the Church of Rome and her clergy. Every where the change appears; and could we but come forth before the eyes of our countrymen with those undeniable marks of an apostolic spirit which can spring only from an apostolic origin, we are persuaded that in a few years our position in the nation would exhibit even a more marvelous change from that which we now have gained, than our present position displays when contrasted with our humiliation a quarter of a century ago. And whatever other causes may have combined to work this wonderful result, to the movement of 1833 it surely must chiefly be attributed. Catholics are now before the eyes of their fellow-countrymen. The conversion of so many Anglicans has brought about a personal contact and familiar intercourse hitherto unknown, except among the very highest and the very poorest. Catholicism appears before the country as an English religion.... Thousands and thousands of minds have caught a glimpse of what a true system of revealed religion *ought* to be; and while they perceive that such Puseyism is *not*, they are daily becoming more and more convinced, that if Jesus Christ *did* give a revelation of doctrine to man, the Church of Rome, and the Church of Rome alone, is in possession of that revelation.

And thus we quit one of the most interesting themes that can occupy an English pen. When we commenced the historical sketch that we are now closing, it was with little expectation that the movement whose progress we proposed to trace would so rapidly *complete* its course. We saw that it had already entered on its second childhood; but how long its effete old age might linger on, no eye could foresee. For many years the self-delusion might linger among the clergy and households of our islands, and persons whom we had no right to condemn as dishonest might please themselves with a vision of the approaching "Catholicising" of the Established Church. But now this cannot be. The race of Puseyism is all but run. As a *movement* it has ceased to be; as the embodiment of a principle it can no longer hold up its head in the national Church; scarcely a name of repute yet lingers in its muster-roll; beyond those of Keble and Pusey, there is perhaps not one leader remaining who *commands* the homage of a single heart; and of these two, the former, as he was a teacher of old-fashioned High-Church doctrines before the movement began, so has he never been thoroughly identified with its progress, or been recognised as a captain in the fields. One alone remains, bound to the fatal shore by (there is too much reason to fear) a hopeless, incurable, deep-seated attachment to the fundamental principle of Protestantism itself —the rejection of all *authority* save his own intellect. How many souls he may be enabled to continue to enthral, crushing alike their reason and their hearts in an Egyptian bondage, no man can say; but if we may form an anticipation from the ordinary course of human things, it is not impossible that Dr. Pusey himself will be the last Puseyite.[136]

As it happened, this was not to be. Puseyism has proven more enduring than anyone—least of all the Puseyites themselves —would have thought possible: proof, perhaps, of Eliot's contention in *Four Quartets* (1944) that "human kind cannot bear very much reality."[137] As for Capes himself, the inopportunist in Newman was doubtless dismayed by the grounds on which the liberal editor apostatized: it was the definition of papal infallibility that impelled him to bolt. Speaking of the Catholic converts who had come into the Church in the nineteenth century after his conversion in 1845, Capes wrote:

> Their influence has gone unquestionably, on the whole, to uphold Ultramontanism, and they have, some of them, been among the most vehement and successful Italianisers of the English Catholic body. That they have materially assisted in the propagation of Catholicism in the country generally, there can be no doubt. And considering the eccentricities of some of them, and the startling force with which their ways and ideas must have dashed into the midst of the quiet conservatism of the old Catholic body, it is, in my humble judgment, not a little creditable to that body that the converts were altogether not

---

[136] J.M. Capes, "The Rise, Progress and Result of Puseyism," *The Rambler*, vol. 7 (London, Burns & Lambert, 1851): 243–8.

[137] This is from the first section of "Burnt Norton," the first of Eliot's *Four Quartets* (1944).

merely so sincerely welcomed, but, with exceptions, so implicitly trusted.

As for myself, setting aside the opposition and the hostility, especially episcopal, which the expression of liberal views naturally provoked against me, I have again and again almost wondered at the cordiality I have met with, the countenance that has been afforded me, and the support with which I have been aided. And in ceasing, now more than twelve years ago, to regard myself as any longer in communion with the Roman Church, it was, as it still is, a source of deepest pain to me to reflect on the distress and disappointment which my inability to remain a Catholic must have caused in many kind and hopeful hearts.[138]

The Spectator

The Spectator (31 August 1850) ran a long review of the publication of *Lectures on Certain Difficulties Felt by Anglicans in Submitting to the Catholic Church*, which praised its style but found its reasoning Jesuitical and unconvincing. "These lectures are not addressed to sceptics, or Protestants, or zealous members of the Established Church," the reviewer writes; "and therefore they do not touch upon the broad principles of Christianity, or enter into the differences between the Romish and Protestant Churches, unless it be incidentally and in passing. Their object is to call upon those doubting or dissatisfied members of the Establishment who call themselves 'Anglicans' and whom others call Tractarians, to take refuge from the difficulties besetting them, in the bosom of the Catholic Church, where alone salvation is to be secured, at least by them."

Here are the most pertinent passages from the review:

The purpose of the author limits the extent of his topics, and to some degree their interest. There is no occasion to discuss the authority of tradition as an exponent of or addition to Scripture; none to criticize the character and authority of the Fathers, or to weigh the practices of primitive Christianity; for on all these

---

[138] J.M. Capes, *Reasons for Returning to the Church of England* (Strahan & Co: London, 1871), 216–18.

questions the lecturer and those he addresses are at one, so far as lay Tractarians understand them. As little need is there to question the merits of the Saints or the lawfulness of worshiping them; and perhaps Mariolatry is in the same predicament. There is little or no difference between them upon the supernatural powers of the church, the spiritual claims of the priesthood, and those practices of celibacy, confession, the "mummeries" of the service, and priestly interference, which probably are more distasteful to Englishmen than any of the Romish dogmas or doctrines, unless it be transubstantiation. In fact, with the Tractarian views and opinions on church power, government, discipline, and doctrines, there does not seem much difference between the dissatisfied Anglicans and the Catholics save in unimportant or quite secondary matters,—always excepting, as Father Newman does not fail to remark, in the most courteous style and with the most tender defence of their position, the habits, connexions, and livings of his dear brethren. But if the purpose of the lecturer narrows his scope, it gives a freshness and a living interest to much of the lectures. His matter generally is not dug out of books, but gathered fresh from the life around us at home and abroad; even when he refers to history or theology, the references are mostly vivified by a connexion with contemporaries or contemporary events. His very commencement is based upon the actual condition of affairs. It may seem, he says, an ill-chosen time to invite men to disturb the Church by leaving it, when the Universities with all their abuses, and the Church with all its errors, act as a bulwark against worse evils than themselves—against Liberalism, and Dissent, and Infidelity. But, independently of religious considerations, the Tractarians can do no good by remaining where they are. The Church, as late events have shown, is a national church, altogether dependent upon the national will, just as the Ministry and Parliament are dependent upon it, and must shape its course accordingly: Individuals can do no good by remaining; and if they do remain, they will inevitably be carried along with its changes according to the temper of the time. The Church, he declares, is as little bound by what it said or did formerly, as this morning's newspaper by its former numbers, except as it is bound by the law; and while it is upheld by the law it will not be weakened by the subtraction of those individuals nor fortified by their continuance. Its life is an act of Parliament. It will not be able to resist the Arian, Sabellian, or

Editor's Introduction

Unitarian heresies now, because Bull or Waterland resisted them a century or two before; nor will it be unable to resist them—though its more orthodox theologians were presently to leave it. It will be able to resist them while the State gives the word; it would be unable when the State forbids it. Elizabeth boasted that she 'tuned its pulpits'; Charles forbade discussions on Predestination; George on the Holy Trinity; Victoria allows differences on Holy Baptism. While the nation wishes an establishment, it will remain, whatever individuals are for it or against it; and that which determines its existence will determine its voice. Of course the presence or departure of individuals will be one out of various disturbing causes, which may delay or accelerate by a certain number of years a change in its teaching; but, after all, the change depends on events broader and deeper than these; it depends on changes in the nation. As the nation changes its political so may it change its religions views; the causes which earned the Reform Bill and Free Trade may make short work with orthodoxy.

Having touched upon the history of the English Church, and exhibited its present state from the high priestly point of view; with great skill, power, and delicacy, Father Newman proceeds in four lectures to consider the religious or Providential direction of the Tractarian movement, as in two previous lectures he had examined its more popular effects. By reference to facts, and to the writings of himself and others, he affirms that the movement was neither towards the Church, nor towards a party in the Church; that neither by its nature or its intent was it directed to establish a branch church, or a sect; in fact, he seems clearly to make out the charges of his former opponents, that while the Tractarians were wearing the uniform and receiving the pay of the English Church, they were, unconsciously or consciously, doing the work of Rome. In two more lectures, the author describes the political and religious state of Roman Catholic countries, with a view of showing that no argument can be based on the alleged results of Catholicism in prejudice to the sanctity of the Church. But it seems difficult to suppose that a scholar and logician could fancy that his arguments could meet even a Tractarian's objection on that score, temporal though it might be: Father Newman's arguments only prove how very unsuccessful even the Church is in saving souls. In the tenth chapter, "Differences among Catholics no prejudice to the Unity of the Church," it seems hard to suppose that the author could fancy himself reasoning at all: he evades altogether the main points at issue, even as he has stated them. The eleventh lecture aims at showing from Scripture and history that the existence of the Greek and Asiatic Churches is no prejudice to the Catholicity of the true Church, any more than the existence of heresies, or the various sects of Protestants. The last lecture is to prove that Christian history is not prejudicial to the Apostolicity of the Church. The reader who expects to find in it any explanation of the worldly and too often the horribly wicked character of the Popedom and its hierarchy, judged even by the lowest Worldly standard, or any allusion to its bloody persecutions and ambitious wars, will be disappointed. It consists chiefly of an endeavour to identify the English Church, and its moderation with the Erastianism and semi-Arianism which Constantine and his successor aimed at enforcing when Christianity became the established religion of the Roman Empire.

What effects these lectures may have on Tractarian one cannot tell: their master ought to know his disciples well enough to have chosen arguments adapted to their nature. As a piece of reasoning, it seems to be, speaking generally, poor even to disappointment. The exposition of the present state of affairs in the Establishment is indeed done with refined sarcasm; but this is only attack. In like manner, the want of tangible results from the Tractarian movements, and the inconsistency of Tractarian views with those of the Establishment, are well put but the arguments to lure the Tractarians to Rome seem of the weakest, unless the Tractarians are Romanists already, and deterred from avowing it by secular considerations; while the lecturer overlooks the stimulus which the Tractarian movement really has given to the English Church, and possibly to Dissenting bodies. A kind of jesuitical casuistry may be found in the work, but it strikes us as too flimsy and transparent to convince, or even to puzzle. In a literary point of view, the lectures are not equal to some of Newman's other works. They have not so much tenderness and religious unction as he has elsewhere exhibited; and the subject, as he has handled it, is not very favorable to breadth and largeness. Still the lectures possess great literary merit. As delicate in their sarcasm as a lady's malice, they have nothing of bitterness or passion. "My brethren," even among schismatics or heretics, are handled as old Isaac Walton directs the living bait to be impaled—tenderly, as if you loved him. The style is often slightly prolix, but it is the prolixity of a scholar and casuist, who has matter in his prolixity, and is compelled to be full to convey his shades of meaning. There is a grace, an ease, and a flow in his diction. Without force, or effort, or iteration, or any attempt at condensation, the composition has a vital strength arising from the living power of genius. How skillfully the weak points of the Anglican and indeed of any State Church are selected ... and with what easy vigour they are presented! Of course it was not the writer's cue to point out that the clergy are as dependent in a Voluntary system..... One rare accomplishment of a controversialist Newman possesses: he does not aim at proving more than his case requires, and he admits all merit in his opponent except that which is decisive of the question. We do not hear from him that the Church is altogether dead; there is life, only it is not Catholic life.

Dublin Review
If Newman's detractors have always taken it into their heads to imagine that detraction, *per se*, is somehow synonymous with criticism, the Catholic *Dublin Review* shows how sympathy can yield more fruitful insights into an author's work, granted, of course, that the author under consideration merits sympathy. (Chesterton's criticism is a good example of this.) The best thing about this sympathetic review of *Lectures on Certain Difficulties Felt by Anglicans in Submitting to the Catholic Church*, which appeared in the paper in September of 1850, is its appreciation of how seamlessly—and revealingly—Newman introduced autobiography into the fabric of his lectures, which foreshadows how he would turn the autobiographical to account in his *Apologia*. In the earlier book, Newman recognized that the best way to tackle such material was critically, indeed, unsparingly, without any eye to self-vindication, and he would follow this same *modus operandi* in the later book. Thus, the reviewer recognizes that while autobiography presented Newman with his greatest formal challenge in the writing of *Anglican Difficulties*, it also made possible the book's greatest formal achievement, which consisted in his successfully tackling that challenge. "It is often said, that the history of a scholar is the history of his books," the reviewer writes.

There are few writers, and especially few theological writers, of whom this is more true, than of the distinguished author of the *Lectures on Anglican Difficulties*. Even in the absence of the key to certain passages of private history which these Lectures supply, it would be impossible for anyone at all intimately acquainted with Dr. Newman's writings, not to perceive that they all bear a clear and definite personal relation to the author, and that each of them represents some new and distinct reality in the development of his mind. It is not merely that he will recognise them, at a glance, as steps of a regularly progressive series, commencing, at least as far as principles are concerned, with what may almost be called the foundation, of the Christian faith, and following it up into all the minutest details of its dogmatical completeness. To trace out such a progress as this, would be, in itself, a very curious and interesting study. But in Dr. Newman's case, it possesses peculiar attractions. The interest of all, even the most purely and abstractly dogmatical of his publications, is heightened by the evidence of genuineness and reality which they all present. There is an air of earnestness and truth in every thing which he has written, that brings the writer, in his own person, before us, in every page. We cannot help constantly feeling, in what is addressed to ourselves, the workings of his own mind, even where there is not the remotest personal allusion; and as each new view is developed in succession, we are led on, step by step, with the full consciousness that our guide has traced for himself the way by which he leads us.

And it is eminently, and indeed avowedly, so in these *Lectures upon Anglican Difficulties*. In these, however, the personal relation is retrospective. The author himself relates in many most interesting passages, the progress of that mental history which the several works practically reveal. His argumentation is addressed, in great part, not so to his hearers as to his former self. The "difficulties" which he combats, are those which had beset his own course; the obstacles which he removes from the paths of others, are those which it has been the reward of his own long and painful struggle to overcome. Indeed, the very necessity of dealing thus with such a subject has formed, by his own avowal, one of his greatest embarrassments in the undertaking. The apprehension, or rather the certainty, that in treating it at all he would be "compelled to speak of himself," made him sensitively unwilling to undertake the course of

Lectures. He foresaw that he "could not address his audience on the subjects which he proposed, without introducing himself into the discussion;" he could not refer to the past, without alluding to matters in which he had had a part; he could not show that interest in his hearers' state of mind and course of thought which he really felt, "without showing that he therefore understood it, because he had before now experienced it himself:" and he was haunted by the anticipation, doubly painful to a mind so modest as his, that "in drawing out the events of former years, and the motives of past transactions, and the operation of common principles, and the complexion of old habits and opinions, he should be, in no slight degree, constructing, what he has ever avoided, a defence of himself" [322].

It is only just to add that, as may be inferred from such principles as these, the difficulty here anticipated has been most successfully overcome.

The reasons the reviewer cites as to why Newman succeeded in overcoming this core difficulty are persuasive:

We never remember to have seen the trying subject of "self" treated with so much judgment and so much taste as in these Lectures. There is a graceful union of modesty and frankness in the tone of all that relates to the author's own person, removed alike from arrogance and from affected reserve, which, while it excites our interest in the highest degree, and imparts a character of life and reality to the narrative, yet never jars upon that instinctive sensitiveness by which we shrink from every undue exhibition of egotism, however skilfully disguised. There is another most pleasing characteristic of these Lectures which may of course be traced to the same source—the tone which pervades them of trustful confidence in the principles by which the author himself had been influenced, and of affectionate tenderness for those with whom he once held them in common; for the difficulties by which they are surrounded; for the prejudices which hold them back; for the manifold and distracting ties from which he is now set free, but which still fetter their every movement.

Reading this, one is reminded of Newman's sermon "Personal Influence the Means of Propagating Truth" (1832) in his *Fifteen Sermons Preached before the University of Oxford*

(1843), in which he says that the "propagation of Truth" is always beset with "difficulties" not only because of "its want of instruments, as an assailant of the world's opinions," but "the keenness and vigour of the weapons producible against it, when itself in turn is to be attacked." And this prompts him to ask himself a question that must have occurred to him often in the course of his long catechetical life.

> How, then, after all, has [Truth] maintained its ground among men, and subjected to its dominion unwilling minds, some even bound to the external profession of obedience, others at least in a sullen neutrality, and the inaction of despair? I answer, that it has been upheld in the world not as a system, not by books, not by argument, nor by temporal power, but by the personal influence of such men … who are at once the teachers and the patterns of it…. Here, first, is to be taken into account the natural beauty and majesty of virtue, which is more or less felt by all but the most abandoned. I do not say virtue in the abstract,—virtue in a book. Men persuade themselves, with little difficulty, to scoff at principles, to ridicule books, to make sport of the names of good men; but they cannot bear their presence: it is holiness embodied in personal form, which they cannot steadily confront and bear down: so that the silent conduct of a conscientious man secures for him from beholders a feeling different in kind from any which is created by the mere versatile and garrulous Reason.[139]

One achievement of the *Anglican Difficulties* lectures is that Newman so interjects himself into them that the reader can see—in his honesty, his humility, his self-criticism, his solicitude for his old friends—that he did make of himself the "teacher and pattern" of the Truth he wished to impart. The reviewer in the *Dublin Review* quotes a passage from the last lecture of the series to exemplify Newman's solicitude for the spiritual well-being of his Anglo-Catholic friends, a solicitude which does not shy away from admitting the laughter and scorn to which he has sometimes resorted to get his friends' attention:

---

[139] *OS*, 91–2.

"It needed no prophetical gift, he feelingly avows," in his closing Lecture, "to be sure, that others must take ultimately the course which I had taken, though I could not foretell the time or the occasion; no gift to foresee that those who did not choose to plunge into the gulf of scepticism must at length fall back upon the Catholic Church. Nor did it require in me much faith in you, my dear brethren, much love for you, to be sure that, though there were close around you men who look like you but are not, that you, the children of the movement, were too conscientious, too much in earnest, not to be destined by that God, who made you what you are, to greater things. Others may have scoffed at you, but I never; others may have made light of your principles, or your sincerity, but never I; others may have predicted evil of you, I have only felt vexed at the prediction. I have laughed indeed, I have scorned, and scorn and laugh I must, when men set up an outside instead of the inside of religion—when they affect more than they can sustain—when they indulge in pomp or in minutiæ, which are only then becoming when there is something to be proud of, something to be anxious for. If I have been excessive here, if I have confused what is defective with what is hollow, or have mistaken aspiration for pretence, or have been severe upon infirmities, towards which self-knowledge would have made me tender, I wish it otherwise. Still, whatever my faults in this matter, I have ever been trustful in that true Catholic spirit which has lived in the movement of which you are partakers. I have been steady in my loyalty to that supernatural influence among you, which made me what I am, — which, in its good time, shall make you what you shall be."
[323–4]

The reviewer's gloss on this will strike most readers as just: "It would be hard to find a writer better qualified than Dr. Newman, not only by positive acquirements, but also and even more, by the character of his mind and his peculiar habits of ... thought, for the examination of the great questions involved in these fundamental discussions." The reviewer then itemizes the habits of thought that makes his examination of these matters so compelling: "The singular union of depth and acuteness which characterizes all his views; his extraordinary power of analysis; his instinctive faculty of detecting and tracing out the analogies of reason and of revelation; his wonderful capacity for illustration; and, rarer still, the beautifully simple, natural, and persuasive order into which all his varied materials fall, apparently without an effort, seem to point him out as especially qualified for the investigation of questions which resolve themselves ultimately into the foundations of faith."

The reviewer then concludes where he had begun: with a consideration of the autobiographical element of the book, and why this is so instrumental to its success:

> Considered in a personal point of view, however, there is none of the Lectures so interesting as the twelfth and concluding one. It is, in truth, a history of the author's own progress in the gradual discovery of Catholic truth, told with exceeding simplicity and modesty, and yet with the most perfect unreserve. We have no hesitation in saying, that although it is but the merest outline—hardly even a sketch—the impression which it gives us of the author's powers of mind, of his extraordinary familiarity with even the most obscure of the ancient controversies, his faculty of seizing all the strong points of a precedent and applying them to the case which may be under consideration, has been almost greater than that produced by the most elaborate of his former publications: we can hardly even except the Athanasius itself, the most wonderful of them all, and not inferior to the most successful efforts of the Maurists in their proudest days. The comparison of the *Via Media* of the movement of 1833, with the *Via Media* attempted in the controversy upon the Trinity, and again, in that upon the Incarnation, is one of the most interesting historical parallels we ever remember to have read; and although it is little more than hinted at in the Lecture; though the author has not attempted to carry it out into the later stages of the history; to contrast the Report of our modern Privy Council with the Henoticon of Zeno, or to compare Mr. Gorham with Eutyches, or Archbishop Sumner with Acacius of Constantinople: yet the points which are touched, are brought out in such a way as to produce an irresistible effect, even upon those who are most wedded to the high hopes with which the originators of the *Via Media* of Anglicanism first mapped it out for their followers. We can only make room for the general observations with which he closes this portion of the subject, and which are doubly interesting as

containing a brief but lucid statement of his favourite theory of Doctrinal Development.

> Recollect, my brethren, I am going into these details, not as if I thought of convincing you on the spot by a view of history which convinced me after careful consideration, nor as if I called on you to be convinced by what convinced me at all (for the methods of conviction are numberless, and one man approaches the Church by this road, another by that), but merely in order to show you how it was that Antiquity, instead of leading me from the Holy See, as it leads many, on the contrary drew me on to submit to its claims. But, even had I worked out for you these various arguments ever so fully, I should have brought before you but a secondary portion of the testimony, which the ancient Church seemed to me to supply to its identity with the modern. What was far more striking to me than the ecclesiastical phenomena which I have been drawing out, remarkable as they are, is a subject of investigation which is not of a nature to introduce into a popular Lecture; I mean, the history of the doctrinal definitions of the Church. It is well known that, though the creed of the Church has been one and the same from the beginning, yet it has been so deeply lodged in her bosom as to be held by individuals more or less implicitly, instead of being delivered from the first in those special statements, or what are called definitions, under which it is now presented to us, and which preclude mistake or ignorance. These definitions, which are but the expression of portions of the one dogma which has ever been received by the Church, are the work of time; they have grown to their present shape and number in the course of eighteen centuries, under the exigency of successive events, such as heresies and the like, and they may of course receive still further additions as time goes on. Now this process of doctrinal development, as you might suppose, is not of an accidental or random character; it is conducted upon laws, as every thing else which comes from God; and the study of its laws and of its exhibition, or, in other words, the science and history of the formation of theology, was a subject which had interested me more than any thing else from the time I first began to read the Fathers, and which had engaged my attention in a special way. Now it was gradually brought home to me, in the course of my reading, so gradually, that I cannot trace the steps of my conviction, that the decrees of later Councils, or what Anglicans call the Roman corruptions, were but instances of that very same doctrinal law which was to be found in the history of the early Church; and that in the sense in which the dogmatic truth of the prerogatives of the Blessed Virgin may be said in the lapse of centuries to have grown upon the consciousness of individuals, in that same sense did in the first age the mystery of the Blessed Trinity also gradually shine out

and manifest itself more and more completely before their minds. Here was at once an answer to the objections urged by Anglicans against the present teaching of Rome; but not only an answer to objections, but a positive argument in its favour; for the immutability and uninterrupted action of the laws in question throughout the course of Church history is a plain note of identity between the Catholic Church of the first ages and that which now goes by the name: — just as the argument from the analogy of natural and revealed religion is at once an answer to difficulties in the latter, and a direct proof that Christianity has the same Author as the physical and moral world. But the force of this, to me ineffably cogent argument, I cannot hope to convey to another. [320–2]

Finally, the reviewer observes:

But we have no hope of being able by these few extracts, which we have selected almost at random, or by the brief outline which we have attempted of their contents, to give anything like an accurate notion of these memorable Lectures, the delivery of which may well be regarded as one of the great epochs in this auspicious movement. There are few more pregnant writers than Dr. Newman. His style, even as much as his matter, is eminently suggestive. He is one of that class of thinkers to whom he alludes in one of his Lectures, whom no one can approach without being himself set thinking, and whose thoughts must therefore necessarily suffer bypassing through the hands of an interpreter. His Lectures must be read in their integrity, in order to be fully appreciated; and we are sure there is not one, whether friend or foe, who will not rise from their perusal, prepared to unite with us in the earnest hope that he may soon be induced to resume them, and to complete in a similar course, the tempting list of subjects to which he alludes in his preface, and which are hardly inferior in interest or importance to those which form the matter of his present volume.[140]

Edward Healy Thompson

Edward Healy Thompson (1813–91), Roman Catholic convert and writer, was educated at Oakham School and Emmanuel College, Cambridge. After taking Anglican orders, he obtained a curacy at Calne. Thereafter he was Anglican

---

[140] *Dublin Review*, vol. xxix, no. lvi (September 1850): 208–12, 223–5.

minister at Marylebone, Ramsgate. He converted to Catholicism in 1846, largely as the result of Newman's work. He was a friend of Hope and Badeley, and the latter wrote to Newman on 3 April 1846, when Thompson was on the verge of conversion to Roman Catholicism: "He is really almost a Pupil of yours, having been tutored and instructed mainly by your writings."[141] For the rest of his life, which he spent in Cheltenham, Thompson devoted himself to religious literature. *The Life and Glories of St. Joseph* (1888) is one of his more popular titles, being still in print. He married Harriet Diana Calvert, daughter of Nicholson Calvert of Humsden. On her husband's conversion, she also joined the Catholic Church and, like him, devoted herself to literary work, producing, among other things, a life of St. Charles Borromeo. Her husband was a regular correspondent of Newman over the years. In a letter to the editor of the *Weekly Register* (4 April 1857), Thompson wrote of himself and his fellow Anglo-Catholic converts:

We do not take the same view as Mr. Phillipps[142] of the character and prospects of the National Church. We do not hope for its restoration to Catholic Unity, for the simple reason that we do not believe it has the sort of existence Mr. Phillipps attributes to it. For my own part I honestly declare that I do not hope and I do not even pray for the Anglican Church in its corporate capacity. I hope and pray for England, for all my countrymen; I hope and pray for the members of the Anglican Church, and especially for those who profess the principles which were the occasion of my own conversion, and who are sincerely seeking the Truth, or earnestly acting upon such truths as they already possess, careless of consequences. But for the Anglican Church as an

---

[141] *LD*, viii, note 4, 55.

[142] Ambrose Lisle Phillipps (1809–78), an indefatigable advocate of union between the Roman Catholic Church and the Anglican Church, formed the Association for the Unity of Christendom in 1857, from which Catholics were ordered to withdraw in 1864. For Newman's view of corporate reunion, see letters of 1, 4, 9, 13, and 30 July 1857 to A.L. Phillipps in *LD*, xviii. See also Mark D. Chapman, *The Fantasy of Reunion: Anglicans, Catholics and Ecumenism, 1833–1882* (Oxford: Oxford University Press, 2014).

ecclesiastical body, or as a body at all, I have no sort of feeling whatever. Nor ought this to shock or surprise Mr. Phillipps when he recollects what has been written by the very leader of the movement, by him to whom the children of the movement looked up as their master and teacher. It is curious to compare the language used by Mr. Phillipps in his letter to the *Union*, with that employed by Father Newman in his "Lectures on Anglican Difficulties."[143]

Newman's reply to Thompson's letter was amusingly grateful: "I am glad to see from the Register and Union that you, or at least your argumentative powers, are in so good case—and I shall be glad to know that I am right in believing it of your whole man, that is, your body, which was the ailing portion of it. I have heard nothing definite about you for a long time. But what I write to you about especially is to congratulate you on fixing A. Phillipps on a spit, if he is made to see it. I wanted it to come out as the turning point of the controversy—viz that we did not pray for the conversion of the Church of England as such, any more than we pray for the Fishmongers Company as such, because we did not allow its religious existence. This is the sole difference between you and him—will he accept it? will he maintain that the Church of E has a religious existence? and if so, will he give you on paper *what* the notes are of its religious existence?"[144]

Something of the same toughmindedness that Thompson brought to his reading of *Anglican Difficulties* can be seen in his memorable introduction to his convert friend Henry Bedford's *Life of St Vincent de Paul*, in which he gave an unsparing account of the state of the Church in France in the seventeenth century. The first page contained a quotation from Adrien Bourdoise, Saint Vincent's associate in the work of reform: "The world is sick enough, but the clergy is not less so: frivolity, impurity, immodesty, are everywhere paramount.... The majority of our priests stand with their arms

---

[143] *LD*, xviii, note 2, 12.
[144] Newman to Edward Healy Thompson (6 April 1857), *LD*, xviii, 11–12.

folded; God is forced to raise up laymen—cutlers and haberdashers—to do the work of these lazy ecclesiastics."[145]

Richard Holt Hutton

In his classic short biography, *Cardinal Newman* (1890), Richard Holt Hutton (1826–97), the good friend of Walter Bagehot and editor of the *Spectator*, whose own Christian faith was deeply influenced and enriched by Newman, called attention to the literary merits of the lectures. Hutton refers to them as a "landmark" in Newman's history as a Roman Catholic, though, as a High Church Anglican, he was not persuaded entirely of Newman's charge of Erastianism against the National Church, nor was he comfortable with the fact that Newman did not more expressly address the issue of infallibility in the lectures—a sticking point for him personally when it came to considering the claims of the Roman Church. Since Hutton attended all of the lectures as a young man, his view of them in his biography of Newman has to be seen as retrospective, though also informed by a lifetime's close reading of Newman's work.

> In matter and style alike these lectures were marked by all the signs of his singular literary genius. They were simpler and less ornate than the *Sermons addressed to Mixed Congregations*, and more exquisite in form as well as more complete in substance than the *Essay on Development*, which was written under the heavy pressure of the dreaded and anticipated rupture between himself and the Church of his baptism. I think the *Lectures on Anglican Difficulties* was the first book of Newman's generally read amongst Protestants, in which the measure of his literary power could be adequately taken. In the Oxford sermons there had been of course more room for the expression of religious feeling of a higher type, and frequently there had been more evidence of depth and grasp of mind; but here was a great subject with which Newman was perfectly intimate, giving the fullest scope to his powers of orderly and beautiful exposition, and opening a far greater range to his singular genius for gentle and delicate irony than any thing which he had previously

[145] *LD*, xvii, note 1, 450.

written. It is a book, however, which adds but little to our insight into his mind, though it adds much to our estimate of his powers, and I must pass it by with only brief notice.... As he described the growth of his disillusionment with the Church of England, and compared it to the transformation which takes place in fairy tales when the magic castle vanishes, the spell is broken, "and nothing is seen but the wild heath, the barren rock, and the forlorn sheep-walk" [6], no one could have doubted that he was describing with perfect truth the change that had taken place in his own mind. "So it is with us," he said, "as regards the Church of England, when we look in amazement on that we thought so unearthly, and find so commonplace or worthless. Then we perceive that aforetime we have not been guided by reason, but biased by education, and swayed by affection. We see in the English Church; I will not merely say, no descent from the first ages, and no relationship to the Church in other lands, but we see no body politic of any kind; we see nothing more or less than an establishment, a department of government, or a function or operation of the State—without a substance,—a mere collection of officials, depending on and living in the supreme civil power. Its unity and personality are gone, and with them its power of exciting feelings of any kind. It is easier to love or hate an abstraction than so tangible a framework or machinery." [6]

This is, of course, an exaggerated view. It is not true that the State can do what it pleases with the English Church, can modify its theology or change its liturgy at will; but it is still less true that the Church can do as she will without the consent of the State.... Indeed this whole lecture delivers one of the most powerful attacks ever opened on the Anglican theory of the Church as independent of the State. Not less powerful was Newman's delineation, in the fifth lecture, of the collapse of the Anglican theory of the Church when applied to practice. The Anglicans, he said, "had reared a goodly house, but their foundations were falling in. The soil and the masonry both were bad. The Fathers would protect 'Romanists' as well as extinguish Dissenters. The Anglican divines would misquote the Fathers and shrink from the very doctors to whom they appealed. The Bishops of the seventeenth century were shy of the Bishops of the fourth, and the Bishops of the nineteenth were shy of the Bishops of the seventeenth" [151]....

The lectures were much more powerful in attack than in defence. Those of which it was the object to show that the

Anglican Church was essentially Erastian, and was not one which could ever satisfy the ideal of the Tractarians, were simply demonstrative; the lectures of which it was the intention to remove the objections felt towards the Roman Catholic communion were partly defective, partly inadequate. They did not deal at all with what seems to me the greatest of all objections to the Roman Catholic Church, the indifference she shows to reasonable criticisms, even in her most solemn acts, such as the sanction given to utterly unhistorical facts in the feast of the Assumption of the Virgin Mary, and the sanction given to the doctrine of the plenary inspiration of the Scriptures in the decrees of the Council of Trent and (subsequently) of the Council of the Vatican. On the other hand, the eighth and ninth lectures on the "Political state of Catholic countries no prejudice to the sanctity of the Church," and the "Religious character of Catholic countries no prejudice to the sanctity of the Church," raise, I think, at least as many difficulties as they remove. And in effect they almost concede that comparative want of self-reliance and self-control in matters both political and religious which certainly characterizes Catholic countries, as distinguished from those Catholic communities which exist in the heart of Protestant countries, and which are surrounded on all sides by religious opponents. Newman's apology for the political and religious state of Ireland as given in 1850 seems even less effective, indeed much less effective, when read in 1890 than it seemed then. Almost all that Ireland has gained since 1850, she has gained by the resolute ignoring of Catholic principles; and all that she has lost, she has lost by the resolute ignoring of Catholic principles. And though the gain may be considerable politically, I fear the moral loss far outweighs the political gain.[146]

Augustine Birrell

Augustine Birrell (1850–1933), the son of a Baptist minister, began his career in Liverpool as an articled clerk. After going on to Trinity College, Cambridge, he became, first, a Chancery lawyer and, then Queen's Counsel. He was also the epitome of a bookman, when essayists and litterateurs were in

---

[146] Richard Holt Hutton, *Cardinal Newman* (London: Methuen, 1891), 206–12.

great demand for the instruction and entertainment of a pre–WW I mass reading public undistracted by film and the wireless.[147] Birrell's love of books came, in part, from the solace they gave him after the death of his wife and their baby in childbirth, thirteen months after the couple had married. Birrell also had the unenviable distinction of being Chief Secretary for Ireland when the insurrectionists of the Easter Rebellion knocked poor Dublin silly. His political bad timing notwithstanding, his essays abound in lively literary judgments, proof that his ability to interest the denizens of Rotten Row in literature was neither inconsiderable nor accidental.[148]

The bookman in him wrote of Dr. Johnson and Edmund Burke, Hazlitt and Lamb, Walter Bagehot and Matthew Arnold with infectious *brio*. But the would-be believer in him, the critic who was neither Anglican nor Catholic, was also fascinated by Newman. In a number of his essays, he wrote perceptively of Newman, usually from the standpoint of style.[149] "Newman's books have long had a large and

---

[147] For a fascinating overview of the now vanished literary landscape of the bookmen, see Philip Waller's magnificent *Writers, Readers, and Reputations: Literary Life in Britain 1870–1918* (Oxford: Oxford University Press, 2006).

[148] Apropos Birrell's appeal for society readers, Ensor noted how the "fascinating style" and "small bulk" of his "breakthrough" book of essays, *Obiter Dicta* (1884) "made it easy to carry [the book] about from country house to country house and discuss under the trees on a fine afternoon." *DNB*.

[149] The subject of style in Newman's work has not received anything like the attention it deserves, though a few commentators have had worthwhile things to say about it. See John Holloway, *The Victorian Sage: Studies in Argument* (London: Macmillan, 1953) and Ronald Begley, "Metaphor in the *Apologia* and Newman's Conversion" in *Newman and Conversion*, ed. Ian Ker (Indiana: Notre Dame, 1997), 59-74. See also Ian Ker's "Newman the Satirist," in *Newman After a Hundred Years* ed. Ian Ker and Alan G. Hill (Oxford: Oxford University Press, 1990). In his essay (p. 9), Ker quotes Newman on the private life of the English cleric, biblical scholar and author Thomas Newton (1704-82) admittedly distinguished for his "kindness of heart" and "amiableness" but "a man so idolatrous of comfort, so liquorish of preferment, whose most fervent aspiration apparently was that he might ride in a carriage and sleep on down, whose keenest sorrow

increasing sale," he wrote in the extract that I include here. "They stand on all sorts of shelves, and wherever they go a still, small voice accompanies them. They are speaking books." This is particularly true of *Anglican Difficulties*, which reproduces not only Newman's voice, but those of Eusebians, Arians, semi-Arians, Eutychians, John Jewel and the Reformers, the Caroline divines, the Non-Jurors, Bishop Warburton, John Wesley, Richard Whatley, Tractarians, popes, heretics, saints, statesmen, emperors, poets, Anglo-Catholics—the list goes on and on, though always, intermingled with these are the voices of the King James Bible, an inalienable part of Newman's heart and mind. Of course, style may not be something that our own age either understands or prizes, but Birrell reminds readers of how essential an understanding of style is to understanding Newman. In a piece about Newman that Birrell wrote two years after the Cardinal's death, included in his essay collection, *Res Judicatae* (1892), he touches on *Anglican Difficulties* in the context of his entire career. In addition to his well-taken points about Newman's style, Birrell shows how Newman was still being judged in death by the same criteria that he had written *Anglican Difficulties* in life to mock — the criteria of an unreal Establishment. Over a hundred years later, this state of affairs has not changed, though Newman's "minimizers" (to use Birrell's word) now include not only liberal Protestants of various stripes but Modernist Catholics as well, many of whose notions of Christianity are indistinguishable.

Rather than comment myself on Birrell's commentary, I shall only add one trenchant comment offered by a reader of mine, which can serve to preface the extracts. In responding to my typescript, Father Carleton Jones, O.P., wrote: "I won't

---

was that he could not get a second appointment without relinquishing the first, who cast a regretful look back upon his dinner while he was at supper, and anticipated his morning chocolate in his evening muffins, who will say that this is the man, not merely to unchurch, but to smite, to ban, to wither the whole of Christendom for many centuries, and the greater part of it even in his own day…" *Ess*, ii, 138-9

go into any detail, but when I finished your Introduction, I was surprised to find that my favorite commentator in your array of commentators was Augustine Birrell. A couple of his sentences show his appreciation for Newman's holiness. Here is an example (not to imply that Burke is a saint): 'I have elsewhere ventured upon a comparison between Burke and Newman,' Birrell wrote. 'Both men, despite their subtlety and learning and super-refinement, their love of fine points and their splendid capacity for stating them in language so apt as to make one's admiration breathless, took very broad, common-sense, matter-of-fact views of humanity, and ever had the ordinary man and woman in mind as they spoke and wrote.' In other words, Newman had in mind the salvation of souls." This is true; it also confirms the point I made earlier that there is a straightforwardness to the lectures, which has always colored responses to them: readers either wholeheartedly embrace or reject them.

Here, then, are the extracts from Birrell's essay:

There are some men whose names are inseparably and exclusively associated with movements; there are others who are forever united in human memories with places; it is the happy fortune of the distinguished man whose name is at the top of this page [Cardinal Newman] to be able to make good both titles to an estate in our minds and hearts; for whilst his fierce intellectual energy made him the leader of a great movement, his rare and exquisite tenderness has married his name to a lovely place. Whenever men's thoughts dwell upon the revival of Church authority in England and America during this century, they will recall the Vicar of St. Mary's, Oxford, who lived to become a Cardinal of Rome, and whenever the lover of all things that are quiet and gentle and true in life and literature visits Oxford, he will find himself wondering whether snap-dragon still grows outside the windows of the rooms in Trinity where once lived the author of the "Apologia."... A strong personal attachment of the kind which springs up from reading an author, which is distilled through his pages, and turns his foibles, even his follies, into pleasant things we would not for the world have altered, is apt to cause the reader who is thus affected to exaggerate the importance of any intellectual movement with which the author happened to be associated. There are, I know, people who think this is notably so in Dr. Newman's case. Crusty men are to be met with, who rudely say they have heard enough of the Oxford movement, and that the time is over for penning ecstatic paragraphs about Dr. Newman's personal appearance in the pulpit at St. Mary's. I think these crusty people are wrong. The movement was no doubt an odd one in some of its aspects—it wore a very academic air indeed; and to be academic is to be ridiculous, in the opinion of many. Our great Northern towns lived their grimy lives, amidst the whirl of their machinery, quite indifferent to the movement. Our huge Nonconformist bodies knew no more of the University of Oxford in those days than they did of the University of Tübingen. This movement sent no missionaries to the miners, and its tracts were not of the kind that are served suddenly upon you in the streets like legal process, but were, in fact, bulky treatises stuffed full of the dead languages. London, of course, heard about the movement, and, so far as she was not tickled by the comicality of the notion of anything really important happening outside her cab radius, was irritated by it. Mr. Henry Rogers poked heavy fun at it in the *Edinburgh Review*. Mr. Isaac Taylor wrote two volumes to prove that ancient Christianity was a drivelling and childish superstition, and in the opinion of some pious Churchmen succeeded in doing so. But for the most part people left the movement alone, unless they happened to be Bishops....

But notwithstanding this aspect of the case, it was a genuine thought-movement in propagating which these long-coated parsons, with their dry jokes, strange smiles, and queer notions were engaged. They used to drive about the country in gigs, from one parsonage to another, and leave their tracts behind them. They were not concerned with the flocks—their message was to the shepherds. As for the Dissenters, they had nothing to say to them, except that their very presence in a parish was a plenary argument for the necessity of the movement. The Tractarians met with the usual fortune of those who peddle new ideas. Some rectors did not want to be primitive—more did not know what it meant; but enough were found pathetically anxious to read a meaning into their services and offices, to make it plain that the 'Tracts' really were 'for' and not 'against' the times. The great plot, plan, or purpose, call it what you will, of the Tractarian movement was to make Churchmen believe with a personal conviction that the Church of England was not a mere National Institution, like the House of Commons or the game of cricket, but a living branch of that Catholic Church which God had, from the beginning, endowed with sacramental gifts and graces, with a Priesthood apostolically descended, with a creed, precise and specific, which it was the Church's duty to teach and man's to believe, and with a ritual and discipline to be practised and maintained with daily piety and entire submission....

It cannot be denied that the Tractarians had their work before them. But they had forces on their side.

It is always pleasant to rediscover the meaning of words and forms which have been dulled by long usage. This is why etymology is so fascinating. By the natural bent of our minds we are lovers of whatever things are true and real. We hanker after facts. To get a grip of reality is a pleasure so keen—most of our faith is so desperate a 'make-believe,' that it is not to be wondered at that pious folk should have been found who rejoiced to be told that what they had been saying and doing all the years of their lives really had a meaning and a history of its own. One would have to be very unsympathetic not to perceive that the time we are speaking of must have been a very happy one for many a devout soul. The dry bones lived—formal devotions were turned into joyous acts of faith and piety. The Church became a Living Witness to the Truth. She could be interrogated—she could answer. The old calendar was revived, and Saint's Day followed Saint's Day, and season season, in the sweet procession of the Christian Year. Pretty girls got up early, made the sign of the Cross, and, unscared by devils, tripped across the dewy meadows to Communion. Grave men read the Fathers, and found themselves at home in the Fourth Century....

What has come of the movement? It is hard to say. Its great leader has written a book of fascinating interest to prove that it was not a genuine Anglican movement at all; that it was foreign to the National Church, and that neither was its life derived from, nor was its course in the direction of, the National Church. But this was after he himself had joined the Church of Rome. Nobody, however, ventured to contradict him, nor is this surprising when we remember the profusion of argument and imagery with which he supported his case.

A point was reached, and then things were allowed to drop. The Church of Rome received some distinguished converts with her usual well-bred composure, and gave them little things to do in their new places. The *Tracts for the Times*, neatly bound, repose on many shelves. Tract No. 90, that fierce bomb-shell which once scattered confusion through clerical circles, is perhaps the only bit of Dr. Newman's writing one does not, on thinking of, wish to sit down at once to re-read. The fact is that the movement, as a movement with a *terminus ad quem*, was fairly beaten by a power fit to be matched with Rome herself— John Bullism. John Bull could not be got to assume a Catholic demeanour. When his judges denied that the grace of baptism was a dogma of his faith, Bull, instead of behaving as did the people of Milan when Ambrose was persecuted by an Arian Government, was hugely pleased, clapped his thigh, and exclaimed, through the mouth of Lord John Russell, that the ruling was 'sure to give general satisfaction,' as indeed it did.

The work of the movement can still be seen in the new spirit that has descended upon the Church of England and in the general heightening of Church principles; but the movement itself is no longer to be seen, or much of the temper or modes of thought of the Tractarians. The High Church clergyman of today is no Theologian—he is an Opportunist. The Tractarian took his stand upon Antiquity—he laboured his points, he was always ready to prove his Rule of Faith and to define his position. His successor, though he has appropriated the results of the struggle, does not trouble to go on waging it. He is as a rule no great reader—you may often search his scanty library in vain for the works of Bishop Jackson. Were you to ask for them, it is quite possible he would not know to what bishop of that name you were referring. He is as hazy about the Hypostatic Union as are many laymen about the Pragmatic Sanction. He is all for the People and for filling his Church. The devouring claims of the Church of Rome do not disturb his peace of mind. He thinks it very rude of her to dispute the validity of his orders —but, then, foreigners are rude! And so he goes on his hard-working way, with his high doctrines and his early services, and has neither time nor inclination for those studies that lend support to his priestly pretensions.

This temper of mind has given us peace in our time, and has undoubtedly promoted the cause of Temperance and other good works; but some day or another the old questions will have to be gone into again, and the Anglican claim to be a Church, Visible, Continuous, Catholic, and Gifted, investigated—probably for the last time.

Cynics may declare that it will be but a storm in a teacup—
a dispute in which none but 'women, priests, and peers' will be
called upon to take part—but it is not an obviously wise policy
to be totally indifferent to what other people are thinking about
—simply because your own thoughts are running in other
directions.

But all this is really no concern of mine. My object is to call
attention to Dr. Newman's writings from a purely literary point
of view.

The charm of Dr. Newman's style necessarily baffles
description: as well might one seek to analyze the fragrance of a
flower, or to expound in words the jumping of one's heart when
a beloved friend unexpectedly enters the room. It is hard to
describe charm.... One can, of course, heap on words. Dr.
Newman's style is pellucid, it is animated, it is varied; at times
icy cold, it oftener glows with a fervent heat; it employs as its
obedient and well-trained servant a vast vocabulary, and it does
so always with the ease of the educated gentleman, who by a
sure instinct ever avoids alike the ugly pedantry of the book-
worm, the forbidding accents of the lawyer, and the stiff conceit
of the man of scientific theory. Dr. Newman's sentences
sometimes fall upon the ear like well-considered and final
judgments, each word being weighed and counted out with
dignity and precision; but at other times the demeanour and
language of the judge are hastily abandoned, and, substituted for
them, we encounter the impetuous torrent—the captivating
rhetoric, the brilliant imagery, the frequent examples, the
repetition of the same idea in different words, of the eager and
accomplished advocate addressing men of like passions with
himself.

Dr. Newman always aims at effect, and never misses it. He
writes as an orator speaks, straight at you. His object is to
convince, and to convince by engaging your attention, exciting
your interest, enlivening your fancy. It is not his general practice
to address the pure reason. He knows (he well may) how little
reason has to do with men's convictions. 'I do not want,' he
says, 'to be converted by a smart syllogism.' In another place he
observes: 'The heart is commonly reached not through the
reason—but through the imagination by means of direct
impressions, by the testimony of facts and events, by history and
by description. Persons influence us, voices melt us, books
subdue us, deeds inflame us.'

Editor's Introduction

I have elsewhere ventured upon a comparison between Burke and Newman. Both men, despite their subtlety and learning and super-refinement, their love of fine points and their splendid capacity for stating them in language so apt as to make one's admiration breathless, took very broad, common-sense, matter-of-fact views of humanity, and ever had the ordinary man and woman in mind as they spoke and wrote.

Politics and Religion existed, in their opinion, for the benefit of plain folk, for Richard and for Jane, or, in other words, for living bundles of hopes and fears, doubts and certainties, prejudices and passions. Anarchy and Atheism are in their opinion the two great enemies of the Human Race. How are they to be frustrated and confounded, men and women being what they are? Dr. Newman, recluse though he is, has always got the world stretched out before him; its unceasing roar sounds in his ear as does the murmur of ocean in the far inland shell. In one of his Catholic Sermons, the sixth of his *Discourses to Mixed Congregations*, there is a gorgeous piece of rhetoric in which he describes the people looking in at the shop windows and reading advertisements in the newspapers. Many of his pages positively glow with light and heat and colour. One is at times reminded of Fielding. And all this comparing, and distinguishing, and illustrating, and appealing, and describing, is done with the practised hand of a consummate writer and orator. He is as subtle as Gladstone, and as moving as Erskine; but whereas Gladstone is occasionally clumsy, and Erskine was frequently crude, Newman is never clumsy, Newman is never crude, but always graceful, always mellowed.

Humour he possesses in a marked degree. A quiet humour, of course, as befits his sober profession and the gravity of the subjects on which he loves to discourse. It is not the humour that is founded on a lively sense of the incongruous. This kind, though the most delightful of all, is apt, save in the hands of the great masters, the men whom you can count upon your fingers, to wear a slightly professional aspect.

It happens unexpectedly, but all the same we expect it to happen, and we have got our laughter ready. Newman's quiet humour always takes us unawares, and is accepted gratefully, partly on account of its intrinsic excellence, and partly because we are glad to find that the

'Pilgrim pale with Paul's sad girdle bound'

has room for mirth in his heart.

In sarcasm Dr. Newman is pre-eminent. Here his extraordinary powers of compression, which are little short of marvellous in one who has also such a talent for expansion, come to his aid and enable him to squeeze into a couple of sentences pleadings, argument, judgment, and execution. Had he led the secular life, and adopted a Parliamentary career, he would have been simply terrific, for his weapons of offence are both numerous and deadly. His sentences stab—his invective destroys. The pompous high-placed imbecile mouthing his platitudes, the wordy sophister with his oven full of half-baked thoughts, the ill-bred rhetorician with his tawdry aphorisms, the heartless hate-producing satirist, would have gone down before his sword and spear. But God was merciful to these sinners: Newman became a Priest and they Privy Councillors.

And lastly, all these striking qualities and gifts float about in a pleasant atmosphere. As there are some days even in England when merely to go out and breathe the common air is joy, and when, in consequence, that grim tyrant, our bosom's lord,

'Sits lightly in his throne,'

so, to take up almost any one of Dr. Newman's books, and they are happily numerous—between twenty and thirty volumes—is to be led away from 'evil tongues,' and the 'sneers of selfish men,' from the mud and the mire, the shoving and pushing that gather and grow round the pig-troughs of life, into a diviner ether, a purer air, and is to spend your time in the company of one who, though he may sometimes astonish, yet never fails to make you feel (to use Carlyle's words about a very different author), 'that you have passed your evening well and nobly, as in a temple of wisdom, not ill and disgracefully as in brawling tavern supper-rooms with fools and noisy persons.'

The tendency to be egotistical noticeable in some persons who are free from the faintest taint of egotism is a tendency hard to account for—but delightful to watch.

'Anything,' says glorious John Dryden, though 'ever so little, which a man speaks of himself—in my opinion, is still too much.' A sound opinion most surely, and yet how interesting are the personal touches we find scattered up and down Dryden's noble prefaces. So with Newman—his dignity, his self-restraint, his taste, are all the greatest stickler for a stiff upper lip and the consumption of your own smoke could desire, and yet

Editor's Introduction

the personal note is frequently sounded. He is never afraid to strike it when the perfect harmony that exists between his character and his style demands its sound, and so it has come about that we love what he has written because he wrote it, and we love him who wrote it because of what he has written.

I now approach by far the pleasantest part of my task, namely, the selection of two or three passages from Dr. Newman's books by way of illustrating what I have taken the liberty to say are notable characteristics of his style....

For examples of what may be called Newman's oratorical rush, one has not far to look—though when torn from their context and deprived of their conclusion they are robbed of three-fourths of their power. Here is a passage from his second lecture addressed to the Anglican Party of 1833. It is on the Life of the National Church of England.

> Doubtless the National religion is alive. It is a great power in the midst of us, it wields an enormous influence; it represses a hundred foes; it conducts a hundred undertakings; it attracts men to it, uses them, rewards them; it has thousands of beautiful homes up and down the country where quiet men may do its work and benefit its people; it collects vast sums in the shape of voluntary offerings, and with them it builds churches, prints and distributes innumerable Bibles, books, and tracts, and sustains missionaries in all parts of the earth. In all parts of the earth it opposes the Catholic Church, denounces her as anti-Christian, bribes the world against her, obstructs her influence, apes her authority, and confuses her evidence. In all parts of the world it is the religion of gentlemen, of scholars, of men of substance, and men of no personal faith at all. If this be life, if it be life to impart a tone to the Court and Houses of Parliament, to Ministers of State, to law and literature, to universities and schools, and to society, if it be life to be a principle of order in the population, and an organ of benevolence and almsgiving towards the poor, if it be life to make men decent, respectable, and sensible, to embellish and reform the family circle, to deprive vice of its grossness and to shed a glow over avarice and ambition; if, indeed, it is the life of religion to be the first jewel in the Queen's crown, and the highest step of her throne, then doubtless the National Church is replete, it overflows with life; but the question has still to be answered: 'life of what kind?' [47] ...

If I may suppose this paper read by someone who is not yet acquainted with Newman's writings, I would advise him, unless he is bent on theology, to begin not with the Sermons, not even with the *Apologia*, but with the *Lectures on the Present Position of Catholics in England.* Then let him take up the Lectures on the *Idea of a University*, and on *University Subjects*. These may be followed by *Discussions and Arguments*, after which he will be well disposed to read the *Lectures on the Difficulties felt by Anglicans.* If after he has despatched these volumes, he is not infected with what one of those charging Bishops called 'Newmania,' he is possessed of a devil of obtuseness no wit of man can expel....

To the inveterate truth-hunter there has been much of melancholy in the very numerous estimates, hasty estimates no doubt, but all manifestly sincere, which the death of Cardinal Newman has occasioned.

The nobility of the pursuit after truth wherever the pursuit may lead has been abundantly recognized. Nobody has been base enough or cynical enough to venture upon a sneer. It has been marvellous to notice what a hold an unpopular thinker, dwelling very far apart from the trodden paths of English life and thought, had obtained upon men's imaginations. The 'man in the street' was to be heard declaring that the dead Cardinal was a fine fellow. The newspaper-makers were astonished at the interest displayed by their readers. How many of these honest mourners, asked the *Globe*, have read a page of Newman's writings? It is a vain inquiry. Newman's books have long had a large and increasing sale. They stand on all sorts of shelves, and wherever they go a still, small voice accompanies them. They are speaking books; an air breathes from their pages....

No one's plummet since Pascal's had taken deeper soundings of the infirmity—the oceanic infirmity—of the intellect. What actuary, he asks contemptuously, can appraise the value of a man's opinions? In how many a superb passage does he exhibit the absurd, the haphazard fashion in which men and women collect the odds and ends, the bits and scraps they are pleased to place in the museum of their minds, and label, in all good faith, their convictions! Newman almost revels in such subjects. The solemn pomposity which so frequently dignifies with the name of research or inquiry feeble scratchings amongst heaps of verbosity had no more determined foe than the Cardinal.

But now the same measure is being meted out to him, and we are told of a thinker's life—it is nought.

He thought he had constructed a way of escape from the City of Destruction for himself and his followers across the bridge of that illative sense which turns conclusions into assents, and opinions into faiths—but the bridge seems no longer standing.

The writer in the *Guardian*,[150] who attributes Newman's restlessness in the English Church to the smug and comfortable life of many of its clergy rather than to any special craving after authority, no doubt wrote with knowledge.

A married clergy seemed always to annoy Newman. Readers of *Loss and Gain* are not likely to forget the famous 'pork chop' passage, which describes a young parson and his bride bustling into a stationer's shop to buy hymnals and tracts. What was once only annoyance at some of the ways of John Bull on his knees, soon ripened into something not very unlike hatred. Never was any invention less *ben trovato* than that which used to describe Newman as pining after the 'incomparable liturgy' or the 'cultured society' of the Church of England. He hated *ex animo* all those aspects of Anglicanism which best recommend it to Erastian minds. A church of which sanctity is not a note is sure to have many friends.

The *Saturday Review* struck up a fine, national tune:

> An intense but narrow conception of personal holiness, and personal satisfaction with dogma ate him (Newman) up—the natural legacy of the Evangelical school in which he had been nursed, the great tradition of Tory churchmanship, *of pride in the Church of England as such*, of determination to stand shoulder to

---

[150] Richard William Church (1815–90), essayist, historian, and eventually Dean of St. Paul's. His history of the Oxford Movement is still the best. He also wrote a number of good essays on Newman in the *Guardian* newspaper, which are collected in his two-volume *Occasional Papers* (1897). Newman corresponded with him regularly while composing his *Apologia pro Vita Sua*, knowing that Church's memory of Tractarian matters was reliable. They were close allies during the Tractarian era, Newman confiding in Church throughout the movement's twists and turns. As one can see in his letters, the Dean stood up for the Tractarians when it became fashionable in Jowett's liberal Oxford to disparage them. "Poor Tractarians! Jowett attacks them for want of literature, another man for deficiency in Biblical exegesis, another man for want of German philosophy, and ignorance of Kant. It seems that they were expected to exhaust all important subjects in the few years when they were mostly fighting for their lives. It is odd that such a poor lot should have been able to leave such a mark behind them." Church to Wilfrid Ward (22 January 1889), in *Life and Letters of Dean Church*, ed. Mary C. Church (London: MacMillan & Co, 1897), 403.

shoulder in resisting the foreigner, whether he came from Rome or from Geneva, from Tübingen, or from Saint Sulpice, of the union of all social and intellectual culture with theological learning—the idea which, alone of all such ideas, has made education patriotic, and orthodoxy generous, made insufficient appeal to him, and for want of it he himself made shipwreck.

Here is John Bullism, bold and erect. If the Ark of Peter won't hoist the Union Jack, John Bull must have an Ark to himself, with patriotic clergy of his own manufacture tugging at the oar, and with nothing foreign in the hold save some sound old port. 'It will always be remembered to Newman's credit,' says this same reviewer, 'that he knew good wine if he did not drink much. Mark the 'if'; there is much virtue in it.

We are now provided with two causes of Newman's discomfort in the Church of England—its too comfortable clergy, and its too frequent introduction of the lion and the unicorn amongst the symbols of religion—both effective causes, as may be proved by many passages; but to say that either or both availed to drive him out, and compelled him to seek shelter at the hands of one whom he had long regarded as a foe, is to go very far indeed.

It should not be overlooked that these minimizers of Newman's influence are all firmly attached for different reasons to the institution Newman left. Their judgments therefore cannot be allowed to pass unchallenged. What Disraeli meant when he said that Newman's secession had dealt the Church of England a blow under which it still reeled, was that by this act Newman expressed before the whole world his profound conviction that our so-called National Church was not a branch of the Church Catholic. And this really is the point of weakness upon which Newman hurled himself. This is the damage he did to the Church of this island. Throughout all his writings, in a hundred places, in jests and sarcasms as well as in papers and arguments, there crops up this settled conviction that England is not a Catholic country, and that John Bull is not a member of the Catholic Church.

This may not matter much to the British electorate; but to those who care about such things, who rely upon the validity of orders and the efficacy of sacraments, who need a pedigree for their faith, who do not agree with Emerson that if a man would be great he must be a Nonconformist—over these people it would be rash to assume that Newman's influence is spent. The general effect of his writings, the demands they awaken, the spirit they breathe, are all hostile to Anglicanism. They create a profound dissatisfaction with, a distaste for, the Church of England as by law established. Those who are affected by this spirit will no longer be able comfortably to enjoy the maimed rites and practices of their Church. They will feel their place is elsewhere, and sooner or later they will pack up and go. It is far too early in the day to leave Newman out of sight.

But to end where we began. There has been scant recognition in the Cardinal's case of the usefulness of devoting life to anxious inquiries after truth. It is very noble to do so, and when you come to die, the newspapers, from the *Times* to the *Sporting Life*, will, in the first place, point out, after their superior fashion, how much better was this pure-minded and unworldly thinker than the soiled politician, full of opportunism and inconsistency, trying hard to drown the echoes of his past with his loud vociferations, and then proceed in a few short sentences to establish how out of date is this Thinker's thought, how false his reasoning, how impossible his conclusions, and lastly, how dead his influence.

It is very puzzling and difficult, and drives some men to collect butterflies and beetles. Thinkers are not, however, to be disposed of by scratches of the pen. A Cardinal of the Roman Church is not, to say the least of it, more obviously a shipwreck than a dean or even a bishop of the English establishment. Character, too, counts for something. Of Newman it may be said:

'Fate gave what chance shall not control, His sad lucidity of soul.'

But the truth-hunter is still unsatisfied.[151]

Christopher Dawson

With Newman's *Anglican Difficulties* lectures in mind, the Catholic historian Christopher Dawson (1889–1970) wrote of the predicament of the Anglo-Catholics in his *Spirit of the Oxford Movement* (1933) with a prophetic accuracy second only to Newman's own.

---

[151] Augustine Birrell, "Cardinal Newman" (1892), in *Res Judicatae* (London: Elliot Stock, 1892), 128–64. The verse is from M. Arnold's "To Fausta" (1849).

When the Liberal movement was sweeping everything before it, and when it had on its side the weight of popular opinion and the most brilliant minds of the age, the founders of Anglo-Catholicism stood out against it and anathematized it. Today [1933], when Liberalism is a spent force, when hardly anyone believes in Progress, and when modern civilization seems self-dedicated to destruction, we find the heirs of the Oxford Movement (or some of them at least) surrendering their post to an enemy that is in full retreat. But the ultimate cause of this contradiction is to be found in the later history of the Oxford Movement itself. No movement can live by Tradition alone, even if it be the tradition of Keble and Pusey. It needs positive intellectual principles. But the men who gave the Movement its intellectual character were just those who left it for Rome. Keble and Pusey were great moral forces, but they were not thinkers. By their personal influence they saved the Anglo-Catholic tradition for the Church of England. But they were unable to supply the place of Newman. His departure left an intellectual void which was left unfilled or filled with improvised and heterogenous material. This has remained the weak spot in the later development of the Movement, and it explains the intrusion of an intellectual element that is entirely incongruous with its original spirit. Nevertheless, it is difficult to see how such an element can be permanently incorporated with the Anglo-Catholic tradition. One of them must ultimately expel the other. Either the existence of the Tractarian tradition will provide the basis for a return to Catholic intellectual principles, or the Movement will become so penetrated by modernist elements that it will no longer possess any fundamental opposition to Liberal Protestantism.[152]

Owen Chadwick

Owen Chadwick (1916–2015) is a good example of the sort of Anglo-Catholic beneficiary of the Establishment's plums that Newman had in mind when writing *Anglican Difficulties*. To put it mildly, he was never a disinterested critic of Newman, possessing as he did, and necessarily wishing to retain, all of

---

[152] Christopher Dawson, *The Spirit of the Oxford Movement* with a biographical note by Mrs. Christina Scott (London: St. Austin Press, 2001), 140–1.

the worldly advantages that the Establishment could bestow – advantages that Newman fairly mocks. The *Oxford Dictionary of National Biography* duly trots out the long list of honors bestowed upon the Anglican paladin:

> With Chadwick's eminence came other calls on his time. He was president of the British Academy from 1981 to 1985, a trustee of the National Portrait Gallery from 1978 to 1984, a member of the Royal Commission on Historical Manuscripts from 1984 to 1991, and president of the Ecclesiastical History Society in 1988–9. Shortly after his retirement he was invited to serve as chancellor of the University of East Anglia, which he did from 1985 to 1994. There were many honorary degrees, including honorary DDs from St Andrews and Oxford universities, and an honorary LittD from Cambridge. He was made a KBE in 1982, though as a clergyman he did not conventionally use the title "Sir"; in 1983 he was awarded the rare distinction of the Order of Merit.

One distinction not listed here is the fact that for many years Chadwick was the doyen of Newman detractors. Many of his books are strewn with falsehoods about Newman and his work, including *From Bossuet to Newman* (1987), *The Spirit of the Oxford Movement* (1990) and *Newman* (1990), a little book in Oxford University Press's Past Masters series.[153] In his comprehensive history, *The Victorian Church* (1966), Chadwick insinuates that Newman was given his honorary doctorate of divinity from Rome in return for abusing the Anglican Establishment, which, of course, is false. But he also says that *Anglican Difficulties* "was the only book by Newman which many Anglicans found it impossible to forgive," which is probably true.[154]

---

[153] See Ian Ker's witty refutation of Chadwick's characteristically false claim that Newman was in search of an "ideal church" in "Catholic Christianity," Ian Ker, *Newman and the Fullness of Christianity* (Edinburgh: T&T Clark, 1993), 103-22.

[154] Owen Chadwick, *The Victorian Church* (Oxford: Oxford University Press, 1966), I, 89.

John Griffin

In a paper entitled "Newman's Difficulties Felt by Anglicans: History or Propaganda?" (1983) for the *Catholic Historical Review*,[155] John Griffin, then professor of English at the University of Southern Colorado (Pueblo), argued that Newman's lectures constituted "a valid history of the origins, development, and *telos* of the religious revival of 1833, or what we now call the Oxford Movement, and an accurate portrait of the Anglo-Catholics in 1850," while conceding that "the *Difficulties* text is perhaps the most controversial of all of Newman's work." Accordingly, citing the work of Wilfrid Ward, Meriol Trevor, and J. Derek Holmes, he remarked that "Catholic scholars are embarrassed at Newman's satiric portrait of the Church of England and seek to defend him by suggesting that he was working under orders from Nicholas Wiseman in a process 'distasteful' to himself. The result of such a process was a volume obviously 'too polemical in intent'[156] [as Marvin O'Connell charged in his *Oxford Conspirators*] to be of any use as a history of the revival." However, Professor Griffin refuted these criticisms by confirming that Newman did not choose or execute his theme "under orders" from Wiseman and that his intent was not solely polemical. Professor Griffin also cited Owen Chadwick's aforementioned claim that the lectures constituted a book that "many Anglicans found impossible to forgive," only adding: "More important than the infrequent mention of the text is the curious silence which has enveloped the work. In spite of the enormous body of writings about the Oxford Movement, I have found only one study which even mentions *Difficulties*."[157]

---

[155] John Griffin, "Newman's Difficulties Felt by Anglicans: History or Propaganda?" *Catholic Historical Review* 69, no. 3 (July 1983): 371–83. Professor Griffin wrote before Ian Ker published his magisterial biography, which, as I note, includes a detailed discussion of the lectures.

[156] Marvin O'Connell, *Oxford Conspirators* (New York: Macmillan & Co., 1969), ix.

[157] Griffin, "Newman's Difficulties Felt by Anglicans," 371.

Professor Griffin drew on the work of Keble's biographer, Georgina Battiscombe, and others to argue that "the validity of Newman's account of the 'Puseyites' in 1850 is stronger, perhaps, than Newman knew, for Keble's various biographers invariably describe him as the 'saint of Anglicanism'[158] because of his steadfast loyalty to the church in spite of all the opposition from bishops, statesmen, and others."[159]

Griffin also defended the accuracy of Newman's reading of the Anglo-Catholic party by showing its consonance with his other subsequent writings on the party:

> Further evidence of the accuracy of the *Difficulties* text is to be found in its general consistency with Newman's other writings about the Church of England and the anomalous position of the Anglo-Catholics within that church. Far from the text being "the only example of aggressive controversy" of Newman's Catholic years [as Holmes and Ward had erroneously claimed], the lectures are consistent with all of his writings on the Church of England. The *Essay on Development* is, of course, a defense of the Tridentine church; but every one of the "notes" that Newman sets forward as the test of an orthodox doctrine could be employed against the teachings of the Anglo-Catholics, especially the fifth note of a valid development.... It was Newman's argument that Anglo-Catholicism could survive only through a repudiation of the past, notably the events of the sixteenth century. In an essay of 1846, "John Keble," Newman commented on the abysmal state of the Establishment and its clergy and the dream-like quality of Keble's image of that church; and most important, the extreme difference of doctrinal beliefs that separated Keble from his professed religion. [*Ess.*, ii, 421]

Griffin also cited Newman's essay "Characteristics of the Popes: Saint Gregory the Great" in his historical essays (*HS*, iii, 130), the *Apologia* (492), the *Letter to the Duke of Norfolk* (the Notre Dame edition, ed. A. Ryan, (98–120), and his *Letters and Diaries* (xvi, 108; xx, 495) to argue the

---

[158] See Georgina Battiscombe, *John Keble: A Study in Limitations* (London: Constable, 1963), 334.
[159] Griffin, "Newman's Difficulties Felt by Anglicans," 381–2.

consistency of his pastoral approach to the plight of the Anglo-Catholics. He also cited the introduction to Newman's *Letter to Dr. Pusey* in response to Pusey's *Eirenicon*, in which the convert reiterated what he had said sixteen years earlier in his King William Street lectures: "I cannot pay them [the Anglo-Catholic party] a greater compliment than to tell them they ought to be Catholics, nor do them a more affectionate service than to pray that they may one day become such" (*Diff.*, ii, 3).[160]

Professor Griffin's concluding paragraph in defense of the accuracy of Newman's reading is worth quoting in its entirety, confirming as it does not only the inability of the Anglo-Catholic party to thwart the Anglican Church from descending into ever more incoherent liberalism but the true pastoral force of Newman's urging the Anglo-Catholics to join the true Church.

A final defense of the *Difficulties* text is to be found in its prophetic element, that the Anglo-Catholics could not influence or change the Church of England. In spite of the Anglican insistence that the Oxford Movement was "full of life" because it had endured from 1833 to 1932[161] and Eugene Fairweather's comments on the victories of the later Anglo-Catholic priests in their "skirmishes against Parliament, Privy Council, and the Crown," the later trials of Anglo-Catholic doctrines and practice record no such victories. Edwin Hutton attacked at length Newman's insistence that the doctrinal authority of the national church was lodged in the state, but the ecclesiastical trials of 1850 and beyond gave verdicts that were against an Anglo-Catholic belief or practice; and it is almost irrelevant for historians of the post-1845 revival to say that Pusey and his friends "refused to accept" such verdicts, for the verdicts became the law of the land. In addition, it should be noted that the episcopal appointments of 1848 (Hampden) and later were given to men of an increasingly liberal cast of theology in the pervasive reaction of the Establishment against "Puseyism." The petitions, essays and letters to the Anglo-Catholic press did

---

[160] Ibid, 381-2.
[161] Professor Griffin cites Charles Clarke's book *The Oxford Movement and After* (London, 1932).

nothing to change the Establishment. But Newman's intent in the *Difficulties* lecture was not to satirize the Establishment simply for the sake of humor or to endear himself to the Catholic hierarchy. He believed throughout his Catholic years, that there was but "one ark of salvation," [4] and he used every occasion that presented itself to drive home that unpopular fact.[162]

Ian Ker

Ian Ker's discussion of the lectures in his definitive biography of Newman is worth reading *in toto*. It remains one of the best things ever written about the lectures. Here, I have only showcased a portion of his detailed, witty, trenchant commentary on lectures that are still either ignored, dismissed, or misunderstood.

> The lectures are specifically intended not to prove Catholicism, but to remove difficulties in the way of Anglo-Catholics. Newman admits that they are necessarily incomplete as not touching on a whole range of disputed questions. More than half of them, which form the first part of the work, are concerned exclusively with the relation between the Established Church and what Newman calls 'the movement of 1833'. Although the argument is more detailed and explicit than in *Loss and Gain*, it is directed and underpinned by much the same general principles. The contrast, in particular, between reality and unreality is central. Indeed, it is the first consideration that Newman presses on the high Anglicans:
>
> > We must not indulge our imagination, we must not dream: we must look at things as they are ... we must not indulge our imagination in the view we take of the National Establishment. If, indeed, we dress it up in an ideal form, as if it were something real ... as if it were in deed and not only in name a Church, then indeed we may feel interest in it, and reverence towards it, and affection for it, as men have fallen in love with pictures, or knights in romance do battle for high dames whom they have never seen. Thus it is that students of the Fathers, antiquaries, and poets, begin by assuming that the body to which they belong is that of which they read in times past, and then proceed to decorate it with that majesty and beauty of which history tells, or which their genius creates. [4–5]

---

[162] Griffin, "Newman's Difficulties Felt by Anglicans," 383.

This, of course, was how Newman himself, as 'a student of the Fathers', had once tried to picture the Church of England.

> But at length, either the force of circumstances or some unexpected accident dissipates it; and, as in fairy tales, the magic castle vanishes when the spell is broken, and nothing is seen but the wild heath, the barren rock, and the forlorn sheep-walk, so is it with us as regards the Church of England, when we look in amazement on that we thought so unearthly and find so commonplace or worthless. [6]

It is true that Newman says that on such occasions we find 'we have not been guided by reason' [6], but this does not mean that imagination or idealism, or even 'romance', is rejected. Far from it. If there were no place for such, Newman himself would never have become a Catholic:

> Even when I was a boy, my thoughts were turned to the early Church, and especially to the early Fathers, by the perusal of the Calvinist [Joseph] Milner's Church History, and I have never lost, I never have suffered a suspension of the impression, deep and most pleasurable, which his sketches of St. Ambrose and St. Augustine left on my mind. From that time the vision of the Fathers was always, to my imagination, I may say, a paradise of delight… [370–1]

Newman certainly allows a very special place for imagination, but the object of the imaginative vision must be a real one, and it is reason that helps to determine and locate this reality. He argues that it is not the picture of the early Church that is a fantasy, but it is the imaginative effort to identify this picture with the Church of England that is fantastic; for the picture is in fact a picture of the Roman Catholic Church. In the end, for Newman himself it was 'the living picture' which the study of 'history presents to us' [379] that opened his eyes to the identity of the Church of the Fathers with the Roman Catholic Church.[163]

Robert Pattison

In his study of Newman's lifelong evisceration of liberalism, *The Great Dissent: John Henry Newman and the Liberal*

---

[163] Ian Ker, *John Henry Newman: A Biography* (Oxford: Oxford University Press, 1988), 351–2.

Heresy, Robert Pattison gets to the heart of Newman's exposure of the radical absurdity of the Anglo-Catholic position within the Established Church, which *Anglican Difficulties* takes as its starting point:

> No one understood the failure of the Oxford Movement to influence the English Church better than Newman. How could "a thing without a soul" [7] respond to living apostolic truths or one whose life "is an Act of Parliament" [9] adopt Catholic principles? "As a nation changes its political, so may it change its religious views: the causes which carried the Reform Bill and free trade may make short work with orthodoxy" [35]. This is not Mill or Bagehot, but Newman in the 1850 lectures, *Certain Difficulties Felt by Anglicans*. Here is a cold-blooded appreciation of what Keble and Pusey, Liddon and Church could not grasp, that those Tractarians who remained in the established church were in the anomalous position of Peel's Tory followers who supported the anti–Corn Law legislation. They maintained their party only by betraying their principles. What sense was there in preaching the independence and indefectibility of Catholic truth within a church subordinate to the state and committed to toleration? To Newman, Catholicism offered clear-headed Tractarians the only refuge from the predicament in which English liberalism had placed them.[164]

Stanley L. Jaki

A Benedictine priest with degrees in physics and theology, Stanley Jaki (1924–2009) was an impassioned devotee of Newman. His own edition of *Anglican Difficulties*, from which I have benefited, is worth reading. It is full of perspicuity. It also exhibits sympathy—critical sympathy— for the Catholic apologist in Newman. Here is the conclusion of his editor's introduction, which captures the pastoral, indeed providential, character of Newman's autobiographical writings, so many samples of which can be found in *Anglican Difficulties*. Newman's detractors like to characterize those sympathetic to Newman's work as "hagiographers" in a

---

[164] Robert Pattison, *The Great Dissent: John Henry Newman and the Liberal Heresy* (Oxford: Oxford University Press, 1991), 30–1.

vulgar, disparaging sense;[165] but, of course, there is a sense in which writers faithful to the work of Newman must be hagiographers in order to do justice to its saintly marrow, and Jaki was one of them.

> The author of the *Difficulties of Anglicans* never lived up so well to his dictum, "logic is a stern master" as when he told his Anglo-Catholic listeners that if the Son of God came to save the souls of men, He hardly came for nothing. For only if he takes the mystery of the Incarnation with the utmost seriousness will the mystery of the Church appear with its four Notes shining like daylight. In instructing Anglo-Catholics on their way to the One True Fold, the Catholic Newman told them again and again of his puzzlement about his having failed to see those Notes much sooner than he did and act accordingly. He suffered a delay only to help speed up the steps of others towards this Fold and firm up the stance of those already there.[166]

"You were born to be Catholics, refuse not the unmerited grace of your bountiful God," Newman told his Anglo-Catholic friends in the course of his lectures, and Jaki's response to them never loses sight of the paramount importance of that heartfelt, fraternal, faithful summons.

---

[165] See Eamon Duffy, "The Reception of Turner's Newman: A Reply to Simon Skinner," in *Journal of Ecclesiastical History*, 63, no. 3 (July 2012).
[166] Stanley L. Jaki, introduction to *Anglican Difficulties* (Pinckney: Real View Books, 2004), xiii.

TWELVE LECTURES ADDRESSED TO THE PARTY

OF THE RELIGIOUS MOVEMENT OF 1833

WILLIAM BERNARD ULLATHORNE,[1]

D.D., O.S.B.,

BISHOP OF HETALONA,

AND VICAR-APOSTOLIC OF THE CENTRAL DISTRICT

MY DEAR LORD,

In gaining your Lordship's leave to place the following Volume under your patronage, I fear I may seem to the world to have asked what is more gracious in you to grant, than becoming or reasonable in me to have contemplated. For what assignable connection is there between your Lordship's name, and a work, not didactic, not pastoral, not ascetical, not devotional, but for the most part simply controversial, directed, moreover, against a mere transitory phase in an accidental school of opinion,

---

[1] *William Bernard Ullathorne*: (1806-89), Vicar Apostolic of the Western District and first Bishop of Birmingham, was born in the East Riding of Yorkshire, the eldest son of an Old Catholic recusant distantly related to Thomas More. After helping to establish the Church in Australia, he took charge of the Benedictine mission at Coventry in 1841, and the Western District in 1846. Transferred to the Central District in 1848, he became the first Bishop of Birmingham two years later. After what Newman nicely styled "preliminary boxing bouts," the bishop and his Oratorian subordinate became good friends. For Judith Champ, Ullathorne's biographer, the bishop's "most lasting achievement" was his "sympathetic encouragement of Newman." See *ODNB*.

and for that reason, both in its matter and its argument, only of local interest and ephemeral importance?

Such a question may obviously be put to me; nor can I answer it, except by referring to the well-known interest which your Lordship has so long taken in the religious party to which I have alluded, and the joy and thankfulness with which you have welcomed the manifestations of God's grace, as often as first one and then another of their number has in his turn emerged from the mists of error into the light and peace of Catholic truth.

Whatever, then, your Lordship's sentiments may be of the character of the Work itself, I persuade myself that I may be able suitably to present it to you, in consideration of the object it has in view; and that you, on your part, will not repent of countenancing an Author, who, in the selection of his materials, would fain put the claims of charity above the praise of critics, and feels it is a better deed to write for the present moment than for posterity.

Begging your Lordship's blessing,
I am, my dear Lord,

Your Lordship's faithful and grateful Servant,

JOHN H. NEWMAN,
OF THE ORATORY.

July 14, 1850.

PREFACE

———

IT may happen to some persons to feel surprise, that the Author of the following Lectures, instead of occupying himself on the direct proof of Catholicism, should have professed no more than to remove difficulties from the path of those who have already admitted the arguments in its favour.[1] But, in the first place, he really does not think that there is any call just now for an Apology in behalf of the divine origin of the Catholic Church. She bears her unearthly character on her brow, as her enemies confess, by imputing her miracles to Beelzebub. There is an instinctive feeling of curiosity, interest, anxiety, and awe, mingled together in various proportions, according to the tempers and opinions of individuals, when she makes her appearance in any neighbourhood, rich or poor, in the person of her missioners or her religious communities. Do what they will, denounce her as they may, her enemies cannot quench this emotion in the breasts of others, or in their own. It is their involuntary homage to the Notes of the Church; it is their spontaneous recognition of her royal descent and her imperial claim; it is a specific feeling, which no other religion tends to excite. Judaism, Mahometanism, Anglicanism, Methodism, old religions and [viii] young, romantic and commonplace, have not this spell.[2] The

———

[1] *proof of Catholicism ...* : Newman was always leery of touting proofs of Christianity, convinced, as he was, that "A mutilated and defective evidence suffices for persuasion where the heart is alive, but dead evidences, however perfect, can but create a dead faith." *U.S.*, 200.

[2] *... have not this spell*: "The more *obvious* reasons for believing the Church to come from God are its great notes as they are called — such as its antiquity, universality, its unchangeableness through so many

presence of the Church creates a discomposure and
restlessness, or a thrill of exultation, wherever she comes.
Meetings are held, denunciations launched, calumnies
spread abroad, and hearts beat secretly the while. The babe
leaps in Elizabeth's womb, at the voice of her in whom is
enshrined and lives the Incarnate Word.[3] Her priests appeal
freely to the consciences of all who encounter them, to say
whether they have not a superhuman gift, and that multitude
by silence gives consent. They look like other men; they
may have the failings of other men; they may have as little
worldly advantages as the preachers of dissent; they may
lack the popular talents, the oratorical power, the imposing
presence, which are found elsewhere; but they inspire
confidence, or at least reverence, by their very word. Those
who come to jeer and scoff, remain to pray.

There needs no treatise, then, on the Notes of the
Church, till this her mysterious influence is accounted for
and destroyed; still less is it necessary just at this time,
when the writings and the proceedings of a school of
divines in the Establishment have, against their will and
intention, done this very work for her as regards a multitude
of our countrymen.[4] What treatise indeed can be so
conclusive in this day as the history, carried out before their
eyes, of the religious teaching of the school in question, a
teaching simple and intelligible in its principles, persuasive
in its views, gradually developed, adjusted, and enlarged,
gradually imbibed and mastered, in a course of years; and
now converging in many minds at once to one issue, and in

---

revolutions and controversies, its adaptation to our wants. The more you
think on these subjects, the more, under God's grace, will you be led to
see that the Catholic Church is God's *guide* to you. How ignorant we are!
do we not *want* a guide?" *LD*, xiv, 292-3. See also *Essay on the
Development of Christian Doctrine* (1845).
[3] Luke 1:41-44
[4] *a school of divines*: the Tractarian school, which Newman founded with
his Oriel friends John Keble and Hurrell Froude in 1833 in the wake of
Keble's Assize Sermon on 'National Apostasy.' Devoting itself to
locating some Apostolical legitimacy in the National Church, it led
instead to a number of Newman's compatriots converting to Rome.

some of them already reaching it, and that issue the divinity of the Catholic Religion? Feeling, then, that an exhibition of [ix] the direct Evidences in favour of Catholicism is not the want of the moment, the Author has had no thoughts of addressing himself to a work, which could not be executed by any one who undertook it, except at leisure and with great deliberation. At present the thinking portion of society is either very near the Catholic Church, or very far from her.[5] The first duty of Catholics is to house those in, who are near their doors; it will be time afterwards, when this has been done, to ascertain how things lie on the extended field of philosophy and religion, and into what new position the controversy has fallen: as yet the old arguments suffice. To attempt a formal dissertation on the Notes of the Church at this moment, would be running the risk of constructing what none would need today, and none could use tomorrow.[6]

Those surely who are advancing towards the Church would not have advanced so far as they have, had they not had sufficient arguments to bring them still further. What retards their progress is not any weakness in those arguments, but the force of opposite considerations, speculative or practical, which are urged, sometimes against the Church, sometimes against their own submitting to her

---

[5] *either very near the Catholic Church, or very far from her*: Newman, like the agnostic Thomas Huxley, believed that there were but two poles when it came to religion, with atheism at the one end and Roman Catholicism at the other. See *GA*, 495-501.

[6] *To attempt a formal dissertation …* : This is an arresting comment in light of Newman's having written his own rather brilliant dissertation on the Notes of the Church in his *Essay on Development* in 1845. Why he made no reference to the book may be attributable to the self-deprecatory modesty with which he tended to refer to his writings, which was a mark of his humility. In the *Apologia Pro Vita Sua* (1864), for example, he said of the monograph that many consider his most scintillating contribution to theology: "That work, I believe, I have not read since I published it, and I do not doubt at all I have made many mistakes in it;— partly, from my ignorance of the details of doctrine, as the Church of Rome holds them, but partly from my impatience to clear as large a range for the *principle* of doctrinal Development... as was consistent with the strict Apostolicity and identity of the Catholic Creed." *Apo*, 79-80.

authority. They would have no doubt about their duty, but for the charges brought against her, or the remonstrances addressed to themselves; charges and remonstrances which, whatever their logical cogency, are abundantly sufficient for their purpose, in a case where there are so many inducements, whether from wrong feeling, or infirmity, or even error of conscience, to listen to them.[7] Such persons, then, have a claim on us to be fortified in their right [x] perceptions and their good resolutions, against the calumnies, prejudices, mistakes, and ignorance of their friends and of the world, against the undue influence exerted on their minds by the real difficulties which unavoidably surround a religion so deep and manifold in philosophy, and occupying so vast a place in the history of nations. It would be wonderful, indeed, if a teaching which embraces all spiritual and moral truth, from the highest to the least important, should present no mysteries or apparent inconsistencies; wonderful if, in the lapse of eighteen hundred years, and in the range of three-fourths of the globe, and in the profession of thousands of millions of souls, it had not afforded innumerable points of plausible attack; wonderful, if it could assail the pride and sensuality which are common to our whole race, without rousing the hatred, malice, jealousy, and obstinate opposition, of the natural man; wonderful, if it could be the object of the jealous and unwearied scrutiny of ten thousand adversaries, of the coalition of wit and wisdom, of minds acute, far-

---

[7] *charges and remonstrances ...:* Gerard Manley Hopkins (1844-99) was one notable Anglican who managed to disregard such "charges and remonstrances"—in his case, those of his father, the dons of Balliol and Henry Parry Liddon, Pusey's biographer. For Benjamin Jowett, the Regius Professor of Greek at Balliol, seeing young undergraduates like Hopkins succumbing to Roman Catholicism was like living amidst "the Roman epidemic." Jowett, *Dear Miss Nightingale: Letters to Florence Nightingale 1860-93*, (Oxford, 1987), 37. How much of Newman Hopkins read is uncertain, though it is likely he read *Anglican Difficulties.* In any case, English literature lost what might have been an inspired dissertation when Newman dissuaded Hopkins from writing a gloss on his *Grammar of Assent* (1870).

seeing, comprehensive, original, and possessed of the deepest and most varied knowledge, yet without some sort of case being made out against it; and wonderful, moreover, if the vast multitude of objections, great and small, resulting from its exposure to circumstances such as these, acting on the timidity, scrupulousness, inexperience, intellectual fastidiousness, love of the world, or self-dependence of individuals, had not been sufficient to keep many a one from the Church, who had, in spite of them, good and satisfactory reasons for joining her communion. Here is the plain reason why so many are brought near to the Church, and then go back, or are so slow in submitting to her.

Now, as has been implied above, where there is [xi] detachment from the world, a keen apprehension of the Unseen, and a simple determination to do the Divine Will, such difficulties will not commonly avail, if men have had sufficient opportunity of acquainting themselves with the Notes or Evidences of the Church. In matter of fact, as we see daily, they do not avail to deter those whose hearts are right, or whose minds are incapable of extended investigations, from recognizing the Church's Notes and acting upon them. They do not avail with the poor, the uneducated, the simple-minded, the resolute, and the fervent; but they are formidable, when there are motives in the background, amiable or unworthy, to bias the will. Every one is obliged, by the law of his nature, to act by reason; yet no one likes to make a great sacrifice unnecessarily; such difficulties, then, just avail to turn the scale, and to detain men in Protestantism, who are open to the influence of tenderness towards friends, reliance on superiors, regard for their position, dread of present inconvenience, indolence, love of independence, fear of the future, regard to reputation, desire of consistency, attachment to cherished notions, pride of reason, or reluctance to go to school again. No one likes to take an awful step, all by himself, without feeling sure he is right; no one likes to remain long in doubt whether he should take it or not; he wishes to be settled, and he readily catches at objections, or listens to dissuasives, which allow of his giving over the inquiry, or postponing it *sine die*. Yet those very same persons who would willingly hide the truth from their eyes by objections and difficulties, nevertheless, if [xii] actually forced to look it in the face, and brought under the direct power of the Catholic arguments, would often have strength and courage enough to take the dreaded step, and would find themselves, almost before they knew what they had done, in the haven of peace.

These were some of the reasons for the particular line of argument which the Author has selected; and in what he has been saying in explanation, he must not be supposed to forget that faith depends upon the will, not really on any process of reasoning, and that conversion is a simple work of divine grace. He aims at nothing more than to give free play to the conscience, by removing those perplexities in the proof of Catholicity, which keep the intellect from being touched by its cogency, and give the heart an excuse for trifling with it. The absence of temptation or of other moral disadvantage, though not the direct cause of virtuous conduct, still is a great help towards it; and, in like manner, to clear away from the path of an inquirer objections to Catholic truth, is to subserve his conversion by giving room for the due and efficacious operation of divine grace. Religious persons, indeed, do what is right in spite of temptation; persons of sensitive and fervent minds go on to believe in spite of difficulty; but where the desire of truth is languid, and the religious purpose weak, such impediments suffice to prevent conviction, and faith will not be created in the mind, though there are abundant reasons for its creation. In these circumstances, it is quite as much an act of charity to attempt the removal of objections to the truth, which, without excusing, are made the excuse for unbelief, as to remove the occasion of sin in any other department of duty.

[xiii] It is plain that the Author is rather describing what his Lectures were intended to be, than what they have turned out. He found it impossible to fulfil what he contemplated within the limits imposed upon him by the circumstances

under which they were written. The very first objection which he took on starting, the alleged connection of the Movement of 1833 with the National Church, has afforded matter for the greater part of the course; and, before he had well finished the discussion of it, it was getting time to think of concluding, and that, in any such way as would give a character of completeness to the whole. Else, after the seventh Lecture, it had been his intention to proceed to the consideration of the alleged claim of the National Church on the allegiance of its members; of the alleged duty of our remaining in the communion in which we were born; of the alleged danger of trusting to reason; of the alleged right of the National Church to forbid doubt about its own claims; of the alleged uncertainty which necessarily attends the claims of any religion whatever; of the tests of certainty; of the relation of faith to reason; of the legitimate force of objections; and of the matter of Catholic evidence. He is ashamed to continue the list much further, lest he should seem to have been contemplating what was evidently impracticable; all he can say in extenuation is, that he never aimed at going more fully into any of the subjects of which he was to treat, than he has done in the sketches which now he presents to the reader. Lastly, he had proposed to end his course with a notice of the objections made by Protestants to particular doctrines, as Purgatory, Intercession of the Saints, and the like.

Incomplete, however, as the Lectures may be with [xiv] reference to the idea with which they were commenced, or compared with what might be said upon each subject which is successively treated, of course he makes no apology for the actual matter of them; else he should not have delivered or published them. It has not been his practice to engage in controversy with those who have felt it their duty to criticise what at any time he has written; but that will not preclude him, under present circumstances, from elucidating what is deficient in them by further observations, should questions be asked, which, either from the quarter whence they proceed, or from their intrinsic weight, have, according to his judgment, a claim upon his attention.

BIRMINGHAM, *July* 14, 1850.

PART I

COMMUNION WITH THE ROMAN SEE THE LEGITIMATE
ISSUE OF THE RELIGIOUS MOVEMENT OF 1833

———————

LECTURE I

*ON THE RELATION OF THE NATIONAL CHURCH TO THE
NATION*

THERE are those, my brethren, who may think it strange, and even shocking, that, at this moment, when the liberalism of the age, after many previous attempts, is apparently at length about to get possession of the Church and Universities of the nation, any one like myself, who is a zealous upholder of the dogmatic principle in all its bearings,[1] should be doing what little in him lies to weaken, even indirectly, Institutions which, with whatever shortcomings or errors, are the only political bulwarks of that principle left to us by the changes of the sixteenth century. For to help forward members of the Established Church towards the Catholic Religion, as I propose to do in these Lectures, what is this but, so far, to co-operate with a levelling party, who are the enemies of God, and truth, and virtue? The Institutions in question, it may be said, [2] uphold what is right and what is holy as far as they go,

———————

[1] *a zealous upholder of the dogmatic principle*: "From the age of fifteen, dogma has been the fundamental principle of my religion: I know no other religion; I cannot enter into the idea of any other sort of religion; religion, as a mere sentiment, is to me a dream and a mockery." *Apo*, 49

13

and, moreover, the duty of upholding it; they do not in their genuine workings harm the Church; they do but oppose themselves to sectarianism, free-thinking, infidelity, and lawlessness. They are her natural, though they may be her covert, allies; they are the faithful nurses and conservators of her spirit; they are glad, and proud, as far as they are allowed to do so, to throw her mantle over themselves, and they do her homage by attempting a mimic Catholicism. They have preserved through bad times our old churches, our forms, our rites, our customs, in a measure, our Creed; they are taunted by our enemies for their Catholic or Papistical tendency;[2] and many of those who are submitted to their teaching, look wistfully to us, in their forlorn struggle with those enemies of ours, for encouragement and sympathy.[3] Certainly, reviewing the history of the last three centuries, we cannot deny that those Institutions have uniformly repressed the extravagance, and diluted the virulence, of Protestantism. To the divines, to whom they have given birth, our country is indebted for Apologies in behalf of various of the great doctrines of the faith: to Bull for a defence of the Creed of Nicæa, nay, in a

---

[2] *taunted by our enemies ...*: John Spurgin, vicar of Hockham, Norfolk warned his fellow Anglicans in one of his "Anti-Tractarian Tracts" (1848) that: "The teaching of the Tractarians is but a slight modification of Popery. Let them try to hide or disguise the cloven foot as they may... yet it cannot but be seen ... They would Doubtless overturn the Whole Fabric of the Church!—Let British Christians, then, nail their Colours to the Mast and Swear eternal Enmity to Popery, and to every Modification of it."

[3] *many of those ...* : Charles Crawley (1788–1871), the Littlemore country gentleman with whom Newman became friendly, is a good example of the many aggrieved Anglo-Catholics who looked to the former Tractarian leader for support against their shared enemies. See their correspondence, before and after Newman's conversion, in *LD*, x, 428-9 and *LD*, xix, 452-3.

measure, of the true doctrine of justification, which the
most accomplished Catholic theologians of this day, as
well as of his own, treat with great consideration;[4] to
Pearson[5] for a powerful argument in behalf of the [3]
Apostolical origin of Episcopacy; to Wall for a proof
of the primitive use of Infant Baptism;[6] to Hooker for a
vindication of the great principle of religious order and
worship;[7] to Butler for a profound investigation into
the connection of natural with revealed religion;[8] to

---

[4] *Bull ...* : In *Defensio Fidei Nicaene* (1685), the Anglican theologian
Bishop George Bull (1634-1710) argued, *pace* the Jesuit Petavius, that
the doctrine of the Trinity was fully developed before the Council of
Nicea (325), which won the approval of both the French preacher and
controversialist J.B. Bossuet and the French clergy at their Synod at St.
Germain (1686).

[5] *Pearson*: John Pearson (1613-86), Bishop of Chester, reaffirmed the
apostolic origin of episcopacy in *An Exposition of the Creed* (1659).

[6] *Wall*: The Anglican theologian William Wall (1647-1728) wrote his
two-volume *History of Infant Baptism* (1705) to refute the objections of
the Baptists to the doctrine, learnedly showing how the early Fathers
promulgated it.

[7] *Hooker*: In *Treatise on the Laws of Ecclesiastical Polity* (1594-7 and
1648), the Anglican apologist Richard Hooker (c. 1554-1600) defended
the Elizabethan Settlement (1558) by reaffirming the principle of
episcopacy against the *sola scriptura* Puritans. While not all Puritans
were Presbyterians, the more radical Puritans certainly were. Hooker was
intent on defending and prospering the 'top down' structure of the
Elizabethan church against the 'bottom up' Presbyterian structure of
these radical Puritans.

[8] *Butler*: In *The Analogy of Religion* (1736) Joseph Butler (1692-1752),
Bishop of Durham, drew on natural theology to argue the probability,
rather than the evidential proof, of Christianity, convinced, as he said,
that "probability is the very guide of life." For Butler's considerable
influence on Newman, see *Apo*, 22-3. Despite this, Newman saw the
dangers of a theory of probability that could seem to undercut the
"absolute certainty" of Christian faith. See *Apo*. 30. In 1871, Newman
wrote a correspondent that: "it is the tendency of anglican writers, even
Bishop Butler and Keble, to say that we cannot get beyond probabilities
and opinions — *but they don't act upon their theory.* I almost think that
Keble somewhere speaks as if faith was only a probability, and I think I
have somewhere said myself that the being of God is a strong probability,
but neither Keble nor I (I hope) ever felt a practical doubt as to the object

Paley and others for a series of elaborate evidences of the divinity of Christianity.[9] It is cruel, it is impolitic, to cast off, if not altogether friends, yet at least those who are not our worst foes; nor can we afford to do so. If they usurp our name, yet they proclaim it in the ears of heretics all about; they have kept much error out of the country, if they have let much in; and if Neo-Platonism,[10] though false, is more honourable than the philosophy of the academy or of the garden, by the same rule, surely, we ought, in comparison with other sects, to give our countenance to the Anglican Church to compassionate her in her hour of peril, "and spare the meek usurper's hoary head."[11]

Well, and I do not know what natural inducement there is to urge me to be harsh with her in this her hour: I have only pleasant associations of those many years when I was within her pale; I have no theory to put forward, nor position to maintain; and I am come to a time of life, when men desire to be quiet and at peace;—moreover, I am in a communion which

---

of faith." *LD*, xxv, 266. Newman wrote his *Grammar of Assent* (1870) to show how certainty is possible in Christian faith, even though one might shy away from offering any formal proof of the certainty.

[9] *Paley*: In his *View of the Evidences of Christianity* (1794) the theologian and philosopher William Paley (1743-1805) argued for the persuasiveness of the evidences of Christianity. For Newman, Paley's argument was "clear, clever and powerful, and there is something which looks like charity in going out into the highways and hedges, and compelling men to come in..." *GA*, 425.

[10] *Neo-Platonism*: "A philosophical and religious system based on Platonic ideas and originating with Plotinus in the 3rd century, which emphasizes the distinction between an eternal world accessible to thought and the changing physical world accessible to the senses, and combines this with a mystical belief in the possibility of union with a supreme being from which all reality is held to derive." (*OED*)

[11] *"and spare the meek usurper's hoary head."*: The actual line from Thomas Gray's Pindaric ode, "The Bard" (1757), about Edward I's alleged slaughtering of the Welsh bards during the conquest of Wales in 1283 is: "And spare the meek usurper's holy head."

satisfies its members, and draws them into itself, and, by the objects which it presents to faith, and the influences which it exerts over the heart, leads them to [4] forget the external world, and look forward more steadily to the future. No, my dear brethren, there is but one thing that forces me to speak,—and it is my intimate sense that the Catholic Church is the one ark of salvation,[12] and my love for your souls; it is my fear lest you ought to submit yourselves to her, and do not; my fear lest I may perchance be able to persuade you, and not use my talent. It will be a miserable thing for you and for me, if I had been instrumental in bringing you but half-way, if I have cooperated in removing your invincible ignorance,[13] but am able to do no more. It is this keen feeling that my life is wearing away,[14] which overcomes the lassitude which possesses me, and scatters the excuses which I might plausibly urge to myself for not meddling with what I have left for ever, which subdues the recollection of past times, and

---

[12] *the one ark of salvation*: "Gladly would I serve the Lady in whom you are so much interested," Newman wrote to a fellow priest in 1867. "With the convictions she has, it is her clear duty to submit herself to the Church at once; for who that knows he is external to it can for a moment delay, when he knows in his heart that the Catholic Church is the fold of Christ and the Ark of Salvation and that Rome is the necessary centre of it. She had better go to the nearest Priest. She need not be afraid of being received hastily, for he will take care that she is well acquainted with the Catholic Catechism, and is otherwise properly prepared for reception." *LD*, xxiii, 47.

[13] *invincible ignorance*: "Ignorance is said to be invincible when a person is unable to rid himself of it notwithstanding the employment of moral diligence ... Such ignorance is obviously involuntary and therefore not imputable." *Catholic Encyclopedia.* See also Thomas Aquinas, *Summa Theol.* lxxvi. §2. It was precisely because the Lady referred to in the previous note could not claim invincible ignorance that Newman was so intent that she enter the One True Fold of the Redeemer *instanter*.

[14] *my life is wearing away*: Newman often took a kind of theatrical delight in portraying himself as older than he actually was: when he wrote this he was scarcely fifty.

which makes me do my best, with whatever success, to bring you to land from off your wreck, who have thrown yourselves from it upon the waves, or are clinging to its rigging, or are sitting in heaviness and despair upon its side. For this is the truth: the Establishment, whatever it be in the eyes of men, whatever its temporal greatness and its secular prospects, in the eyes of faith is a mere wreck. We must not indulge our imagination, we must not dream: we must look at things as they are; we must not confound the past with the present, or what is [5] substantive with what is the accident of a period. Ridding our minds of these illusions, we shall see that the Established Church has no claims whatever on us, whether in memory or in hope; that they only have claims upon our commiseration and our charity whom she holds in bondage, separated from that faith and that Church in which alone is salvation. If I can do aught towards breaking their chains, and bringing them into the Truth, it will be an act of love towards their souls, and of piety towards God.

1.

I have said, we must not indulge our imagination in the view we take of the National Establishment. If, indeed, we dress it up in an ideal form, as if it were something real, with an independent and a continuous existence, and a proper history, as if it were in deed and not only in name a Church, then indeed we may feel interest in it, and reverence towards it, and affection for it, as men have fallen in love with pictures, or knights in romance do battle for high dames whom they have never seen. Thus it is that students of the Fathers, antiquaries, and poets, begin by assuming that the body to which they belong is that of which they read in times past, and then proceed to decorate it with that majesty and beauty of which history tells, or which their genius creates. Nor is it by an easy process or a light effort that their minds are disabused of this error. It is an error for many reasons too dear to them to be readily relinquished. But at [6] length, either the force of circumstances or some unexpected accident dissipates it; and, as in fairy tales, the magic castle vanishes when the spell is broken, and nothing is seen but the wild heath, the barren rock, and the forlorn sheep-walk, so is it with us as regards the Church of England, when we look in amazement on that we thought so unearthly, and find so commonplace or worthless. Then we perceive, that aforetime we have not been guided by reason, but biassed by education and swayed by affection. We see in the English Church, I will not merely say no descent from the first ages, and no relationship to the Church in other lands, but we see no body politic of any kind; we see nothing more or less than an Establishment, a department of Government, or a function or operation of the State,— without a substance,—a mere collection of officials, depending on and living in the supreme civil power.[15] Its unity and personality are gone, and with them its power of exciting feelings of any kind. It is easier to love or hate an abstraction, than so commonplace a framework or mechanism. We regard it neither with anger, nor with aversion, nor with contempt, any more than with respect or interest. It is but one aspect of the State, or mode of civil governance; it is responsible for nothing; it can appropriate neither praise nor blame;

---

[15] Hooker's achievement was to give the ineradicably Erastian relationship between the English State and its National Church at least the semblance of ecclesiastical respectability. As Evelyn Waugh said of style in *Helena* (1950): "...it has the Egyptian secret of the embalmers."

but, whatever feeling it raises is to be referred on, by [7] the nature of the case, to the Supreme Power whom it represents, and whose will is its breath. And hence it has no real identity of existence in distinct periods, unless the present Legislature or the present Court can affect to be the offspring and disciple of its predecessor. Nor can it in consequence be said to have any antecedents, or any future; or to live, except in the passing moment. As a thing without a soul, it does not contemplate itself, define its intrinsic constitution, or ascertain its position. It has no traditions; it cannot be said to think; it does not know what it holds, and what it does not;[16] it is not even conscious of its own existence. It has no love for its members, or what are sometimes called its children, nor any instinct whatever, unless attachment to its master, or love of its place, may be so called. Its fruits, as far as they are good, are to be made much of, as long as they last, for they are transient, and without succession; its former champions of orthodoxy are no earnest of orthodoxy now; they died, and there was no reason why they [8] should be reproduced. Bishop is not like bishop, more than king is like king, or ministry like ministry; its Prayer-Book is an Act of Parliament of two centuries ago, and its cathedrals and its chapter-houses are the spoils of Catholicism.

---

[16] This fact is strikingly brought out in Archbishop Sumner's correspondence with Mr. Maskell. "You ask me," he says, "whether you are to conclude that you ought not to teach, and have not authority of the Church to teach any of the doctrines spoken of in your five former questions, in the *dogmatical* terms there stated? To which I reply, Are they contained in the word of God? St. Paul says, 'Preach the word.' ... Now, whether the doctrines concerning which you inquire are contained in the Word of God, and can be proved thereby, you have the same means of discovering as myself, and I have no special authority to declare." The Archbishop at least would quite allow what I have said in the text, even though he might express himself differently. [N]

I have said all this, my brethren, not in declamation, but to bring out clearly to you, why I cannot feel interest of any kind in the National Church, nor put any trust in it at all from its past history, as if it were, in however narrow a sense, a guardian of orthodoxy. It is as little bound by what it said or did formerly, as this morning's newspaper by its former numbers, except as it is bound by the Law; and while it is upheld by the Law, it will not be weakened by the subtraction of individuals, nor fortified by their continuance. Its life is an Act of Parliament. It will not be able to resist the Arian, Sabellian, or Unitarian heresies[17] now, because Bull or Waterland[18] resisted them a century or two before; nor on the other hand would it be unable to resist them, though its more orthodox theologians were presently to leave it. It will be able to resist them while the State gives the word; it would be unable, when the State forbids it. Elizabeth boasted that she "tuned her pulpits;"[19]   Charles   forbade   discussions   on

---

[17] *Arian, Sabellian, or Unitarian heresies*: The Arian heresy (4th c.) denied the true divinity of Christ; the Sabellian heresy (3rd c.) held that the Father, Son and Holy Spirit are simply 'masks' of the one God, rather than Persons; and the Unitarian heresy (18th c.) denied the Trinity, the divinity of Christ, the Atonement, and Hell.

[18] *Waterland*: The High Church Anglican theologian Daniel Waterland (1683-1740), Fellow and Master of Magdalene College, Cambridge engaged in controversy against Deists on the divinity of Christ, the Trinity, and the Eucharist. For a good balanced overview of the Tory reaction to Deism in the early 18th century, as well as the gathering challenges of Dissent, see J. Hoppitt, *A Land of Liberty? England 1689-1727* (Oxford, 2000), 207-41.

[19] *"tuned her pulpits;"*: Peter Heylyn, Archbishop Laud's biographer, relates how King Charles would often emulate Queen Elizabeth, who, when seeking to secure her people's support, "used to tune the pulpits, as her saying was" by having ministers in and around London commend her wishes from their public pulpits. P. Heylyn, *Cyprianus Anglicus* (1668), 161.

predestination;[20] George on the Holy Trinity;[21] Victoria allows differences on Holy Baptism.[22] While the nation wishes an Establishment, it will remain, whatever individuals are for it or against it; and that which determines its existence will determine its voice. Of [9] course the presence or departure of individuals will be one out of various disturbing causes, which may delay or accelerate by a certain number of years a change in its teaching: but, after all, the change itself depends on events broader and deeper than these; it depends on changes in the nation. As the nation changes its political, so may it change its religious views; the causes which carried the Reform Bill[23] and Free Trade[24] may make short work with orthodoxy.[25]

---

[20] *Charles forbade discussions ...* : When King Charles' proclamation against disturbers of the peace in church and state was flouted by Puritan divines, he had the Book of Articles reprinted on June 16, 1626 with the declaration that they were the true Articles of the Anglican faith and no modifications should be made, especially with respect to predestination. See Heylyn, 187-8. See also Godfrey Davies, "English Political Sermons 1603-1640," *Huntington Library Quarterly*, Vol. 3, No. 1 (Oct. 1939), 14.

[21] *George on the Holy Trinity*: George I (1660-1727) became concerned about divines making heterodox statements about the Holy Trinity in the wake of the theologian Samuel Clarke writing of it in Socinian terms in *The Scripture Doctrine of the Trinity* (1712). Although no theologian himself, George saw the dangers of Socinian principles subverting the national religion. The English classical scholar Richard Bentley (1662-1742) nicely catalogued these principles thus: "That the soul is material, Christianity a cheat, Scripture a falsehood, hell a fable, heaven a dream, our life without providence, and our death without hope—such are the items of the glorious gospel of these evangelists." Bentley quoted in P. Langford, *A Polite and Commercial People: England 1727-1783* (Oxford, 1989), 240.

[22] *Victoria allows differences on Holy Baptism*: Newman is referring here to Queen Victoria's Privy Council overruling the Anglican Church's settled doctrine regarding Holy Baptism in the Gorham Case.

[23] *the Reform Bill*: The first Reform Act (1832) disfranchised pocket boroughs and enfranchised large towns and new London districts, including Birmingham, Bradford, Brighton, Manchester, Sheffield, Leeds, and Wolverhampton. Although the bill infuriated the Tories, it

2.

The most simple proof of the truth of this assertion will be found in considering what and how much has been hitherto done by the ecclesiastical movement of 1833, towards heightening the tone of the Established Church—by a movement extending over seventeen years and more, and carried on with great energy, and (as far as concerns its influence over individuals) with surprising success.[26] Opinions which, twenty years ago, were not held by any but Catholics, or at most only in fragmentary portions by isolated persons, are now the profession of thousands. Such success ought to have acted on the Establishment itself; has it done so? or rather, is not that success simply and only in expectation and in hope, like the conversion of heathen nations by the various Evangelical societies? The Fathers have catholicised the Protestant Church at home, pretty much as the Bible has evangelised the Mahometan or Hindoo religions abroad. There have [10] been recurring vaticinations and promises of good; but little or no actual fulfilment. Look back year after year, count up the exploits of the movement party, and

---

was nothing as radical as the three subsequent reform bills. Newman's response to the Bill's passage was not sanguine: "For the gradual development of a democratic government without religion, without subordination, and without stability, we must therefore, I suppose, prepare." *LD*, iii, 34.

[24] *Free Trade*: The repeal of the Corn Laws in 1846 was seen by its critics as another radical measure, since lifting the tariffs on grain adversely affected the agricultural interests of the landed aristocracy. The increasingly imperial character of nineteenth-century Britain, however, made free trade irresistible.

[25] See what Newman has to say himself about how the forces behind the Reform Bill and Free Trade affected orthodoxy. *Diff*, I, 8-9, 304

[26] *the ecclesiastical movement of 1833*: The Tractarian or Oxford Movement began in 1833 and fizzled out in 1843 after Newman's *Tract 90* (1841) incurred the concerted opposition of Oxford's Heads of Houses.

consider whether it has had any effect at all on the religious judgment of the nation, as represented by the Establishment. The more certain and formidable is the growth of its adherents and well-wishers, so much the more pregnant a fact is it, that the Establishment has steadily gone on its own way, eating, drinking, sleeping, and working, fulfilling its nature and its destiny, as if that movement had not been; or at least with no greater consciousness of its presence, than any internal disarrangement or disorder creates in a man who has a work to do, and is busy at it.

The movement, I say, has formed but a party after all, and the Church of the nation has pursued the nation's objects, and executed the nation's will, in spite of it. The movement could not prevent the Ecclesiastical Commission, nor the Episcopal mismanagement of it.[27] Its zeal, principle, and clearness of view, backed by a union of parties, did not prevent the royal appointment of a theological Professor, whose sentiments were the expression of the national idea of religion. Nor did its protest even succeed in preventing his subsequent elevation to the Episcopal bench.[28] Nor did it succeed in preventing the

[27] *the Ecclesiastical Commission*: In 1835 Parliament set up the Ecclesiastical Commission to manage the estates and revenues of the Church of England.

[28] *a theological Professor*: Newman led the unavailing Tractarian attack against R. D. Hampden (1793-1868), after the liberal Oriel Fellow published his Bampton Lecture, *The Scholastic Philosophy considered in its relation to Christian Theology* (1832), which attacked the dogmatic principle of which Newman was so solicitous. Oxford's High Church and Evangelical parties were also opposed to Hampden, deploring his views not only on Christian dogma but the admission of Dissenters to Oxbridge. Despite this opposition, Hampden was made Regius Professor of Divinity and, later, Bishop of Hereford. See R. Brent's entry in the *ODNB*, as well as his Editor's Introduction to R.W. Church, *The Oxford Movement* (Chicago, 1970), xxv.

establishment of a sort of Anglo-Prussian, half-Episcopal, half-Lutheran See at Jerusalem; nor the [11] selection of two individuals of heretical opinions to fill it in succession.[29] Nor did it prevent the intrusion of the Establishment on the Maltese territory;[30] nor has it prevented the systematic promotion at home of men heterodox, or fiercely latitudinarian, in their religious views, or professedly ignorant of theology, and glorying in their ignorance.[31] Nor did the movement prevent the promotion of Bishops and others who deny or explain away the grace of Baptism.[32] Nor has it hindered the two Archbishops of England from concurring in the royal decision, that within the national communion baptismal regeneration is an open question.[33] It has not heightened the theology of the

---

[29] *See at Jerusalem*: The Jerusalem Bishopric, the brainchild of the anglophile Baron Bunsen, was a joint bishopric established in 1841 to serve both Lutherans and Anglicans in Syria, Chaldea, Egypt and Abyssinia. The scheme went *kaput* in 1886 after Lutherans decided that they had had enough of episcopacy.

[30] *Maltese territory*: In June of 1841, the Anglican Church appointed a Bishop of Malta or Valetta to the ancient Catholic see of Malta. See *LD*, viii, 203.

[31] *men heterodox ...*: The number of men to whom Newman might have been referring here is too numerous to fit within the confines of a note. However, he was always appreciative of how susceptible the Anglican ministry was to the corruption of the social order to which it ministered. "Christianity is of faith, modesty, lowliness, subordination," he wrote his mother in 1829, "but the spirit at work against it is one of latitudinarianism, indifferentism, republicanism and schism, a spirit which tends to overthrow doctrine ...". Indeed, for Newman, "the talent of the day is against the Church." *LD*, ii, 129-30.

[32] *the grace of Baptism*: Newman's conviction on this point can be seen in a letter he wrote to his sister Jemima in 1837: "[T]his I hold most decidedly, that where Catholic Truth is denied (where it is, when men deny the grace of Baptism) any one, layman, woman, child, has a right to hold up the standard of the faith against Bishops, Archdeacons, and Clergy." *LD*, vi, 127

[33] *baptismal regeneration*: In the Gorham Case (1847), J.B Sumner, the Archbishop of Canterbury ruled "that a clergyman of the Church of

Universities or of the Christian Knowledge Society,[34] nor afforded any defence in its hour of need to the National Society for Education.[35] What has it done for the cause it undertook?[36] It has preserved the Universities to the Established Church for fifteen years;[37] perhaps it prevented certain alterations in the Prayer-Book; it has secured at Oxford the continuance of the Oath of Supremacy against Catholics for a like period; it has hindered the promotion of high-minded liberals, like the late Dr. Arnold, at the price of the advancement of second-rate men who have shared his opinions.[38] It has built Churches and Colleges,[39] and

---

England need not believe in baptismal regeneration." Newman's argument throughout this first lecture is that if the English state could rule against so central a doctrine as baptismal regeneration, the English national church to which the Anglo-Catholic party attached itself could have no claim on its continued loyalty.

[34] *the Christian Knowledge Society*: The Society for Promoting Christian Knowledge (SPCK) was founded in 1698 to provide religious literature for those without access to libraries.

[35] *the National Society for Education*: The National Society for the Education of the Poor in the Principles of the Established Church was founded in 1811.

[36] *... for the cause it undertook?*: Readers might query Pusey House.

[37] *... for fifteen years*: After the Tractarians were shown the door in Oxford, the liberals took possession, which did not redound to the interests of the Anglican Church. See R.W. Church, *The Oxford Movement* (London, 1891), 392-3.

[38] *the late Dr. Arnold*: Thomas Arnold of Rugby (1795-1842), a Liberal Anglican, was one of Newman's favorite whipping boys, though here he shows that he could occasionally find nice things to say about his controversial opponents. For Newman's objections to Arnold, see *Apo*, 42. For Arnold's view of Newman and the Tractarians, especially as it relates to the Hampden fracas, see T. Arnold, "The Oxford Malignants and Dr. Hampden," *Edinburgh Review*, 63 (1836), 225-39. See also M.D. Chapman, "Liberal Anglicanism," *The Oxford History of Anglicanism* ed. R. Strong (Oxford, 2017), III, 212-31. Apropos the muscular Christian, Sydney Smith had nothing but praise: "I have been reading Arnold's Life by Stanley," he wrote. "Arnold seems to have been a very pious, honest, learned, and original man." *A Memoir of the Reverend Sydney Smith by his daughter Lady Holland* (London, 1855), ii, 493.

endowed Sees,[40] of which its enemies in the Establishment have gladly taken or are taking possession; it has founded sisterhoods[41] or enforced confessions, the fruits of which are yet to be seen. On [12] the other hand, it has given a hundred educated men to the Catholic Church;[42] yet the huge creature, from which they went forth, showed no consciousness of its loss, but shook itself, and went about its work as of old time—as all parties, even the associates they had left, united, and even glorified, in testifying. And lastly, the present momentous event, to which I have already

---

[39] *built Churches*: St. Saviour's, Leeds, consecrated in 1842 and completed in 1845, is perhaps the best example of the vexed contributions that the Tractarians made to the life of parishes in the Anglican Church. See G. P. Grantham, *A History of St. Saviour's, Leeds* (London, 1872). Following suggestions by R. H. Froude, Pusey had wished to endow colleges on an extensive scale but little came of it beyond St. Saviour's. See H. P. Liddon, *Life of Edward Bouverie Pusey* (London, 1893), ii, 36-40, as well as the entry on the vicar of St Saviour's, W. F. Hook in the *ODNB*. See also F. Knight, "The Influence of the Oxford Movement in the Parishes: A Reassessment," *From Oxford to the People* (Leominster, 1996), as well as J. Tolhurst, "Introduction," John Henry Newman, *Tracts for the Times* ed. J. Tolhurst (Leominster, 2013).

[40] *endowed Sees*: In 1847, the Tractarian Edward Coleridge (1800-83), Fellow of Eton and Vicar of Mapledurham cajoled Baroness Angela Georgina Burdett Coutts (1814-1906) into donating £35,000 to endow the sees of Adelaide and Cape Town. See Austin Cooper, "Forgotten Australian Anglican: Edward Coleridge" *Pacifica: Australasian Theological Studies,* vol. 3, issue 3, 1990. For a profile on the Baroness, see the *ODNB.*

[41] *sisterhoods*: For the varied work that Edward Pusey did to promote sisterhoods, thanks to his mother's inheritance, see the *ODNB*.

[42] *a hundred educated men*: A brief list of those whose conversion to Roman Catholicism was influenced by Tractarianism would include Thomas Allies, Edward Badeley, Edward Bellasis, Emily Bowles, William Copeland, John Dalgairns, William Dodsworth, Frederick Faber, Catherine Froude, Lady Georgiana Fullerton, Mary Holmes, James Hope-Scott, William Lockhart, the Marchioness of Lothian, Henry Edward Manning, William Maskell, Frederick Oakeley, Augustus Pugin, George William Ward and Henry and Robert Wilberforce.

alluded, bearing upon the doctrine of Baptism, which is creating such disturbance in the country, has happened altogether independent of the movement, and is unaffected by it. Those persons who went forward to Catholicism have not caused it; those who have stayed neither could prevent it, nor can remedy it. It relates to a question previous to any of those doctrines which it has been the main object of the movement to maintain. It is caused, rather it is willed, by the national mind; and, till the grace of God touches and converts that mind, it will remain a fact done and over, a precedent and a principle in the Establishment.

3.

This is the true explanation of what is going on before our eyes, as seen whether in the decision of the Privy Council, or in the respective conduct of the two parties in the Establishment with relation to it. It may seem strange, at first sight, that the Evangelical section [13] should presume so boldly to contravene the distinct and categorical teaching of the national formularies on the subject of Baptism; strange, till it is understood that the interpreter of their sense is the Nation itself, and that that section in the Establishment speaks with the confidence of men who know that they have the Nation on their side. Let me here refer to the just and manly admissions on this subject, of a high-principled writer, which have lately been given to the public:—

"There is" a "consideration," he says, "which, for some time, has pressed heavily and painfully upon me. As a fact, the Evangelical party plainly, openly, and fully declare their opinions upon the doctrines which they contend the Church of England holds; they tell their people continually, what they ought, as a matter of duty towards God and towards themselves, both to believe and practise. Can it be pretended that we, as a party, anxious to teach the truth, are equally open, plain, and unreserved? ... And it is not to be alleged, that only the less important duties and doctrines are so reserved: as if it would be an easy thing to distinguish and draw a line of division between them ... We do reserve vital and essential truths; we often hesitate and fear to teach our people many duties, not all necessary, perhaps, in every case or to every person, but eminently practical, and sure to increase the growth of the inner, spiritual life; we differ, in short, as widely from the Evangelical party in the manner and openness, as in the matter and details of our doctrine ... [14] All this seems to me to be, day by day and hour by hour, more and more hard to be reconciled with the real spirit, mind, and purpose of the English Reformation, and of the modern English Church, shown by the experience of three hundred years ... People often say it is wrong to use such terms as 'the spirit of the Reformed English Church;' or 'its intention,' 'purpose,' and the like. And is it really so? was the Reformation nothing? did it effect nothing, change nothing, remove nothing? ... No doubt the Reformed Church of England claims to be a portion of the Holy Catholic Church; and it has been common for many of our own opinions, to add also the assertion, that she rejects and condemns, as being out of the Church Catholic, the Reformed Churches abroad, Lutheran, Genevan, and others, together with the Kirk of Scotland, or the Dissenters at home. Upon our principles, nay, on any consistent Church principle at all, such a corollary must follow. But there is a strangeness in it; it commends itself perhaps to our intellect, but not to the eye or ear; nor, it may be, to the heart or conscience."[43]

These remarks are as true as they are candid; and it is, I hope, no disrespect to the Author, if, taking them from their context, I use them for my own argument, which is not indeed divergent, though distinct from his own. Whether, then, they prove that the Evangelical [15] party is as much at home in the *National Prayer-Book* as the Anglican, I will not pronounce; but at least they prove that that party is far more at home in the *National Establishment*; that it is in cordial and intimate sympathy with the sovereign Lord and Master of the Prayer-Book, its composer and interpreter, the Nation itself,—on the best terms with Queen and statesmen, and practical men, and country gentlemen, and respectable tradesmen, fathers and mothers, school-masters, churchwardens, vestries, public societies, newspapers, and their readers in the lower classes. The Evangelical ministers of the Establishment have, in comparison with their Anglican rivals, the spirit of the age with them; they are congenial with the age; they glide forward rapidly and proudly down the stream; and it is this fact, and their consciousness of it, which carries them over all difficulties. Jewell[44] was triumphant over Harding, and Wake over Atterbury[45] or

---

[43] Maskell's Second Letter, pp. 57-69. [N]

[44] *Jewell*: John Jewell (1522-71), Bishop of Salisbury, and one of the principal architects of the Elizabethan Settlement (1558), entered into controversy with the defender of the papacy's position, Thomas Harding (1516-72) after publishing his *Apologia Ecclesiae Anglicanae* (1562). One of the signal contributions that Jewell made to Elizabeth's 'hedge priests,' as she called them on her deathbed, was to prepare Hooker for university.

[45] *Wake over Atterbury*: William Wake (1657-1737), Archbishop of Canterbury, wrote his history of the synods of the English Church, *State of the Church and Clergy in England* (1703) to rebut the Tory High Church champion of Convocation, Francis Atterbury (1662-1732),

Leslie,[46] with the terrors or the bribes of a sovereign to back them; and their successors in this day have, in like manner, the strength of public opinion on their side. The letter of enactments, pristine customs, ancient rights, is no match for the momentum with which they rush along upon the flood of public opinion, which rules that every conclusion is absurd, and every argument sophistical, and every maxim untrue, except such as it recognises itself.

4.   [16]

How different has it been with the opposite party? Confident, indeed, and with reason, of the truth of its great principles, having a perception and certainty of its main tenets, which is like the evidence of sense compared with the feeble, flitting, and unreal views of doctrine held by the Evangelical body, still, as to their application, their adaptation, their combination, their development, it has been miserably conscious that it has had nothing to guide it but its own private and

---

Bishop of Rochester. Although Wake's response to Atterbury was seen as masterly, by the time it appeared "the ministry had conceded a sitting convocation and the debate had moved on. Wake played no further role in the convocation controversy, but his exchange with Atterbury had established him as the hero of the Whig clergy" – not a distinction that would have endeared him to Newman, though as N. Sykes, Wake's biographer, points out, the Archbishop believed that the 39 Articles were framed so that 'they may, without an equivocation, have more senses than one fairly put upon them.'" *ODNB*.

[46] *Leslie*: Charles Leslie (1650-1722), non-juror and controversialist, with whom Wake crossed swords. See W. Frank, "Charles Leslie and Theological Politics in Post-Revolutionary England" Ph.D. Thesis, McMaster University (February, 1983). Newman had occasion to quote one of Leslie's jibes in a letter of 1837: "I grudge not the office of a scavenger, and the Herculean labour of cleansing so foul a stable; a sink and complication of the vilest heresies that have ever been broached in the Christian church ..." *LD*, vi, 52. Anglicans who complain of the occasional acerbity of Newman's controversial writings should revisit their own rather more vitriolic tradition.

unaided judgment.[47] Dreading its own interpretation of Scripture and the Fathers, feeling its need of an infallible guide, yet having none; looking up to its own Mother, as it called her, and finding her silent, ambiguous, unsympathetic, sullen, and even hostile to it; with ritual mutilated, sacraments defective, precedents inconsistent, articles equivocal, canons obsolete, courts Protestant, and synods suspended; scouted by the laity, scorned by men of the world, hated and blackened by its opponents; and moreover at variance with itself, hardly two of its members taking up the same position, nay, all of them, one by one, shifting their own ground as time went on, and obliged to confess that they were in progress; is it wonderful, in the words of the Pamphlet already referred to, that these men have exhibited "a conduct and a rule of a religious life," "full of shifts, and compromises, and [17] evasions, a rule of life, based upon the acceptance of half one doctrine, all the next, and none of the third, upon the belief entirely of another, but not daring to say so?" After all, they have not been nearly so guilty "of shifts, and compromises, and evasions," as the national formularies themselves; but they have had

---

[47] *its own private and unaided judgment*: Since Newman as a Tractarian spent years remonstrating with liberal Anglicans for indulging in what he regarded as their 'private judgement,' turning the same criticism against his Tractarian friends was fairly ruthless, which was not lost on W. E. Gladstone, who would later tell the historian Lord Acton after Newman's death: "He was trained (as I was) in the Evangelical School, which is beyond all others ... the school of private judgment. By private judgment he excogitated the scheme of doctrine and thought which he taught in his Anglican works. By private judgment he grew sore with the manifold abuses and defects of the English Church; but then, also by private judgment, he measured the corruptions of the Roman, and recoiled from them. It is wonderful, and shows the loyalty of his affection, that, leaving nothing but rags and shreds to hang on by, he remained in the English Church until 1845." *Correspondence on Church and Religion of William Ewart Gladstone* ed. Lathbury (London, 1910), i, 406.

none to support them, or, if I may use a familiar word, to act the bully for them, under the imputation. There was no one, with confident air and loud voice, to retort upon their opponents the charges urged against them, and no public to applaud though there had been. Whether they looked above or below, behind or before, they found nothing, indeed, to shake or blunt their faith in Christ, in His establishment of a Church, in its visibility, continuance, catholicity, and gifts, and in the necessity of belonging to it: they despised the hollowness of their opponents, the inconsequence of their arguments, the shallowness of their views, their disrelish of principle, and their carelessness about truth, but their heart sunk within them, under the impossibility, on the one hand, of their carrying out their faith into practice, *there*, where they found themselves, and of realising their ideas in fact,—and the duty on the other, as they were taught it, of making the best of the circumstances in which they were placed. Such were they; I trust they are so still: I will not allow myself to fancy that secret doubts on the one hand, that self-will, disregard of authority, an unmanly, disingenuous bearing, and the spirit of party on the other, have deformed a body of persons whom I have loved, revered, and sympathised with. I speak of those [18] many persons whom I admired; who, like the hero in the epic, did not want courage, but encouragement; who looked out in vain for the approbation of authority; who felt their own power, but shrank from the omen of evil, the hateful raven, which flapped its wings over them; who seemed to say with the poet—

—Non me tua fervida terrent

Dicta, ferox; Dii me terrent, et Jupiter hostis.[48]

But their very desire of realities, and their fear of deceiving themselves with dreams, was their insurmountable difficulty here. They could not make the Establishment what it was not, and this was forced on them day after day. It is a principle, in some sense acknowledged by Catholic theologians, that the spirit of an age modifies its inherited professions. Moralists lay down, that a law loses its authority which the lawgiver knowingly allows to be infringed and put aside; whatever, then, be the abstract claims of the Anglican cause, the fact is that the living community to which they belong has for centuries ignored and annulled them. It was a principle parallel to this which furnished one of the reasons on which the judges of the Queen's Bench the other day acted, when they refused to prohibit the execution of the Royal decision, in the appeal made from the Bishop of Exeter.[49] His counsel [19] urged certain provisions in statutes of the reign of Henry VIII., which had not been discussed in the pleadings. "Were the language of 25 Henry VIII. c. 9, obscure instead of clear," observed the Chief Justice, "we should not be justified in differing from the

---

[48] *...et Jupiter hostis*: Virgil, *Aeneid*, XII, 894-5. "Your fierce words do not frighten me, you wild man/The gods frighten me, and the hostile Jupiter." Stanley Jaki's gloss is worth quoting; "The irony intended by Newman consists in the fact that he lets the Anglican authorities use these words of Turnus, Aeneas' ignoble adversary, against the Tractarians." See Stanley L. Jaki's edition of *Anglican Difficulties* (Michigan, 1995), 267.

[49] In 1847, Henry Phillpotts (1778-1869), Bishop of Exeter, refused to institute G. C. Gorham, who had been presented to the living of Brampford, after Gorham refused to subscribe Baptismal Regeneration, which gave rise to the Gorham Case, in which the Privy Council overruled the Bishop in favour of Gorham, thus undermining the long-standing Anglican doctrine of baptismal regeneration. See Editor's Introduction.

construction put upon it by contemporaneous and long-continued usage. There would be no safety for property or liberty if it could be successfully contended, that all lawyers and statesmen have been mistaken for centuries as to the true meaning of the Act of Parliament." Whatever becomes of the general question, this was at least the language of reason and common sense; as physical life assimilates to itself, or casts off, whatever it encounters, allowing no interference with the supremacy of its own proper principles, so is it with life social and civil. When a body politic grows, takes definite shape, and matures, it slights, though it may endure, the vestiges and tokens of its rude beginnings. It may cherish them as curiosities, but it abjures them as precedents. They may hang about it, as the shrivelled blossom about the formed fruit; but they are dead, and will be sure to disappear as soon as they are felt to be troublesome. Common sense tells us these appendages do not apply to things as they are; and, if individuals attempt to insist on them, they will but bring on themselves the just imputation of vexatiousness and extravagance. So it is with the Anglican formularies; they are but the expression of the national sentiment, and therefore are necessarily modified by it. Did the nation grow into [20] Catholicity, they might easily be made to assume a Catholic demeanour; but as it has matured in its Protestantism, they must take, day by day, a more Evangelical and liberal aspect. Of course I am not saying this by way of justifying individuals in professing and using doctrinal and devotional forms from which they dissent; nor am I denying that words have, or at least ought to have, a definite meaning which must not be explained away; I am merely stating what takes place in matter of fact, allowably in some cases, wrongly in others, according to the strength, on the one hand, of the wording of the formulary, and of the diverging opinion on the other.

I say, that a nation's laws are a nation's property, and have their life in the nation's life, and their interpretation in the nation's sentiment: and where that living intelligence does not shine through them, they become worthless and are put aside, whether formally or on an understanding. Now Protestantism is, as it has been for centuries, the Religion of England; and since the semi-patristical Church, which was set up for the nation at the Reformation, is the organ of that religion, it must live for the nation; it must hide its Catholic aspirations in folios, or in college cloisters; it must call itself Protestant, when it gets into the pulpit; it must abjure Antiquity; for woe to it, if it attempt to thrust the wording of its own documents in its master's path, [21] if it rely on a passage in its Visitation for the Sick,[50] or on an Article of the Creed,[51] or on the tone of its

---

[50] *Visitation for the Sick*: Since the Anglican Article of Faith pertaining to the Visitation of the Sick makes repeated reference to Confession, Anglo-Catholics might have to ignore such references in order to remain in good standing with a national religion calling itself Protestant. The difficulties inherent in Anglo-Catholics trying to introduce Confession into Anglicanism are well-documented. See W. Gresley, *The Ordinance of Confession* (London, 1851) and J. M. Neale, *Lectures principally on the Church Difficulties of the Present Time* (London, 1852) and *Confession and Absolution* (London, 1854). The most eloquent testimony to this difficulty, however, is from Newman, who wrote Keble in 1842: "As to reminding my People about Confession, it is the most dreary and dismal thought which I have about my Parish that I dare do so little, or rather nothing. I have long thought it would hinder me ever taking another cure. Confession is the life of the Parochial charge—without it all is hollow—and yet I do not see my way to say that I should not do more harm than good by more than the more distant mention of it." *LD*, ix, 175.

[51] *the Creed*: This was a prophetic reference to the Athanasian Creed in light of the many Anglicans who would forswear its articles in the 19th century, though Newman was pleased that his erstwhile assailant C. Kingsley came out in favor of them. See *LD*, xxvii, 220.

Collects, or on a catena of its divines,[52] when the age has determined on a theology more in keeping with the progress of knowledge! The antiquary, the reader of history, the theologian, the philosopher, the Biblical student may make his protest; he may quote St. Austin,[53] or appeal to the canons, or argue from the nature of the case; but *la Reine le veut*;[54] the English people is sufficient for itself; it wills to be Protestant and progressive; and Fathers, Councils, Schoolmen, Scriptures, Saints, Angels, and what is above them, must give way. What are they to it? It thinks, argues, and acts according to its own practical, intelligible, shallow religion; and of that religion its Bishops and divines, will they or will they not, must be exponents.[55]

5.

In this way, I say, we are to explain, but in this way most naturally and satisfactorily, what otherwise would

---

[52] *a catena*: Newman had compiled a catena of Anglican divines in his long letter of March, 1841 to R.W. Jelf (1798-1871), Canon of Christ Church, in the wake of the controversy arising from Tract 90. See *LD*, viii, 78-90.

[53] *Austin*: St Augustine (d. 604 or 605), first Archbishop of Canterbury. Pope St Gregory the Great sent the Italian Benedictine monk to Kent in 597 to convert the pagan English.

[54] *la Reine le veut:* The Norman-French phrase – 'The Queen wills it' – is spoken in the English parliament to confirm that a public bill has received the royal assent.

[55] "It is not the practice for Judges to take up points of their own, and, *without argument*, to decide a case upon them. Lord Eldon used to say, that oftentimes hearing an argument in support of an opinion he had so taken up, convinced him he had been wrong—a great authority in favour of the good sense of the practice, which the Queen's Bench has disregarded in this case. In the Hampden case, the whole practice of the Court for two hundred and fifty years was set at naught by Lord Denman. In this case a course has been taken which has never hitherto been followed in questions of a mandamus to a railway, or a criminal information against a newspaper. *And both are Church cases.*"— *Guardian*, May 1, 1850. [N]

[22] be startling, the late Royal decision to which I have several times referred. The great legal authorities, on whose report it was made, have not only pronounced, that, as a matter of fact, persons who have denied the grace of Baptism had held the highest preferments in the National Church, but they felt themselves authorised actually to interpret its ritual and its doctrine, and to report to her Majesty that the dogma of baptismal regeneration is not part and parcel of the national religion. They felt themselves strong enough, in their position, to pronounce "that the doctrine held by" the Protestant clergyman, who brought the matter before them,[56] "was not contrary or repugnant to the declared doctrine of the Church of England, as by law established." The question was not whether it was true or not,—as they most justly remarked,—whether from heaven or from hell; they were too sober to meddle with what they had no means of determining; they "abstained from expressing any opinion of their own upon the theological correctness or error of the doctrine" propounded: the question was, not what God had said, but what the English nation had willed and allowed; and, though it must be granted that they aimed at a critical examination of the letter of the documents, yet it must be granted on the other hand too, that their criticism was of a very national cast, and that the national sentiment was of great use to them in helping them to their conclusions. What was it to the

[23] nation or its lawyers whether Hooker used the word "charity" or "piety" in the extract which they adduced from his works, and that "piety" gave one sense to the passage, and "charity" another? Hooker must speak as

---

[56] *the Protestant clergyman*: This is another reference to Henry Phillpotts (1778-1869), Bishop of Exeter. For an excellent, barbed profile of the bishop, see the entry in the *ODNB* by A. Burns.

the existing nation speaks, if he is to be a national authority. What though the ritual categorically deposes to the regeneration of the infant baptized? The Evangelical party, who, in former years, had had the nerve to fix the charge of dishonesty on the explanations of the Thirty-nine Articles, put forth by their opponents, could all the while be cherishing in their own breasts an interpretation of the Baptismal Service, simply contradictory to its most luminous declarations. Inexplicable proceeding, if they were professing to handle the document in its letter; but not dishonourable, not dishonest, not hypocritical, but natural and obvious, on the condition or understanding that the Nation, which imposes the document, imposes its sense,—that by the breath of its mouth it had, as a god, made Establishment, Articles, Prayer-Book, and all that is therein, and could by the breath of its mouth as easily and absolutely unmake them again, whenever it was disposed.

Counsel, then, and pamphleteers may put forth unanswerable arguments in behalf of the Catholic interpretation of the Baptismal service; a long succession of Bishops, an unbroken tradition of writers, may have faithfully and anxiously guarded it. In vain has the Caroline school[57] honoured it by ritual observance; in vain has the Restoration[58] illustrated it by varied learning; in vain did the Revolution[59] retain it [24]

---

[57] *Caroline school*: The Caroline divines were those Anglican divines from the reign of Charles I to Charles II whose works constitute what is generally regarded as the golden age of Anglican theology. Their number includes Lancelot Andrewes (1555-1628), John Bramhall (1594-1663), Thomas Ken (1637-1711), and Jeremy Taylor (1612-67).

[58] *Restoration:* Reestablishment of the monarchy in 1660.

[59]*Revolution*: The Revolution of 1688 saw the overthrow of the Catholic King James II, who was replaced by his Protestant daughter Mary and her Dutch husband, William of Orange. The revisionist historian S. Pincus

as the price for other concessions; in vain did the eighteenth century use it as a sort of watchword against Wesley;[60] in vain has it been persuasively developed

---

depicts the Revolution as "the culmination of a long and vitriolic argument about how to transform England into a modern nation." S. Pincus, *1688: The First Modern Revolution* (New Haven, 2009), 486. This secularist reading flouts what Macaulay had to say of the two "renowned factions" who were involved in the Revolution, neither of whom, *pace* Pincus, took a greater interest in economics, trade and foreign policy than in their deep-seated religious and constitutional convictions. See T. B. Macaulay, *The History of England* (London, 1913), I, 76. The old reading of the Revolution is still the most cogent: 1688 "ended monarchical absolutism, established the primacy of Parliament, and preserved the Protestant religion." R. Tombs, *The English and their History* (London, 2014), 263. Pincus is also wrong to see the Revolution as somehow a European event. It may have had ramifications beyond England's shores but it highlighted the distinctness of England in a Europe where "confessionalization, the identification of a state and its people with a single religion" had become the norm. In England, by contrast, "Disunity was institutionalized, both in religion, the dominant cultural arena, and in 'Whig' and 'Tory' political identities." Tombs, 263. Again, Macaulay's reading may be laced with Whig triumphalism but at least he accurately identified the antagonists: Whigs and Tories precipitated the Revolution, not such abstractions as 'secularization' and 'modernity.' Jonathan Clark is good on this matter: "... secularization is not a process, but a project; not something happening autonomously within the phenomena, like ocean currents or hurricanes, but a project urged by some individuals who seek historical validation for a cause." J. C. D. Clark, "Secularization and Modernization: The Failure of a 'Grand Narrative,'" *The Historical Journal*, Vol. 55, No. 1 (March, 2012), p. 190.

[60] *Wesley*: John Wesley (1763-91), founder of the Methodist Movement, was not only an influential preacher but a crack organizer. An indefatigable man, he is said to have traveled some 250,000 miles on horseback over fifty years and although barred from most Anglican pulpits he managed to extend his Evangelical faith throughout the country, even to the prisons. The turnkey at Clerkenwell, for example, told Tobias Smollett that since his Methodist character Humphry Clinker entered the prison, there had been "nothing but canting and praying... [and] the gentlemen get drunk with nothing but your damned religion." See B. Williams, *The Whig Supremacy 1714-1760* (Oxford, 1960), 97. Such eighteenth-century critics as Bishop Lavington (see below) took issue with Wesley for, among other things, taking liberties with the doctrine of baptismal regeneration. Lavington, for example, cited a

and fearlessly proclaimed by the movement of 1833; all this is foreign to the matter before us. We have not to enquire what is the dogma of a collegiate, antiquarian religion, but what, in the words of the Prime Minister, will give "general satisfaction;" what is the religion of Britons. May not the free-born, self-dependent, animal mind of the Englishman, choose his religion for himself? and have lawyers any more to do than to state, as a matter of fact and history, what that religion is, and for three centuries has been? are we to obtrude the mysteries of an objective, of a dogmatic, of a revealed system, upon a nation which intimately feels and has established, that each individual is to be his own judge in truth and falsehood in matters of the unseen world? How is it possible that the National Church, forsooth, should be allowed to dogmatize on a point which so immediately affects the Nation itself? Why, half the country is unbaptized; it is difficult to say for certain who are baptized; shall the country unchristianize itself? it has not yet advanced to indifference on such a matter. Shall it, by a suicidal act, use its own Church against itself, as its instrument whereby to cut itself off from the hope of another life? Shall it confine the Christian promise within limits, [25] and put restrictions upon grace, when it has thrown open trade, removed disabilities, abolished monopolies, taken off agricultural protection, and enlarged the franchise?—Such is the thought, such the

---

reference in Wesley's *Journal* to "blind leaders of the blind who speak of the new birth, as if it were no more than baptism." (*Journal*, 82) For a witty comparison between Wesley and Newman, see R. Knox, *Enthusiasm: A Chapter in the History of Religion* (Oxford, 1950), 422-3. For Newman's own grudging tribute to Wesley and the Wesleyans, see below *Diff*, i, 90-1.

language of the England of today.[61] What a day for the defenders of the dogma in bygone times, if those times had anything to do with the present! What a day for Bishop Lavington, who, gazing on Wesley preaching the new birth at Exeter, pronounced Methodism as bad as "Popery"![62] What a portentous day for Bampton Lecturers and divinity Professors! What a day for Bishop Mant[63] and Archbishop Lawrence,[64] and Bishop

---

[61] *the England of today*: Here, Newman answers his own question as to what effect Free Trade and the Reform Bill mentality might have on Anglican orthodoxy. See *Diff*, i, 8-9.

[62] *Lavington*: George Lavington (1684–1762), Bishop of Exeter, was a fierce opponent of Wesley and his Methodism, though no fonder of Catholicism, calling it in one of his sermons "that *scandal and scourge of the Christian world.*" According to the *ODNB*, Lavington's *The Enthusiasm of Methodists* (1749-51) "was learned and wide ranging but also rambling, crude, and sometimes caustic. ... Thus the Methodists' personal mortifications, ecstatic raptures, vainglory, and other perceived characteristics were ridiculed and castigated. So was their undutiful behaviour towards the civil powers. Enthusiasm was '*Religion run mad*' (ibid., 81) ... Lavington's *Enthusiasm* can be dismissed as a brutal diatribe but it should be remembered that Methodism was attacked from many quarters in its early years. Nor were all the charges contained in the *Enthusiasm*, or its central premise, far from the mark."

[63] *Mant*: Richard Mant (1776-1848), Bishop of Down, Connor and Dromore, gave the Bampton Lecture for 1812, *An Appeal to the Gospel*. He also published an edition of the Bible with notes from Protestant divines (1814), an annotated edition of the *Book of Common Prayer* (1820), and a *History of the Church of Ireland* (1840). In a letter to Hurrell Froude of January, 1830, Newman referred to one of Mant's other publications – *A Clergyman's Obligations* (Oxford, 1830) – as "twaddling." *LD*, ii, 185. In his Bishop's Charge of June, 1842, Mant responded to favorable references that Newman had made to the Church of Rome in his "Letter to Dr. Jelf by the author of No. 90" thus: "Your reflections, my brethren, will readily furnish the counterpart of this picture; and, together with the flattering features of the portrait, you will remember others of a very different cast, which distinguish the Roman communion: the adoration paid to our common saints, and the multitudinous addition of her own, with their meritorious and miraculous actions; the 'blasphemous fables and dangerous deceits' by which her most holy truths and practices are desecrated and profaned; her real disagreements under the semblance of universal union; her discipline disgraced by tyranny; her devotions sullied by superstition; her ritual

Van Mildert,[65] and Archbishop Sutton,[66] and, as we may trust, what a day had it been for Archbishop Howley,[67] taken away on its very dawning! The giant ocean has suddenly swelled and heaved, and majestically yet masterfully snaps the cables of the

---

abounding in occasions of offence, and representing our Saviour's sacrifice as aided by the merits of her saints; her monastic institutions supplied by fraud, supported by injustice and violence, teeming with profligacy, and too grievous to be borne; her edifices erected professedly to God's honour, but abounding in abominations which dishonour God; her implacable animosity towards us, and her anathemas and execrations perpetually poured on us from her altars." *LD*, ix, 621. Such vituperative impatience with the Roman Church notwithstanding, Mant, as Newman told his brother Charles, did have the distinction of being the last Trinity man to become an Oriel Fellow before Newman himself. *LD*, i, 131.

[64] *Lawrence*: Richard Laurence (1760-1838), Regius Professor of Hebrew (1814-22) and, thereafter, Archbishop of Cashel. In 1804, Laurence took Evangelicals to task for attempting to misrepresent the 39 Articles in his Bampton lectures aptly entitled: *An Attempt to illustrate those Articles of the Church of England which the Calvinists improperly consider Calvinistical.*

[65] *Van Mildert*: William Van Mildert (1765-1836) gave the Bampton lecture for 1814, *The General Principles of Scripture-Interpretation.* Appointed Regius Professor of Divinity in 1813, Van Mildert was made Bishop of Llandaff in 1819, Dean of St. Paul's in 1820 and Bishop of Durham in 1826. He produced a 10-volume edition of the works of Daniel Waterland (1823-8). See *LD*, v, 33.

[66] *Sutton*: Charles Manners-Sutton (1755–1828), Archbishop of Canterbury from 1805 to 1828.

[67] *Howley:* William Howley (1766-1848). Appointed Regius Professor of Divinity in 1809, he became Archbishop of Canterbury in 1828. High Church, he opposed religious liberalism as fiercely as political reform. However, in 1836, when the appointment of the Divinity Professorship was being broached, Howley inadvertently betrayed these loyalties by accepting (to his later chagrin) R. D. Hampden, who had been recommended to Lord Melbourne by the feckless Noetics R. Whately and E. Copleston. Like them, Hampden had been a Fellow in Oriel's Senior Common Room. See *LD*, v, 216, Note 1. "[T]he *Noetic* school... [maintained] around them a continuous dialectical ferment – Oriel Common Room *stunk* of logic, was the complaint of easy-going guests – and ... [provoked] by their political and ecclesiastical liberalism the great revolt of the Newmania." W. Tuckwell, *Reminiscences of Oxford* (London, 1900), 17.

smaller craft which lie upon its bosom, and strands them upon the beach. Hooker, Taylor, Bull, Pearson, Barrow,[68] Tillotson,[69] Warburton,[70] and Horne,[71] names mighty in their generation, are broken and wrecked before the power of a nation's will. One vessel alone

---

[68] *Barrow*: Isaac Barrow (1630-77), Anglican preacher and mathematician. Charles II made him his chaplain and, in 1673, Master of Trinity College, Cambridge. According to the *ODCC*, "The precision of a mathematician's thought is reflected in his theology, and his *Treatise on the Pope's Supremacy* (1680, posthumous) remains a work of outstanding ability." Newman admired his English style. *LD*, iii, 31. A polymath, Barrow wrote on optics and geometry, as well as papal supremacy, and is perhaps most well-known for inspiring his famous pupil, Isaac Newton, for whom he gave up the Lucasian chair in 1660. *Companion to British History*.

[69] *Tillotson*: John Tillotson (1630-94), Archbishop of Canterbury. "Archbishop Tillotson set the tone for Georgian moderate Anglicanism [throughout the 18th century] by thus characterizing Christ: 'His Virtues were shining without Vanity, Heroical without anything of Transport, and very extraordinary without being in the least extravagant.'" R. Porter, *England in the 18th Century* (London, 1990), 159.

[70] *Warburton*: William Warburton (1698-1779), English churchman, editor and polemicist. Preacher of Lincoln's Inn (1746), prebendary of Gloucester (1753), king's chaplain (1754), prebendary of Durham (1755), dean of Bristol (1757), and Bishop of Gloucester 1759), Warburton took issue with Hume, Voltaire and Wesley, edited Shakespeare and became Pope's literary executor. Apropos *The Alliance between Church and State* (1736), his defence of the Erastianism of the English Church, Newman wrote to John Bowden in 1834: "It is a remarkable fact ... that of the *concessions* mutually made on Warburton's Theory by Church and State, the State has resumed all hers, yet *retained* all the Church's." *LD*, iv, 190. After the bishop praised Samuel Johnson's "manly spirit in rejecting [the] condescensions of Lord Chesterfield...," the lexicographer and critic always retained a high opinion of him. J. Boswell, *Life of Johnson* ed. Chapman (Oxford, 1953), 186. See also Johnson's generous character of the learned bishop in his *Lives of the English Poets*. ed. Lonsdale (Oxford), iv, 40-1. In addition to his literary and ecclesiastical writings, Warburton took issue with the slave trade as early as 1766.

[71] *Horne*: George Horne (1730-92), Bishop of Norwich. A High Church critic of Newton, Hume and William Law, the apologist whose *Serious Call* (1728) managed to get Samuel Johnson out of bed before noon, Horne nevertheless sympathized with the Wesleyans and would not bar Wesley from preaching in his diocese. His *Commentary on the Psalms* (1771) was his most significant work.

can ride those waves; it is the boat of Peter, the ark of God.

6.

And now, my brethren, it is plain that this doctrine does not stand by itself:—if the grace of Baptism is not to be taught dogmatically in the National Church, if it [26] be not a heresy to deny it, if to hold it and not to hold it be but matters of opinion, what other doctrine which that Church professes stands on a firmer or more secure foundation? The same popular voice which has explained away the wording of the Office for Baptism, may of course in a moment dispense with the Athanasian Creed altogether. Who can doubt, that if that symbol be not similarly dealt with in course of law in years to come, it is because the present judgment will practically destroy its force as efficaciously, and with less trouble to the lawyers? No individual will dare to act on views which he knows to a certainty would be overruled as soon as they are brought before a legal tribunal. As to the document itself, it will be obvious to allege that the details of the Athanasian Creed were never intended for reception by national believers; that all that was intended (as has before now been avowed) was to uphold a doctrine of a Trinity, and that, provided we hold this "scriptural fact," it matters not whether we be Athanasians,[72] Sabellians,

---

[72] *Athanasians*: These were adherents of the doctrines of Athanasius (c. 295-373), Archbishop of Alexandria. A pellucid theologian and stalwart opponent of Arianism, Athanasius was steeped in Scripture and the Fathers, as well as such classical authors as Homer, Euripides, and Plato. As a young man, in addition to teaching catechumens, he spent time in the desert with St. Anthony. After attending the Council of Nicea, he defended not only the Trinity but the Incarnation and the Holy Spirit. On this score, Gibbon paid him a memorably double-edged compliment: "We have seldom an opportunity of observing, either in active or speculative life, what effect may be produced, or what obstacles may be surmounted, by the force of a single mind, when it is inflexibly applied to

Tritheists,[73] or Socinians,[74] or rather we shall be neither one nor the other of them. Precedents on the other hand

---

the pursuit of a single object. The immortal name of Athanasius will never be separated from the catholic doctrine of the Trinity, to whose defence he consecrated every moment and every faculty of his being." Gibbon, *Decline & Fall*, ii, 383. In addition, St. Athanasius upheld the autonomy of the Church. In his unflagging fight against various Arian and anti-Nicene factions within the Church, he endured no less than five exiles, and it was for his uncompromising pertinacity that he became known as *Athanasius contra mundum*. His written works include: *De Incarnatione Verbi* (373); *De Virginitate* (357), and *Contra Arianos* (362). A good sense of the high esteem in which Newman held Athanasius can be found in the *Apologia* where he says: "I believe the whole revealed dogma as taught by the Apostles, as committed by the Apostles to the Church, and as declared by the Church to me. I receive it, as it is infallibly interpreted by the authority to whom it is thus committed, and (implicitly) as it shall be, in like manner, further interpreted by that same authority till the end of time. ... Also, I consider that, gradually and in the course of ages, Catholic inquiry has taken certain definite shapes, and has thrown itself into the form of a science, with a method and a phraseology of its own, under the intellectual handling of great minds, such as St. Athanasius, St. Augustine, and St. Thomas; and I feel no temptation at all to break in pieces the great legacy of thought thus committed to us for these latter days." *Apo.*, 250-1. For Athanasius, as for Newman, there was one sure riposte to heresy: "This is not the faith of the Catholic Church, this is not the faith of the Fathers." Altogether fittingly, Newman was often referred to as the "English Athanasius." See *The Saints: A Concise Biographical Dictionary* ed. J. Coulson (New York, 1958), 57-8.

[73] *Tritheists*: These were "heretics who divide the Substance of the Blessed Trinity. Those who are usually meant by the name were a section of the Monophysites, who had great influence in the second half of the sixth century, but have left no traces save a few scanty notices in John of Ephesus, Photus, Leontius, etc. Their founder is said to be a certain John Ascunages, head of a Sophist school at Antioch." See *Catholic Encyclopedia*.

[74] *Socinians:* These were 16th-century Antitrinitarian heretics. According to the papal condemnations of Pope Paul IV (1555) and Clement VIII (1603), the Socinians held: "that there was no Trinity; that Christ was not consubstantial with the Father and Holy Spirit; that He was not conceived of the Holy Spirit, but begotten by St. Joseph; that His Death and Passion were not undergone to bring about our redemption; and finally that the Blessed Virgin was not the Mother of God, neither did she retain her virginity." Deism and Unitarianism are offshoots of Socinianism. *Catholic Encyclopedia*.

are easily adducible of Arian, Sabellian, and Unitarian Bishops and dignitaries, and of divines who professed that Trinitarianism was a mere matter of opinion, both in former times and now. Indeed it might with much reason be maintained, were the question before a court, that, looking at the matter historically, Locke gave the death-blow to the Catholic phraseology on that [27] fundamental doctrine among the Anglican clergy;[75] and it is surely undeniable, that such points as the Eternal Generation of the Son,[76] the Homoüsion,[77] and the

---

[75] *Locke*: John Locke (1632-1704), English philosopher, "gave the death-blow to the Catholic phraseology" of the Trinity by arguing in his *Essay concerning Human Understanding* (1690) that all of our ideas come from experience, i.e., our senses and our rational knowledge, not 'innate ideas,' as Plato had argued. Here was the dubious counsel of his celebrated '*tabula rasa*.' A Deist, Locke thought reasonableness the basis of Christianity, not Revelation. Newman was predictably critical of the rationalist savant. "He takes a view of the human mind," Newman wrote in his *Grammar of Assent*, "... which to me seems theoretical and unreal. ... Instead of going by the testimony of psychological facts, and thereby determining our constitutive faculties and our proper condition, and being content with the mind as God has made it, he would form men as he thinks they ought to be formed, into something better and higher, and calls them irrational and indefensible, if (so to speak) they take to the water instead of remaining under the narrow wings of his own arbitrary theory." *GA*, 164. Most of Newman's contemporary critics shared Locke's notions about the relationship between faith and reason. For Newman, three hundred years of Protestant Christianity in England had not been without grave metaphysical consequences. Locke's malign influence notwithstanding, for a generous defense of the rationalist philosopher, see Jonathan Clark: "John Locke has been misinterpreted if presented as a philosopher seeking to demote faith to opinion, for he argued both that God's existence was 'the most obvious Truth that Reason discovers', and that the evidence for God's existence was '(if I mistake not) equal to mathematical Certainty." J. C. D Clark, "Secularization and Modernization: The Failure of a 'Grand Narrative,'" *The Historical Journal*, Vol. 55, No. 1 (March, 2012), 186.

[76] *Eternal Generation of the Son*: "The Trinity is the term employed to signify the central doctrine of the Christian religion — the truth that in the unity of the Godhead there are Three Persons, the Father, the Son, and the Holy Spirit, these Three Persons being truly distinct one from another. Thus, in the words of the Athanasian Creed: "the Father is God,

Hypostatic Union,[78] have been silently discarded by the many, and but anxiously and apologetically put

---

the Son is God, and the Holy Spirit is God, and yet there are not three Gods but one God." In this Trinity of Persons the Son is begotten of the Father by an eternal generation, and the Holy Spirit proceeds by an eternal procession from the Father and the Son. Yet, notwithstanding this difference as to origin, the Persons are co-eternal and co-equal: all alike are uncreated and omnipotent. This, the Church teaches, is the revelation regarding God's nature which Jesus Christ, the Son of God, came upon earth to deliver to the world: and which she proposes to man as the foundation of her whole dogmatic system." *Catholic Encyclopedia*. See also life of Alexander, bishop of Alexandria (from 313); born Alexandria ca.250, died there 18 April 328. "His first task as bishop was to deal with the Meletian Schism. Most of his reign, however, was concerned with his major adversary, Arius. Although condemned and excommunicated by a synod convened by Alexander ca.321, Arius refused to abandon his teaching. This led to the convocation of the First Council of Nicaea (325) in which Alexander, accompanied by his deacon Athanasios (future bishop of Alexandria), played an important role. Of his voluminous correspondence, only three letters survive. In these he reveals himself as an active and persistent supporter of the Orthodox position concerning the Son's perfect consubstantiality and eternal generation from the Father. Fragments of sermons ascribed to him are also preserved in Coptic and Syriac." *The Oxford Dictionary of Byzantium*.

[77] *Homoüsion*: Term, from the Greek meaning 'of one substance,' used by Augustine to express the identity of the substance of the persons of the Trinity; the principal doctrine affirmed in the Athanasian Creed, drawn up to confute the Arian heresy. The word should not be confused with *homoiousion*, which derives from the Greek, meaning 'of like substance' and signifies of similar but not identical essence or substance; a seemingly small but actually big difference between the belief that the persons of the Trinity are of one substance (*homoousion*) and the belief that they are of different substances. *The Oxford Dictionary of Philosophy*. The similarity of the two words amused the scoffer in Gibbon, who delighted in the fact "that the profane of every age have derided the furious contests which the difference of a single diphthong excited between the Homoousians and the Homoiousians." Gibbon, *Decline and Fall*, ii, 373.

[78] *Hypostatic Union*: "The union of the Divine and human natures in the One Person ('Hypostasis') of Jesus Christ. The doctrine was elaborated by St Cyril of Alexandria and formally accepted by the Church in the Definition of Chalcedon (451)."

forward by the few.[79] With this existing disposition in the minds of English Churchmen towards a denial of the Catholic doctrine of the Trinity, I surely am not rash in saying, that the recent judgment has virtually removed it from their authoritative teaching altogether.

Nor can eternal punishment be received as an Anglican dogma, against the strong feeling of the age, with so little in its favour in the national formularies; nor original sin, considering that the national suspicion of it is countenanced and defended by no less an authority of past times than Bishop Jeremy Taylor.[80] And much less the inspiration of Scripture, and the existence of the evil spirit, doctrines which are not mentioned in the Thirty-nine Articles at all. Yet, plain though this be, at this moment the Evangelical members of the Establishment are extolling the recent judgment, and are transported at the triumph it gives

---

[79] *such points*: For a reliable explanation of these vital but complicated matters, see the article on "The Real Presence of Christ in the Eucharist" in the *Catholic Encyclopedia*.

[80] *Taylor*: Jeremy Taylor (1613-67), Anglican Bishop, chaplain of King Charles, and writer of devotional prose. The book to which Newman refers is *Unum Necessarium* (1655), Taylor's treatise on sin and repentance. In the Textual Appendix of the critical edition of *The Idea of a University* (1873), one can see Newman's amusing stricture against what he regarded as Taylor's meretricious learning, which he left out of his final edition. "I am almost ashamed to trespass on your indulgence, Gentlemen, with a fresh catalogue of names; yet I should not do justice to the marvellous availableness of this writer's erudition for enforcing truisms and proving proverbs, unless I told you that to this new subject he devotes near a dozen pages more, using for his purpose, not any common-sense principles or clear broad rules, but Juvenal, St. Chrysostom, Antidamus (?), Terence, St. Ambrose, Martial, Dio, Seneca, Homer, Aristotle, Horace, Boethius, and others, leaving the subject pretty much as he found it. Such is learning, when used, not as a means, but as an end, less dignified even than the 'sonitus spinarum ardentium sub ollâ', of Ecclesiastes, 'the crackling of thorns under a pot', for they at least make the water boil, but nothing comes of pedantry." J. H . Newman, *The Idea of a University* ed. I. T. Ker (Oxford, 1976), 526.

them, as if it might not, or would not, in time to come, be turned against themselves; as if, while it directly affected the doctrine of baptismal grace, it had no bearing upon those of predestination, election, satisfaction, justification, and others, of which they [28] consider themselves so especially the champions. Poor victims! do you dream that the spirit of the age is working for you, or are you indeed secretly prepared to go further than you avow? At least some of you are honest enough to be praising the recent judgment on its own account, and blind enough not to see what it involves; and so you contentedly and trustfully throw yourselves into the arms of the age. But it is "today for me, tomorrow for thee!" Do you really think the age is stripping Laud[81] or Bull of his authority, in order to set

---

[81] *Laud*: William Laud (1573-1645), Archbishop of Canterbury. In imposing strict ritual uniformity and discountenancing evangelical piety. Laud sought to purge the national church of its Calvinist alloy. "Of all the prelates of the Anglican Church," Macaulay wrote in his famous history, "Laud had departed furthest from the principles of the Reformation, and drawn nearest to Rome." As Chancellor of Oxford, he worked diligently to reform the university, "extremely sunk [as he said] from all discipline, and fallen into all licentiousness." He instituted more efficient statutes, established chairs of Hebrew and Arabic, and made many gifts of manuscripts and books to the Bodleian. See K. Fincham, "Early Stuart Policy," *The History of the University of Oxford*, (Oxford, 1997), iv, 179-210. G.M. Trevelyan credited him with being "The founder of Anglo-Saxon supremacy in the new world," so many emigrants did his harrying of the Puritans create, not to mention his robust abuse of the Star Chamber. G.M. Trevelyan, *England under the Stuarts* (London, 1996), 154. Unsurprisingly, by acquiescing in the introduction of a version of the English Prayer Book into Scotland, Laud precipitated the king's and his own downfall. After being impeached by the Long Parliament, he was imprisoned, tried, and beheaded under an unconstitutional attainder on Tower Hill. At his trial, he insisted that "Unity cannot long continue in the Church, when Uniformity is shut out at the Church door." *CBH.* Certainly, he went to his grave protesting his Protestantism. *OCBH.* In Tractarian Oxford, the memory of Laud might have been inconvenient but it was inexpellable. "I say, old gentleman," an Oxford friend wrote to Newman in March of 1839, "I don't see your name among the

up Whittaker[82] or Baxter?[83] or with what expedient are you to elude a power, whose aid you have already invoked against your enemies?[84]

7.

For us, Catholics, my brethren, while we clearly recognise how things are going with our countrymen and while we would not accelerate the march of [29]

---

subscribers to the Ridley and Latimer memorial (I can't afford it)—You must be a bit of a papist—Pray is Laud to be included among the list of Martyrs? What would I not give to have seen the effect produced by an amendment to that effect at the public meeting—" *LD*, vii, 45. After converting, Newman paid tribute to Laud's influence: "I was confident in the truth of a certain definite religious teaching… viz., that there was a visible Church, with sacraments and rites which are the channels of invisible grace," he wrote of himself at the outset of the Movement of 1833. "I put this ecclesiastical doctrine on a broader basis, after reading Laud…" *Apo.*, 55.

[82] *Whitaker*: William Whitaker (1548-95), Regius Professor of Divinity at St. John's College, was a strict Calvinist and impassioned anti-Romanist who spent his last days drafting the Lambeth Articles.

[83] *Baxter*: Richard Baxter (1615-91), Puritan divine, whose rejection of episcopacy was typical of those who opposed Laud, though he also found Oliver Cromwell insufferable. He joined the Parliamentary Army during the Civil War and preached at Alcester on the day of the Battle of Edgehill (23 October 1642).

[84] The Oxford tutors are more sharp-sighted; understanding the mental state of the junior portion of the University, they see that a decision like that of the Privy Council is fitted to destroy at once what little hold the old Anglican system has on them, and to give entrance among them to a scepticism on all points of religion. In a strong and spirited protest, they quote against the Archbishop the very words he used on another occasion, eight or nine years since. Yet his evasive interpretation of the Baptismal service is not the fault of the Archbishop, but of the Reformers. No member of the Establishment can believe in a system of theology of any kind, without doing violence to the formularies. Those only go easily along Articles and Prayer-book, who do not think. It is remarkable, the Archbishop's book on apostolical Preaching first brought the present writer to a belief in baptismal regeneration in 1824. He has the copy still, with his objections marked on the side, given him for the purpose of convincing him by a dignitary whom he has ever loved amid the gravest differences, Dr. Hawkins. [N]

infidelity if we could help it, yet we are more desirous that you should leave a false church for the true, than that a false church should hold its ground. For if we are blessed in converting any of you, we are effecting a direct, unequivocal, and substantial benefit, which out-weighs all points of expedience—the salvation of your souls. I do not undervalue at all the advantage of institutions which, though not Catholic, keep out evils worse than themselves. Some restraint is better than none; systems which do not simply inculcate divine truth, yet serve to keep men from being utterly hardened against it, when at length it addresses them; they preserve a certain number of revealed doctrines in the popular mind; they familiarize it to Christian ideas; they create religious associations; and thus, remotely and negatively, they may even be said to prepare and dispose the soul in a certain sense for those inspirations of grace, which, through the merits of Christ, are freely given to all men for their salvation, all over the earth. It is a plain duty, then, not to be forward in destroying religious institutions, even though not Catholic, if we cannot replace them with what is better; but, from fear of injuring them, to shrink from saving the souls of the individuals who live under them, would be worldly wisdom, treachery to Christ, and uncharitableness to His redeemed.

As to the Catholic Church herself, no vicissitude of [30] circumstances can hurt her which allows her fair play. If, indeed, from the ultimate resolution of all heresies and errors into some one form of infidelity or scepticism, the nation was strong enough to turn upon her in persecution, then indeed she might be expelled from our land, as she has been expelled before now. Then persecution would do its work, as it did three centuries ago. But this is an extreme case, which is not to be anticipated. Till the nation becomes thus unanimous in unbelief, Catholics are secured by the collision and balance of religious parties, and are sheltered under that claim of toleration which each sect prefers for itself. But give us as much as this, an open field, and we ask no favour; every form of Protestantism turns to our advantage. Its establishments of religion remind the world of that archetypal Church of which it is a copyist; its Creeds contain portions of our teaching; its quarrels and divisions serve to break up its traditions, and rid its professors of their prejudices; its scepticism makes them turn in admiration and in hope to her, who alone is clear in her teaching and consistent in its transmission; its very abuse of her makes them inquire about her. She fears nothing from political parties; she shrinks from none of them; she can coalesce with any. She is not jealous of progress nor impatient with conservatism, if either be the national will. Nor is there anything for us to fear (except for the moment and for the sake of individuals) in that movement towards Pantheism,[85] in the Protestant world,[86] which excites the [31]

---

[85] *Pantheism*: According to the *OED*, Pantheism is "The religious belief or philosophical theory that God and the universe are identical (implying a denial of the personality and transcendence of God); the doctrine that God is everything and everything is God," which often issues in the sentimental worship of nature and, by extension, the self. The word was coined by the Deist John Toland in 1705, though the thing itself goes back to ancient times. The *OED* cites Daniel Waterland (1732) for its first illustration of the word: "Pantheism ... and Hobbism are scandalously bad, scarce differing from the broadest Atheism." In *Tract 85* (1838), Newman spoke of the "symptoms" of "a spread of a Pantheistic spirit, that is, the religion of beauty, imagination, and philosophy, without constraint moral or intellectual, a religion speculative and self-indulgent. Pantheism, indeed, is the great deceit which awaits the Age to come." *DA*, 233.

special anxiety of many; for, in truth, there is something so repugnant to the feelings of man, in systems which deprive God of His perfections, and reduce Him to a name, which remove the Creator to an indefinite distance from His creatures, under the pretence of bringing them near to Him, and refuse Him the liberty of sending mediators and ordaining instruments to connect them with Him, which deny the existence of sin, the need of pardon, and the fact of punishment, which maintain that man is happy here and sufficient for himself, when he feels so keenly his own ignorance and desolateness,—and on the other hand, the sects and parties round about us are so utterly helpless to remedy his evils, and to supply his need,— that the preachers of these new ideas from Germany[87]

---

[86] I am aware that the name of Pantheism is repudiated by several writers of the school I allude to, but I think it will be found to be the ultimate resolution of its principles. [N]

[87] *new ideas from Germany*: These derived, principally, from the theologian and New Testament critic, F.C. Baur (1792-1860), who applied methods of historical research to the study of early Christianity. For J. Zachhuber, Prof. of Historical Theology at Trinity College, Oxford: "The historicist-idealist concept of theology as *Wissenschaft* ['science'] was first conceived and executed in the 1820s by the Tübingen theologian ... Baur. His own work and the writing of his numerous students, who together comprise the Tübingen School, dominated historical theology until the 1850s even though the fundamental tension of their conception had been exposed when in 1835 Friedrich David Strauss, one of Baur's students, published *The Life of Jesus* ... ". J. Zachhuber, *Theology as Science in Nineteenth-Century Germany: from F.C. Bauer to Ernst Troeltsch* (Oxford, 2013), 19. Strauss (1808-74), who was critically influenced by the anti-dogmatic theologian F. D. E. Schleiermacher (1768-1834), was sacked from his post at Tübingen when it was found that *Leben Jesu* denied the divinity of Christ. More specifically, the book "denied the historical foundation of all supernatural elements in the Gospels, which were assigned to an unintentionally creative legend (the 'myth'), developed between the death of Christ and the writing of the Gospels in the 2nd century. The growth of primitive Christianity was to be understood in terms of the Hegelian dialectic. The work, which exercised a deep influence on subsequent

and America[88] are really, however much against their will, like Caiphas,[89] prophesying for us. Surely they will find no resting-place anywhere for their feet, and the feet of their disciples, but will be tumbled down from one depth of blasphemy to another, till they arrive at sheer and naked atheism, the *reductio ad absurdum* of their initial principles. Logic is a stern master; they feel it, they protest against it; they profess to hate it, and would fain dispense with it; but it is the law of their intellectual nature. Struggling and [32] shrieking, but in vain, will they make the inevitable descent into that pit from which there is no return, except through the almost miraculous grace of God, the grant of which in this life is never hopeless. And Israel, without a fight, will see their enemies dead upon the seashore.[90]

I will but observe in conclusion, that, in thus explaining the feeling under which I address myself to members of the Anglican communion in these

---

German Protestant theology, roused a storm of indignation … " *ODCC*. In English rationalist circles, however, Strauss's historicist ideas on Christianity, after *Leben Jesu* was translated by the novelist George Eliot, were received with open arms, though Eliot herself confessed that "dissecting the beautiful story of the crucifixion" made her "Strauss-sick." P. Davis, *The Victorians* (Oxford, 2002), 111. Much of Newman's work can be seen as a response to the rationalist undermining of Christianity inherent in the "new ideas from Germany" epitomized by the Tübingen school.

[88] *America*: See Newman's essay, "The Anglo-American Church," (1841) in the first volume of his *Essays Critical and Historical* (1871) for his discussion of the Pelagian view of sin that he encountered in his insightful reading of and about America's Episcopalians.

[89] *Caiaphas, prophesying*: John 11:50-1, Caiaphas, the Jewish High Priest before whom Christ was tried and condemned prophesied that "one man should die for the people, and that the whole nation should not perish … Jesus should be put to death for the nation."

[90] *Israel*: "And Israel saw the Egyptians dead upon the seashore." Exodus 14:30.

Lectures, I have advanced one step towards fulfilling the object with which I have undertaken them. For it is a very common difficulty which troubles men, when they contemplate submission to the Catholic Church, that perhaps they shall thus be weakening the communion they leave, which, with whatever defects, they see in matter of fact to be a defence of Christianity against its enemies. No, my brethren, you will not be harming it; if the National Church falls, it falls because it *is* national; because it left the centre of unity in the sixteenth century, not because you leave it in the nineteenth. Cranmer,[91] Parker,[92] Jewell, will complete their own work; they who made it, will be its destruction.

---

[91] *Cranmer*: Thomas Cranmer (1489-1556), Archbishop of Canterbury. After the death of Henry VIII, Cranmer, who is often referred to as the 'Father of English Protestantism,' compiled Edward VI's First Prayer Book (1549) and drew up what became the defining 39 Articles of the new national religion. He also had a presiding hand over the drafting of the Second Prayer Book (1552), about which the historian P. Williams writes: "The prayer for the Church in 1549 had rendered praise and thanksgiving for the virtues of the Virgin Mary, the patriarchs, prophets, apostles, and martyrs: these words were omitted from the 1552 book." P. Williams, *The Later Tudors: England 1547-1603* (Oxford, 1995), 73. In addition, "any hint of transubstantiation" was removed, an excising which would cause E. B. Pusey a good deal of grief in 1843 when he was suspended from preaching for two years by Oxford's Vice Chancellor and six Doctors of Divinity after publishing a university sermon entitled *The Holy Eucharist, a Comfort to the Penitent*.

[92] *Parker*: Matthew Parker (1504-75), Archbishop of Canterbury. He revised the 39 articles drafted by Cranmer, which were passed in Convocation in 1562.

LECTURE II

THE MOVEMENT OF 1833 FOREIGN TO THE NATIONAL CHURCH

1.

MY object in these Lectures, my brethren, is not to construct any argument in favour of Catholicism, for there is no need. Arguments exist in abundance, and of the highest cogency, and of the most wonderful variety, provided severally by the merciful wisdom of its Divine Author,[1] for distinct casts of mind and character;—so much so, that it is often a mistake in controversy to cumulate reasons for what is on many considerations so plain already, and the evidence of which is only weakened to the individual inquirer, when he is distracted by fresh proofs,[2] consistent indeed with those

---

[1] *Any argument in favour of Catholicism*: The demurral with which Newman thus begins his second lecture echoes the demurral with which he begins the Introduction of his *Lectures on the Prophetical Office of the Church* (1837). "Unhappy is it that we should be obliged to discuss and defend what a Christian people were intended to enjoy, to appeal to their intellects instead of 'stirring up their pure minds by way of remembrance,' to direct them towards articles of faith which should be their place of starting, and to treat as mere conclusions what in other ages have been assumed as first principles. Surely life is not long enough to prove everything which may be made the subject of proof; and, though inquiry is left partly open in order to try our earnestness, yet it is in great measure, and in the most important points, superseded by Revelation..." *Lectures on the Prophetical Office of the Church* (London, 1837), 1.

[2] *fresh proofs*: Newman would always look askance at any enterprise that sought to bring about conversion by an appeal to the intellect alone and even admitted that his own conversion had been unduly delayed by his inordinate need for intellectual certainty. "Having myself been called to the Church late in life," he told a correspondent in 1849, "when my best days were gone, I feel for those who persevere in losing what cannot be recalled. You say that, 'though you feel this' (the ground on which you rest your position,) 'in a dry argumentative way, you constantly feel your

which have brought conviction to him, but to him less convincing than his own, and at least strange and unfamiliar. Every inquirer may have enough of positive proof to convince him that the Catholic Religion is divine: it is owing to the force of counter-objections that his conviction remains in fact either defective or inoperative. I consider, then, that I shall be ministering in my measure to [34] the cause of truth, if I do ever so little towards removing the difficulties, or any of them, which beset the mind, when it is urged to accept Catholicism as true. It is with this view that I have insisted on the real character of the Established Church, and its relation to the nation; for, if it be mainly as I have represented it, a department of government under the temporal sovereign, one at least is struck off from the catalogue of your objections. You fear to leave it lest you should, by your secession throw it into the hands of a latitudinarian party; but it never has been in your hands, nor ever under your influence. It is in the hands of the nation; it is mainly what the nation is: such is it, while you are in it; such would it be, if you left it. I do not deny you may by your presence somewhat retard its downward career, but you are not of the real importance to it, which you fancy.

Now, in the course of the argument I made a remark, which I shall today pursue. I spoke of the movement which began in the Establishment in 1833, or shortly before; and I dwelt on the remarkable fact, that in nearly twenty years that movement, though certainly it exerted great influence over the views of individuals, nevertheless has created a mere party in the National Church, having had the least possible influence over the National Church itself; and no wonder, if that Church be simply an organ or department of [35] the State, for in that case, all ecclesiastical acts really

---

position to be most painful.' Others have had and have the same feeling. is not this a reductio ad absurdum of that ground? is it not the witness of heart and conscience, of the whole man, that that argument will not work, and therefore cannot be true, difficult as it may be to find what is the intellectual flaw in what seems so specious? It will serve as an excuse for the insincere, not as a stay for the earnest." *LD*, xiii, 295.

proceeding from the supreme civil government, to influence the Establishment, is nothing else than to influence the State, or even the Constitution.

Now I shall pursue the argument. I shall, by means of one or two suggestions, try to bring home to you the extreme want of congeniality which has existed between the movement of 1833 and the nation at large; and then assuming that you, my brethren, owe your principles to that movement, and that your first duty is to your principles, I shall infer your own want of congeniality with the national religion, however you may wish it otherwise; I shall infer that you have no concern with that national religion, have no place in it, have no reason for belonging to it, and have no responsibilities towards it.

I am then to point out to you, that, what is sometimes called, or rather what calls itself, the Anglo-Catholic teaching, is not only a novelty in this age (for to prove a thing new to the age, is not enough in order to prove it uncongenial), but that, while it is a system adventitious and superadded to the national religion, it is, moreover, not supplemental, or complemental, or collateral, or correlative to it,—not implicitly involved in it, not developed from it,— nor combining with it,—nor capable of absorption into it; but, on the contrary, most uncongenial and heterogeneous, floating upon it, a foreign substance, like oil upon the water. And my proof shall consist, first, of what was augured of it [36] when it commenced; secondly, what has been fulfilled concerning it during its course.

2.

As to the auguries with which it started, we need not go beyond the first agents of the movement, in order to have a tolerably sufficient proof that it had no lot, nor portion, nor parentage in the Established Church; for when those who first recommended to her its principles and doctrines are found themselves to have doubted how far these were congenial with her, when the very physicians were anxious as to what would come of their own medicines, who shall feel confidence in them? Such, however, was the case: its originators confessed that they were forcing upon the Establishment doctrines from which it revolted, doctrines with which it never had given signs of coalescing, doctrines which tended they knew not whither. This is what they felt, this is what with no uncertain sound they publicly proclaimed.

For instance, one, who, if any, is the author of the movement altogether, and whose writings were published after his death, says in one of his letters, "It seems agreed among the wise, that we must begin by laying a foundation." Again he writes to a friend, "I am getting more and more to feel, what you tell me, about the impracticability of making sensible people," that is, the [37] High Church party of the day, "enter into our ecclesiastical views; and, what is most discouraging, I hardly see how to set about leading them to us." Elsewhere he asks, "How is it we are so much in advance of our generation?" And again, "The age is out of joint." And again, "I shall write nothing on the subject of Church grievances, till I have a tide to work with." Further he calls the Establishment "an incubus upon the country," and, "a upas tree:" and, lastly, within three or four months of his death, his theological views still expanding and diverging from the existing state of things, he exclaims, "How mistaken we may ourselves be on many points, that are only gradually opening on us!"[3]

---

[3] Froude's Remains, vol. i. [N] *Remains of the Late Reverend Richard Hurrell Froude, M.A., Fellow of Oriel* eds. Keble and Newman 2 vols. (London, 1838), i, 321, 396, 329, 401, 396, 405, 422. Richard Hurrell Froude (1803-36), one of Newman's closest friends, was a key founding member of the Oxford Movement. As brilliant as he was unbiddable, he poured scorn on the English reformers and was pivotal in opening Newman's eyes to the hollowness of the Anglican Establishment. It is a mark of Newman's loyalty to his discriminating friend that he should have drawn on his papers to make the points that he makes here in Lecture II, though it is also a mark of how well-placed that loyalty was. "That bright and beautiful Froude," was the way Newman's sister Harriet referred to him. M. Ward, *Young Mr. Newman* (New York, 1948), 147. See also Pier Brendon's *Hurrell Froude and the Oxford Movement* (London, 1974). Apropos the *Remains*, Brendon observes in the *ODNB*:

Avowals of a like character are made with the utmost frankness in the very work which in 1837 professed formally to lay down and defend the new doctrines. The writer (that is, myself) begins by allowing that he is "discussing rather than teaching, what was *meant* to be simply an article of faith," viz., belief in "the Catholic Church," alleging in excuse that "the teaching of the Apostles concerning it is, in a good measure, withdrawn," and that, "we are, so far, left to make the best of our way to the promised land by our natural resources."[4] The preaching of the doctrines of the movement is compared, in its strangeness, to the original preaching of Christianity, and this only alleviation is suggested, if it be any, that they who are startled at those doctrines, could not be *more* startled than "the outcasts to whom the Apostles preached in the beginning."[5] Nay, it is categorically stated, that "these doctrines are in one sense as entirely new as Christianity when first preached."[6] He continues, "Protestantism and Popery" (by Popery he means the popular Catholic system) "are real religions; no one can doubt about them; they have furnished the mould in which nations have been cast; but the Via Media, viewed as an integral system, has scarcely had existence except on paper."[7] Presently he continues, "It still remains to be tried, whether what is called Anglo-Catholicism, the religion of Andrewes,[8] Laud, Hammond,[9]

[38]

"Denounced by low-churchmen as papistical, it alarmed the bishops and embarrassed the 'high-and-dry' clergy who had been hitherto the lukewarm allies of the Tractarians. The *Remains* by no means proved that Froude would have converted to Rome, although some of its admirers—including W. G. Ward and Frederick Oakeley—did; indeed, some of its readers—such as J. B. Mozley and R. W. Church—were to be important liberal Anglo-Catholics." Calling Mozley and Church 'liberals' is stretching matters, but the rest of what Brendon says is true enough.

[4] Prophetical Office of the Church. Vid. Via Media, vol. i., ed. 1877. [N] *VM*, i. 5.

[5] Ibid, 15

[6] Ibid, 16

[7] Ibid, 17

[8] *Andrewes*: Lancelot Andrewes (1555-1626), Bishop of Winchester, patristic scholar, preacher and devotional writer. T. S. Eliot thought "his

Butler, and Wilson,[10] is capable of being professed, acted on, and maintained in a large sphere of action, and through a sufficient period; or whether it be a mere modification or transition state, either of Romanism or of popular Protestantism, according as we view it."[11] "It may be argued," he adds, and, as he does not deny, argued with plausibility, "that the Church of England, as established by law, and existing in fact, has never represented a certain doctrine, or been the development of a principle; that it has been but a name, or a department of the State, or a political party in which religious opinion was an accident, and therefore has been various."[12] And this prospectus, as it may [39] be called, of a new system ends by stating that, "it is proposed to offer helps towards the formation of a recognised Anglican theology in one of its departments."[13] … "We require a recognised theology," he insists, "and, if the present work, instead of being what it is meant to be, a first approximation to the required solution, in one

---

prose ... not inferior to that of any sermons in the language, unless it be some of Newman's." T. S. Eliot, "Lancelot Andrewes," *Selected Essays*, (London, 1951), 353. In translating Andrewes' devotions from the Greek, Newman captured something of his own devotions' austere beauty. L. Bouyer went so far as to say that Andrewes' habit of weaving "sentences from the Bible, the Fathers, and the ancient liturgies should be considered the fundamental inspiration of all Newman's devotional writings," which overstates matters, even though Newman did find Andrewes' work deeply sympathetic. See J. H. Newman, *Prayers, Verses and Devotions* (San Francisco, 1989), xvii.

[9] *Hammond*: Henry Hammond (1605-60), Fellow of Magdalen. Chaplain to King Charles, Hammond was a prolific writer best known for his *Practical Catechism* (1644).

[10] *Wilson*: Thomas Wilson (1665-1755), Bishop of Sodor and Man. Newman edited his *Sacra Privata* (1838). A critic of the Erastian character of the English church, Wilson managed to perform his own church duties on the Isle of Man with vigor and aplomb, personifying something Samuel Johnson once told a young parson: "A clergyman's diligence always makes him venerable." *The Letters of Samuel Johnson* ed. Redford (Princeton, 1992), iii, 313.

[11] *VM*, i, 17.

[12] Ibid, 18.

[13] Ibid, 24.

department of a complicated problem, contains, after all, but a series of illustrations demonstrating our need, and supplying hints for its removal; such a result, it is evident, will be quite a sufficient return for whatever anxiety it has cost the writer to have employed his own judgment on so serious a subject."[14]

I must add, in justice to this writer, and it is not much to say for him, that he did not entertain the presumptuous thought of creating, at this time of day, a new theology himself; he considered that a theology true in itself, and necessary for the position of the Anglican Church, was to be found in the writings of Andrewes, Laud, Bramhall, Stillingfleet,[15] Butler, and other of its divines, but had never been put together,—as he expressly declares. Nor, in spite of his misgivings, was he without a persuasion that the theological system contained in those writers, and derived, as he believed, from the primitive Fathers, not only ought to be, but might be, and, as he hoped, would be, acknowledged and acted upon by the Establishment. On the other hand, I allow, of course, and am not loth to allow, that, had he seen clearly that Antiquity and the Establishment were [40] incompatible with each other, he would promptly have given up the Establishment, rather than have rejected Antiquity. Moreover, let it be observed, in evidence of his misgivings on the point, that, when he gets to the end of his volume, instead of their being removed, they return in a more definite form, and he confesses that "the thought, with which we entered upon the subject, is apt to recur, when the excitement of the inquiry has subsided, and weariness has succeeded, that what has been said is but a dream, the

---

[14] Ibid, 25.

[15] *Stillingfleet*: Edward Stillingfleet (1635-99) Bishop of Worcester. Controversialist, preacher and antiquary, Stillingfleet was a favorite of Charles II, who made him not only Archdeacon of London but Dean of St Paul's. Under James II, his favoured status abated but he was still made Bishop of Worcester. His major work was *Origines Britannicae* (1685), a study of the origins of British church history. His *Irenicum* (1659) advocated a union between Episcopalians and Presbyterians. His sermons were his most popular work. (*ODCC*)

wanton exercise, rather than the practical conclusions, of the intellect."[16]

3.

These auguries speedily met with a response, though in a less tranquil tone, in every part of the Establishment, and by each of the schools of opinion within it,—the High Church[17] section, the Evangelical,[18] and the Latitudinarian.[19] They

---

[16] *VM*, i, 331.

[17] *High Church:* The *OED* defines a 'High Churchman' as "a member of the Church of England holding opinions which give a high place to the authority and claims of the Episcopate and the priesthood, the saving grace of the sacraments, and, generally, to those points of doctrine, discipline, and ritual, by which the Anglican Church is distinguished from the Calvinistic churches of the Continent, and the Protestant Nonconformist churches of England."

[18] *Evangelical:* "From 18th c. applied to that school of Protestants which maintains that the essence of 'the Gospel' consists in the doctrine of salvation by faith in the atoning death of Christ, and denies that either good works or the sacraments have any saving efficacy. Other features of the theology of this school are: a strong insistence on the totally depraved state of human nature consequent on the Fall; the assertion of the sole authority of the Bible in matters of doctrine, and the denial of any power inherent in the Church to supplement or authoritatively interpret the teaching of Scripture; the denial that any supernatural gifts are imparted by ordination; and the view that sacraments are merely symbols, the value of which consists in the thoughts which they are fitted to suggest. As a distinct party designation, the term came into use in England at the time of the Methodist revival; and it may be said, with substantial accuracy, to denote the school of theology which that movement represents, though its earlier associations were rather with Calvinistic than the Arminian branch of the movement. In the early part of the 19th c. the words 'Methodist' and 'Evangelical' were, by adversaries, often used indiscriminately, and associated with accusations of fanaticism and 'puritanical' disapproval of social pleasures. The portion of the 'evangelical' school which belongs to the Anglican church is practically identical with the 'Low Church' party. In the Church of Scotland during the latter part of the 19th c. the two leading parties were the 'Evangelical' and the 'Moderate' party." *OED*

[19] *Latitudinarian:* "One who practises or favours latitude in thought, action or conduct, esp. in religious matters; spec. one of those divines of the English Church in the 17th century who, while attached to episcopal government and forms of worship, regarded them as things indifferent; hence, one who, though not a sceptic, is indifferent as to particular creeds and forms of church government or worship." Joseph Butler quipped that

condemned, not only the attempt, but the authors of it. The late Dr. Arnold, a man who always spoke his mind, avowed that his feelings towards a Roman Catholic were quite different from his feelings to the author of the above work. "I think the one," he continued, "a fair enemy, the other a treacherous one. The one is the Frenchman in his own uniform, the other is the Frenchman disguised in a red coat. I should honour the first and hang the second."[20] For the Evangelical party, it is scarcely necessary to make the following extracts from the work of even a cautious and [41] careful writer:—"If," says the writer of "Essays on the Church," "the grievances and warfare of Dissenters against it have greatly diminished in interest, a new and gigantic evil has arisen up in their room ... Popery, not indeed of the days of Hildebrand or Leo the Tenth, but Popery as it first established itself in the seventh and eighth centuries, is already among us ... Popery has anew arisen up among us, in youthful vigour and in her youthful attractions. Such is the chief, the greatly preponderating peril, which besets the Church of England at the present day. It has in it all the essential features of Popery; but, apart from this, and were it never to proceed beyond the perils to which it has now reached, it is fraught with the fearful evil of a withering, parching, blighting operation, drying-up and banishing all spiritual life and influence from the Church."[21]

Lastly, a theological professor of the High Church section, in an attack which he delivered from the pulpit, viewed the movement from another point of view, yet in perfect accordance of judgment with the two writers who have been already cited: "Instead of quietly acquiescing," he says, "in what they cannot change, submitting in silence

---

"A Latitudinarian ... believes that the Way to Heaven is never the better for being strait." *OED*

[20] *"... honour the first and hang the second."*: Thomas Arnold quoted in A.P. Stanley, *Life and Correspondence of Thomas Arnold* (London, 1844), ii, 285.

[21] Essays on the Church, by a Layman, 1838, pp. 270, 299, 300. Ditto, 1840, p. 401. [N]

to their imagined privations, and patiently enduring this 'meagreness of Protestantism,' by a species of
[42] 'ecclesiastical agitation,' unexampled in obtrusiveness and perseverance, they are unsettling the faith of the weak, blinding the judgment of the sober-minded, raising the hopes of the most inveterate advocates of our Reformed and Protestant Church, and, as far as a small knot of malcontents can well be supposed capable, they are compromising her character and disturbing her peace."[22]

---

[22] Faussett's Sermon, 1838, Preface to Third Edition. [N] G. Faussett, *The Revival of Popery: a sermon preached before the University of Oxford St. Mary's on Sunday, May 20, 1838* 3rd. ed. (Oxford, 1838), xvi. Godfrey Faussett (1780 or 1-1853), entered Corpus Christi College in 1797, B.A. 1801, and gained a Fellowship at Magdalen in 1802. He was appointed Lady Margaret Professor of Divinity in 1827, and a Canon of Christ Church in 1840. He preached the sermon, as G. Tracey points out, in response to Newman's and Keble's edition of Froude's *Remains*. "The response to the *Remains* fulfilled the worst of Newman's fears. People did not bother to look further than the first volume, which contained the Journal and the letters, with their revelation of the schemes of the Oxford men, and Froude's vitriolic denunciation of the Reformers. Evangelicals and Low Churchmen declared war, moderate Anglicans were disgusted, and the loyalty of the more cautious and conservative of the adherents of the Movement was strained. The only positive response came from a few of the younger, more extreme Tractarians, such as Frederick Oakeley and W. G. Ward, whose allegiance was to a large extent decided by the work. The *Edinburgh Review* and other journals were caustic in their criticism. Lord Morpeth raised the matter in the House of Commons, and Gladstone came to the defence of Newman and Keble. Godfrey Faussett, Lady Margaret Professor of Divinity, protested against what he termed the 'Revival of Popery' in the pulpit of St Mary's. It was widely rumoured that the *Remains* were the cause of the testimonial for a memorial to Cranmer, Latimer, and Ridley, which was started later in the year." *LD*, vi, xviii. However disappointing the initial response might have been to the *Remains*, the fortunes of the Tractarians in 1838 were at their 'zenith.' *LD*, vi, 248. Moreover, Newman, after publishing his response to Faussett, "had the 'satisfaction' of finding that his own pamphlet sold 750 copies against 500 copies of Faussett's sermon." I. Ker, *John Henry Newman: A Biography* (Oxford, 1988), 163. By June, 1843, however, the Tractarians' star had begun to fade; that very month Pusey was suspended from preaching for two years after delivering a sermon on the Eucharist; and Newman could not have been entirely surprised when he

Yet even at this date, in spite of the success which for five years had attended him, the author whom I have already quoted felt no greater confidence than before in his own congeniality with the National Church; and, on occasion of the last-mentioned attack upon him, scrupled not to avow the fact. "Sure I am," said he, "that the more stir is made about those opinions which you censure, the wider they will spread. Whatever be the faults or mistakes of their advocates, they have that root of truth in them, which, as I do firmly believe, has a blessing with it. *I do not pretend to say they will ever become widely popular*, that is another matter: truth is never, or at least never long, popular; nor do I say they will ever gain that powerful external influence over the many which truth, vested in the few, cherished, throned, energising in the few, often has possessed; nor that they are not destined, as truth has often been destined, to be cast away, and at length *trodden under foot as an odious thing*: but of this I am sure, that, at this juncture, in proportion as they are known, they will make [43] their way through the community, *picking out their own*, seeking and obtaining refuge in the hearts of Christians, high and low, here and there, with this man and that, as the case may be; doing their work in their day, and raising a memorial and a witness to this *fallen generation* of what once has been, of what God would ever have, of what one day shall be in perfection; and that, not from what they are in themselves, because, viewed in the concrete, they are mingled, as everything human must be, with error and infirmity, but by reason of the spirit, the truth, the old Catholic life and power which is in them."[23]

---

learned that the prelate responsible for denouncing the Canon of Christ Church to the Vice-Chancellor as 'heretical' was Faussett. *Ker*, 276.

[23] The author's "Letter to Dr. Faussett." Vid. Via Media. vol. ii. [N] *VM*, ii, 197-98. With the exception of this letter, Newman made a point of eschewing controversy with Faussett. As he told one of his friends in December of 1840: "I think it allowable to speak, as I often do, of the great Chess player, who uses us most wonderfully as his pawns. What could be a bolder stroke in order to give us free scope in Oxford,—than, whereas there were two divinity professors, Hampden and Faussett, to

4.

What was it, then, which the originators of the movement of 1833 demanded or desiderated in its behalf, in the communion for whose benefit it was intended? How came they to dread lest the principles of St. Athanasius[24] and of St. Ambrose[25] should fail to take root in the minds of

---

knock down the former, and to leave the other, like a fat old watchman, to waddle after us as best he could." *LD*, vii, 465-6. According to T. Mozley, Faussett was ill-read and lazy, though "a clever writer and a telling preacher." T. Mozley, *Reminiscences Chiefly of Oriel College and the Oxford Movement* 2 vols. (London, 1882), i, 441-2.

[24] *St. Athanasius*: Here, it might be well to quote something Newman said in his *Essay on Development* about St. Athanasius and St. Ambrose: "Did St. Athanasius, or St. Ambrose, come suddenly to life, it cannot be doubted what communion he would take to be his own. All surely will agree that these Fathers, with whatever opinions of their own, whatever protests, if we will, would find themselves more at home with such men as St. Bernard, or St. Ignatius Loyola, or with the lonely priest in his lodgings, or the holy sisterhood of mercy, or the unlettered crowd before the altar, than with the teachers or with the members of any other creed. And may we not add, that were those same Saints, who once sojourned, one in exile, one on embassy, at Treves, to come more northward still, and to travel until they reached another fair city, seated among groves, green meadows, and calm streams, the holy brothers would turn from many a high aisle and solemn cloister which they found there, and ask the way to some small chapel, where mass was said, in the populous alley or the forlorn suburb? And, on the other hand, can any one who has but heard his name, and cursorily read his history, doubt for one instant, how, in turn, the people of England, in turn, 'we, our princes, our priests, and our prophets,' Lords and Commons, Universities, Ecclesiastical Courts, marts of commerce, great towns, country parishes, would deal with Athanasius,—Athanasius, who spent his long years in fighting against kings for a theological term?" *Dev*, 97-8

[25] *St. Ambrose*: One of the four Latin Doctors of the Church, together with St. Augustine, St. Gregory the Great and St. Jerome, St. Ambrose (334 – 397) was born at Augusta Treverorum (what is now Trier in the Moselle wine region, near the Luxembourg border), the son of a praetorian prefect and thus a member of the senatorial aristocracy. While practicing law in the Roman courts, he was appointed governor of the province of Amelia and Liguria, whose capital was Milan. In 374 Ambrose was appointed Bishop of Milan by acclamation, though only a catechumen, an office he would hold till death. Since Milan was the capital of the western empire, Ambrose was charged not only with diplomatic duties but instructing new and disabusing older converts led

their brethren, and to spread through the laity? In truth, when they feared that the good seed would fall, not on a congenial soil, but on hard, or stony, or occupied ground, they were fearing that the National Church, though they did not use the word, had no *life*. Life consists or manifests itself in activity of principle. There are various kinds of life, and each kind is the influence or operation in a body of [44] those principles upon which the body is constituted. Each kind of life is to be referred, and is congenial, to its own principle. Principles, distinct from each other, will not take root and flourish in bodies to which respectively they are foreign. One principle has not the life of another. The life of a plant is not the same as the life of an animated being, and the life of the body is not the same as the life of the intellect; nor is the life of the intellect the same in kind as the life of grace; nor is the life of the Church the same as the life of the State. When, then, these writers doubted whether

---

astray by Arianism. Deeply learned in Scripture, Ambrose was instrumental in the conversion of Augustine. In addition, he "seems to have realized that the Roman world was plunging into darkness; within a few years of his death all the western provinces were overrun by the barbarians. More than any other man he handed on to the middle ages the legacy of Rome; the conception of objective justice and law, the sense of responsibility of office, pride in integrity... He christened Seneca and Cicero in his *De Officiis* and made their teaching part of the mediaeval heritage." *The Saints* ed. J. Coulson (New York, 1958). Ambrose also wrote on the Eucharist, Baptism and Confirmation. He was the first catechist to make hymns engines of catechesis. His own hymns include *Aeterne Rerum Conditor* and *Veni Redemptor Omnium*. When visiting Milan for the first time, the new convert in Newman spoke movingly of his affection for the great saint, writing to his sister Jemima in October of 1846: "I will not leave Milan ... without sending you a line. ... it is so great a thing to be in the city of St Ambrose. I never was in a city which has so enchanted me. To stand before the tombs of such great saints as St Ambrose and St Carlo — and to see the places where St Ambrose repelled the Arians, where St Monica kept watch through the night with the 'pia plebs' as St Augustine calls them, and where St Augustine himself was baptized. Our oldest Churches in England are nothing in antiquity to those here, and then the ashes of the Saints have been scattered to the four winds. It is so great a thing to be where the 'primordia,' the cradle, as it were, of Christianity is still existing." *LD*, xi, 264.

Apostolical principles,[26] as they called them, would spread through the laity of England, they were doubting whether that laity lived, breathed, energised, in Apostolical principles; whether Apostolical principles were the just expression and the constituent element of the national sentiment; whether the intellectual and moral life of the nation was not distinct from the life of the Apostolical age; and, if the Establishment professed to be built upon the principles and to partake of the life of the Apostolical age, as they knew ought to be the case, then they were doubting whether it really had those principles and that life, in spite of its professions.

There was no doubt at all, there is no doubt at all, that the Establishment has *some* kind of life. No one ever doubted it; and one of its dignitaries triumphantly proves it [45] in a passage which I will quote:— "Surely, my dear friend," says this accomplished writer,[27] with a reference to the

---

[26] *Apostolic principles*: In speaking of the force of these "Apostolic principles" to his brother Francis in November, 1840, Newman previewed what would become his discussion of the notes of the Church in his *Essay on the Development of Christian Doctrine* (1845). "From the first," he wrote, "running up into the obscurity of the Apostolic century, there has been a large body called the Church, claiming the exclusive dispensation of the gospel; and there has been but one such,—large, continuous and commanding. ... This body, in centuries iv and v, is known to have been of a certain temper, cast of principle, system of doctrine, and character of conduct; in a word of a certain *religion* ... This temper, cast of principle, doctrine, conduct, are singularly consistent with each other, or *one*; so that the existence of e.g. the temper, makes the co-existence of the doctrine at least not improbable. ... The *temper and principles* of the Church have been precisely the same from first to last, from the Apostolic age to this; viz what her enemies call dogmatic, mystical, credulous, superstitious, bigotted, legal. I consider no persons doubt this great fact." *LD*, vii, 440. For a good critical discussion of Newman's understanding of the notes of the Church, see I. Ker, *Newman on Vatican II* (Oxford, 2014), 41-43, 52-5, 62-70.
[27] Archdeacon Hare, in *Record* Newspaper. [N] Newman is referring here to J. C. Hare, *A Letter to the Hon. Richard Cavendish on the Recent Judgment of the Court of Appeal as Affecting the Doctrine of the Church* (London, 1850), 12-13. Julius Charles Hare (1795-1855), English churchman and controversialist. Born near Vincenza and educated at Charterhouse and Trinity College, Cambridge, Hare wrote a number of

present controversy, "it requires an inordinate faith in one's own logical dreams, an idolising worship of one's own opinions, to believe that the Church of England, blest as she has been by God for so many generations, raised as she has been by Him to be the mother of so many Churches, with such a promise shining upon her, and brightening every year, that her daughters should spread round the earth, that she, who has been chosen by God to be the instrument of so many blessings, and the presence of the Lord and His Spirit with whom was never more manifest than at this day, should forfeit her office and authority, as a witness of the truth, should be cut off from the body of Christ's Church, and should no longer be able to dispense the grace of the sacraments, because her highest law court has not condemned a proposition asserted by one of her ministers, concerning a very obscure and perplexing question of dogmatical theology. Surely this would be an extraordinary delusion; ... for, whatever the dogmatical value of the opinion" in question "may be, the error is not one which indicates any want of personal faith and holiness, or any decay of Christian life in the Church."

No, I grant it would be very difficult to the imagination to receive it as a dogma, that there was no "life" in the [46] National Church, or indeed no "faith." The simple question is, What is meant by "life" and faith"? Will the Archdeacon

---

rather eccentric books, which show his broad church affinities, including *Guesses at Truth* (1827) and *The Unity of the Church* (1845) in the latter of which Gladstone found "many horrors but many parts of truth also." Before converting as the result of the Gorham Case, H. E. Manning befriended Hare, about whom he wrote to Gladstone in 1844: "As to Hare ... I have a sincere feeling of affection for him: & he has for me much more than I deserve. He has in some ways the mind of a Poet: and a gift of beautiful English, in which when not deformed by conceits, I delight. He has also some great truths and axioms of truth (as in the thing you are reading) with which I go all lengths. But there are two things in which his defects are almost unequalled in any man I know, I mean in logical connection of reasoning, and in practical judgment. My close intimacy personal & official has given me abundant opportunities of knowing this." *The Correspondence of Henry Edward Manning and William Ewart Gladstone* ed. Erb (Oxford, 2013), ii, 62, 64.

tell us whether he does not mean by faith a something very vague and comprehensive? Does he mean, as he might say, the faith of Marcus Antoninus,[28] St. Austin, and Peter the Hermit,[29] of Luther,[30] Rousseau,[31] Washington,[32] and Napoleon Bonaparte?[33] Faith has one meaning to a Catholic, another to a Protestant. And life,—is it the religious "life" of England, or of Prussia, that he means, or is it Catholic life, that is, the life which belongs to Catholic principles? Else he will be arguing in a circle, if he is to prove that Protestants have that life, which manifests "the presence of the Spirit," on the ground of their having, as they are sure to have, a life congenial and in conformity to Protestant principles. If then "life" means strength, activity, energy, and well-being of any kind whatever, in that case doubtless the national religion is alive. It is a great power in the midst of us; it wields an enormous influence; it represses a hundred foes; it conducts a hundred undertakings. It attracts men to it, uses them, rewards them; it has thousands of beautiful homes up and down the country, where quiet men may do its work and benefit its people; it collects vast sums in the shape of voluntary offerings, and with them it builds churches, prints and distributes innumerable Bibles, books, and tracts and sustains missionaries in all parts of the earth.

[47] In all parts of the earth it opposes the Catholic Church, denounces her as antichristian, bribes the world against her, obstructs her influence, apes her authority, and confuses her evidence. In all parts of the world it is the religion of

---

[28] *Marcus Antoninus*: Marcus Aurelius Antoninus (121-80), Roman emperor.

[29] *Peter the Hermit*: Peter of Amiens (c. 1050-1115), French monk and preacher of the First Crusade.

[30] *Luther*: Martin Luther (1483-1546), German founder of the Reformation.

[31] *Rousseau*: Jean Jacques Rousseau (1712-78): French political philosopher fond of touting the benefits of family life while putting his own numerous illegitimate children into the Enfants-Trouvé.

[32] *Washington*: George Washington (1732-99), first president of the United States of America.

[33] *Napoleon*: Napoleon Bonaparte (1769-1821), emperor of France.

gentlemen, of scholars, of men of substance, and men of no personal faith at all. If this be life,—if it be life to impart a tone to the court and houses of parliament, to ministers of state, to law and literature, to universities and schools, and to society,—if it be life to be a principle of order in the population, and an organ of benevolence and almsgiving towards the poor,—if it be life to make men decent, respectable, and sensible, to embellish and refine the family circle, to deprive vice of its grossness, and to shed a gloss over avarice and ambition,—if indeed it is the life of religion to be the first jewel in the Queen's crown, and the highest step of her throne, then doubtless the National Church is replete, it overflows with life; but the question has still to be answered, Life of what kind? Heresy has its life, worldliness has its life. Is the Establishment's life merely national life, or is it something more? Is it Catholic life as well? Is it a supernatural life? Is it congenial with, does it proceed from, does it belong to, the principles of Apostles, Martyrs, Evangelists, and Doctors, the principles which the movement of 1833 thought to impose or to graft upon it, or does it revolt from them? If it be Catholic and Apostolic, it will endure Catholic and Apostolic principles; [48] no one doubts it can endure Erastian;[34] no one doubts it can be patient of Protestant; this is the problem which was started by the movement in question, the problem for which, surely, there has been an abundance of tests in the course of twenty years.

5.

But the passage I have quoted suggests a second observation. I have spoken of the *tests*, which the last twenty years have furnished, of the real character of the Establishment; for I must not be supposed to be inquiring

---

[34] *Erastian*: Adherent of the doctrines of Erastus, subordinating ecclesiastical to secular power. Erastus or Liebler was a physician of Heidelberg in the 16th century, to whom has been attributed the theory of state supremacy in ecclesiastical affairs. *OED*. In Lecture VI of *Anglican Difficulties*, Newman refers to 'Erastianism' as "the fruitful mother of all heresies," *Diff*, i, 172.

whether the Establishment has been unchurched during that period, but whether it has been proved to have been no Church from the first.[35] The want of congeniality which now exists between the sentiments and ways, the moral life of the Anglican communion, and the principles, doctrines, traditions of Catholicism—this uncongeniality I am speaking of in order to prove something done and over long

---

[35] *from the first*: Newman had occasion to elaborate on this point in a letter to the convert Francis Richard Wegg-Prosser (1824-1911), who, after attending Eton and Balliol, succeeded to his family's property at Belmont in Herefordshire. MP for Herefordshire (1847-52), he converted in 1852 and later became a prominent member of the Society of St. Vincent de Paul, as well as one of Newman's correspondents. "I know well you do not ask frivolous or captious questions," Newman wrote to the benefactor of the Benedictine church and monastery at Belmont. "As to your present, I do not suppose that a formal anathema is necessary to cut off a country from Catholic unity, any more than a formal disease is necessary for death. Did a person faint long enough, he would die. Partial interruptions of communion are most serious things, but they are but beginnings. And not only are they short, but they have not the intensity of a schism—e.g. Antioch, and Africa (if Africa must be taken) or Cappadocia was in unity and communion with one part of the Church while in disunion with another. As to the precise moment at which the disunion becomes formal schism, it is very difficult at times to determine. I have made some remarks on this in the second of a set of Lectures on Anglican Difficulties I published two years ago. Difficult as the minute may be to determine, there *is* a time at which one may safely say the Rubicon has been passed; just as you are sure a person is dead, though you could not make out the moment when his soul departed. As to England, the King, the country, the Establishment, distinctly cast off all connexion, all reverence towards the Holy See. If there could be a declaration of war, the English people made one. The feeling was so strong down to near the beginning of the 17th century that Hooker got into trouble for allowing a Papist could be saved. There is a work emphatically named the Church of E's [England's] Apology—I mean, Jewell's. Consider how it speaks of the Roman Communion. Consider the Homilies again, appointed to be read in Churches, think of the Canons of 1603—nay Laud's in (I think) 1644 or a little earlier. The heretic is said to be 'self condemned,' and is sometimes represented with his head in his hand—Did not England simply and absolutely cut off itself, by a succession of formal acts, from the Latin Church?" Newman to F.R. Wegg-Prosser (29 August 1852), *LD*, xv, 156-7. In the same letter Newman thanked his correspondent for supporting him during the Achilli trial.

ago before the movement, in order to show that that movement of 1833 was from its very beginning engaged in propagating an unreality. The eloquent writer just quoted, in ridicule of the protest made by twelve very distinguished men against the Queen's recent decision concerning the sacrament of baptism, contrasts "logical dreams" and "obscure and perplexing questions of dogmatic theology" with "the promise" in the Establishment of a large family "of daughters, spread round the earth, shining and [49] brightening every year." Now, I grant that it has a narrow and technical appearance to decide the Catholicity of a religious body by particular words, or deeds, or measures, resulting from the temper of a particular age, accidentally elicited, and accomplished in minutes or in days. I allow it and feel it;—that a particular vote of parliament, endured or tacitly accepted by bishops and clergy, or by the Metropolitans, or a particular appointment, or a particular omission, or a particular statement of doctrine, should at once change the spiritual character of the body, and *ipso facto* cut it off from the centre of unity and the source of grace, is almost incredible. In spite of such acts, surely the Anglican Church might be today what it was yesterday, with an internal power and a supernatural virtue, provided it had not already forfeited them, and would go about its work as of old time. It would be today pretty much what it was yesterday, though in the course of the night it had allowed an Anglo-Prussian See to be set up in Jerusalem, and had disavowed the Athanasian Creed.

This is the common sense of the matter, to which the mind recurs with satisfaction, after zeal and ingenuity have done their utmost to prove the contrary. Of course, I am not saying that individual acts do not tend towards, and a succession of acts does not issue in, the most serious spiritual consequences; but it is so difficult to determine the [50] worth of each ecclesiastical act, and what its position is relatively to acts before and after it, that I have no intention of urging any argument deduced from such acts in particular. A generation may not be long enough for the completion of an act of schism or heresy. Judgments admit of repeal or reversal; enactments are liable to flaws and informalities; laws require promulgation; documents admit of explanation; words must be interpreted either by context or by circumstances; majorities may be analysed; responsibilities may be shifted. I admit the remark of another writer in the present controversy, though I do not accept his conclusion: "The Church's motion," he says, "is not that of a machine, to be calculated with accuracy, and predicted beforehand; where one serious injury will disturb all regularity, and finally put a stop to action. It is that of a living body, whose motions will be irregular, incapable of being exactly arranged and foretold, and where it is nearly impossible to say how much health may co-exist with how much disease." And he speaks of the line of reasoning which he is opposing, as being "too logical to be real. Men," he observes, "do not, in the practical affairs of life, act on such clear, sharp, definite theories. Such reasoning can never be the cause of any one leaving the Church of England. But it looks well on paper, and therefore may, perhaps, be put forward as a theoretical argument by those [51] who, from some other feeling, or fancy, or prejudice, or honest conviction, think fit to leave us."[36]

Truly said, except in the imputation conveyed in the concluding words. I will grant that it is by life without us, by life within us, by the work of grace in our communion and in ourselves, that we are all of us accustomed practically to judge whether that communion be Catholic or

---

[36] Neal's Few Words of Hope, pp. 11, 12. [N] Newman is referring to J.M. Neale, *A Few Words of Hope on the Present Crisis* (London, 1850), 11-12. In response to the Gorham case, Neal counselled patience. Speaking of past scrapes in which the National Church had found itself, he wrote: "It is not as in the adoption of the Second Prayer Book of Edward VI—in the recognition of the Synod of Dort,—in the foundation of the Jerusalem Bishopric. There she sinned: here she only suffers.—And is this the time that her sons choose to forsake her? If they leave her because she has offended, they should, as I said, have gone before: if they leave her now, it is simply because she is afflicted. Clearly is it their duty to wait." Neal, 20.

not; not by this or that formal act or historical event. I will grant it, though of course it requires some teaching, and some discernment, and some prayer, to understand what spiritual life is, and what is the working of grace. However, at any rate, let the proposition pass;—I will here allow it, at least for argument's sake; for, my brethren, I am not here going to look out, in the last twenty years, for dates when, and ways in which, the Establishment fell from Catholic unity, and lost its divine privileges. No; the question before us is nothing narrow or technical; it has no cut-and-dried premisses, and peremptory conclusions; it is not whether this or that statute or canon at the time of the Reformation, this or that "further and further encroachment" of the State, this or that "Act of William IV.," constituted the Establishment's formal separation from the Church; not whether the Queen's recent decision binds it to heresy; but, whether these acts, and abundant others, are not one and all evidences, in one out of a hundred heads of evidence, that, [52] whatever were the acts which constituted, or the moment which completed the schism, or rather the utter disorganisation of the National Church, cut off and disorganised it is. No sober man I suppose, dreams of denying, that, if that Church be un-apostolical and impure now, it has had no claim to be called "pure and apostolical" last year, or twenty years back, or for any part of the period since the Reformation.

We have, then, this simple question before us: What evidence is there, that the doctrines and principles proclaimed to the world in 1833 had then, or have now, any congeniality with the Establishment in which they were propagated, and that they could or can live in that Establishment; whether they can move or work, whether they can breathe and live in it, better than a being with lungs in an exhausted receiver? It was doubted, as we have seen, by their first preachers; how has it been determined by the event? Now, then, to give one or two specimens and illustrations of a fact too certain, as I think, to need much dwelling on.

6.

We know that it is the property of life to be impatient of any foreign substance in the body to which it belongs. It will be sovereign in its own domain, and it conflicts with what it cannot assimilate into itself, and is irritated and [53] disordered till it has expelled it. Such expulsion, then, is, emphatically, a test of uncongeniality, for it shows that the substance ejected, not only is not one with the body that rejects it, but cannot be made one with it; that its introduction is not only useless, or superfluous, or adventitious, but that it is intolerable. For instance, it is usual for High Churchmen to speak of the Establishment as patient, in matter of fact, both of Catholic and Protestant principles;—truly said as regards Protestant, and it will illustrate my point to give instances of it. No one will deny, then, that neither Lutheranism nor Calvinism is the exact doctrine of the Church of England, and yet either heresy readily coalesces with it in matter of fact. Persons of Lutheran and Calvinistic, and Luthero-Calvinist bodies, are and have been chosen without scruple by the English people for husbands and wives, for sponsors, for missionaries, for deans and canons, without any formal transition from communion to communion. The Anglican Prelates write complimentary letters to what they call the foreign Protestant Churches, and they attend, with their clergy and laity, Protestant places of worship abroad.[37] William III.[38]

---

[37] *The Anglican Prelates*: The evangelical controversialist William Goode (1801-68) supplied a useful overview of the tune to which Anglican divines sought union with their continental counterparts in a book entitled *Brotherly Communion with The Foreign Protestant Churches Desired and Cultivated by The Highest and Best of The Divines of The Church of England. An Address Delivered at Cambridge at A Private Meeting of Some of The Senior Members of The University, And Published at Their Request.* (Cambridge, 1859). A few excerpts will corroborate Newman's point that if the National Church was averse to Roman Catholicism, it had no such aversion to continental Protestantism. "No sooner was the Reformation established in this country in the reign of Edward VI," Goode writes, "than our first Protestant Archbishop Cranmer endeavoured to bring about a union of all the Protestant Churches. So early as the year 1548 Archbishop Cranmer proposed to Bullinger,

Calvin, and Melancthon, that for the better uniting of all the Protestant Churches a Synod should be held in England of the leading Protestant divines, in which a common Confession of faith should be drawn up in which all might unite'. 'Our adversaries,' says Cranmer, in his letter to Calvin, dated March 20, 1552, 'have their Councils at Trent, that they may establish their errors; and shall we neglect to convene a religious Synod that we may be able to refute their errors, and reform their doctrines and propagate the truth'? The design was warmly responded to by the foreign divines to whom the Archbishop wrote, Calvin in particular expressing his great regret that the Protestant Churches were so divided from one another, and that he would willingly pass over ten seas, if it were necessary, to assist in such a work". *Goode*, 4-6. In a subsequent passage, Goode writes: "For the next, that is, the 18th century, we may content ourselves with the testimonies of the four well-known Archbishops, Dr Sharp of York, and Drs Tenison, Wake and Secker of Canterbury, and the Oxford Convocation. In the debate in the House of Lords on Occasional Conformity in 1702, Dr Sharp, Archbishop of York, stated, that 'if he were abroad, he would willingly communicate with the Protestant Churches, where he should happen to be.' In the debate on the Union with Scotland in 1707, Dr Tenison, Archbishop of Canterbury, said, 'he thought the narrow notions of all churches had been their ruin, and that he believed the Church of Scotland to be as true a Protestant Church as the Church of England, though he could not say it was as perfect'. This of course applies equally to the similarly constituted churches of the Continent." Ibid, 30-1. Goode quotes Wake to the same effect: "The Reformed Churches, though differing in some points from our English Church, I willingly embrace. I could have wished indeed that the Episcopal form of government had been retained by all of them.... Meanwhile far be it from me that I should be so iron-hearted as to believe, that, on account of such a defect (let me be permitted without offence to call it so), any of them ought to be cut off from our communion, or with certain mad writers among us, to declare that they have no true and valid sacraments, and thus are scarcely Christians." Ibid, 33. Goode then quotes "the late Archbishop Howley, in 1835, addressing a letter, in the name of himself and his 'brother bishops,' to 'the Moderator of the company of pastors at Geneva,' expressing their 'high respect for the Protestant Churches on the Continent,' and speaking of the Genevan Reformation as a 'noble achievement, which brought light out of darkness, and rescued your Church from the shackles of Papal domination and the tyrannical imposition of a corrupt faith and a superstitious ritual,' wrought by 'illustrious men, who, under the direction of Almighty God, were the instruments of this happy deliverance,' 'an event not less glorious to Geneva than conducive to the success of the Reformation.'" Ibid., 34.

was called to the throne, though a Calvinist, and George I., though a Lutheran, and that in order to exclude a family who adhered to the religion of Rome.[39] The national religion, then, has a congeniality with Lutheranism and Calvinism, which it has not, for instance, with the Greek religion, or the Jewish. Other religions, as they come, whatever they be, are not indifferent to it; it takes up one, it precipitates another; it, as every religion, has a life, a spirit, a genius of its own, in which doctrines lie implicit, out of which they are developed, and by which they are attracted into it from without, and assimilated to it.

[54]

There is a passage in Moehler's celebrated work on Symbolism,[40] so much to the point here, that I will quote it:

---

[38] *William III*: (1650-1702), king of England, Scotland (as William II) and Ireland (1689-1702), prince of Orange.

[39] *William III. was called to the throne*: Here is Newman's pithy reading of the 'Glorious' Revolution and its aftermath.

[40] *Moehler*: Johann Adam Möhler (1796-1838) Roman Catholic historian and theologian. Ordained in 1819, he served as lecturer at Tübingen from 1823 to 1826; professor 1826-35; and professor at Munch from 1835 until his untimely death in 1838. The significance of Mohler's work at the famous historicist academy in Tübingen is that it would eventually expose the peculiar unreality of Protestant historicism. According to the *Catholic Encyclopedia*, Mohler's *Symbolik* (1832), a study of the dogmatic differences between Catholicism and Protestantism, "demonstrated that there could be no incompatibility between what was truly rational and what was truly Christian, both finding their sole, direct, and entirely adequate expression in Catholic dogma. He showed also how Catholic doctrine held the middle course between the extremes of Protestantism, e.g., between a supernaturalist pietism that denied the rights of reason, and a naturalism and rationalism that rejected absolutely the supernatural. ... He was persuaded that a knowledge of the real character of great religious conflict, based on the genuine and original documents, was a necessary preliminary to any definite appeal to the tribunal of truth. Such investigations seemed to him important, not only for theologians, but also for every true scholar, the truth being nowhere so important as in matters of faith. The work was enthusiastically received, and went through five editions in six years. An English translation by James Burton Robertson appeared in London in 1843 under the title 'Symbolism; or Exposition of Doctrinal Differences between Catholics and Protestants, as evidenced lay their Symbolical Writings' ..." (*Catholic Encyclopaedia*). For the historian G.P. Gooch, *Symbolik* was "the most formidable attack on the Reformation since Bossuet. Its

"Each nation," he says, "is endowed with a peculiar character, stamped on the deepest, most hidden parts of its being, which distinguishes it from all other nations, and manifests its peculiarity in public and domestic life, in art and science; in short, in every relation. In every general act of a people, the national spirit is infallibly expressed; and should contests, should selfish factions occur, the element destructive to the vital principle of the whole will most certainly be detected in them, and the commotion excited by an alien spirit either miscarries or is expelled; as long as the community preserves its self-consciousness, as long as its peculiar genius yet lives and works within it ... Let us contemplate the religious sect founded by Luther himself. The developed doctrines of his Church, consigned as they are in the symbolical books, retain, on the whole, so much of his spirit, that, at the first view, they must be recognised by the observer as genuine productions of Luther. With a sure vital instinct, the opinions of the Majorists,[41] the

---

aim was to prove from patristic literature that Protestantism was unfaithful to the teaching of the primitive Church. His colleague Baur wrote a pointed criticism," to which Mohler replied that "his opponent argued his case from the standpoint of Schleiermacher and Hegel, not of the Reformers, and that he only defended Protestantism by misstating its teaching." G.P. Gooch, *History and Historians of the Nineteenth Century* (London, 1913), 550. O. Chadwick says that Mohler drew "a sharp line between Baur's evolutionary and Hegelian historicism and his own theories of tradition." O. Chadwick, *From Bossuet to Newman* (Cambridge, 1987), 110. Yet Mohler's respect for tradition was based on his study of Catholic doctrine, not his "own theories." Mohler's preoccupation with doctrine and national identity is important for readers of *Anglican Difficulties* because it was an equally judicious study of doctrine and national identity that led Newman to recognize that there could be no difference between what English Protestants were fond of calling the 'Primitive Church' and Roman Catholicism.

[41] *Majorists*: Adherents of Georg Major (1502-74), German theologian, who studied theology under M. Luther and P. Melancthon. Believing that good works are necessary to salvation, Major ran afoul of the strict Lutherans, who would brook no modifying of the Lutheran doctrine of justification by faith. As a compromise, Major taught that while faith alone might be essential to salvation, good works were still necessary as a corollary of faith. His Lutheran opponents countered that good works

[55]   Synergists,[42] and others, were rejected as deadly, and indeed (from Luther's point of view) as untrue, by that community whose soul, whose living principle, he was."[43]

We have the most vivid and impressive illustrations of the truth of these remarks in the history of the Church. The religious life of a people is of a certain quality and in a certain direction, and this quality and this direction are tested by the mode in which it encounters the various opinions, customs, and institutions which are submitted to it. Drive a stake into a river's bed, and you will at once ascertain which way it is running, and at what speed; throw up even a straw upon the air, and you will see which way the wind blows; submit your heretical and your Catholic principle to the action of the multitude, and you will be able to pronounce at once whether that multitude is imbued with Catholic truth or with heretical falsehood.

7.

Take, for example, a passage in the history of the fourth century; let the place be Milan; the date the Lent of 384,

---

might actually be impediments to salvation. The doctrines advocated by Major were adjudged heretical in the *Corpus doctrinae Prutenicnum,* and rejected by the compilers of the *Formula Concordiae.* The *Catholic Encyclopaedia* offers a useful critical assessment of the Lutheran understanding of Justification. "By stating that fiduciary faith alone suffices for obtaining both justification and eternal happiness, [Luther] minimized our moral faculties to such an extent that charity and good works no longer affect our relations with God. By this doctrine Luther opened a fundamental breach between religion and morality, between faith and law, and assigned to each its own distinct sphere of action in which each can attain its end independent of the other." This antinomian incoherence was one persistent feature of the liberalism that Newman opposed throughout his long life: indeed, it is still with us.

[42] *Synergists*: Adherents of Synergism, the teaching of P. Melancthon, according to which, in conversion, the human will can cooperate with the Holy Spirit and God's grace. By insisting that the primary cause of such conversion is the Holy Spirit and not the will, Melancthon sought to parry the charge of Pelagianism levelled against him by his opponents. See *ODCC.*

[43] Robertson's Transl., vol. ii. pp. 36-39. [N]

385; the reigning powers Justina[44] and her son Valentinian,[45] and St. Ambrose the Archbishop. The city is in an uproar; there is a mob before the imperial residence; the soldiery interferes in vain, and Ambrose is despatched by the court to disperse the people. A month elapses; Palm Sunday is come; the Archbishop is expounding the Creed to the [56] catechumens, when he is told that the people are again in commotion. A second message comes, that they have seized one of the empress's priests. The court makes reprisals on the tradesmen, some of whom are fined, some thrown into prison, while men of higher rank are threatened. We are arrived at the middle of Holy Week, and we find soldiers posted before one of the churches, and Ambrose has menaced them with excommunication. His threat overcomes them, and they join the congregation to whom he is preaching. The court gives way, the guards are withdrawn to their quarters, and the fines are remitted. What does all this mean? There evidently has been a quarrel between the

---

[44] *Justina:* The empress Justina was an avowed Arian, despite her husband Valentinian I (364–75) insisting that she subscribe to the Nicene Creed. When her four-year old son Valentinian II was proclaimed joint emperor of the West together with his fifteen-year-old brother Gratian, Justina became empress regent. Her Arianism put her in direct conflict with the uncompromising Ambrose. As Gibbon nicely put it, "Justina was persuaded that a Roman emperor might claim, in his own dominions, the public exercise of his religion; and she proposed to the archbishop, as a moderate and reasonable concession, that he should resign the use of a single church, either in the city or in the suburbs of Milan. But the conduct of Ambrose was governed by very different principles." *Decline and Fall*, iii, 165. In the midst of resisting Justina and her troops, Ambrose exhibited holy relics excavated from underneath the cathedral, which caused even Gibbon to acknowledge the striking unanimity between Ambrose and his flock. "The reason of the present age," Gibbon writes, "may possibly approve the incredulity of Justina and her Arian court; who derided the theatrical representations ... of the archbishop. Their effect, however, on the minds of the people was rapid and irresistible; and the feeble sovereign of Italy found himself unable to contend with the favourite of heaven." *Ibid,* 169. After Justina 's death Valentinian repudiated Arianism and placed himself under the guidance of Ambrose.

[45] *Valentinian*: Valentinian II, Roman Emperor (A.D. 375-92).

court and the Archbishop, and the Archbishop, aided by the popular enthusiasm, has conquered. A year passes, and there is a second and more serious disturbance. Soldiers have surrounded the same church; yet, dreading an excommunication, they let the people enter, but refuse to let them pass out. Still the people keep entering; they fill the church, the courtyard, the priests' lodgings; and there they remain with the Archbishop for two or three days, singing psalms, till the soldiers, overcome by the music, sing psalms too, and the blockade melts away, no one knows how. And now, what was the cause of so enthusiastic, so dogged an opposition to the court, on the part of the population of [57] Milan? The answer is plain; it was because they loved Christ so well, and were so sensitive of the doctrine of His divinity, that they would not allow the reigning powers to take a church from them, and bestow it on the Arians. I conceive, then, that Catholicism was emphatically the religion of Milan, or that the life of the Milanese Church was a Catholic life.[46]

---

[46] *a Catholic life*: Cf. Gibbon's account of Ambrose's thwarting Justina's attempt to force Arianism on the Church in Milan in *Decline and Fall*, iii, 166-69. "A large body of Goths had marched to occupy the Basilica which was the object of the dispute: and it might be expected from the Arian principles and barbarous manners of these foreign mercenaries that they would not entertain any scruples in the execution of the most sanguinary orders. They were encountered, on the sacred threshold, by the archbishop, who, thundering against them a sentence of excommunication, asked them, in the tone of a father and a master, Whether it was to invade the house of God that they had implored the hospitable protection of the republic? The suspense of the Barbarians allowed some hours for a more effectual negotiation; and the empress was persuaded, by the advice of her wisest counsellors, to leave the Catholics in possession of all the churches of Milan; and to dissemble, till a more convenient season, her intentions of revenge." *Decline and Fall*, iii, 167. Newman based his account on those given by St. Ambrose himself, his biographer Paulinus and St. Augustine in his *Confessions*. For Ambrose's own account, see *HS*, i, 350. In the *Confessions*, St. Augustine confirms the talent Ambrose had for impressing upon others the majestic appeal of the Faith. "I heard him 'rightly preaching the word of truth' (2 Tim. 2:15) among the people," Augustine recalled. "More and more my conviction grew that all the knotty problems and clever

84

And so, in like manner, when in St. Giles' Church, Edinburgh, in July 1635, the dean of the city opened the service-book, in the presence of Bishop and Privy Council, and "a multitude of the meanest sort, most of them women," clapped their hands, cursed him, cried out, "A pope! a pope! antichrist! stone him;"[47] and one flung a stool at the Bishop, and others threw stones at doors and windows, and at Privy-seal and Bishop on their return, and this became the beginning of a movement which ended in obtaining the objects at which it aimed,—this, I consider, shows clearly enough that the religious life at Edinburgh at that day was not Catholic, not Anglican, but Presbyterian and Puritan.

And, to take one more instance, when the seven Bishops[48] were committed to the Tower, and were proceeding "down the river to their place of confinement, the banks were covered with spectators, who, while they knelt and asked their blessing, prayed themselves for a blessing on them and their cause. The very soldiers who guarded them, and some even of the officers to whose [58] charge they were committed, knelt in like manner before them, and besought their benediction." When they were brought before the Court of King's Bench, they "passed through a line of people who kissed their hands and their garments, and begged their blessing;" and when they were admitted to bail, "bonfires were made in the streets, and healths drunk to the Seven Champions of the Church."

---

calumnies which those deceivers of ours had devised against the divine books could be dissolved." St Augustine, *Confessions* trans. H. Chadwick (Oxford, 1991), 93.

[47] Hume. Charles the First. [N] D. Hume, *History of England* (1828), iii, 422. When King Charles sought to introduce a new Prayer Book on the English model in Scotland, the Scots vehemently rejected it, which led to the Bishops Wars (1639-40), and, subsequently, the downfall of both Charles and his Archbishop.

[48] *seven Bishops*: When James II issued the decree that his "Declaration of Indulgence," proclaiming full liberty of worship, be read out in all churches on 20 and 27 May, 1688, William Sancroft, Archbishop of Canterbury and six other bishops drew up a petition protesting the decree. Subsequently, on June 8th, the seven bishops were arrested for sedition and imprisoned in the Tower. After being tried, they were all acquitted.

Lastly, when they were acquitted, the verdict "was received with a shout which seemed to shake the hall ... All the churches were filled with people; the bells rang from every tower, every house was illuminated, and bonfires were kindled in every street. Medals were struck in honour of the event, and portraits hastily published and eagerly purchased, of men who were compared to the seven golden candlesticks, and called the seven stars of the Protestant Church."[49] Now here again are signs of life, religious life, doubtless, but they have nothing to do with Catholicism; they are indubitable, unequivocable tokens what the national religion was and is, affording a clear illustration of the congeniality existing between the spirit and character of a system and its own principles, and not with their opposites.

8.

Let a people, then, Catholic or not, be little versed in doctrine—let them be a practical, busy people, full of their secular matters—let them have no keen analytical view of the principles which govern them,—yet they will be

[59]

---

[49] Southey's Book of the Church. [N] Newman is referring to R. Southey, *The Book of the Church* (1824), which he wrote to defend England's Protestant order, even though he was not a believer himself in any of the articles of the National Church. In pitching the book to his publisher John Murray, Southey wrote: "Two such books if they could be put into the hands of the rising generation would go far towards inspiring that ardent and devoted patriotism of which the ancients had so much and we have so little." W. A. Speck, *Robert Southey: Entire Man of Letters* (London, 2006), 148. It was Southey's readiness to ingratiate himself with the Establishment that Newman mocks in *Anglican Difficulties* that made him so loathsome to Lord Byron, who nicknamed him "dry Bob." F. MacCartney, *Byron: Life and Legend* (London, 2002), 349. W. Hazlitt was more charitable, saying of the poet in an essay in 1825: "No man in our day ... has led so uniformly and entirely the life of the scholar, from boyhood to the present hour, devoting himself to learning with the enthusiasm of an early love... [but] well would it have been if he had confined himself to this, and not undertaken to pull down or to patch up the State!" W. Hazlitt, *The Spirit of the Age* (Oxford, 1904), 129. Newman thought Southey's epic poem "Thabala the Destroyer" (1801), which the English composer Sir Granville Bantock would set to music in 1899, "the most sublime of English poems." *LD*, xiii, 449.

spontaneously attracted by those principles and irritated by their contraries, in such sort as they can be attracted or irritated by no other. Their own principles or their contraries, when once sounded in their ears, thrill through them with a vibration, pleasant or painful, with sweet harmony or with grating discord; under which they cannot rest quiet, but relieve their feelings by gestures and cries, and startings to and fro, and expressions of sympathy or antipathy towards others, and at length by combination, and party manifestos, and vigorous action. When, then, the note of Catholicism, as it may be called, was struck seventeen years since, and while it has sounded louder and louder on the national ear, what has been the response of the national sentiment? It had many things surely in its favour; it sounded from a centre which commanded attention—it sounded strong and full; nor was it intermitted, or checked, or lowered by the opposition nor drowned by the clamour, which it occasioned while, at length, it was re-echoed and repeated from other centres with zeal, and energy, and sincerity, and effect, as great as any cause could even desire or could ask for. So far, no movement could have more advantages attendant on it than it had; and, as it proceeded, it did not content itself with propagating an abstract theology, but it took a part in the public events of the day; it [60] interfered with court, with ministers, with University matters, and with counter-movements of whatever kind.

And, moreover, which is much to the purpose, it appealed to the people, and that on the very ground that it was Apostolical in its nature. It made the experiment of this appeal the very test of its Apostolicity. "I shall offend many men," said one of its organs, "when I say, we must look to the people; but let them give me a hearing. Well can I understand their feelings. Who, at first sight, does not dislike the thoughts of gentlemen and clergymen depending for their maintenance and their reputation on their flocks? of their strength, as a visible power, lying, not in their birth, the patronage of the great, or the endowments of the Church, as hitherto, but in the homage of a multitude? But, in truth, the prospect is not so bad as it seems at first sight. The chief and obvious objection to the clergy being thrown on the people lies in that probable lowering of Christian views, and that adulation of the vulgar, which would be its consequence; and the state of dissenters is appealed to as an evidence of the danger. But let us recollect that we are an Apostolical body; we were not made, nor can be unmade, by our flocks; and, if our influence is to depend on them, yet the Sacraments are lodged with us. We have that with us which none but ourselves possess, the mantle of the

[61] Apostles; and this, properly understood and cherished, will ever keep us from being the creatures of a population."[50]

Here, then, was a challenge to the nation to decide between the movement and its opponents; and how did the nation meet it? When clergymen of Latitudinarian theology were promoted to dignities, did the faithful of the diocese, or of the episcopal city, rise in insurrection? Did parishioners blockade a church's doors to keep out a new incumbent, who refused to read the Athanasian Creed? Did vestries feel an instinctive reverence for the altar-table, as soon as that reverence was preached? Did the organs of public opinion pursue with their invectives those who became dissenters or Irvingites?[51] Was it a subject of

---

[50] Church of the Fathers. [N] Newman is quoting here from "What Does Ambrose Say About It?" one of the papers of "Church of the Fathers," which as he wrote in the Prefatory Notice to the first volume of *Historical Sketches*, "appeared in the *British Magazine* in the years 1833-36 and ... published afterwards in one volume with additions in 1840." Newman also noted that "The date of their composition is a sufficient indication of the character of the theology which they contain. They were written under the assumption that the Anglican Church has a place, as such, in Catholic communion and Apostolic Christianity. This is a question of fact, which the Author would now of course answer in the negative ..." The piece was later republished in the first of three volumes under the heading "Primitive Christianity" in *Historical Sketches* in 1872. See *HS*, i, 340-1.

[51] *Irvingites*: Adherents of Edward Irving (1792-1834), Scottish preacher. Irving inspired a large congregation in Hatton Garden, London to speak in tongues while awaiting Christ's second coming. Irving's first love was Jane Welsh, whom he tutored as a girl when she was "the belle of

popular indignation, discussed and denounced in railway trains and omnibuses and steamboats, in clubs and shops, in episcopal charges and at visitation dinners, if a clergyman explained away the baptismal service, or professed his intention to leave out portions of it in ministration? Did it rouse the guards or the artillery to find that the Bishop, where they were stationed, was a Sabellian? Was it a subject for public meetings if a recognition was attempted of foreign Protestant ordinations? Did animosity to heretics of the day go so far as to lead speakers to ridicule their persons and their features, amid the cheers of sympathetic hearers? Did petitions load the tables of the Commons from [62] the mothers of England or Young Men's Associations, because the Queen went to a Presbyterian service,[52] or a high minister of state was an infidel?[53] Did the Bishops cry

---

Haddington," but after he married someone else, the acid Mrs. Carlyle told a friend: 'There would have been no tongues if Irving had married me.'" See J.A. Froude, *Thomas Carlyle: A History of his Life in London: 1834-1881* (London, 1882), i, 162.

[52] *Presbyterian service*: Newman appears to be referring to Queen Victoria attending Presbyterian services when in Balmoral, Scotland, though as Colin Matthew points out "She was herself, by necessity and inclination, 'Protestant to the very *heart's core*' [as she said in one of her letters], her personal preference was for extremely simple services, and she argued for greater unity among the different protestant churches. (She took communion at a Presbyterian service at Crathie kirk for the first time on 3 November 1873, having previously held back from scruple as to her position at the head of the episcopalian church.)" *ODNB* The impeccably Protestant Samuel Wilberforce was her favourite preacher. See E. Longford, *Queen Victoria* (London, 1964), 159. In a letter to E. Pusey in December of 1841, W.G. Ward noted how "members of our Church are I believe constantly in the habit of attending the Presbyterian worship in Scotland, without any censure or remonstrance." *LD*, viii, 366.

[53] *an infidel*: It is unclear to whom Newman is referring here – there were a number of men who could be regarded as 'infidels' serving as 'high ministers of state' at the time, though if one had to choose one might venture Lord Brougham, Lord Chancellor in Melbourne's First Cabinet (formed July 1834); Sir Robert Peel, Prime Minister and Chancellor of the Exchequer in his First Cabinet (formed in December, 1834) and Prime Minister in his Second Cabinet (formed in September, 1841), while instituting the Tamworth Reading Room with Lord Brougham (See *DA*,

out and stop their ears on hearing that one of their body denied original sin or the grace of ordination? Was there nothing in the course of the controversy to show what the nation thought of that controversy, and of the parties to it?

9.

Yes, I hear a cry from an episcopal city; I have before my eyes one scene, and it is a sample and an earnest of many others. Once in a way, there were those among the authorities of the Establishment who made certain recommendations concerning the mode of conducting divine worship: simple these in themselves, and perfectly innocuous, but they looked like the breath, the shadow of the movement; they seemed an omen of something more to come; they were the symptoms of some sort of ecclesiastical favour bestowed in one quarter on its adherents. The newspapers, the organs of the political, mammon-loving community, of those vast multitudes of all ranks who are allowed by the Anglican Church to do nearly what they will for six, if not seven days in the week,—who, in spite of the theological controversies rolling over their heads, could, if they would, buy, and sell, and manufacture, and trade at their pleasure,—who might be unconcerned, [63] and go their own way, for no one would interfere with them, and might "live and let live,"—the organs, I say, of these multitudes kindle with indignation, and menace, and revile, and denounce, because the Bishops in question suffer their clergy to deliver their sermons, as well as the prayers, in a surplice.[54] It becomes a matter of popular interest. There are

---

254-305); or Viscount Palmerston, Foreign Secretary in Russell's First Cabinet (formed in July 1846).

[54] *surplice*: The wearing of the surplice by Church of England divines – which, as Newman says, constituted the "faintest, wannest expression" of "Apostolical principles" – offended the sectarian sensibilities of both Presbyterians and Anglicans at various times throughout the history of the National Church. Outrage, for example, met the Rev. Mr. Courtenay on a number of occasions when he wore the surplice in St. Sidwell's Church, Exeter, after Bishop Phillpotts had instructed his priests to wear it. See accounts in *The Times* for 31 December 1844 and 20 January 1845

mobs in the street, houses are threatened, life is in danger, because only a gleam of Apostolical principles, in their faintest, wannest expression, is cast inside a building which is the home of the national religion. The very moment that Catholicism ventures out of books, and cloisters, and studies, towards the national house of prayer, when it lifts its hand or its very eyebrow towards this people so tolerant of heresy, at once the dull and earthly mass is on fire. It would be little or nothing though the minister baptized without water, though he chucked away the consecrated wine, though he denounced fasting, though he laughed at virginity, though he interchanged pulpits with a Wesleyan or a Baptist, though he defied his Bishop; he might be blamed, he might be disliked, he might be remonstrated with; but he would not touch the feelings of men; he would not inflame their minds;—but, bring home to them the very thought of Catholicism, hold up a surplice, and the religious building is as full of excitement and tumult as St. Victor's at Milan in the cause of orthodoxy, or St. Giles', Edinburgh, for the Kirk.

"The uproar commenced," says a contemporary account, [64] "with a general coughing down; several persons then moved to the door making a great noise in their progress; a young woman went off in a fit of hysterics, uttering loud shrieks, whilst a mob outside besieged the doors of the building. A cry of 'fire' was raised, followed by an announcement that

---

In the latter account, *The Times* Exeter correspondent wrote: "About two thousand persons were assembled to hoot Mr. Courtenay as he left the church. Gibes, and shouts, and laughter rang through the air. The Rev. gentleman was again surrounded by a party of his friends to protect him as he left the church. A strong body of the police made a lane through the crowd for him, and then formed in close file round him to keep off the crowd. ... The indignation of the people is certainly excusable, for the cause of all the mischief was Mr. Courtenay and a white gown. It was generally rumoured that the Mayor had called on Mr. Courtenay before the afternoon service, and represented to him the danger to the peace of the town, and the great probability of a fight with the police if he persevered, and had put it to him as a clergyman if he thought it proper to run the risk of such a result by persisting in the line of conduct he was pursuing." *The Times* (20 January 1845).

the church doors were closed, and a rush was made to burst them open. Some cried out, 'Turn him out,' 'Pull it off him.' In the galleries the uproar was at its height, whistling, cat-calls, hurrahing, and such cries as are heard in theatres, echoed throughout the edifice. The preacher still persisted to read his text, but was quite inaudible; and the row increased, some of the congregation waving their hats, standing on the seats, jumping over them, bawling, roaring, and gesticulating, like a mob at an election. The reverend gentleman, in the midst of the confusion, despatched a message to the mayor, requesting his assistance, when one of the congregation addressed the people, and also requested the preacher to remove the cause of the ill-feeling which had been excited. Then another addressed him in no measured terms, and insisted on his leaving the pulpit. At length the mayor, the superintendent of the police, several constables, also the chancellor and the archdeacon, arrived. The mayor enforced silence, and, after admonishing the people, requested the clergy-man to leave the pulpit for a [65] few minutes, which he declined to do,—gave out his text, and proceeded with his discourse. The damage done to the interior of the church is said to be very considerable."[55] I believe I am right in supposing that the surplice has vanished from that pulpit from that day forward. Here, at length, certainly are signs of life, but not the life of the Catholic Church.

And now to draw my conclusion from what I have been following out, if I have not sufficiently done so already. If, my brethren, your reason, your faith, your affections, are indissolubly bound up with the holy principles which you have been taught, if you know they are true, if you know their life and their power, if you know that nothing else is true; surely you have no portion or sympathy with systems which reject them. Seek those principles in their true home.

---

[55] *very considerable*: Newman's quotation from *The Times* refers to a second anti-surplice row involving St. Sidwell's and Courtenay dated 29 October 1848. See *LD*, xiii, 468.

If your Church rejects your principles, it rejects you;—nor dream of indoctrinating it with them by remaining; everything has its own nature, and in that nature is its identity. You cannot change your Establishment into a Church without a miracle. It is what it is, and you have no means of acting upon it; you have not what Archimedes[56] looked for, when he would move the world,—the fulcrum of his lever,—while you are one with it. It acts on you, while you act on it; you cannot employ it against itself. If you would make England Catholic, you must go forth on your mission *from* the Catholic Church. You *have* duties [66] towards the Establishment; it is the duty, not of owning its rule, but of converting its members. Oh, my brethren! life is short, waste it not in vanities; dream not; halt not between two opinions; wake from a dream, in which you are not profiting your neighbour, but imperilling your own souls.

---

[56] *Archimedes*: Archimedes (c. 287-212 BC) Greek mathematician. One of the most astute mathematicians of all time, he is quoted as having said: "Give me a lever long enough and a fulcrum on which to place it, and I shall move the world." After a life full of mathematical epiphany and discovery, he was killed by a Roman soldier at the siege of Syracuse while pondering a mathematical problem.

LECTURE III

THE LIFE OF THE MOVEMENT OF 1833 NOT DERIVED
FROM THE NATIONAL CHURCH

1.

I AM proposing, my brethren, in these Lectures, to answer several of the objections which are urged against quitting the National Communion for the Catholic Church. It has been a very common and natural idea of those who belong to the movement of 1833, as it was the idea of its originators, that, the Nation being on its way to give up revealed truth, all those who wish to receive that truth in its fulness, and to resist its enemies, are called on to make use of the National Church, to which they belong, whose formularies they receive, as their instrument for that purpose. I answer them, that their attempt is hopeless, because the National Church is strictly part of the Nation, in the same way that the Law or the Parliament is part of the Nation; and therefore, as the Nation changes, so will the National Church change. That Church, then, cannot be used against the spirit of the age, except as a drag on a wheel; for nothing can really resist the Nation, except what stands on a basis independent of the Nation. It must say and will say just what the Nation says, though it may be some time in saying it. Next, having thus shown that the National Church is absolutely one with the Nation, I proceeded further to show that, on the other hand, the National Church is absolutely heterogeneous from the Apostolic or Anglo-Catholic party of 1833; so that, while the National Church is part of the Nation, the movement, on the contrary, has no part or place in the National Church. To aim, then, at making the Nation Catholic by means of the Church of England, was something like evangelizing Turkey by means of Islamism; and, as the Turks would feel serious resentment at hearing the Gospel in the mouths of their Muftis and Mollahs, so was, and is, the English Nation provoked, not persuaded, by Catholic preaching in the Establishment.[1]

And I rest the proof of these two statements on incontrovertible facts going on during the last twenty years, and now before our eyes; for, first, the National Church *has* changed and *is* changing with the Nation; and secondly, the Nation and Church have been indignant, and are indignant, with the movement of 1833. I conceive that, except in imagination and in hope, there are no symptoms whatever of the National Church preventing those changes of Progress,[2] as it is called, whether in the Nation or in itself,

---

[1] *evangelizing Turkey*: What Newman is saying here is that the Anglo-Catholic party would have as much chance of making the Established Church Catholic as the mullahs and muftis would have of convincing the Sultan and the Ottoman Turks of adopting the Gospel. It is true that the Tanzimat (or 'Reorganization') was being carried out in the Ottoman Empire from 1839 to 1876, a series of Westernizing reforms aimed at reversing the empire's decline by putting its different religious and ethnic groups, including Christians, on some more equitable footing, but "...the bulk of the Muslim population ... [was] outraged by this emancipation of the infidel, which struck right at the roots of their traditional conception of the absolute superiority of Islam and the inferiority of all other religions." Lord Kinross, *The Ottoman Empire* introduced by Norman Stone (London, 2003), 466. The great difference between the Sultan and his court and the mullahs and muftis, on the one hand, and the Establishment and the Anglo-Catholic party, on the other, is that "the bulk of the Muslim population" were united with the mullahs and muftis in their embrace of Islam. The Anglo-Catholic party could never rely on any comparable support from the bulk of the English people when it came to the Gospel, let alone Anglo-Catholicism.

[2] *Progress*: Newman, unlike so many of his contemporaries, was unimpressed by the allure of the suppositious advances of Progress. In September of 1832, he wrote his friend Samuel Francis Wood: "Now, I fear, nothing but the reality of severe suffering will bring us to a right estimate of what we are — and rouse us from this indolent contemplation of our advances in the useful arts and the experimental sciences, to the thought and practice of our duties as immortal beings. The country seems to me to be in a dream — being drugged with this fallacious notion of its superiority to other countries and times. — And I think from this another mistake follows. Men see that those parts of the national system, (and those, of course, far the most important and comprehensive) which really

though it may retard them: nor any symptoms whatever of
[69] its welcoming those retrograde changes, to which it is
invited under the name of primitive and Apostolical truth.
The National Church is the slave of the Nation, and it is the
opponent of the Movement; which, after all, has done no
more than form a party in the one to the annoyance of the
other.

And now I come to a second objection, which shall be
my subject today. An inquirer, then, may say, "This is a
very unfair and one-sided view of the matter. I grant—
indeed I cannot deny—that the movement has but formed a
party in the National Church. I grant it has no hold on the
Church, that it does not coalesce with it, that it hangs loose
of it: nay, I grant that this want of congeniality comes out
clearer and clearer year by year, so that the Anglican party
has never appeared more distinct from the Establishment,
and foreign to it, than at this moment, when State and
Bishops and people have cast it off, and its efforts, whether
to alter the constitution of the Establishment, or to preserve
its doctrine, have failed and are failing. I grant all this; I am
forced in fairness to grant it;—or rather, whether I grant it
or no, it will be taken for granted by all men without
waiting for my granting. But still, so far is undeniable, that
that movement of 1833 issued forth *from* the National
Church; this, at least, is an incontrovertible fact: whatever
light, life, or strength it has possessed, or possesses, from
[70] the National Church was it derived. To the Sacraments, to
the ordinances, to the teaching of the national Church, the
movement owes its being and its continuance; and, if it be
its offspring, it belongs to it, it is cognate to it, and cannot
be really alien from it; and great sin and undutifulness,

---

depend on personal and private virtue do not work well — and, not
seeing [where] the deficiency lies, viz. in want of personal virtue, they
imagine they can put things right by applying their scientific knowledge
to the improvement of the existing system — Hence political economy is
to supersede morality — again, hence we are promised laws which shall
prevent bribery and corruption — and hence the projects of reform in the
Church." *LD*, iii, 90.

ingratitude, presumption, and cruelty, there must be committed by those who, belonging to the movement, abandon the Church." This is a consideration which is urged with great force against affectionate and diffident minds, and acts as an insurmountable difficulty in the way of their becoming Catholics. It is pressed upon them—"The National Church is the Church of your baptism, and therefore to leave it is to abandon your Mother."[3]

Now, then, let us examine what is the real state of the case.

2.

We see then, certainly, a multitude of men all over the country, who, in the course of the last twenty years, have been roused to a religious life by the influence of certain principles professing to be those of the Primitive Church,[4] and put forth by certain of the National Clergy. Every year has added to their number; nor has it been a mere profession of opinion which was their characteristic, or certain exercises of the intellect; not a fashion or taste of the hour, but a rule of life. They have subjected their wills, they have

---

[3] *your Mother*: Cf. "No man can justly blame me for honoring my spiritual Mother, the Church of England, in whose womb I was conceived, at whose breasts I was nourished, and in whose bosom I hope to die. Bees, by the instinct of nature, do love their hives, and birds their nests. But, God is my witness, that, according to my uttermost talent and poor understanding, I have endeavored to set down the naked truth impartially, without favour or prejudice ... My desire hath been to have Truth for my chiefest friend, and no enemy but error." Quoted in *VM*, i, xii-xiii, from *The Works of ... John Bramhall, D.D.* (1-vol. ed., Dublin, 1677), 141.

[4] *the Primitive Church*: This was the preferred term used by Anglo-Catholics when recommending their Anglo-Catholicism against the Erastian National Church of the Establishment. But it was also the term used by Anglo-Catholics and Anglicans alike when making invidious comparisons between the early and the later Church, the presumption being that the latter was guilty of unwarrantable accretions to the former. The fundamental point of Newman's idea of doctrinal development was to show how the 'Primitive' Church and the Roman Catholic Church were one and the same. The notion that Newman articulated his idea of doctrinal development to try to smuggle heretical innovations into the Church as 'developments' is a Modernist fantasy.

chastened their hearts, they have subdued their affections, they have submitted their reason. Devotions, communions, [71] fastings, privations, almsgiving, pious munificence, self-denying occupations, have marked the spread of the principles in question; which have, moreover, been adorned and recommended in those who adopted them by a consistency, grace, and refinement of conduct nowhere else to be found in the National Church. Such are the characteristics of the party in question; and, moreover, its members themselves expressly attribute their advancement in the religious life to the use of the ordinances of that National Church.

They have found, they say, as a matter of fact, that as they attended those ordinances, they became more strong in obedience and dutifulness, had more power over their passions, and more love towards God and man. "If, then," they may urge, "you confront us with those external facts, which have formed the subjects of your first and second Lectures, here are our internal facts to meet them; our own experience, serious, sober, practical, outweighs a hundredfold representations which may be logical, dazzling, irrefragable; but which still, as we ourselves know better than any one, whatever be the real explanation of them, are, after all, fallacious and untrue."

Here, then, we are brought to the question of the internal evidence, which is alleged in favour of a real, however recondite, connection of the (so-called) Anglo-Catholic party with the National Church.[5] It is said that, however you [72] are to account for it, there is the fact of a profound intimate relationship, a spiritual bond, between the one and the other; that party has actually risen out of what seems so earthly, so inconsistent, so feeble, and is sustained by it; and, in fact

---

[5] *The National Church:* What follows is a good example of how barristerial a polemicist Newman could be, putting his opponents' arguments in as sympathetic a light as possible before exposing their manifold flaws, though here he takes not just his Anglo-Catholic friends to task but his own role in their religious development, since he was one of the chief architects of the party whose thinking he means to repudiate.

does but illustrate the great maxim of the Gospel, that the weak shall be strong, and the despised shall be glorious. Taking their stand on this evangelical promise and principle, the persons of whom I speak are quite careless of argument, which silences them without touching them. "Their opponents may triumph, if they will; but, after all, there certainly must be some satisfactory explanation of the difficulties of their own position, if they did but know what it was. The question is deeper than argument, while it is very easy to be captious and irreverent. It is not to be handled by intellect and talent, or decided by logic. They are undoubtedly in a very anomalous state of things, a state of transition; but they must submit for a time to be without a theory of the Church, without an intellectual basis on which to plant themselves. It would be an utter absurdity for them to leave the Establishment, merely because they do not at the moment see how to defend their staying in it. Such accidents will from time to time happen in large and complicated questions; they have light enough to guide them practically,—first, because even though they wished to move ever so much, they see no place to move into; and next, because, however it comes to pass, however contrary [73] it may seem to be to all the rules of theology and the maxims of polemics, to Apostles, Scripture, Fathers, Saints, common-sense, and the simplest principles of reason,— though it ought not to be so in the way of strict science,— still, so it is, they are, in matter of fact, abundantly blest where they are.

"Certainly it is vexatious that the Privy Council should have decided as it has done; vexatious not to know what to say about the decision; vexatious, inconvenient, perplexing, but nothing more. It is not a real difficulty, but only an annoyance, to be obliged to say something to quiet their people, and not to have a notion what. However, they must do their best; and, though it is true one of their friends uses one argument, another another, and these arguments are inconsistent with one another, still that is an accidental misery of their position, and it will not last for ever.

Brighter times are coming; meanwhile they must, with resignation, suffer the shame, scorn of man, and distrust of friends, which is their present portion; a little patience, and the night will be over; their Athanasius will come at length, to defend and to explain the truth, and their present constancy will be their future reward."[6]

3.

Now, as truth is the object which I set before me in the inquiry which I am prosecuting, I will not follow their [74] example in considering only one side of the question. I will not content myself, on my part, with insisting merely upon the external view of it, which is against them, leaving them in possession of that argument from the inward evidences of grace, on which they especially rely. I have no intention at all of evading their position,—I mean to attack it. I feel intimately what is strong in it, and I feel where it halts; so, to state their argument fairly, I will not extemporize words of my own, but I will express it in the language of a writer, who, when he so spoke, belonged to the Established Church.

"Surely," he says, "as the only true religion is that which is seated within us,—a matter not of words, but of things, so the only satisfactory test of religion is something within us. If religion be a personal matter, its reasons also should be personal. Wherever it is present in the world or in the heart, it produces an effect, and that effect is its evidence. When we view it as set up in the world, it has its external proofs;

---

[6] *their future reward*: The reasoning set out here in quotation marks and subsequently echoes J.M. Neale's spirited call to Anglicans to abide the storm of the Gorham Case and to remain faithful to the Anglican ship. "[H]aving had more opportunities than most of my brethren for examining the present revival of our Church in nearly every part of England," Neal wrote in *A Few Words of Hope in the Present Crisis of the English Church* (1850), "I am convinced that, while there is every call for exertion there is absolutely no cause for despair; that, if we may be excused for sometimes trembling, we are bound to acknowledge that every thing is as yet full of hope: that our LORD is only asleep in the vessel, not that He has left it." Neal, 5.

when as set up in our hearts, it has its internal; and that, whether we are able to elicit them ourselves, and put them into shape, or not. Nay, with some little limitation and explanation, it might be said, that the very fact of a religion taking root within us is a proof so far that it is true. If it were not true, it would not take root. Religious men have, in their own religiousness, an evidence of the truth of their religion. That religion is true which has power, and so far as it has power; nothing but what is divine can renew the heart. [75] And this is the secret reason *why* religious men believe,— whether they are adequately conscious of it or no,—whether they can put it into words or no—viz., their past experience that the doctrine which they hold is a reality in their minds, not a mere opinion, and has come to them, 'not in word but in power.' And in this sense the presence of religion in us is its own evidence."[7]

Again:—

"If, then, we are asked for 'a reason of the hope that is in us,' why we are content, or rather thankful, to be in that Church in which God's providence has placed us, would not the reasons be some one or other of these, or rather all of them, and a number of others besides, which these may suggest, deeper than they?

"First, I suppose a religious man is conscious that God has been with him, and given him whatever he has of good within him. He knows quite enough of himself to know how fallen he is from original righteousness, and he has a conviction, which nothing can shake, that without the aid of his Lord and Saviour, he can do nothing aright. I do not say he need recollect any definite season when he turned to God, and gave up the service of sin and Satan; but in one sense, every season, every year, is such a time of turning. I mean, he ever has experience, just as if he had hitherto been living in the world, of a continual conversion; he is ever [76]

---

[7] The author's Sermons on Subjects of the Day, pp. 345, 346. [N] John Henry Newman, "Grounds for Steadfastness in Our Religious Profession" (1841), *Sermons Bearing on Subjects of the Day* (London, 1843), 345, 346.

taking advantage of holy seasons, and new providences, and beginning again. The elements of sin are still alive within him; they still tempt and influence him, and threaten when they do no more; and it is only by a continual fight against them that he prevails; and what shall persuade him that his power to fight is his own, and not from above? And this conviction of a divine presence with him is stronger, according to the length of time during which he has served God, and to his advance in holiness. The multitude of men, nay, a great number of those who think themselves religious, do not aim at holiness, and do not advance in holiness; but consider, what a great evidence it is that God is with us, so far as we have it! Religious men, really such, cannot but recollect in the course of years that they have become very different from what they were ... In the course of years a religious person finds that a mysterious unseen influence has been upon and changed him. He is indeed very different from what he was. His tastes, his views, his judgments are different. You will say that time changes a man as a matter of course; advancing age, outward circumstances, trials, experience of life. It is true; and yet I think a religious man would feel it little less than sacrilege, and almost blasphemy, to impute the improvement of his heart and conduct, in his moral being, with which he has been favoured in a certain sufficient period, to outward or [77] merely natural causes. He will be unable to force himself to do so—that is to say, he has a conviction, which it is a point of religion with him not to doubt, which it is a sin to deny, that God has been with him. And this is, of course, a ground of hope to him that God will be with him still; and if he, at any time, fall into religious perplexity, it may serve to comfort him to think of it."[8]

And again:—

"I might go on to mention a still more solemn subject, viz., the experience, which, at least, certain religious persons have of the awful sacredness of our sacraments and

---

[8] Ibid., pp. 348-350. [N]

other ordinances. If these are attended by the presence of Christ, surely we have all that a Church can have in the way of privilege and blessing. The promise runs, 'Lo, I am with you always, even unto the end of the world.' That is a Church where Christ is present; this is the very definition of the Church. The question sometimes asked is, Whether our services, our holy seasons, our rites, our sacraments, our institutions, really have with them the presence of Him who thus promised? If so, we are part of the Church; if not, then we are but performers in a sort of scene or pageant, which may be religiously intended, and which God in His mercy may visit; but if He visits, will in visiting go beyond His own promise. But observe, as if to answer to the challenge, and put herself on trial, and to give us a test of her Catholicity, our Church boldly declares of her most solemn [78] ordinance, that he who profanes it incurs the danger of judgment. She seems, like Moses, or the Prophet from Judah, or Elijah, to put her claim to issue, not so openly, yet as really, upon the fulfilment of a certain specified sign. Now she does not speak to scare away the timid, but to startle and subdue the unbelieving, and withal to assure the wavering and perplexed; and I conceive that in such measure as God wills, and as is known to God, these effects follow. I mean, that we really have proofs among us, though, for the most part, they will be private and personal, from the nature of the case, of clear punishment coming upon profanations of the holy ordinance in question; sometimes very fearful instances, and such as serve, while they awe beholders, to comfort them;—to comfort them, for it is plain, if God be with us for judgment, surely He is with us for mercy also; if He punishes, why is it but for profanation? And how can there be profanation if there is nothing to be profaned? Surely He does not manifest His wrath except where He has first vouchsafed His grace?"[9]

---

[9] Ibid., pp. 353-355. [N]

I might quote much more to the same purpose; if I do not, it is not that I fear the force of the argument, but the length to which it runs.

4.

Now in this preference of internal evidences to those [79] which are simply outward, there is a great principle of truth; it requires much guarding, indeed, and explaining, but I suppose, in matter of fact, that the notes of the Church, as they are called, are chiefly intended, as this writer says, as guides and directions into the truth, for those who are as yet external to it, and that those who are within it have *primâ facie* evidences of another and more personal kind. I grant it, and I make use of my admission; for one inward evidence at least Catholics have, which this writer had not,—certainty. I do not say, of course, that what seems like certainty is a sufficient evidence to an individual that he has found the truth, for he may mistake obstinacy or blindness for certainty; but, at any rate, the *absence* of certainty is a clear proof that a person has *not* yet found it, and at least a Catholic knows well, even if he cannot urge it in argument, that the Church is able to communicate to him that gift. No one can read the series of arguments from which I have quoted, without being struck by the author's clear avowal of *doubt*, in spite of his own reasonings, on the serious subject which is engaging his attention. He longed to have faith in the National Church, and he could not. "What *want we*," he exclaims, "*but* faith in our Church? With faith we can do everything; without faith we can do nothing."[10] So all these inward notes which he enumerates, whatever their *primâ* [80] *facie* force, did not reach so far as to implant conviction even in his own breast; they did not, after all, prove to him that connection between the National Church and the spiritual gifts which he recognised in his party, which he fain would have established, and which they would fain establish to whom I am now addressing myself.

---

[10] Ibid., p. 380. [N]

But to come to the gifts themselves. You tell me, my brethren, that you have the clear evidence of the influences of grace in your hearts, by its effects sensible at the moment or permanent in the event. You tell me, that you have been converted from sin to holiness, or that you have received great support and comfort under trial, or that you have been carried over very special temptations, though you have not submitted yourselves to the Catholic Church. More than this, you tell me of the peace, and joy, and strength which you have experienced in your own ordinances. You tell me, that when you began to go weekly to communion you found yourselves wonderfully advanced in purity. You tell me that you went to confession, and you never will believe that the hand of God was not over you at the moment when you received absolution. You were ordained, and a fragrance breathed around you; you hung over the dead, and you all but saw the happy spirit of the departed. This is what you say, and the like of this; and I am not the person, my dear brethren, to quarrel with the truth of what you say. I am not the person to be jealous of such facts, nor to wish you to [81] contradict your own memory and your own nature, nor am I so ungrateful to God's former mercies to myself, to have the heart to deny them in you. As to miracles, indeed, if such you mean, that of course is a matter which might lead to dispute; but if you merely mean to say that the supernatural grace of God, as shown either at the time or by consequent fruits, has overshadowed you at certain times, has been with you when you were taking part in the Anglican ordinances, I have no wish, and a Catholic has no anxiety, to deny it.

Why should I deny[11] to your memory what is so pleasant in mine? Cannot I too look back on many years past, and

---

[11] *Why should I deny*: On 5 November 1862, Newman wrote a correspondent on this matter of what might appear his inconsistency in his view of the National Church when he was an Anglican and when he was a Catholic: "I have lately said: 'The Thought of the Anglican Service makes me shiver.' [*LD*, xx, 216] But in 1840 I published the following passage in Volume V of my *Parochial Sermons*: 'How great is our privilege etc .... we are full.' ["How great is our privilege, my brethren! —every one of us enjoys the great privilege of daily Worship and weekly

many events, in which I myself experienced what is now your confidence? Can I forget the happy life I have led all my days, with no cares, no anxieties worth remembering; without desolateness, or fever of thought, or gloom of mind, or doubt of God's love to me and providence over me? Can I forget,—I never can forget,—the day when in my youth I first bound myself to the ministry of God in that old church of St. Frideswide, the patroness of Oxford? nor how I wept most abundant, and most sweet tears, when I thought what I then had become; though I looked on ordination as no sacramental rite, nor even to baptism ascribed any supernatural virtue? Can I wipe out from my memory, or

---

Communion. This great privilege God has given to me and to you,—let us enjoy it while we have it. Not any one of us knows how long it may be his own. Perhaps there is no one among us all who can reckon upon it for a continuance. Perhaps, or rather probably, it is a bright spot in our lives. Perhaps we shall look upon these days or years, time hence; and then reflect, when all is over, how pleasant they were; how pleasant to come, day after day, quietly and calmly, to kneel before our Maker,—week after week, to meet our Lord and Saviour. How soothing will then be the remembrance of His past gifts! we shall remember how we got up early in the morning, and how all things, light or darkness, sun or air, cold or freshness, breathed of Him,—of Him, the Lord of glory, who stood over us, and came down upon us, and gave Himself to us, and poured forth milk and honey for our sustenance, though we saw Him not. Surely we have all, and abound: we are full." "Present Blessings" (1839), *P.S.* v, 282-3] I am asked how these two frames of mind and expressions of feeling are consistent with each other. Whether consistent or not, I certainly feel them both at this very time; and I felt them both in 1840—or at least soon after. 1. When at St Mary's, I and others thought the Church Service clumsy and dreary, though our own devotions in Church might be pleasant. 2. And now I look back with the greatest tenderness upon those years, when I was at St Mary's and Littlemore, as a most happy time of my life, though I still feel nevertheless an extreme distaste and dislike of the Order of Morning Prayer and the Communion Service in the Church of England. ... For this purpose, I think it enough to refer to the following passage in my third Lecture on Anglican Difficulties, published in 1850, five years after I became a Catholic. There at pp 68, 69 I write as follows:—'Why should I deny' etc.... So much then generally, by way of suggesting to a candid inquirer, that it is one thing to shiver at the Anglican Service, quite another to take delight in the Devotion of which it was the occasion; and that the one feeling does not interfere with the other." *LD*, xx, 339-40.

wish to wipe out, those happy Sunday mornings, light or dark, year after year, when I celebrated your communion-rite, in my own church of St. Mary's; and in the pleasantness and joy of it heard nothing of the strife of tongues which surrounded its walls? When, too, shall I not feel the soothing recollection of those dear years which I spent in retirement, in preparation for my deliverance from Egypt, asking for light, and by degrees gaining it, with less of temptation in my heart, and sin on my conscience, than ever before? O my dear brethren, my Anglican friends! I easily give you credit for what I have experienced myself. Provided you be in good faith, if you are not trifling with your conscience, if you are resolved to follow whithersoever God shall lead, if the ray of conviction has not fallen on you, and you have shut your eyes to it; then, anxious as I am about you for the future, and dread as I may till you are converted, that perhaps, when conviction comes, it will come in vain; yet still, looking back at the past years of my own life, I recognise what you say, and bear witness to its truth. Yet what has this to do with the matter in hand? I admit your fact; do you, my brethren, admit, in turn, my explanation of it. It is the explanation ready provided by the Catholic Church, provided in her general teaching, quite independently of your particular case, not made for the occasion, only applied when it has arisen;—listen to it, and see whether you admit it or not as true if it be not sufficiently probable, or possible if you will, to invalidate [83] the argument on which you so confidently rely.

[82]

5.

Surely you ought to know the Catholic teaching on the subject of grace, in its bearing on your argument, without my insisting on it:—*Spiritus Domini replevit orbem terrarum.*[12] Grace is given for the merits of Christ all over the earth; there is no corner, even of Paganism, where it is

---

[12] *Spiritus Domini replevit orbem terrarium*: 'The Spirit of the Lord has filled the whole world.' (Wis. 1:7).

not present, present in each heart of man in real sufficiency for his ultimate salvation. Not that the grace presented to each is such as at once to bring him to heaven; but it is sufficient for a beginning. It is sufficient to enable him to plead for other grace; and that second grace is such as to impetrate a third grace; and thus the soul may be led from grace to grace, and from strength to strength, till at length it is, so to say, in very sight of heaven, if the gift of perseverance does but complete the work. Now here observe, it is not certain that a soul which has the first grace will have the second; for the grant of the second at least depends on its use of the first. Again, it may have the first and second, and yet not the third; from the first on to the nineteenth, and not the twentieth. We mount up by steps towards God, and alas! it is possible that a soul may be courageous and bear up for nineteen steps, and stop and faint at the twentieth. Nay, further than this, it is possible to [84] conceive a soul going forward till it arrives at the very grace of contrition—a contrition so loving, so sin-renouncing, as to bring it at once into a state of reconciliation, and clothe it in the vestment of justice; and yet it may yield to the further trials which beset it, and fall away.

Now all this may take place even outside the Church; and consider what at once follows from it. This follows, in the first place, that men there may be, not Catholics, yet really obeying God and rewarded by Him—nay, I might say (at least by way of argument), in His favour, with their sins forgiven, and in the enjoyment of a secret union with that heavenly kingdom to which they do not visibly belong—who are, through their subsequent failure, never to reach it. There may be those who are increasing in grace and knowledge, and approaching nearer to the Catholic Church every year, who are not in the Church, and never will be. The highest gifts and graces are compatible with ultimate reprobation.[13] As regards, then, the evidence of sanctity in

---

[13] *reprobation*: Reprobation in its theological sense means: "Rejection by God; the state of being so rejected or cast off, and thus ordained to eternal misery." *OED*. In Johnson's Dictionary, which Newman would have

members of the National Establishment, on which you insist, Catholics are not called on to deny them. We think such instances are few, nor so eminent as you are accustomed to fancy; but we do not wish to deny, nor have any difficulty in admitting such facts as you have to adduce, whatever they be. We do not think it necessary to carp at every instance of supernatural excellence among Protestants when it comes before us, or to explain it away; all we know is, that the grace given them is intended ultimately to bring [85] them into the Church, and if it is not tending to do so, it will not ultimately profit them; but we as little deny its presence in their souls as they do themselves; and as the fact is no perplexity to us, it is no triumph to them.

And, secondly, in like manner, whatever be the comfort or the strength attendant upon the use of the national ordinances of religion, in the case of this or that person, a Catholic may admit it without scruple, for it is no evidence to him in behalf of those ordinances themselves. It is the teaching of the Catholic Church from time immemorial, and

---

consulted, the word is defined as "The act of abandoning or the state of being abandoned to eternal destruction" and illustrated by one passage from Shakespeare's Othello: "This sight would make him do a desperate turn/Yea curse his better angel from his side/And fall to reprobation" and another from the clergyman and minor poet and dramatist Jasper Mayne (1604-72) whose surname Johnson spells 'Maine:' "God, upon a true repentance, is not so fatally tied to the spindle of absolute reprobation, as not to keep his promise, and seal merciful pardons." Newman's use of this unusual word was not adventitious: he converted, after all, as he told his sister Jemima, because he feared reprobation. Speaking of his decision to leave Littlemore, to leave Oxford, to join a despised and reviled Church, and to leave so many friends and loved ones behind, Newman wrote: "With what conscience could I have remained? how could I have answered it at the last day, if, having opportunities of knowing the Truth which others have not, I had not availed myself of them? What a doom would have been mine, if I had kept the Truth a secret in my own bosom, and when I knew which the One Church was, and which was not part of the One Church, I had suffered friends and strangers to die in an ignorance from which I might have relieved them! impossible. One may not act hastily and unsettle others when one has not a clear view—but when one has, it is impossible not to act upon it." *LD*, xi, 16.

independently of the present controversy, that grace is given in a sacred ordinance in two ways, viz.—to use the scholastic distinction, *ex opere operantis*, and *ex opere operato*.[14] Grace is given *ex opere operato*, when, the proper

---

[14] *distinction*: Since the matter Newman broaches here is complicated – and has an important bearing on the claims made by the Anglo-Catholics for the validity of their party – the lucid and authoritative explication of it in the *Catholic Encyclopedia* is useful. "Against all innovators the Council of Trent declared: 'If anyone say that the sacraments of the New Law do not contain the grace which they signify, or that they do not confer grace on those who place no obstacle to the same, let him be anathema' (Sess. viii, can.vi). 'If anyone say that grace is not conferred by the sacraments *ex opere operato* but that faith in God's promises is alone sufficient for obtaining grace, let him be anathema' (ibid., can. viii; cf. can. iv, v, vii). The phrase *ex opere operato*, for which there is no equivalent in English, probably was used for the first time by Peter of Poitiers (d. 1205), and afterwards by Innocent III (d. 1216; de myst. missae, III, v), and by St. Thomas (d. 1274; IV Sent., dist. 1, Q.i, a.5). It was happily invented to express a truth that had always been taught and had been introduced without objection. It is not an elegant formula but, as St. Augustine remarks (*Enarration on Psalm 138*): It is better that grammarians should object than that the people should not understand. '*Ex opere operato*, i.e. by virtue of the action, means that the efficacy of the action of the sacraments does not depend on anything human, but solely on the will of God as expressed by Christ's institution and promise. *Ex opere operantis*, i.e. by reason of the agent, would mean that the action of the sacraments depended on the worthiness either of the minister or of the recipient (see Pourrat, *Theology of the Sacraments*, tr. St. Louis, 1910, 162 sqq.). Protestants cannot in good faith object to the phrase as if it meant that the mere outward ceremony, apart from God's action, causes grace. It is well known that Catholics teach that the sacraments are only the instrumental, not the principal, causes of grace. Neither can it be claimed that the phrase adopted by the council does away with all dispositions necessary on the part of the recipient, the sacraments acting like infallible charms causing grace in those who are ill-disposed or in grievous sin. The fathers of the council were careful to note that there must be no obstacle to grace on the part of the recipients, who must receive them *rite*, i.e. rightly and worthily; and they declare it a calumny to assert that they require no previous dispositions (Sess. XIV, de poenit., cap.4). Dispositions are required to prepare the subject, but they are a condition (*conditio sine qua non*), not the causes, of the grace conferred. In this case the sacraments differ from the sacramentals, which may cause grace *ex opere operantis*, i.e. by reason of the prayers of the Church or the good, pious sentiments of those who use them."

dispositions being supposed in the recipient, it is given through the ordinance itself; it is given *ex opere operantis*, when, whether there be outward sign or no, the inward energetic act of the recipient is the instrument of it. Thus Protestants say that justification, for instance, is gained by faith as by an instrument—*ex opere operantis*; thus Catholics also commonly believe that the benefit arising from the use of holy water accrues, not *ex opere operato*, or by means of the element itself, but, *ex opere operantis*, through the devout mental act of the person using it, and the prayers of the Church. So again, the Sacrifice of the Mass [86] benefits the person for whom it is offered *ex opere operato*, whatever be the character of the celebrating priest; but it benefits him more or less, *ex opere operantis*, according to the degree of sanctity which the priest has attained, and the earnestness with which he offers it. Again, baptism, whether administered by man or woman, saint or sinner, heretic or Catholic, regenerates an infant *ex opere operato*; on the other hand, in the case of the baptism of blood, as it was anciently called (that is, the martyrdom of unbaptized persons desiring the sacrament, but unable to obtain it), a discussion has arisen, whether the martyr was justified *ex opere operato* or *ex opere operantis*—that is, whether by the physical act of his dying for the faith, considered in itself, or by the mental act of supreme devotion to God, which caused and attended it. So again, contrition of a certain kind is sufficient as a disposition or condition, or what is called matter, for receiving absolution in Penance *ex opere operato* or by virtue of the sacrament; but it may be heightened and purified into so intense an act of divine love, of hatred and sorrow for sin, and of renunciation of it, as to cleanse and justify the soul, without the sacrament at all, or *ex opere operantis*. It is plain from this distinction, that, if we would determine whether the Anglican ordinances are attended by divine grace, we must first determine whether the effects which accompany them arise *ex opere operantis* or *ex opere operato*—whether out of the religious acts, the [87] prayers, aspirations, resolves of the recipient, or by the direct power of the ceremonial act itself,—a nice and difficult question, not to be decided by means of those effects themselves, whatever they be.

Let me grant to you, then, that the reception of your ordinances brings peace and joy to the soul; that it permanently influences or changes the character of the recipient. Let me grant, on the other hand, that their profanation, when men have been taught to believe in them, and in profaning are guilty of contempt of that God to whom they ascribe them, is attended by judgments; this properly shows nothing more than that, by a general law, lying, deceit, presumption, or hypocrisy are punished, and prayer, faith, contrition rewarded. There is nothing to show that the effects would not have been precisely the same on condition of the same inward dispositions, though another ordinance, a love-feast or a washing of the feet, with no pretence to the name of a Sacrament, had been in good faith adopted. And it is obvious to any one that, for a member of the Establishment to bring himself to confession, especially some years back, required dispositions of a very special character, a special contrition and a special desire of the Sacrament, which, as far as we may judge by outward signs, were a special effect of grace, and would fittingly receive from God's bounty a special reward, some further and higher grace, and even, at least I am not bound to deny it, remission of sins. And again, when a member of the Establishment, surrounded by those who scoffed at the doctrine, accepted God's word that He would make Bread His Body, and honoured Him by the fact that he accepted it, is it wonderful, is it not suitable to God's mercy, if He rewards such a special faith with a *quasi* sacramental grace, though the worshipper unintentionally offered to a material substance that adoration which he intended to pay to the present, but invisible, Lamb of God?

[88]

6.

But this is not all, my dear brethren; I must allow to others what I allow to you. If I let you plead the sensible effects of supernatural grace, as exemplified in yourselves, in proof that your religion is true, I must allow the plea to others to whom by your theory you are bound to deny it. Are you willing to place yourselves on the same footing with Wesleyans?[15] yet what is the difference? or rather, have they not more remarkable phenomena in their history, symptomatic of the presence of grace among them, than you can show in yours? Which, then, is the right explanation of your feelings and your experience,—mine, which I have extracted from received Catholic teaching; or yours, which is an expedient for the occasion, and cannot be made to tell for your own Apostolical authority without telling for those who are rebels against it? Survey the rise of Methodism, [89] and say candidly, whether those who made light of your ordinances, abandoned them, or at least disbelieved their virtue, have not had among them evidences of that very same grace which you claim for yourselves, and which you consider a proof of your acceptance with God. Really I am obliged in candour to allow, whatever part the evil spirit had in the work, whatever gross admixture of earth polluted it, whatever extravagance there was to excite ridicule or disgust, whether it was Christian virtue or the excellence of unaided man, whatever was the spiritual state of the subjects of it, whatever their end and their final account, yet there were higher and nobler vestiges or semblances of grace and truth in Methodism than there have been among you. I give

---

[15] *Wesleyans*: Wesleyan: a follower of John Wesley and his Wesleyan Methodism, which the *OED* defines as "The system of Arminian theology introduced and taught by John Wesley." An Arminian is "an adherent of the doctrine of Arminius, Dutch Protestant theologian, who opposed the views of Calvin, especially on predestination." *OED*. More specifically, while Wesley "preached the total depravity of man," he also preached that "he becomes justified by his free will co-operating with the grace of God." As regards the Bible, Wesley was *sola scriptura*, though he did not reject all Tradition, accepting the Trinity, the Incarnation, the Atonement, and the Passion and Resurrection of Our Lord. His insistence on personal holiness – an insistence he shared with Newman – derived from his admiration for *The Imitation of Christ* of Thomas à Kempis. See *A Catholic Dictionary* ed. Attwater (London, 1958), 524.

you credit for what you are, grave, serious, earnest, modest, steady, self-denying, consistent; you have the praise of such virtues; and you have a clear perception of many of the truths, or of portions of the truths, of Revelation. In these points you surpass the Wesleyans; but if I wished to find what was striking, extraordinary, suggestive of Catholic heroism—of St. Martin,[16] St. Francis,[17] or St. Ignatius[18]—I

---

[16] *St. Martin*: Martin, (315-97), Bishop of Tours, was a most effective missionary, whose evangelizing extended from Ireland to Africa and the East. He was also the father of monasticism. One of the first men to be declared a saint who had not been a martyr, he was an inspired preacher and revered wonderworker. For Saint Pope Gregory the Great, Martin epitomized the communion of saints. As P. Brown points out: "In defending... the resurrection of the dead, Gregory brought the distant past into his own age. The souls of those who would be resurrected at the end of time were ... fully active both in the other world and this world ... [T]he past was never past. Long-dead saints were still present and, active at their shrines, they constantly intervened to show their existing power. ... Past, present, and future came together. The power of Christ, first displayed by the miracles in the Gospels, reached directly into the present through the saints in whom He 'dwelt.' This was particularly the case of Gregory's hero, Saint Martin. Martin had been the charismatic bishop of Tours but for Gregory, Martin was far from dead. Up to the present, Christ's mighty hand lay behind the hand of Saint Martin as it reached out from his tomb at Tours to heal the sick." P. Brown: *The Ransom of the Soul: Afterlife and Wealth in Early Western Christianity* (Cambridge, MA, 2015), 161. In invoking the saints throughout *Anglican Difficulties*, Newman calls his readers' attention not only to the Christian understanding of time but the providential presence of the saints in the travails of the living.

[17] *St. Francis*: St. Francis of Assis (c. 1181-1226), Founder of the Friars Minor. The son of a draper, Francis came to the Faith by renouncing his dandyism and embracing 'Lady Poverty,' though he would always retain his delight in the beauty of the created universe. At the Church of St. Damiano, Our Lord exhorted the new convert: "Francis, rebuild my fallen house." In response, Francis founded the Franciscan Order, which remade Christendom by recalling it to renewed penitence and sanctity. In 1224, while praying on Monte La Verna in the Apennines he received the five wounds of the crucified Christ, or *stigmata*, with which, two years later, he would go to his grave. In addition to inspiring those giants, Giotto and Dante, St. Francis coaxed a hagiography out of Chesterton, in which the Fleet Street sage said what will always need saying about this often misunderstood saint: "The first fact to realise about St. Francis is ... that when he said from the first that he was a Troubadour, and said later that

should betake myself far sooner to them than to you. "In our own times," says a writer in a popular Review, speaking of the last-mentioned Saint and his companions, "in our own times much indignation and much alarm are thrown away on innovators of a very different stamp. From the ascetics of [90] the common room, from men whose courage rises high enough only to hint at their unpopular opinions, and whose belligerent passions soar at nothing more daring than to worry some unfortunate professor, it is almost ludicrous to fear any great movement on the theatre of human affairs. When we see these dainty gentlemen in rags, and hear of them from the snows of the Himalaya, we may begin to tremble."[19] Now such a diversion from the course of his

---

he was a Troubadour of a newer and nobler romance, he was not using a mere metaphor, but understood himself much better than the scholars understand him. He was, to the last agonies of asceticism, a Troubadour. He was a Lover. He was a lover of God and he was really and truly a lover of men; possibly a much rarer mystical vocation." G. K. Chesterton, *St. Francis of Assisi* (London, 1924), 20. That Newman should have said that Wesley put one in mind of St. Francis was a generous compliment and shows how generous and, indeed, fair he could be to Evangelicals generally.

[18] *St. Ignatius*: St. Ignatius of Loyola (1491-1556), Founder of the Society of Jesus, whose *Spiritual Exercises* encouraged Newman when he was undergoing the ordeal of conversion. As late as December of 1844, less than a year before his conversion, Newman confided to his dear friend Keble: "No one could have a more unfavourable view than I have of the present state of the Roman Catholics—so much so that any who joined them would be like the Cistercians at Fountains, living under trees till their house was built ..." *LD*, x, 476. Despite these doubts, Newman's Catholic faith was becoming stronger by the day and during the long period in which he feared that his doubts might be the result of sinfulness—a fear Anglicans inclined to Rome were encouraged to feel by an Establishment Church naturally hostile to conversions to Rome— he undertook St. Ignatius's Spiritual Exercises, which, he told Keble, he found of "extreme utility." For Newman, Loyola "and his followers after him, seem to have reduced the business of self-discipline to a science— and since our enemy's warfare upon us proceeds doubtless on system, every one, I suppose, must make a counter system for himself, or take one which experience has warranted." *LD*, ix, 307-8 See also E. Short, *Newman and his Contemporaries* (London, 2011), 104.

[19] *tremble*: This is from Sir James Stephen, "Ignatius Loyola and his Associates," *Edinburgh Review*, LXXV (July 1842), 358, which was

remarks upon St. Ignatius and his companions, I must say, was most uncalled for in this writer,[20] and not a little ill-natured; for we had never pretended to be heroes at all, and should have been the first to laugh at any one who fancied us such; but they will serve to suggest the fact, which is undeniable, that even when Anglicans approach in doctrine nearest to the Catholic Church, still heroism is not the line of their excellence. The Established Church may have preserved in the country the idea of sacramental grace, and the movement of 1833 may have spread it; but if you wish to find the shadow and the suggestion of the supernatural qualities which make up the notion of a Catholic Saint, to Wesley you must go, and such as him. Personally I do not like him, if it were merely for his deep self-reliance and self-conceit; still I am bound, in justice to him, to ask, and you in consistency to answer, what historical personage in

[91] the Establishment, during its whole three centuries, has

---

republished unrevised as "The Founders of Jesuitism" in Sir James Stephen, *Essays in Ecclesiastical Biography,* (London 1849), 187. In a letter of July, !853, Newman wrote Stephen, with whom he had had a pleasant dinner: "I have never forgotten the kind hospitality you showed me at Kensington in January 1836, and am glad of this opportunity of bringing it to your memory." He also enclosed a copy of Lecture III of *Anglican Difficulties* and signed off thanking the evangelical civil servant for saying "flattering" things about him to Mr. Wilberforce. As Charles Dessain points out in a note, at the dinner to which Newman refers Stephen urged his young guest to develop a philosophy of Christianity "to meet the age." *LD*, xv, 394-5.

[20] Sir James Stephen. [N] Sir James Stephen (1789-1859), civil servant at the Colonial Office, whose sons James Fitzjames Stephen and Lesley Stephen became virulent critics of Newman. See the forthcoming E. Short, *Newman and his Critics* (Bloomsbury). Nicknamed 'Mr Mother-Country," Stephen, like Edmund Burke, was convinced that trying to run colonial affairs strictly from London would only "terminate in defeat;" the imperial government was best advised to delegate to local governors. Although an inveterate writer of *memoranda*—being too shy to confront his staff face-to-face—Stephen had, again like Burke, "no very exalted opinion of the virtue of paper government," a trait which doubtless disinclined him to approve the paper religion of the Anglo-Catholics. An impassioned Evangelical, for all of his delight in irony, Stephen had difficulty passing on his Christian faith to his obdurately rationalist sons. *ODNB*.

approximated in force and splendour of conduct and achievements to one who began by innovating on your rules, and ended by contemning your authorities? He and his companions, starting amid ridicule at Oxford, with fasting and praying in the cold night air, then going about preaching, reviled by the rich and educated, and pelted and dragged to prison by the populace, and converting their thousands from sin to God's service—were it not for their pride and eccentricity, their fanatical doctrine and untranquil devotion, they would startle us, as if the times of St. Vincent Ferrer[21] or St. Francis Xavier[22] were come again in a Protestant land.

Or, to turn to other communions, whom have you with those capabilities of greatness in them, which show themselves in the benevolent zeal of Howard the philanthropist,[23] or Elizabeth Fry?[24] Or consider the almost

---

[21] *Ferrer*: St. Vincent Ferrer (c. 1350-1419), Missionary. Born in Valencia, his father was an Englishman and his mother Spanish. Vincent joined the Dominican Friars in 1367 and later taught philosophy in the Dominican House of Studies before becoming an influential preacher, especially amongst the Jews and Moors of Spain During the Avignon schism, he supported the Avignon claimant to the papacy, Peter de Luna (Benedict XIII), whose counsellor and confessor he became, though he would later repudiate Benedict for failing to end the schism, especially after the Council of Constance (1414-18) recommended that he resign. Vincent's missionary field primarily comprised France and Spain, where he attracted large numbers of penitents, who, moved by his faithful witness, followed him from place to place. The itinerant quality of St. Vincent's apostolate certainly recalls the equestrian evangelist in Wesley.

[22] *Xavier*: St. Francis Xavier (1506-52), Missionary. Born in the Spanish kingdom of Navarre, St. Francis Xavier, like St. Ignatius, spoke Basque. A disciple of Ignatius, he dedicated himself to converting the Mussulmen, Brahmins and Buddhists of India, as well as the people of the East Indies, Malacca, the Moluccas, and Japan. An exuberantly faithful man, he dedicated himself to prayer and to caring for the sick and poor. Like St. Francis Assisi and Newman's patron saint, St. Philip Neri, St Francis Xavier spread joy wherever he went. After his death, Pope Gregory XV canonized him with St. Ignatius on March 12th, 1662.

[23] *Howard*: John Howard (1726-90) philanthropist and early English prison reformer.

miraculous conversion and subsequent life of Colonel
Gardiner.[25] Why, even old Bunyan,[26] with his vivid dreams
when a child, his conversion, his conflicts with Satan, his
preachings and imprisonments, however inferior to you in
discipline of mind and knowledge of the truth, is, in the
outline of his history, more Apostolical than you. "Weep
not for me," were his last words, as if he had been a Saint,
"but for yourselves. I go to the Father of our Lord Jesus
Christ, who doubtless, through the mediation of His Son,
will receive me, though a sinner, when we shall erelong
[92] meet, to sing the new song and be happy for ever!"[27]
Consider the deathbeds of the thousands of those, in and out
of the Establishment, who, with scarcely one ecclesiastical
sentiment in common with you, die in confidence of the
truth of their doctrine, and of their personal safety. Does the
peace of their deaths testify to the divinity of their creed or

---

[24] *Fry*: Elizabeth Fry (1780-1845), English Quaker and prison reformer,
whose disapproval of teetotalism endeared her to the bibulous
misfortunates she served.

[25] *Gardiner*: Given over to what his biographer styled "criminal
sensualities," Colonel James Gardiner was apparently miraculously cured
of his besetting sin after converting to Christianity. P. Doddridge, *Life of
James Gardiner* (London, 1813), 60.

[26] *old Bunyan*: John Bunyan (1628-88), English preacher and writer. The
son of a tinker, Bunyan was a prolific author, whose works include *The
Holy City* (1665), *The Resurrection of the Dead* (1665) and *Grace
Abounding* (1666). His most famous and popular work, *The Pilgrim's
Progress* (1678) won unusually high praise from no less a critic than
Samuel Johnson. As Bowell attests: "Johnson praised John Bunyan
highly. 'His Pilgrim's Progress has great merit, both for invention,
imagination, and the conduct of the story; and it has had the best evidence
of its merit, the general and continued approbation of mankind. Few
books, I believe, have had a more extensive sale. It is remarkable that it
begins very much like the poem of Dante; yet there was no translation of
Dante when Bunyan wrote. There is reason to think that he had read
Spenser.'" Boswell, *Life of Johnson*, ii, 238. Converted by his wife,
Bunyan took to preaching in Bedford out of deep conviction. Although
his nonconformism landed him in jail for a good portion of his life, the
county jail gave him a considerable amount of leisure, without which he
might never have become so productive an author.

[27] Bunyan quoted in Robert Philip, *The Life, Times and Characteristics of
John Bunyan* (London, 1839), 476.

of their communion? Does the extreme earnestness and reality of religious feeling, exhibited in the sudden seizure and death of one who was as stern in his hatred of your opinions as admirable in his earnestness, who one evening protested against the sacramental principle, and next morning died nobly with the words of Holy Scripture in his mouth—does it give any sanction to that hatred and that protest?[28] And there is another, a Calvinist, one of whose special and continual prayers in his last illness was for perseverance in grace, who cried, "O Lord, abhor me not, though I be abhorrible, and abhor myself!" and who, five minutes before his death, by the expression of his countenance, changing from prayer to admiration and calm peace, impressed upon the bystanders that the veil had been removed from his eyes, and that, like Stephen, he saw things invisible to sense;—did he, by the circumstances of his death-bed, bear evidence to the truth of what you, as well as I, hold to be an odious heresy?[29] "Mr. Harvey resigned his meek soul into the hands of his Redeemer, saying, 'Lord, now lettest Thou Thy servant depart in [93] peace.'"[30] "Mr. Walker, before he expired, spoke nearly

[28] Dr. Arnold. [N] See previous note page 31.

[29] Mr. Scott of Ashton Sandford. [N] *The Life of the Reverend Thomas Scott, Rector of Aston Sandford* (London, 1834), 581. That Newman chose to list Scott's last words in this deathbed catalogue shows the extent to which he was personally invested in *Anglican Difficulties*. Thomas Scott (1747-1821), a convert from Unitarianism to Calvinism and Biblical commentator, had an influence on the young Newman that held him in good stead for the rest of his life. In the *Apologia* he praises him as someone "to whom (humanly speaking) I almost owe my soul" and confesses that for years "I used almost as proverbs what I considered to be the scope and issue of his doctrine, 'Holiness rather than peace,' and 'Growth the only evidence of life.'" *Apo*, 18. If this man could go to his grave imagining the "odious heresy" of Calvinism pleasing to God, what confidence could the Anglo-Catholic party have that they would not be equally deluded in going to theirs professing Anglo-Catholicism?

[30] *depart in peace*: Luke 2:29. Edwin Sidney, *Life of Sir. Richard Hill, Bart.* (London, 1839), 519. The Rev. James Hervey, (1714-58), Rector of Weston Favel in Northamptonshire was an Evangelical clergyman, preacher, and poet. In 1733 he joined the Oxford Methodists and came under the influence of John Wesley, though he was against Wesley

these words: 'I have been on the wings of the cherubim; heaven has in a manner been opened to me; I shall be there soon.'"[31] "Mr. Whitfield rose at four o'clock on the Sabbath day, went to his closet, and was unusually long in private; laid himself on his bed for about ten minutes, then went on his knees and prayed most fervently he might that day finish his Master's work." Then he sent for a clergyman, "and before he could reach him, closed his eyes on this world without a sigh or groan, and commenced a Sabbath of everlasting rest."[32] Alas! there was another, who for three months "lingered," as he said, "in the face of death." "O my God," he cried, "I know Thou dost not overlook any of Thy creatures. Thou dost not overlook me. So much torture ... to kill a worm! have mercy on me! I cry to Thee, knowing I cannot alter Thy ways. I cannot if I would, and I would not if I could. If a word would remove these sufferings, I would not utter it." "Just life enough to suffer," he continued; "but I submit, and not only submit, but rejoice." One morning he woke up, "and with firm voice and great sobriety of manner, spoke only these words: 'Now I die!' He sat as one in the

---

separating from the Anglican Church. At Lincoln College, he was a member of the Holy Club, which met to deepen their religious life with readings from devotional books and the Greek New Testament. By 1800, his *Meditations Among the Tombs: Tending to Reform the Vices of The Age, And to Promote Evangelical Holiness* (1746) had gone into no less than 26 editions. Since he gave what he made from his books to the poor, his eleemosynary giving was not negligible: The *Meditations* alone brought in £700. An influence on Horace Walpole's *The Castle of Otranto* (1764), he helped usher in the Gothic mode. He was also admired by the poet Blake. See V. H. H. Green, "Religion in the Colleges 1715-1800," *The History of the University of Oxford* eds. Sutherland and Mitchell (Oxford, 1986), v., 447-8, 452, 454. See also *ODNB*.
[31] *I shall be there soon*: Sidney, 520. The Rev. Samuel Walker of Truro (1714-61), was an Evangelical Church of England clergyman and associate of John Wesley.
[32] Sidney's Life of Hill. [N] *Ibid*, 522. George Whitefield (1714-70) Methodist evangelist. A fiery preacher, Whitefield conducted large open-air Methodist meetings around the country where he made many conversions to his Calvinist faith. With Selina, Countess of Huntingdon, he opened a Tabernacle in Tottenham Court Road, London and made several visits to America.

attitude of expectation; and about two hours afterwards, it was as he had said." And he was a professed infidel, and worse than an infidel—an apostate priest![33]

No, my dear brethren, these things are beyond us. Nature can do so much, and go so far; can form such rational notions of God and of duty, without grace, or merit, or a future hope; good sense has such an instinctive apprehension of what is fitting; intellect, imagination, and feeling can so take up, develop, and illuminate what nature has originated; education and intercourse with others can so insinuate into the mind what really does not belong to it; grace, not effectual, but inchoate, can so plead, and its pleadings look so like its fruits; and its mere visitations may so easily be mistaken for its indwelling presence, and its vestiges, when it has departed, may gleam so beautifully on the dead soul, that it is quite impossible for us to conclude, with any fairness of argument, that a certain opinion is true, or a religious position safe, simply on account of the confidence or apparent excellence of those who adopt it. Of course, we think as tenderly of them as we can; and may

---

[33] *an apostate priest!*: Here is another poignantly autobiographical addition to Newman's catalogue, for these piteous words were uttered by J. B. White (1775-1841), the writer and Noetic, whom Newman befriended when he was at Oriel. *The Life of the Rev. Joseph Blanco White: Written by Himself* ed. J.H. Thom (London, 1845), iii, 302-3, 310. Born in Seville, the son of an Irish Catholic father and Spanish noblewoman, White left the Catholic priesthood for Anglicanism and then Anglicanism for Unitarianism. Coleridge, perhaps after a night of too much opium, thought White's poem, "Night and Death" (1825) the "finest and most grandly conceived sonnet" in the language. By all accounts a lovable and gifted man, White intrigued Newman not only because of his brush with continental Catholicism but his ability to enter into his love of music, particularly Beethoven's sonatas. Blanco, like Newman, was a fiddler, with a fine, discerning ear. When Newman learned that his old friend had abandoned the Christian faith for Unitarianism, he was dismayed, and White, for his part, was convinced that Newman's conversion was misguided. See M. Murphy's life, *Blanco White: Self-Banished Spaniard* (New Haven, 1989), as well as his entry on White in the *ODNB*.

fairly hope that what we see is, in particular instances, the work of grace, wrought in those who are not responsible for their ignorance; but the claim in their behalf is unreasonable and exorbitant, if it is to the effect that their state of mind is to be taken in evidence, not only of promise in the individual, but of truth in his creed.

[95]   And should this view of the subject unsettle and depress you, as if it left you no means at all of ascertaining whether God loves you, or whether anything is true, or anything to be trusted, then let this feeling answer the purpose for which I have impressed it on you. I wish to deprive you of your undue confidence in self; I wish to dislodge you from that centre in which you sit so self-possessed and self-satisfied. Your fault has been to be satisfied with but a half evidence of your safety; you have been too well contented with remaining where you found yourselves, not to catch at a line of argument, so indulgent, yet so plausible. You have thought that position impregnable; and growing confident, as time went on, you have not only said it was a sin to ascribe your good thoughts, and purposes, and aspirations to any but God (which you were right in saying), but you have presumed to pronounce it blasphemy against the Holy Ghost to doubt that they came into your hearts by means of your Church and by virtue of its ordinances. Learn, my dear brethren, a more sober, a more cautious tone of thought. Learn to fear for your souls. It is something, indeed, to be peaceful within, but it is not everything. It may be the stillness of death. The Catholic, and he alone, has within him that union of external with internal notes of God's favour, which sheds the light of conviction over his soul, and makes him both fearless in his faith and calm and thankful in his hope.

LECTURE IV

THE PROVIDENTIAL COURSE OF THE MOVEMENT OF 1833 NOT IN THE DIRECTION OF THE NATIONAL CHURCH

1.

IT is scarcely possible to fancy that an event so distinctive in its character as the rise of the so-called Anglo-Catholic party in the course of the last twenty years, should have no scope in the designs of Divine Providence. From beginnings so small, from elements of thought so fortuitous, with prospects so unpromising, that in its germ it was looked upon with contempt, if it was ever thought of at all, it suddenly became a power in the National Church, and an object of alarm to her rulers and friends. Its originators would have found it difficult to say what they aimed at of a practical kind; rather they put forth views and principles for their own sake, because they were true, as if they were obliged to say them; and though their object certainly was to strengthen the establishment, yet it would have been very difficult for them to state precisely the intermediate process, or definite application, by which, in matter of fact, their [97] preaching was to arrive at that result. And, as they might be themselves surprised at their earnestness in proclaiming, they had as great cause to be surprised at their success in propagating, the doctrines which have characterised their school. And, in fact, they had nothing else to say but that those doctrines were in the air; that to assert was to prove, and that to explain was to persuade; and that the movement in which they were taking part, was the birth of a crisis rather than of a place. I do not mean to say, that they did not use arguments on the one hand, nor attempt to associate themselves with things as they were on the other; but that, after all, their doctrine went forth rather than was delivered, and spoke rather than was spoken; that it was a message rather than an argument; that it was the master, not the creature of its proclaimers, and seemed to be said at random, because uttered with so indistinct an aim; and so, with no advantage except that of position, which of course is not to be undervalued, it spread and was taken up no one knew how. In a very few years a school of opinion was formed, fixed in its principles, indefinite and progressive in their range; and it extended into every part of the country. If, turning from the contemplation of it from within, we inquire what the world thought of it, we have still more to raise our wonder; for not to mention the excitement it [98] caused in England, the movement and its party-names were known to the police of Italy and the back-woodsmen of America. So it proceeded, getting stronger and stronger every year, till it has come into collision with the Nation, and that Church of the Nation, which it began by professing especially to serve; and now its upholders and disciples have to look about, and ask themselves where they are, and which way they are to go, and whither they are bound.

Providence does nothing in vain; so much earnestness, zeal, toil, thought, religiousness, success, as has a place in the history of that movement, must surely have a place also in His scheme, and in His dealings towards His Church in this country, if we could discern what that place was. He has excited aspirations, matured good thoughts, and prospered pious undertakings arising out of them: not for nothing surely[1]—then for what? Wherefore?

---

[1] *not for nothing*: Cf. "God has created me to do Him some definite service; He has committed some work to me which He has not committed to another. I have my mission—I never may know it in this life, but I shall be told it in the next. Somehow I am necessary for His purposes, as necessary in my place as an Archangel in his—if, indeed, I fail, He can raise another, as He could make the stones children of Abraham. Yet I have a part in this great work; I am a link in a chain, a bond of connexion between persons. He has not created me for naught. I shall do good, I shall do His work; I shall be an angel of peace, a preacher of truth in my own place, while not intending it, if I do but keep His commandments and serve Him in my calling. Therefore I will trust Him. Whatever, wherever I am, I can never be thrown away. If I am in sickness, my

The movement certainly is one and the same to all who have been influenced by it; the principles and circumstances, which have made them what they are, are one and the same; the history of one of you, my brethren, is pretty much the history of another—the history of all. Is it meant that you should each of you end in his own way, if your beginnings have been the same? The duty of one of you, is it not the duty of another? Are you not to act together? In other words, may I not look at the movement as integrally one, and thus investigate what is its bearing and its legitimate issue? and may not, in consequence, that [99] direction and scope of the movement, if such can be ascertained, be taken as a suggestion to you how you should act, distinct from, and in addition to, the intimations of God's will, which come home to you personally and individually? The movement has affected us in a certain way: at one time we have felt urged perhaps, with some of those who took part in it, to go forward; at another, to remain where we are; then to retire into lay-communion, if we were in the Established ministry; then to collapse into a sect external to its pale. We have tried to have faith in the sacraments of the National Church; for a time we have succeeded, and then we have failed; we have felt ourselves drawn, we have felt ourselves repelled by the Catholic Church;—we have felt difficulties in her faith, counter-difficulties in rejecting it, complications of difficulty on difficulty, concurrent or antagonist, till we could ascertain neither their mutual relation nor their combined issue, and could neither change nor remain where we were without scruple.

---

sickness may serve Him; in perplexity, my perplexity may serve Him; if I am in sorrow, my sorrow may serve Him. My sickness, or perplexity, or sorrow may be necessary causes of some great end, which is quite beyond us. He does nothing in vain; He may prolong my life, He may shorten it; He knows what He is about. He may take away my friends, He may throw me among strangers, He may make me feel desolate, make my spirits sink, hide the future from me—still He knows what He is about." *MD*, 301-2. Here is a good example of how the prose stylist in Newman delighted in the idiomatic genius of the language.

Under such a trial it would be some guidance, a sort of token or note of the course destined for us by Providence, if the movement itself, whose principles we have drunk in, with which we are so intimately one, had, from the nature of the case, its own natural and necessary termination. Before now, when a Protestant, I have said more or less to others [100] who were in anxiety, "Watch the movement; it is made up of individuals, but it has an objective being, proceeds on principles, is governed by laws, and is swayed and directed by external facts. We are apt to be attracted or driven this way or that; each thinks for himself and judges differently from others; each fears to decide; but may we not ascertain and follow the legitimate and divinely intended course of that, whose children we are?" A great Saint was accustomed to command his sons, when they had to determine some point relatively to themselves and their Society, to throw themselves in imagination out of themselves, and to look at the question externally, as if it were not personal to them, and they were deciding for a stranger. In like manner it has been sometimes recommended in the solution of public questions, to look at them as they will show in history, and as they will be judged of by posterity. Now in some such way should I wish, at this moment, to regard the movement of 1833, and to discover what is its proper, suitable, legitimate termination. This, then, is the question I shall consider in the present Lecture;—here is a great existing fact before our eyes—the movement and its party. What is to become of it? What ought to become of it? Is it to melt away as if it had not been? Is it merely to subserve the purposes of Liberalism, in breaking up establishments by weakening them, and in making dogma ridiculous by [101] multiplying sects? or is it of too positive a character, both in its principles and its members, to anticipate for it so disappointing an issue.

2.

I say, it has been definite in its principles, though vague in their application and their scope. It has been formed on one idea, which has developed into a body of teaching, logical in the arrangement of its portions, and consistent with the principles on which it originally started. That idea, or first principle, was ecclesiastical liberty; the doctrine which it especially opposed was in ecclesiastical language, the heresy of Erastus, and in political, the Royal Supremacy.[2] The object of its attack was the Establishment, considered simply as such.

When I thus represent the idea of the movement of which I am speaking, I must not be supposed to overlook or deny to it its theological, or its ritual, or its practical aspect;

---

[2] *the Royal Supremacy*: Act of Supremacy, 1534 (26 Hen. VIII c.1), made King Henry VIII Supreme Head of the Church of England. The act was repealed during the reign of Mary I in 1554-5 but reasserted during the reign of Elizabeth I, who styled herself 'Supreme Governor' of the Church. "[C]ommissioners," writes David Knowles in his magisterial history, "toured the country in the second half of 1534 demanding adherence on oath from members of chapters, monastic communities, colleges and hospitals to a series of assertions and undertakings, of which the first was the acceptance in perpetuity of the king as Supreme Head of the Church and the second a declaration that the bishop of Rome, who had usurped the title of pope, had no more scriptural warranty for exercising any jurisdiction over England than any other foreign bishop. ... Something over one hundred certificates of this oath-taking by religious houses are preserved, and there can be little doubt that the absence of the remainder is purely accidental. No doubt many acted against the grain, and as a concession to present evils, and hoped for the day when England would once more acknowledge the pope. It is not for the historian to say how many or how few were thus disposed. It is, however, within his province to record the facts. In the words of More's apologue, they were first deflowered that they might afterwards be devoured. It was not a question of conciliarist or Gallican opinion. By this action of compliance, which was not taken blindly or on a sudden impulse of fear, the monks did in fact admit a lay ruler to supreme power in spiritual matters and thus cut themselves off from the Roman Catholic Church of which the pope was head, and when we have no evidence of any expression of remorse or any word of recantation we have no grounds for supposing that they returned to the fold." David Knowles, *The Religious Orders in England* 2nd ed. (Cambridge, 1971) iii, 178-9. All of Newman's insistence on the inescapably Erastian character of the Church of England is here confirmed. Knowles' account of the significance of the Royal Supremacy should also be borne in mind when considering the Anglo-Catholic claim that the Church of England is somehow a 'branch' of the Roman Catholic Church.

but I am speaking of what may be called its *form*. If I said that the one doctrine of Luther was justification by faith only,[3] or of Wesley the doctrine of the new birth,[4] I should not be denying that those divines respectively taught many other doctrines, but merely should mean that the one doctrine or the other gave a shape and character to its teaching. In like manner, the writers of the Apostolical party of 1833 were earnest and copious in their enforcement of the high doctrines of the faith, of dogmatism, of the sacramental principle, of the sacraments (as far as the [102] Anglican Prayer Book admitted them), of ceremonial observances, of practical duties, and of the counsels of perfection; but, considering all those great articles of teaching to be protected and guaranteed by the independence of the Church, and in that way alone, they viewed sanctity, and sacramental grace, and dogmatic fidelity, merely as subordinate to the mystical body of

---

[3] *one doctrine of Luther*: "Justification: (*Theol.*) The action whereby man is justified, or freed from the penalty of sin, and accounted or made righteous by God; the fact or condition of being so justified. Protestant theologians regard justification as an act of grace in which God accounts man righteous, not owing to any merit of his own, but through imputation of Christ's righteousness, as apprehended and received by faith Roman Catholic theologians hold that it consists in man's being made really righteous by infusion of grace, such justification being a work continuous and progressive from its initiation." *OED*

[4] *new birth*: According to J. Wesley: "If any doctrines within the whole compass of Christianity may be properly termed fundamental, they are doubtless these two, — the doctrine of justification, and that of the new birth: The former relating to that great work which God does for us, in forgiving our sins; the latter, to the great work which God does in us, in renewing our fallen nature." Wesley based his doctrine of the new birth on John's Gospel: "Ye must be born again." John 3.7. "Be you baptized or unbaptized, 'you must be born again;' otherwise it is not possible you should be inwardly holy; and without inward as well as outward holiness, you cannot be happy, even in this world, much less in the world to come. Do you say, 'Nay, but I do no harm to any man; I am honest and just in all my dealings; I do not curse, or take the Lord's name in vain; I do not profane the Lord's day; I am no drunkard; I do not slander my neighbour, nor live in any wilful sin.' If this be so, it were much to be wished that all men went as far as you do. But you must go farther yet, or you cannot be saved: Still, 'you must be born again.'" J. Wesley, Sermon 45.

Christ, and made them minister to her sovereignty, that she might in turn protect them in their prerogatives. Dogma would be maintained, sacraments would be administered, religious perfection would be venerated and attempted, if the Church were supreme in her spiritual power; dogma would be sacrificed to expedience, sacraments would be rationalized, perfection would be ridiculed if she was made the slave of the State. Erastianism, then, was the one heresy which practically cut at the root of all revealed truth; the man who held it would soon fraternise with Unitarians,[5] mistake the bustle of life for religious obedience, and pronounce his butler to be as able to give communion as his priest. It destroyed the supernatural altogether, by making most emphatically Christ's kingdom a kingdom of the world. Such was the teaching of the movement of 1833. The whole system of revealed truth was, according to it, to be carried out upon the anti-Erastian or Apostolical basis. The independence of the Church is almost the one subject of three out of four volumes of Mr. Froude's Remains;[6] it is, in one shape or other, the prevailing subject of the early [103]

---

[5] *Unitarians*: In the *OED*, 'Unitarian' is defined as "one who affirms the unipersonality of the Godhead, especially as opposed to an orthodox Trinitarian." In other words, Unitarians deny the divinity of Christ: they are Socinians. Murray cites the *Church Quarterly Review* (1889) to illustrate the word's meaning: "We may roughly state three conceptions [of Christianity] as (1) the Unitarian, which conceives of Christ as an exalted human teacher merely, (2) the Protestant ... 3) the Catholic."

[6] *Froude's Remains*: "Calvinism, such as it existed in the 16th century, amidst all its errors had two truths. Though its Articles of Faith were erroneous, yet it asserted that a true faith was necessary to salvation: and though its discipline was a human invention, yet it asserted that Church authority was from God. Against these two truths of Calvinism were forged the doctrines of Arminius and Erastus; the former asserting that mere opinions were matters of indifference, the latter that the Church was a mere creature of the State. It is a remarkable fact, that from the restoration of Charles II. to the present day, Calvinism, Erastianism, and Arminianism, have, like Herod and Pontius Pilate, been made friends together to carry on a joint war against Apostolical Christianity." Froude, *Remains*, i, 394.

numbers of the "Tracts for the Times,"[7] as well as of other publications which might be named. It was for this that the writers of whom I speak had recourse to Antiquity, insisted upon the Apostolical Succession, exalted the Episcopate, and appealed to the people, not only because these things were true and right, but in order to shake off the State; they introduced them, in the first instance, as means towards the inculcation of the idea of the Church, as constituent portions of that great idea, which, when it once should be received, was a match for the world.

"Our one tangible object," it was said, in a passage too long to be extracted at length, "is to restore the connection, at present broken, between Bishops and people; for in this everything is involved, directly or indirectly, for which it is a duty to contend … We wish to maintain the faith, and bind men together in love. We are aiming, with this view, at that commanding moral influence which attended the early Church, which made it attractive and persuasive, which manifested itself in a fascination sufficient to elicit out of Paganism and draw into itself all that was noblest and best from the mass of mankind, and which created an internal system of such grace, beauty, and majesty, that believers were moulded thereby into martyrs and evangelists … If master-minds are ever granted to us, they must be [104] persevering in insisting on the Episcopal system, the Apostolical Succession, the ministerial commission, the power of the keys, the duty and desirableness of Church discipline, the sacredness of Church rites and ordinances. But, you will say, how is all this to be made interesting to the people? I answer, that the topics themselves which they are to preach are of that attractive nature, which carries with it its own influence. The very notion that representatives of the Apostles are now on earth, from whose communion we may obtain grace, as the first Christians did from the Apostles, is surely, when admitted, of a most transporting

---

[7] *Tracts*: See J.H. Newman, *Tracts for the Times* ed. J. Tolhurst (Leominster, 2013).

and persuasive character. Clergymen are at present subject to the painful experience of losing the more religious portion of their flocks, whom they have tutored and moulded as children, but who, as they come into life, fall away to the Dissenters. Why is this? They desire to be stricter than the mass of Churchmen, and the Church gives them no means; they desire to be governed by sanctions more constraining than those of mere argument, and the Church keeps back those doctrines, which, to the eye of faith, give reality and substance to religion. One who is told that the Church is the treasure-house of spiritual gifts, comes for a definite privilege ... Men know not of the legitimate priesthood, and, therefore, are condemned to hang upon the judgment of individuals and self-authorised preachers; they put up with legends of private Christians, in the place of the men of God, the meek martyrs, the saintly [105] pastors, the wise and winning teachers of the Catholic Church."[8]

3.

Passages such as this, which is but a portion of a whole, show to me, my brethren, clearly enough, that these men understood the nature of the Church far better than they understood the nature of the religious communion which they sought to defend. They saw in that religion, indeed, a contrariety to their Apostolic principles, but they seem to have fancied that such contrariety was an accident in its constitution, and was capable of a cure. They did not understand that the Established Religion[9] was set up in

---

[8] British Magazine, April 1836—[Discussions and Arguments, pp. 34-38.] [N] John Henry Newman, "How To Accomplish It" (1836), *Discussions and Arguments* (London, 1872), 34-39. *Apropos* the dialogue, Newman's prefatory note explains: "[The discussion in this Paper is carried on by two speculative Anglicans, who aim at giving vitality to their Church, the one by uniting it to the Roman See, the other by developing a nineteenth-century Anglo-Catholicism. The narrator sides on the whole with the latter of these.]" *Ibid*, 1.

[9] We must not forget, however, Mr. Froude's upas-tree. [N] "Would that the waters would throw up some Acheloides, where some new Bishop

Erastianism, that Erastianism was its essence, and that to destroy Erastianism was to destroy the religion. The movement, then, and the Establishment, were in simple antagonism from the first, although neither party knew it; they were logical contradictories; they could not be true together; what was the life of the one was the death of the other. The sole ambition of the Establishment was to be the creature of Statesmen; the sole aspiration of the movement was to force it to act for itself. The movement went forth on the face of the country; it read, it preached, it published; it [106] addressed itself to logic and to poetry; it was antiquary and architect; only to do for the Establishment what the Establishment considered the most intolerable of disservices. Every breath, every sigh, every aspiration, every effort of the movement was an affront or an offence to the Establishment. In its very first tract, it could wish nothing better for the Bishops of the Establishment than martyrdom; and, as the very easiest escape, it augured for them the loss of their temporal possessions. It was easy to foresee what response the Establishment would make to its officious defenders, as soon as it could recover from its surprise; but experience was necessary to teach this to men who knew more of St. Athanasius than of the Privy Council or the Court of Arches.[10]

---

might erect a see beyond the blighting influence of our upas tree." *Remains*, i, 405.

[10] *Privy Council or the Court of Arches*: It was in the Court of Arches that the Gorham case was heard and it was the Privy Council that ruled upon it. "The Court of Arches, so called from the fact that it was anciently held in the Church of St. Mary le Bow (Sancta Maria de Arcubus), in Cheapside, was the chief and most ancient court and consistory of the jurisdiction of the Archbishop of Canterbury. Originally the judge of this court, the official Principal of the Arches, took cognizance of causes throughout the ecclesiastical province, and by his patent was invested with the right of hearing appeals from the Dean of the Arches. This latter exercised jurisdiction over a 'peculiar,' consisting of thirteen parishes including St. Mary le Bow, within the diocese, but exempt from the jurisdiction of the Bishop of London. ... Suits are conducted by means of citation, production of libel (accusation), answer to libel, arguments of advocates, and the judge's decree. This court

"Why should any man in Britain," asks a Tract, "fear or hesitate boldly to assert the authority of the Bishops and pastors of the Church on grounds strictly evangelical and spiritual?" "Reverend Sir," answered the Primate to a protest against a Bishop-elect, accused of heresy, "it is not within the bounds of any authority possessed by me to give you an opportunity of proving your objections; finding, therefore, nothing in which I could act in compliance with your remonstrance, I proceeded, in the execution of my office, to obey Her Majesty's mandate for Dr. Hampden's consecration in the usual form."

"Are we contented," asks another Tract, "to be accounted the mere creation of the State, as school-masters [107] and teachers may be, as soldiers, or magistrates, or other public officers? Did the State make us? Can it unmake us? Can it send out missionaries? Can it arrange dioceses?" "William the Fourth," answers the first magistrate of the State, "by the grace of God, of the united kingdom of Great Britain, and Ireland, King, Defender of the Faith, to all to whom these presents shall come, greeting: We, having great confidence in the learning, morals, and probity of our well-beloved and venerable William Grant Broughton,[11] do name

---

exercises appellate jurisdiction from each of the diocesan courts within the province of Canterbury. It may also take original cognizance of causes by letters of Request from such courts. It latterly sat in the hall belonging to the College of Civilians (Doctors' Commons) until the ecclesiastical courts were thrown open to the bar and to solicitors generally, and all probate and divorce business taken away (1857), since when it sits at Lambeth or Westminster." *Catholic Encyclopedia.*

[11] *William Grant Broughton*: W.G. Broughton (1788-1853), Church of England colonial bishop. Educated at The King's School, Canterbury, he was a King's scholar from 1798. Through the influence of his paternal uncles and the Cecil family he gained a clerkship in the Treasury department of the East India Co.; then in 1814 a legacy enabled him to go to Cambridge where he was a scholar of Pembroke Hall. In 1818 he was ordained deacon and, later, priest. In 1835 he was nominated to the new see of Australia. At first he had been reluctant to accept. opposed as he was to the religious and educational policy of the Anglican Church in Australia; he particularly feared that in an episcopal capacity he would be required 'to act in concert with Sir Richard Bourke [the Irish Anglican Governor, 1831-7] in giving public support to three separate forms of

and appoint him to be Bishop and ordinary pastor of the see
of Australia, so that he shall be, and shall be taken to be,
Bishop of the Bishop's see, and may, by virtue of this our
nomination and appointment, enter into and possess the said
Bishop's see as the Bishop thereof, without any let or
impediment of us; and we do hereby declare, that if we, our
heirs and successors, shall think fit to recall or revoke the

religion [i.e., the English, Scottish and Roman Catholic], and possibly
also to every congregation of dissenters and Jews upon the same
principle.' The Colonial Office disavowed an 'intention to impose any
condition upon your acceptance of the bishopric, or to fetter the free
exercise of your judgment ... either in your episcopal or legislative
capacity.' Broughton's doubts were resolved and he was consecrated
bishop of Australia on 14 February 1836 in Lambeth Palace chapel by
Archbishop Howley. Broughton arrived back in Sydney in the *Camden*
on 2 June and was enthroned in St James's Church three days later.
According to the *Dictionary of Australian Biography*, from which the
preceding has been gratefully plucked: "In 1835 Broughton first met the
work of the Tractarians. Until the publication of Tract 90 he was their
consistent supporter and after 1840 he remained an admirer of Pusey and
Keble. Broughton came of an older school of High Churchmen and was
never a Tractarian, but the movement helped him to solve, to his own
satisfaction, some of the problems that he met after the passing of the
Church Act. Its emphasis upon the historical continuity of the national
church and the apostolic succession of its bishops strengthened his
resistance to the growth of the Roman Catholic Church. In 1843
Broughton protested formally against the creation of the Roman Catholic
archdiocese of Sydney ... and in 1850 against the elevation of Dr
Wiseman to the new archbishopric of Westminster. In his controversy
with Wiseman, Broughton tried to define royal supremacy and to deny
that it involved the subordination of the church to the secular state. But he
had always expressed reservations about the degree of practical control
exercised by the government over the chaplains and the clash of
jurisdictions that this might, and in Van Diemen's Land did, involve."
See Newman's comment regarding the authority of colonial bishops to S.
Wilberforce in May of 1837: "Is there any precedent in the English
Church of a Bishop being sent among the heathen? Could not the
difficulty be met by getting Daniel Wilson and his Colleagues to
consecrate; if the consent of the Calcutta etc Government was requisite, I
suppose they might gain it. But one should like to try the power of at least
Colonial Bishops to do without the State. Is Calcutta a Metropolitan See,
or under Canterbury? if the former, it is free to act without the English
Church; at least I assume Canterbury would not claim such patriarchal
dominion over it." *LD*, vi, 68.

appointment of the said Bishop of Australia, or his successors, that every such Bishop shall, to all intents and purposes, cease to be Bishop of Australia."

"Confirmation is an ordinance," says the Tract, "in which the Bishop witnesses for Christ. Our Lord and Saviour confirms us with the spirit of all goodness; the Bishop is His figure and likeness when he lays his hands on the heads of children. Then Christ comes to them, to confirm in them the grace of baptism." "And we do hereby [108] give and grant to the said Bishop of Australia," proceeds His Majesty, "and his successors, Bishops of Australia, full power and authority to confirm those that are baptized and come to years of discretion, and to perform all other functions peculiar and appropriate to the office of Bishop within the limits of the said see of Australia."

"Moreover," says the Tract, "the Bishop rules the Church here below, as Christ rules it above; and is commissioned to make us clergymen God's ministers. He is Christ's instrument." "And we do by these presents give and grant to the said Bishop and his successors, Bishops of Australia, full power and authority to admit into the holy orders of deacon and priest respectively, any person whom he shall deem duly qualified, and to punish and correct chaplains, ministers, priests, and deacons, according to their demerits."

"The Bishop speaks in me," says the Tract, "as Christ wrought in him, and as God sent Christ; thus the whole plan of salvation hangs together;—Christ the true Mediator; His servant the Bishop His earthly likeness; mankind the subjects of His teaching; God the author of salvation." And the Queen answers, "We do hereby signify to the Most Reverend Father in God, William, Lord Archbishop of Canterbury,[12] our nomination of the said Augustus,[13]

---

[12] *William*: Willam Howley (1766-48), Archbishop of Canterbury.
[13] *Augustus*: Augustus Short (1802-83), Anglican bishop of Adelaide. Educated at Westminster and Christ Church, he was ordained priest in 1827. He wrote but did not publish a defence of Newman's Tract No. 90. In 1846, he published his Bampton lectures, *The Witness of the Spirit*

[109] requiring, and, by the faith and love whereby he is bound unto us, commanding the said Most Reverend Father in God, to ordain and consecrate the said Augustus." And the consecrated prelate echoes from across the ocean, "Augustus, by the grace of God and the favour of Queen Victoria, Bishop."

"You will, in time to come," says the Tract, [14] "honour us with a purer honour than men do now, as those who are intrusted with the keys of heaven and hell, as the heralds of mercy, as the denouncers of woe to wicked men, as intrusted with the awful and mysterious privilege of dispensing Christ's Body and Blood." And a first Episcopal Charge replies in the words of the Homily, "Let us diligently search the well of life, and not run after the stinking puddles of tradition, devised by man's imagination." [15] A second, "It is a subject of deep concern

---

with Our Spirit, which did not address the controversial issues broached by Newman and the Tractarians. "In 1845 Short was given the choice of either the Adelaide or Newcastle diocese. He chose Adelaide and on 29 June 1847 was consecrated bishop in Westminster Abbey. He arrived in the *Derwent* on 28 December. His vast diocese, which included Western Australia, had only eight clergy, four church buildings, with five under construction, one parsonage and one school ... As a high churchman Short frequently clashed with his predominantly Evangelical flock and with the province's Nonconformists. In 1850 at a bishops' conference in Sydney he supported the doctrine of baptismal regeneration; he provoked protest from the South Australian Church Society and the formation of a vigilant committee to petition the archbishop of Canterbury for protection from episcopal interference with doctrine. Short was unperturbed and assured his flock of his dislike of most of the Tractarian beliefs. In 1848 Governor Frederick Robe had granted land in Victoria Square as a cathedral site, but in 1855 the Supreme Court ruled the grant illegal: eventually in 1869 Short laid the foundation stone of St Peter's Cathedral in North Adelaide. In 1858 he created a furore by refusing to allow the Congregationalist divine Thomas Binney to preach in an Anglican Church. His precedence as bishop of Adelaide was regarded by many as repugnant to the foundation principles of the colony and in 1872 Short voluntarily surrendered his claim." *Dictionary of Australian Biography*

[14] *the Tract*: *Tracts for the Times*, XXXV, "The People's Interests in their Minister's Commission," (8 May 1834) p. 3 [A.P. Perceval]

[15] *"... man's imagination."*: From: Homily Entitled "A Fruitful Exhortation to the Reading and Knowledge of Holy Scripture" (1587), in

that any of our body should prepare men of ardent feelings and warm imaginations for a return to the Roman Mass-book."[16] And a third, "Already are the foundations of apostasy laid; if we once admit another Gospel, Antichrist is at the door. I am full of fear; everything is at stake; there seems to be something judicial in the rapid spread of these opinions."[17] And a fourth, "It is impossible not to remark upon the subtle wile of the Adversary; it has been signally and unexpectedly exemplified in the present day by the revival of errors which might have been supposed buried for ever."[18] And a fifth, "Under the spurious pretence of deference to antiquity and respect for primitive models, the [110] foundations of our Protestant Church are undermined by

---

J. F. Russell, *The Judgment of the Anglican Church (Posterior to the Reformation) on the Sufficiency of Holy Scripture, and the Authority of the Holy Catholic Church in Matters of Faith as Contained in her Authorized Formularies, and Illustrated by the Writings of her Elder Masters and Doctors.* (London, 1838), 1. "Here have we two authoritative declarations of the Church; the first affirming the perfect sufficiency of Scripture for information on points affecting justification and salvation, and dehorting from the use of Tradition; the second repudiating the doctrine that Catholic Tradition was an authoritative teacher. With such declarations before us, we cannot allow ourselves to believe that we have mistaken the import of the Articles, or the mind of their compilers." Archibald Boyd, *England, Rome and Oxford Compared as to Certain Doctrines* (London, 1846), 11.

[16] *Roman Mass-book*: From "The Bishop of London's Charge" (1842), *The Churchman: A Magazine in Defence of the Church and Constitution*, vol. vii July to December 1842 (London, 1842), 359. C.J. Blomfield (1786-1857), had a brilliant career at Trinity College, Cambridge. He was Bishop of Chester from 1824-28, and was then translated to London where he remained until 1856. ... He condemned the extreme elements in Tractarianism, but appreciated much of the Oxford Movement's work." *LD*, vi, 385.

[17] *opinions*: From: Review of "Oxford Tracts," *Christian Observer* (January, 1842). The *Christian Observer* was a London evangelical paper whose editor from 1816 to 1849 was Samuel Charles Wilks.

[18] From: J.B. Sumner, *A Charge delivered to the Clergy of the Diocese of Chester, at the Visitation in June, MDCCCXLI*. According to the editor of the *LD*, G. Tracey: "Newman took the strongest exception to the Charge of the Bishop of Chester (considering that it amounted to heresy virtually) ..." See *LD*, viii, 569.

men who dwell within her walls, and those who sit in the Reformer's seat are traducing the Reformation."[19] "Our glory is in jeopardy," says a sixth.[20] "Why all this tenderness for the very centre and core of corruption?"[21] asks a seventh.

---

[19] *for ever*: From: The Bishop of Chester's Charge, (1841). "In the 1830s, Bishop J.B. Sumner of Chester, who became the first Evangelical Archbishop of Canterbury, pointed to what he regarded as the threat to the Church of England of those who denied the importance of the Reformation: 'Under the spurious pretence of deference to antiquity and respect for primitive models, the foundations of our Protestant Church are undermined by men who dwell within her walls, and those who sit in the Reformer's seat are traducing the Reformation'. On such a picture, which was not wholly removed from the truth, as Newman's notorious Tract XC of 1841 revealed, the Tractarians were little less than fifth columnists seeking to remove the inheritance of the sixteenth century. This was noted by many at the time. For instance, after reading a review of this final Tract, which sought to explain the Thirty-Nine Articles of Religion quite differently from how their framers had intended, the broad churchman Charles Kingsley wrote to his mother in 1841: 'Whether wilful or deceived, these men are Jesuits, taking the oath to the Articles with moral reservations, which allow them to explain them away in senses utterly different from those of their authors – All the worst doctrinal features of Popery Mr Newman professes to believe in'" M.D. Chapman, *Anglican Theology* (London, 2012), 17-18.

[20] *a sixth*: From: the Bishop of Winchester's *Charge* (1841), 29, 30. "The Bishop of Winchester, referring to the Tractarian Doctrines, as tending to sully the purity and simplicity of the Gospel, and to defraud the Church of her spiritual glories, asks: — 'Are we then, as a Church, in risk of incurring any such danger? Is our glory in any jeopardy? Is there heard, as it were, something of a confused sound of noises at a distance, which might make some Eli, sitting in the gate, to tremble for the Ark of God? There is reason for fearing injury to the distinctive principles of our Church.'" J. B. Clifford, *The Church's Last Struggle: A Sermon* (Bristol, 1842), 10. C. R. Sumner (1790-1874), Bishop of Winchester opposed R. D. Hampden but "was vehement against the 'papal aggression' crisis of 1850 when the Roman Catholic hierarchy in England was restored. He sought to prevent any action on the Gorham judgment on the part of his clergy which might lead to an abridgement of traditional liberty in the interpretation of the article on baptism, but fully sympathized with the agitation against *Essays and Reviews* in 1860–61 and against Colenso in 1863. He was also hostile to the recurrence of revivalism after the manner of Wesley and Whitefield in the church." *ODNB*

[21] *core of corruption*: From: Bishop of Llandaff's Charge (1842), W.S. Bricknell, *The Judgement of the Bishops upon Tractarian Theology: A Complete Analytical Arrangement of the Charges delivered by the*

"Among other marvels of the present day," says an eighth, "may be accounted the irreverent and unbecoming language applied to the chief promoters of the Reformation in this land. The quick and extensive propagation of opinions, tending to exalt the claims of the Church and of the Clergy, can be no proof of their soundness."[22] "Reunion with Rome has been rendered impossible," says a ninth, "yet I am not without hope that more cordial union may, in time, be effected among all Protestant Churches."[23] "Most of the Bishops," says a tenth, "have spoken in terms of disapproval of the 'Tracts for the Times,' and I certainly believe the system to be most pernicious, and one which is calculated to produce the most lamentable schism in a Church already fearfully disunited."[24]

"Up to this moment," says an eleventh, "the movement is advancing under just the same pacific professions, and the same imputations are still cast upon all who in any way impede its progress. Even the English Bishops, who have officially expressed any disapprobation of the principles or proceedings of the party, have not escaped such [111] animadversions."[25] "Tractarianism is the masterpiece of Satan,"[26] says a twelfth.

Prelates of the Anglican Church, from 1837 to 1842 inclusive; so far as they relate to the Tractarian Movement. (London, 1845), 488.

[22] *their soundness*: From: [T. Musgrave], *A Charge to the Clergy of the Diocese of Hereford. June 1842, at the second Visitation of Thomas, Lord Bishop of Hereford.* See *LD*, ix 625. T. Musgrave (1788-1860), Bishop of Hereford.

[23] *Protestant Churches*: From: Howley, Archbishop of Canterbury (1840), *Bricknell*, 473.

[24] *fearfully disunited*: From: The Bishop of Rochester's Charge (1843), in *The Court, Lady's Magazine: A Family Journal* (November, 1843), 37.

[25] *animadversions*: From: Dr. Pusey's Letter to Archbishop of Canterbury (1841), *Bricknell*, 117.

[26] *the masterpiece of Satan*: "That the danger of a renewal of the Popish superstition has occurred to others besides the opponents of Tractarianism is evident from the scope of the Bishop of Oxford's Charge. Indeed the fact that the Tractarians have a leaning towards Rome, and that several of their doctrines and opinions are essentially Popish, and quite foreign from the principles of our Reformed Church, is now pretty well acknowledged by nearly all parties in the Church. Thus

4.

But there was a judgment more cruel still, because it practically told in their favour; but it was the infelicity of the agents in the movement, that, the National Church feeling both in its rulers and its people as it did, their teaching could not escape animadversion except at the expense of their principles. "A Bishop's lightest word, *ex Cathedrâ*,[27] is heavy," said a writer of the "Tracts for the

---

Bishop Mant asserts, that "a disposition may be perceived to revert to the once by-gone fancies of Romish superstition, and thence to bring forward obsolete notions and practices, which, in common with others from the same repository of error, she (the Church of England) had disallowed and repudiated." And the same authority, in his recent episcopal charge, felt it incumbent on him to inculcate the caution "that we abstain from the use of all such language as may tend to indicate in our own minds, or to implant on others, an indifference to the errors and corruptions of the Romish Church, and to encourage, on the other hand, a favourable contemplation of her, by putting forward and commending her better qualities, and by obscuring and keeping out of sight her peculiar abominations." Popery is acknowledged to have been the great masterpiece of Satan in his hostile assaults upon the Church of Christ. It is no wonder, therefore, that he should so often, as it were, repeat himself." F.T. Hill, *A Letter to the Laity of the Church of England, on some points connected with the Tractarian controversy.* (London, 1842), 100-1.

[27] *"ex Cathedrâ"*: "Literally 'from the chair,' a theological term which signifies authoritative teaching and is more particularly applied to the definitions given by the Roman pontiff. Originally the name of the seat occupied by a professor or a bishop, *cathedra* was used later on to denote the magisterium, or teaching authority. The phrase *ex cathedra* occurs in the writings of the medieval theologians, and more frequently in the discussions which arose after the Reformation in regard to the papal prerogatives. But its present meaning was formally determined by the [First] Vatican Council, Sess. IV, Const. de Ecclesiâ Christi, c. iv: 'We teach and define that it is a dogma Divinely revealed that the Roman pontiff when he speaks *ex cathedra*, that is when in discharge of the office of pastor and doctor of all Christians, by virtue of his supreme Apostolic authority, he defines a doctrine regarding faith or morals to be held by the universal Church, by the Divine assistance promised to him in Blessed Peter, is possessed of that infallibility with which the Divine Redeemer willed that his Church should be endowed in defining doctrine regarding faith or morals, and that therefore such definitions of the Roman pontiff are of themselves and not from the consent of the Church irreformable.'" *Catholic Encyclopaedia.*

Times." "His judgment on a book cannot be light; it is a rare occurrence."[28] And an Archbishop answered from the other side of St. George's Channel, "Many persons look with considerable interest to the declarations on such matters that from time to time are put forth by Bishops in their Charges, or on other occasions. But on most of the points to which I have been alluding, a Bishop's declarations have no more weight, except what they derive from his personal character, than any anonymous pamphlet would have. The points are mostly such as he has no official power to decide, even in reference to his own diocese; and as to legislation for the Church, or authoritative declarations on many of the most important matters, neither any one Bishop, nor all collectively, have any more right of this kind, than the ordinary magistrates have to take on themselves the [112] functions of Parliament."[29]

However, it is hardly necessary to prolong the exhibition of the controversy, or to recall to your recollection the tone of invective in which each party relieved the keen and vehement feelings which its opponents excited;—how the originators of the movement called Jewell "an irreverent Dissenter;"[30] were even "thinking worse and worse of the Reformers;" "hated the Reformation and the Reformers more and more;"[31] thought them the false prophets of the

---

[28] *a rare occurrence*: See Newman's letter to Archdeacon Clerke (16 August 1838), *LD*, vi, 29.

[29] *the functions of Parliament*: Richard Whately, *A Charge to the Clergy of Dublin and Glandelagh, Delivered in St. Patrick's Cathedral, June, 1843* (London, 1843), 22.

[30] *"an irreverent Dissenter"*: "As to the Reformers, I think worse and worse of them. Jewell was what you would in these days call an irreverent dissenter. His 'Defence of his Apology' disgusted me more than almost any work I have read. Bishop Hickes and Dr. Brett I see go all lengths with me in this respect, and I believe Laud did. The preface to the Thirty-nine Articles was certainly intended to disconnect us from the Reformers." *Remains*, p. 379-80.

[31] *more*: "Really I hate the Reformation and the Reformers more and more, and have almost made up my mind that the rationalist spirit they set afloat is the ψευδοπροφήτης [false prophet] of the Revelations." *Ibid*, 389.

Apocalypse; described the National Church as having "blasphemed Tradition and the Sacraments;"[32] were "more and more indignant at the Protestant doctrine of the Eucharist;" thought the principle on which it was founded "as proud, irreverent, and foolish, as that of any heresy, even Socinianism;"[33] and considered the Establishment their "upas-tree," "an incubus on the country;"[34] and its reformed condition, "a limb badly set, which must be broken before it could be righted."[35] And how they were called in turn, "superstitious,"[36] "zealots,"[37] "mystical,"[38] "malignants,"[39]

---

[32] "...*the Sacraments*": "One of the Tracts for the Times speaks of the Millennium being ushered in by mutual confessions on the part of all branches of the Church. If so, we should cut the worst figure of all, after the way we have blasphemed Tradition and the Sacraments," *Ibid*, 438.

[33] "... *Socinianism*": Ibid, 391.

[34] "*an incubus on the country*": "Any Churches they might build, any endowment they might make, would be as likely as not to become in another generation propagandas of liberalism. ... The present Church is an incubus on the country. It spreads its arms in all directions. Claiming the whole surface of the earth for its own, and refusing a place to any subsidiary system to spring upon. Would that the waters would throw up some Alcheloides, where some Bishop might erect a see beyond the blighting influence of our upas tree." *Ibid*, 404-05.

[35] "... *righted.*": "The Reformation was a limb badly set – it must be broken again in order to be righted." *Ibid*, 438.

[36] "*superstitious,*": No note could possibly cover the instances in which the Tractarians were called "superstitious" by their opponents in the Church of England. However, there is a striking use of the word in a charge against the Tractarians by Bishop Wilson of Calcutta (1838): "It is to me, I confess, a matter of surprise and shame, that in the nineteenth century we should really have the fundamental position of the whole system of Popery virtually reasserted in the bosom of that very Church, which was reformed so determinately three centuries since from this self-same evil, by the doctrine, and labours, and martyrdom of Cranmer and his noble fellow-sufferers. ... The whole system, indeed, goes to generate, as I cannot but think, an inadequate, and superficial, and superstitious religion. The mere admissions of the inspiration and paramount authority of Holy Scripture will soon become a dead letter; due humiliation before God, under a sense of the unutterable evil of sin, will be less and less understood; a conviction of the need of the meritorious Righteousness of the incarnate Saviour, as the alone ground of Justification, will be only faintly inculcated; the operations of the Holy Ghost in creating man anew will be more and more forgotten; the nature

"Oxford heretics,"[40] "Jesuits in disguise,"[41] "tamperers with Popish idolatry,"[42] "agents of Satan,"[43] "a synagogue of

---

of those good works which are acceptable to God in Christ will be lost sight of; and 'another Gospel,' framed on the Traditions of men, will make way for an apostacy in our own Church, as in that of Rome—unless, indeed, the evangelical piety, the reverence for Holy Scripture, the theological learning, and the forethought and fidelity of our Divines of dignified station and established repute at home interpose by distinct cautions to prevent it..." *Bricknell*, 627-8. See also, D. Wilson's *The Sufficiency of Holy Scripture as the Rule of Faith. A Sermon ... at an Ordination, holden on Sunday, May 2, 1841,* London 1841, pp. 59-61. In addition to these pages, some of Wilson's eight Appendices sharply criticize Newman and the Tractarians.

[37] *"zealot"*: In 1841, Bishop Maltby of Durham remonstrated with the Tractarians for introducing "a fresh element of discord" into the Church by insisting on "the authority of the Fathers," and then went on to say: "But in quitting this very unpleasant subject it may not be unseasonable, if I add a few general remarks upon the consequences of misplaced zeal. ... The zealot, who feels secure in his honesty of purpose, complains that he is treated unjustly; while others, who do not share the same extent of error, still think that, where a fault is only in excess, it should be protected by the excellence of the motive. But neither of these parties is aware of the deceitfulness of the human heart; nor how unconsciously feelings of pride and selfishness mix themselves up with designs originally good." *Bricknell*, 631. "The sole active whig among the episcopate—Bathurst of Norwich was eighty-seven and incapacitated—Maltby, branded a 'black swan', met the other bishops' hostility with plainspoken resolve to do his duty 'equally regardless of their smiles or their frowns.'" (J. Grant, *Random Recollections of the House of Lords* (1836), 401–3). A former schoolfellow at Winchester, Sydney Smith ... regarded ... [Maltby] as an 'excellent man and a great fool' (P. Virgin, *Sydney Smith*, 1994, 27)." *ODNB.*

[38] *"mystical"*: "We do not mean to apply personally to the Oxford Tract writers any one word that is offensive: their devoutness, though somewhat mystical, is intense; and, as an example of their love of good works, we need only notice Professor Pusey's munificent donation of 5000*l.* to the Bishop of London's church-building fund, under the anonymous title of 'One who seeks Treasure in Heaven.'" *The Christian Observer,* 423, 1837 (March), 197. 29. See also, *LD*, vi, 39.

[39] *"malignant"*: For Thomas Arnold's famous slur, see previous note.

[40] *"Oxford heretics"*: G.P. de Sancta Trinitate, *The True State of the Case Considered: The Oxford Tracts, the Public Press and the Evangelical Party* (London, 1839), 43.

[41] *"Jesuits in disguise"*: For Charles Kingsley's jibe, see previous note.

Satan,"[44] "snakes in the grass,"[45] "walking about our beloved Church, polluting the sacred edifice, and leaving

[42] *"... Popish idolatry"*: "Who can witness without grief and amazement that awful tampering with Popish idolatry, exhibited in the republication of the abominations of the Roman Breviary." This was the Rev. J. Scholepield's decided reaction to Newman's *Tract for the Times*, No. 75, "On the Roman Breviary As Embodying the Substance of the Devotional Services of the Church Catholic" (24 June 1836). See *Scriptural Grounds of Union, considered in Five Sermons. Preached before the University of Cambridge in the month of November, 1840. By the Rev. James Scholepield, A.M., Regius Professor of Greek* (London,1840).

[43] *"agents of Satan"*: In November of 1841, a correspondent had asked Newman if his criticisms of the Anglican Church left Anglicans no choice but to consider seceding to Rome, to which Newman replied: "... you need have no fear of any intimate friend of mine going to Rome at this time — But I must say candidly, that if the Bishops will not let us use Church weapons for the Church, they will be used by the R C's against her. I do not ask them to adopt these arms — I only asked to be allowed to use them myself — I do not ask for sanction but sufferance. I ask that liberty of prophesying which has ever existed in the reformed Church — ... But instead of that we have a new thing in the English Church — while the so called evangelical principles are left unnoticed in Episcopal charges, when all sorts of irregularities are committed as to the Church Services weekly, while (as at Bristol) a man in the pulpit alluding to Pusey says 'You have lately had the hellborn heresy of Puseyism here in person,' and another taking up a volume of the Tracts holds it out to his congregation saying 'I denounce the authors of this volume as agents of Satan,' the Bishops employ themselves in a series of charges against us as 'Angels from heaven' preaching another gospel. And the rest keep silence — Not one has dared to praise us... for 8 years — ... Will not men ask, Is this indeed a Church? Its authorities deny those very things which we are taught are notes of the Church. And then comes the Bishop of Chester with a charge which contains flat heresy. And, in cumulum, we are doing a new thing in the East, fraternizing with Lutherans and Calvinists — About this last matter some Protests are going about — and I suppose I must have one myself." *LD*, viii, 319-20.

[44] *"a synagogue of Satan"*: In his *Letter to Faussett* (1836), Newman wrote: "Another question on which we may be fairly indulged in a liberty of opinion is, whether or not the Church of Rome is 'the mother of harlots,' and the Pope St. Paul's 'man of sin.' ... How those divines who hold the Apostolical Succession can maintain the affirmative, passes my comprehension; for in holding the one and other point at once, they are in fact proclaiming to the world that they come from 'the synagogue of Satan' and (if I may so speak) have the devil's orders." *Letter to Faussett*, 31.

their slime about her altars;" "whose head," it was added, "may God crush!"[46]

Is it not then abundantly plain, that, whatever be the [113] destiny of the movement of 1833, there is no tendency in it towards a coalition with the Establishment? It cannot strengthen it, it cannot serve it, it cannot obey it. The party may be dissolved, the movement may die—that is another matter; but it and its idea cannot live, cannot energize, in the National Church. If St. Athanasius could agree with Arius, St. Cyril with Nestorius, St. Dominic with the Albigenses, or St. Ignatius with Luther,[47] then may two parties coalesce,

---

[45] *"snakes in the grass"*: "As the Tractarian party—now that the tide of popularity seems turning against them in Belgravia, and that they can no longer assume the haughty and domineering position which they formerly held—are endeavouring to excite sympathy for the Rev. Mr. Liddell, by representing that those of the parishioners who feel desirous to have purity and simplicity of worship established in the Churches of St. Paul and St. Barnabas are actuated by motives of personal hostility towards the reverend gentleman, and that they are not justified in carrying on what is termed 'a system of persecution' against him; it is right that the public should know that the Parishioners are not influenced by such unworthy and narrow motives, and that they are acting upon much broader and higher principles. Their sole aim is to eradicate the system of spurious Popery which, unfortunately, has been so firmly rooted and established in their district, and which has already inflicted so great an amount of injury both there and elsewhere; making divisions and dissensions in families previously happy and united, and creating in the Church a most painful and most dangerous schism." *Puseyism, The Snake in the Grass at St. Paul's and St. Barnabas by A Belgravian* (London, 1855), 3-4.

[46] *"may God crush!"*: This quotation is from a source – perhaps a bishop's charge or other episcopal lament – that the editor could not locate, despite much searching and researching.

[47] *If*: "If St. Athanasius could agree with Arius, St. Cyril with Nestorius, St. Dominic with the Albigenses, or St. Ignatius with Luther …" In other words, there is no likelihood whatever of these settled opponents agreeing with one another. St. Athanasius could never agree with Arius that Christ was not divine; St. Cyril could never agree with Nestorius that Mary was not the Mother of God; St. Dominic could never agree with the Albigenses that Neo-Manicheanism was somehow orthodox; and St. Ignatius could never agree with Luther that the German heresiarch's Protestantism was a legitimate reform of the one holy catholic and apostolic Church. Similarly, the Establishment of the Church of England could never agree with the Anglo-Catholic party that their Romish faith

in a certain assignable time, or by certain felicitously gradual approximations, or with dexterous limitations and concessions, who mutually think light darkness and darkness light. "Delenda est Carthago;"[48] one or other must perish. Assuming, then, that there is a scope and limit to the movement, we certainly shall not find it in the dignities and offices of the National Church.

5.

If then, this be not the providential direction of the movement, let us ask, in the next place, is it intended to remain just what it is at present, not in power or authority, but as a sort of principle or view of religion, found here and there with greater or less distinctness, with more or fewer followers, scattered about or concentrated, up and down the Establishment; with no exact agreement between man and man in matters of detail or in theoretical basis, but as an influence, sleeping or rousing, victorious or defeated, from [114] time to time, as the case may be? This state of things is certainly supposable, at least for a time, for a generation; and various arguments may be adduced in its behalf. It may be urged, "that if you cannot do any positive good to the nation, yet at least in this way you may prevent evil; that to be a drag upon the career of unbelief, if you are nothing else, is a mission not to be despised; moreover, if it be not a heroic course of action, or look well in history, still so much

---

accorded with the 39 Articles; and the Anglo-Catholics could never agree with the Establishment that their Erastian faith accorded with Apostolical principles. If it were possible for such opponents to agree, Newman concludes, "then may two parties coalesce, in a certain assignable time, or by certain felicitously gradual approximations, or with dexterous limitations and concessions, who mutually think light darkness and darkness light." The good Noetic in Whately would have appreciated the logic of this droll, satirical sally.

[48] *"Delenda est Carthago"*: "Carthage must be destroyed." The phrase originates from debates in the Roman Senate prior to the Third Punic War (149–146 BC) between Rome and Carthage; Cato uttered it at the end of all of his speeches to persuade the Romans to go to war. It has since come to denote a call for total war.

the more does such an office become those who are born in
a fallen time, and who wish to be humble."

Again, though it is good to be humble, still, on the other
hand, "there is a chance," it may be whispered by others,
"of a nobler and higher function opening on you, if you are
but patient and dutiful for a time." This is the suggestion of
those who cannot, will not, look at things as they are; who
think objects feasible because they are desirable, and to be
attempted because they are tempting. These persons go on
dwelling upon the thought of the wonderful power of the
British people, at this day, all over the world, till at length
they begin to conjecture what may possibly be the design of
Providence in raising it up. They feel that Great Britain
would be a most powerful instrument of good, if it could be
directed aright; and then they argue that if it *is* to be
influenced, what else ought naturally and obviously to
influence it but the National Church? The National Church,
then, is to be God's instrument for the conversion of the [115]
world. But in order to this, of course it is indispensable that
the National Church should have a clear and sufficient hold
of Apostolical doctrine and usage; but then, who is to
instruct the National Church in these necessary matters, but
that Apostolical movement to which they themselves
belong? And thus, by a few intermediate steps, they have
attained the conclusion, that, because the nation is so
powerful, the movement must succeed. Accordingly, they
bear any degree of humiliation and discomforture; nay, any
argumentative exposure, any present stultification of their
principles, any, however chronic, disorganization, with an
immovable resolve, as a matter of duty and merit, because
they are sanguine about the future. They seem to feel that
the whole cause of truth, the reform of the Establishment,
the catholicizing of the nation, the conversion of the world,
depends at this moment on their faithfulness to their
position; on their own steadfastness the interests of
humanity are at stake, and where they now are, there they
will live and die. They have taken their part, and to that part
they will be true.

Moreover, there are those among them who have very little grasp of principle, even from the natural temper of their minds. They see that this thing is beautiful, and that is in the Fathers, and a third is expedient, and a fourth pious; but of their connection one with another, their hidden [116] essence and their life, and the bearing of external matters upon each and upon all, they have no perception or even suspicion. They do not look at things as parts of a whole, and often will sacrifice the most important and precious portions of their creed, or make irremediable concessions in word or in deed, from mere simplicity and want of apprehension.[49] This was in one way singularly exemplified in the beginning of the movement itself. I am not saying that every word that was used in the "Tracts for the Times" was matter of principle, or that the doctrines to be enforced were not sometimes unnecessarily coloured by the vehemence of the writer; but still it not seldom happened that readers took statements which contained the very point of the argument, or the very heart of the principle, to be mere intemperate expressions, and suggested to the authors their removal. They said "they went a great way with us, but they really could not go such lengths. Why speak of the Apostolic Succession, instead of Evangelical truth and Apostolical order? It gave offence, it did no manner of good. Why use the word 'altar,' if it displeased weak brethren? The word 'sacrifice' was doubtless a misprint for 'sacrament;' and to talk with Bishop Bull of 'making the body of Christ,' was a most extravagant, unjustifiable way of describing the administration of the Lord's Supper."[50]

[117] Things are changed now at the end of twenty years, but characters and intellects are the same. Such persons, at the

---

[49] Since writing the above, the author finds it necessary to observe, that, in writing it, it had no reference to persons, and he would be pained if it seemed to refer to actual passages in the controversy now in progress. [N]

[50] ... *Lord's Supper.*": The Church of England has always inclined to regard the use of such words as 'altar,' 'sacrifice,' and 'the body of Christ' as "intemperate" because such words are expressive of the Roman Catholic understanding of transubstantiation, which the Church of England disavows.

present moment, do not formally profess any intention of giving up any of the doctrines of the movement; but they think it possible and expedient to divide portion from portion, and are rash and inconsistent in their advice and their conduct, from mere ignorance of what they are doing. So, too, they think it a success, and are elated accordingly, if any measure whatever, which happens to have been contemplated by the movement, is in any shape conceded by the Establishment or by the State; heedless altogether whether such measure be capable or not of coalescing with a foreign principle, and whether, instead of modifying, it has not been changed into that against which, in the minds of the writers of the Tracts, it was directed. For instance, the movement succeeded in gaining an increase in the number of Episcopal sees at home and abroad; well, a triumph this certainly is, if any how to succeed in a measure which one has advocated may be called by that name. But, be it recollected, measures derive their character and their worth from the principle which animates them; they have little meaning in themselves; they are but material facts, unless they include in them their scope and enforce their object; nay, they readily assume the *animus* and drift, and are taken up into the *form*, of the system by which they are adopted. If the Apostolical movement desired to increase the [118] Episcopate, it was with a view to its own Apostolical principles; it had no wish merely to increase the staff of Government officers in England or in the colonies, the patronage of a ministry, the erection of country palaces, or the Latitudinarian votes in Parliament. Has it, for instance, done a great achievement at Manchester, if it has planted there a chair of liberalism, and inaugurated an anti-Catholic tradition?[51]

---

[51] *Manchester*: Manchester in the mid-19th century was a liberal stronghold, due, in large measure, to its industry and the German influences that colored its commercial and intellectual development. "In fact," as A.J.P. Taylor wrote, "you could really say that the Germans of Manchester were the German liberals who had failed in Germany itself, but who succeeded here in England and did so much to help Manchester

6.

A policy, then, resting on such a temper of mind as I have been describing,—viz., a determination to act as if the course of events itself would, in some way or other, work for Apostolical truth, sooner or later, more or less; to let things alone, to do nothing, to make light of every triumph of the enemy from within or without, to waive the question

---

liberalism to have its special character; one was Friedrich Engels." A.J.P. Taylor, "Manchester," *From Napoleon to the Second International: Essays on Nineteenth-Century Europe* ed. C Wrigley (London, 1993), 398-9. Engels (1820-95) was not the only person who gave Manchester its liberal élan. Another German, Nathan Rothschild (1777-1836) also got his start there. Free Trade, not incipient communism, animated the city's Victorian vitality. For Rothschild's early career in Manchester, see B. Hilton, *Mad, Bad, and Dangerous to Know: England 1783-1846* (Oxford, 2006), 155. As for the Church of England in Manchester, its first Anglican bishop, James Prince Lee (1804-69), consecrated in 1848, was representative of the "chair of liberalism" and "anti-Catholic tradition" to which Newman refers. "A low-churchman, who attacked both 'papal aggression' in 1851 and ritualistic practices, Lee had Erastian tendencies (he approved of the Gorham judgment), which further alienated high-churchmen. His suppression of high-church innovations at Ringley Chapel, described in a pamphlet by Edward Fellows, assistant curate, was followed by an attack on the 'popish' fittings in the chancel of Broughton church, which drew a sharp reply from A. J. Beresford Hope (1851). Lee's charges (1851, 1855) showed a preference for evangelical styles of worship (Mark Smith, *Religion in Industrial Society*, 1994, 90). His headmasterly method of ruling his diocese, using rural deans to inform on his clergy, and his rather cold manner led to much opposition and distrust. His role in a dispute over the property of the dean and canons of Manchester Cathedral permanently harmed his relations with the chapter and he was rarely seen in the cathedral. The success of his episcopate lay in his organization of spiritual provision: he consecrated 110 new churches, created 163 new parishes and ecclesiastical districts, attached schools to new churches, and ordained some 500 clergy." *ODNB* In May of 1850, Newman wrote his Anglo-Irish friend W. Monsell, later Lord Emly: "Somehow I do not feel the force of what you say about Colonial Bishops — for it is but a perpetuation of the miserable State system. It is curious that, just before your letter came, Papers about Dr. Broughton and Australia, moved for, I believe, by Sir R. H. Inglis, were put into my hands as signal *corroborations* of what I had been saying [in Lecture IV of *Diff*.]. E.g. what *gain* to the Catholic cause in the Anglican Church is it to have gained a see at Manchester, if Dr. Lee is to fill it? —" *LD*, xiii, 472.

of ecclesiastical liberty, to remain where you are, and go about your work in your own place, either contented to retard the course of events, or sanguine about an imaginary future,—this is simply to abandon the cause of the movement altogether. It is simply to say that there is no providential destiny or object connected with it at all. You may be right, my brethren; this may be the case; perhaps it is so. You have a right to this opinion, but understand what you are doing. Do not deceive yourselves by words; it is not a biding your time, as you may fancy, if you surrender the [119] idea and the main principle of the movement; it is the abandonment of your cause. You remain, indeed, in your place, but it is no moral, no intellectual, but a mere secular, visible position which you occupy. Great commanders, when in war they are beaten back from the open country, retire to the mountains and fortify themselves in a territory which is their own. You have no place of refuge from the foe; you have no place from which to issue in due season, no hope that your present concessions will bring about a future victory. Your retreat is an evacuation. You will remain in the Establishment in your own persons, but your principles will be gone.

I know how it will be—a course as undignified as it will be ineffectual. A sensation and talk whenever something atrocious is to be done by the State against the principles you profess; a meeting of friends here or there, an attempt to obtain an archidiaconal meeting; some spirited remarks in two or three provincial newspapers; an article in a review; a letter to some Bishop; a protest signed respectably; suddenly the news that the anticipated blow has fallen, and *causa finita est.*[52] A pause, and then the discovery that

---

[52] *causa finita est*: This is from the palmary saying of St. Augustine: *Roma locuta, causa finita est,* "Rome has spoken: the case is closed." In advising that the pope had ratified the condemnations of the Pelagian heresy pronounced at the councils of Milevi and Carthage, Augustine exclaimed: "The two councils sent their decrees to the Apostolic See and the decrees quickly came back. The cause is finished; would that the error had been as quickly resolved!" (Sermon 131:10)

things are not so bad as they seemed to be, and that after all your Apostolical Church has come forth from the trial even stronger and more beautiful than before. Still a secret dissatisfaction and restlessness; a strong sermon at a [120] visitation; and a protest after dinner, when his lordship is asked to print his Charge; a paragraph to your great satisfaction in a hostile newspaper, saying how that most offensive proceedings are taking place in such and such a Tractarian parish or chapel, how that there were flowers on the table, or that the curate has tonsured himself, or has used oil and salt in baptizing, or has got a cross upon his surplice, or that in a benefit sermon the bigoted Rector unchurched the Society of Friends, or that Popery is coming in amain upon our venerable Establishment, because a parsonage has been built in shape like a Trappist monastery. And then other signs of life; the consecration of a new church, with Clergy walking in gown and bands, two and two, and the Bishop preaching on decency and order, on the impressive performance of divine Service, and the due decoration of the house of God. Then a gathering in the Christian Knowledge Rooms about some new book put upon the Society's list, or some new liberalizing regulation; a drawn battle, and a compromise. And every now and then a learned theological work, doctrinal or historical, justifying the ecclesiastical principles on which the Anglican Church is founded, and refuting the novelties of Romanism. And lastly, on occasion of a contested election or other political struggle, theology mingled with politics; the liberal candidate rejected by the aid of the High-Church Clergy on some critical question of religious policy; the Government annoyed or embarrassed; and a sanguine hope entertained of [121] a ministry more favourable to Apostolical truth. My brethren, the National Church has had experience of this, *mutatis mutandis*, once before: I mean in the conduct of the Tory Clergy at the end of the seventeenth, and beginning of the following century. Their proceedings in Convocation were a specimen of it; their principles were far better than those of their Bishops; yet the Bishops show to advantage and the Clergy look small and contemptible in the history of that contest. Public opinion judged, as it ever judges, by such broad and significant indications of right and wrong; the Government party triumphed, and the meetings of the Convocation were suspended.

It is impossible, in a sketch such as this, to complete the view of every point which comes into consideration; yet I think I have said enough to suggest the truth of what I am urging to those who carefully turn the matter in their minds. Is the influence of the movement to be maintained adequately to its beginnings and its promise? Many, indeed, will say—certainly many of those who hated or disapproved of it—that it was a sudden ebullition of feeling, or burst of fanaticism, or reaction from opposite errors; that it has had its day, and is over. It may be so; but I am addressing those who, I consider, are of another opinion; and to them I appeal, whether I have yet proposed anything plausible about the providential future of the movement. It is surely not intended, either to rise into the high places of the [122] Establishment, or to sink into a vague, amorphous faction at the foot of it. It cannot rise and it ought not to sink.

7.

And now I am in danger of exceeding the limits which I have proposed to myself, though another more important head of consideration lies before me, could I hope to do justice to it. I have urged that you will be most inconsistent, my brethren, with your principles and views, if you remain in the Establishment; I say with your principles and views, for you may give them up, and then you will not be inconsistent. You may say, "I do not hold them so strongly as to make them the basis and starting-point of any course of action whatever. I have believed in them, it is true; but I have never contemplated the liabilities you are urging upon me. I cannot, under any supposition, contemplate an abandonment of the National Church. I am not that knight-errant to give up my position, which surely is given me by Providence, on a theory. I am what I am. I am where I am.

My reason has followed the teaching of the movement, and I have assented to it; so far I grant. But it is a new idea to me quite, which I have never contemplated at starting, which I cannot contemplate now, that possibly it might [123] involve the most awful, most utter of sacrifices. I have ten thousand claims upon me, urging me to remain where I am. They are real, tangible, habitual, immutable; nothing can shake or lessen them from within. A distinct call of God from without would, of course, overcome them, but nothing short of it. Am I as sure of those Apostolical principles which I have embraced as I am of these claims? Moreover, I am doing good in my parish and in my place. The day passes as usual. Sunday comes round once a week; the bell rings, the congregation is met, and service is performed. There is the same round of parochial duties and charities; sick people to be visited, the school to be inspected. The sun shines, and the rain falls, the garden smiles, as it used to do; and can some one definite, external event have changed the position of this happy scene of which I am the centre? Is not that position a self-dependent, is it a mere relative position? What care I for the Privy Council or the Archbishop, while I can preach and catechize just as before? I have my daily service and my Saints' day sermons, and I can tell my people about the primitive Bishops and martyrs, and about the grace of the Sacraments, and the power of the Church, how that it is Catholic, and Apostolic, and Holy, and One, as if nothing had happened; and I can say my hours, or use [124] my edition of Roman Devotions, and observe the days of fasting, and take confessions, if they are offered, in spite of all gainsayers."

It is true, my dear brethren, you *may* knowingly abandon altogether what you have once held, or you may profess to hold truths without being faithful to them. Well, then, you are of those who think that the movement has come to an end; if in your conscience you think so—that it was a mere phantom, or deceit, or unreality, or dream, which has taken you in, and from which you have awakened,—I have not a word to say. If, however, as I trust is the case, God has not in vain unrolled the pages of antiquity before your eyes, but has stamped them upon your hearts; if He has put into your minds the perception of the truth which, once given, can scarcely be lost, once possessed, will ever be recognized; if you have by His grace been favoured in any measure with the supernatural gift of faith, then, my brethren, I think too well of you, I hope too much of you, to fancy that you can be untrue to convictions so special and so commanding. No; you are under a destiny, the destiny of truth—truth is your master, not you the master of truth—you must go whither it leads. You can have no trust in the Establishment or its Sacraments and ordinances. You must leave it, you must secede; you must turn your back upon, you must renounce, what has—not suddenly become, but has now been proved to you to have ever been—an imposture. You must take up [125] your cross and you must go hence. But whither? That is the question which it follows to ask, could I do justice to it. But you will rather do justice to it in your own thoughts. You must betake yourselves elsewhere—and "to whom shall you go?"[53]

---

[53] *"to whom shall you go?"*: "Then Simon Peter answered him, Lord, to whom shall we go? thou hast the words of eternal life." John 6:68.

LECTURE V

THE PROVIDENTIAL COURSE OF THE MOVEMENT OF 1833
NOT IN THE DIRECTION OF A PARTY IN THE NATIONAL
CHURCH

1.

I KNOW how very difficult it is to persuade others of a point which to one's self may be so clear as to require no argument at all; and, therefore, I am not at all sanguine, my brethren, that what I said in my last Lecture has done as much as I wished it to do. It is not an easy thing to prove to men that their duty lies just in the reverse direction to that in which they have hitherto placed it; that all they have hitherto learned and taught, that all their past labours, hopes, and successes, that their boyhood, youth, and manhood, that their position, their connections, and their influence, are, in a certain sense, to go for nothing; and that life is to begin with them anew. It is not an easy thing to attain to the conviction, that, with the Apostle, their greatest gain must be counted loss; and that their glory and their peace must be found in what will make them for a while the wonder and [127] the scorn of the world. It is true I may have shown you that you cannot coalesce with the National Church; that you cannot wed yourselves to its principles and its routine, and that it, in turn, has no confidence at all in you;—and, again, that you cannot consistently hang about what you neither love nor trust, cumbering with your presence what you are not allowed to serve; but still, nevertheless, you will cling to the past and present, and will hope for the future against hope; and your forlorn hope is this, that it is, perhaps, possible to remain as an actual party in the Establishment, nay, an avowed party; not, on the one hand, rising into

156

ecclesiastical power, yet not, on the other, disorganized and contemptible; but availing yourselves of your several positions in it individually, and developing, with more consistency and caution, the principles of 1833. You may say that I passed over this obvious course in my foregoing Lecture, and decided it in the negative without fair examination; and you may argue that such a party is surely allowable in a religious communion like the Establishment, which, as the Committee of Privy Council implies, is based upon principles so comprehensive, exercises so large a toleration, and is so patient of speculatists and innovators, who are even further removed from its professed principles than yourselves.

Thus I am led to take one more survey of your present position; yet I own I cannot do so without an apology to others, who may think that I am trifling with a serious [128] subject and a clear case, and imagining objections in order to overthrow them. Such persons certainly there may be; but these I would have consider, on the other hand, that my aim is to bring before those I am addressing, really and vividly, where they are standing; that this cannot be done, unless they are induced steadily to fix their minds upon it; that the discussion of imaginary cases brings out principles which they cannot help recognizing, when they are presented to them, and the relation, moreover, of those principles to their own circumstances and duty; and that even where a view of a subject is imaginary, if taken as a whole and in its integral perfection, yet portions of it may linger in the mind, unknown to itself, and influence its practical decisions.

With this apology for a proceeding which some persons may feel tedious, I shall suppose you, my brethren, to address me in the following strain: "The movement has been, for nearly twenty years, a party, and why should it not continue a party as before? It has avowedly opposed a contrary party in the National Church; it has had its principles, its leaders, its usages, its party signs, its publications: it may have them still. It was once, indeed, a point of policy to deny our party character, or we tried to

[129] hide the truth from ourselves, but a party we were. The National Church admits of private judgment,[1] and where there is private judgment, there must be parties. We are, of course, under a disadvantage now, which then did not lie upon us; we have, at the present time, the highest ecclesiastical authorities in distinct and avowed opposition to our doctrines and our doings; but we knew their feelings before they expressed them. This misfortune is nothing new; we always reckoned on an uphill game; it is better that every one should speak out; we now know the worst; we know now where to *find* our spiritual rulers; they are not more opposed to us than before, but they have been obliged openly to commit themselves, which we always wished them to do, though, of course, we should have preferred their committing themselves on our side. But, anyhow, we cannot be said to be in a worse case than before; and, if we were allowably and hopefully a party before, we surely have as ample allowance to agitate, and not less hope of success, now."

2.

You think, then, my brethren, that today can be as yesterday, that you were a party then and can remain a party

---

[1] *private judgement*: The *OED* defines private judgement as "personal opinion (esp. in religious matters), as opposed to the acceptance of a statement or doctrine on authority ..." In a piece in the *British Critic* entitled "Private Judgment" (July 1841), Newman explained why such "personal opinion" in religious matters exercised him. "There is this obvious, undeniable difficulty in the attempt to form a theory of Private Judgment, If, indeed, there be no religious truth, or at least no sufficient means of arriving at it, then the difficulty vanishes: for where there is nothing to find, there can be no rules for seeking, and contradiction in the result is but a *reductio ad absurdum* of the attempt. But such a conclusion is intolerable to those who search, else they would not search; and therefore on them the obligation lies to explain, if they can, how it comes to pass, that Private Judgment is a duty, and an advantage, and a success, considering it leads the way not only to their own faith, whatever that may be, but to opinions which are diametrically opposite to it; considering it not only leads them right, but leads others wrong, landing them as it may be in the Church of Rome, or in the Wesleyan Connexion, or in the Society of Friends." *Ess*, ii, 336.

now, that your present position is your old one, that you can be faithful to the movement, yet continue just what you were. My brethren, you do not bear in mind that a movement is a thing that moves; you cannot be true to it and remain still. The single question is, What is the limit or scope of that which once had a beginning and now has a progress? Your principles, indeed, are fixed, but [130] circumstances are not what they were. If you would be true to your principles, you must remove from a position in which it is not longer possible for you to fulfil them.

Observe:—your movement started on the ground of maintaining ecclesiastical authority, as opposed to the Erastianism of the State. It exhibited the Church as the one earthly object of religious loyalty and veneration, the source of all spiritual power and jurisdiction, and the channel of all grace. It represented it to be the interest, as well as the duty, of Churchmen, the bond of peace and the secret of strength, to submit their judgment in all things to her decision. And it taught that this divinely founded Church was realized and brought into effect in our country in the National Establishment, which was the outward form or development of a continuous dynasty and hereditary power which descended from the Apostles. It gave, then, to that Establishment, in its officers, its laws, its usages, and its worship, that devotion and obedience which are correlative to the very idea of the Church. It set up on high the bench of Bishops and the Book of Common Prayer, as the authority to which it was itself to bow, with which it was to cow and overpower an Erastian State.

It is hardly necessary to bring together passages from the early numbers of the "Tracts for the Times" in support of this statement. Each Tract, I may say, is directed, in one [131] way or other, to the defence of the existing documents or regulations of the National Church. No abstract ground is taken in these compositions; conclusions are not worked out from philosophical premisses, nor conjectures recommended by poetical illustrations, nor a system put together out of eclectic materials; but emphatically and strenuously it is maintained, that whatever is is right, and must be obeyed. If the Apostolic succession is true, it is not simply because St. Ignatius[2] and St. Cyprian[3] might affirm it, though Fathers are adduced also, but because it is implied in the Ordination Service. If the Church is independent of the State in things spiritual, it is not simply because Bishop Pearson has extolled her powers in his Exposition of the Creed,[4] though divines are brought forward as authorities

---

[2] *St. Ignatius*: St Ignatius of Antioch (d. 6 July 108), bishop and martyr. He is a vital source for our understanding of the early Church. Before being thrown to the lions in the Colosseum, Ignatius told a correspondent in his delightful letters not to bother trying to attain a reprieve; instead, he wrote: "Let me follow the example of the suffering of my God." For Newman's interest in the jubilant martyr, see his essay, "The Theology of St. Ignatius" (1839), *Ess*, i, 222-61. A. Nash, in his introduction to the critical edition of the first volume of Newman's essays, observes how "... the whole essay has a more personal background for Newman than might be imagined on first reading," particularly since it "describes how people can misunderstand the early Fathers of the Church by reading them through the prism of Protestant doctrine." J.H. Newman, *Essays Critical and Historical* (Leominster, 2019), i, xxxvii.

[3] *St Cyprian*: St. Cyprian (c. 200–58), Bishop and Martyr. Beheaded by the Emperor Valerian for refusing to pay obeisance to the gods of Rome, Cyprian, as Bishop of Carthage, led the African Church during the persecution of Decius from hiding, and proved, before and after his banishment, a gentle, courteous, faithful man, about whom even Gibbon had a good word, assuring his readers that Cyprian "possessed every quality which could engage the reverence of the faithful or provoke the ... resentment of the Pagan magistrates." *Decline and Fall*, ii, 105. Newman reminded his readers of what an exemplary bishop Cyprian had been. "While exhorting to alms giving, he is already an example of voluntary poverty; if he praises virginity, he has himself embraced the single life; he insists on the nothingness of things earthly, having first chosen contempt and reproach; he denounces the heathen magistrate, with the knowledge that he is braving his power; and he is severe with the Lapsed, because he himself is to be a Martyr." J. H. Newman, Preface to "The Treatises of S. Cæcilius Cyprian, Bishop of Carthage, and Martyr," *A Library of Fathers of the Holy Catholic Church, Anterior to the Division of the East and West* (London, 1872), xxiii.

[4] *Creed*: John Pearson (1613-86), Bishop of Chester, "perhaps the most erudite and profound divine of a learned and theological age," published his *Exposition of the Creed*, exhibiting his "remarkable knowledge" of the Fathers, in 1659. *ODCC*.

too; but by reason of "the force of that article of our belief, the one Catholic and Apostolic Church."[5] If the mysterious grace of the Episcopate is insisted on, it is not merely as contained in Holy Scripture, though Scripture is appealed to again and again; but as implied in "that ineffable mystery, called in the Creed, the Communion of Saints."[6] Scripture was copiously quoted, the Fathers[7] were boldly invoked, and Anglican divines were diligently consulted; but the immediate, present, and, as the leaders of the movement hoped, the living authority, on which they based their theological system, was what was called the "Liturgy," or Book of Common Prayer.

This "Liturgy," as the instrument of their teaching, was, [132] on that account, regarded as practically infallible. "Attempts are making to get the Liturgy altered," says a Tract; "I beseech you consider with me, whether you ought not to resist the alteration of even one jot or tittle of it."[8] Then as to the burial service: "I frankly own," says another Tract, "it is sometimes distressing to use it; but this must ever be in the nature of things, wherever you draw the line."[9] Again, it was said that "there was a growing feeling that the Services were too long," and ought to be shortened, but it was to be

---

[5] *Apostolic Church*: J. H. Newman, *Tract 2, The Catholic Church* (8 September 1833).

[6] *Communion of Saints*: J. Morison, *Homilies for the Times; Or Rome and her Allies: A Plea for the Reformation* (London, 1841), 284.

[7] *the Fathers*: Cf. "I have to-day received a very valuable present of books from many of my new friends and pupils, consisting of 36 volumes of the Fathers; among these are the works of Austin, Athanasius, Cyril Alexandrinus, Epiphanius, Gregory Nyssen, Origen, Basil, Ambrose, and Irenæus. They are so fine in their outsides as to put my former ones to shame, and the editions are the best. Altogether, I am now set up in the patristical line..." JHN to Mrs. Newman (24 October 1831), *LD*, ii, 369.

[8] *"... tittle of it"*: Tract 3, *Thoughts Respectfully Addressed to the Clergy on Alterations in the Liturgy* (9 September 1833).

[9] *"...draw the line"*: *Ibid*, this is from the "Burial Service" section of Tract 3.

"arrested" by "certain considerations"[10] offered in a third. "There were persons who wished certain Sunday Lessons removed from the Service;"[11] but, according to a fourth, there was reason the other way, in the very argument which was "brought in favour of the change." Another project afloat was that of leaving out "such and such chapters of the Old Testament," and "assigning proper Lessons to every Sunday from the New;"[12] but it was temperately and ingeniously argued in a fifth, that things were best just as they were. And as the Prayer Book, so too was the Episcopate invested with a sacred character, which it was a crime to affront or impair. "Exalt our Holy Fathers," said a sixth Tract, "as the representatives of the Apostles, and the Angels of the Churches."[13] "They stand in the place of the Apostles," said a seventh, "as far as the office of ruling is concerned; and he that despiseth them despiseth the Apostles."[14]

[133]

3.

Now, why do I refer to these passages? Not for their own sake, but to show that the movement was based on submission to a definite existing authority, and that private judgment was practically excluded. I do not mean to say that its originators thought the Prayer Book inspired, any more than the Bishops infallible, as if they had nothing to

---

[10] *"certain considerations"*: R. H. Froude, *Tract 9, On Shortening the Church Service* (31 October 1833)

[11] *"removed from the Service"*: J. Keble, *Tract 13, Sunday Lessons: The Principle of Selection* (5 December 1833)

[12] *"from the New"*: *Ibid.*, "Among projected alterations in the Liturgy, not the least popular seems to be a very considerable change in the selection of the Sunday Lessons. People do not see, first of all, why such and such chapters are chosen out of the Old Testament, in preference to others which they think more edifying. Secondly, they see no reason why the Church should not assign Proper Lessons to every Sunday from the New Testament as well as from the Old. One who hopes that he should not be found froward,"

[13] *"the Angels of the Churches"*: J. H. Newman, *Tract 1, Thoughts on the Ministerial Commission* (9 September 1833)

[14] *"despiseth the Apostles"*: J. H. Newman, *Tract 10, Heads of a Weekday Lecture* (4 November 1833)

do but accept and believe what was put into their hands. They had too much common sense to deny the necessary exercise of private judgment, in one sense or another. They knew that the Catholic Church herself admitted it, though she directed and limited it to a decision upon the question of the organ of revelation; and they expressly recognized what they had no wish to deny. "So far," they said, "all parties must be agreed, that without private judgment there is no responsibility ... even though an infallible guidance be accorded, a man must have a choice of resisting it or not."[15] But still, not denying this as an abstract truth, they determined that, as regards the teaching of the Liturgy, or the enunciations of the Bishops—which is the point immediately under our consideration—all differences of opinion existing between members of the Establishment could be but minor ones, which might profitably, and [134] without effort, be suppressed; that is, these were such as ought to be inwardly discredited and rejected, as less probable than the authoritative rule or statement, or at most must only be entertained at home, not published or defended. The matters in debate could not be more than matters of opinion, not of doctrine. Thus, with respect to alterations in the Prayer Book, the Tract says, "Though most of you would wish some immaterial points altered, yet not many of you agree in those points, and not many of you agree what is and what is not immaterial. If all your respective emendations are taken, the alterations in the Service will be extensive; and, though each will gain something he wishes, he will lose more in consequence of those alterations which he did not wish. How few would be pleased by any given alterations and how many pained!"[16] Though, then, the Prayer Book was not perfect, it had a sort of practical perfection; and, though it was not unerring, it was a sure and sufficient safeguard against error. It was dangerous to question any part of it. "A taste for criticism

---

[15] Proph. Off., p. 157. [N] *VM*, i, 130.
[16] *"many pained"*: *Tract 3.*

grows upon the mind," said a Tract. "This unsettling of the mind is a frightful thing, both for ourselves, and more so for our flocks."[17] The principle, then, of these writers was this: An infallible authority is necessary; we have it not, for the Prayer Book is all we have got; but since we have nothing [135] better, we must use it as if infallible. I am not justifying the logic of this proceeding; but if it be deficient, much more clearly does it, for that very reason, bring out the strength with which they held the principle of authority itself, when they would make so great an effort to find for it a place in the National Religion, and would rather force a conclusion than give up their premiss.

The Prayer Book, then, according to the first agents in the movement, was the arbiter, and limit, and working rule of the ten thousand varying private judgments of which the community was made up, which could not all be satisfied, which could not all be right, which were, every one of them, less likely to be right than it. It was the immediate instrument by means of which they professed to make their way, the fulcrum by which they were to hoist up the Establishment, and set it down securely on the basis of Apostolical Truth. And thus it was accepted by the party, not only as essentially and substantially true, but also as eminently expedient and necessary for the time.

"To do anything effectually," said a speaker in a dialogue of mine, who is expressing the philosophy (so to call it) of the movement in answer to a Romanizing friend, "we must start from recognized principles and customs. Any other procedure stamps a person as wrong-headed, ill-judging, or eccentric, and brings upon him the contempt and ridicule of those sensible men by whose opinions society is [136] necessarily governed. Putting aside the question of truth and falsehood (which, of course, is the main consideration), even as aiming at success, we must be aware of the great error of making changes on no more definite basis than their abstract fitness, alleged scripturalness, or adoption by the

---

[17] *"... our flocks"*: Tract 3.

ancients. Such changes are rightly called innovations;— those which spring from existing institutions, opinions, and feelings, are called developments, and may be recommended, without invidiousness, as improvements. I adopt then, and claim as my own, that position of yours, that 'we must take and use what is ready to our hands.' To do otherwise is to act the *doctrinaire*, and to provide for failure. For instance, if we would enforce observance of the Lord's Day, we must not, at the outset, rest it on any theory, however just, of Church authority, but on the authority of Scripture. If we would oppose the State's interference with the distribution of Church property, we shall succeed, not by urging any doctrine of Church independence, or by citing decrees of general councils, but by showing the contrariety of that measure to existing constitutional and ecclesiastical precedents among ourselves. Hildebrand found the Church provided with certain existing means of power; he vindicated them, and was rewarded with the success which attends, not on truth as such, but on this prudence and tact in conduct. St. Paul observed the same rule, whether in preaching at Athens or persuading his countrymen. It was the gracious condescension of our Lord Himself, not to [137] substitute Christianity for Judaism by any violent revolution, but to develope Judaism into Christianity, as the Jews might bear it."[18]

---

[18] British Mag., April 1836. [N] J.H. Newman, "How to Accomplish It" (1836), *DA*, 29-30. In the dialogue, Basil, the speaker who opposes his "Romanizing friend," Ambrose goes on to argue that "... Popery is not here ready to our hands; on the contrary, we find among us, at this day, an intense fear and hatred of Popery; and that, ill-instructed as it confessedly is, still based upon truth. It is mere headstrong folly, then, to advocate the Church of Rome. It is to lose our position as a Church, which never answers to any, whether body or individual. If, indeed, salvation were not in our Church, the case would be altered ; as it is, were Rome as pure in faith as the Church of the Apostles, which she is not, I would not join her, unless those about me did so too, lest I should commit schism. Our business is to take what we have received, and build upon it: to accept, as a legacy from our forefathers, this 'Protestant' spirit which they have bequeathed us, and merely to disengage it from its errors,

4.

Now all this was very well, if expedience was the end, and not merely a reason, of their extolling the Episcopate and the Prayer Book; but if it was a question of truth (and as such they certainly considered it), then it was undeniable, that Prayer Book and Episcopate could not support themselves, but required some intellectual basis; and what was that to be? Here again, as before (and this is the point to which all along I wish to direct your attention), these writers professed to go by authority, not by private judgment; for they fell back upon the divines of the Anglican Church, as their channels for ascertaining both what Anglicanism taught and why. It is scarcely necessary to remind any one who has followed the movement in its course, how careful and anxious they were, as soon as they got (what may be called) under weigh, at once to collect and arrange Catenas of Anglican authorities, on whom their own teaching might be founded, and under whose name it might be protected.[19] Accordingly the doctrines, especially of the Apostolical succession, of Baptismal Regeneration, of the Eucharistic sacrifice, and of the Rule of Faith, were made the subject of elaborate collections of extracts from the divines of the Establishment. And so in like manner, when a formal theory or idea was attempted of the Anglican system, the writer said, and believed, that "he had endeavoured, in all important points of doctrine, to guide himself by our standard divines; and, had space admitted, would have selected passages from their writings, in evidence of it. Such a collection of testimonies," he continued, "is almost a duty on the part of every author, who professes, not to strike

[138]

---

purify it, and make it something more than a negative principle; thus only have we a chance of success." *Ibid*, 30-1.

[19] *protected*: See J.H. Newman, "Letter to Dr. Jelf in Explanation of the Remarks, 1841," *VM*, ii, 365-93 for an example of Newman's own catena of Anglican authorities in answer to the charges of several bishops against his Tract 90.

out new theories, but to build up and fortify what has been committed to us."[20]

5.

But now a further question obviously arises: by what rule will you determine what divines are authoritative, and what are not? for it is obvious, unless you can adduce such, private judgment will come in at last upon your ecclesiastical structure, in spite of your success hitherto in keeping it out. This answer, too, was ready—Scripture itself suggested to them the rule they should follow, and it was a rule external to themselves. They professed, then, to take simply those as authorities whom "all the people accounted prophets."[21] As it was no private judgment, but the [139] spontaneous sentiment of a whole people, that canonized the Baptist, as the ancient saints are raised over our altars by the acclamation of a universal immemorial belief; so, according to these writers, the popular voice was to be consulted, and its decision simply recorded and obeyed, in the selection of the divines on whom their theology was to be founded. They professed to put aside individual liking; they might admire Hooker, or they might think him obscure; they might love Taylor, or they might feel a secret repugnance to him; they might delight in the vigour of Bull, or they might be repelled by his homeliness and his want of the supernatural element; these various feelings they had, but they did not wish to select their authorities by any such private taste or reason, in which they would differ from each other, but by the voice of the community. For instance, Davenant[22] is a far abler writer than Hammond,[23] but how

---

[20] Proph. Off. p. vi. [N] J.H. Newman, "Advertisement to the First and Second Editions," *Lectures on the Prophetical Offices of the Church Viewed Relatively to Romanism and Popular Protestantism, VM*, i, xii.

[21] Viz., the text prefixed to the Catenas, Tract 74. There was another obvious rule also, but still not a private one. They had recourse to those Anglican divines who alone contemplated, and professed to provide, an *idea, theory, or intellectual position,* for their Church, as Laud and Stillingfleet. [N]

[22] *Davenant*: John Davenant (1597-1670), Puritan divine. After graduating from Oxford with his brother Christopher, who converted to

few have heard of him? Horne or Wilson is far inferior in learning, power, or originality to Warburton, yet their works have a popularity which Warburton's have not, and have, in consequence, a higher claim to the formal title of Anglican divinity. Such was the principle of selection on which the authors of the movement proceeded; and if you say they were untrue to their principles in the Catenas they drew out, [140] and, after all, selected partially, and on private judgment, I repeat, so much the more for my purpose. How clearly must the principle of an ecclesiastical and authoritative, not a private judgment, have been the principle of the movement, when those who belonged to it were obliged to own that principle, at the very time that it was inconvenient to them, and when they were driven, whether consciously or not, to misuse or evade it!

6.

Such, then, was the principle on which they professed to select the authorities they were to follow; nor was their anxiety in consulting them less than their carefulness in ascertaining them. Here again, I am not going into the question whether they deceived themselves in consulting, as well as in ascertaining these divines; whether they followed them where they agreed with themselves, and, where they stopped short, went forward without them: I am not aware that they did, but, whether they did or no, they tried not to do so; they wished to make the Anglican divines real

---

Rome and became chaplain, successively, to Queens Henrietta Maria and Catherine of Braganza, Davenant founded the Quinnipiac colony in the Colony of New Haven. A prolific author, his works include *A Catechism containing the Chief Heads of the Christian Religion* (1659) and *The Power of Congregational Churches Asserted and Vindicated* (1672). *ODCC*.

[23] *Hammond*: Henry Hammond (1605-60), Anglican divine. Forced to leave his living at Penhurst during the Civil War, he returned to Oxford, where he had been educated at Magdalen, and composed his *Practical Catechism* (1645), which commanded a wide readership. Deprived of his own ministry, he looked after penurious, and arranged for the instruction of future Anglican clergy. *ODCC*.

vouchers and sanctions of their own teaching, and they used their words rather than their own. They shrank from seeming to speak without warrant, even on matters which in no sense were matters of faith, and I can adduce an instance of it, which is more to the point, for the very reason it was singularly misunderstood; and, though it may seem to [141] require some apology that I should again refer to an author from whom I have made several extracts already, I mean myself, I have an excuse for doing so in the circumstance, that I naturally know his works better than those of others, and I can quote him without misrepresenting him or hurting his feelings. In a Retractation, then, which he published in the year 1843, of some strong statements which he had made against the Catholic Church, these words occur:—"If you ask me how an individual could venture, *not simply to hold but to publish* such views of a communion so ancient, so wide-spreading, so fruitful in Saints, I answer, that I said to myself, '*I am not speaking my own words*, I am but following almost a *consensus* of the divines of my Church. They have ever used the strongest language against Rome, even the most able and learned of them. I wish to throw myself into their system. While I say what they *say*, I am safe. Such views, too, are necessary for our position.'"[24] Now, this passage has been taken to mean, that the writer spoke from expediency what he did not believe; but this is false in fact, and inaccurate in criticism. He spoke what he felt, what he thought, what at the time he held, and nothing but what he held with an internal assent; but still, though he internally thought it, he would not have dared to say it—he would have shrunk, as well he might, from standing up, *on his own private judgment*, an accuser against the great [142] Roman communion, and unless in doing so he felt he had been doing simply what his own Church *required* of him, and what was *necessary* for his Church's cause, and what all his Church's divines had ever done before him. This

---

[24] *"... for our position"*: J. H. Newman, "To the Editor of the *Oxford Conservative Journal*" (12 December 1842), *LD*, ix, 171.

being the case, he "could venture, not simply to *hold* but to *publish*;" he was not "speaking his own *words*," though he *was* expressing his own *thoughts*; and, as using those words, he was behind "a system" received by his Church, as well as by himself. He felt "safe," because he spoke after, and "throwing himself into," he was sheltering himself according to its teaching and its teachers. It had, indeed, been one sin that he had thought ill of the Catholic Church; it had been another and greater, that he had uttered what he thought; and there was just this alleviation of his second sin, that he had not said it wantonly, and that he had said what others had said before him. There is nothing difficult or unnatural, surely, in this state of mind; but it is not wonderful that to the mass of Protestants it was incomprehensible that any one should shrink from the display of that private judgment in which they themselves so luxuriated, that any one should think of clearing himself from what in their eyes was simply a virtue, or should be shocked at having the credit given him of making use of a special privilege.

7.

But I have not yet arrived at the ultimate resolution of faith, in the judgment of the theological party of 1833: the Anglican divines, it seems, were to be followed, but, after all, were they inspired more than the Prayer Book? else, on what are we to say that their authority in turn depended? Again, the answer was ready: The Anglican divines are sanctioned by that authority, to which they themselves refer, the Fathers of the Church. Thus spoke the party: now at length, you will say, they are brought to a point, when private judgment must necessarily be admitted; for who shall ascertain what is in the Fathers and what is not, without a most special and singular application of his own powers of mind, and his own personal attainments, to the execution of so serious an undertaking? But not even here did they allow themselves to be committed to the Protestant instrument of inquiry, though this point will require some

170

little explanation. It must be observed, then, that they were accustomed to regard theology generally, much more upon its anti-Protestant side than upon its anti-Roman; and, from the circumstances in which they found themselves, were far more solicitous to refute Luther[25] and Calvin[26] than Suarez[27]

---

[25] *Luther*: One of the chief architects of the Reformation, Martin Luther (1483-1546) entered the monastery of the Augustinian hermits in 1505. He was ordained a priest in 1507. In 1510, he visited Rome, where the morbidly scrupulous young German found the papacy of Pope Julius II scandalous, especially its altogether salutary practice of granting indulgences in return for alms, without which there should have been no 'bricks and mortar' Christendom. As a doctor of philosophy in the university at Wittenberg, Luther succumbed to the fashionable nominalism of the time and, concurrently, the gloomy view of nature and grace held by the Augustinians, a poisonous cocktail, which his own lugubrious nature could only worsen. Between 1512 and 1513, he came to the conclusion that the key to the Gospel was that faith alone justifies without works—the heretical misunderstanding of nature and grace which would animate all of his subsequent disavowals of Catholic doctrine. Ironically, by insisting that works were immaterial to salvation, Luther paved the way for the very Erastian Christianity in which the English Reformation would culminate, one in which the state, not the church dictated faith and morals, and this despite the fact that Henry VIII had been a fierce critic of Luther before the 'great matter' of his divorce arose.

[26] *Calvin:* John Calvin (1509-64), French theologian and heresiarch. Calvin refined on the Erastian character of Luther's ideas by setting up a theocracy in Geneva, in which all the affairs of the city and its citizens were dictated by his heterodox views. The Calvinism that ensued beguiled the obduracy of human depravity with the self-complacencies of election. As the good Whig historian, H. A. L. Fisher observed, "among the European peoples none have been sterner in the practice of religion or more ruthless in the pursuit of wealth than the professors of a doctrine which seems to make all human effort unavailing and to invite to a life of apathy and ease." Fisher, *A History of Europe* rev. ed. (London, 1938), ii, 110. Apropos Calvin's impact on England, Fisher is equally clear-eyed: "it exercised an influence over the Thirty-Nine Articles ... the declared creed of the national Church, so palpable that Queen Elizabeth, little as she sympathized with the spirit of Geneva, was excommunicated as a Calvinist." *Ibid*, 111.

[27] *Suarez*: Francesco de Suarez (1548-1617), Spanish Jesuit theologian. His interest in matters of church and state and the Church and the law animate both his *De Virtute et Statu Religionis* (1608-09) and *De Legibus* (1612). In addition, Suarez published *Defensio Fidei*, a critique of the

or Bellarmine.[28] Protestantism was a present foe; Catholicism, or Romanism as they called it, was but a possible adversary; "it was not likely," they said, "that [144] Romanism should ever again become formidable in England;" and they engaged with it accordingly, not from any desire to do so, but because they could not form an ecclesiastical theory without its coming in their way, and challenging their notice. It was "necessary for their position" to dispose of Catholicism, but it was not a task of which they acquitted themselves with the zeal or interest which was so evident in their assaults upon their Protestant brethren. "Those who feel the importance of that article of the Creed," the holy Catholic Church, says a work several times quoted, "and yet are not Romanists, are *bound* on several accounts to show why they are not Romanists, and how they differ from them. They are bound to do so, in order to remove the prejudice with which an article of the Creed is at present encompassed. From the circumstances, then, of the moment, the following Lectures are chiefly engaged in examining and exposing certain tenets of Romanism."[29] The author's feeling, then, seems to have

---

Church of England which met with an indignant bonfire in London. If Aquinas is the greatest theologian produced by the Order of Preachers, Suarez is the greatest produced by the Society of Jesus. In October of 1850, Newman advised a fellow convert: "Nothing can be better than ... [Suarez's] Treatise on Grace [*Varia Opuscula Theologica* (1599)] ... St. Thomas himself would be most instructive. But any how go to a real thorough thinker, though a partisan, not to a mere expounder of wealth, or an eschewer of scholastic quarrels, as Perrone, useful and accurate as he is. The fault of Suarez is his great length." *LD*, xiv, 96.

[28] *Bellarmine*: Roberto Bellarmine (1542-1621), Italian Jesuit, cardinal, saint and Doctor of the Church. A key figure of the Counter-Reformation, he is best known for his 3-voume *Disputantiones de Controversiis Christianae Fidei adversus hujus temporis Haereticos* (1586-93). The definitive Newman biographer, I. Ker expects that Newman will be made a Doctor of the Church precisely because "he is likely to be seen as the counterpart, in the Church of the Second Vatican Council, of St. Robert Bellarmine, the Doctor *par excellence* of the Tridentine Church." Ker, *Newman on Vatican II*, 161.

[29] Proph. Office, p. 7. I am not unmindful of the following "ground" for publishing the Translations of the Fathers, contained in the prospectus:—"

been,—I should have a perfect case against this Protestantism but for these inconvenient "Romanists," [145] whose claims I do not admit indeed, but who, controversially, stand in my way.

But now, with this explanation, to the point before us:— The consequence of this state of mind was, that the persons in question were not very solicitous (if I dare speak for others) *how far* the Fathers *seemed* to tell for the Church of Rome or not; on the whole, they were sure they did not tell materially for her; but it was no matter, though they partially seemed to do so; for their great and deadly foe, their scorn, and their laughing-stock, was that imbecile, inconsistent thing called Protestantism; and there could not be a more thorough refutation of its foundation and superstructure than was to be found in the volumes of the Fathers. There was no mistaking that the principles professed, and doctrines taught by those holy men, were utterly anti-Protestant; and, being satisfied of this, which was their principal consideration, it did not occur to them accurately to determine the range and bounds of the teaching of the early Church, or to reflect that, perhaps, they had as yet a clearer view of what it did not sanction, than of what it did. They saw, then, that there simply was no opportunity at all for private judgment, if one wished to exercise it ever so much, as regards the question of the anti-Protestantism of the Fathers; it was a patent fact, open to all, written on the face of their works, that they were anti-Protestant; you might defer to them, you might reject them, [146]

II. The great danger in which the Romanists are of lapsing into secret infidelity, not seeing how to escape from the palpable errors of their own Church, without falling into the opposite errors of ultra-Protestants. It appeared an act of especial charity to point out to such of them as are dissatisfied with the state of their own Church, a body of ancient Catholic truth, free from the errors alike of modern Rome, and of ultra-Protestantism." I have nothing to say in explanation, but that this passage was not written by me, and that I do not consider it to have expressed my own feelings, or those of the movement. [N] See R.W. Pfaff, "The Library of the Fathers: The Tractarians as Patristic Translators," *Studies in Philology* 70 (1973), 329-44.

but you could as little deny that they were essentially anti-Protestant, as you could deny that "the Romanists" were anti-Protestants. It was a matter of fact, a matter of sense, which Protestants themselves admitted or rather maintained; and here, in this public and undeniable fact, we have arrived at what the movement considered the ultimate resolution of its faith. It argued, for instance, "A private Christian may put what meaning he pleases on many parts of Scripture, and no one can hinder him. If interfered with, he can promptly answer, that it is his own opinion, and may appeal to his right of private judgment. But he cannot so deal with Antiquity: history is a record of facts; and facts, according to the proverb, are stubborn things."[30] And accordingly, these writers represented the Church as they conceived of it, as having no power whatever over the faith; her Creed was simply a public matter of fact, which needed as little explanation, as little interpretation, as the fact of her own existence. Hence they said: "The humblest and meanest among Christians may defend the faith against the whole Church, if the need arise. He has as much stake in it, and as much right to it, as Bishop or Archbishop; ... all that learning has to do for him is to ascertain the fact, what is the meaning of the Creed in particular points, since matter of

[147] opinion it is not, any more than the history of the rise and spread of Christianity itself."[31]

Accordingly, as their first act, when they were once set off, had been to publish Catenas of the Anglican divines, so their second was to publish translations of the Fathers—viz., in order to put the matter out of their own hands, and throw the decision upon the *private* judgment of no one, but on the common judgment of the whole community, Anglicans and Protestants at once. They considered that the Fathers had hitherto been monopolised by controversialists, who treated them merely as magazines of passages which might be brought forward in argument, mutilated and garbled for the

---

[30] Proph. Office, p. 45. [N]
[31] P. 292. [N]

occasion; and that the greatest service to their own cause was simply to publish them.[32] "A main reason," it was said, "of the jealousy with which Christians of this age and country adhere to the notion that truth of doctrine can be gained from Scripture by individuals is this, that they are unwilling, as they say, to be led by others blindfold. They can possess and read the Scriptures; whereas, of traditions they are not adequate judges, and they dread priestcraft. I am not here to enter into the discussion of this feeling, whether praiseworthy or the contrary. However this be, it does seem a reason for putting before them, if possible, the principal works of the Fathers, translated as Scripture is; [148] that they may have by them what, whether used or not, will at least act as a check upon the growth of an undue dependence on the word of individual teachers, and will be a something to consult, if they have reason to doubt the Catholic character of any tenet to which they are invited to accede."[33]

By way, then, of rescuing the faith from private teaching on the one hand, and private judgment on the other, it was proposed to publish a Library of the Fathers translated into English. And let it be observed, in pursuance of this object, the Translations were to be presented to the general reader without note or comment. It was distinctly stated in the Prospectus, that "the notes shall be limited to the explanation of obscure passages, or the removal of any misapprehension which might not improbably arise." And this was so strictly adhered to at first, that the translation of St. Cyril's Catechetical Lectures was criticised in a Catholic

---

[32] See this brought out in an article on the Apostolical Fathers, in the *British Critic* of January 1839. [*Vide* the author's "Essays Critical and Historical," No. 5.] [N] J.H. Newman, "Apostolical Tradition," *Ess*, i, 102-37.

[33] Proph. Office, p. 203. This passage, moreover, negatives the charge, sometimes advanced against the agents in the movement, that they wished *every individual Christian* to gain his faith for himself by study of the Fathers. They have enough to bear without our imagining absurdities. [N]

Review on this very ground;[34] and it was asked why his account of the Holy Eucharist was not *reconciled* by the Editor with the Anglican formularies, when the very idea of [149] the Editor had been to bring out *facts*, and leave the result to a judgment more authoritative than his own, and favourable on the whole, as he hoped, in the event, to the Church to which he belonged. "We can do no more," he had said in the Preface, "than have patience, and recommend patience to others; and with the racer in the Tragedy, look forward steadily and hopefully to the event, 'in the end relying,'[35] when, as we trust, all that is inharmonious and anomalous in the details, will at length be practically smoothed."[36]

8.

Such, then, was the clear, unvarying line of thought, as I believed it to be, on which the movement of 1833 commenced and proceeded, as regards the questions of Church authority and private judgment. It was fancied that no opportunity for the exercise of private judgment could arise in any public or important matter. The Church declared, whether by Prayer Book or Episcopal authority, what was to be said or done; and private judgment either had no objection which it could make good, or only on those minor matters where there was a propriety in its yielding to authority. And the present Church declared what her divines had declared; and her divines had declared what

---

[34] Viz., the "Dublin Review." The rule of publishing without note or comment was, in consequence of such objections, soon abandoned. [N] *The Dublin Review*, No. xiii. (August, 1839), 24. See also, J.H. Browne, *Strictures of Some Parts of the Oxford Tract System, especially as it is Developed in the 80th and 83rd Tracts. A Charge, Delivered to The Clergy of the Archdeaconry of Ely, At A Visitation, Held in the Parish Church of St. Michael's, Cambridge, On Thursday, May the 21st, 1840.* (London, 1840), 8.

[35] *the racer in the Tragedy* ... : "Orestes had been driving last and holding/his horses back, putting his trust in the finish." Sophocles, *Electra* translated by D. Grene, 734-5. *The Complete Tragedies* eds. Grene and Lattimore (Chicago, 1992), ii, 365.

[36] Page xi. [N]

the Fathers had declared; and what the Fathers had declared was no matter of private judgment at all, but a matter of fact, cognizable by all who chose to read their writings. [150] Their testimony was as decisive and clear as Pope's Bull or Definition of Council, or catechisings or direction of any individual parish priest. There was no room for two opinions on the subject; and, as Catholics consider that the truth is brought home to the soul supernaturally, so that the soul sees it and no longer depends on reason, so in some parallel way it was supposed, in the theology of the movement, that that same truth, as contained in the Fathers, was a natural fact, recognised by the natural and ordinary intelligence of mankind, as soon as that intelligence was directed towards it.

The idea, then, of the divines of the movement was simply and absolutely submission to an external authority; to such an authority they appealed, to it they betook themselves; there they found a haven of rest; thence they looked out upon the troubled surge of human opinion and upon the crazy vessels which were labouring, without chart or compass, upon it. Judge then of their dismay, when, according to the Arabian tale,[37] on their striking their

---

[37] *the Arabian tale*: Newman alludes to "The Story of the Lady of the Beautiful Hair" in the *Arabian Nights*. "By degrees, the point to which he had directed his eyes, seemed to him like a floating island, of capacity enough to block up the harbour towards which it seemed to be bearing. With a precipitate flight, he hastened to inform Dorathil-goase of what he had beheld. He described the motion he had discovered in the waters; the island which seemed gradually to rise from its bosom; its approach towards their coasts; and farther, that he had beheld living beings on its surface. "In other respects," said he, "Abarikas seems to have called off his forces to the black island, where their multitude seems to darken the day. There is nothing menacing in the appearance of the island which approaches; but as it must have been the produce of enchantment, your sagacity must be careful to prevent and subdue its effects." Dorathil-goase immediately sent for her two ministers, and her grandfather, Il-Hatrous-habous, and in a moment, the coasts were lined with all the warriors of the country." *Arabian Tale; or, A Continuation of the Arabian Nights Entertainments. Consisting of Stories, Related by The Sultana of the Indies, To Divert her Husband from the Performance of a Rash Vow.* (London, 1794), 333-4.

anchors into the supposed soil, lighting their fires on it, and fixing in it the poles of their tents, suddenly their island began to move, to heave, to splash, to frisk to and fro, to dive and at last to swim away, spouting out inhospitable jets of water upon the credulous mariners who had made it their [151] home. And such, I suppose, was the undeniable fact: I mean, the time at length came, when first of all turning their minds (some of them, at least) more carefully to the doctrinal controversies of the early Church, they saw distinctly that in the reasonings of the Fathers, elicited by means of them, and in the decisions of authority, in which they issued, were contained at least the rudiments, the anticipation, the justification of what they had been accustomed to consider the corruptions of Rome. And if only one, or a few of them, were visited with this conviction, still even one was sufficient, of course, to destroy that cardinal point of their whole system, the objective perspicuity and distinctness of the teaching of the Fathers. But time went on, and there was no mistaking or denying the misfortune which was impending over them. They had reared a goodly house, but their foundations were falling in. The soil and the masonry both were bad. The Fathers *would* protect "Romanists" as well as extinguish Dissenters. The Anglican divines *would* misquote the Fathers, and shrink from the very doctors to whom they appealed. The Bishops of the seventeenth century were shy of the Bishops of the fourth; and the Bishops of the nineteenth were shy of the Bishops of the seventeenth. The ecclesiastical courts upheld the sixteenth century against the seventeenth, and, regardless of the flagrant irregularities of Protestant clergymen, chastised the mild misdemeanours of Anglo-Catholic. Soon the living rulers of the Establishment [152] began to move. There are those who, reversing the Roman's maxim,[38] are wont to shrink from the contumacious, and to

---

[38] *"Parcere subjectis, et debellare superbos:"* It may be right here to say, that the author never can forget the great kindness which Dr. Bagot, at that time Bishop of Oxford, showed him on several occasions. He also has to notice the courtesy of Dr. Thirwall's language, a prelate whom he

be valiant towards the submissive; and the authorities in question gladly availed themselves of the power conferred on them by the movement against the movement itself. They fearlessly handselled their Apostolic weapons upon the Apostolical party. One after another, in long succession, they took up their song and their parable against it. It was a solemn war-dance, which they executed round victims, who by their very principles were bound hand and foot, and could only eye with disgust and perplexity this most unaccountable movement, on the part of their "holy Fathers, the representatives of the Apostles, and the Angels of the Churches." It was the beginning of the end.

My brethren, when it was at length plain that primitive Christianity ignored the National Church, and that the

---

has never had the honour of knowing. [N] The ironic Latin reference is to Virgil, *Aeneid*, 6.853. 'To show mercy to the conquered and to subdue the proud.' When the bishops moved to attack Tract 90, they showed little mercy to the 'conquered' Tractarian in Newman. Dr. Bagot, Bishop of Oxford was an exception. Yes, he first asked Newman that he comply with the suppression of the Tract, but he later thought better of it and decided against suppression, declaring in his charge that while he was 'against all interpretations which made the Articles mean every thing or nothing,' he did not see why the Tractarians should not be granted the same liberty of interpretation as the Evangelicals. In all events, Newman thanked him for his 'kindness.' See I. Ker, *John Henry Newman: A Biography* (Oxford, 1988), 248. In the *Apologia*, Newman recalled the bemusement with which he found himself 'posted up by the marshall on the buttery-hatch of every College of my University, after the manner of discommoned pastry-cooks.' *Apo*, 88. In his charge, Connop Thirwall, the Bishop of St. David wrote: "I am aware, my Reverend Brethren, that the language of moderation is commonly least welcome where it is most needed.... Be on your guard against the illusions of names and phrases, and against the influence of authority in this matter etc." Newman had not seen the charge when he made his reference to Thirwall in his lectures, but explained many years later to a friend who claimed that the Bishop had been one of those who had wished to "hound" Newman out of Oxford at the time: "I am not aware that he made any *protest* against the hounding — or did anything to hinder it — but of course he may have done so in private, for what one knows. In his charge at the time I think he took a distinct part against me, but in a very temperate and gentlemanlike way." Newman to M. Maccoll (13 December 1872), *LD*, xxvi, 214.

National Church cared little for primitive Christianity, or for those who appealed to it as her foundation; when Bishops spoke against them, and Bishops' courts sentenced them, and Universities degraded them, and the people rose against them, from that day their "occupation was gone." Their [153] initial principle, their basis, external authority, was cut from under them; they had "set their fortunes on a cast;"[39] they had lost; henceforward they had nothing left for them but to shut up their school, and retire into the country. Nothing else was left for them, unless, indeed, they took up some other theory, unless they changed their ground, unless they ceased to be what they were, and became what they were not; unless they belied their own principles, and strangely forgot their own luminous and most keen convictions; unless they vindicated the right of private judgment, took up some fancy-religion, retailed the Fathers, and jobbed theology.[40] They had but a choice between doing nothing at all, and looking out for truth and peace elsewhere.

---

[39] *on a cast*: "I have set my life upon a cast/And I will stand the hazard of the die." Shakespeare, *King Richard III*, Act V, Sc. iv, 9-10.

[40] *jobbed theology*: Newman is using 'job' in the sense of "To hire (less usually let out on hire) for a particular job ..." *OED*. The Church of England let out theology on hire to its bishops for the particular job of serving the interests of the Establishment. Many of the biographical profiles of Anglican divines included in these annotations will abundantly (indeed, in some cases, comically) show this. If, as Newman says in his 12th lecture, he does not scoff at these divines, he does "scorn and laugh" at them. *Diff*, i, 398. Apropos the bishops of the Georgian Church, the historian R Porter confirms Newman's characterization of the jobbery implicit in the Erastian church when he points out that "Most bishops were business-like diocesan managers, efficient at conducting visitations and holding mass confirmations. Above all, the higher clergy served their political masters well. 'He resides as much as any bishop in his diocese,' Viscount Percival complimented Bishop Wilcocks of Gloucester in 1730, 'at least four months in the year, and keeps a very generous and hospitable table, which makes amends for the learning he is deficient in. Though no great scholar nor a deep man, he is a very frequent preacher and this with his zeal for the government, good humour and regular life, makes him very well liked by the government and all that know him.'" R Porter, *England in the Eighteenth Century* (London, 1998), 162-3.

9.

And now, at length, I am in a condition to answer the question which you have proposed for my consideration. You ask me whether you cannot now continue what you were. No, my brethren, it is impossible, you cannot recall the past; you cannot surround yourselves with circumstances which have simply ceased to be. In the beginning of the movement you disowned private judgment, but now, if you would remain a party, you must, with whatever inconsistency, profess it;—then you were a party only externally, that is, not in your wishes and feelings, but merely because you were seen to differ from others in matter of fact, when the world looked at you, whether you [154] would or no; but now you will be a party knowingly and on principle, intrinsically, and will be erected on a party basis. You cannot be what you were. You will no longer be Anglo-Catholic, but Patristico-Protestants. You will be obliged to frame a religion for yourselves, and then to maintain that it is that very truth, pure and celestial, which the Apostles promulgated. You will be induced of necessity to put together some speculation of your own, and then to fancy it of importance enough to din it into the ears of your neighbours, to plague the world with it, and, if you have success, to convulse your own Communion with the imperious inculcation of doctrines which you can never engraft upon it.

For me, my dear brethren, did I know myself well, I should doubtless find I was open to the temptation, as well as others, to take a line of my own, or what is called, to set up for myself; but whatever might be my real infirmity in this matter, I should, from mere common sense and common delicacy, hide it from myself, and give it some good name in order to make it palatable. I never could get myself to say, "Listen to me, for I have something great to tell you, which no one else knows, but of which there is no manner of doubt." I should be kept from such extravagance from an intense sense of the intellectual absurdity, which, in my feelings, such a claim would involve; which would

[155]

shame me as keenly, and humble me in my own sight as utterly, as some moral impropriety or degradation. I should feel I was simply making a fool of myself, and taking on myself in figure that penance, of which we read in the Lives of the Saints, of playing antics and making faces in the market-place. Not religious principle, but even worldly pride, would keep me from so unworthy an exhibition. I can understand, my brethren, I can sympathise with those old-world thinkers, whose commentators are Mant and D'Oyly,[41] whose theologian is Tomline,[42] whose ritualist is Wheatly,[43] and whose canonist is Burns;[44] who are proud of

---

[41] *D'Oyly*: George D'Oyly (1778–1846), Church of England clergyman and theologian. Well known in his day as a theologian, D'Oyly was also "an admirable parish priest, and while he was rector of Lambeth thirteen places of worship were added to the church establishment of the parish. He was treasurer to the Society for Promoting Christian Knowledge, a member of the London committee of the Society for the Propagation of the Gospel, and one of the principal promoters of the establishment of King's College, London. ... He assisted Richard Mant in the preparation of the annotated *Bible* published by the SPCK and known as *'D'Oyly and Mant's Bible'* (1814 and later edns)." *ODNB*. Newman was unimpressed with their handiwork: "The Society's outlines from Mant's Bible are wretched," he told a correspondent in 1840. *LD*, vii, 253.

[42] *Tomline*: Sir George Pretyman Tomline, fifth baronet (1750–1827), Bishop of Winchester and political adviser. In *A Refutation of Calvinism* (1818), Tomline "consolidated and extended the message of many of the charges to his clergy, assembling a formidable collection of quotations from the fathers to demonstrate their opposition to Calvinist doctrines and, in chapter 6, argued from detailed evidence that the opinions of many heretics resembled Calvinism. He concluded: 'Our Church is not Lutheran—it is not Calvinistic—it is not Arminian—It is Scriptural: it is built upon the Apostles and Prophets, Jesus Christ himself being the chief corner-stone' (3rd edn, 1811, 590). The *Refutation* achieved considerable success, reaching an eighth edition in 1823, and provoked replies of a high quality, notably from Thomas Scott." *ODNB*. In March of 1831, H.J. Rose wrote Newman of "the great [theological] deficiencies of the books in common use (especially Bishop Tomline's ...)" *LD*, ii, 321.

[43] *Wheatly*: Charles Wheatly (1686–1742), Church of England clergyman and liturgical scholar. "Arguably the most influential liturgical scholar of his generation, Wheatly is best remembered for *The Church of England Man's Companion, or, A Rational Illustration of ... the Book of Common Prayer* (1710; 8th edn, 1759). This ... remained the standard work on its subject for over 100 years. Markedly High-Church in emphasis, it drew

their Jewels and their Chillingworths,[45] whose works they have never opened, and toast Cranmer and Ridley,[46] and

---

on deep patristic learning to uphold the Church of England's claims to a spiritual commission independent of any reliance upon the State; to assert the indispensable nature of the apostolic succession in the ministry; and to justify the use of external ceremonies in the conduct of public worship. Much of its teaching, particularly in relation to eucharistic theology, was identical to that of 'usager' nonjurors. However, Wheatly rejected Jacobitism, arguing in the *Rational Illustration* and elsewhere in favour of allegiance to the *de facto* powers." *ODNB*

[44] *Burns*: Richard Burn (1709–85), legal writer and Church of England clergyman. "His first book, *The justice of the peace and parish officer, upon a plan entirely new, and comprehending all the law to the present time* (2 vols., 1755), became a classic because it fulfilled the promise of its title. Before Burn, justices' manuals had arbitrarily subdivided the myriad matters with which justices dealt, and then simply listed the laws uniquely concerned with each arbitrarily defined topic. Burn instead constructed coherent categories for the discussion of the matters subject to the powers of justices and parish officers; and within each category he presented, in the order in which they arose in the performance of the justice's or officer's duty, the steps a justice or officer would take in dealing with each matter, and the law relevant to each step … *Ecclesiastical Law* (2 vols.), which like his justices' manual was a great success, presented the law relevant to matters arising in ecclesiastical courts. … This manual reached its ninth and final edition in 1842." *ODNB*.

[45] *Chillingworth*: William Chillingworth (1602–44), Anglican controversialist. Having converted to Catholicism and reconverted to Anglicanism, Chillingworth was a useful deterrent to Anglicans inclined to pope. As the *ODNB* remarks: "Chillingworth's consistent stance was one of rational scepticism, a distrust of dogmatic certainty." As he wrote in *The Religion of Protestants* (1637), he was "not willing … to take any thing upon trust, and to believe it without asking my selfe why; no, nor able to command my selfe (were I never so willing) to follow, like a sheepe, every sheepheard that should take upon him to guide me; or every flock that should chance to goe before me: but most apt and most willing to be led by reason to any way, or from it.' Chillingworth is best known today, and was often cited by Newman for his incisive recognition that "The Bible and the Bible only is the religion of Protestants."

[46] *Ridley*: Nicholas Ridley (c. 1502–1555), Bishop of London. Arrested for treason after the accession of Mary I, Ridley was burnt at the stake with Hugh Latimer in Oxford on 16 October 1555. J. Foxe fashioned his famous account of Latimer's dying words, 'Be of good comfort Master Ridley, and play the man: we shall this day light such a candle by God's

William of Orange, as the founders of their religion. In these times three hundred years is a respectable antiquity; and traditions, recognized in law courts, and built into the structure of society, may well without violence be imagined to be immemorial. Those also I can understand, who take their stand upon the Prayer Book; or those who honestly profess to follow the *consensus* of Anglican divines, as the voice of authority and the standard of faith. Moreover, I can quite enter into the sentiment with which members of the liberal and infidel school investigate the history and the documents of the early Church. They profess a view of Christianity, truer than the world has ever had; nor, on the assumption of their principles, is there anything shocking to good sense in this profession. They look upon the Christian [156] Religion as something simply human; and there is no reason at all why a phenomenon of that kind should not be better understood, in its origin and nature, as years proceed. It is, indeed, an intolerable paradox to assert, that a revelation, given from God to man, should lie unknown or mistaken for eighteen centuries, and now at length should be suddenly deciphered by individuals; but it is quite intelligible to assert, and plausible to argue, that a human fact should be more philosophically explained than it was eighteen hundred years ago, and more exactly ascertained than it was a thousand. History is at this day undergoing a process of revolution; the science of criticism, the disinterment of antiquities, the unrolling of manuscripts, the interpretation of inscriptions, have thrown us into a new world of thought; characters and events come forth transformed in the process; romance, prejudice, local tradition, party bias, are no longer accepted as guarantees of truth; the order and mutual relation of events are readjusted; the springs and the scope of action are reversed. Were Christianity a mere work of man, it, too, might turn out something different from what it has hitherto been considered; its history might

---

grace in England, as (I trust) shall never be put out' (Foxe, 1583, 1770), from Eusebius's account of the death of Polycarp.

require rewriting, as the history of Rome, or of the earth's strata, or of languages, or of chemical action. A Catholic neither deprecates nor fears such inquiry, though he abhors the spirit in which it is too often conducted. He is willing that infidelity should do its work against the Church, [157] knowing that she will be found just where she was, when the assault is over. It is nothing to him, though her enemies put themselves to the trouble of denying everything that has hitherto been taught, and begin with constructing her history all over again, for he is quite sure that they will end at length with a compulsory admission of what at first they so wantonly discarded. Free thinkers and broad thinkers, Laudians and Prayer-Book Christians, high-and-dry and Establishment-men, all these he would understand; but what he would feel so prodigious is this,—that such as you, my brethren, should consider Christianity given from heaven once for all, should protest against private judgment, should profess to transmit what you have received, and yet from diligent study of the Fathers, from your thorough knowledge of St. Basil[47] and St. Chrysostom,[48] from living,

---

[47] *St. Basil*: Basil the Great (c. 330-79), Bishop of Caesarea and Doctor of the Church. One of the four great Greek Doctors of the Church, he defended the Church against the Arian assaults of the Emperor Valens by founding a number of monasteries and preaching the doctrine adopted by the Church at the Council of Nicaea. Thanks to his efforts, Arianism was largely stamped out two years after his death. Newman had great respect for the passionate saint, about whom he wrote: "Basil, from his multiplied trials, may be called the Jeremiah or Job of the fourth century, though occupying the honoured place of a ruler in the Church at a time when heathen violence was over. He had a sickly constitution, to which he added the rigour of an ascetic life. He was surrounded by jealousies and dissensions at home; he was accused of heterodoxy abroad; he was insulted and roughly treated by great men; and he laboured, apparently without fruit, in the endeavour to restore unity to Christendom and stability to its Churches. If temporal afflictions work out for the saints 'an exceeding weight of glory,' who is higher in the kingdom of heaven than Basil?" *HS*, ii, 12.

[48] *St. Chrysostom*: John Chrysostom (c. 347- 407), Bishop and Doctor of the Church. One of the four great Greek Doctors of the Church, he was preeminently known as a great preacher, especially on Scripture and St. Paul. For Newman, Chrysostom's appeal lay "in his intimate sympathy

as you say, in the atmosphere of Antiquity, that you should come forth into open day with your new edition of the Catholic faith, different from that held in any existing body of Christians anywhere, which not half-a-dozen men all over the world would honour with their *imprimatur*; and then, withal, should be as positive about its truth in every part, as if the voice of mankind were with you instead of being against you.

[158] You are a body of yesterday; you are a drop in the ocean of professing Christians; yet you would give the law to priest and prophet; and you fancy it an humble office, forsooth, suited to humble men, to testify the very truth of Revelation to a fallen generation, or rather to almost a long bi-millenary, which has been in unalleviated traditionary error. You have a mission to teach the National Church, which is to teach the British empire, which is to teach the world; you are more learned than Greece; you are purer than Rome; you know more than St. Bernard; you judge how far St. Thomas was right, and where he is to be read with caution, or held up to blame. You can bring to light juster views of grace, or of penance, or of invocation of saints, than St. Gregory or St. Augustine,—

---

and compassionateness for the whole world, not only in its strength but in its weakness; in the lively regard with which he views everything that comes before him ..." Newman was also moved by "the discriminating affectionateness with which he accepts every one for what is personal in him and unlike others. I speak of his versatile recognition of men, one by one, for the sake of that portion of good, be it more or less, of a lower order or a higher, which has severally been lodged in them; his eager contemplation of the many things they do, effect, or produce, of all their great works, as nations or as states; nay, even as they are corrupted or disguised by evil, so far as that evil may in imagination be disjoined from their proper nature, or may be regarded as a mere material disorder apart from its formal character of guilt. I speak of the kindly spirit and the genial temper with which he looks round at all things which this wonderful world contains; of the graphic fidelity with which he notes them down upon the tablets of his mind, and of the promptitude and propriety with which he calls them up as arguments or illustrations in the course of his teaching as the occasion requires." *HS*, ii, 286.

"qualia vincunt
Pythagoran, Anytique reum, doctumque Platonia."[49]

This is what you can do; yes, and when you have done all, to what have you attained? to do just what heretics have done before you, and, as doing, have incurred the anathema of Holy Church. Such was Jansenius;[50] for of him we are told, "From the commencement of his theological studies, when he began to read, with the schoolmen, the holy Fathers, and especially Augustine,[51] he at once saw, as he confessed, that most of the schoolmen went far astray from that holy Doctor's view, in that capital article of grace and free will. He sometimes owned to his friends, that he had read over more than ten times the entire works of Augustine, with lively attention and diligent annotation, and his books against the Pelagians[52] at least thirty times from [159]

---

[49] *Qualia vincunt ... :* "of a character surpassing those of Pythagoras, Socrates or the learned Plato." Horace, Book II, Satire IV. Anytus' false accusation put Socrates to death.

[50] *Jansenius*: Cornelius Jansen (1585-1638), Dutch theologian, Bishop of Ypres in Flanders, from whose works sprang the heretical movement of Jansenism, which warped the Roman Catholic understanding of nature, grace, sin and free will. Extant in the Church in the 17th and 18th centuries, the Jansenists and their heresies were condemned by several popes, including Clement X in his bull, *Unigenitus* (1713). Apropos Jansen, Newman admitted to Father Faber in 1851: "Were I a Bishop, I should be a Jansenist in forbidding pretty maidservants in clerical establishments, et id genus omne." *LD*, xiv, 196.

[51] *Augustine*: It was, initially, a misreading of the anti-Pelagian works of St. Augustine (354–430), Bishop of Hippo and Doctor of the Church, that led Jansen to misunderstand the Church's understanding of nature, grace, sin and free will.

[52] *Pelagians*: Adherents of the British monk Pelagius (354-418), who refused to credit the doctrine of original sin. "As all his ideas were chiefly rooted in the old, pagan philosophy, especially in the popular system of the Stoics, rather than in Christianity, he regarded the moral strength of man's will (*liberum arbitrium*), when steeled by asceticism, as sufficient in itself to desire and to attain the loftiest ideal of virtue. The value of Christ's redemption was, in his opinion, limited mainly to instruction (*doctrina*) and example (*exemplum*), which the Saviour threw into the balance as a counterweight against Adam's wicked example, so that nature retains the ability to conquer sin and to gain eternal life even

beginning to end. He said that no mind, whether Aristotle or Archimedes, or any other under the heavens, was equal to Augustine ... I have heard him say more than once, that life would be most delightful to him, though on some ocean-isle or rock, apart from all human society, had he but his Augustine with him. In a word, after God and Holy Scripture, Augustine was his all in all. However, for many years he had to struggle with his old opinions, before he put them all off, and arrived at the intimate sense of St. Augustine ... For this work, he often said, he was specially born; and that, when he had finished it, he should be most ready to die."[53] Such, too, was another nearer home, on whom Burnet bestows this panegyric:—"Cranmer," says he, "was at great pains to collect the sense of ancient writers upon all the heads of religion, by which he might be directed in such an important matter. I have seen two volumes in folio, written with his own hand, containing, upon all the heads of religion, a vast heap of places of Scripture, and quotations out of ancient Fathers, and later doctors and schoolmen, by which he governed himself in that work."[54]

10.

And now, my brethren, will it not be so, as I have said, of simple necessity, if you attempt at this time to perpetuate in the National Church a form of opinion which the National Church disowns? You do not follow its Bishops; you disown its existing traditions; you are discontented with its divines; you protest against its law courts; you shrink from its laity; you outstrip its Prayer Book. You have in all respects an eclectic or an original religion of your own. You dare not stand or fall by Andrewes, or by Laud, or by

[160]

without the aid of grace. ... It was due to the intervention of St. Augustine and the Church, that greater clearness was gradually reached in the disputed questions and that the first impulse was given towards a more careful development of the dogmas of original sin and grace." *Catholic Encyclopaedia.*

[53] Synops, Vit. ap. Opp. 1643. [N]

[54] *Burnet*: G. Burnet, *The History of the Reformation* 4 vols. (London, 1837), i, 280.

Hammond, or by Bull, or by Thorndike,[55] or by all of them together. There is a *consensus* of divines, stronger than there is for Baptismal Regeneration or the Apostolical Succession, that Rome is, strictly and literally, an anti-Christian power: —Liberals and High Churchmen in your Communion in this agree with Evangelicals; you put it aside. There is a *consensus* against Transubstantiation, besides the declaration of the Article; yet many of you hold it notwithstanding. Nearly all your divines, if not all, call themselves Protestants, and you anathematize the name. Who makes the concessions to Catholics which you do, yet remains separate from them? Who, among Anglican

---

[55] *Thorndike*: Herbert Thorndike (1598-1672), Biblical scholar and theologian. "Thorndike's major publication of the interregnum, *An Epilogue to the Tragedy of the Church of England*, used what he called 'the Present Calamity of the Church of England' as the basis for discussing a wide range of theological issues: scripture and tradition, the Trinity, justification, predestination, the sacraments, and relations between church and state. His intention was evidently to lay a foundation not only for the restoration of the Church of England but also for the bringing together of the major Western churches. Reason was the means of resolving differences, but it was to be guided by the scriptures as understood by the 'whole Church, from the beginning' (bk 1, pp. 1–3, 35). In the section entitled *'The covenant of grace'* he combined a doctrine of justification by grace through faith with a doctrine of the church as the body of the baptized who sought to be obedient to God's commands and were nurtured by the word and sacraments. The *'Epilogue'* expressed both a protestant soteriology and a largely Catholic ecclesiology. Thorndike regarded the Roman Catholic church as 'a true Church' which 'continueth the same visible body, by the succession of Pastors and Lawes' from the apostles' days, but considered that it was corrupt in many ways and had made unwarranted additions to the historic Christian faith. He saw a mean between the extremes of Roman Catholicism and the radical protestant sects as the surest way to salvation. The work was not universally well received by Anglican loyalists: Edward Hyde reacted sharply in May 1659 to news of the book's publication, expressing dismay that Thorndike had cast doubt on the English church's prospects for survival and had thus aided its enemies." *ODNB*. While sharply averse to Socinianism, Thorndike took exception to the Roman Catholic doctrine of transubstantiation. In summing up the work of this strenuously eclectic figure, the *ODCC* remarks: "Thorndike's significance was for long forgotten, until he was rediscovered by the Tractarians."

authorities, would speak of Penance as a Sacrament, as you do? Who of them encourages, much less insists upon, auricular confession, as you? or makes fasting an obligation? or uses the crucifix and the rosary? or reserves the consecrated bread? or believes in miracles as existing in your communion? or administers, as I believe you do, Extreme Unction? In some points you prefer Rome, in [161] others Greece, in others England, in others Scotland; and of that preference your own private judgment is the ultimate sanction.

What am I to say in answer to conduct so preposterous? Say you go by any authority whatever, and I shall know where to find you, and I shall respect you. Swear by any school of Religion, old or modern, by Ronge's Church,[56] or the Evangelical Alliance,[57] nay, by Yourselves, and I shall know what you mean, and will listen to you. But do not come to me with the latest fashion of opinion which the world has seen, and protest to me that it is the oldest. Do not come to me at this time of day with views palpably new, isolated, original, *sui generis*, warranted old neither by Christian nor unbeliever, and challenge me to answer what I really have not the patience to read. Life is not long enough

---

[56] *Ronge's Church*: Johannes Ronge (1813–87), was the founder of the *Frei Germeinde* (Free Community) in Hamburg in 1847, and known as "the modern Luther." A former Roman Catholic priest from Upper Silesia, Ronge was defrocked after denouncing the Bishop of Trier for exhibiting the 'Holy Coat of Trier.' In the wake of the 1848 revolutions, Ronge met Karl Marx in London and thereafter went into exile with his wife Bertha in England, where they joined forces with Unitarians and established the first kindergarten in Manchester and then Leeds. "The victim of priestly hate," one observer said of Ronge, he had been "driven from the Church of his fathers by its sham and lies," and he was consequently "shy of Churches and sceptical as to creeds." R. Ashton, *Victorian Bloomsbury* (New Haven, 2012), 16, 209, 274 -9, 307.

[57] *Evangelical Alliance*: Formed in 1846, the Evangelical Alliance was an Evangelical Protestant society that sponsored No Popery speakers for the Protestant lecture circuit. One of the speakers they engaged was Giovanni Giacinto Achilli (1803-60), the defrocked Italian Dominican, who joined cause with England's Evangelicals and later sued Newman for libel after the convert called attention to his serial rape of women on the Continent and elsewhere.

for such trifles. Go elsewhere, not to me, if you wish to make a proselyte. Your inconsistency, my dear brethren, is on your very front. Nor pretend that you are but executing the sacred duty of defending your own Communion: your Church does not thank you for a defence, which she has no dream of appropriating. You innovate on her professions of doctrine, and then you bid us love her for your innovations. You cling to her for what she denounces; and you almost anathematise us for taking a step which you would please her best by taking also. You call it restless, impatient, undutiful in us, to do what she would have us do; and you [162] think it a loving and confiding course in her children to believe, not her, but you. She is to teach, and we are to hear, only according to your own private researches into St. Chrysostom and St. Augustine. "I began myself with doubting and inquiring," you seem to say; "I departed from the teaching I received; I was educated in some older type of Anglicanism; in the school of Newton,[58] Cecil,[59] and Scott, or in the Bartlett's-Building School,[60] or in the

---

[58] *Newton*: John Newton (1725-1807), an Anglican clergyman, abolitionist and hymn writer. Going to sea as a young man, Newton worked on slave ships for several years before converting to Christianity, when he became an impassioned abolitionist. He was ordained as a Church of England clergyman and served as parish priest at Olney, Buckinghamshire for two decades. An Evangelical, he also wrote hymns, including "Amazing Grace" and "Glorious Things of Thee Are Spoken." Asked to condemn the papacy, Newton replied:" I have read of many Popes but the worst Pope I ever encountered was Pope Self." Newton quoted in A. Fraser, *The King and the Catholics: England, Ireland and the Fight for Religious Freedom 1780-1829* (New York, 2018), 11-12.

[59] *Cecil*: Richard Cecil (1748-1810): Evangelical Anglican divine. A member of the Clapham Sect with Z. Macaulay and W. Wilberforce, Cecil was a founding member and leader of the Eclectic Society, an evangelical abolitionist society which he started with J. Newton atop a pub in 1783 and later moved to the vestry at Bedford Row in 1784.

[60] *Bartlett's Building School*: This appears to refer to one of the schools of University College London, founded in 1828, which was Unitarian in its religious leanings and dedicated to the 'march of mind,' or what Thackeray characterized as "proof of the 'intelligence of the working classes' and the meritorious efforts of the schoolmaster abroad." *Victorian Bloomsbury*, 80. In January of 1836, Newman wrote Pusey of

Liberal Whig School.[61] I was a Dissenter, or a Wesleyan, and by study and thought I became an Anglo-Catholic. And then I read the Fathers, and I have determined what works are genuine, and what are not; which of them apply to all times, which are occasional; which historical, and which doctrinal; what opinions are private, what authoritative; what they only seem to hold, what they ought to hold; what are fundamental, what ornamental. Having thus measured and cut and put together my creed by my own proper intellect, by my own lucubrations, and differing from the whole world in my results, I distinctly bid you, I solemnly warn you, not to do as I have done, but to accept what I have found, to revere that, to use that, to believe that, for it is the teaching of the old Fathers, and of your Mother the Church of England. Take my word for it, that this is the very truth of Christ; deny your own reason, for I know better than you, and it is as clear as day that some moral

---

the place: "I do not look at things so sadly as you do — that is, doubtless we shall have a great deal to distress us, but it will rather be the bringing to light of what seems fair and is not.... Surely we have been for years in a very unsatisfactory deceptive state. We cannot regret, however ... that we should see ourselves as we are. Men like Ogilvie or others of the old Bartlett Building School are worthy of all reverence and gratitude — but these have been the few. The mass of those called High Church have had no principles — their turning round now shows it. Can we say Blomfield etc etc. ever were fixed, ever saw the Truth? they go by expedience, because they have not ascertained, in those respects in which they veer about, any other guide. Is it not very clear that the English Church subsists *in the State,* and has no internal consistency (in matter of fact, I do not say in theory) to keep it together? is bound into one by the imposition of articles and the inducement of State protection, not by ἦθος and a common faith?" *LD*, v, 213-14. Charles Atmore Ogilvie (1793-1873) was looked upon as the leader of the High Church party in Oxford but refrained from supporting the Tractarians; he was also one of the six doctors of divinity at Christ Church who censured Pusey in 1843 for his sermon on the Eucharist.

[61] *Liberal Whig School*: This school consisted of a broad range of political and religious figures, from Lord Brougham to Thomas Arnold, whose readiness to encroach upon the prerogatives and to alter the doctrinal character of the Anglican Church was one factor that instigated the founding of the Movement of 1833.

fault in you is the cause of your differing from me. It is [163] pride, or vanity, or self-reliance, or fulness of bread. You require some medicine for your soul; you must fast; you must make a general confession; and look very sharp to yourself, for you are already next door to a rationalist or an infidel."

Surely, I have not exaggerated, my brethren, what you will be obliged to say, if you take the course which you are projecting; but the point immediately before us is something short of this; it is, whether a party in the Establishment formed on such principles (and as things are now it can be formed on no other) can in any sense be called a genuine continuation of the Apostolical party of twenty years ago? The basis of that party was the professed abnegation of private judgment; your basis is the professed exercise of it. If you are really children of it as it was in 1833, you must have nothing to say to it as it is in 1850.

LECTURE VI

THE PROVIDENTIAL COURSE OF THE MOVEMENT OF 1833 NOT IN THE DIRECTION OF A BRANCH CHURCH

1.

THERE are persons who may think that the line of thought which I pursued in my last two Lectures had somewhat of a secular and political cast, and was deficient in that simplicity which becomes an inquiry after religious truth. We are inquiring, you may say, whether the National Church is in possession of the Sacraments, whether we can obtain the grace of Christ, necessary for our salvation, at its hands? On this great question depends our leaving its communion or not; but you answer us by simply bidding us consider which course of action will look best, what the world expects of us, how posterity will judge of us, what termination is most logically consistent with our commencement, what are to be the historical fortunes in prospect of a large body of men, variously circumstanced, and subject to a variety of influences from without and [165] within. It is a personal, an individual, question to each inquirer; but you would have us view it as a political game, in which each side makes moves, and just now it is our turn, not, as it really is, a matter of religious conviction, duty, and responsibility.

But thus to speak is mistaking the argument altogether. First, I am not addressing those who have no doubt whatever about the divine origin of the Established Church. I am not attempting to rouse, or, as some would call it, unsettle them. If there be such—for, to tell the truth, I almost doubt their existence—I pass them by. I am contemplating that not inconsiderable number, who are, in a true sense, though in various degrees, and in various modes, inquirers; who, on the one hand, have no doubt at all of the great Apostolical principles which are stamped upon the face of the early Church, and were the life of the movement of 1833; and who, on the other hand, have certain doubts about those principles being the property and the life of the National Church—who have fears, grave anxieties or vague misgivings, as the case may be, lest that communion be not a treasure-house and fount of grace—and then all at once are afraid again, that, after all, perhaps it *is*, and that it is their own fault that they are blind to the fact, and that it is undutifulness in them to question it;—who, after even their most violent doubts, have seasons of relenting and compunction; and who at length are so perplexed by reason [166] of the clear light pouring in on them from above, yet by the secret whisper the while, that they ought to doubt their own perceptions, because (as they are told) they are impatient, or self-willed, or excited, or dreaming, and have lost the faculty of looking at things in a natural, straightforward way, that at length they do not know what they hold and what they do not hold, or where they stand, and are in conflict within, and almost in a state of anarchy and recklessness.

2.

Now, to persons in this cruel strife of thought, I offer the consideration on which I have been dwelling, as a sort of diversion to their harassed minds; as an argument of fact, external to themselves, and over which they have no power, which is of a nature to arbitrate and decide for them between their own antagonist judgments. You wish to know whether the Establishment is what you began by assuming it to be—the grace-giving Church of God. If it be, you and your principles will surely find your position there and your home. When you proclaim it to be Apostolical, it will smile on you; when you kneel down and ask its blessing, it will stretch its hands over you; when you would strike at heresy, it will arm you for the fight; when you wind your dangerous

[167]

way with steady tread between Sabellius,[1] Nestorius,[2] and Eutyches,[3] between Pelagius and Calvin, it will follow you with anxious eyes and a beating heart; when you proclaim its relationship to Rome and Greece, it will in transport embrace you as its own dear children; you will sink happily into its arms, you will repose upon its breast, you will recognise your mother, and be at peace. If, however, on the contrary, you find that the more those great principles which you have imbibed from St. Athanasius and St. Augustine, and which have become the life and the form of your moral and intellectual being, vegetate and expand within you, the more awkward and unnatural you find your position in the Establishment, and the more difficult its explanation; if

---

[1] *Sabellius*: Sabellius was a priest, probably of the city of Ptolemais, and is first heard of at Rome in the time of St. Zephyrinus (d. 217). "His adherents, known as Sabelleians, were heretics, who regarded God the Father and God the Son as one person and later interpreted the Blessed Trinity as one God in his three different relations (or as Modernists would now say, aspects) to man, as Creator, Incarnate Redeemer and Sanctifier. Sabellius was condemned by Pope St. Callistus I." *Catholic Dictionary*.

[2] *Nestorius*: Nestorius, Patriarch of Constantinople (d. 451). Nestorians were a Christian sect that originated in Asia Minor and Syria stressing the independence of the divine and human natures of Christ and, in effect, suggesting that they are two persons loosely united. The schismatic sect formed following the condemnation of Nestorius and his teachings by the ecumenical councils of Ephesus (431) and Chalcedon (451). Nestorius was anathematized at the former Council for denouncing the use of the title Θεοτόκος ("Mother of God") for Mary, since this compromised the reality of Christ's human nature. While Eusebius of Dorylaeum was the first to accuse Nestorius of heresy, it was Cyril of Alexandria who brought the charge most effectively at the Council of Ephesus.

[3] *Eutyches*: Eutyches (c. 378-454), Archimandrite of a monastery housing 300 monks outside the walls of Constantinople. He was charged with asserting that Christ has but one nature after the Incarnation and thus lent his name to the Eutychian, or the Monophysite heresy. In July of 1839, Newman wrote to his friend Rogers: "I have got up the history of the Eutychian controversy, got hold of the opinions of Eutyches , and the turning point of the controversy (no easy matter … in theology … but now that I am in the Monophysite controversy, I think I shall read through it, and then back to the Nestorian, before I go to him. I should not wonder if this opened other questions …" *LD*, vii, 105. Shortly, thereafter, Newman would experience what he called "the great revolution of mind" that led to his conversion. *Apo.* 92.

there is no lying, or standing, or sitting, or kneeling, or stooping there, in any possible attitude; if, as in the tyrant's cage,[4] when you would rest your head, your legs are forced out between the Articles, and when you would relieve your back, your head strikes against the Prayer Book; when, place yourselves as you will, on the right side or the left, and try to keep as still as you can, your flesh is ever being punctured and probed by the stings of Bishops, laity, and nine-tenths of the Clergy buzzing about you; is it not as plain as day that the Establishment is not your place, since it is no place for your principles? Those principles are not there professed, they are not there realised. That mystical sacramental system on which your thoughts live, which was once among men, as you know well—and therefore must be always with them—is not the inheritance of Anglicanism, [168] but must have been bequeathed to others; it must be sought elsewhere. You have doubts on the point already; well, here is the confirmation of them. I have no wish, then, to substitute an external and political view for your personal serious inquiry. I am but assisting you in that inquiry; I am deciding existing doubts, which belong to yourselves, by an

---

[4] *the tyrant's cage*: Newman might have been thinking here of Walter Scott's account of Louis XI's iron cages for prisoners at Loches, a prison which, as Scott describes it, "fell like a death-toll upon the ear of the young Scotchman. He had heard it described as a place destined to the workings of those secret acts of cruelty with which even Louis shamed to pollute the interior of his own residence. There were in this place of terror dungeons under dungeons, some of them unknown even to the keepers themselves — living graves, to which men were consigned with little hope of farther employment during the rest of their life than to breathe impure air and feed on bread and water. At this formidable castle were also those dreadful places of confinement called 'cages,' in which the wretched prisoner could neither stand upright nor stretch himself at length — an invention, it is said, of the Cardinal Balue." W. Scott, *Quentin Durward* (1823). The cages were 8 feet long and about 7 feet high. Philippe de Comines was confined in one of them for eight months; Balue himself was imprisoned in one of the cages for 11 years. See Comines, *Memoirs* (1524). Jean Balue (c. 1421–91) was a French cardinal and minister of Louis XI. Philippe de Comines (1447–1511) was a writer and diplomat in the courts of Burgundy and France.

external fact, which is as admissible, surely, in such a matter, as the allegation of miracles would be, or any other evidence of the kind; for the same God who works in you individually, is working in the public and historical course of things also.

I think, then, that in my last Lectures I have proved, not adequately, for it would take many words to do justice to a proof so abundant in materials, but as far as time allowed, and as was necessary for those who would pursue the thought, that the movement to which you and I belong, looks away from the Establishment, that "Let us go hence" is its motto. I cannot doubt you would agree with me in this, did you not belong to it, did you disbelieve its principles, were you merely disinterested, dispassionate lookers-on; in that case you would decide that you must join some other communion: judge then as disbelieving, act as believing. If the movement be a providential work, it has a providential scope; if that scope be not in the direction of the Establishment, as I have been proving, in what direction is [169] it? Does it look towards Greece, or towards America, or towards Scotland, or towards Rome? This is the subject which has next to be considered, and to which, in part, I shall address myself today.

Here then, when you are investigating whither you shall go for your new succession and your new priesthood, I am going to offer you a suggestion which, if it approves itself to you, will do away with the opportunity, or the possibility, of choice altogether. It will reduce the claimants to one. Before entering, then, upon the inquiry, whither you shall betake yourselves, and what you shall be, bear with me while I give you one piece of advice; it is this—While you are looking about for a new Communion, have nothing to do with a "Branch Church."[5] You have had enough experience

---

[5] *"Branch Church"*: For Anglo-Catholics, the 'Universal Church' consists of three branches: the Roman, the Eastern Orthodox and the Anglican. One of the more prominent champions of the branch theory was William Palmer (1803-85), Fellow of Worcester College and pre-eminent Anglo-Catholic theologian, who argued that Newman's idea of

of branch churches already, and you know very well what they are. Depend upon it, such as is one, such is another. They may differ in accidents certainly; but, after all, a branch is a branch, and no branch is a tree. Depend on it, my brethren, it is not worth while leaving one branch for another. While you are doing so great a work, do it thoroughly; do it once for all; change for the better. Rather than go to another branch, remain where you are; do not put yourselves to trouble for nothing; do not sacrifice this world without gaining the next. Now let us consider this point attentively.

3.

[170]

By a Branch Church is meant, I suppose, if we interpret the metaphor, a Church which is separate from its stem; and if we ask what is meant by the stem, I suppose it means the

---

development, which made no allowance for the branch theory, was rationalistic. *LD*, xi, 281. "Nothing can be more dissimilar, certainly, than the results to which the theory of development has led Mr. Newman's adherents and the German rationalists," Palmer wrote; "yet the same principle is at the root of both, the only difference being, that the former are anxious to evade the conclusions which the latter, by a bolder and more consistent course of argument, have arrived at. The whole system of tests, and of a developing authority, devised by Mr. Newman, is utterly and miserably powerless to arrest the march of reason to an infidel theory of development." W. Palmer, *The Doctrine of Development and Conscience considered in relation to the Evidences of Christianity and of the Catholic System* (London, 1846), 133. Twenty years later, Newman remarked in his *Apologia*: "Mr Palmer had a certain connexion, as it may be called, in the Establishment, consisting of high Church dignitaries... [who] were far more opposed than even he was to the impossible action of individuals. Of course their *beau ideal* in ecclesiastical action was a board of safe, sound, sensible men. Mr. Palmer was their organ ... and he wished for a Committee ... with rules and meetings, to protect the interests of the Church in its existing peril." *Apo*, 47. Another supporter of the branch theory was William Palmer (1811-79) of Magdalen College, who made several unavailing attempts to have the Church of England admitted as a branch of the Russian Orthodox Church, after which, in 1855, he converted to Rome. Newman, a friend of Palmer, agreed to serve as the executor of his correspondence. See R.D. Middleton, "William Palmer," *Magdalen Studies* (London, 1936), 97-124, and the *ODNB*.

"Universal Church," [6] as you are accustomed to call it. The Catholic Church, indeed, as understood by Catholics, is one kingdom or society, divisible into parts, each of which is in inter-communion with each other and with the whole, as the members of a human body. This Catholic Church, as I suppose you would maintain, has ceased to exist,[7] or at least

---

[6] *"Universal Church"*: For Palmer of Worcester: "All articles of faith, according to the Anglo catholic doctrine, are proved by scripture, and by a universal tradition establishing the right interpretation, and corroborating the testimony of scripture. This is certainly a much more reasonable system, and much more probable in the abstract, than that which imagines that God would have left some of his Revelation to be proved from tradition only." W. Palmer, *A Treatise on the Church of Christ* 2 vols. (London, 1839), ii, 9. As to what basis he had for arguing for this 'universal tradition' different from the tradition of the Catholic Church, Palmer stated that he argued for it as "a matter of fact, which is to be established on the same sort of evidence as proves any other historical fact. The question is, what were the tenets of the religious community called Christian, from the beginning? This is evidently to be proved only by authentic documents, monuments, and facts: and we accordingly adduce the creeds or professions of faith acknowledged by the universal church, in proof of her faith on certain points up to the period when she made them, the creeds and liturgies of particular churches, as evidence of their belief as far back as those creeds and liturgies can be traced." *Ibid*, ii, 48.

[7] *ceased to exist*: In 1862, Newman responded to the letter of a Liverpool stock broker, whom he characterized as a "clever young Puseyite," who had argued that the "the Anglican clings to the original theory of Catholicity, on the ground of its being apparently obsolete." For Newman, this is why the Anglican claims that what he fancies the disunity of the Catholic Church renders her unentitled to the claim of Catholicity. "Here the 'original theory' I suppose means this: 'What and where is the True Church? that is the true Church, *whose parts are in intercommunion* — whose dioceses are so one that each Bishop is a repetition of the rest, so that there is but unus episcopatus.' This I *suppose* is the definition of the Church referred to; viz the Sacramentum Unitatis… Now I am surprised that it should be said we have given this theory up; and I am surprised that Anglicans should be said to cling to it. All this is quite new to me. On the contrary we hold to this definition entirely, but Anglicans give it up. We form a large polity in all quarters of the world bound together by nothing but religious ties — Anglicanism on the contrary is not a polity at all. Its only bond is an external one, Acts of Parliament. The Established Church would break into at least three

is in *deliquium*,[8] for you will not give the name to us, nor do you take it yourselves, and scarcely ever use the phrase at all, except in the Creed; but a "Universal Church" you think there really is, and you mean by it the whole body of professing Christians all over the world, whatever their faith, origin, and traditions, provided they lay claim to an Apostolical Succession,[9] and this whole is divisible into portions or branches, each of them independent of the whole, discordant one with another in doctrine and in ritual, destitute of mutual intercommunion, and more frequently in

---

communions if unestablished." Newman to Daniel Radford (15 October 1862), *LD*, xx, 305.

[8] *deliquium*: The *OED* defines the word as "Failure of the vital powers; a swoon, fainting fit;" from the Latin *dēliquium* failure, want.

[9] *Apostolical Succession*: The claim to Apostolical Succession that Palmer makes for the Church of England is set out in his *Treatise on the Church of Christ*: "All our churches were originally founded by the labours of holy missionaries," Palmer writes, "who, in obedience to the divine command, having received their commission from the church of Christ, came into these lands, and gathered churches of Christ from amidst their heathen inhabitants. The societies thus formed by peaceful derivation from the Christian body, or by incorporation with it, and in no case by separation from a more ancient Christian society, have in all ages, without interruption, continued visibly to profess Christ, to administer Christian rites and sacraments, to be guided by a ministry professing to be Christian and apostolical, and to add continually new members to themselves by baptism. No other Christian societies formerly existed in these countries, from which our churches separated themselves originally, and acquired existence by the act of separation. The church of Canterbury has continued as a Christian society in unbroken succession for more than twelve centuries; that of Armagh has existed for fourteen centuries; those of Menevia and others in Wales, for at least the same time; and all these churches were derived by spiritual descent, and fraternal association, from the still more ancient and apostolical churches of Britain, Gaul, and Rome. It may be objected, indeed, that our churches departed from their ancient faith, or were separated from the rest of the catholic church at the Reformation. That is a different question, and must be separately considered: but the fact is beyond all possibility of dispute: it is as certain as the truth of Christianity itself, that these churches have always continued as visible societies, in unbroken succession from the very earliest ages of Christianity." *A Treatise on the Church of Christ*, i, 217-18.

actual warfare,[10] portion with portion, than in a state of neutrality. Such is pretty nearly what you mean by a Branch, allowing for differences of opinion on the subject; such, for instance, is the Russian Branch, which denounces the Pope as a usurper; such the Papal, which anathematises the Protestantism of the Anglican; such the Anglican, which reprobates the devotions and scorns the rites of the Russian; such the Scotch, which has changed the Eucharistic service of the Anglican; such the American, which has put aside its Athanasian Creed.

Such, I say, is a Branch Church, and, as you will see at once, it is virtually synonymous with a National; for though it may be in fact and at present but one out of many communions in a nation, it is intended, by its very mission, as preacher and evangelist, to spread through the nation; nor has it done its duty till it has so spread, for it must be supposed to have the promise of success as well as the mission. On the other hand, it cannot extravagate beyond the nation, for the very principle of demarcation between Branch and Branch is the distinction of Nation or State; to the Nation, then, or State it is limited, and beyond the Nation's boundaries it cannot properly pass. Thus it is the normal condition of a Branch Church to be a National Church; it tends to nationality as its perfect idea; till it is national it is defective, and when it is national it is all it can be, or was meant to be. Since, then, to understand what any

[171]

---

[10] *actual warfare*: The High Church solution to this "actual warfare" had at least the advantage of a certain simplicity, as James Pereiro relates. "The Church universal, founded by Christ, was constituted by [sic] three branches – Anglican, Orthodox and Roman – which had preserved apostolic succession and the fundamentals of the faith. The breaches of the original unity, resulting from diverse historical circumstances, without destroying the unity of the Church, had, however, brought about a weakening in each of the branches' hold on its divine endowments and impaired their mission. It was imperative, as a result, to work for re-establishment of the original unity. Traditional High Churchmanship considered that the Church of Rome should reform itself on the model of the Church of England before reunion was to be possible." J. Pereiro, "The Oxford Movement and Anglo-Catholicism," *The Oxford History of Anglicanism* ed. R. Strong (London, 2017), iii, 205.

being is, we must contemplate it, not in its rudiments or commencements, any more than in its decline, but in its maturity and its perfection, it follows that, if we would know what a Branch Church is, we must view it as a National Church, and we shall form but an erroneous estimate of its nature and its characteristics, unless we [172] investigate its national form.

Recollect, then, that a Branch Church is a National Church, and the reason why I warn you against getting your orders from such a Church, or joining such a Church, as, for instance, the Greek, the Russian, or some Monophysite Church, is that you are in a National Church already, and that a National Church ever will be and must be what you have found your own to be,—an Erastian body. You are going to start afresh. Well, then, I assert, that if you do not get beyond the idea of Nationalism in this your new beginning, you are just where you were. Erastianism, the fruitful mother of all heresies, will be your first and your last. You will have left Erastianism to take Erastianism up again,—that heresy which is the very badge of Anglicanism, and the abomination of that theological movement from which you spring.

I here assert, then, that a Branch or National Church is necessarily Erastian, and cannot be otherwise, till the nature of man is other than it is; and I shall prove this from the state of the case, and from the course of history, and from the confession, or rather avowal, of its defenders.[11] The

---

[11] *its defenders*: In the 8th section of this lecture, Newman shares with his readers the tell-tale defence of Erastianism mounted by Bishop W. Warburton in *The Alliance of Church and State* (1736) – the same Warburton who once observed: "Our *Grandees* have at last found their way back into the Church. I only wonder they have been so long about it. ... The Church has been of old the cradle and the throne of the younger nobility." Warburton quoted in R. Porter, *England in the Eighteenth Century* rev. ed. (London, 1990), 61. Another defender of English Erastianism was the historian and Queen's Counsel Sir Spencer Walpole (1839-1907), who wrote, among other books, the authorized biography of Lord John Russell. In his history of England, Walpole observed: "In England, indeed, as in Scotland, High Churchmen are accustomed to

English Establishment is nothing extraordinary in this respect; the Russian Church is Erastian,[12] so is the Greek;[13] such was the Nestorian;[14] such would be the Scotch

---

condemn Erastianism, as they are accustomed to condemn Arianism and Nestorianism. But the masses of the English nation, if they were acquainted with the whole condition of the question, would certainly declare that Erastus was right as against Beza, just as they would conclude that Arius was right as against Athanasius, and Nestorius was right as against Cyril. It is only the universal ignorance of the people on the nature of these struggles which induces them to regard Arianism, Nestorianism, and Erastianism as terms of reproach." S. Walpole, *A History of England from the Great War of 1815* (London, 1886), v, 330. Theodore Beza (1519-1605) was the French Calvinist who rebutted Thomas Erastus's *Explicatio gravissimae quaestionis utrum excommunicatio* (1589), arguing that ecclesiastical, not civil authorities should be authorized to excommunicate. Walpole, like Newman, had his portrait drawn in crayon by George Richmond, RA. Home Secretary in 1852 in the Derby government, he received a letter from Newman enquiring about the scope of the restrictions for the wearing of cassocks in public. *LD*, xv, 102-3.

[12] *the Russian Church is Erastian*: Founded in the 9th century by Greek missionaries from Byzantium, the Orthodox Church in Russia did not become fully Erastian until fairly late in its history. In 1700, upon the death of Patriarch Adrian, Peter I prevented a successor from being named. In 1721, the patriarchate of Moscow was replaced with the Most Holy Governing Synod to govern the Church. The Holy Governing Synod was modelled after the state-controlled synods of the Lutheran Church of Sweden and in Prussia and was tightly intertwined with the state. The Synod remained the supreme church body in the Russian Church for almost two centuries.

[13] *so is the Greek*: The Church of Greece is organized as a state church according to the pattern adopted in Russia under Peter the Great. Supreme authority is vested in the synod of all the bishops under the presidency of the archbishop of Athens and all Greece. During the Byzantine Empire and the subsequent Turkish occupation of Greece (1453-1832), the Christian church in Greece was under the administration of the ecumenical patriarch of Constantinople. After the Greek War of Independence (1821–32), the national assemblies of free Greece began making their Church independent of the patriarch. In 1833, the Greek Parliament set up a Holy Directing Synod after the Russian model. In 1850, the patriarch grudgingly acknowledged the Greek synod, which meets in Athens under the presidency of the metropolitan. Four other bishops are appointed by the Greek state as members for a year by vote.

[14] *Nestorian*: Although the Nestorian Church operated within the Byzantine and Eastern form of church-state relations, its own more far-

Episcopal,[15] such the Anglo-American,[16] if ever they became commensurate with the nation. And now for my reasons for [173] saying so.

4.

You hold, and rightly hold, that the Church is a sovereign and self-sustaining power, in the same sense in which any temporal State is such. She is sufficient for herself; she is absolutely independent in her own sphere; she has irresponsible control over her subjects in religious matters; she makes laws for them of her own authority, and enforces obedience on them as the tenure of their membership with her. And you know, in the next place, that the very people, who are her subjects, are in another relation

---

flung ecclesiastical interests tended to elude imperial control. "Christianity flourished where it had become, not just an ally of power … but also the heart and inspiration of a social complex," the church historian J. McManners points out. "This never happened with the Nestorian Church, which in the tenth century had fifteen metropolitan provinces from the Caspian Sea to the Persian Gulf, whose missionaries reached China, Samarkand, and India, and whose scholars translated works of the Greek philosophers into Arabic. It did not integrate with Persian civilization, lost the Mongols to Islam, and finally, amid barbarous invasions from the East, was reduced to a few scattered communities." John McManners, "Introduction," *The Oxford Illustrated History of Christianity* ed. McManners (Oxford, 1990), 7-8.

[15] *Scotch Episcopal*: According to the *ODCC*: "The overwhelming majority of the population of Scotland belong to the Church of Scotland, which is Presbyterian, national, endowed and free." However, "From those who adhered to Episcopacy at the Revolution settlement (1690) arose the Episcopal Church in Scotland which after years of repression and suspicion, largely owing to its Jacobite predilections is now free to make its distinctive contribution to Scottish religious life. It is in full communion with the C. of E., but is autonomous, has its own Prayer Book and is governed by bishops." Precisely because the Scotch Episcopal, like the RC Church, is a minority church in Scotland, it is not Erastian.

[16] *Anglo-American*: Since the Episcopal Church in America never became "commensurate with the nation," especially after the influx of Catholic immigrants from central and southern Europe starting in the 1820s, the question of whether it was Erastian never arose. Moreover, the founders' pronounced opposition to church establishments would have prevented such Erastianism, even if Episcopalians had become more representative of America's overall population.

the State's subjects, and that those very matters which in one aspect are spiritual, in another are secular. The very same persons and the very same things belong to two supreme jurisdictions at once, so that the Church cannot issue any order, but it affects the persons and the things of the State; nor can the State issue any order, without its affecting the persons and the things of the Church. Moreover, though there is a general coincidence between the principles on which civil and ecclesiastical welfare respectively depend, as proceeding from one and the same God, who has given power to the Magistrate as well as to the Priest, still there is no necessary coincidence in their particular application and resulting details, in the one and in the other polity, just as the good of the soul is not always [174] the good of the body; and much more is this the case, considering there is no divine direction promised to the State, to preserve it from human passion and human selfishness. You will, I think, agree with me in judging, that under these circumstances it is morally impossible that there should not be continual collision, or chance of collision, between the State and the Church; and, considering the State has the power of the sword, and the Church has no arms but such as are spiritual, the problem to be considered by us is, how the Church may be able to do her divinely appointed work without let or hindrance from the physical force of the State.

And a difficulty surely it is, and a difficulty which Christianity for the most part brought into the world. It can scarcely be said to have existed before; for, if not altogether in Judaism, yet certainly in the heathen polities, the care of public worship, of morals, of education, was mainly committed, as well as secular matters, to the civil magistrate. There was once no independent jurisdiction in religion; but, when our Lord came, it was with the express object of introducing a new kingdom, distinct and different from the kingdoms of the world, and He was sought after by

Herod,[17] and condemned by Pilate,[18] on the very apprehension that His claims to royalty were inconsistent with their prerogatives. Such was the Church when first introduced into the world, and her subsequent history has been after the pattern of her commencement; the State has ever been jealous of her, and has persecuted her from [175] without and bribed her from within.

I repeat, the great principles of the State are those of the Church, and, if the State would but keep within its own province, it would find the Church its truest ally and best benefactor. She upholds obedience to the magistrate; she recognises his office as from God; she is the preacher of peace, the sanction of law, the first element of order, and the safeguard of morality, and that without possible vacillation or failure; she may be fully trusted; she is a sure friend, for she is indefectible and undying. But it is not enough for the State that things should be done, unless it has the doing of them itself; it abhors a double jurisdiction, and what it calls a divided allegiance; *aut Cæsar aut nullus*,[19] is its motto, nor does it willingly accept of any compromise. All power is founded, as it is often said, on public opinion; for the State to allow the existence of a collateral and rival authority, is to weaken its own and, even though that authority never showed its presence by collision, but never concurred and cooperated in the acts of the State, yet the divinity with which the State would fain hedge itself would, in the minds of men, be concentrated on that Ordinance of God which has the higher claim to it.

5.

Such being the difficulty which ever has attended, and [176]

---

[17] *Herod*: "And when they were departed, behold, the angel of the Lord appeareth to Joseph in a dream, saying, Arise, and take the young child and his mother, and flee into Egypt, and be thou there until I bring thee word: for Herod will seek the young child to destroy him." Matthew 2:13
[18] *Pilate*: Luke, 23: 1-24
[19] *aut Caesar aut nullus*: 'either Caesar or nothing.' Gaius Julius Caesar (100–42 BC), Roman general, statesman and historian.

ever will attend, the claims and the position of the Catholic Church in this proud and ambitious world, let us see how, as a matter of history, Providence has practically solved or alleviated it. He has done so by means of the very circumstance that the Church *is* Catholic, that she is one organised body, expanded over the whole earth, and in active intercommunion part with part, so that no one part acts without acting on and acting with every other. He has broken the force of the collisions, which ever must be, between Church and State, by the circumstance that a large community, such as the Church, necessarily moves slowly; and this will particularly be the case when it is subject to distinct temporal rulers, exposed to various political interests and prepossessions, and embarrassed by such impediments to communication (physical or moral, mountains and seas, languages and laws) as separation into nations involves. Added to this, the Church is composed of a vast number of ranks and offices, so that there is scarcely any of her acts that belongs to one individual will, or is elaborated by one intellect, or that is not rather the joint result of many co-operating agents, each in his own place, and at his appointed moment. And so fertile an idea as the Christian faith, so happy a mother as the Catholic Church, is necessarily developed and multiplied into a thousand various powers and functions; she has her Clergy and laity,

[177] her seculars and regulars, her Episcopate and Prelacy, her diversified orders, congregations, confraternities, communities, each indeed intimately one with the whole, yet with its own characteristics, its own work, its own traditions, its graceful rivalry, or its disgraceful jealousies, and sensitive, on its own ground and its own sphere, of whatever takes place anywhere else. And then again, there is the ever-varying action of the ten thousand influences, political, national, local, municipal, provincial, agrarian, scholastic, all bearing upon her; the clashing of temporal interests, the apprehension of danger to the whole or its parts, the necessity of conciliation, and the duty of temporising. Further, she has no material weapons of attack

or defence, and is at any moment susceptible of apparent defeat from local misfortune or personal misadventure. Moreover, her centre is one, and, from this very circumstance, sheltered from secular inquisitiveness; sheltered, moreover, in consequence of the antiquated character of its traditions, the peculiarity of its modes of acting, the tranquillity and deliberateness of its operations, as well as the mysteriousness thrown about it both from its picturesque and imposing ceremonial, and the popular opinion of its sanctity. And further still, she has the sacred obligation on her of long-suffering, patience, charity, of regard for the souls of her children, and of an anxious anticipation of the consequences of her measures. Hence, though her course is consistent, determinate, and simple, when viewed in history, yet to those who accompany the [178] stages of its evolution from day to day as they occur, it is confused and disappointing.

How different is the bearing of the temporal power upon the spiritual! Its promptitude, decisiveness, keenness, and force are well represented in the military host which is its instrument. Punctual in its movements, precise in its operations, imposing in its equipments, with its spirits high and its step firm, with its haughty clarion and its black artillery, behold, the mighty world is gone forth to war, with what? with an unknown something, which it feels but cannot see? which flits around it, which flaps against its cheek, with the air, with the wind. It charges and it slashes, and it fires its volleys, and it bayonets, and it is mocked by a foe who dwells in another sphere, and is far beyond the force of its analysis, or the capacities of its calculus. The air gives way, and it returns again; it exerts a gentle but constant pressure on every side; moreover, it is of vital necessity to the very power which is attacking it. Whom have you gone out against? a few old men, with red hats and stockings, or a hundred pale students, with eyes on the ground, and beads in their girdle; they are as stubble;[20] destroy them;—then there will be other old men; and other pale students instead of them. But we will direct our rage against one; he flees; what is to be done with him? Cast him out upon the wide world! but nothing can go on without him. Then bring him back! but he will give us no guarantee for the future. Then leave him alone; his power is gone, he is at an end, or he will take a new course of himself: he will take part with the State or the people. Meanwhile the multitude of interests in active operation all over the great Catholic body rise up, as it were, all around, and encircle the combat, and hide the fortune of the day from the eyes of the world; and unreal judgments are hazarded, and rash predictions, till the mist clears away, and then the old man is found in his own place, as before, saying Mass over the tomb of the Apostles. Resentment and animosity succeed in the minds of the many, when they find their worldly wisdom quite at fault, and that the weak has over-mastered the strong. They accuse the Church of craft. But, in truth, it is her very vastness, her manifold constituents, her complicated structure, which gives her this semblance, whenever she wears it, of feebleness, vacillation, subtleness, or dissimulation. She advances, retires, goes to and fro, passes to the right or left, bides her time, by a spontaneous, not a deliberate action. It is the divinely-intended method of her coping with the world's power. Even in the brute creation, each animal which God has made has its own instincts for securing its subsistence, and guarding against its foes; and, when He sent out His own into the world, as sheep among wolves,[21] over and above the harmlessness and wisdom with which He gifted them, He lodged the security of His truth in the very fact of its Catholicity. The Church

[179]

[180]

---

[20] *they are as stubble*: "Behold, they shall be as stubble; the fire shall burn them; they shall not deliver themselves from the power of the flame: *there shall* not *be* a coal to warm at, *nor* fire to sit before it." Isaiah 47:14

[21] *sheep among wolves*: "Behold, I send you forth as sheep in the midst of wolves: be ye therefore wise as serpents, and harmless as doves." Matthew 10:16.

triumphs over the world's jurisdiction everywhere, because, though she is everywhere, for that very reason she is in the fulness of her jurisdiction nowhere. Ten thousand subordinate authorities have been planted round, or have issued from, that venerable Chair where sits the plenitude of Apostolical power. Hence, when she would act, the blow is broken, and concussion avoided, by the innumerable springs, if I may use the word, on which the celestial machinery is hung. By an inevitable law of the system, and by the nature of the case, there are inquiries, and remonstrances, and threatenings, and first decisions, and appeals, and reversals, and conferences, and long delays, and arbitrations, before the final steps are taken in its battle with the State, if they cannot be avoided, and before the proper authority of the Church shows itself, whether in definition, or bull, or anathema, or interdict, or other spiritual instrument; and then, if, after all, persuasion has failed, and compromise with the civil power is impossible, the world is prepared for the event; and even in that case the Sovereign Pontiff, as such, is spared any direct collision with it, for the reason that he is no subject in matters temporal of the State with which he is at variance, whatever it be, being temporal Sovereign in his own home, and treating with the States of the earth only through his secular representatives and ministers.

6. [181]

The remarks I have been making are well illustrated by the history of our own great St. Thomas,[22] in his contest with King Henry II. Deserted by his suffragans, and threatened with assassination, he is forced to escape, as he

---

[22] *St. Thomas*: For an excellent account of the struggles of Archbishop Thomas Becket (1118-70) with King Henry II, and his relations with King Louis VII of France and Pope Alexander III, see David Knowles's Raleigh Lecture, "Archbishop Thomas Beckett: A Character Study" (1949) in *The Historian and Character* (Cambridge, 1963), 98-128. See also John Guy, *Thomas Becket: Warrior, Priest, Rebel* (New York, 2012).

can, to the Continent. He puts his cause before the Pope, but with no immediate result, for the Pope is in contest with the Emperor, who has supported a pretender to the Apostolic See. For two years nothing is done; then the Pope begins to move, but mediates between Archbishop and King, instead of taking the part of the former. The King of France comes forward on the Saint's side, and his friends attempt to gain the Empress Matilda[23] also. Strengthened by these demonstrations, St. Thomas excommunicates some of the King's party, and threatens the King himself, not to say his realm, with an interdict. Then there are appeals to Rome on the part of the King's Bishops, alarmed at the prospect of such extremities, while the Pope on the other hand gives a more distinct countenance to the Saint's cause. Suddenly, the face of things is overcast; the Pope has anathematised

---

[23] *Empress Matilda*: Matilda, called the "Empress Maude" (1102-67), English princess, the only daughter of Henri I. In 1128, she married Geoffrey Plantangenet of Anjou, by whom she had a son, "Henry FitzEmpress," the future Henry II of England. In an attempt to reconcile Archbishop Thomas Becket to her son, after they had fallen out, she wrote to the Archbishop: "My lord Pope sent to me, enjoining me, for the remission of my sins, to interfere to renew peace and concord between you and the king, my son, and to try to reconcile you to him. You, as you well know, have asked the same thing from me, wherefore, with the more goodwill, for the honour of God and the Holy church, I have begun and carefully treated of that affair. But it seems a very hard thing to the king, as well as to his barons and council seeing he so loved and honoured you, and appointed you lord of his whole kingdom and of all his lands, and raised you to the highest honours in the land, believing he might trust you rather than any other; and especially so, because he declares that you have, as far as you could, roused his whole kingdom against him; nor was it your fault that you did not disinherit him by main force. Therefore I send you my faithful servant, Archdeacon Laurence, that by him I may know your will in these affairs, and what sort of disposition you entertain towards my son, and how you intend to conduct yourself, if it should happen that he fully grants my petition and prayer on your behalf. One thing I plainly tell you, that you cannot recover the king's favour, except by great humility, and most evident moderation. However what you intend to do in this matter signify to me by my messenger and your letters." See Susan Abernethy, "Letter from Empress Matilda to Thomas Becket, Archbishop of Canterbury, 1165," *Medieval History* (16 June 2017).

the Emperor, and has his hands full of his own matters; Henry's agents at Rome obtain a Legatine Commission, under the presidency of a Cardinal favourable to his cause.

The quarrel lingers on; two years more have passed, and then the Commission fails. Then St. Thomas rouses himself [182] again, and is proceeding with the interdict, when news comes that the King has overreached the Pope, and the Archbishop's powers are altogether suspended for a set time. The artifice is detected by the good offices of the French Bishops, the Pope sends comminatory letters to the King, but, then again, does not carry them out. There is a reconciliation between the Kings of England and France, at the expense of St. Thomas; but, by this time, the suspension is over, and the Saint excommunicates the Bishop of London. In consequence, he receives a rebuke from the Pope, who, after absolving the Bishop, takes the matter into his own hands, himself excommunicates the Bishop, and himself threatens the kingdom with an interdict. Then St. Thomas returns, and is martyred, winning the day by suffering, not by striking.

Seven years are consumed in these transactions from first to last, and they afford a sufficient illustration of the subject before us. If I add the remarks made on them by the editor of the Saint's letters, in Mr. Froude's "Remains," it is for the sake of his general statement, which is as just as it is apposite to my purpose, though I may not be able to approve of the tone or the drift of it. Speaking of St. Thomas, he says, "His notions, both as regarded the justice and policy to be pursued in the treatment of Henry, had suggested this course [the interdict] to him from the first opening of the contest; and he seems always to have had such a measure before him, only the interruptions [183] occasioned by embassies from Rome, and appeals to Rome, and other temporary suspensions of his ecclesiastical powers, had prevented him from putting his purpose into effect; these having, in fact, taken up almost the whole of the time. For an embassy, it must be observed, from the first day of its appointment, suspended the Archbishop's movements, who could do nothing while special and higher judges were in office ... In this way, there being so much time, both before and after the actual holding of the conferences, during which the Archbishop's hands were tied, he may be said to have been almost under one sentence of suspension from the first, only rendered more harassing and vexatious from the promise afforded by his short intervals of liberty, and the alternations, in consequence, of expectation and disappointment. It was a state of confinement, which was always approaching its termination, and never realising it. With a clear line of action before him from the first, and with resolution and ability to carry it out, the Archbishop was compelled to keep pace, step by step, with a court that was absolutely deficient in both these respects; and found himself reduced throughout to a state of simple passiveness and endurance."[24] Of course;—a Branch Church indeed, with the Catholic dogma and with Saints in it, cannot be; but, supposing the English Church had been such at the time of [184] that contest, it would, humanly speaking, have been inevitably shattered to pieces by its direct collision with the civil power; or else, its Saints got rid of, its Erastianising Bishops made its masters, and ultimately its dogma corrupted, and the times of Henry VIII. anticipated;[25]—this

---

[24] Froude's Remains, vol. iv. p. 449. [N]

[25] *Henry VIII. anticipated*: While it is widely known that St. Thomas of Canterbury staved off the Erastianism of the Henrician Reformation for a few centuries, it may not be so well known what became of his shrine in the wake of that Reformation, a fate which needs to be borne in mind when reading Anglican theologians like Palmer of Worcester expatiate on what they regarded as the continuity between the national and the ancient Church. According to the historian John Guy: "In September 1538, the shrine would be demolished and its rich treasures despoiled, carried off in two large chests, 'such as six or eight men could but convey out of the church.' Henry had the ruby known as the 'regal of France' made into a thumb ring. Becket was declared a traitor: his bones would be ignominiously burned. Iconoclasts would obliterate his image with hammers, knives or whitewash in cathedrals and parish churches all over England, smashing many of the stained-glass windows containing the stories of his miracles. Even his very name would be carefully excised

would have been the case, but for its intercommunion with the rest of Christendom and the supremacy of Rome.

7.

This, however, is what has been going on, in one way or another, for the whole eighteen centuries of Christian history. For even in the ante-Nicene period, the heretic Patriarch of Antioch[26] was protected by the local sovereign against the Catholics, and was dispossessed by the authority and influence with the Imperial Government of the See of Rome. And since that time, again and again would the civil power, humanly speaking, have taken captive and corrupted each portion of Christendom in turn, but for its union with the rest, and the noble championship of the Supreme Pontiff.[27] Our ears ring with the oft-told tale, how the temporal sovereign persecuted, or attempted, or gained, the local Episcopate, and how the many or the few faithful fell back on Rome. So was it with the Arians in the East and St. Athanasius; so with the Byzantine Empress and St. Chrysostom;[28] so with the Vandal Hunneric and the

---

from missals, Psalters, and the calendar of saints." J. Guy, *Thomas Becket: Warrior, Priest, Rebel* (London, 2012), 348.

[26] *Patriarch of Antioch*: Leontius the Eunuch (344–358), subscribed to the Arian heresy.

[27] *Supreme Pontiff*: The Swiss theologian Hans Urs von Balthasar (1905-88) quoted from this passage to show his agreement with Newman's argument that it was only "the noble championship of the Supreme Pontiff" that prevented Christendom from being held captive and corrupted by the civil power. "Newman's patristic studies," the theologian wrote, "reinforced his view that state influence on the Church was the fundamentally baneful feature of church history." H. U. von Balthasar, *The Office of Peter and the Structure of the Church* 2nd ed. (San Francisco, 1989), 293-4. Balthasar is worth reading on Newman's reading of Erastianism and the papacy.

[28] *St. Chrysostom*: St. John Chrysostom's "combination of honesty, asceticism, and tactlessness, esp. in relation to the Empress Eudoxia, who with some reason took all attempts at moral reform as a censure of herself, was sufficient to work his ruin. When Chrysostom sheltered the Tall Brothers who had fled from Egypt after the condemnation of Origenism, Theophilus, Patriarch of Alexandria, seized the opportunity to humiliate the see of Constantinople. At the Synod of the Oak (403),

[185] Africans;[29] so with the 130 Monophysite Bishops at Ephesus and St. Flavian;[30] so was it in the instance of the 500 Bishops, who, by the influence of Basilicus,[31] signed a

---

carefully packed by Theophilus, Chrysostom was condemned on 29 charges. He was removed from his see, but shortly afterwards recalled by the court. Very soon, however, his plain speaking brought the displeasure of the Empress on him again, and his enemies saw their opportunity, and secured his banishment on a charge of unlawfully reassuming the duties of a see from which he had been canonically deposed (404). Even the support of the people of Constantinople, of the Pope (Innocent I), and of the entire Western Church, failed to save him. He was exiled at first to near Antioch, and when it became clear that in spite of his enfeebled health he would not die there soon enough, he was moved to Pontus, and finally deliberately killed by enforced travelling on foot in severe weather. His chief claim to remembrance, apart from his personal holiness, rests on his preaching and exegesis." *ODCC*.

[29] *Africans*: Octavianus, a 5th-century Carthaginian saint, was put to death with several thousand companions by the Asiatic Vandal king Hunneric.

[30] *St. Flavian*: "Flavian, bishop of Constantinople (July 446—between 8 and 11 Aug. 449); died Lydian Hypaepa Aug. 449 or Feb. 450. Elected as successor of Proklos, Flavian immediately entered into a conflict with the court: the eunuch Chrysaphios, favourite of Theodosios II, reprimanded Flavian for not sending presents of gold to the emperor on the occasion of his election, but the bishop refused to yield (Theoph. 98.11–19). Then, in 448, with Pope Leo I's support, Flavian dismissed Bassianos, the popular bishop of Ephesus, whose election had been approved by Theodosios II and Proklos. A crisis erupted when in 448 Flavian condemned and deposed the Monophysite archimandrite Eutyches, a protégé of Chrysaphios. Following an appeal by Eutyches, Theodosios II convoked the 'Robber' Council of Ephesus (449), which deposed Flavian. The mood in Ephesus was evidently hostile to Flavian; even its bishop Stephen voted for Flavian's condemnation. Flavian was banished and probably died en route to exile, even though shortly afterward the legend arose that he had been murdered by his enemies. Emperor Marcian ordered that Flavian's remains be brought to Constantinople and buried in the Church of the Holy Apostles. Emp. Leo I and the Council of Chalcedon praised Flavian in 451 as a victim of the Monophysites." *ODB*

[31] *Basilicus*: "In the Fifth Century, the Emperor Zeno was dispossessed, and driven into Isauria by Basilicus, who, by Usurpation, mounted the Imperial Throne: And yet after he was settled in it, had so general a Submission, that we find no less than 500 Bishops, and amongst them, Three of the Four Eastern Patriarchs, subscribing to Basilicus's Circular Letters, for anathematizing the Council of Chalcedon, and Leo's Tome. It must be confess'd, that these Bishops, who discover'd such Pusillanimity,

216

declaration against the Tome of St. Leo;[32] so in the instance
of the Henoticon of Zeno;[33] and so in the controversies both
of the Monothelites[34] and of the Iconoclasts.[35] Nay, in some

---

and Levity, in condemning the Council of Chalcedon, are not to be set up
for Examples." W. Higden, *A View of the English Constitution with
Respect to the Sovereign Authority of the Prince and the Allegiance of the
Subject* 3rd ed. (London, 1710), 108.

[32] *Tome of St. Leo*: The Tome of St. Leo is "The letter sent by Pope Leo I
(Ep. 28) to Flavian, Patriarch of Constantinople, on 13 June 449, also
called Epistola Dogmatica. Basing himself on the teaching of the Fathers,
esp. Tertullian and St Augustine, St Leo expounds with remarkable
clarity, precision, and vigour the Christological doctrine of the Latin
Church. Acc. to it Jesus Christ is One Person, the Divine Word, in whom
are two natures, the Divine and the human, permanently united, though
unconfused and unmixed. Each of these exercises its own particular
faculties, but within the unity of the Person. Hence follows the
'communicatio idiomatum', so that it can truly be said that the Son of
Man descended from heaven, and that the Son of God was crucified. The
letter, which was directed esp. against the heresy of Eutyches, was given
formal authority by the Council of Chalcedon (451) as the classic
statement of the Catholic doctrine of the Incarnation: 'Peter has spoken
through Leo'. Later it was constantly used in the controversies with the
Monophysites." *ODCC*

[33] *Henoticon of Zeno*: The Union of Henotikon, issued by Emperor Zeno
in 482 to reconcile those who accepted Chalcedon's definition of the
nature of Our Lord's nature and person and those who opposed it.
Rejecting Monophysism, the Council declared: 'We confess one and the
same Jesus Christ, the only-begotten, in who we acknowledge two
natures without mixture, without change, without separation, without
division ...' Furthermore, as H. Chadwick points out: "It affirmed the
supreme authority of the Nicene creed of 325 confirmed at
Constantinople (381) and followed by the Council of Ephesus (431);
pronounced anathema on both Nestorius and Eutyches at either extreme;
accepted the twelve anathemas attached to the third letter of Cyril of
Alexandria to Nestorius; insisted on the unqualified unity of the person of
Christ incarnate of the Holy Spirit and Mary the mother of God
(*Theotókos*)] and finally anathematized any who had held or now holds a
different doctrine, 'whether at Chalcedon or any other synod." See H.
Chadwick, *East and West: The Making of a Rift in the Church: From
Apostolic Times to the Council of Florence* (Oxford, 2003), 52.

[34] *Monothelites*: Monothelitism (from the Greek, "one will") teaches that
Jesus Christ had two natures but only one will. This is contrary to the
orthodox interpretation of Christology, which teaches that Jesus Christ
has two wills (human and divine) corresponding to his two natures.
Monothelitism is a development of the Monophysitism position in

of those few instances which are brought in controversy, as derogatory to the constancy of the Roman See, the vacillation, whatever it was, was owing to what, as I have shown is ordinarily avoided,—the immediate and direct pressure of the temporal power. As, among a hundred Martyr and Confessor Popes, St. Peter and St. Marcellinus for an hour or a day denied their Lord,[36] so if Liberius[37] and

---

Christological debates. It enjoyed considerable support in the seventh century before being rejected as heretical at the Sixth Ecumenical Council in 680.

[35] *Iconoclasts*: "In 726 the Byzantine emperor Leo III issued a ban on Christian religious imagery and its veneration, thus initiating the policy of iconoclasm. ...The chronicler Theophanes links the inauguration of iconoclasm with a volcanic eruption in the Cyclades which threw up a new island between the islands of Thera and Therasia, themselves of volcanic origin, and says that Leo's initial act of iconoclasm was to order the removal of the icon of Christ from above the Chalke, the bronze gate at the entrance to the palace." Its removal "caused a riot, and many protesters were severely punished: the beginning of the persecution of those who resisted the imperial edict, the iconodules or iconophiles. ... Iconoclasm soon became settled policy, and was to hold sway in the Byzantine Empire for more than a century: until the death of the last iconoclast emperor, Theophilos, in 842, apart from a period when the icons were restored between 787 and 815. The period of iconoclasm was critical for the Byzantine Empire. It can be seen as the last of the religious reactions to the loss of the eastern provinces in the early seventh century, first to the Persians, and then, permanently, to the Arabs. ... As such, iconoclasm is one of a number of measures by which the Byzantines responded to the spectre of defeat, measures that swept away much of the administrative and military system they had inherited from the Roman Empire, to replace it with a centralized bureaucracy, permanently located in the capital city, Constantinople, combined with the organization of the rest of the Empire into areas known as 'themes', governed by a military commander. The final defeat of iconoclasm in the ninth century was heralded as the 'Triumph of Orthodoxy', and was celebrated by a public ceremony in which the *Synodikon of Orthodoxy* was proclaimed. This *Synodikon* was issued by the synod held in 843 under the presidency of the patriarch Methodios, and reaffirmed the decrees of the Seventh Oecumenical Synod, held in Nicaea [under Pope Hadrian] in 787, and the oecumenicity of that synod." A Louth, *St John Damascene: Tradition and Originality in Byzantine Theology* (Oxford, 2002). 194-5.

[36] *denied their Lord*: St Peter denied knowing Our Lord three times (Matt. 26: 69-75), though he afterwards wept bitterly (Luke 22:62) and

Vigilius[38] gave a momentary scandal to the cause of orthodoxy, it was when they were no longer in their proper place, as the keystone of a great system, and as the correlative of a thousand ministering authorities, but mere individuals, torn from their see and prostrated before Cæsar.

In later and modern times we see the same truth irresistibly brought out; not only, for instance, in St. Thomas's history, but in St. Anselm's,[39] nay, in the whole course of English ecclesiastical affairs, from the Conquest[40]

---

was the first to enter the tomb (Luke 24:12). During the Diocletian persecution, in 303, Pope Marcellinus decreed that sacrifice be made to the gods in the law courts, though after being beheaded on Diocletian's orders, he was revered as a martyr.

[37] *Liberius*: Pope Liberius (352-66), was elected pope when the Arians were in the ascendancy and the Emperor Constantius II (337-61) was urging the western empire to anathematize St. Athanasius, the champion of Nicene orthodoxy, and to accept the Arian heresy. Pope Liberius duly acquiesced in the anathematization of St. Athanasius as well as the First Creed of Sirmium (which omitted the Nicene reference to 'one in being with the Father'). Later, he sought to make amends by reaffirming the Nicene Creed.

[38] *Vigilius*: Vigilius (537-55) passed himself off as a Monophysite to ingratiate himself with the Empress Theodora in order to secure the papacy at a time when the court of Constantinople was Monophysite. Once installed as pope, he acquiesced in the emperor Justinian's attempt to appease the Monophysites and to repudiate the Council of Chalcedon, if only obliquely, by signing a condemnation of the anti-Monophysite 'Three Chapters.' Towards the end of his life after attempting to reaffirm Chalcedon, Vigilius clashed with Justinian, who published correspondence revealing the full extent of the pope's treachery. In response, before dying, Pope Vigilius published a series of retractions, which did not prevent the papacy suffering grave disrepute as a result of his manifold betrayals. He died, with a becoming ingloriousness, of gallstones. See E. Duffy, *Saints and Sinners: A History of the Popes* (London, 2006), 59-64.

[39] *Anselm*: Anselm (1093-1109), Archbishop of Canterbury. In addition to being a brilliant theologian, St. Anselm protected the interests of his archbishopric by reminding William II, Henry I and Rufus that his primary obedience as archbishop was to the pope, not English kings.

[40] *Conquest*: The Norman Conquest was the military conquest of England by William, duke of Normandy, initiated by his victory at the Battle of Hastings (October 14, 1066), which resulted in profound linguistic, political, administrative, and social changes in the British Isles.

to the sixteenth century, and, not with least significancy, in the primacy of Cranmer. Moreover, we see it in the tendency of the Gallicanism of Louis XIV.,[41] and the Josephism of Austria.[42] Such, too, is the lesson taught us in the recent policy of the Czar towards the United Greeks,[43]

---

[41] *Gallicanism of Louis XIV*: Gallicanism is "the distinctive epithet of the ancient Church of Gaul or France, and of its characteristic usages, liturgies, etc. as compared with those of other national Churches of the Roman communion. Hence applied to that of school of French Roman Catholics of which Bossuet was the leader, which maintains the right of the French Church to be in certain important respects self-governing, and free from papal control; opposed to *Ultramontane*." *OED*. "The Concordat of Bologna (1516), by conceding to the French Crown the right to nominate to major benefices, disposed her monarchs to seek accommodation rather than a break with Rome. It also dictated the (unsuccessful) strategy of J. Calvin and T. Beza, which aimed to capture the support of the Crown so that the whole Gallican Church could be transformed on Protestant principles. Until the adoption of the RC faith by Henry IV in 1593 the Huguenots hoped this might be achieved. After prolonged civil wars during the second part of the 16th century, culminating in the St Bartholomew's Day Massacre in 1572 (retrospectively chronicled by the Protestant Agrippa d'Aubigné (1552–1630) in *Les Tragiques*), the Huguenots gained limited protection under the Edict of Nantes (1598), but this was eroded and finally removed by its Revocation (1685). Their numbers declined and RC Christianity was invigorated by post-Tridentine piety. Louis XIV (reigned 1643–1715) affirmed the power of the Crown not only against the Protestants but also against the Papacy, inducing the clergy to publish the Gallican Articles in 1682." *ODCC*.

[42] *Josephism of Austria*: *Josephism* refers to the wide-ranging reforms imposed by Joseph II of Austria on the Roman Catholic Church in the Habsburg Empire, which included barring Austrian bishops from having any formal contact with the pope or international Catholic organizations; making changes to the Catholic liturgy; cutting the number of feast days; abolishing religious brotherhoods; regulating religious processions and burial practices; and regulating marriage as a civil contract. "Marriage among Christians remained a religious sacrament celebrated by a priest or pastor, but now the state stepped in to regulate an institution that had previously been regulated solely by the church." P.M. Judson, *The Habsburg Empire: A New History* (Princeton, 2016), 70.

[43] *United Greeks*: Czar Nicholas (1795-1855), before and after the Polish uprising of 1830, took control of and despoiled the Roman Catholic properties of the United Greeks in Poland and elsewhere in the Russian empire to strengthen and enrich the Russian Greek Church.

and in the present bearing of the English Government [186] towards the Church of Ireland.[44] In all these instances, it is a struggle between the Holy See and some local, perhaps distant, Government, the liberty and orthodoxy of its faithful people being the matter in dispute; and while the temporal power is on the spot, and eager, and cogent, and persuasive, and dangerous, the strength of the assailed party lies in its fidelity to the rest of Christendom and to the Holy See.

Well, this is intelligible; we see why it should be so, and we see it in historical fact; but how is it possible, and where are the instances in proof, that a Church can cast off Catholic intercommunion without falling under the power of the State? Could an isolated Church do now, what, humanly speaking, it could not have done in the twelfth century, though a Saint was its champion? Do you hope to do, my brethren, what was beyond St. Thomas of Canterbury? Truly is it then called a Branch Church; for, as a branch cannot live of itself, therefore, as soon as it is lopped off from the Body of Christ, it is straightway grafted of sheer necessity upon the civil constitution, if it is to preserve life of any kind. Indeed, who could ever entertain such a dream, as that a circumscribed religious society, without the awfulness of a divine origin, the sacredness of immemorial custom, or the authority of many previous successes, while standing on its own ground, and simply subordinate as regards its constituent members to the civil [187] power, should be able to assert ecclesiastical claims, which are to impede the free action of that same sovereign power, and to insult its majesty?—a subject hierarchy, growing out of a nation's very soil, yet challenging it, standing breast to breast against it, breathing defiance into its very face, striking at it full and straight,—why, as men are constituted, such a nuisance, as they would call it, would be intolerable.

---

[44] *Church of Ireland*: The Erastian relationship between the English government and the Church of Ireland only succeeded in making the majority of the Irish more devoted to the Roman Catholic religion and the Holy See.

The rigid, unelastic, wooden contrivance would be shivered into bits by the very recoil and jar of the first blow it was rash enough to venture. But matters would not go so far; the blandishments, the alliances, the bribes, the strong arm of the world, would bring it to its senses, and humble it in its own sight, ere it had opportunity to be valiant. The world would simply over-master the presumptuous claimant to divine authority, and would use for its own purposes the slave whom it had dishonoured. It would set her to sweep its courts, or to keep the line of its march, who had thought to reign among the stars of heaven.

For, it is evident enough, a National or Branch Church can be of the highest service to the State, if properly under control. The State wishes to make its subjects peaceful and obedient; and there is nothing more fitted to effect this object than religion. It wishes them to have some teaching about the next world, but not too much: just as much as is [188] important and beneficial to the interests of the present. Decency, order, industry, patience, sobriety, and as much of purity as can be expected from human nature,—this is its list of requisites; not dogma, for it creates the *odium theologicum*;[45] not mystery, for it only serves to exalt the priesthood. Useful, sensible preaching, activity in benevolent schemes, the care of schools, the superintendence of charities, good advice for the thoughtless and idle, and "spiritual consolation" for the dying—these are the duties of a National or Branch Church.

---

[45] *odium theologicum*: 'theological hatred,' referring to "the hatred which proverbially characterizes theological dissensions." The *OED* cites A.J. Froude's *History of England* (1856) to illustrate the word: "The *odium theologicum* is ever hotter between sections of the same party which are divided by trifling differences, than between the open representatives of antagonist principles." Newman's explanation for this often unseemly theological brawling is worth quoting: "Religion is so deeply interesting and sovereign a matter and so possesses the whole man, when it once gains its due entrance into the mind, that it is not wonderful, that, as worldly men quarrel fiercely about worldly things, so, through the weakness of human nature, particular theologians have had unchristian disputes about Christian truths." *LD*, xxiv, 6.

The parochial clergy are to be a moral police; as to the Bishops, they are to be officers of a State-religion, not shepherds of a people; not mixing and interfering in the crowd, but coming forward on solemn occasions to crown, or to marry, or to baptize royalty, or to read prayers to the House of Peers, or to consecrate churches, or to ordain and confirm, or to preach for charities, and to be but little seen in public in any other way. Synods are unnecessary and dangerous, for they convey the impression that the Establishment is a distinct body, and has rights of its own. So is discipline, or any practical separation of Churchmen and Dissenters; for nationality is the real bond, and Churchmanship is but the accident, of Englishmen. Churches and churchyards are national property, and open to all, whatever their denomination, for marriage and for burial, when they will. Nor must the Establishment be in the eye of the law a corporation, even though its separate incumbents and chapters be such, lest it be looked upon as [189] politically more than a name, or a function of State.

8.

Now, in order to show that this is no exaggeration, I will, in conclusion, refer in evidence to the celebrated work of a celebrated man, in defence of the Establishment; a work, too, which disowns Erastianism, and, in a certain sense, is written against it, and which, moreover, is, in breadth of doctrine, behind what would be maintained or taken for granted by statesmen now. For all these reasons, if I would illustrate what I have been saying of the certainty of a theoretical Branch Church becoming, in fact, and in the event, a Branch of the State, and of the liking of the State for Branch Churches and nothing else, I could not take a work fairer to the National Church, than "The Alliance of Church and State" of Bishop Warburton. A few extracts will be sufficient for my purpose.

In this Treatise he tells us, that the object of the State in this alliance is, not the propagation of the truth, but the wellbeing of society. "The true end," he says, "for which

[190] religion is established," by the State, "is not to provide for the true faith, but for civil utility."[46] This is "the key," he observes, "to open the whole mystery of this controversy, and to lead" a man "safe through all the intricacies, windings, and perplexities in which it has been involved." Next, religion is to be used for the benefit of that civil power, which, it seems, does not in any true sense provide for religion. "This use of religion to the State," he says, "was seen by the learned, and felt by all men of every age and nation. The ancient world particularly was so firmly convinced of this truth, that the greatest secret of the sublime art of legislation consisted in this—how best religion might be applied to serve society."[47]

---

[46] Bp. Warburton's "Alliance of Church and State," p. 148, ed. 1741. [N]

[47] Bp. Warburton's "Alliance of Church and State," p. 18. [N] Apropos Warburton's *Alliance of Church and State* (1736), the intellectual historian B.W. Young writes in the *ODNB*: "Warburton argued that religion alone can supply the rewards necessary to ensure that individual virtue continues to underpin the proper function of civil government. The magistrate was to oversee the government of the body, the church that of the soul. Fundamental to the alliance so formed was the influence that the church could give to the service of the state, and the support and protection that the state could in turn give to the church. Above all the church was to oversee that popular measure of the early and mid-eighteenth-century Church of England, the 'reformation of manners'. Warburton argued that an established denomination provided moral security for the state, and that it should therefore be composed by the majority confession of the nation, thereby standing clear of any multiplication and fragmentation into sectarianism. Sectarianism he identified as the source of contention and internal wars. Reflection on the legacy of the civil war, a subject on which he had planned to write a history, comprised a major part of his thinking on such matters. He read most of the political pamphlets produced between 1640 and 1660, and his very full annotations to Clarendon's *History* were finally published by the Clarendon Press in 1826. While he argued that the civil magistrate could not coerce opinions, he also declared that such opinions should always give way to civil peace. Utility was absolutely central to his argument, but it was a utility that led to knowledge of divine truth through the proper, tolerant practice of Christianity as a revealed religion. Hobbes and Roman Catholicism represented the two extremes to be avoided ..." According to Paul Langford, a more authoritative chronicler of these matters, Warburon's *Alliance* "offered a realistic defence of the position of the Church, one which abandoned all pretensions to an independent

Well, so far we might tolerate him; such statements, if not simply true, are not absolutely unheard of or paradoxical; but next he makes a startling step in advance. "Public utility and truth coincide,"[48] he says; nay, further still, he distinctly calls public utility "a sure rule and measure of truth;"[49] so that he continues, by means of it the State "will be much better enabled to find out truth, than any speculative inquirer with all the aid of the philosophy of the schools."[50] "From whence it appears," he continues, "that while a State, in union with the Church, hath so great an interest and concern with true religion, and so great a capacity for discovering what is true, religion is likely to thrive much better than when left to itself." The State, then, it would appear, out of compassion to Religion, takes it out of the schools, and adapts it to its own purposes to keep it pure and make it perfect.

He does not scruple to bring out this very sentiment in the most explicit statements, that there may be no mistake about his meaning. He considers conformity to objects of State, the simple rule of truth, of purity, of exaggeration, of excess, of perversity, and of dangerousness in doctrinal teaching. "Of whatever use," he says, "an alliance may be thought for preserving the being of religion, the necessity of it for preserving its *purity* is most evident ... Let us consider the danger religion runs, when left in its natural state to itself, of deviating from truth. In those circumstances, the men who have the greatest credit in the Church are such as are famed for greatest sanctity. Now, Church sanctity has been generally understood to be then most perfect, when most estranged from the world and all its habitudes and relations. But this being only to be acquired by secession [191]

---

authority. ... In time it came to be seen as the classic statement of complacent Georgian Erastianism and a mark of the stable relationship between religion and politics in mid-eighteenth-century England." P. Langford, *A Polite and Commercial People: England 1727-1783* (Oxford, 1998), 43-4.

[48] Ibid. p. 147. [N]
[49] Ibid. p. 135. [N]
[50] Ibid. [N]

and retirement from human affairs, and that secession rendering man ignorant of civil society and its rights and interests, in place of which will succeed, according to his natural temper, all the follies of superstition or fanaticism, we must needs conclude, that religion, under such directors and reformers (and God knows these are generally its lot), will deviate from truth, and *consequently* from a capacity, in proportion, of serving civil society ... Such societies we have seen, whose religious doctrines are so little serviceable to civil society, that they can prosper only on the ruin and [192] destruction of it. Such are those who preach up the sanctity of celibacy, asceticism, the sinfulness of defensive war, of capital punishments, and even of civil magistracy itself. On the other hand, when Religion is in alliance with the State, as it then comes under the magistrate's direction (those holy leaders having now neither credit nor power to do mischief), its purity must needs be reasonably well supported and preserved. For, truth and public utility coinciding, the civil magistrate, as such, will see it for his interest to seek after and promote the truth in religion; and, by means of public utility, which his office enables him so well to understand, he will never be at a loss to know where such truth is to be found."[51]

He takes delight in this view of the subject, and enforces it as follows:—"The means of attaining man's happiness here," he says, "is civil society; the means of his happiness hereafter is contemplation. If, then, opinions, the result of contemplation, obstruct the effects of civil society, it follows that they must be restrained. Accordingly, the ancient masters of wisdom, who, from these considerations, taught that man was born for action, not for contemplation, universally concurred to establish it as a maxim, founded on the nature of things, that *opinions should always give way to civil peace*."[52] And he proceeds to defend it as follows: [193] "God so disposed things, that the means of attaining the

---

[51] Bp. Warburton's "Alliance of Church and State," p. 58. [N]
[52] Ibid. p. 126. [N]

happiness of one state [of existence] should not cross or obstruct the means of attaining the happiness of the other. From whence we must conclude, that where the supposed means of each—viz., opinions and civil peace—do clash, there one of them is not the true means of happiness. But the means of attaining the happiness peculiar to that state in which the man at present exists, being *perfectly and infallibly known* by man, and the means of the happiness of his future existence, as far as relates to the discovery of truth, but *very imperfectly known* by him, it necessarily follows that, *wherever opinions clash with civil peace, those opinions are no means of future happiness*, or, in other words, are either no truths, or truths of no importance." Behold the principle of the reasonings of the Committee of Privy Council,[53] and the philosophy of the Premier's

---

[53] *Privy Council*: Apropos the Erastianism that Newman mocks so splendidly here, Peter Nockles claims that Newman "did much to perpetuate a misconception of Orthodox teaching on church and state;" indeed, his very use of the word 'Erastian' was a "catch-all rhetorical device;" to say that the National Church was Erastian, or worse, to say that Anglican clergymen were, in effect, little more than agents of the state, showed a "lack of discrimination;" the true relationship between church and state in the 18th-century English National Church being what Dr. Nockles styles the "Hookerian understanding of church-state theory in terms of an organic union of two interrelated divinely-ordained powers;" after all, "parliament still represented the church as a lay synod, as Hooker envisaged." To try to substantiate this risible claim, Dr. Nockles quotes the High Churchman Godfrey Faussett, who "assailed the error 'of those who wholly confound their idea of the Church of Christ with that of a political establishment.'" P. Nockles, *The Oxford Movement in Context: Anglican High Churchmanship 1860-1857* (Cambridge, 1994), 55, 56, 63, 64-5. In other words, not only Warburton and Newman but everyone was wrong about church and state in England who saw Erastianism in the relations between the National Church and England's political Establishment. *Pace* Dr. Nockles, a more reliable guide to this fundamental aspect of English history is the wonderful old popular historian J.R. Green, who wrote: "A large number of prelates were mere Whig partisans with no higher aim than that of promotion. The levees of the ministers were crowded with lawn sleeves." *A Short History of the English People* (London, 1874), 747. As for Faussett, Dr. Nockles' dubious authority on these matters, Newman wrote to Pusey in 1838: "Fausett to-day has fired off a sermon against us, as leading to Popery…

satisfaction thereupon! Baptismal regeneration is determined to be true or not true, not by the text of Scripture, the testimony of the Fathers, the tradition of the Church, nay, not by Prayer Book, Articles, Jewell, Usher,[54] Carleton,[55] or Bullinger,[56] but by its tendency to minister to

---

The time was now come to speak out a great deal against what he considered a quasi Transubstantiation — he took a miserably low view. A great deal about Rome being Antichrist..." *LD*, vi, 246.

[54] *Usher*: James Ussher (1581-1656), Archbishop of Armagh, scholar, controversialist. According to the *ODNB*: "Whatever the disputes over Ussher's administrative abilities as a bishop, there is no argument over his standing as a scholar and churchman. His long-term legacy includes the first detailed academic treatment of the early Irish church, the creation of an identity myth for Irish protestantism, the identification of the genuine Ignatian epistles, and even, in extreme fundamentalist circles, the defence of creationism. In terms of his contemporaries he was also noted for his pastoral and spiritual skills. Deeply prayerful, he was repeatedly approached for spiritual advice, comfort, and assistance during his career. His expertise as a controversialist made him the natural choice to rescue Roman Catholics for the protestant faith—this was, after all, the foundation of his friendship with the countess of Peterborough. His spiritual sensitivity similarly recommended him as counsellor for those who were dying. Thus in 1655, when Elizabeth, the wife of Sir Hugh Cholmley, was asked whom she wished to attend her on her deathbed, she chose Ussher."

[55] *Carleton*: George Carleton (1557-1628), Bishop of Chichester, biographer and controversialist. According to the *ODNB*: "Carleton's earliest writing was a laudatory piece for Queen Elizabeth, *Carmen panegyricum*. ... As he began to bid for higher preferment Carleton wrote a series of conformist pamphlets, vindicating tithes (1606) and attacking the Church of Rome (1610, 1613), in the latter case with somewhat equivocal results. In April 1614 Dudley Carleton wrote to George from Venice, warning him that his writings were capable of being misconstrued, and also censuring him for confining ordination to bishops only. Carleton took the position—summarized in his 1615 *Directions to Know the True Church*—that the Church of Rome had remained true in doctrine until the time of Luther, a position in which he was later seconded by [among others] ... James Ussher." He also wrote a celebrated biography of Bernard Gilpin (1517-83), the "Apostle of the North," who made many converts to the new Protestant religion in the North of England.

[56] *Bullinger*: Johann Heinrich Bullinger (1504-75) Swiss Reformer and, according to the ODCC, "something of an oracle among many of the English higher clergy." Elizabeth turned to Bullinger to help her

the peace and repose of the community, to the convenience and comfort of Downing Street, Lambeth, and Exeter Hall.[57]

If the Bishop makes doctrine depend upon political expedience, it is not wonderful that he should take the same measure of the Sacraments and Orders of his Church. [194] "Hence," he says, "may be seen the folly of those Christian sects, which, under pretence that Christianity is a spiritual religion, fancy it cannot have rites, ceremonies, public worship, a ministry or ecclesiastical policy. *Not reflecting* that *without* these *it could never have become national*, and consequently, could not have done that *service* to the State that it, of all religions, is most capable of performing."[58] And then in a note, on occasion of Burnet's statement, that "Sidney's notion of Christianity was, that it was like a divine philosophy in the mind, without public worship or anything that looked like a Church," he adds, "that an ignorant monk, who had seen no further than his cell, or a mad fanatic, who had thrown aside his reason, should talk thus is nothing; but that the great Sidney, a man so superlatively skilled in the science of human nature and civil policy, and who *so well knew* what religion *was capable* of doing for the State, should fall into this extravagant error, is, indeed, very surprising."

Accordingly, he mentions some of the details in which ecclesiastical ceremonies are serviceable to the State; and in quoting his list and reasons of them, I shall conclude my extracts from his very instructive volume. "There are peculiar junctures," he says, "when the influence of religion

---

manage the Puritans in her new religion and to reply to Pope Pius V after the Holy Father excommunicated England.

[57] *the convenience and comfort of Downing Street, Lambeth and Exeter Hall*: Downing Street is the London residence of the English prime minister; Lambeth is the London residence of the archbishops of Canterbury; and Exeter Hall is the building in the Strand used, from 1830, as a venue for Evangelical and ultra-Protestant religious, polemical and philanthropic assemblies. Achilli, for example, Newman's *bête noir*, harangued Newman's contemporaries on the monstrosities of Roman Catholicism from the platform of Exeter Hall.

[58] Bp. Warburton's "Alliance of Church and State," p. 104. [N]

is more than ordinarily serviceable to the State, and these the civil magistrate only knows. Now, while a Church is in [195] its natural state of independency, it is not in his power to improve these conjunctures to the advantage of the State by a proper application of religion; but when the alliance is made, and, consequently, the Church under his direction, he has the authority to prescribe such public exercises of religion, as days of humiliation, fasts, festivals, exhortations and dehortations, thanksgivings and depreciations, and in such a manner as he finds the exigencies of State require."[59]

9.

And now I think I have shown you, my brethren, as far as I could hope to do so in the course of a Lecture, that if your first principle be, as it was the first principle of the movement of 1833, that the Church should have absolute power over her faith, worship, and teaching, you must not be contemplating an ecclesiastical body, local and isolated, or what you have been accustomed to call a Branch Church. The fable of the bundle of sticks[60] especially applies to those who have no weapons of flesh and blood,—to an unarmed hierarchy, who have to contend with the pride of intellect and the power of the sword. Look abroad, my brethren, and

---

[59] Bp. Warburton's "Alliance of Church and State," p. 63. [N]

[60] *The fable of the bundle of sticks*: This is a reference to the fable by Aesop, the ancient storytelling moralist. "A certain Father had a family of Sons, who were forever quarreling among themselves. No words he could say did the least good, so he cast about in his mind for some very striking example that should make them see that discord would lead them to misfortune. One day when the quarreling had been much more violent than usual and each of the Sons was moping in a surly manner, he asked one of them to bring him a bundle of sticks. Then handing the bundle to each of his Sons in turn he told them to try to break it. But although each one tried his best, none was able to do so. The Father then untied the bundle and gave the sticks to his Sons to break one by one. This they did very easily. 'My Sons,' said the Father, 'do you not see how certain it is that if you agree with each other and help each other, it will be impossible for your enemies to injure you? But if you are divided among yourselves, you will be no stronger than a single stick in that bundle.' *In unity is strength.*"

see whether this union of many members, divided in place and circumstances, but one in heart, is not most visibly the very strength of the Catholic Church at this very time. Then only can you resist the world, when you belong to a [196] communion which exists under many governments, not one; or should it ever be under some empire commensurate with itself (which is not conceivable), a communion which has, at least, an immovable centre to fall back upon. But if this be the state of the case, if you must, on the one hand, leave the existing Establishment, yet, on the other, not seek or form a Branch Church instead of it, I have brought you by a short, but I hope, not an abrupt or unsafe path, to the conclusion that you must cease to be an Anglican by becoming a Catholic. Indeed, if the movement, of which you are the children, had any providential scope at all, I do not see how you can disguise from yourselves that Catholicism is it. The Catholic Church, and she alone, from the nature of the case, is proof against Erastianism.

LECTURE VII

THE PROVIDENTIAL COURSE OF THE MOVEMENT OF 1833 NOT IN THE DIRECTION OF A SECT

IT was my object yesterday to show that such persons as are led by the principles of the anti-Erastian movement of 1833 to quit the Establishment, are necessarily called upon, as by one and the same act, to join the Catholic Church; for the case is not supposable in reason, of their quitting the one without their joining the other. The only other course which lies open to them is either that of joining the communion of some other National or Branch Church, or, on the other hand, that of founding a Sect;[1] but a Branch or National Church is inevitably Erastian. This point I argued out at considerable length; and now I come to the second alternative, viz., that of founding a Sect, or as it is sometimes familiarly called, setting up for one's self. And I shall show today that, bad as it is for a man to take the State for his guide and master in religion, or to become an

---

[1] *Sect*: According to the *OED*, one definition of *Sect* is: "A system of belief or observance distinctive of one of the parties or schools into which the adherents of a religion are divided; sometimes *spec.*, a system differing from what is deemed the orthodox tradition; a heresy. A body of persons who unite in holding certain views differing from those of others who are accounted to be of the same religion; a party or school among the professors of religion; sometimes applied *spec.* to parties that are regarded as heretical, or at least as deviating from the general tradition." To exemplify this meaning of the word, the Dictionary defines the *Clapham Sect* as "a name applied derisively early in the 19th century to a coterie of persons of Evangelical opinions and conspicuous philanthropic activity, some of whom lived at Clapham; among the chief members of whom were Wilberforce, Zachary Macaulay, and Henry Thornton." Another illustration given by the *OED* for the word is this: "1788 Gibbon *Decl. & F.* I. V. 170 The church was distracted by the Nestorian and Monophysite sects."

Erastian, it is worse still to become a Sectarian, that is, to be his own Doctor and his own Pope.

What is really meant by a "Church," is a religious body [198] which has jurisdiction over its members, or which governs itself; whereas, according to the doctrine of Erastus, it has no such jurisdiction, really is not a body at all, but is simply governed by the State, and is one department of the State's operations. This is one error, and a great one; it is an error, my brethren, which you have from the first withstood; but now I wish to show you that, if you will not accept of the Catholic Church, and submit yourselves to her authority, this said Erastianism is the least and the most tolerable error you can embrace; that your best and most religious of courses, which are all bad and irreligious, is to acquiesce in Erastianism at once; to give up the principles on which you set out, and to tell the world that the movement of 1833 was a mistake, and that you have grown wiser.

1.

I would have you recollect, then, that the civil power is a divine ordinance;[2] no one doubts it. It is prior in history to

---

[2] *civil power… a divine ordinance*: "Medieval scholars used scripture to develop theories of ecclesiastical power and, in particular, the division of power into secular and ecclesiastical, royal and sacerdotal, temporal and spiritual (Ullmann, 1970; Watt, 1988). Such theories had canonical implications, but they were based in theology. Although medieval theories of the two realms are in a tradition leading to modern theories of church and state, medieval scholars divided the church, the *res publica christiana*, into two hierarchies: spiritual and secular. Three resources from scripture were fundamental to the theology of power: Matthew 22:21, where Jesus uses a coin to teach that one should render to God what is God's and to the emperor what is the emperor's; Romans 13:1–7, where Paul teaches that all authority comes from God and should be obeyed; and the texts on Melchizedek, the high priest and king (Gen 14:18–20; Ps 110:4; Heb 5:6, 10; 6:20; 7:1, 10–11, 15, 17, 21). Despite, or perhaps because of, how little the Hebrew Bible says about Melchizedek, he has been the subject of much speculation among Jewish scholars (Kuehn, 2010). Paul teaches in Hebrews that Jesus Christ was the successor of Melchizedek. Whereas the first resource (Matt 22:21) suggests that there are two independent authorities, the others suggest that a single divine power diverges into the secular and ecclesiastical

ecclesiastical power. The Jewish lawgivers,[3] judges, prophets, kings, had some sort of jurisdiction over the priesthood, though the priesthood had its distinct powers and duties. The Jewish Church was not a body distinct from the State. In a certain sense, then, the civil magistrate is

---

powers. Moreover, if all power is divine in origin (Rom 13:1–7), one might expect the church to control how the power flows from Christ to the temporal prince. All theories of the division of powers were versions of the Gelasian doctrine, so called because it was articulated in a letter that Pope Gelasius I sent to the Emperor Anastasius in 494. Gelasius posits two powers, respectively royal and priestly. The priestly power is superior inasmuch as its ministers are responsible for the eternal well-being of everyone, including kings, whereas kings are responsible only for their subjects' temporal well-being. Nevertheless, neither authority should intrude upon the domain of the other. Kings should not interfere in the work of those who dispense the 'mysteries of religion,' but nor should priests interfere in secular matters. The model implies that the priestly authority is inferior to the secular authority in the secular domain." *The Oxford Encyclopaedia of the Bible and Law.*

[3] *The Jewish lawgivers*: "Historically, Jewish law has largely functioned as the religious law of Jews rather than as the law of a state. Its range is far greater than that of secular legal systems, since it includes the whole of the ritual law (even though the latter is largely left to divine enforcement). Although there are some conceptual differences between 'ritual' and 'civil' law, for most purposes the two are treated as a unified whole, and thus arguments by analogy may be made from one sphere to the other. As for 'civil' (here including criminal) law, Jewish law is comparable in extent to any other system of private law. Thus, there is a Jewish contract law, tort law, commercial law, succession law, and family law. Succession and family law, however, are regarded as having important religious connotations, and Orthodox Jews seek to regulate their marriages and wills in ways compatible with both Jewish law and the secular law of the host country. Both the term 'Jewish law' (*mishpat ivri*) and its historical (as opposed to dogmatic and philosophical-theological) analysis are of modern vintage and reflect the use of modern secular models to describe what the Jewish tradition calls *Torah* (instruction) or *Halacha* (the way [of life]). In the latter, the 'law' is just one part of divine revelation, albeit the part that revelation seeks to have enforced, in varying degrees, by human agencies. Whereas *mishpat ivri* may seek to analyze the law in terms of authoritative sources and institutions, the tradition itself understands the issues against the background of different forms of revelation (e.g., prophecy, charismatic authority) and the strength claimed for them in different historical periods." *The Oxford International Encyclopedia of Legal History*

what divines call, "in possession;" the *onus probandi* lies
with those who would encroach upon his power. He was in [199]
possession in the age when Christ came; he is in possession
now in the minds of men, and in the *primâ facie* view of
human society. He is in possession, because the benefits he
confers on mankind are tangible, and obvious to the world
at large. And he is recognised and sanctioned in Scripture in
the most solemn way; nay, the very instrument of his power,
by which he is strong, the carnal weapon itself, is formally
committed to him. "Let every soul," says St. Paul, "be
subject to the higher powers; for there is no power but from
God; and those that are," the powers that be, "are ordained
of God. Therefore he that resisteth the power, resisteth the
ordinance of God; and they that resist, purchase to
themselves damnation. For princes are not a terror to the
good work, but to the evil. Wilt thou, then, not be afraid of
the power? Do that which is good, and thou shalt have
praise from the same. For he is God's minister to thee for
good. But if thou do that which is evil, fear, for he beareth
not the sword in vain. For he is God's minister, an avenger
to execute wrath upon him that doth evil."[4]

It is difficult to find a passage in Scripture more solemn
and distinct than this—distinct in the duty laid down, and in
the sin of transgressing it, and solemn in the reasons on
which the duty is enforced. The civil magistrate is a
minister, or, in a certain sense, a priest of the Most High;
for, as is well known, the word in the original Greek is one [200]
which commonly is appropriated to denote the sacerdotal
office and function.[5] He is, moreover, "an avenger to

---

[4] *"… to execute wrath upon him that doth evil"*: Romans 13
[5] *the sacerdotal office and function*: For confirmation of Newman's
etymological point, see the *OED* entry for 'priest.' "Etymologically *priest*
represents Greek πρεσβύτερος, Latin *presbyter*, elder n.[3]; but by the late
2nd or early 3rd cent. a.d. (Tertullian), and thus long before the Latin or
Romance word was taken into English, the Latin word *sacerdos*,
originally, like Greek ἱερεύς, applied to the sacrificing priests of the
heathen gods, and also, in the translations of the Scriptures, to the Jewish
priests, had come to be applied to the Christian ministers also, and thus to
be a synonym of *presbyter* (compare sacerdos n.). In Old English, Latin

execute wrath;" he is the representative and image on earth of that awful attribute of God, His justice, as fathers are types and intimations of His tenderness and providence towards His creatures. Nor is this a solitary recognition of the divine origin and the dignity of the civil power:—when Divine Wisdom, in the book of Proverbs, would enlarge upon her great works on the earth, she finds one principal and special instance of them to consist in her presence and operation in the rulers of the people. "By me," she says, "kings reign, and lawgivers decree just things: by me princes rule, and the mighty decree justice." And let it be observed, that the function here ascribed to the civil magistrate, and requiring a peculiar gift, is one of those which especially enters into the idea of the times of the promised Messias. "Behold," says the Prophet, "a king shall reign in justice, and princes shall rule in judgment."[6] Such is the civil power, the representative, and oracle, and instrument, of the eternal law of God, with the power of life and death, the awful power of continuing or cutting short the probation of beings destined to live eternally. To it are committed all things under heaven; it is the sovereign lord of the wide earth and its various fruits, and of men who till it or traverse it; and it allots, and distributes, and maintains, [201] the one for the benefit of the other. And as it is sacred in its origin, so may it be considered irresponsible in its acts, and treason against it, in some sort, rebellion against the Most High.

---

presbyter was usually represented by *prēost*; Latin *sacerdos*, applied to a heathen or Jewish priest, was usually rendered by *sacerd* (regularly so in the Hexateuch, Psalms, and Gospels); sometimes, when applied to a Jewish or Christian priest, by *prēost*. Old English *prēost* was used as a generic term including all clergymen, not necessarily in priest's, or even deacon's, orders (compare sense [3]); the fuller term *mæsse-prēost* mass-priest *n.* was often used to distinguish a priest in full orders, qualified to teach and celebrate mass (compare sense [1]). By the early Middle English period, *sacerd* had become obsolete, and *prest*, like Old French *prestre*, became the current word alike for *presbyter* and *sacerdos*."

[6] *"a king ... in judgment."*: Isaiah 32:1

236

Now, such being the office of the temporal power, and considering the manifold temporal blessings of which it is the source and channel, and the cruelty of disturbing the settled order of society, and the madness of the attempt, surely a man has to think twice, and ought to be quite sure what he is doing, and to have a clear case to produce in his behalf, before he sets up any rival society to embarrass and endanger it. Pause before you decide on such a step, and make sure of your ground. Surely it is not likely that God should undo His own work for nothing. He does not revoke His ordinances except when they have failed of their mission. He does not supersede them or innovate on them, except when He is about to commence a higher work than He has already committed to them. Judaism was supplanted by Christianity, because its law was unprofitable, and because the Gospel was a definite revelation and doctrine from above, which required a more perfect organ for its promulgation. An institution was formed upon a new idea, and to it was transferred a portion of that authority which hitherto had centred in the State, and independence was bestowed on it; but surely only because it was able to do something which ancient philosophy and statesmanship had not dreamed of. Unless the duties of the Church had been different, or if they had been but partially different, from the [202] duties of the State, it is obvious to ask, for what conceivable reason should two societies be set up to do the work of one? Is it likely that Almighty Wisdom would have set up a second without recalling the first? would have continued the commission to the first, yet sent forth a second upon the same field? Such a course would simply have been adapted to kindle perpetual strife, and, if we may judge by appearances, to defeat the very purposes for which the civil power was appointed, and therefore is, in the highest degree, improbable, prior to some very clear proof to the contrary. This surely approves itself to the common sense of mankind. Either no Church has been set up in the world, or it is not set up for nothing; it must have a mission and a message of its own. Everything is defined, or made specific by its object: if the duties of the Church, its functions, its teaching, its working, be not specially distinct from those of the State, why, it will be impossible to resist the conclusion, that it was meant to be amalgamated with the State, to join on to it, to be a part of it, to be subordinate to it. We do not form two guilds for the same trade. Either assign to the Church its own craft, or do not ask that it should be chartered. Its object is its claim.

This consideration is a sufficient exposure of the theory of Alliance between Church and State, of which I was led to speak yesterday. Warburton maintains that each power, the [203] Church and the State, does substantially just one and the same thing; the Church preaches truth, the State pursues expediency; but Christian truth is identical with political expediency. There is no possible thesis which a preacher can put forth, or a synod could define as true, but is infallibly determined to be such ("infallible" is his word) by the political expedience and experience of the State. But if this be really so, what is the use of this second Society, which you put forth as naturally independent of the State, and as so high and mighty an ally of it? I do not say that to preach is not a function different from speaking in Parliament, or reading prayers to a congregation from sitting in a police court; the functions are different, and the functionaries will be different. But in like manner the function of a police magistrate is different from the function of a speaker in Parliament; but you do not have a distinct society, divine in its origin, independent in its constitution, to exercise jurisdiction over members of Parliament or of the Police. I repeat, unless the Church has something to say and something to do, very different from what the State says and does, Erastianism is the doctrine of common sense, and must be very clearly negatived in Scripture if it is to be discarded.

2.

I will refer to another author in illustration. There was an [204] anonymous work published, apparently in the character of a Scotch Episcopalian, some years before the movement of

1833; which, on supposed principles of Scripture, advocated a Branch or National Church, though the author would, I suppose, have preferred the words, "free," "independent," or "unestablished." Judging from the internal evidence, the world identified him with a vigorous and original thinker, whom none could approach without being set thinking also, whether with him or contrary to him, and who has since risen to the very highest rank of the Anglican hierarchy.[7] He wrote, partly in answer to Warburton, and partly to exhibit a counter-view of his own; but, if he will pardon me in saying it, he is an instance of the same unreality and inconsistency which I have just been imputing to Warburton himself.

"The supreme head on earth," he says, "of each branch of Christ's Church should evidently be some *spiritual* officer or body. Whether the governor of the English Church were the primate, or the convocation, or both conjointly, or any other man or body of men, holding *ecclesiastical* authority, not attached to any civil office, nor in the gift of any civil governor, in either case the non-secular character of Christ's kingdom would be preserved. The king, in conjunction with the other branches of the legislature, ought to have a distinctly defined *temporal* authority over every one of his subjects, of whatever persuasion; and, of consequence, over the ministers and all [205] other members, both of the Church of England and of every other religious community, Christian, Jewish, or Pagan,

---

[7] Dr. Whately. [N] Richard Whately (1787–1863), Anglican Archbishop of Dublin from 1831. According to the *ODCC*: "At Oxford [Oriel College] he was one of the best-known of the 'Noetics', an anti-Erastian, and an anti-Evangelical. His writing influenced J. H. Newman, who at one time assisted him [by contributing to what became his classic textbook on logic, *The Elements of Logic* (1827)]. Later Whately opposed the Tractarians. In Dublin he was active in the political life of Ireland and did valuable work as a Commissioner of National Education." Readers of the 7th lecture of *Anglican Difficulties* can see for themselves the quality of Whately's anti-Erastianism. For Newman's generous portrait of Whately, see *Apo*, 20-1. If lecture VII is largely given over to an attack on his former Oriel colleague's feeble anti-Erastianism, it also exhibits the logic that Newman learned from the logician in Whately.

within his dominions; but neither he, nor any other civil power, should interfere with articles of faith, liturgy, Church discipline, or any other spiritual matters. The kingdom of Heaven has no king but Christ; and He delegated His authority to Apostles, and through them to Bishops and Presbyters; not to any secular magistrates. These, therefore, ought not, by virtue of their civil offices, to claim the appointment to any office in the Church."[8] You see, my brethren, what clear views this anonymous writer has of the jurisdiction of the Church; they are identical with your own, or rather they go beyond you.

In consequence he speaks of its "degrading" the sacred character of Articles and Liturgy, "that they should stand upon the foundation of Acts of Parliament; that the spiritual rulers cannot alter them when they may need it; and that the secular power can, whether they need it or not. "And accordingly," he continues, "it is almost a proverbial reproach, that yours is a 'parliamentary religion;' that you worship the Almighty as the Act directs; and that you are bound to seek for salvation 'according to the law in that [206] case made and provided' by kings, lords, and commons; under the directions of the ministers of State; of persons," he adds, with a prophetic eye towards 1850, "who may be eminently well fitted for their *civil* offices, and who may indeed *chance* to be not only exemplary Christians, but sound divines, but who certainly are not appointed to their respective offices with any sort of view to their spiritual functions, who cannot even pretend that any sort of qualification for the good regulation of the Church is implied by their holding such stations as they do. Can this possibly be agreeable to the designs and institutions of Christ and His Apostles? If any one will seriously answer in the affirmative, he is beyond my powers of argumentation."[9]

Presently he observes, "The English Government seems to have a delight and a pride, in not only making the clergy

---

[8] Letters on the Church, p. 181. Dr. Whately never, I believe, owned to the authorship of this work. [N]

[9] p. 119. [N]

do as much as possible in return for the protection they enjoy, but in enforcing their services in the most harsh and mortifying way. Like the ancient Persian soldiers, they are brought into the field under the lash of perpetual penalties, which serve to keep your ministers in a state of degradation as well as of dependence on the State, which I defy you to parallel in any other Christian Church that ever existed."[10] He then compares certain of the clergy to the dog in the fable, who mistook the clog round his neck for a badge of honourable distinction. He continues, "Altogether, indeed, I cannot but say, if I must speak out, there is another fable [207] respecting a dog, of which the condition of your Church strongly reminds me. Your American brethren,[11] for instance, and some others, might say to you, as the lean and hungry wolf did to the well-fed mastiff, 'you are fat and sleek, indeed, while I am gaunt and half-famished, but what means that mark round your neck?' You must do this, under a penalty; and you must not do that under a penalty; you must comply with the rubric, and yet, at the same time, you must not comply with the rubric ... In short, you are fettered and crippled and disabled in every joint, by your alliance with a body of a different character, which could not, even with the best intentions, fail to weaken instead of aiding you; but which, in fact, aims chiefly at making a tool of you. But some of you seem so habituated to this dependence of the Church on the State, and so fond of it, as to have even solicited interference in a case which could not concern the civil community, and which the secular magistrate was likely to care about as little as Gallio.[12] An English bishop

---

[10] p. 125. [N]

[11] *Your American brethren*: See Newman's essay, "The Anglo-American Church," *Ess*, i, 310-378.

[12] *Gallio*: Lucius Junius Gallio. Brother of Seneca the philosopher; mentioned in Acts 18: 12–17 as proconsul of Achaia and judge in the case brought by the Jews against Paul. He dismissed the disputants, which became proof of what has become his proverbial indifference. An inscription discovered at Delphi mentions Gallio and provides a date for his time in Corinth and so also for Paul's foundation of the Church there,

did not dare to ordain an American to officiate in a country not under British dominion, without asking and obtaining permission of his government, which had just as much to do with the business as the government of Abyssinia."[13]

[208] Now all this is very ably put, and very true; but the question comes upon the reader, What is the meaning and object of the sweeping ecclesiastical changes which are advocated by this author? We must not take to pieces the constitution and rewrite the law for nothing. What would be gained by his recommendations practically? And what are they intended to accomplish or secure? Is it a gymnastical display or "agonism,"[14] as the heathen author calls it, from the Academy or the Garden, or a clever piece of irony which he presents to our perusal, or is it the grave and earnest sermon of one who would practise what he preaches, and would not partake of what he condemns? Now I will do the writer the justice to confess, that he does not agree with Warburton in considering that truth is measured by political expediency. He is too honest, too generous, too high-minded, too sensible, for so miserable a paradox; but, considering the far higher views he takes of the position of the Church, how he frets under her humiliation, how nobly zealous he is for her liberty, certainly he will be guilty of a different, indeed, but a not less startling paradox himself, if he has such exalted notions of the Church, and yet gives her nothing to do. Warburton recognises the Church in order to destroy it; he thinks it never has existed, or rather never ought to have existed in its proper nature, but, from its first moment of creation, ought to have been dissolved into the constitution of the State. But our author makes much ado about ecclesiastical rights and privileges, which he considers divinely bestowed, [209] and, therefore, indefeasible. He thinks the Church so pure and celestial, as to be insulted, defiled, by any communion

---

51–2 AD. Before the Romans took it into their heads to persecute the Christians, they, like Gallio, were largely indifferent to them.

[13] p. 129. [N]

[14] *agonism*: The victor's prize in a contest. *OED*

with things simply secular. "My kingdom is not of this world,"[15] said our Lord, and, therefore, it seems, no ecclesiastical person must, as such, have a seat in Parliament, and, on the other hand, neither King nor Parliament, as such, must be able to appoint a fast day. "It was," he says, "Satan who first proposed an alliance between the Christian Church and the State, by offering temporal advantages in exchange for giving up some of the 'things that be God's,' and which we ought to 'render unto God,'—for not 'serving Him only,' whom only we ought to serve. The next, I am inclined to think, who proposed to himself this scheme, and endeavoured to bring it about, was Judas Iscariot."[16]

Well, then, if the Church be a kingdom, or government, not of this world, I do trust you have provided for her a message, a function, not of this world,—something distinct, something special, something which the world cannot do, which "eye hath not seen, nor ear heard, nor heart of man conceived." It is not enough to give her morality to preach about; why a heaven-appointed Society for that? With the Bible in his hands, if that be all, I do not see why one man, if properly educated, should not preach morality as well as another, without any disturbance of the rights of the magistrate or the order of civil society. It is sometimes said [210] in bitterness that the Church's work is priestcraft;[17] I have already accepted the word; it *is* a craft, a craft in the same sense that goldsmiths' work, or architecture, or legal science is a craft; it must have its teaching, its intellectual and moral

---

[15] *"My kingdom is not of this world,"*: John 18:36.

[16] p. 97. [N]

[17] *priestcraft*: Samuel Johnson defines this as: "Religious frauds; management of wicked priests to gain power." The *OED* defines it as: "The maintenance or extension of priestly power and influence; the practices and policy supporting this; priestly scheming, guile, or deceit." One of its illustrations points to the basis for the charge. "1692 C. Gildon *Post-boy rob'd of his Mail* I. lxix. 204 Prithee, if thou wouldst leave Bigottry, leave it for good, and all, and rail not at it in this, or that, and caress it in another thing. It was no Crime, when natural Religion rul'd the World, till State-Politics, and Priest-Craft made it so."

habits, its long experience, its precedents, its traditions; nay, it must have all these in a much higher sense than crafts of this world, if it is to claim to come from above.[18] The more certainly the Church is a kingdom of heaven, and, as the author is so fond of saying, "not of this world," the more certain is it that she must have simply a heavenly work also, which the world cannot do for itself.

3.

Now, I fear, I must say, I see no symptoms at all of the writer in question intending to make his pattern-Church answer to this most reasonable expectation. There is nothing in his book to show that he entrusts his Church with any special doctrine or work of any kind. Whatever he may say, there is nothing to show why a lawyer, or a physician, or a scientific professor, or a country gentleman, or any one who has his evenings to himself, and is of an active turn, should not do everything which he ascribes to his heaven-born society. If, for instance, religion has its mysteries, if it has its fertile dogmas and their varied ramifications, if it has its [211] theology, if it has its long line of momentous controversies, its careful ventilation of questions, and its satisfactory and definite solutions; if, moreover, it has its special work, its substantial presence in the midst of us, its daily gifts from heaven, and its necessary ministries thence arising, then we shall see the meaning, we shall adore the wisdom, of the Divine Governor of all, in having done a new thing upon the earth when Christ came, in having withdrawn a jurisdiction He had once given to the State, and having bestowed it on a

---

[18] *to come from above*: For a brilliant essay showing how keenly Evelyn Waugh understood this matter of the unworldly, practical craft of the priest, see I. Ker, "Evelyn Waugh: The Priest as Craftsman," *The Catholic Revival in English Literature 1845-1961* (Notre Dame, 2003), 149-202, probably the single best critical essay ever written about the Catholic writer in Waugh, in one passage of which, apropos *A Handful of Dust* (1934), Ker observes: "As usual in Waugh, the Anglican clergyman is portrayed as totally ineffectual: he doesn't have a proper job to do, like a Catholic priest, and what he does attempt to say accomplishes nothing." 173.

special ordinance created for a special purpose. But in proportion as this author fails in this just anticipation, and disappoints the common sense of mankind, if he has nothing better to tell us than that one man's opinion is as good as another's; that Fathers and Schoolmen, and the greater number of Anglican divines, are puzzled-headed or dishonest; that heretics have at least this good about them, that they are in earnest, and do not take doctrines for granted; that religion is simple, and theologians have made it hard; that controversy is on the whole a logomachy; that we must worship in spirit and in truth; that we ought to love truth; that few people love truth for its own sake; that we ought to be candid and dispassionate, to avoid extremes, to eschew party spirit, to take a rational satisfaction in contemplating the works of nature, and not to speculate about "secret things;" that our Lord came to teach us all this, and to gain us immortality by His death, and the [212] promise of spiritual assistance, and that this is pretty nearly the whole of theology; and that at least all is in the Bible, where every one may read it for himself—(and I see no evidence whatever of his going much beyond this round of teaching)—then, I say, if the work and mission of Christianity be so level in its exercise to the capacities of the State, surely its ministry also is within the State's jurisdiction. I cannot believe that Bishops, and clergymen, and councils, and convocations have been divinely sent into the world, simply or mainly to broach opinions, to discuss theories, to talk literature, to display the results of their own speculations on the text of Scripture, to create a brilliant, ephemeral, ever-varying theology, to say in one generation what the next will unsay; else, why were not our debating clubs and our scientific societies ennobled with a divine charter also? God surely did not create the visible Church for the protection of private judgment: private judgment is quite able to take care of itself. This is no day for what are popularly called "shams." Many as are its errors, it is aiming at the destruction of shadows and the attainment of what is either sensibly or intellectually tangible. Why, then, should we have so much bustle and turmoil about "supremacy," and "protection," and "alliance," and "authority;" and "indefeasible rights," and [213] "encroachments," and "usurpations,"[19] after the manner of this writer, if all the effort and elaboration is to be in its result but a mountain in labour bringing forth nothing?[20]

The State claims the allegiance of its subjects on the ground of the tangible benefits of which it is the instrument towards them. Its strength lies in this undeniable fact, and its subjects endure and maintain its coercion and its laws, because the certainty of this fact is ever present to their minds. What mean the array and the pomp which surround the Sovereign,—the strict ceremonial, the minute etiquette, the almost unsleeping watchfulness which eyes her every motion, which follows her into her garden and her chamber, which notes down every shade of her countenance and every variation of her pulse? Why do her soldiers hover about her, and officials line her anterooms, and cannon and illumination carry forward the tiding of her progresses among her people? Is this all a mockery? Is it done for nothing? Surely not; in her is centred the order, the security, the happiness of a great people. And, in like manner, the Church must be the guardian of a fact; she must have something to produce; she must have something to do. It is not enough to be keeper of even an inspired book: for there is nothing to show that her protection of it is necessary at this day. The State might fairly commit its custody to the art of printing, and dissolve an institution whose occupation [214] was no more. She must, in order to have a meaning, do that which otherwise cannot be done, which she alone can do.

---

[19] *"supremacy ... usurpations"*: These were the approved buzzwords in the Anglo-Catholics' unreal literature of anti-Erastianism, to which Whatley contributed so revealingly.

[20] *a mountain in labour bringing forth nothing*: Having demolished poor Whatley here – however deservedly – Newman felt compunctious once the archbishop went to his reward and, with the magnanimity that he often showed his controversial opponents, eulogized him as "a man who, whatever were his faults, was in generosity, in boldness of speech, and in independence of mind a prince." *AW*, 84.

She must have a benefit to bestow, in order to be worth her existence; and the benefit must be a fact which no one can doubt about. It must not be an opinion, or matter of opinion, but a something which is like a first principle, which may be taken for granted, a foundation indubitable and irresistible. In other words, she must have a dogma[21] and Sacraments;[22]—it is a dogma and Sacraments, and nothing else, which can give meaning to a Church, or sustain her against the State; for by these are meant certain facts or acts which are special instruments of spiritual good to those who receive them. As we do not gain the benefits of civil society unless we submit to its laws and customs, so we do not gain the spiritual blessings which the Church has to bestow upon us, unless we receive her dogmas and her Sacraments.

---

[21] *dogma*: The *Catechism of the Catholic Church* defines the word thus: "The Church's Magisterium exercises the authority it holds from Christ to the fullest extent when it defines dogmas, that is, when it proposes truths contained in divine Revelation or also when it proposes in a definitive way truths having a necessary connection with them. There is an organic connection between our spiritual life and the dogmas. Dogmas are lights along the path of faith; they illuminate it and make it secure. Conversely, if our life is upright, our intellect and heart will be open to welcome the light shed by the dogmas of faith. The mutual connections between dogmas, and their coherence, can be found in the whole of the Revelation of the mystery of Christ. 'In Catholic doctrine there exists an order or hierarchy of truths, since they vary in their relation to the foundation of the Christian faith.'" (89-90)

[22] *Sacraments*: *The Catechism of the Catholic Church* defines the word thus: "'Adhering to the teaching of the Holy Scriptures, to the apostolic traditions, and to the consensus ... of the Fathers,' we profess that 'the sacraments of the new law were ... all instituted by Jesus Christ our Lord.' Jesus' words and actions during his hidden life and public ministry were already salvific, for they anticipated the power of his Paschal mystery. They announced and prepared what he was going to give the Church when all was accomplished. the mysteries of Christ's life are the foundations of what he would henceforth dispense in the sacraments, through the ministers of his Church, for 'what was visible in our Savior has passed over into his mysteries.' Sacraments are 'powers that comes forth' from the Body of Christ, which is ever-living and life-giving. They are actions of the Holy Spirit at work in his Body, the Church. They are 'the masterworks of God' in the new and everlasting covenant." (1116)

This, you know, is understood by every fanatic who would collect followers and form a sect. Who would ever dream of collecting a congregation, and having nothing to say to them? No! they think they have that to offer to the world which cannot otherwise be obtained. They do not bring forward mere opinions; they do not preach a disputable doctrine; but they assert, boldly and simply, that he who believes them will be saved. They announce, for instance, that every one must undergo the new birth, and for [215] this they organise their society; viz., in order to preach and to testify, to realise and to perpetuate in the world this great and necessary fact,—the new birth of the soul.[23] Or, again, they have a commission to do miracles, or they can prophesy, or they are sent to declare the end of the world. Something or other they do, which the existing establishments of Church and State do not, and cannot do.

---

[23] *new birth of the soul*: "The Holy Ghost, I have said, dwells in body and soul, as in a temple. Evil spirits indeed have power to possess sinners, but His indwelling is far more perfect; for He is all-knowing and omnipresent, He is able to search into all our thoughts, and penetrate into every motive of the heart. Therefore, He pervades us (if it may be so said) as light pervades a building, or as a sweet perfume the folds of some honourable robe; so that, in Scripture language, we are said to be in Him, and He in us. It is plain that such an inhabitation brings the Christian into a state altogether new and marvellous, far above the possession of mere gifts, exalts him inconceivably in the scale of beings, and gives him a place and an office which he had not before. In St. Peter's forcible language, he becomes 'partaker of the Divine Nature,' and has 'power' or authority, as St. John says, 'to become the son of God.' Or, to use the words of St. Paul, 'he is a new creation; old things are passed away, behold all things are become new.' His rank is new; his parentage and service new. He is 'of God,' and 'is not his own,' 'a vessel unto honour, sanctified and meet for the Master's use, and prepared unto every good work.' This wonderful change from darkness to light, through the entrance of the Spirit into the soul, is called Regeneration, or the New Birth; a blessing which, before Christ's coming, not even Prophets and righteous men possessed, but which is now conveyed to all men freely through the Sacrament of Baptism." J. H. Newman, "The Indwelling Spirit" (1834), *PP* ii, 19, 222-23.

4.

This being the state of the case, consider how entirely the reasonable anticipation of our minds is fulfilled in the professions of the Catholic Church. A Protestant wanders into one of our chapels; he sees a priest kneeling and bowing and throwing up a thurible, and boys in cottas going in and out, and a whole choir and people singing amain all the time, and he has nothing to suggest to him what it is all about; and he calls it mummery, and he walks out again. And would it not indeed be so, my brethren, if this were all? But will he think it mummery when he learns and seriously apprehends the fact, that, according to the belief of a Catholic, the Word Incarnate, the Second Person of the Eternal Trinity, is there bodily present,—hidden, indeed, from our senses, but in no other way withheld from us? He may reject what we believe; he will not wonder at what we do. And so, again, open the Missal, read the minute directions given for the celebration of Mass,—what are the fit dispositions under which the Priest prepares for it, how [216] he is to arrange his every action, movement, gesture, utterance, during the course of it, and what is to be done in case of a variety of supposable accidents. What a mockery would all this be, if the rite meant nothing! But if it be a fact that God the Son is there offered up in human flesh and blood by the hands of man, why, it is plain that no rite whatever, however anxious and elaborate, is equal to the depth of the overwhelming thoughts which are borne in upon the mind by such an action.[24] Thus the usages and

---

[24] *by such an action*: "'I declare, to me,' he said, and he clasped his hands on his knees, and looked forward as if soliloquising,—'to me nothing is so consoling, so piercing, so thrilling, so overcoming, as the Mass, said as it is among us. I could attend Masses for ever and not be tired. It is not a mere form of words, —it is a great action, the greatest action that can be on earth. It is, not the invocation merely, but, if I dare use the word, the evocation of the Eternal. He becomes present on the altar in flesh and blood, before whom angels bow and devils tremble. This is that awful event which is the scope, and is the interpretation, of every part of the solemnity. Words are necessary, but as means, not as ends; they are not

ordinances of the Church do not exist for their own sake; they do not stand of themselves; they are not sufficient for themselves; they do not fight against the State their own battle; they are not appointed as ultimate ends; but they are dependent on an inward substance; they protect a mystery; they defend a dogma; they represent an idea; they preach good tidings; they are the channels of grace. They are the outward shape of an inward reality or fact, which no Catholic doubts, which is assumed as a first principle, which is not an inference of reason, but the object of a spiritual sense.

Herein is the strength of the Church; herein she differs from all Protestant mockeries of her. She professes to be built upon facts, not opinions; on objective truths, not on variable sentiments; on immemorial testimony, not on private judgment; on convictions or perceptions, not on [217] conclusions. None else but she can make this profession. She makes high claims against the temporal power, but she has that within her which justifies her. She merely acts out what she says she is. She does no more than she reasonably should do. If God has given her a specific work, no wonder she is not under the superintendence of the civil magistrate in doing it. If her Clergy be Priests, if they can forgive sins, and bring the Son of God upon her altars, it is obvious they cannot, considered as such, hold of the State. If they were not Priests, the sooner they were put under a minister of public instruction, and the Episcopate abolished, the better. But she has not disturbed the world for nothing. Her precision and peremptoriness, all that is laid to her charge as intolerance and exclusiveness, her claim entirely to understand and to be able to deal with her own deposit and her own functions; her claim to reveal the unknown and to communicate the invisible, is, in the eye of reason (so far from being an objection to her coming from above), the very tenure of her high mission,—just what would be sure

---

mere addresses to the throne of grace, they are instruments of what is far higher, of consecration, of sacrifice …'" *LG*, 327-8.

to characterise her if she had received such a mission. She cannot be conceived without her message and her gifts. She is the organ and oracle, and nothing else, of a supernatural doctrine, which is independent of individuals, given to her once for all, coming down from the first ages, and so deeply and intimately embosomed in her, that it cannot be clean torn out of her, even if you should try; which gradually and majestically comes forth into dogmatic shape, as time goes [218] on and need requires, still by no private judgment, but at the will of its Giver, and by the infallible elaboration of the whole body;—and which is simply necessary for the salvation of every one of us. It is not a philosophy, or literature, cognisable and attainable at once by those who cast their eyes that way; but it is a sacred deposit and tradition, a mystery or secret, as Scripture calls it, sufficient to arrest and occupy the whole intellect, and unlike anything else; and hence requiring, from the nature of the case, organs special to itself, made for the purpose, whether for entering into its fulness, or carrying it out in deed.

5.

And now, my brethren, you may have been some time asking yourselves how all this bears upon the particular subject on which these Lectures are engaged; and yet I think it bears upon it very closely and significantly. For, perhaps, you may have said, in answer to my Lecture of yesterday, "We do not aim at forming a Branch Church; we put before us a really humble work. We have no ambition, no expectation of spreading through the nation, or of spreading at all. We do but mean to preserve for future times what we hold to be the truth. As books are consigned to some large library, with a simple view to their security, not let out to the world, and apparently useless, but yet with a definite [219] object and benefit,—'though for no other cause, yet for this,' as Hooker says, 'that posterity may know we have not loosely through silence permitted things to pass away as in a dream,'[25]—so, we care not to be successful in our day; we are willing to be despised; we do but aim at transmitting Catholic doctrine in its purest and most primitive form to posterity. We are willing to look like a small sect at the gate of the National Church, when really we are the heirs of the Apostles. We do not boast of this; we do not wish to inflict it upon the world; leave us to ourselves quietly and unostentatiously to transmit our burden to posterity in our own way."

I say, in reply, my brethren, that so far you are right, that you at least profess to have something to transmit; but be you sure withal that you have it, and know what it is. It will not do to have only a vague idea of it, if it is to form the basis of a communion; you must be at home with it, and must have surveyed it in its various aspects, and must be clear about it, and be prepared to state decisively to all inquirers its ground, its details, and its consequences, and must be able to say, unequivocally, that it comes from heaven;—or it will not serve your purpose. I am not sanguine that you will be able to do this even as regards the Sacrament of Baptism; differences have already risen among you as to the relative importance, at least under circumstances, of separate portions of the doctrine; and [220] when you come to define the consequences of sin after it, and the remedies of that sin, your variations and uncertainties will be greater still. And much more of other doctrines; there is hardly one of which you will be able to take a clear and complete view. I say, then, Do not set up a sect, till you are quite sure what is to be its creed.

6.

In the commencement of the movement of 1833, much interest was felt in the Non-jurors.[26] It was natural that

---

[25] *dream*: This is the first sentence of Hooker's Preface to his *Of the Laws of Ecclesiastical Polity* (1594).

[26] *non-jurors*: Judith Champ, Bishop Ullathorne's biographer, defines the word thus: "Non-jurors were the high churchmen of the late 17th-cent. Church of England, who refused the oath of allegiance to William and

inquirers who had drawn their principles from the primitive Church, should be attracted by the exhibition of any portion of those principles anywhere in, or about, an Establishment which was so emphatically opposed to them. Therefore, in their need, they fixed their eyes on a body of men who were not only sufferers for conscience' sake, but held, in connection with their political principles, a certain portion of Catholic truth. But, after all, what *is*, in a word, the history of the Non-jurors, for it does not take long to tell it? A party composed of seven Bishops and some hundred Clergy, virtuous and learned, and, as regards their leaders, even popular, for political services lately rendered to the nation, is hardly formed but it begins to dissolve and come to nought, and that, simply because it had no sufficient object, represented no idea, and proclaimed no dogma. What should keep it together? why should it exist? To form an association is to go out of the way, and ever requires an [221] excuse or an account of so pretentious a proceeding. Such were the ancient apologies put forward for the Church in her first age; such the Apologies of the Anglican Jewell, and the Quaker Barclay.[27] What was the apology of the Non-jurors? Now their secession, properly speaking, was based on no theological truth at all; it arose simply because, as their name signifies, certain Bishops and Clergy could not take the oaths to a new King. There is something very venerable

---

Mary after their accession in 1688. They held to the doctrine of the divine right of kings and believed, therefore, that the Stuarts remained the legitimate monarchs. Eight bishops (including Sancroft of Canterbury), 400 priests, and a few laymen refused the oath. They were dispossessed and tried to keep an alternative church in existence with illegal services in their churches, but were divided among themselves over the correctness of this. Their links with the Stuarts and the fears of restoration made them unpopular in early Hanoverian England. They were linked in belief and religious principles to the Caroline divines of the 17th cent. and the Oxford Movement of the 19th century." *The Oxford Companion to British History*.

[27] *the Quaker Barclay*: Robert Barclay (1648–90), Scottish Quaker whose *Apology for the True Christian Divinity* (1678) is a reasoned defence of Quakerism. His collected works, *Truth Triumphant*, with a preface by William Penn, were published in 1692.

and winning in Bishop Ken;[28] but this arises in part from the very fact that he was so little disposed to defend any position, or oppose things as they were. He could not take the oaths, and was dispossessed; but he had nothing special to say for himself; he had no message to deliver; his difficulty was of a personal nature, and he was unwilling that the Non-juring Succession should be continued. It was against his judgment to perpetuate his own communion. But look at the body in its more theological aspect, and its negative and external character is brought out even more strikingly. Its members had much more to say against the Catholic Church, like Protestants in general, than for themselves. They are considered especially high in their Doctrine of the Holy Eucharist; yet, I do not know anything in Dr. Brett's whole Treatise on the Ancient liturgies, which fixes itself so vividly on the reader's mind, as his assertion, that the rubrics of the Roman Missal are "corrupt, [222] dangerous, superstitious, abominably idolatrous, theatrical, and utterly unworthy the gravity of so sacred an institution."[29]

---

[28] *Bishop Ken*: Thomas Ken (1637–1711), Nonjuror. In 1683, he refused the use of his house to Nell Gwyn, the royal mistress, and Charles II, far from showing him any spite, rewarded his audacity by making him Bishop of Bath and Wells. (Allegedly Charles declared 'Odd's fish! Who shall have Bath and Wells but the little fellow who would not give poor Nelly a lodging?'). Ken was one of the Seven Bishops who refused to read James II's *Declaration of Indulgence* in 1688, but he declined to take the oath to William and Mary and was deposed from his see. Chastened, he opposed the consecration of further Nonjuring bishops. His writings include the hymns 'Awake my soul, and with the sun' and 'Glory to Thee, my God, this night.' In his will, before his death, he declared: "I die in the holy catholic and apostolic faith, professed by the whole church before the disunion of east and west; more particularly I die in the communion of the Church of England, as it stands distinguished from all papal and puritan innovations, and as it adheres to the doctrine of the cross." The *ODNB* sums up his dedication to the *via media* thus: "A moderate in all his dealings, his opposition to the new oaths was tempered by his paramount desire for the peace, unity, and welfare of the church."

[29] *so sacred an institution*: See Dr. Thomas Brett, *A Collection of the Principal Liturgies: used in the Christian church in the celebration of the*

The Non-jurors were far less certain what they did hold, than what they did not. They were great champions of the Sacrifice, and wished to restore the ancient Liturgies; yet, they could not raise their minds to anything higher than the sacrifice of the material bread and wine, as representatives of One, who was not literally present but absent; as symbols of His Body and Blood, not in truth and fact, but in virtue and effect. Yet, while they had such insufficient notions of the heavenly gift committed to the ordinance, they could, as I have said, be very jealous of its outward formalities, and laid the greatest stress on a point, important certainly in its place, but not when separated from that which gave it meaning and life, the mixing of the water with the wine; and

---

Holy Eucharist (London, 1838), 395-6. Such comical fulminations notwithstanding, the Nonjuror Dr. Thomas Brett (1667–1743) was highly regarded in Georgian England, and even after his death. For the irreproachably Anglican historian, J.H. Overton, "There was no lack then [in the eighteenth century] of great divines; in fact, it may be doubted whether there ever was a time when the general truths of Christianity were more powerfully defended; but liturgical knowledge was not one of their strong points; indeed it was hardly regarded as a matter of study at all. Good Churchmen were content to praise 'our incomparable Liturgy' as they praised 'our happy Establishment in Church and State,' as if the last word had been said; lax Churchmen who were dissatisfied with the Prayer Book as it stood could only suggest modern innovations of their own. But Brett had really studied antiquity, especially the ancient liturgies; and his writings [his *Collection of the Principal Liturgies* was first published in 1720] are authorities on the subject, even to the present day. He was, in my opinion, far and away the best authority in his own day ..." J. H. Overton, *The Nonjurors: Their Lives, Principles and Writings* (London, 1902), 142. See also the *ODNB*: Apropos Brett's *Some Remarks on Dr. Waterland's Review of the Doctrine of the Eucharist* (1736), Robert D. Cornwall observes that: "the work challenged Daniel Waterland's refusal to use the language of material sacrifice in the eucharist, though Waterland recognized that the liturgy had sacrificial implications." This neatly corroborates what Newman styled the tradition of 'semi-Arianism' in Anglo-Catholicism. See Lecture XII. For a good, witty, discriminating sense of how nineteenth-century English Protestants commonly regarded the Roman Catholic Mass as little more than a piece of bad Italianate theatre, see J. Pemble, "Abominations of the Earth," *The Mediterranean Passion: Victorians and Edwardians in the South* (Oxford, 1987), 210-27.

upon this, and other questions, of higher moment indeed, but not of a character specifically different, they soon divided into two communions. They broke into pieces, not from external causes, not from the hostility or the allurements of a court, but simply because they had no common heart and life in them. They were safe from the civil sword, from their insignificancy; they had no need of falling back on a distant centre for support; all they needed was an idea, an object, a work to make them one.

But I have another remark to make on the Non-jurors.
[223] You recollect, my brethren, that they are the continuation and heirs of the traditions, so to call them, of the High-Church divines of the seventeenth century. Now, how high and imposing do the names sound of Andrewes, Laud, Taylor, Jackson, Pearson, Cosin,[30] and their fellows? I am not speaking against them as individuals, but viewing them as theological authorities. How great and mysterious are the doctrines which they teach and how proudly they appeal to

---

[30] *Cosin*: John Cosin (1594–1672), Bishop of Durham. "He was a member of a wealthy family of Norwich and educated at Caius College, Cambridge. After holding several other benefices, he was collated to a canonry at Durham in 1625 and became rector of Brancepeth in Co. Durham in 1626. He was a personal friend of W. Laud and R. Montague, and as such incurred the hostility of the Puritan party. This was increased when he published, in 1627, his famous *Collection of Private Devotions*, a book of prayers compiled at the instigation of Charles I for the use of Queen Henrietta Maria's English maids of honour. In 1635 he was elected master of Peterhouse, whose chapel he decorated according to High Church principles, and in 1640 he was appointed Dean of Peterborough. The Long Parliament deprived him of all his benefices and in 1644 he was ejected from the mastership of Peterhouse. In the same year he went to Paris, where he became chaplain to the C of E members of the Queen's household. He showed sympathy for the Huguenots, and engaged in bitter controversy with the RCs, disinheriting his son on his reception into the RC Church. After the Restoration he returned to England and was made Bishop of Durham in 1660. ... Most of his literary works are of a controversial nature, being directed esp. against RC doctrine. He attacked transubstantiation in his *Historia Transubstantiationis Papalis* (written 1656, pub. 1675), and the inclusion of the so-called Apocrypha in the RC Canon of the Scriptures in *A Scholastical History of the Canon of Holy Scripture* (1657)." *ODCC*.

primitive times, and claim the ancient Fathers! Surely, as some one says, "in Laud is our Cyprian, and in Taylor is our Chrysostom, and all we want is our Athanasius." Look on, my brethren, to the history of the Non-jurors, and you will see what these Anglican divines were worth. There you will see that it was simply their position, their temporal possessions, their civil dignities, as standing round a King's throne, or seated in his great council, and not their principles, which made them what they were.[31] Their genius, learning, faith, whatever it was, would have had no power to stand by themselves; these qualities had no substance, for, as we see, when the State abandoned them, they shrank at once and collapsed, and ceased to be. These qualities were not the stuff out of which a Church is made, though they looked well and bravely when fitted upon the Establishment. And, indeed, they did not, in the event, wear better in the Establishment than out of it; for since the Establishment at the Revolution had changed its make and altered its position, the old vestments would not fit it, and [224] fell out of fashion. The Nation and the National Church had got new ideas, and the language of the ancient Fathers could not express them. There were those, who, at the era in question, took the oaths; they could secure their positions; could they secure their creed? The event answers the question. There is some story of Bull and Beveridge, who were two of the number, meeting together, I think in the House of Lords, and mourning together over the degeneracy of the times.[32] The times certainly *were* degenerate; and if

---

[31] *which made them what they were*: Many of the biographical profiles of the Anglican divines to whom Newman refers included in the annotations of the present edition bear this out.

[32] *some story of Bull and Beveridge*: "The Bishop [George Bull, Bishop of St. David's] took his seat in the House of Lords in a most critical conjuncture, even in that memorable Session, when the Bill for uniting both Kingdoms passed into a law [the first of the Acts of Union of England and Scotland, 1706]; and when not a few were in the greatest apprehensions concerning our Church, and were for considering thence the best methods of securing it to posterity, together with the Union. Wherefore, upon a debate in the House, in relation to the said Bill, a

learning could have restored them, there was enough in those two heads to have done the work of Athanasius, Leo,[33]

---

certain noble Lord, of a very eminent character, moved in a speech, That since the Parliament of Scotland had given a character of their Church, by extolling the "purity of its worship," their Lordships should not be behind hand in giving a character of the "best-constituted Church in the world." 'For,' saith he, (turning himself towards the bench of Bishops,) 'My Lords, I have been always taught by my Lords, the Bishops, from my youth, that the Church of England is the best constituted Church in the world, and most agreeable to the Apostolical institution.' Upon which, Bishop Bull, who sate very near his Lordship, apprehending how upon such an appeal to the Bishops, it was necessary for them to say something, stood up and said: 'My Lords, I do second what that noble Lord hath moved, and do think it highly reasonable, that in this Bill a character should be given of our most excellent Church. For, my Lords, whosoever is skilled in primitive antiquity, must allow it for a certain and evident truth, that the Church of England is, in her Doctrine, Discipline, and Worship, most agreeable to the primitive and Apostolical institution.' The Bishop of St. David's coming out of the House, Bishop Beveridge and another Bishop thanked his Lordship for his excellent speech; and said Bishop Beveridge, 'My Lord, If you and I had the penning of the Bill, it should be in the manner your Lordship hath moved.' Upon which, Bishop Bull made such a reply, as represented the necessity he lay under of thus discharging his duty, when so solemnly called upon in the greatest court of the nation. And it is certainly at all times the indispensable obligation of all the Bishops and Pastors of the Church, to behave themselves with an holy boldness and undaunted resolution, in the affairs of God and religion, without being awed or biassed by the torrent of the times, or made sordidly to crouch to a prevailing power of worldly politicians, who are for carrying on their own sinister designs at any rate, though always under the most specious pretexts." R. Nelson, *The Life of George Bull, D.D.* (London, 1840), 238-9.

[33] *Leo:* That Bull or Beveridge had anything like the practical good sense or courage of St. Athanasius, St. Leo the Great or Pope Gregory VII is dubious. Here, Newman takes his accustomed generosity to opponents to an extreme. In any case, J.N.D. Kelly is good on St. Leo's extraordinary courage: "Declared a doctor of the church by Benedict XIV, Leo [b. late 4th century – d. 461] was a lucid codifier of accepted orthodoxy rather than an original or profound theologian. Although concerned for and accomplished in liturgy, he was not responsible for the so-called Leonine Sacramentary (6th/7th century). His surviving sermons (96) and letters (143) … are marked by clarity, terseness, and rhythmic prose; content and form are admirably united in them. But Leo was a man whose personality and courage impressed more than churchmen. In 452 near Mantua as one of the senatorial legates despatched by Rome he

and the seventh Gregory;[34] but learning never made a body live. The High Church party died out within the Establishment, as well as outside of it, for it had neither dogma to rest upon, nor object to pursue.

---

confronted Attila the Hun, then ravaging north Italy and pressing southwards, and after the meeting Attila withdrew; in 455 he personally, and acting on his own authority, met the Vandal Gaiseric outside the walls of Rome and, if he could not prevent him from seizing and looting the city over fourteen days, he at least induced him to spare it from fire, torture, and massacre. When he died he was buried in the porch of St Peter's, his remains being translated to the interior in 688." *Oxford Dictionary of Popes*

[34] *the seventh Gregory VII*: Pope Gregory VII (before 1029?–1085). Born into a Tuscan peasant family, Hildebrand, one of the greatest of the popes. In 1073, upon the death of Alexander II, Hildebrand was made pope. From the first, he showed his commitment to reform, decreeing against prelates found out in simony or concubinage and condemning a large number of bishops. He also forbade secular authorities from making gifts of bishoprics. On 24 Jan 1076, when an assembly of German bishops declared the pope unfit for his papal office, Gregory deposed and excommunicated their instigator, the emperor Henry IV. Fearing an *entente* between Gregory and the princes, Henry resolved to reconcile with Gregory and accordingly stood in the snow outside Canossa, the Countess Matilda's castle in the garb of a penitent. After vowing to accept Gregory's arbitration, the emperor was restored to the Church, though his hostility to Gregory remained. Indeed, he subsequently sacked Rome, which forced the pope to flee. An eventual prisoner in the Castel Sant'Angelo, the pope was freed by the Norman adventurer Robert Guiscard, whom he had previously excommunicated. Gregory then left the city and took refuge first on Monte Cassino and later at Salerno, where he died on 25 May 1085, uttering the famous apothegm: "I have loved justice and hated iniquity, therefore I die in exile." See also D. Knowles and D. Obololensky, *The Christian Centuries: Vol. 2: The Middle Ages* (New York, 1968) 177-78, and E. Duffy, *Saints & Sinners: A History of the Popes* rev. ed. (New Haven, 2006), 130-8. Duffy is worth quoting: "No one in eleventh-century Europe thought of Church and State as separable entities. There was only one Christendom, and the conflicts between pope and emperor arose from conflicting claims to spiritual headship within that single entity. Gregory's achievement was to stake out, in the starkest terms and with a new clarity, the spiritual claims of the Church." Ibid., 136-7. See also R. Southern, *The Making of the Middle Ages* (London: Hutchinson, 1953), 139-41. Gregory, like Newman, despite every failure, restored the glory of the Apostles.

All this is your warning, my brethren; you too, when it comes to the point, will have nothing to profess, to teach, to transmit. At present you do not know your own weakness. You have the life of the Establishment in you, and you fancy it is your own life; you fancy that the accidental *congeries*[35] of opinions, which forms your creed, has that unity, individuality, and consistency, which allows of its developing into a system, and perpetuating a school. Look into the matter more steadily; it is very pleasant to decorate your chapels, oratories, and studies now, but you cannot be doing this for ever. It is pleasant to adopt a habit or a [225] vestment; to use your office book or your beads; but it is like feeding on flowers, unless you have that objective vision in your faith, and that satisfaction in your reason, of which devotional exercises and ecclesiastical regulations are the suitable expression. Such will not last, on the long run, as are not commanded and rewarded by divine authority; they cannot be made to rest on the influence of individuals. It is well to have rich architecture, curious works of art, and splendid vestments, when you have a present God; but oh! what a mockery, if you have not! If your externals surpass what is within, you are, so far, as hollow as your evangelical opponents who baptize, yet expect no grace; or, as the latitudinarian writer I have been reviewing, who would make Christ's kingdom not of this world, in order to do little more than the world's work. Thus your Church becomes, not a home, but a sepulchre; like those high cathedrals, once Catholic, which you do not know what to do with, which you shut up and make monuments of, sacred to the memory of what has passed away.

7.

Therefore, I say now,—as I have said years ago, when others have wished still to uphold their party, after their arguments had broken under them—Find out first of all where you stand, take your position, write down your creed,

---

[35] congeries: disorderly collections, jumbles (*OED*)

draw up your catechism. Tell me why you form your party, [226] under what conditions, how long it is to last, what are your relations to the Establishment, and to the other branches (as you speak) of the Universal Church, how you stand relatively to Antiquity, what is Antiquity, whether you accept the *Via Media*, whether you are zealous for "Apostolical order," what is your rule of faith, how you prove it, and what are your doctrines. It is easy for a while to be doing merely what you do at present; to remain where you are, till it is proved to you that you must go; to refuse to say what you hold and what you do not, and to act only on the offensive; but you cannot do this for ever. The time is coming, or is come, when you must act in some way or other for yourselves, unless you would drift to some form of infidelity, or give up principle altogether, or believe or not believe by accident. The *onus probandi* will be on your side then. Now you are content to be negative and fragmentary in doctrine; you aim at nothing higher than smart articles in newspapers and magazines, at clever hits, spirited attacks, raillery, satire, skirmishing on posts of your own selecting; fastening on weak points, or what you think so, in Dissenters or Catholics; inventing ingenious retorts, evading dangerous questions; parading this or that isolated doctrine as essential, and praising this or that Catholic practice or Catholic saint, to make up for abuse, and to show your impartiality; and taking all along a high, eclectic, patronising, indifferent tone; this has been for some time [227] past your line, and it will not suffice; it excites no respect, it creates no confidence, it inspires no hope.[36]

And when, at length, you have one and all agreed upon your creed, and developed it doctrinally, morally, and

---

[36] Here Newman nicely captures the donnish inconsequence of the Anglo-Catholics, about which John Ruskin was so clear-eyed when he said of their leader Edward Pusey, the Canon of Christ Church that "he was not in the least a picturesque or tremendous figure, but only a sickly and rather ill put together English clerical gentleman, who never looked one in the face, or appeared aware of the state of the weather." John Ruskin, *Praeterita* intro. K. Clark (Oxford, 1978), 190.

polemically, then find for it some safe foundation, deeper and firmer than private judgment, which may ensure its transmission and continuance to generations to come. And, when you have done all this, then, last of all, persuade others and yourselves, that the foundation you have formed is surer and more trustworthy than that of Erastianism, on the one hand, and of immemorial and uninterrupted tradition, that is, of Catholicism, on the other.

PART II

DIFFICULTIES IN ACCEPTING THE COMMUNION OF
ROME AS ONE, HOLY, CATHOLIC, AND APOSTOLIC

LECTURE VIII

THE SOCIAL STATE OF CATHOLIC COUNTRIES NO
PREJUDICE TO THE SANCTITY OF THE CHURCH

1.

I HAVE been engaged in many Lectures in showing that
your place, my brethren, if you own the principles of the
movement of 1833, is nowhere else but the Catholic
Church. To this you may answer, that, even though I had
been unanswerable, I should not have done much, for my
argument has, on the whole, been a negative one; that there
are difficulties on both sides of the controversy; that I have
been enlarging on the Protestant difficulty, but there are not
a few Catholic difficulties also; that, to be sure, you are not
very happy in the Establishment, but you have serious
misgivings whether you would be happier with us. [230]
Moreover, you might mention the following objection, in
particular, as prominent and very practical, which weighs
with you a great deal, and warns you off the ground whither
I am trying to lead you. You are much offended, you would
say, with the bad state of Catholics abroad, and their
uninteresting character everywhere, compared with
Protestants. Those countries, you say, which have retained
Catholicism are notoriously behind the age; they have not

263

kept up with the march of civilization; they are ignorant, and, in a measure, barbarous; they have the faults of barbarians; they have no self-command; they cannot be trusted.[1] They must be treated as slaves, or they rebel; they emerge out of their superstitions in order to turn infidels. They cannot combine and coalesce in social institutions; they want the very faculty of citizenship. The sword, not the law, is their ruler. They are spectacles of idleness, slovenliness, want of spirit, disorder, dirt, and dishonesty. There must, then, be something in their religion to account for this; it keeps them children, and then, being children, they keep to it. No man in his senses, certainly no English gentleman, would abandon the high station which his country both occupies and bestows on him in the eyes of man, to make himself the co-religionist of such slaves, and the creature of such a Creed.

[231]   I propose to make a suggestion in answer to this objection; and, in making it, I shall consider you, my brethren, not as unbelievers, who are careless whether this objection strikes at Christianity or no; nor as Protestants proper, who have no concern about so expressing themselves, as to compromise the first centuries of the Church; but as those who feel that the Catholic Church was in the beginning founded by our Lord and His Apostles; again, that the Establishment is not the Catholic Church; that nothing *but* the Church of Rome can be; that, if the Church of Rome is not, then the Catholic Church is not to be found in this age, or in this part of the world; for this is what I have been proving in my preceding Lectures. What, then, you are saying comes, in fact, to this: We would rather deny our initial principles, than accept such a development of them as the communion of Rome, viewed as it is; we would rather believe Erastianism, and all its train of

---

[1] *they cannot be trusted*: The impression that Thackeray came away with of Maynooth College is typical of what Newman is speaking of here: "Ruin so needless, filth so disgusting, such a look of lazy squalor, no Englishman who has not seen can conceive" W. M. Thackeray, *Irish Sketch Book* (London, 1843), 342.

consequences, to be from God, than the religion of such countries as France and Belgium, Spain and Italy. This is what you must mean to say, and nothing short of it.

2.

I simply deny the justice of your argument, my brethren; and, to show you that I am not framing a view for the occasion, and, moreover, in order to start with a principle, which, perhaps, you yourselves have before now admitted. I will quote words which I used myself twelve years ago:— [232] "If we were asked what was the object of Christian preaching, teaching, and instruction; what the office of the Church, considered as the dispenser of the Word of God, I suppose we should not all return the same answer. Perhaps we might say that the object of Revelation was to enlighten and enlarge the mind, to make us act by reason, and to expand and strengthen our powers: or to impart knowledge about religious truth, knowledge being power directly it is given, and enabling us forthwith to think, judge, and act for ourselves; or to make us good members of the community, loyal subjects, orderly and useful in our station, whatever it be; or to secure, what otherwise would be hopeless, our leading a religious life,—the reason why persons go wrong, throw themselves away, follow bad courses, and lose their character, being, that they have had no education, that they are ignorant. These and other answers might be given; some beside, and some short of, the mark. It may be useful, then, to consider with what end, with what expectation, we preach, teach, instruct, discuss, bear witness, praise, and blame; what fruit the Church is right in anticipating as the result of her ministerial labours. St. Paul gives us a reason ... different from any of those which I have mentioned. He laboured more than all the Apostles. And why? Not to civilize the world, not to smooth the face of society, not to facilitate the movements of civil government, not to spread [233] abroad knowledge, not to cultivate the reason, not for any great worldly object, but 'for the elect's sake' ... And such is the office of the Church in every nation where she sojourns; she attempts much; she expects and promises little."[2]

I do not, of course, deny that the Church does a great deal more than she promises: she fulfils a number of secondary ends, and is the means of numberless temporal blessings to any country which receives her. I only say, she is not to be estimated and measured by such effects; and if you think she is, my brethren, then I must rank you with such Erastians as Warburton, who, as I have shown you in a former Lecture, considered political convenience to be the test and standard of truth.

I thus begin with a consideration which, you see, I fully recognised before I was a Catholic; and now I proceed to another, which has been forced on me, as a matter of fact and experience, most powerfully ever since I was a Catholic, as it must be forced on every one who is in the communion of the Church; and which, therefore, like the former, has not at all originated in the need, nor is put forth for the occasion to meet your difficulty.

[234] The Church, you know, is in warfare; her life here below is one long battle. But with whom is she fighting? For till we know her enemy we shall not be able to estimate the skill of her tactics, the object of her evolutions, or the success of her movements. We shall be like civilians, contemplating a field of battle, and seeing much dust, and smoke, and motion, much defiling, charging, and manœuvring, but quite at a loss to tell the meaning of all, or which party is getting the better. And, if we actually mistake the foe, we shall criticise when we should praise, and think that all is a defeat, when every blow is telling. In all undertakings we must ascertain the end proposed, before we can predicate their success or failure; and, therefore, before we so freely speak against the state of Catholic countries, and reflect upon the Church herself in consequence, we must have a clear view what it is that the Church has

---

[2] Paroch. Serm., vol. iv. [N] "The Visible Church for the Sake of the Elect" (1836)

proposed to do with them and for them. We have, indeed, a right to blame and dissent from the end which she sets before her; we may quarrel with the mission she professes to have received from above; we may dispense with Scripture, Fathers, and the continuous tradition of 1800 years. That is another matter; then, at least, we have nothing to do with the theological movement which has given occasion to these Lectures; then we are not in the way to join the Catholic Church; then we must be met on our own ground: but I am speaking to those who go a great way with me; who admit my principles, who almost admit my conclusion; who are all but ready to submit to the Church, but who are frightened by the present state of Catholic [235] countries;—to such I say, Judge of her fruit by her principles and her object, which you yourselves also admit; not by those of her enemies, which you renounce.

The world believes in the world's ends as the greatest of goods; it wishes society to be governed simply and entirely for the sake of this world. Provided it could gain one little islet in the ocean, one foot upon the coast, if it could cheapen tea by sixpence a pound, or make its flag respected among the Esquimaux or Otaheitans,[3] at the cost of a hundred lives and a hundred souls, it would think it a very good bargain. What does it know of hell? it disbelieves it; it spits upon, it abominates, it curses its very name and notion. Next, as to the devil, it does not believe in him either. We next come to the flesh, and it is "free to confess" that it does not think there is any great harm in following the instincts of that nature which, perhaps it goes on to say, God has given. How could it be otherwise? who ever heard of the world fighting against the flesh and the devil? Well, then, what is its notion of evil? Evil, says the world, is whatever

---

[3] *Otaheitans*: This is the obsolete word for 'Tahitians.' The *OED* cites Becky Sharp's creator to illustrate the word: "1840 W. M. Thackeray *Shabby Genteel Story* ii. 685 I love to examine the customs of natives of all countries, and upon my word there are some barbarians in our own; less known, and more worthy of being known, than Hottentots, wild Irish, Otaheiteans, or any such savages."

is an offence to me, whatever obscures my majesty, whatever disturbs my peace. Order, tranquillity, popular contentment, plenty, prosperity, advance in arts and sciences, literature, refinement, splendour, this is my millennium, or rather my elysium,[4] my swerga;[5] I acknowledge no whole, no individuality, but my own; the

[236] units which compose me are but parts of me; they have no perfection in themselves; no end but in me; in my glory is their bliss, and in the hidings of my countenance they come to nought.

3.

Such is the philosophy and practice of the world;—now the Church looks and moves in a simply opposite direction. It contemplates, not the whole, but the parts; not a nation, but the men who form it; not society in the first place, but in the second place, and in the first place individuals; it looks beyond the outward act, on and into the thought, the motive, the intention, and the will; it looks beyond the world, and detects and moves against the devil, who is sitting in ambush behind it. It has, then, a foe in view; nay, it has a battle-field, to which the world is blind; its proper battle-field is the heart of the individual, and its true foe is Satan.

My dear brethren, do not think I am declaiming in the air or translating the pages of some old worm-eaten homily; as I have already said, I bear my own testimony to what has been brought home to me most closely and vividly as a matter of fact since I have been a Catholic; viz., that that mighty world-wide Church, like her Divine Author, regards, consults for, labours for the individual soul; she looks at the souls for whom Christ died, and who are made over to her; and her one object, for which everything is sacrificed—

[237] appearances, reputation, worldly triumph—is to acquit herself well of this most awful responsibility. Her one duty

---

[4] *elysium*: Elysium: "The supposed state or abode of the blessed after death in Greek mythology." *OED*.

[5] *swerga*: Swarga: *Hinduism*. "Heaven, paradise; *spec.* the heaven presided over by Indra, where virtuous souls reside before reincarnation." *OED*.

is to bring forward the elect to salvation, and to make them as many as she can:—to take offences out of their path, to warn them of sin, to rescue them from evil, to convert them, to teach them, to feed them, to protect them, and to perfect them. Oh, most tender loving Mother, ill-judged by the world, which thinks she is, like itself, always minding the main chance; on the contrary, it is her keen view of things spiritual, and her love for the soul, which hampers her in her negotiations and her measures, on this hard cold earth, which is her place of sojourning. How easy would her course be, at least for a while, could she give up this or that point of faith, or connive at some innovation or irregularity in the administration of the Sacraments! How much would Gregory have gained from Russia could he have abandoned the United Greeks![6] how secure had Pius been upon his throne, could he have allowed himself to fire on his people![7]

---

[6] *United Greeks*: The diplomacy Pope Gregory XIII (1502–85) conducted with Russia to protect the Catholic interests of the United Greeks – especially those in Poland – may have been more successful if he had abandoned those interests, though it enabled him to advance the broader interests of the Counter Reformation. Newman was well-versed in the history of Gregory's diplomacy, not least because the champion of the Council of Trent approved the foundation of St. Philip Neri's Oratorians (1575).

[7] *his people*: Pope Pius IX, Bl, pope from 16 June 1846 - 7 Feb. 1878. To the chagrin of conservatives like Metternich, Pius began his pontificate favorably disposed to liberal reform, granting amnesty to political prisoners and exiles, calling for two-chamber government of the papal states, lifting the disabilities against the Jews, and giving his blessing to the building of railroads, which his predecessor Gregory XVI had regarded as "roads of hell." However, when his first minister Pelegrino Rossi was murdered in 1848, and he had to flee Rome to escape a revolutionary mob in the Quirinal, on whom he would not fire, Pius's well-meaning flirtation with liberal reform came to an end. Yet, as Newman foresaw, his loss of the papal states enhanced his moral authority, even though Romans would later regret abandoning papal rule for "the disasters of Crispi's foreign policy" and "the fearful sufferings" of Italy in the Great War. E.E.Y. Hales, *Pio Nono: A Study in European Politics and Religion in the Nineteenth Century* (London, 1954), 165-6. Despite his travails, Pius became one of the most beloved popes in the history of the papacy. The Anglican patristic scholar, J. N. D. Kelly makes a fair assessment of his pontificate in his *Oxford Dictionary of Popes*:

"Politically Pius' pontificate, the longest in history, might seem to have been a disaster, but viewed ecclesiastically it was full of positive achievements. In the old and new worlds he founded over two hundred new dioceses and vicariates apostolic, notably in the USA and the British colonies; and he re-established the hierarchies in England (1850) and the Netherlands (1853). He restored the Latin patriarchate in Jerusalem (1847). He concluded concordats with numerous states, such as Russia (1847, never fully implemented and repudiated by Russia in 1866), Spain (1851), Austria (1855), and Latin American republics (1852–62), and gave strong support to the Catholic Union in Germany and the Central Party in Prussia (1852). A feature of the reign was an increasing centralization of authority, facilitated by modern means of transport but encouraged by the bishops' loss of political power and their consequent need to work closely with the pope; it helped to eliminate the last vestiges of Gallicanism and Josephinism. Pius carried out an unprecedented number of canonizations and beatifications, and consecrated (16 June 1875) the Catholic world to the Sacred Heart of Jesus (the feast of which he had extended to the entire church in 1856). But three events stand out as particularly significant. The first was his definition of the Immaculate Conception of the BVM, i.e. of her freedom from original sin, on 8 Dec. 1854. Made after lengthy consultation with bishops around the world but without mention of episcopal approbation, this gave a powerful stimulus to Marian devotion, and opened fresh possibilities of theological development. Because it was based on papal authority alone it can be seen as a forerunner of papal infallibility. Secondly, after repeated condemnations of teaching deemed unsound and calls for a return to that of St Thomas Aquinas (d. 1274), he published (8 Dec. 1864) the encyclical *Quanta cura*, with the 'Syllabus of Errors' attached, which denounced 'the principal errors of our times', including the view that the pope 'can or should reconcile himself to, or agree with, progress, liberalism, and modern civilization'. This dealt a fatal blow to liberal Catholicism, and affirmed the autonomy of the church in relation to the religiously neutral modern state. Thirdly, he summoned the First Vatican (Twentieth General) Council (1869–70), which, in the constitution *Pastor aeternus* (18 July 1870), declared the formal definitions of the pope in faith and morals to be infallible in their own right, not as a result of the consent of the church, thereby completing the doctrinal development of centuries and removing all conciliarist interpretations of the role of the papacy. This owed much to Pius' personal intervention; but the Council's constitution on faith (*Dei filius*: 24 Apr. 1870), deploring contemporary pantheism, materialism, and atheism, defining the spheres of reason and faith, and basing positive Catholic doctrine firmly on revelation, was no less representative of his programme. Pius was the first pope to identify himself wholeheartedly with ultramontanism, i.e. the tendency to centralize authority in church government and doctrine in the holy see,

No, my dear brethren, it is this supernatural sight and supernatural aim, which is the folly and the feebleness of the Church in the eyes of the world, and would be failure but for the providence of God. The Church overlooks everything in comparison of the immortal soul.

Good and evil to her are not lights and shades passing over the surface of society, but living powers, springing from the depths of the heart. Actions in her sight are not [238] mere outward deeds and words, committed by hand or tongue, and manifested in effects over a range of influence wider or narrower, as the case may be; but they are the thoughts, the desires, the purposes of the solitary responsible spirit. She knows nothing of space or time, except as secondary to will; she knows no evil but sin, and sin is a something personal, conscious, voluntary; she knows no good but grace, and grace again is something personal, private, special, lodged in the soul of the individual. She has one and one only aim—to purify the heart; she recollects who it is who has turned our thoughts

---

but its triumph at Vatican I not only extended the Old Catholic schism in Holland to other countries but led to an outbreak of anticlericalism in Europe generally, culminating in the abrogation (1874) of the concordat by Austria and Bismarck's repressive attack on the church in Germany (the *Kulturkampf*), which Pius denounced in the encyclical *Quod nunquam* (5 Feb. 1875). Yet when he died, he had effectively created the modern papacy, stripped (as he never ceased to deplore) of its temporal dominion, but armed with vastly enhanced spiritual authority in compensation." It is also worth noting that Pius made Newman a 'Doctor of Divinity' after his *Essay on the Development of Christian Doctrine* was recognized as orthodox, a distinction, which as Father Charles Dessain remarked, "would not have been done for a holder of suspect theories." Dessain, "The Reception Among Catholics of Newman's Doctrine of Development," *Newman Studien* 6 (1964), 185. While unsure whether his papacy was always animated by what he called the "gift of sagacity," Newman was not averse to Pius's papacy *per se*: he was averse to certain individuals within his papacy forming what he called "an aggressive insolent faction" in order to promote an extreme definition of papal infallibility. *AW*, 320; Newman to Bishop Ullathorne (28 January 1870), *LD*, xxv, 19. See also I. Ker. *John Henry Newman: A Biography* (Oxford, 1988), 651-3 and J. H. Newman, "The Pope and the Revolution" (1866) in *OS*, 281-316.

from the external crime to the inward imagination; who said, that "unless our justice abounded more than that of Scribes and Pharisees, we should not enter into the kingdom of Heaven;"[8] and that "out of the heart proceed evil thoughts, murders, adulteries, fornications, thefts, false testimonies, blasphemies. These are the things that defile a man."[9]

Now I would have you take up the sermons of any preacher, or any writer on moral theology, who has a name among Catholics, and see if what I have said is not strictly fulfilled, however little you fancied so before you make trial. Protestants, I say, think that the Church aims at appearance and effect; she must be splendid, and majestic, and influential: fine services, music, lights, vestments, and then again, in her dealings with others, courtesy, smoothness, cunning, dexterity, intrigue, management—[239] these, it seems, are the weapons of the Catholic Church. Well, my brethren, she cannot help succeeding, she cannot help being strong, she cannot help being beautiful; it is her gift; as she moves, the many wonder and adore;—"Et vera incessu patuit Dea."[10] It cannot be otherwise, certainly; but it is not her aim; she goes forth on the one errand, as I have said, of healing the diseases of the soul. Look, I say, into any book of moral theology you will; there is much there which may startle you: you will find principles hard to digest; explanations which seem to you subtle; details which distress you; you will find abundance of what will make excellent matter of attack at Exeter Hall;[11] but you will find

---

[8] *... the kingdom of Heaven"*: Matthew 5:20

[9] *... defile a man."*: Matthew 15:19

[10] *"Et vera incessuit patuit Dea*: Vergil, Aeneid, i, 405: 'And in her tread was revealed a very goddess.'

[11] *... at Exeter Hall*: Sin, as Newman had occasion to confirm in one of his anonymous reviews in the *British Critic*, was not a paramount concern of Exeter Hall. "Aged bishops are said, of old time, to have exerted an arm of force, and to have compelled others to enjoy the privileges, and undertake the duties of the Christian Church;—but now-a-days, bright eyes and tasteful bonnets are found more effective, and, though we do not pretend to be connoisseurs in the matter ourselves, we

from first to last this one idea—(nay, you will find that very matter of attack upon her is occasioned by her keeping it in view; she would be saved the odium, she would not have thus bared her side to the sword, but for her fidelity to it)— the one idea, I say, that sin is the enemy of the soul; and that sin especially consists, not in overt acts, but in the thoughts of the heart.

4.

This, then, is the point I insist upon, in answer to the objection which you have today urged against me. The Church aims, not at making a show, but at doing a work. She regards this world, and all that is in it, as a mere

---

certainly have read in the public prints that, whatever their advantage in the ball-room our charming countrywomen never look so well as in a morning dress. And, while the bazaar is the realm of feminine beauty, the platform is the region of manly eloquence, and still with the same object of propagating religion by means not religious. The societies which are there advocated are engaged always in benevolent, often in the most sacred and serious religious objects; this should be attentively considered. The Bible Society is formed for giving to individuals the sacred volume, which moreover it considers to be the one means of spiritual life. The Church Missionary Society is for the conversion of the heathen; the Jews, as its name denotes, for that of the once chosen people; the Reformation Society for withstanding errors which their agents in their printed papers declare to be worse than paganism. Objects higher and more momentous cannot be conceived; and individual speakers confess that they are such, and treat them accordingly; and yet, on the whole, strange to say, the anniversary and other meetings, which are the most formal image of these societies, are essentially not religious. They cannot be made religious, for the attempt to make them so would be the signal for private judgment to insist through a thousand separate voices upon a thousand separate varieties of creed or form; and they *will* not be made religious, because their supporters hold that what inspires respect is a degradation of religion, a superstition and a mummery, and that forms are only safe when variable and secular. The temple of this new system is Exeter Hall; its holytide is 'the London season;' its chancel is a platform; its cathedral throne is the chairman's seat; its ministers are the speakers; for holy salutations it uses 'Ladies and Gentlemen;' for benedictions it has "cheers;" for a creed it maintains the utility of combination; and for holy services and godly discipline it proclaims civil and religious liberty throughout the world." Review of *Random Recollections of Exeter Hall in 1834-1837* By one of the Protestant Party (London, 1838). British Critic, vol. 24, July, 1838, 197-8.

shadow, as dust and ashes, compared with the value of one [240] single soul. She holds that, unless she can, in her own way, do good to souls, it is no use her doing anything; she holds that it were better for sun and moon to drop from heaven, for the earth to fail, and for all the many millions who are upon it to die of starvation in extremest agony, so far as temporal affliction goes, than that one soul, I will not say, should be lost, but should commit one single venial sin, should tell one wilful untruth, though it harmed no one, or steal one poor farthing without excuse.[12] She considers the action of this world and the action of the soul simply incommensurate, viewed in their respective spheres; she would rather save the soul of one single wild bandit of Calabria, or whining beggar of Palermo, than draw a hundred lines of railroad through the length and breadth of Italy, or carry out a sanitary reform, in its fullest details, in every city of Sicily, except so far as these great national works tended to some spiritual good beyond them.

Such is the Church, O ye men of the world, and now you know her. Such she is, such she will be; and, though she aims at your good, it is in her own way,—and if you oppose her, she defies you. She has her mission, and do it she will, whether she be in rags, or in fine linen; whether with awkward or with refined carriage; whether by means of uncultivated intellects, or with the grace of accomplishments. Not that, in fact, she is not the source of numberless temporal and moral blessings to you also; the [241] history of ages testifies it; but she makes no promises; she is sent to seek the lost; that is her first object, and she will fulfil it, whatever comes of it.

And now, in saying this, I think I have gone a great way towards suggesting one main solution of the difficulty which I proposed to consider. The question was this:—How is it, that at this time Catholic countries happen to be behind

---

[12] ... *without excuse*: This is one of the passages to which Charles Kingsley objected in his pamphlet, "What, Then, Does Dr. Newman Mean?" (London, 1864). See Editor's Introduction.

Protestants in civilization?[13] In answer, I do not at all
determine how far the fact is so, or what explanation there
may be of the appearance of it; but anyhow the fact,
granting it exists, is surely no objection to Catholicism,
unless Catholicism has professed, or ought to have
professed, directly to promote mere civilization; on the
other hand, it has a work of its own, and this work is, first,
different from that of the world; next, *difficult of attainment*,
compared with that of the world; and, lastly, *secret* from the
world in its details and consequences. If, then, Spain or Italy
be deficient in secular progress, if the national mind in those
countries be but partially formed, if it be unable to develop
into civil institutions, if it have no moral instinct of
deference to a policeman, if the national finances be in
disorder, if the people be excitable, and open to deception
from political pretenders, if it know little or nothing of arts,
sciences, and literature; I repeat, of course, I do not admit
all this, except hypothetically, because it is difficult to draw

---

[13] *... behind Protestants in civilization?*: Although Newman here and
elsewhere concedes that Catholic countries tended to be more backward
than Protestant counties, he was also careful to point out that
Protestantism is the "religion of civilization" precisely because it rejects
conscience, which it sees as primitive and barbaric, and "since this
civilization itself is not a development of man's whole nature, but mainly
of the intellect, recognizing indeed the moral sense, but ignoring the
conscience, no wonder that the religion in which it issues has no
sympathy either with the hopes and fears of the awakened soul, or with
those frightful presentiments which are expressed in the worship and
traditions of the heathen." *GA*, 396. See also, E. Short, *Newman and his
Contemporaries* (London, 2011), 157-9. It is noteworthy here that
Charles Kinglsey, after rejecting what he regarded as the superstitious
character of Newman's Catholic faith, expresses his contempt for it thus:
"The sooner it is civilized off the face of the earth, if this be its teaching,
the better for mankind." *Apo.*, 373. Newman's response to the notion that
Catholicism is untenable because it is not sufficiently civilized can be
found in the last sentence of Lecture VIII: "You tell me, that the political
and civil state of Catholic countries is below that of Protestant: I answer,
that, even though you prove the fact, you have to prove something
besides, if it is to be an argument for your purpose, viz., that the standard
of civil prosperity and political aggrandisement is the truest test of grace
and the largest measure of salvation." *Diff*, i, 259-60.

[242] the line between what is true in it and what is not:—then all I can say is, that it is not wonderful that civil governments, which profess certain objects, should succeed in them better than the Church, which does not. Not till the State is blamed for not making saints, may it fairly be laid to the fault of the Church that she cannot invent a steam-engine or construct a tariff. It is, in truth, merely because she has often done so much more than she professes, it is really in consequence of her very exuberance of benefit to the world, that the world is disappointed that she does not display that exuberance always,—like some hangers-on of the great, who come at length to think they have a claim on their bounty.

5.

Now, let me try to bring out what I mean more in detail; and, in doing so, I hope to be pardoned, my brethren, if my language be now and then of a more directly religious cast than I willingly would admit into disquisitions such as the present; though speaking, as I do, in a place set apart for religious purposes, I am not perhaps called upon to apologize. In religious language, then, the one object of the Church, to which every other object is second, is that of reconciling the soul to God. She cannot disguise from herself, that, with whatever advantages her children commence their course, in spite of their baptism, in spite of their most careful education and training, still the great [243] multitude of them require her present and continual succour to keep them or rescue them from a state of mortal sin. Taking human nature as it is, she knows well, that, left to themselves, they would relapse into the state of those who are not Catholics, whatever latent principle of truth and goodness might remain in them, and whatever consequent hope there might be of a future revival. They may be full of ability and energy, they may be men of genius, men of literature and taste, poets and painters, musicians and architects; they may be statesmen or soldiers; they may be in professions or in trade; they may be skilled in the mechanical arts; they may be a hard-working, money-making community; they may have great political influence; they may pour out a flood of population on every side; they may have a talent for colonization; or, on the other hand, they may be members of a country once glorious, whose day is past; where luxury, or civil discord, or want of mental force, or other more subtle cause, is the insuperable bar in the way of any national demonstration; or they may be half reclaimed from barbarism, or they may be a simple rural population; they may be the cold north, or the beautiful south; but, whatever and wherever they are, the Church knows well, that those vast masses of population, as viewed in the individual units of which they are composed, are in a state of continual lapse from the Centre of sanctity and love, ever falling under His displeasure, and tending to a state of [244] habitual alienation from Him. Her one work towards these many millions is, year after year, day after day, to be raising them out of the mire, and when they sink again to raise them again, and so to keep them afloat, as she best may, on the surface of that stream, which is carrying them down to eternity. Of course, through God's mercy, there are numbers who are exceptions to this statement, who are living in obedience and peace, or going on to perfection; but the word of Christ, "Many are called, few are chosen,"[14] is fulfilled in any extensive field of operation which the Church is called to superintend. Her one object, through her ten thousand organs, by preachers and by confessors, by parish priests and by religious communities, in missions and in retreats, at Christmas and at Easter, by fasts and by feasts, by confraternities and by pilgrimages, by devotions and by indulgences, is this unwearied, ever-patient reconciliation of the soul to God and obliteration of sin. Thus, in the words of Scripture, most emphatically, she knows nought else but "Jesus Christ and Him crucified."[15] It is her ordinary toil, into which her other labours resolve themselves, or towards

---

[14] *... few are chosen"*: Matthew 22;14.

[15] *... and Him crucified"*: "For I determined not to know any thing among you, save Jesus Christ, and him crucified." 1 Corinthians 2:2.

which they are directed. Does she send out her missionaries? Does she summon her doctors? Does she enlarge or diversify her worship? Does she multiply her religious bodies? It is all to gain souls to Christ. And if she [245] encourages secular enterprises, studies, or pursuits, as she does, or the arts of civilization generally, it is either from their indirect bearing upon her great object, or from the spontaneous energy which great ideas, such as hers, exert, and the irresistible influence which they exercise, in matters and in provinces not really their own.

Moreover, as sins are of unequal gravity in God's judgment, though all of whatever kind are offensive to Him, and incur their measure of punishment, the Church's great object is to discriminate between sin and sin, and to secure in individuals that renunciation of evil, which is implied in the idea of a substantial and unfeigned conversion. She has no warrant, and she has no encouragement, to enforce upon men in general more than those habits of virtue, the absence of which would be tantamount to their separation from God; and she thinks she has done a great deal, and exults in her success, does she proceed so far; and she bears as she may, what remains still to be done, in the conviction that, did she attempt more, she might lose all. There are sins which are simply incompatible with contrition and absolution under any circumstances; there are others which are disorders and disfigurements of the soul. She exhorts men against the second, she directs her efforts against the first.

Now here at once the Church and the world part company; for the world, too, as is necessary, has its scale of [246] offences as well as the Church; but, referring them to a contrary object, it classifies them on quite a contrary principle; so that what is heinous in the world is often regarded patiently by the Church, and what is horrible and ruinous in the judgment of the Church may fail to exclude a man from the best society of the world. And, this being so, when the world contemplates the training of the Church and its results, it cannot, from the nature of the case, if for no other reason, avoid thinking very contemptuously of fruits, which are so different from those which it makes the standard and token of moral excellence in its own code of right and wrong.

6.

I may say the Church aims at three special virtues as reconciling and uniting the soul to its Maker:—faith, purity,[16] and charity; for two of which the world cares little or nothing. The world, on the other hand, puts in the foremost place, in some states of society, certain heroic qualities; in others certain virtues of a political or mercantile character. In ruder ages, it is personal courage, strength of purpose, magnanimity; in more civilized, honesty, fairness, honour, truth, and benevolence:—virtues, all of which, of course, the teaching of the Church comprehends, all of which she expects in their degree in all her consistent children, and all of which she enacts in their fulness in her saints; but which, after all, most beautiful as they are, admit [247] of being the fruit of nature as well as of grace; which do not necessarily imply grace at all: which do not reach so far as to sanctify, or unite the soul by any supernatural process to the source of supernatural perfection and supernatural

---

[16] *purity*: In his sermon "Christian Nobleness" (1831), Newman speaks forcefully of the virtue of purity. "… St. Paul, as feeling the majesty of that new nature which is imparted to us, addresses himself in a form of indignation to those who forget it. "What!" he says, "what! know ye not that your body is the temple of the Holy Ghost?" As if he said, "Can you be so mean-spirited and base-minded as to dishonour yourselves in the devil's service? Should we not pity the man of birth, or station, or character, who degraded himself in the eyes of the world, who forfeited his honour, broke his word, or played the coward? And shall not we, from mere sense of propriety, be ashamed to defile our spiritual purity, the royal blood of the second Adam, with deeds of darkness? Let us leave it to the hosts of evil spirits, to the haters of Christ, to eat the dust of the earth all the days of their life. Cursed are they above all cattle, and above every beast of the field; grovelling shall they go, till they come to their end and perish. But for Christians, it is theirs to walk in the light, as children of the light, and to lift up their hearts, as looking out for Him who went away, that He might return to them again." *SD*, 145.

blessedness.[17] Again, as I have already said, the Church contemplates virtue and vice in their first elements, as conceived and existing in thought, desire, and will, and holds that the one or the other may be as complete and mature, without passing forth from the home of the secret heart, as if it had ranged forth in profession and in deed all over the earth. Thus at first sight she seems to ignore bodies politic, and society, and temporal interests: whereas the world, on the contrary, talks of religion as being a matter of such private concern, so personal, so sacred, that it has no opinion at all about it; it praises public men, if they are useful to itself, but simply ridicules inquiry into their motives, thinks it impertinent in others to attempt it, and out of taste in themselves to sanction it. All public men it considers to be pretty much the same at bottom; but what matter is that to it, if they do its work? It offers high pay, and it expects faithful service; but, as to its agents, overseers, men of business, operatives, journeymen, figure-servants, and labourers, what they are personally, what are their principles and aims, what their creed, what their conversation; where they live, how they spend their leisure time, whither they are going, how they die—I am stating a simple matter of fact, I am not here praising or blaming, I am but contrasting,—I say, all questions implying the existence of the soul, are as much beyond the circuit of the world's imagination, as they are intimately and primarily present to the apprehension of the Church.

[248]

The Church, then, considers the momentary, fleeting act of the will, in the three subject matters I have mentioned, to be capable of guiltiness of the deadliest character, or of the most efficacious and triumphant merit. Moreover, she holds that a soul laden with the most enormous offences, in deed as well as thought, a savage tyrant, who delighted in cruelty, an habitual adulterer, a murderer, a blasphemer, who has scoffed at religion through a long life, and corrupted every

---

[17] *... and supernatural blessedness*: Cf. "At this day the 'gentleman' is the creation, not of Christianity but of civilization." *Idea*, 174. See also, 179-81 Newman's celebrated definition of the gentleman.

soul which he could bring within his influence, who has loathed the Sacred Name, and cursed his Saviour,—that such a man can under circumstances, in a moment, by one thought of the heart, by one true act of contrition, reconcile himself to Almighty God (through His secret grace), without Sacrament, without priest, and be as clean, and fair, and lovely, as if he had never sinned. Again, she considers that in a moment also, with eyes shut and arms folded, a man may cut himself off from the Almighty by a deliberate act of the will, and cast himself into perdition. With the world it is the reverse; a member of society may go as near the line of evil, as the world draws it, as he will; but, till he [249] has passed it, he is safe. Again, when he has once transgressed it, recovery is impossible; let honour of man or woman be sullied, and to restore its splendour is simply to undo the past; it is impossible.[18]

---

[18] *it is impossible*: The rules of English society to which Newman refers were undisguisedly cynical, as one of Edward VII's biographers points out. "There can be no advantage in pretending to virtue unless society values it. Hypocrisy only flourishes where standards are high. In permissive ages, where few things are unacceptable, there is little to hide. Because the Victorians made such strenuous moral demands they did not always practice what they preached. The dominating idea of English society was not to cultivate virtue but to avoid scandal. 'Everything was all right,' claimed Lady Warwick, 'if only it was kept quiet, hushed up, covered.' Although it was thought necessary in the nineteenth century to maintain that marriage vows were sacred, affairs were common among fashionable people, and lovers were given adjoining rooms when staying in country houses. But if adultery was reckoned venial its advertisement was mortal: the moment they were discovered romances turned into scandal." When Lady Harriet Mordaunt confessed her infidelity, her husband Sir Charles, Conservative MP for South Warwickshire took the unusual step of serving her with a writ of divorce. Although the subsequent 'Warwickshire Scandal' (1869) ruined her reputation, whether the distraught lady was sane when she made her confession has always been unclear, and, in any case, the letters to her from the Prince of Wales "were such as Prince Albert might have sent to an elderly governess." Giles St. Aubyn, *Edward VII: Prince and King* (New York, 1979), 151, 160. The Prince was represented in the ensuing trial by Sir Alexander Cockburn, who represented Newman in his defense against Achilli's libel charge, a year after Newman delivered his King William Street lectures.

Such being the extreme difference between the Church and the world, both as to the measure and the scale of moral good and evil, we may be prepared for those vast differences in matters of detail, which I hardly like to mention, lest they should be out of keeping with the gravity of the subject, as contemplated in its broad principle. For instance, the Church pronounces the momentary wish, if conscious and deliberate, that another should be struck down dead, or suffer any other grievous misfortune, as a blacker sin than a passionate, unpremeditated attempt on the life of the Sovereign.[19] She considers direct unequivocal consent, though as quick as thought, to a single unchaste desire as indefinitely more heinous than any lie which can possibly be fancied, that is, when that lie is viewed, of course, in itself, and apart from its causes, motives, and consequences. Take a mere beggar-woman, lazy, ragged, and filthy, and not over-scrupulous of truth—(I do not say she had arrived at perfection)—but if she is chaste, and sober, and cheerful, and goes to her religious duties (and I am supposing not at all an impossible case), she will, in the [250] eyes of the Church, have a prospect of heaven, which is quite closed and refused to the State's pattern-man, the just,

---

[19] *life of the Sovereign*: In the course of her long reign, Queen Victoria survived eight assassination attempts. On the evening of June 19th, 1849, the official commemoration of her birthday and a year before Newman's lectures, she was riding through Hyde and Regent's Park with three of her children, including the future King Edward VII, when William Hamilton, a 24-yerar old unemployed bricklayer fired a pistol at the royal carriage as it descended Constitution Hill on its return to Buckingham Palace. Hamilton, who had come from Ireland to London in the 1840s to escape the potato famine, told the police he had fired the gun "for the purpose of getting into prison, as he was tired of being out of work." He only learned later that the pistol was unloaded. Once convicted, the unbalanced Irishman was banished to Gibraltar for seven years. For another example, on July 27, 1850, just two weeks after Newman delivered his lectures, Robert Pate, a retired lieutenant of the 10th Hussars assaulted the Queen with an umbrella when she was in her royal carriage visiting her dying Uncle Adolphous at Cambridge House. The blow above her eye was so violent that it rendered her unconscious, after which onlookers restrained the assailant, who was sentenced to seven years in Tasmania. See E. Longford, *Queen Victoria* (London, 1998), 177, 178-9.

the upright, the generous, the honourable, the conscientious, if he be all this, not from a supernatural power—(I do not determine whether this is likely to be the fact, but I am contrasting views and principles)—not from a supernatural power, but from mere natural virtue.[20] Polished, delicate-minded ladies, with little of temptation around them, and no self-denial to practise, in spite of their refinement and taste, if they be nothing more, are objects of less interest to her, than many a poor outcast who sins, repents, and is with difficulty kept just within the territory of grace.[21] Again, excess in drinking is one of the world's most disgraceful offences; odious it ever is in the eyes of the Church, but if it does not proceed to the loss of reason, she thinks it a far less sin than one deliberate act of detraction, though the matter of it be truth. And again, not unfrequently does a priest hear a confession of thefts, which he knows would sentence the penitent to transportation, if brought into a court of justice, but which he knows, too, in the judgment of the Church, might be pardoned on the man's private contrition, without any confession at all. Once more, the State has the guardianship of property, as the Church is the guardian of the faith:—in the Middle Ages, as is often objected, the Church put to death for heresy; well but, on the other hand, even in our own times, the State has put to death for [251] forgery; nay, I suppose for sheep-stealing. How distinct must be the measure of crime in Church and in State, when so heterogeneous is the rule of punishment in the one and in the other!

My brethren, you may think it impolitic in me thus candidly to state what may be so strange in the eyes of the

---

[20] *mere natural virtue:* "If Newman had his choice of being an English gentleman or a Sicilian beggar, such an English gentleman and such a beggar, he would have chosen without the slightest hesitation to be the scabrous and drunken beggar. Happily these were not the only alternatives ..." A. Dwight Culler, *The Imperial Intellect: A Study of Newman's Educational Ideal* (New Haven, 1955), 241.

[21] *territory of grace*: This is another of the passages to which Charles Kingsley objected in his pamphlet, "What, Then, Does Dr. Newman Mean?" (London, 1864). See Editor's Introduction.

world;—but not so, my dear brethren, just the contrary. The world already knows quite enough of our difference of judgment from it on the whole; it knows that difference also in its results; but it does not know that it is based on principle; it taunts the Church with that difference, as if nothing could be said for her,—as if it were not, as it is, a mere question of a balance of evils,—as if the Church had nothing to show for herself, were simply ashamed of her evident helplessness, and pleaded guilty to the charge of her inferiority to the world in the moral effects of her teaching. The world points to the children of the Church, and asks if she acknowledges them as her own. It dreams not that this contrast arises out of a difference of principle, and that she claims to act upon a principle higher than the world's. Principle is always respectable; even a bad man is more respected, though he may be more hated, if he owns and justifies his actions, than if he is wicked by accident; now the Church professes to judge after the judgment of the [252] Almighty; and it cannot be imprudent or impolitical to bring this out clearly and boldly. His judgment is not as man's: "I judge not according to the look of man," He says, "for man seeth those things which appear, but the Lord beholdeth the heart."[22] The Church aims at realities, the world at decencies; she dispenses with a complete work, so she can but make a thorough one. Provided she can do for the soul what is necessary, if she can but pull the brands out of the burning, if she can but extract the poisonous root which is the death of the soul, and expel the disease, she is content, though she leaves in it lesser maladies, little as she sympathises with them.

7.

Now, were it to my present purpose to attack the principles and proceedings of the world, of course it would be obvious for me to retort upon the cold, cruel, selfish

---

[22] *... beholdeth the heart."*: "But the Lord said to Samuel, 'Do not look at his appearance or at his physical stature, because I have refused him. For *the Lord does* not *see* as man sees; for man looks at the outward appearance, but the Lord looks at the heart.'" 1 Samuel 16:7.

system, which this supreme worship of comfort, decency, and social order necessarily introduces; to show you how the many are sacrificed to the few, the poor to the wealthy, how an oligarchical monopoly of enjoyment is established far and wide, and the claims of want, and pain, and sorrow, and affliction, and guilt, and misery, are practically forgotten. But I will not have recourse to the common-places of controversy when I am on the defensive. All I would say to the world is,—Keep your theories to yourselves, do not inflict them upon the sons of Adam [253] everywhere; do not measure heaven and earth by views which are in a great degree insular, and can never be philosophical and catholic. You do your work, perhaps, in a more business-like way, compared with ourselves, but we are immeasurably more tender, and gentle, and angelic than you. We come to poor human nature as the Angels of God, and you as policemen. Look at your poor-houses, hospitals, and prisons; how perfect are their externals! what skill and ingenuity appear in their structure, economy, and administration! they are as decent, and bright, and calm, as what our Lord seems to name them,—dead men's sepulchres. Yes! they have all the world can give, all but life; all but a heart. Yes! you can hammer up a coffin, you can plaster a tomb; you are nature's undertakers; you cannot build it a home. You cannot feed it or heal it; it lies, like Lazarus, at your gate, full of sores. You see it gasping and panting with privations and penalties; and you sing to it, you dance to it, you show it your picture-books, you let off your fireworks, you open your menageries. Shallow philosophers! is this mode of going on so winning and persuasive that we should imitate it?

Look at your conduct towards criminals, and honestly say, whether you expect a power which claims to be divine, to turn copyist of you? You have the power of life and death committed to you by Heaven; and some wretched being is sentenced to fall under it for some deed of treachery and [254] blood. It is a righteous sentence, re-echoed by a whole people; and you have a feeling that the criminal himself ought to concur in it, and sentence himself. There is an universal feeling that he ought to resign himself to your act, and, as it were, take part in it; in other words, there is a sort of instinct among you that he should make confession, and you are not content without his doing so. So far the Church goes along with you. So far, but no further. To whom is he to confess? To me, says the Priest, for he has injured the Almighty. To me, says the world, for he has injured me. Forgetting that the power to sentence is simply from God, and that the sentence, if just, is God's sentence, the world is peremptory that no confession shall be made by the criminal to God, without itself being in the secret. It is right, doubtless, that that criminal should make reparation to man as well as to God; but it is not right that the world should insist on having precedence of its Maker, or should prescribe that its Maker should have no secrets apart from itself, or that no divine ministration should relieve a laden breast without its meddling in the act. Yet the world rules it, that whatever is said to a minister of religion in religious confidence is its own property. It considers that a clergyman who attends upon the culprit is its own servant, and by its boards of magistrates, and by its literary organs, it insists on his revealing to its judgment-seat what was uttered before [255] the judgment-seat of God. What wonder, then, if such forlorn wretches, when thus plainly told that the world is their only god, and knowing that they are quitting the presence of that high potentate for ever, steel themselves with obduracy, encounter it with defiance, baffle its curiosity, and inflict on its impatience such poor revenge as is in its power? They come forth into the light, and look up into the face of day for the last time, and, amid the jests and blasphemies of myriads, they pass from a world which they hate into a world which they deny. Small mercies, indeed, has this world shown them, and they make no trial of the mercies of another!

8.

Oh, how contrary is the look, the bearing of the Catholic Church to these poor outcasts of mankind! There was a time, when one who denied his Lord was brought to repentance by a glance; and such is the method which His Church teaches to those nations who acknowledge her authority and her sway. The civil magistrate, stern of necessity in his function, and inexorable in his resolve, at her bidding gladly puts on a paternal countenance, and takes on him an office of mercy towards the victim of his wrath. He infuses the ministry of life into the ministry of death; he afflicts the body for the good of the soul, and converts the penalty of human law into an instrument of everlasting [256] bliss. It is good for human beings to die as infants, before they have known good or evil, if they have but received the baptism of the Church; but next to these, who are the happiest, who are the safest, for whose departure have we more cause to rejoice, and be thankful, than for theirs, who, if they live on, are so likely to relapse into old habits of sin, but who are taken out of this miserable world in the flower of their contrition and in the freshness of their preparation;—just at the very moment when they have perfected themselves in good dispositions, and from their heart have put off sin, and have come humbly for pardon, and have received the grace of absolution, and have been fed with the bread of Angels, and thus amid the prayers of all men have departed to their Maker and their Judge? I say, "the prayers of all:" for oh the difference, in this respect, in the execution of the extreme sentence of the law, between a Catholic State and another! We have all heard of the scene of impiety and profaneness which attends on the execution of a criminal in England; so much so, that benevolent and thoughtful men are perplexed between the evil of privacy and the outrages which publicity occasions.[23] Well, England

---

[23] *... which publicity occasions*: On November 13, 1849 a crowd of over 30,000 people gathered outside Horsemonger Gaol in South London to witness the public execution of Marie and Frederick Manning, a married couple, who had recently murdered Marie's wealthy former lover, Patrick O'Connor. Since this was the first married couple hanged in over a century, the hanging attracted great publicity, including the following letter from Charles Dickens to the editor of *The Times*. "Sir, I was a witness of the execution at Horsemonger Lane this morning. ... I believe

surpasses Rome in ten thousand matters of this world, but never would the Holy City tolerate an enormity which powerful England cannot hinder. An arch-confraternity was instituted there at the close of the fifteenth century, under

---

that a sight so inconceivably awful as the wickedness and levity of the immense crowd collected at that execution this morning could be imagined by no man, and could be presented in no heathen land under the sun. The horrors of the gibbet and of the crime which brought the wretched murderers to it faded in my mind before the atrocious bearing, looks, and language of the assembled spectators. When I came upon the scene at midnight, the shrillness of the cries and howls that were raised from time to time, denoting that they came from a concourse of boys and girls already assembled in the best places, made my blood run cold. As the night went on, screeching, and laughing, and yelling in strong chorus of parodies on negro melodies, with substitutions of 'Mrs. Manning' for 'Susannah' and the like, were added to these. When the day dawned, thieves, low prostitutes, ruffians, and vagabonds of every kind, flocked on to the ground, with every variety of offensive and foul behaviour. Fightings, faintings, whistlings, imitations of Punch, brutal jokes, tumultuous demonstrations of indecent delight when swooning women were dragged out of the crowd by the police, with their dresses disordered, gave a new zest to the general entertainment. When the sun rose brightly—as it did—it gilded thousands upon thousands of upturned faces, so inexpressibly odious in their brutal mirth or callousness, that a man had cause to feel ashamed of the shape he wore, and to shrink from himself, as fashioned in the image of the Devil. When the two miserable creatures who attracted all this ghastly sight about them were turned quivering into the air, there was no more emotion, no more pity, no more thought that two immortal souls had gone to judgement, no more restraint in any of the previous obscenities, than if the name of Christ had never been heard in this world, and there were no belief among men but that they perished like the beasts. I have seen, habitually, some of the worst sources of general contamination and corruption in this country, and I think there are not many phases of London life that could surprise me. I am solemnly convinced that nothing that ingenuity could devise to be done in this city, in the same compass of time, could work such ruin as one public execution, and I stand astounded and appalled by the wickedness it exhibits. I do not believe that any community can prosper where such a scene of horror and demoralization as was enacted this morning outside Horsemonger Lane Gaol is presented at the very doors of good citizens, and is passed by, unknown or forgotten. ... I am, Sir, your faithful Servant. Charles Dickens." Dickens to the *Times* (13 November 1849), *The Selected Letters of Charles Dickens* ed. Jenny Hartley (Oxford, 2012), 205-6.

the invocation of San Giovanni Decollato, that Holy Baptist, [257] who lost his head by a king's sentence, though an unjust one;[24] and it exercises its pious offices towards condemned criminals even now. When a culprit is to be executed, the night preceding the fatal day, two priests of the brotherhood, who sometimes happen to be Bishops or persons of high authority in the city, remain with him in prayer, attend him on the scaffold the next morning, and assist him through every step of the terrible ceremonial of which he is the subject. The Blessed Sacrament is exposed in all the churches all over the city, that the faithful may assist a sinner about to make a compulsory appearance before his Judge. The crowd about the scaffold is occupied in but one thought, whether he has shown signs of contrition. Various reports are in circulation, that he is obdurate, that he has yielded, that he is obdurate still. The women cry out that it is impossible; Jesus and Mary will see to it; they will not believe that it is so; they are sure that he will submit himself to his God before he enters into His presence. However, it is perhaps confirmed that the unhappy man is still wrestling with his pride and hardness of heart, and though he has that illumination of faith which a Catholic cannot but possess, yet he cannot bring himself to hate and abhor sins, which, except in their awful consequences, are, as far as their enjoyment, gone from him

---

[24] *San Giovanni Decollato*: The 'Beheaded John the Baptist' is the name of a Roman Catholic church in Rome on Via di San Giovanni Decollato. The present church stands on the site of an ancient church. In 1488 it was granted to the Archconfraternity of the Beheaded John the Baptist, which began rebuilding the church in 1504, gave it its present dedication and made its main feast day that of the beheading of John the Baptist. The Archconfraternity originated in Florence and was named after the city's patron saint. Its charge, as Newman explains, was to prepare the condemned for death by encouraging them to repent and giving them the last rites. The new church was completed in 1588 and in 1600 pope Clement VIII had a new cloister built for it, in which the mass graves of those condemned to death can still be seen – they are covered in marble and inscribed 'Domine, cum veneris iudicare, noli me condemnare' (Lord, when you come to judge, do not condemn me). The church was restored in 1727 and 1888.

[258] for ever. He cannot taste again the pleasure of revenge or of forbidden indulgence, yet he cannot get himself to give it up, though the world is passing from him. The excitement of the crowd is at its height: an hour passes; the suspense is intolerable, when the news is brought of a change; that before the Crucifix, in the solitude of his cell, at length the—unhappy no longer—the happy criminal has subdued himself; has prayed with real self-abasement; has expressed, has felt a charitable, a tender thought, towards those he has hated; has resigned himself lovingly to his destiny; has blessed the hand that smites him; has supplicated pardon; has confessed with all his heart, and placed himself at the disposal of his Priest, to make such amends as he can make in his last hour to God and man; has even desired to submit here to indignity, to pain, to which he is not sentenced; has taken on himself any length of purgatory hereafter, if thereby he may now, through God's mercy, show his sincerity, and his desire of pardon and of gaining the lowest place in the kingdom of Heaven. The news comes; it is communicated through the vast multitude all at once; and, I have heard from those who have been present, never shall they forget the instantaneous shout of joy which burst forth from every tongue, and formed itself into one concordant act of thanksgiving in acknowledgment of the grace vouchsafed to one so near eternity.[25]

[259] It is not wonderful then to find the holy men who, from time to time, have done the pious office of preparing such

---

[25] *near eternity*: The Italian historian Adriano Prosperi sees the "holy men who have done the pious office ... of preparing such criminals for death" as tools of oppression. "What was played out on the gallows," he writes, "was the triumph of power." Adriano Prosperi, *Crime and Forgiveness: Christianizing Execution in Medieval Europe* trans. J. Carden (Harvard, 2020). 132. Love, repentance, fellow feeling or redemption had nothing to do with the matter. Power is the all-purpose explanation. What can one say to such sloppy unimaginative thinking? Instead of choosing to be another of Foucault's legion parrots, Prosperi might have tried to understand the Catholic faith that animated such confraternities.

criminals for death, so confident of their salvation.[26] "So well convinced was Father Claver of the eternal happiness

---

[26] *their salvation*: *Life of the Venerable Father Peter Claver, Apostle to the West Indies and Memoirs of Cardinal Odescalchi, S.J.* (London, 1849), 140. St. Peter Claver (1580-1654), Spanish Jesuit priest, 'the apostle of the Negroes'. "He was born at Verdu (Catalonia), was educated at Barcelona university, and became a Jesuit in 1600 at Tarragona. He was sent to the college of Palma (Majorca), where he met Alphonsus Rodriguez, who encouraged his desire for missionary work in the New World. He studied theology at Barcelona and was sent to Cartagena (now in Colombia) in 1610, where he was ordained priest five years later. At this time Cartagena was one of the principal centres of the flourishing but iniquitous slave-trade in Negroes from Angola and elsewhere in western Africa, who were shipped in large numbers and often unspeakable conditions across the Atlantic. Cartagena was a convenient clearing-house; it has been estimated that 10,000 reached it every year. Peter devoted himself to them under Fr. Alfonso de Sandoval, who had already spent forty years looking after them. Peter both imitated and surpassed the achievements of his predecessor. When a slave-ship arrived in the port, the slaves were shut up in yards, herded together in the heat without care or medical attention of any kind. Peter would visit them with medicine, food, brandy, lemons, and tobacco. His band of helpers assisted in this distribution and acted as interpreters. With their help and with the use of pictures he would teach the principal truths of Christianity and prepare the slaves for baptism. He also inspired them with some idea of their dignity and worth as men who were redeemed, in contrast with their appalling state of present misery. Eventually the slaves were sent to the mines (where the work was too hard for the native Indians) and to the plantations, which he visited every spring, not always with the approval of their masters. He would also nurse the slaves in conditions which nobody else could endure: he used to call himself 'the slave of the Negroes for ever'. This, however, did not prevent him from caring also for the souls of the more well-to-do members of society and for the traders and visitors (including Moslems and English Protestants) to Cartagena, or for condemned criminals, many of whom he prepared for death. He was also a frequent visitor to the city's hospitals. His apostolate included an annual mission to traders and seamen in the port every autumn. Miracles, prophecies, the gift of reading hearts, and the practice of severe personal penance were all ascribed to him. In 1650 he was taken ill while preaching to the Negroes. Although he recovered, he suffered from paralysis for the remaining four years of his life, broken in health, neglected by the young man who was responsible for looking after him, able to leave his cell only for short visits to the hospital or to friends. He lived long enough to welcome his successor in his apostolate. At his death the civil authorities and the clergy who had thought him indiscreet

of almost all whom he assisted," says this saintly missionary's biographer, "that, speaking once of some persons who had in a bad spirit delivered a criminal into the hands of justice, he said, 'God forgive them; but they have secured the salvation of this man at the probable risk of their own.' Most of the criminals considered it a grace to die in the hands of this holy man. As soon as he spoke to them the most savage and indomitable became gentle as lambs; and, in place of their ordinary imprecations nothing was heard but sighs, and the sound of bloody disciplines, which they took before leaving the prison for execution."

But I must come to an end. I do not consider, my brethren, I have said all that might be said in answer to the difficulty which has come under our consideration; nor have I proposed to do so. Such an undertaking does not fall within the scope of these Lectures; it would be an inquiry into facts. It is enough if I have suggested to you one thought which may most materially invalidate the objection. You tell me, that the political and civil state of Catholic countries is below that of Protestant: I answer, that, even [260] though you prove the fact, you have to prove something besides, if it is to be an argument for your purpose, viz., that the standard of civil prosperity and political aggrandisement is the truest test of grace and the largest measure of salvation.

---

or misguided united in his praise; he was given a civic funeral while Africans and Indians arranged for a Mass of their own. He was canonized in 1888 and declared patron of all missionary enterprises among the Negroes. His feast, 9 September, is on the day after his death; his cult is particularly strong in the United States and Latin America." *Oxford Dictionary of the Saints.*

LECTURE IX

THE RELIGIOUS STATE OF CATHOLIC COUNTRIES NO PREJUDICE TO THE SANCTITY OF THE CHURCH

I CONSIDERED, in the preceding Lecture, the objection brought in this day against the Catholic Church, from the state of the countries which belong to her. It is urged, that they are so far behind the rest of the world in the arts and comforts of life, in power of political combination, in civil economy, and the social virtues, in a word, in all that tends to make this world pleasant, and the loss of it painful, that their religion cannot come from above. I answered, that, before the argument could be made to tell against us, proof must be furnished, not only that the fact was as stated (and I think it should be very closely examined), but especially that there is that essential connection in the nature of things between true religion and temporal prosperity, which the objection took for granted. That there is a natural and ordinary connection between them no one would deny; but it is one thing to say that prosperity ought to follow from religion, quite another to say that it must follow from it. [262] Thus, health, for instance, may be expected from a habit of regular exercise; but no one would positively deny the fact that exercise had been taken in a particular case, merely because the patient gave signs of an infirm and sickly state of the body. And, indeed, there may be particular and most wise reasons in the scheme of Divine Providence, whatever be the legitimate tendency of the Catholic faith, for its being left, from time to time, without any striking manifestations of its beneficial action upon the temporal interests of mankind, without the influence of wealth, learning, civil talent, or political sagacity; nay, as in the days of St.

Cyprian[1] and St. Augustine, with the actual reproach of impairing the material resources and the social greatness of the nations which embrace it:[2] viz., in order to remind the Church, and to teach the world, that she needs no temporal

---

[1] *St. Cyprian*: St Cyprian (200–58), Roman writer and martyr; Bishop of Carthage.

[2] *which embrace it*: Newman would have read what Gibbon had to say of why he thought Christians incurred the reproach of their Roman neighbors for abandoning the beliefs and practices that made Rome's 'material resources' and 'social greatness' possible. "The Jews were a *nation*, the Christians were a *sect*." Gibbon wrote, "and if it was natural for every community to respect the sacred institutions of their neighbours, it was incumbent on them to persevere in those of their ancestors. The voice of oracles, the precepts of philosophers, and the authority of the laws, unanimously enforced this national obligation. By their lofty claim of superior sanctity the Jews might provoke the Polytheists to consider them as an odious and impure race. By disdaining the intercourse of other nations they might deserve their contempt. The laws of Moses might be for the most part frivolous or absurd yet, since they had been received during many ages by a large society, his followers were justified by the example of mankind, and it was universally acknowledged that they had a right to practise what it would have been criminal in them to neglect. But this principle, which protected the Jewish synagogue, afforded not any favour or security to the primitive church. By embracing the faith of the Gospel the Christians incurred the supposed guilt of an unnatural and unpardonable offence. They dissolved the sacred ties of custom and education, violated the religious institutions of their country, and presumptuously despised whatever their fathers had believed as true or had reverenced as sacred. Nor was this apostasy (if we may use the expression) merely of a partial or local kind; since the pious deserter who withdrew himself from the temples of Egypt or Syria would equally disdain to seek an asylum in those of Athens or Carthage. Every Christian rejected with contempt the superstitions of his family, his city, and his province. The whole body of Christians unanimously refused to hold any communion with the gods of Rome, of the empire, and of mankind. It was in vain that the oppressed believer asserted the inalienable rights of conscience and private judgment. Though his situation might excite the pity, his arguments could never reach the understanding, either of the philosophic or of the believing part of the Pagan world. To their apprehensions it was no less a matter of surprise that any individuals should entertain scruples against complying with the established mode of worship than if they had conceived a sudden abhorrence to the manners, the dress, or the language of their native country." Gibbon, *Decline and Fall*, ch. 16.

recommendations who has a heavenly Protector, but can make her way (as they say) against wind and tide.

This, then, was the subject I selected for my foregoing Lecture, and I said there were three reasons why the world is no fit judge of the work, or the kind of work, really done by the Church in any age:—first, because the world's measure of good and scope of action are so different from those of the Church, that it judges as unfairly and as narrowly of the fruits of Catholicism and their value, as the Caliph Omar[3] might judge of the use and the influence of literature, or rather indefinitely more so. The Church, [263] though she embraces all conceivable virtues in her teaching, and every kind of good, temporal as well as spiritual, in her exertions, does not survey them from the same point of view, or classify them in the same order as the world. She makes secondary what the world considers indispensable; she places first what the world does not even recognise, or undervalues, or dislikes, or thinks impossible; and not being able, taking mankind as it is found, to do everything, she is often obliged to give up altogether what she thinks of great indeed, but of only secondary moment, in a particular age or a particular country, instead of effecting at all risks that extirpation of social evils, which, in the world's eyes, is so necessary, that it thinks nothing really is done till it is secured. Her base of operations, from the difficulties of the season or the period, is sometimes not broad enough to enable her to advance against crime as well as against sin, and to destroy barbarism as well as irreligion. The world, in consequence, thinks, that because she has not done the world's work, she has not fulfilled her Master's purpose; and imputes to her the enormity of having put eternity before time.

---

[3] *Omar*: Caliph Omar *c.*581–644, Muslim caliph, who declared, apropos the burning of the library at Alexandria, ad *c.*641: "If these writings of the Greeks agree with the book of God, they are useless and need not be preserved; if they disagree, they are pernicious and ought to be destroyed." See Gibbon *Decline and Fall,* ch. 51.

And next, let it be observed that she has undertaken the more difficult work; it is difficult, certainly, to enlighten the savage, to make him peaceable, orderly, and self-denying; to persuade him to dress like a European, to make him [264] prefer a feather-bed to the heather or the cave, and to appreciate the comforts of the fireside and the tea-table: but it is indefinitely more difficult, even with the supernatural powers given to the Church, to make the most refined, accomplished, amiable men, chaste or humble; to bring, not only his outward actions, but his thoughts, imaginations, and aims, into conformity to a law which is naturally distasteful to him. It is not wonderful, then, if the Church does not do so much in the Church's way, as the world does in the world's way. The world has nature as an ally, and the Church, on the whole, and as things are, has nature as an enemy.[4]

And lastly, as I have implied, her best fruit is necessarily secret: she fights with the heart of man; her perpetual conflict is against the pride, the impurity, the covetousness, the envy, the cruelty, which never gets so far as to come to light; which she succeeds in strangling in its birth. From the nature of the case, she ever will do more in repressing evil than in creating good; moreover, virtue and sanctity, even when realised, are also in great measure secret gifts, known only to God and good Angels; for these, then, and other reasons, the powers and the triumphs of the Church must be hid from the world, unless the doors of the Confessional could be flung open, and its whispers carried abroad on the voices of the winds. Nor indeed would even such disclosures suffice for the due comparison of the Church [265] with religions which aim at no personal self-government, and disown on principle examination of conscience and confession of sin; but in order to our being able to do justice to that comparison, we must wait for the Day when the books shall be opened and the secrets of hearts shall be

---

[4] ... *nature as an enemy*: See Newman's sermon, "Religion a Weariness to the Natural Man" (1828), *PS*, vii-16.

disclosed.[5] For all these reasons, then, from the peculiarity, and the arduousness, and the secrecy of the mission entrusted to the Church, it comes to pass that the world is led, at particular periods, to think very slightly of the Church's influence on society, and vastly to prefer its own methods and its own achievements.

So much I have already suggested towards the consideration of a subject, to which justice could not really be done except in a very lengthened disquisition, and by an examination of matters which lie beyond the range of these Lectures. If then today I make a second remark upon it, I do so only with the object I have kept before me all along, of smoothing the way into the Catholic Church for those who are already very near the gate; who have reasons enough, taken by themselves, for believing her claims, but are perplexed and stopped by the counter-arguments which are urged against her, or at least against their joining her.[6]

1.

Today, then, I shall suppose an objector to reply to what I have said in the following manner: viz., I shall suppose [266] him to say, that "the reproach of Catholicism is, not what it does not do, so much as what it does; that its teaching and its training do produce a certain very definite character on a nation and on individuals; and that character, so far from being too religious or too spiritual, is just the reverse, very like the world's; that religion is a sacred, awful, mysterious, solemn matter; that it should be approached with fear, and named, as it were, *sotto voce*; whereas Catholics, whether in the North or the South, in the Middle Ages or in modern times, exhibit the combined and contrary faults of profaneness and superstition. There is a bold, shallow, hard, indelicate way among them of speaking of even points of

---

[5] *... shall be disclosed*: Cf. "Therefore judge nothing before the time, until the Lord come, who both will bring to light the hidden things of darkness, and will make manifest the counsels of the hearts, and then shall every man have praise of God." 1 Corinthians, 4:5.

[6] *against their joining her*: See Editor's Introduction.

faith, which is, to use studiously mild language, utterly out of taste, and indescribably offensive to any person of ordinary refinement.[7] They are rude where they should be reverent, jocose where they should be grave, and loquacious where they should be silent. The most sacred feelings, the most august doctrines, are glibly enunciated in the shape of some short and smart theological formula; purgatory, hell, and the evil spirit, are a sort of household words upon their tongue; the most solemn duties, such as confession, or saying office, whether as spoken of or as performed, have a business-like air and a mechanical action about them, quite inconsistent with their real nature.[8] Religion is made both

---

[7] *... ordinary refinement*: Cf. "... you must consider the usual lightness of Catholic conversation as contrasted with what serious Protestants may think allowable." Newman to T. F. Knox (5 January 1851), *LD*, xiv, 190.

[8] *their real nature*: Cf., Ian Ker on Evelyn Waugh's treatment of Catholicism's "businesslike matter-of-factness," I. Ker, *The Catholic Revival in English Literature 1848-1961* (Notre Dame, 2003), 169, 183, 191-93, 195-98, 202, 205. See also the description of the businesslike quality of Milan Cathedral that Newman sent to his friend Henry Wilberforce. "I have said not a word about that overpowering place, the Duomo. It has moved me more than St Peter's did — but then, I studiously abstained from all services etc. when I was at Rome, and now of course I have gone when they were going on and have entered into them. And, as I have said for months past that I never knew what worship was, as an objective fact, till I entered the Catholic Church, and was partaker in its offices of devotion, so now I say the same on the view of its cathedral assemblages. I have expressed myself so badly that I doubt if you will understand me; but a Catholic Cathedral is a sort of world every one going about his own business, but that business a religious one; groups of worshippers, and solitary ones — kneeling, standing — some at shrines, some at altars — hearing Mass and communicating — currents of worshippers intercepting and passing by each other — altar after altar lit up for worship, like stars in the firmament — or the bell giving notice of what is going on in parts you do not see — and all the while the canons in the choir going through [[their hours]] matins and lauds [[or Vespers]], and at the end of it the incense rolling up from the high altar, and all this in one of the most wonderful buildings in the world and every day — lastly, all of this without any show or effort, but what every one is used to — every one at his own work, and leaving every one else to his." Newman to H. Wilberforce (24 September 1846), *LD*, ix, 253. "[I]nstead of being something very special and removed from the ordinary, mundane world, Catholicism for all of its supernatural claims – and ever

free and easy, and yet is formal. Superstitions and false [267] miracles are at once preached, assented to, and laughed at, till one really does not know what is believed and what is not, or whether anything is believed at all. The saints are lauded, yet affronted. Take medieval England or France, or modern Belgium or Italy, it is all the same; you have your Boy-bishop at Salisbury, your Lord of Misrule at Rheims, and at Sens your Feast of Asses.[9] Whether in the South now, or in the North formerly, you have the excesses of your Carnival. Legends, such as that of St. Dunstan's fight with the author of all evil at Glastonbury,[10] are popular in

---

since... [his] Mediterranean tour it had always seemed to Newman a much more spiritual religion than that of the Church of England – seemed also, paradoxically, a far more matter-of-fact kind of 'business.' Ker, *Catholic Revival*, 20.

[9] *Feast of Asses*: Another name for the "Feast of Fools, the generic name for the New Year revels in European cathedrals and collegiate churches, when the minor clergy usurped the functions of their superiors and burlesqued the services of the Church. The practice may have arisen spontaneously, as an outlet for high spirits, or may be an echo of the Roman Saturnalia. It appears to have originated in France in about the 12th century, and from the beginning evidently included some form of crude drama. The proceedings opened with a procession headed by an elected 'king'—in schools a boy bishop—riding on a donkey, a detail which was taken over by the liturgical drama for the scenes of Balaam's Ass, the Flight into Egypt, and perhaps Christ's Entry into Jerusalem. The Feast of Fools lingered on in France until the 16th century, by which time the festivities had moved out of the church, and was eventually absorbed into the merrymaking of the *sociétés joyeuses*; but in England, where it is known to have taken place at St Paul's in London as well as at Lincoln, Beverley, and Salisbury, it died out some time in the 14th century. Part of its functions, though without the burlesque church services, survived during the Christmas season at Court and in the colleges of the universities, the 'king' being replaced by an Abbot or Lord of Misrule; at the Inns of Court in London the custom of appointing a Christmas Lord of Misrule lingered on intermittently until the 1660s." *Concise Oxford Companion to the Theatre*.

[10] *St. Dunstan's*: St. Dunstan (909-88) Benedictine monk and reformer, Archbishop of Canterbury. According to one of his hagiographers, Archbishop Dunstan had a number of encounters with the devil, in one of which he pulled the devil by the nose with his blacksmith's tongs. In later life the playwright and poet Ben Jonson kept court in the Apollo Room of the Devil and St Dunstan's Tavern near Temple Bar.

Germany, in Spain, in Scotland, and in Italy; while in Naples or in Seville your populations rise in periodical fury against the celestial patrons whom they ordinarily worship. These are but single instances of a widespread and momentous phenomenon, to which you ought not to shut your eyes, and to which we can never be reconciled;—a phenomenon in which we see a plain providential indication, that, in spite of our certainty,—first, that there *is* a Catholic Church, next, that it is *not* the religious communion dominant in England, or Russia, or Greece, or Prussia, or Holland; in short, that it *can* be nothing else *but* the communion of Rome,—still, that it is our bounden duty to have nothing to do with the Pope, the Holy See, or the Church of which it is the centre." Such is the charge, my [268] brethren, brought against the Catholic Church, both by the Evangelical section of the Establishment, and by your own.

2.

Now I will, on the whole and in substance, admit the fact to be as you have stated it; and next I will grant, that to no national differences can be attributed a character of religion so specific and peculiar. It is too uniform, too universal, to be ascribed to anything short of the genius of Catholicism itself; that is, to its principles and influence acting upon human nature, such as human nature is everywhere found. I admit both your fact and your account of the fact; I accept it, I repeat, in general terms what you have said; but I would add to it, and turn a particular fact into a philosophical truth. I say, then, that such a hard, irreverent, extravagant tone in religion, as you consider it, is the very phenomenon which must necessarily result from a revelation of divine truth falling upon the human mind in its existing state of ignorance and moral feebleness.

The wonder and offence which Protestants feel arises, in no small measure, from the fact that they hold the opinions of Protestants. They have been taught a religion, and imbibed ideas and feelings, and are suffering under disadvantages, which create the difficulty of which they complain; and, to remove it, I shall be obliged, as on some former occasions, against my will, to explain a point of [269] doctrine:—Protestants, then, consider that faith and love are inseparable; where there is faith, there, they think, are love and obedience; and in proportion to the strength and degree of the former, are the strength and degree of the latter. They do not think the inconsistency possible of really believing without obeying; and, where they see disobedience, they cannot imagine there the existence of real faith. Catholics, on the other hand, hold that faith and love, faith and obedience, faith and works, are simply separable, and ordinarily separated, in fact; that faith does not imply love, obedience, or works; that the firmest faith, so as to move mountains, may exist without love,—that is, real faith, as really faith in the strict sense of the word as the faith of a martyr or a doctor. In other words, when Catholics speak of faith they are contemplating the existence of a gift which Protestantism does not even imagine. Faith is a spiritual sight of the unseen; and since in matter of fact Protestantism does not impart this sight, does not see the unseen, has no experience of this habit, this act of the mind—therefore, since it retains the word "faith," it is obliged to find some other meaning for it; and its common, perhaps its commonest, idea is, that faith is substantially the same as obedience; at least, that it is the impulse, the motive of obedience, or the fervour and heartiness which attend good works. In a word, faith is hope or it is love, or it is a mixture of the two. Protestants define or determine faith, not by its [270] nature or essence, but by its effects. When it succeeds in producing good works, they call it real faith; when it does not, they call it counterfeit—as though we should say, a house is a house when it is inhabited; but that a house to let is not a house. If we so spoke, it would be plain that we confused between house and home, and had no correct image before our minds of a house *per se*. And in like manner, when Protestants maintain that faith is not really faith, except it be fruitful, whether they are right or wrong in saying so, anyhow it is plain that the idea of faith, as a habit in itself, as a something substantive, is simply, from the nature of the case, foreign to their minds, and that is the particular point on which I am now insisting.

Now faith, in a Catholic's creed, is a certainty of things not seen but revealed; a certainty preceded indeed in many cases by particular exercises of the intellect, as conditions, by reflection, prayer, study, argument, or the like, and ordinarily, by the instrumental sacrament of Baptism, but caused directly by a supernatural influence on the mind from above. Thus it is a spiritual sight; and the nearest parallel by which it can be illustrated is the moral sense. As nature has impressed upon our mind a faculty of recognising certain moral truths, when they are presented to us from without, so that we are quite sure that veracity, for [271] instance, benevolence, and purity, are right and good, and that their contraries involve guilt, in a somewhat similar way, grace impresses upon us inwardly that revelation which comes to us sensibly by the ear or eye; similarly, yet more vividly and distinctly, because the moral perception consists in sentiments, but the grace of faith carries the mind on to objects. This certainty, or spiritual sight, which is included in the idea of faith, is, according to Catholic teaching, perfectly distinct in its own nature from the desire, intention, and power of acting agreeably to it. As men may know perfectly well that they ought not to steal, and yet may deliberately take and appropriate what is not theirs; so may they be gifted with a simple, undoubting, cloudless belief, that, for instance, Christ is in the Blessed Sacrament, and yet commit the sacrilege of breaking open the tabernacle, and carrying off the consecrated particles for the sake of the precious vessel containing them. It is said in Scripture, that the evil spirits "believe and tremble;"[11] and reckless men, in like manner, may, in the very sight of hell, deliberately sin for the sake of some temporary gratification. Under these circumstances, even though I did

---

[11] *"believe and tremble"*: "Thou believest that there is one God; thou doest well: the devils also believe, and tremble." James 2:19

not assume the Catholic teaching on the subject of faith to be true (which in the present state of the argument I fairly may do, considering whom I am addressing), though I took it merely as an hypothesis probable and philosophical, but not proved, still I would beg you to consider whether, *as* an hypothesis, it does not serve and suffice to solve the [272] difficulty which is created in your minds by the aspect of Catholic countries. This, too, at least I may say: if it shall turn out that the aspect which Catholic countries present to the looker-on is accounted for by Catholic doctrine, at least that aspect will be no difficulty to you when once you have joined the Catholic Church, for, in joining the Church, you will be, of course, accepting the doctrine. Walk forward, then, into the Catholic Church, and the difficulty, like a phantom, will, as a matter of necessity, disappear. And now, assuming the doctrine as an hypothesis, I am going to show its bearing upon the alleged difficulty.

3.

The case with most men is this: certainly it is the case of any such large and various masses of men as constitute a nation, that they grow up more or less in practical neglect of their Maker and their duties to Him. Nature tends to irreligion and vice, and in matter of fact that tendency is developed and fulfilled in any multitude of men, according to the saying of the old Greek, that "the many are bad,"[12] or

---

[12] *"the many are bad"*: While it may have been axiomatic for the Archaic Greeks, choosing as they did to be ruled by aristocratic oligarchies, that the many, or *οἱ πολλοί*, were bad, Pericles took pride in the fact that the fifth-century Athenians were ruled by the many, not the few. "Our form of government does not enter into rivalry with the institutions of others," he declared in Thucydides' great history. "Our government does not copy that of our neighbours, but is an example to them. It is true that we are called a democracy, for the administration is in the hands of the many and not of the few. But while there exists equal justice to all and alike in their private disputes, the claim of excellence is also recognized; and when a citizen is in any way distinguished, he is preferred to the public service, not as a matter of privilege, but as the reward of merit." Thucydides, "Pericles Funeral Oration," *History of the Peloponnesian War*, bk. ii, 37.

according to the Scripture testimony, that the world is at enmity with its Creator.[13] The state of the case is not altered, when a nation has been baptized; still, in matter of fact, nature gets the better of grace, and the population falls into [273] a state of guilt and disadvantage, in one point of view worse than that from which it has been rescued. This is the matter of fact, as Scripture prophesied it should be: "Many are called, few are chosen;"[14] "the kingdom of heaven is like unto a net gathering together of every kind."[15] But still, this being granted, a Catholic people is far from being in the same state in all respects as one which is not Catholic, as theologians teach us. A soul which has received the grace of baptism receives with it the germ or faculty of all supernatural virtues whatever,—faith, hope, charity, meekness, patience, sobriety, and every other that can be named; and if it commits mortal sin, it falls out of grace, and forfeits these supernatural powers. It is no longer what it was, and is, so far, in the feeble and frightful condition of those who were never baptized. But there are certain remarkable limitations and alleviations in its punishment, and one is this: that the faculty or power of faith remains to it.[16] Of course the soul may go on to resist and destroy this

---

[13] *at enmity with its Creator*: "Ye adulterers and adulteresses, know ye not that the friendship of the world is enmity with God? whosoever therefore will be a friend of the world is the enemy of God." James 4:4. Cf., "Did I see a boy of good make and mind, with the tokens on him of a refined nature, cast upon the world without provision, unable to say whence he came, his birth-place or his family connexions, I should conclude that there was some mystery connected with his history, and that he was one, of whom, from one cause or other, his parents were ashamed. Thus only should I be able to account for the contrast between the promise and the condition of his being. And so I argue about the world;—*if* there be a God, *since* there is a God, the human race is implicated in some terrible aboriginal calamity. It is out of joint with the purposes of its Creator." *Apo*, 217-18.

[14] *"... chosen"*: Matthew 22:14.

[15] *"... kind"*: Matthew 13:47.

[16] *remains to it*: In 'A Visit to Morin' (1959), one of Graham Greene's later short stories, a lapsed Catholic novelist declares: "I can tell myself now that my lack of belief is a final proof that the Church is right and the faith is true. I had cut myself off for twenty years from grace and my

supernatural faculty also; it may, by an act of the will, rid itself of its faith, as it has stripped itself of grace and love; or it may gradually decay in its faith till it becomes simply infidel; but this is not the common state of a Catholic people. What commonly happens is this, that they fall under the temptations to vice or covetousness, which naturally and urgently beset them, but that faith is left to them. Thus the many are in a condition which is absolutely novel and strange in the ideas of a Protestant; they have a vivid [274] perception, like sense, of things unseen, yet have no desire at all, or affection, towards them; they have knowledge without love. Such is the state of the many; the Church at the same time is ever labouring with all her might to bring them back again to their Maker; and in fact is ever bringing back vast multitudes one by one, though one by one they are ever relapsing from her. The necessity of yearly confession, the Easter communion, the stated seasons of indulgence, the high festivals, Lent, days of obligation, with their Masses and preaching,—these ordinary and routine observances and the extraordinary methods of retreats, missions, jubilees, and the like, are the means by which the powers of the world unseen are ever acting upon the corrupt mass, of which a nation is composed, and breaking up and reversing the dreadful phenomenon which fact and Scripture conspire to place before us.[17]

---

belief withered as the priests said it would. I don't believe in God and His Son and His angels and His saints, but I know the reason why I don't believe and the reason is—the Church is true and what she taught me is true. For twenty years I have been without the sacraments and I can see the effect. The wafer must be more than wafer." Greene's faith has been disputed by many critics skeptical of his belief, but this is hardly the writing of someone whose faith was factitious. As Samuel Johnson once observed: "… he that is most deficient in the duties of life, makes some atonement for his faults, if he warns others against his own failings, and hinders, by the salubrity of his admonitions, the contagion of his example." Samuel Johnson, *The Rambler* ed. Bate and Strauss, *The Yale Edition of the Works of Samuel Johnson* (Yale, 1969), iii, 76.

[17] … *before us*: Cf. "A good man, of a timorous disposition, in great doubt of his acceptance with God, and pretty credulous, might be glad to be of a church where there are so many helps to get to Heaven. I would

Nor is this all: good and bad are mixed together, and the good is ever influencing and mitigating the bad. In the same family one or two holy souls may shed a light around and raise the religious tone of the rest. In large and profligate towns there will be planted here and there communities of religious men and women, whose example, whose appearance, whose churches, whose ceremonies, whose devotions,—to say nothing of their sacerdotal functions, or their charitable ministrations,—will ever be counteracting [275] the intensity of the poison. Again, you will have vast multitudes neither good nor bad; you will have many scandals; you will have, it may be, particular monasteries in a state of relaxation; rich communities breaking their rule and living in comfort and refinement, and individuals among them lapsing into sin; cathedrals sheltering a host of officials, many of whom are a dishonour to the sacred place; and in country districts, priests who set a bad example to their flock, and are the cause of anxiety and grief to their bishops. And besides, you will have all sorts of dispositions and intellects, as plentiful of course as in a Protestant land: there are the weak and the strong-minded, the sharp and the dull, the passionate and the phlegmatic, the generous and the selfish, the idle, the proud, the sceptical, the dry-minded, the scheming, the enthusiastic, the self-conceited, the strange, the eccentric; all of whom grace leaves more or less in their respective natural cast or tendency of mind. Thus we have before us a confused and motley scene, such as the world presents generally; good and evil mingled together in all conceivable measures of combination and varieties of result; a perpetual vicissitude; the prospect brightening and then overcast again; luminous spots, tracts of splendour, patches of darkness, twilight regions, and the glimmer of day; but in spite of this moral confusion, in one and all a clear intellectual apprehension of the truth.

---

be a Papist if I could. I have fear enough; bur an obstinate rationality prevents me." Samuel Johnson quoted in Boswell, *Life of Johnson*, iv, 289.

Perhaps you will say that this conflict of good and evil is [276] to be seen in a Protestant country in just the same way: that is not the point; but this,—that, in a Catholic country, on the mixed multitude, and on each of them, good or bad, is written, is stamped deep, this same wonderful *knowledge*. Just as in England, the whole community, whatever the moral state of the individuals, *knows* about railroads and electric telegraphs; and about the Court, and men in power, and proceedings in Parliament; and about religious controversies, and about foreign affairs, and about all that is going on around and beyond them: so, in a Catholic country, the ideas of heaven and hell, Christ and the evil spirit, saints, angels, souls in purgatory, grace, the Blessed Sacrament, the sacrifice of the Mass, absolution, indulgences, the virtue of relics, of holy images, of holy water, and of other holy things, are of the nature of *facts*, which all men, good and bad, young and old, rich and poor, take for granted. They are facts brought home to them by faith; substantially the same to all, though coloured by their respective minds, according as they are religious or not, and according to the degree of their religion. Religious men use them well, the irreligious use them ill, the inconsistent vary in their use of them, but all use them. As the idea of God is before the minds of all men in a community not Catholic, so, but more vividly, these revealed ideas confront the minds of a Catholic people, whatever be the moral state of that people, taken one by one. They are facts attested by each to all, and by all to each, common property, primary [277] points of thought, and landmarks, as it were, upon the territory of knowledge.

4.

Now, it being considered, that a vast number of sacred truths are taken for granted as *facts* by a Catholic nation, in the same sense as the sun in the heavens is a fact, you will see how many things take place of necessity, which to Protestants seem shocking, and which could not be avoided, unless it had been promised that the Church should consist of none but the predestinate; nay, unless it consisted of none

307

but the educated and refined. It is the spectacle of supernatural faith acting upon the multitudinous mind of a people; of a divine principle dwelling in that myriad of characters, good, bad, and intermediate, into which the old stock of Adam grafted into Christ has developed. If a man sins grossly in a Protestant country, he is at once exposed to the temptation of unbelief; and he is irritated when he is threatened with judgment to come. He is threatened, not with what to him is a fact, but with what to him is at best an opinion. He has power over that opinion; he holds it today, whether he shall hold it tomorrow he cannot exactly say; it depends on circumstances. And, being an opinion, no one has a right to assume that it is anything more, or to thrust it upon him, and to threaten him with it. This is what is to him

[278] so provoking and irritating. Protestants hold that there is a hell, as the conclusion of a syllogism; they prove it from Scripture; it is from first to last a point of controversy, and an opinion, and must not be taken for granted as immutable. A vicious man is angry with those who hold opinions condemnatory of himself, because those opinions are the creation of the holders, and seem to reflect personally upon him. Nothing is so irritating to others as my own private judgment. But men are not commonly irritated by facts; it would be irrational to be so, as it is in children who beat the ground when they fall down. A bad Catholic does not deny hell, for it is to him an incontestable fact, brought home to him by that supernatural faith, with which he assents to the Divine Word speaking through Holy Church; he is not angry with others for holding it, for it is no private decision of their own. He may indeed despair, and then he blasphemes; but, generally speaking, he will retain hope as well as faith, when he has lost charity. Accordingly, he neither complains of God nor of man. His thoughts will take a different turn; he seeks to evade the difficulty; he looks up to our Blessed Lady; he knows by supernatural faith her power and her goodness; he turns the truth to his own purpose, his bad purpose; and he makes her his patroness and protectress against the penalty of sins which he does not

308

mean to abandon. Such, I say, is the natural effect of having faith and hope without the saving grace of divine love.

Hence, the strange stories of highwaymen and brigands [279] devout to the Madonna. And, their wishes leading to the belief, they begin to circulate stories of her much-coveted compassion towards impenitent offenders; and these stories, fostered by the circumstances of the day, and confused with others similar but not impossible, for a time are in repute. Thus, the Blessed Virgin has been reported to deliver the reprobate from hell, and to transfer them to purgatory; and absolutely to secure from perdition all who are devout to her, repentance not being contemplated as the means. Or men have thought, by means of some sacred relic, to be secured from death in their perilous and guilty expeditions. So, in the middle ages, great men could not go out to hunt without hearing Mass, but were content that the priest should mutilate it and worse, to bring it within limits. Similar phenomena occur in the history of chivalry: the tournaments were held in defiance of the excommunications of the Church, yet were conducted with a show of devotion; ordeals, again, were even religious rites, yet in like manner undergone in the face of the Church's prohibition. We know the dissolute character of the medieval knights and of the troubadours; yet, that dissoluteness, which would lead Protestant poets and travellers to scoff at religion, led them, not to deny revealed truth, but to combine it with their own wild and extravagant profession. The knight swore before Almighty God, His Blessed Mother, and—the ladies; the [280] troubadour[18] offered tapers, and paid for Masses, for his

---

[18] *troubadour*: The troubadours were "poets composing in Occitan (a Romance language spoken in southern France and parts of Italy and Spain) during the 12th and early 13th centuries (and perhaps earlier). They were famous for the complexity of their verse forms, and for the conception of courtly love which their poems to a great extent founded. Guilhem IX (1071–1126), count of Poitou and duke of Aquitaine, is the first known troubadour; Jaufre Rudel (fl.1125–48) developed the theme of 'amor de lonh', love from afar. The most celebrated troubadour love poets are Bernart de Ventadorn (*fl.* 1147–70), Raimbaut d'Aurenga (c.1143–73), Guiraut de Bornelh (c.1165–1212), and Arnaut Daniel (*fl.*

success in some lawless attachment; and the object of it, in turn, painted her votary under the figure of some saint. Just as a heathen phraseology is now in esteem, and "the altar of hymen"[19] is spoken of, and the trump of fame, and the trident of Britannia,[20] and a royal cradle is ornamented with figures of Nox[21] and Somnus;[22] so in a Catholic age or country, the Blessed Saints will be invoked by virtuous and vicious in every undertaking, and will have their place in

---

1180–1200), later admired by Dante and Petrarch, and Ezra Pound. The troubadours flourished in the courts of Spain, Italy, and northern France, as well as in the south of France, and courtly poetry was being written and cultivated in Italy in the later 13th century (see Robert Browning's *Sordello*) when it was disappearing in the Midi. Through their influence on the northern French poets (such as Chrétien de Troyes, and the writers of the Roman de la Rose) and on the German poets (notably the Minnesänger) they had a major effect on the development of European lyric poetry. Love was their major but not their only subject; they also composed moralizing, satirical, and political poems called sirventes (of which Guiraut de Bornelh was the recognized master), and military poems in which Bertran de Born (c.1140–c.1215) excelled. See A. R. Press (ed. and trans.), *Anthology of Troubadour Lyric Poetry* (1971: parallel text); L. T. Topsfield, *Troubadours and Love* (1975)." *Oxford Companion to English Literature*. If the troubadours were inescapably influenced by the Catholic culture in which they moved, Catholics were also influenced by the troubadours. St. Francis is perhaps the most notable example. "His era saw a growing interest in the observation and artistic depiction of nature. He was deeply impressed by the ideal of chivalry and he loved a number of popular French troubadour songs and poems that praised both knightly virtue and the beauty of nature. He came to refer to his friars as "God's troubadours." He may well have heard stories of the lives of Irish saints which commonly depicted even animals as recognizing a saint's gentleness and authority. Francis' decision to become a wandering preacher and frequent hermit meant that he had close and sustained contact with nature and animals." *The Encyclopaedia of Religion and Nature* ed. B. Taylor.

[19] *Hymen*: Hymen is the Greek god of marriage.
[20] *Britannia*: The personification of Britain, usually depicted as a helmeted woman with a shield and trident. The patriotic song 'Rule, Britannia' is from *Alfred: A Masque* (1740), attributed to the Scottish poet James Thomson (1700–48). The trident Britannia holds is an attribute of the sea god Poseidon or Neptune: from this origin it has come to be seen as a symbol of sovereignty over the seas.
[21] *Nox*: the Roman god of night.
[22] *Somnus*: the Roman god of sleep.

every room, whether of palace or of cottage. Vice does not involve a neglect of the external duties of religion. The Crusaders had faith sufficient to bind them to a perilous pilgrimage and warfare; they kept the Friday's abstinence, and planted the tents of their mistresses within the shadow of the pavilion of the glorious St. Louis.[23] There are other pilgrimages besides military ones, and other religious journeys besides the march on Jerusalem; but the character of all of them is pretty much the same, as St. Jerome[24] and

---

[23] *glorious St. Louis*: Louis IX, (1214–70), King of France. "In his austere and prayerful private life, with its close links with the Franciscan and Dominican Orders, his energy, his determination that every man should have his due, and the paramount consideration which he gave to the defence of the Holy Land, Louis embodied the highest ideals of medieval kingship. He reformed the administration of France, frequently meting out justice himself. He built the Sainte-Chapelle in Paris (c. 1245–8) for the Crown of Thorns which he had acquired from the Latin Emperor of Constantinople, Baldwin II, in 1239; he endowed various religious houses and supported the theological college founded by Robert de Sorbon in 1257. He was canonized by Boniface VIII in 1297. Feast day, 25 Aug." *ODCC*.

[24] *St. Jerome*: Jerome (Hieronymus) (c. 341–420), monk and Doctor of the Church. Born at Strido, near Aquileia, in Dalmatia, Jerome had an excellent grounding in rhetoric, his mastery of which distinguishes all of his writing. His fondness for pilgrimages led him to visit the churches and especially the catacombs of Rome. He was baptized some time before 366. "He travelled in Gaul, Dalmatia, and Italy. While at Trier he decided to become a monk; this he did with like-minded friends in Aquileia until, after a quarrel caused by some real or supposed scandal, Jerome left for Palestine. He reached Antioch in 374: two of his companions died, Jerome too was seriously ill. In this state he dreamt that he appeared before God's judgement-seat and was condemned for being a Ciceronian rather than a Christian. For several years he took this experience very seriously. He became a hermit in the desert of Chalcis in Syria for five years, gave up the classics he knew and loved so well, and learnt Hebrew instead to study Scripture in its original language. Already he had learnt Greek, so that, with his mastery of style and rhetoric, he was equipped for his future achievements as writer and translator. Unfortunately Jerome also had a difficult, cantankerous temperament and a sarcastic wit which made him enemies. After being ordained priest in Antioch, although he had no wish for orders and in fact never said Mass, he studied in Constantinople under Gregory of Nazianzus; no doubt Jerome found himself more at home in the sophisticated capital than

among the rustic Syrian monks. ... [In Rome], he produced other scriptural *opuscula*, mainly translations. He then embarked on the enormous task of producing a standard Latin text of the Bible, revised according to the meaning of the original texts, but not, apparently, an entirely new translation. He began on the Gospels and the Psalter; eventually he produced all, or nearly all, the Bible in what was later called the Vulgate version. He also wrote a number of influential commentaries on particular books such as the Prophets and the Epistles; that on Matthew's Gospel became a standard work. His stay in Rome lasted only three years, but during it he became the guide of a group of dedicated Christian ladies, Paula, Marcella, Eustochium, and others, most of whom had been living a semi-monastic life in their widowhood. He gave them much help in their study of Scripture and in their pursuit of a more perfect Christian life apart from the worldly conditions of Rome. ... He left Rome in 385 ... [resolving] to start again, this time at Bethlehem, where Paula established a convent of nuns and Jerome one of monks. There he spent the rest of his life, teaching, writing, and studying. The causes for which he fought were three: the provision of as accurate a text as possible of the Bible through recourse to the original languages and previous translations. The biblical text should be illuminated by sound exegesis. Monastic life should be based on a systematic *lectio divina*, a prayerful but serious study of Scripture and the Fathers. This life is derived from the Counsels of the Gospel and Paul; it finds its best exemplar in the life of the Virgin Mary, especially in her perpetual virginity. In the welter of conflicting theological opinions of his time he believed the See of Rome was the surest guide. His achievement as scholar and controversialist was somewhat marred by his quarrel with his old friend Rufinus. But his immense learning was unmatched by other Christian writers except Augustine, while his passionate devotion and the asceticism which he believed necessary in the following of Christ are manifest. His works in favour of Christian monasticism such as the Lives of Paul of Thebes, Hilarion, and Malchus, and the works against Jovinian were especially influential. His Letters, for both style and content, are reckoned to be the finest of Christian antiquity." *Oxford Dictionary of Saints.* When Dupanloup, the Bishop of Orleans suggested in 1868 that Newman accompany him to the First Vatican Council, Newman wrote their mutual friend William Monsell, later 1st baron Emly: "Now as to the most gracious intention of Mgr Dupanloup, which is the occasion of your letter, I cannot sufficiently thank him. His act is one of a noble independent Bishop, who dares do what he thinks right. Alas, it is an act to which very few of our English Bishops (I except Dr Clifford) would have the spirit to venture on. But I can't accept it — and don't let him propose it to me. *I am too old for it* ... Take a single view of it — I think the Roman diet would most seriously compromise my health. ... Then again there are men, and some of them have been Saints, whose vocation

St. Gregory Nyssen[25] bear witness in the first age of the Church. It is a mixed multitude, some members of it most holy, perhaps even saints; others penitent sinners; but others, again, a mixture of pilgrim and beggar, or pilgrim and robber, or half gipsy, or three-quarters boon companion, or at least, with nothing saintly, and little religious about them. They will let you wash their feet, and serve them at table, and the hosts have more merit for their ministry than [281] the guests for their wayfaring. Yet, one and all, saints and sinners, have faith in things invisible, which each uses in his own way.

5.

Listen to their conversation; listen to the conversation of any multitude of them or any private party: what strange oaths mingle with it! God's heart, and God's eyes, and God's wounds, and God's blood: you cry out, "How profane!" Doubtless; but do you not see, that their special profaneness over Protestant oaths, lies, not in the words, but simply in the speaker, and is the necessary result of that insight into the invisible world, which you have not? You use the vague words "Providence," or "the Deity," or "good-luck," or "nature:" you would use more sacred words did you believe in the things denoted by them: Catholics, on the contrary, whether now or of old, realise the Creator in His supernatural works and personal manifestations, and

---

does not lie in such ecclesiastical gatherings. St Gregory Nazianzen, and St Chrysostom, not to say St Basil, are instances. And I suspect, also St Jerome. I am their disciple. I am too old to learn the ways of other great Saints, as St Athanasius, St Augustine, and St Ambrose, whom I admire, but cannot run with. They are race-horses — I am a broken-kneed poney." *LD*, xxiii, 396.

[25] *St. Gregory Nyssen*: St. Gregory of Nyssa (c. 350 – c. 395), Bishop. The younger brother of Basil, he took a prominent part in the Council of Constantinople (381) and was instrumental in making the thought of Origen better known. His writings against Arian and in defense of Nicea are some of his most forceful. "All [Gregory's] thought is integrated and directed to show the way by which the mind can ascend to God. And that path of individual spiritual progress is not shown in isolation from the sacramental life of the church, but rather as one and the same with it." *The Saints: A Concise Biographical Dictionary.*

speak of the "Sacred Heart,"[26] or of "the Mother of mercies,"[27] or of "our Lady of Walsingham,"[28] or of "St.

---

[26] *Sacred Heart*: The Solemnity of the Sacred Heart of Jesus is celebrated in the Roman Catholic Church on the first Friday after Corpus Christi. Devotion to the wounded heart of Jesus goes back to the 11th century when Christians began meditating on the Five Wounds of Christ. In 1670, the French priest, Fr. Jean Eudes celebrated the first Feast of the Sacred Heart. At the same time, Margaret Mary Alacoque (1647-90) began to report her visions of Jesus Christ. In 1675, she received her 'great apparition,' in which Jesus asked that the Feast of the Sacred Heart be celebrated each year: he wished to have His love and mercy and goodness better known to the world. After St. Margaret Mary's death in 1690, the devotion grew. Once the apparition was approved, the feast was instituted in 1765. On May 8, 1873, the devotion was formally approved by Pope Pius IX; and on July 21, 1899 Pope Leo XIII recommended that all bishops throughout the world observe the feast in their dioceses. "Since there is in the Sacred Heart a symbol and a sensible image of the infinite love of Jesus Christ which moves us to love one another," Leo wrote in his encyclical *Annum Sacrum* (1899), "therefore is it fit and proper that we should consecrate ourselves to His most Sacred Heart – an act which is nothing else than an offering and a binding of oneself to Jesus Christ, seeing that whatever honour, veneration and love is given to this divine Heart is really and truly given to Christ Himself." The first person in England to petition the Holy See for the institution of the feast was Queen Mary, consort of King James II.

[27] *"Mother of Mercies"*: Newman encountered prayers to the 'Mother of Mercy' in his reading of St. Alphonse Liguori (1696-1787), which he began in November, 1842, under the guidance of Father Charles Russell, an Irish professor at Maynooth, whom Newman thought "had, perhaps, more to do with my conversion than anyone else." *Apo*, 176. Although Newman recognized how the ardour of Liguori's devotion to Mary might lead others to 'Mariolatry,' he had his own devotion to Mary deepened by reading the Doctor of the Church. Here is one of Liguori's prayers to the 'Mother of Mercy:' "HAIL most compassionate Mother of Mercy; hail consolation and pardon, Mary most desired. Who shall not love thee? Thou our light in doubt, our consolation in sorrow, our relief in distress, our refuge in perils and temptations, thou, after thy only-begotten Son, art our secure salvation. Blessed are those who love thee, O Lady. Incline, I pray thee, thy ear of mercy to the prayers of this thy servant, this miserable sinner, and dissipate the darkness of my vices by the rays of thy sanctity, that I may please thee." St Alphonse Liguori, *The Glories of Mary*, (New York, 1862), 782. The first work Newman published as a Catholic priest was *Discourses Addressed to Mixed Congregations* (1849), one of the sermons of which, "The Glories of Mary for the Sake of her Son" was modelled after Liguori's impassioned rhetoric.

George, for merry England," or of loving "St. Francis,"[29] or of dear "St. Philip."[30] Your people would be as varied and

---

[28] *Walsingham*: "In the 13th and 14th centuries Lady Chapels were built in cathedral, abbey, and other churches, often but not invariably at the east end. Frequently these were structures of considerable importance and beauty, as at Winchester, Ely, Long Melford, and elsewhere. In very many churches there were shrines of the Blessed Virgin with a statue or painting of her as at Caversham (Oxon.), Westminster, Willesden, Aylesford (Kent), Cardigan, Eynsham, King's Lynn, and elsewhere. Some of these have been revived in modern times, as has England's principal place of Marian pilgrimage, Walsingham (Norfolk). Here was built a replica of what was believed to be the Holy House of Nazareth as early as the 11th century." *Oxford Dictionary of Saints*.

[29] *"St. Francis"*: St. Francis of Assisi (1181-1226), Founder of the Franciscan order, missionary, and poet whose work transformed Christendom. Converted to Christ in his 20s, he forswore the dandyism of his rich, merchant father, and embraced poverty, sanctity and the life of an itinerant preacher. Attracting many disciples, he continued to dedicate himself to the poor and sick. In 1210 the Franciscan way of life won approval from Innocent III, and was confirmed by Honorius III in 1223. Francis preached in Central Italy, and evangelized Muslims in Syria (1212), Morocco (1213–14), and Egypt (1219). Towards the end of his life, he gave voice to his affinity with all creation in his 'Cantico di frate sole', a milestone of Italian literature. He received the stigmata in 1224. He was canonized in 1228. Of the great saint, G. K. Chesterton observed: "St. Francis had a curious and almost uncanny attraction for the Victorians; for the nineteenth century English who seemed superficially to be most complacent about their commerce and their common sense. Not only a rather complacent Englishman like Matthew Arnold, but even the English Liberals whom he criticised for their complacency, began slowly to discover the mystery of the Middle Ages through the strange story told in feathers and flames in the hagiographical pictures of Giotto. There was something in the story of St. Francis that pierced through all those English qualities which are most famous and fatuous, to all those English qualities which are most hidden and human: the secret softness of heart; the poetical vagueness of mind; the love of landscape and of animals. St. Francis of Assisi was the only medieval Catholic who really became popular in England on his own merits. It was largely because of a subconscious feeling that the modern world had neglected those particular merits. The English middle classes found their only missionary in the figure, which of all types in the world they most despised; an Italian beggar." G.K. Chesterton, *Saint Francis of Assisi* (1923), *The Collected Works of G.K. Chesterton* (San Francisco, 1986), ii, 424-5.

[30] '*St. Philip*:' St. Philip Neri (1515–95), Founder of the Oratory and Newman's patron saint. The son of a Florentine notary, Francesco Neri

lost his mother in childhood, though he was brought up lovingly by his stepmother. He was educated in Florence by the Dominicans of San Marco, who also educated Savonarola. Newman compared the two in his sermon, "The Mission of St. Philip" (1850). Savonarola was a holy but censorious man, who could not abide extravagance; Philip, by contrast, "bore with every outside extravagance in those he addressed, so far as it was not directly sinful, knowing well that if the heart was once set right, the appropriate demeanor would follow." *OS*, 236. After leaving school, St. Philip took a job in a firm run by his uncle, who planned to make him his heir. But in 1533 after experiencing a deep conversion, he left the firm and went to Rome, living austerely in a garret, studying philosophy and theology, and paying his rent by giving lessons to his landlord's two sons. He then commenced evangelist, speaking of the faith with bankers and shopkeepers, who were charmed by the faithful young man. He thence gathered converts around him and urged them to join him in visiting churches and caring for the sick. A man of constant prayer, he would sometimes spend the evening in the catacombs or in a church. In 1544 he had a vision in which a ball of fire entered his mouth and enlarged his heart. After his death, the physical effects of this miracle were verified. In 1548 he founded a confraternity to look after the many pilgrims who traveled to Rome, as well as indigent convalescents. In 1551 he was ordained priest and went to live among a community of priests at San Girolamo della Carita. Unlike Savonarola, a fiery preacher, St. Philip, as Newman wrote, "had no vocation, and little affection for the pulpit; he was jealous of what the world calls eloquence." *OS*, 237. Throughout his apostolate, he made the confessional central to his vocation, convinced, as Newman was convinced, that one could only cure souls whom one truly knew. As a result of his solicitude for penitents, St. Philip knew the hearts of his parishioners with an unearthly clairvoyance. Among the people of Rome, it became axiomatic that "St. Philip draws souls as the magnet draws iron." *OS*, 237. Baronius, the great church historian and Palestrina, the great master of polyphony were among St. Philip's friends. Inspired by Francis Xavier, he contemplated going abroad and becoming a missionary, until a wise Cistercian counseled him to make Rome his Indies; and ever afterwards he was known as the 'Apostle of Rome.' Indeed, his Roman apostolate proved so fruitful that it developed into the Congregation of the Oratory. From an oratory over the nave of S. Girolamo, Philip and his priests would call the faithful to prayer by ringing a small bell. In "The Mission of St. Philip," Newman writes: "An earnest enforcement of interior religion, a jealousy of formal ceremonies, an insisting on obedience rather than sacrifice, on mental discipline rather than fasting or hair-shirt, a mortification of the reason, that illumination and freedom of spirit which comes of love; further, a mild and tender rule for the Confessional; frequent confessions, frequent communions, special devotion towards the Blessed Sacrament, these are

fertile in their adjurations and invocations as a Catholic populace, if they had as rich a creed. Again, listen how freely the name of the evil spirit issues from the mouth even of the better sort of men. What is meant by this very off-hand mention of the most horrible object in creation, of one [282] who, if allowed, could reduce us to ashes by the very hideousness of his countenance, or the odour of his breath? Well, I suppose they act upon the advice of the great St. Anthony;[31] he, in the lonely wilderness, had conflicts enough with the enemy, and he has given us the result of his

---

peculiarities of a particular school in the Church, and St. Ignatius and St. Philip are Masters in it." *OS*, 228. Of the devotion shown the saint after his death, Newman writes: "And when he died, a continued stream of people... came to see his body, during the two days that it remained in the church, kissing his bier, touching him with their rosaries or their rings, or taking away portions of his hair, or the flowers which were strewed over him; and, among the crowd, persons of every rank and condition were heard lamenting and extolling one who was so lowly, yet so great; who had been so variously endowed, and had been the pupil of so many saintly masters; who had the breadth of view of St. Dominic, the poetry of St. Benedict, the wisdom of St. Ignatius, and all recommended by an unassuming grace and a winning tenderness which were his own." *OS*, 240.

[31] *St. Anthony*: St Anthony of Padua (1188/95–1231), Preacher and Wonder Worker. Born in Lisbon, he was a canon regular before becoming a Friar Minor. Moved by Franciscan martyrs in Morocco, he resolved to go to Africa to preach, though he became ill and had to return. On his way back, Anthony landed in Italy, where he joined in the Franciscan general chapter of 1221 in Assisi and then went to Romagna. There Anthony revealed not only his considerable learning but his brilliant oratorical skills. Later, he preached against heresy and taught theology in Bologna. After teaching in France between 1224 and 1227, Anthony was elected the minister provincial of Lombardy. In this position, he continued his preaching, collected in his *Sermones*, and went to Padua for the first time. In 1230 he left the provincial appointment and joined the delegation to Pope Gregory IX that discussed the Franciscan Rule. Returning to Padua, he preached against usury and aided insolvent debtors. There he died at the age of thirty-six in 1231. Anthony was canonized in 1232 by Gregory IX and declared a Doctor of the Church in 1946 in recognition of his profound learning. In his sermons, St. Anthony compares the Lord to the Good Shepherd and the Devil to the wolf, whom the very presence of the Lord causes to flee. St. Anthony's "far-famed biographer" was Saint Bonaventure.

long experience. In the sermon which his far-famed biographer puts into his mouth, he teaches his hearers that the devil and his host are not to be feared by those who are within the fold, for the Good Shepherd has put the wolf to flight. Henceforth, the evil spirit could do no more than frighten them with empty noises (except by some particular permission of God), and could only pretend to do what was now really beyond his power. The experience of a saint, I suppose, is imprudently acted on by sinners; not as if Satan's malice were not equal to any assault upon body or soul; but faith accepts the word that his rule over the earth is now broken, and that any child or peasant may ordinarily make sport of him and put him to ridiculous flight by the use of the "Hail Mary!" or holy water, or the sign of the cross.

Once more, listen to the stories, songs, and ballads of the populace; their rude and boisterous merriment still runs upon the great invisible subjects which possess their imagination. Their ideas, of whatever sort, good, bad, and [283] indifferent, rise out of the next world. Hence, if they would have plays, the subjects are sacred; if they would have games and sports, these fall, as it were, into procession, and are formed upon the model of sacred rites and sacred persons. If they sing and jest, the Madonna and the Bambino, or St. Joseph,[32] or St. Peter,[33] or some other saint,

---

[32] *St. Joseph*: Foster-father of Christ and husband of the Blessed Virgin Mary, who died in the first century. See Matthew 1-2 and 13:55; Luke 1-2 and 4:22. St Joseph is the patron saint of fathers, families, children, manual workers (especially carpenters), and a happy death. For Newman's understanding of what such a happy death might look like, see *Diff*, i, 292-4.

[33] *St. Peter*: St. Peter, Apostle (d. c. 64), First pope. "Originally named Symeon, or Simon in Greek, he was a native of Bethsaida, a village on the Sea of Galilee, son of Jonas (Matt. 16: 17), and with his brother Andrew was a fisherman. When Jesus began his mission Simon was married and living at Capernaum with his mother-in-law and Andrew (Mark 1: 29 f.). According to the Synoptic Gospels, it was by the Sea of Galilee that Jesus summoned the two brothers, with James and John, to follow him. St John's Gospel, which places the call in Judaea (1: 37 ff.), represents the earliest disciples, including Simon, as having previously

is introduced, not for irreverence, but because these are the ideas that absorb them. There is a festival in the streets; you look about: what is it you see? What would be impossible here in London. Set up a large Crucifix at Charing Cross; the police would think you simply insane. Insane, and truly: but why? why dare you not do it? why must you not? Because you are averse to the sacred sign? Not so; you have it in your chamber, yet a Catholic would not dare to do so, more than another. It is true that awful, touching, winning Form has before now converted the very savage who gazed upon it; he has wondered, has asked what it meant, has broken into tears, and been converted ere he knew that he

---

been disciples of John the Baptist. All four Gospels agree, with minor differences of emphasis, that from now onwards Simon was leader and spokesman of the group, recognized as such by the Lord. He is mentioned with conspicuous frequency, appears first in all lists of the Twelve, and belonged to the inner group present at such significant events as the raising of Jairus' daughter (Matt. 9: 18–26), the Transfiguration (Matt. 17: 1–8), and the Agony in the Garden (Matt. 26: 37). According to Matt. 16: 13–20, when Jesus asked the disciples whom they took him to be, Simon answered for them all that he was the Messiah, the Son of the living God; in reply Jesus pronounced him blessed because of this inspired insight, bestowed on him the Aramaic name Cephas (= 'rock'), rendered Peter in Greek, and declared that he would build his indestructible church on 'this rock', and would give him 'the keys of the kingdom of heaven' and the powers of 'binding and loosing'. At the Last Supper Jesus charged him to strengthen his brothers (Luke 22: 32). Warm-hearted and impetuous, he was rebuked by Jesus because, after confessing his messiahship, he refused to accept the necessity of his rejection and death (Mark 8: 31–3, etc.); when Jesus was arrested his courage failed, and he thrice denied knowing him (Matt. 26: 69–75, etc.). Nevertheless he was the first disciple to enter the empty tomb (Luke 24: 12), and the first to whom the risen Lord showed himself (Luke 24: 34; 1 Cor. 15: 5). In a later appearance, recorded only by St John (21: 15–17), Peter three times received from the Lord the pastoral charge to feed, i.e. be shepherd of, his sheep. ... Ignatius assumed that Peter and Paul wielded special authority over the Roman church, while Irenaeus claimed that they jointly founded it and inaugurated its succession of bishops. ... They were both executed, according to the historian Eusebius (*c.* 260–*c.* 340), in Nero's reign (54–68), probably in the persecution of 64. Tertullian (*c.* 160–*c.* 225) reports that Peter was crucified, a fact already known to the fourth Gospel (John 21: 18 f.)." *Oxford Dictionary of Popes.*

believed. The manifestation of love has been the incentive
to faith. I cannot certainly predict what would take place, if
a saint appealed to the guilty consciences of those thousand
passers-by, through the instrumentality of the Divine Sign.
But such occurrences are not of every day; what you would
too securely and confidently foretell, my brethren, were
such an exhibition made, would be, that it would but excite
[284] the scorn, the rage, the blasphemy, of the out-pouring
flocking multitude, a multitude who in their hearts are
unbelievers. Alas! there is no idea in the national mind,
supernaturally implanted, which the Crucifix embodies. Let
a Catholic mob be as profligate in conduct as an English,
still it cannot withstand, it cannot disown, it can but worship
the Crucifix; it is the external representation of a fact, of
which one and all are conscious to themselves and to each
other. And hence, I say, in their fairs and places of
amusement, in the booths, upon the stalls, upon the doors of
wine-shops, will be paintings of the Blessed Virgin, or St.
Michael, or the souls in purgatory, or of some Scripture
subject. Innocence, guilt, and what is between the two, all
range themselves under the same banners; for even the
resorts of sin will be made doubly frightful by the
blasphemous introduction of some sainted patron.

6.

You enter into one of the churches close upon the scene
of festivity, and you turn your eyes towards a confessional.
The penitents are crowding for admission, and they seem to
have no shame, or solemnity, or reserve about the errand on
which they are come; till at length, on a penitent's turning
from the grate, one tall woman, bolder than a score of men,
darts forward from a distance into the space he has vacated,
[285] to the disappointment of the many who have waited longer
than she. You almost groan under the weight of your
imagination that such a soul, so selfish, so unrecollected,
must surely be in very ill dispositions for so awful a
sacrament. You look at the priest, and he has on his face a
look almost of impatience, or of good-natured compassion,

at the voluble and superfluous matter which is the staple of her confession. The priests, you think, are no better than the people. My dear brethren, be not so uncharitable, so unphilosophical. Things we thoroughly believe, things we see, things which occur to us every day, we treat as things which *do* occur and *are* seen daily, be they of this world, or be they of the next. Even Bishop Butler should have taught you that "practical habits are strengthened by repeated acts, and passive impressions grow weaker by being repeated upon us."[34] It is not by frames of mind, it is not by emotions, that we must judge of real religion; it is the having a will and a heart set towards those things unseen; and though impatience and rudeness are to be subdued, and are faulty even in their minutest exhibitions, yet do not argue from them the absence of faith, nor yet of love, or of contrition. You turn away half satisfied, and what do you see? There is a feeble old woman, who first genuflects before the Blessed Sacrament, and then steals her neighbour's handkerchief, or prayer-book, who is intent on his devotions. Here at last, you say, is a thing absolutely indefensible and inexcusable. [286] Doubtless; but what does it prove? Does England bear no thieves? or do you think this poor creature an unbeliever? or do you exclaim against Catholicism, which has made her so profane? but why? Faith is illuminative, not operative; it does not force obedience, though it increases responsibility; it heightens guilt, it does not prevent sin; the will is the source of action, not an influence, though divine, which Baptism has implanted, and which the devil has only not eradicated. She worships and she sins; she kneels because she believes, she steals because she does not love; she may be out of God's grace, she is not altogether out of His sight.

You come out again and mix in the idle and dissipated throng, and you fall in with a man in a palmer's dress, selling false relics, and a credulous circle of customers buying them as greedily as though they were the supposed

---

[34] *"... upon us"*: Bishop Butler, *The Analogy of Religion* (1736) in *The Works of Bishop Butler* ed. David E. White (Rochester, 2006), 194.

French laces and India silks of a pedlar's basket. One simple soul has bought of him a cure for the rheumatism or ague, the use of which might form a case of conscience. It is said to be a relic of St. Cuthbert,[35] but only has virtue at sunrise, and when applied with three crosses to the head, arms, and feet. You pass on, and encounter a rude son of the Church, more like a showman than a religious, recounting to the gaping multitude[36] some tale of a vision of the invisible world, seen by Brother Augustine of the Friars Minors, or by a holy Jesuit preacher who died in the odour of sanctity, and sending round his bag to collect pence for the souls in purgatory; or of some appearance of our Lady (the like of which has really been before and since), but on no authority except popular report, and in no shape but that which popular caprice has given it. You go forward, and you find preparations in progress for a great pageant or mystery; it is a high festival, and the incorporated trades have each undertaken their special religious celebration. The plumbers and glaziers are to play the Creation; the barbers, the Call of Abraham; and at night is to be the grandest performance of all, the Resurrection and Last Judgment, played by the carpenters, masons, and blacksmiths. Heaven and hell are represented,—saints, devils, and living men; and the *chef d'ouvre* of the exhibition is the display of fireworks to be let off as the

[287]

---

[35] *St. Cuthbert*: St Cuthbert (d. 687), Bishop of Lindisfarne, whose shrine was in Durham Cathedral, was a popular saint throughout England. "He appears in an oath in *The Reeve's Tale* (I.4127), perhaps appropriately placed in the mouth of a northern clerk." *Oxford Companion to Chaucer*.

[36] *gaping multitude*: Newman was fond of this phrase and uses it elsewhere. Cf. "It does not require many words, then, to determine that, taking human nature as it is actually found, and assuming that there is an Art of life, to say that it consists, or in any essential manner is placed, in the cultivation of Knowledge, that the mind is changed by a discovery, or saved by a diversion, and can thus be amused into immortality,—that grief, anger, cowardice, self-conceit, pride, or passion, can be subdued by an examination of shells or grasses, or inhaling of gases, or chipping of rocks, or calculating the longitude, is the veriest of pretences which sophist or mountebank ever professed to a gaping auditory." J.H. Newman, "The Tamworth Reading Room" (1841), *DA*, 268.

finale. "How unutterably profane!" again you cry. Yes, profane to you, my dear brother—profane to a population which only half believes; not profane to those who, however coarse-minded, however sinful, believe wholly, who, one and all, have a vision within, which corresponds with what they see, which resolves itself into, or rather takes up into itself, the external pageant, whatever be the moral condition of each individual composing the mass. They gaze, and, in drinking in the exhibition with their eyes, they are making one continuous and intense act of faith.

You turn to go home, and, on your way, you pass [288] through a retired quarter of the city. Look up at those sacred windows; they belong to the convent of the Perpetual Adoration,[37] or to the poor Clares,[38] or to the Carmelites of the reform of St. Theresa,[39] or to the nuns of the Visitation.[40] Seclusion, silence, watching, meditation, is their life day and night. The immaculate Lamb of God is ever before the eyes of the worshippers; or at least the invisible mysteries of faith ever stand out, as if in bodily shape, before their mental gaze. Where will you find such a realised heaven upon earth? Yet that very sight has acted otherwise on the mind of a weak sister; and the very keenness of her faith and wild desire of approaching the Object of it, has led her

---

[37] *Convent of the Perpetual Adoration*: Any such convent would house nuns dedicated to the worship of the Blessed Sacrament. The dedication developed in France in the 17th century out of the Forty Hours Devotion and is now undertaken by a number of different orders of nuns in Europe and America.

[38] *Poor Clares*: Nuns of the second order of St. Francis of Assisi, founded by him and St. Clare in 1212.

[39] *Carmelites of the reform of St. Theresa*: The reform of the Carmelites of St. Theresa Avila and St. John of the Cross in the 16th century resulted in the formation of two branches of the order: the Calced or Shod Carmelites and the Discalced or Barefoot Carmelites. The former modified their original rule, as regards fasting, abstinence, and night office but they retain their mediaeval liturgy.

[40] *nuns of the Visitation*: The Order of the Visitation B.V.M, founded in 1610 by St. Francis de Sales and J. Jane Frances de Chantal. In 1856, Newman's friend and frequent correspondent Maria Giberne (1802-85) joined the Order after converting.

to fancy or to feign that she has received that singular favour vouchsafed only to a few elect souls; and she points to God's wounds, as imprinted on her hands, and feet, and side, though she herself has been instrumental in their formation.[41]

7.

In these and a thousand other ways it may be shown, that that special character of a Catholic country, which offends you, my brethren, so much, that mixture of seriousness and levity, that familiar handling of sacred things, in word and deed, by good and bad, that publication of religious thoughts and practices, so far as it is found, is the necessary [289] consequence of its being Catholic. It is the consequence of mixed multitudes all having faith; for faith impresses the mind with supernatural truths, as if it were sight, and the faith of this man, and the faith of that, is one and the same, and creates one and the same impression. The truths of religion, then, stand in the place of facts, and public ones. Sin does not obliterate the impression; and did it begin to do so in particular cases, the consistent testimony of all around would bring back the mind to itself, and prevent the incipient evil. Ordinarily speaking, once faith, always faith. Eyes once opened to good, as to evil, are not closed again; and, if men reject the truth, it is, in most cases, a question whether they have ever possessed it. It is just the reverse among a Protestant people; private judgment does but create opinions, and nothing more; and these opinions are peculiar to each individual, and different from those of any one else. Hence it leads men to keep their feelings to themselves, because the avowal of them only causes in others irritation or ridicule. Since, too, they have no certainty of the doctrines they profess, they do but feel that they *ought* to believe them, and they try to believe them, and they nurse

---

[41] *their formation*: Here, in conceding the occasional devotional excesses of the Roman Catholic faithful, while never altogether censoring them, Newman anticipated his *Letter to the Rev. E. B. Pusey* (1866), which he wrote, partly, to parry the Canon of Christ Church's charging Roman Catholicism *per se* with Mariolatry.

the offspring of their reason, as a sickly child, bringing it out of doors only on fine days. They feel very clear and quite satisfied, while they are very still; but if they turn about their head, or change their posture ever so little, the vision of the Unseen, like a mirage, is gone from them. So [290] they keep the exhibition of their faith for high days and great occasions, when it comes forth with sufficient pomp and gravity of language, and ceremonial of manner. Truths slowly totter out with Scripture texts at their elbow, as unable to walk alone. Moreover, Protestants know, if such and such things *be* true, what *ought* to be the voice, the tone, the gesture, and the carriage attendant upon them; thus reason, which is the substance of their faith, supplies also the rubrics, as I may call them, of their behaviour. This some of you, my brethren, call reverence; though I am obliged to say it is as much a mannerism, and an unpleasant mannerism, as that of the Evangelical party, which they have hitherto condemned. They condemn Catholics, because, however religious they may be, they are natural, unaffected, easy, and cheerful, in their mention of sacred things; and they think themselves never so real as when they are especially solemn.

8.

And now, my brethren, I will only observe, in conclusion, how merciful a providence it has been, that faith and love are separable, as the Catholic creed teaches. I suppose it might have been, as Luther said it is, had God so willed it—faith and love might have been so intimately one, that the abandonment of the latter was the forfeiture of the [291] former. Now, did sin not only throw the soul out of God's favour, but at once empty it of every supernatural principle, we should see in Catholics, what is, alas! so common among Protestants, souls brought back to a sense of guilt, frightened at their state, yet having no resource, and nothing to build upon. Again and again it happens, that, after committing some offence greater than usual, or being roused after a course of sin, or frightened by sickness, a Protestant wishes to repent; but what is he to fall back

upon? whither is he to go? what is he to do? He has to dig
and plant his foundation. Every step is to be learned, and all
is in the dark; he is to search and labor, and after all for an
opinion. And then, supposing him to have made some
progress, perhaps he is overcome again by temptation; he
falls, and all is undone again. His doctrinal views vanish,
and it can hardly be said that he believes anything. But the
Catholic knows just where he is and what he has to do; no
time is lost when compunction comes upon him; but, while
his feelings are fresh and keen, he can betake himself to the
appointed means of cure. He may be ever falling, but his
faith is a continual invitation and persuasive to repent. The
poor Protestant adds sin to sin, and his best aspirations
come to nothing; the Catholic wipes off his guilt again and
again; and thus, even if his repentance does not endure, and
[292] he has not strength to persevere, in a certain sense he is
never getting worse, but ever beginning afresh. Nor does the
apparent easiness of pardon operate as an encouragement to
sin, unless, indeed, repentance be easy, and the grace of
repentance to be expected, when it has already been
quenched, or unless we come to consider past repentance to
avail, when it is not persevered in.

And, above all, let death come suddenly upon him, and
let him have the preparation of a poor hour; what is the
Protestant to do? He has nothing but sights of this world
around him; wife, and children, and friends, and worldly
interests; the Catholic has these also, but the Protestant has
nought but these. He may, indeed, in particular cases, have
got firm hold of his party's view of justification or
regeneration; or it may be, he has a real apprehension of our
Lord's divinity, which comes from divine grace. But I am
speaking, not of the more serious portion of the community,
but of the popular religion; and I wish you to take a man at
random in one of our vast towns, and tell me, has he any
supernatural idea before his mind at all? The minutes hasten
on; and, having to learn everything, supposing him desirous
of learning, he can practise nothing. His thoughts rise up in
some vague desire of mercy, which neither he nor the

bystanders can analyze. He asks for some chapter of the Bible to be read to him, but rather as the expression of his horror and bewilderment, than as the token of his faith; and [293] then his intellect becomes clouded, and he dies.

How different is it with the Catholic! He has within him almost a principle of recovery, certainly an instrument of it. He may have spoken lightly of the Almighty, but he has ever believed in Him; he has sung jocose songs about the Blessed Virgin and Saints, and told good stories about the evil spirit, but in levity, not in contempt; he has been angry with his heavenly Patrons when things went ill with him, but with the waywardness of a child who is cross with his parents. Those heavenly Patrons were ever before him, even when he was in the mire of mortal sin and in the wrath of the Almighty, as lights burning in the firmament of his intellect, though he had no part with them, as he perfectly knew. He has absented himself from his Easter duties years out of number, but he never denied he was a Catholic. He has laughed at priests, and formed rash judgments of them, and slandered them to others, but not as doubting the divinity of their function and the virtue of their ministrations. He has attended Mass carelessly and heartlessly, but he was ever aware what really was before him, under the veil of material symbols, in that august and adorable action. So, when the news comes to him that he is to die, and he cannot get a priest, and the ray of God's grace pierces his heart, and he yearns after Him whom he has neglected, it is with no inarticulate, confused emotion, [294] which does but oppress him, and which has no means of relief. His thoughts at once take shape and order; they mount up, each in its due place, to the great Objects of faith, which are as surely in his mind as they are in heaven. He addresses himself to his Crucifix; He invokes the Precious Blood or the Five Wounds of his Redeemer; he interests the Blessed Virgin in his behalf; he betakes himself to his patron Saints; he calls his good Angel to his side; he professes his desire of that sacramental absolution, which from circumstances he cannot obtain; he exercises himself in acts of faith, hope, charity, contrition, resignation, and other virtues suitable to his extremity. True, he is going into the unseen world; but true also, that that unseen world has already been with him here. True, he is going to a foreign, but not to a strange place; judgment and purgatory are familiar ideas to him, more fully realised within him even than death. He has had a much deeper perception of purgatory, though it be a supernatural object, than of death, though a natural one. The enemy rushes on him, to overthrow the faith on which he is built; but the whole tenor of his past life, his very jesting, and his very oaths, have been overruled, to create in him a habit of faith, girding round and protecting the supernatural principle. And thus, even one who has been a bad Catholic may have a hope in [295] his death, to which the most virtuous of Protestants, nay, my brethren, the most correct and most thoughtful among yourselves, however able, or learned, or sagacious—if you have lived not by faith but by private judgment—are necessarily strangers.

LECTURE X

DIFFERENCES AMONG CATHOLICS NO PREJUDICE TO THE UNITY OF THE CHURCH

I AM going today to take notice of an objection to the claims of that great Communion, into which, my brethren, I am inviting you, which to me sounds so feeble and unworthy, that I am loth to take it for my subject; for an answer, if corresponding to it, must be trifling and uninteresting also, and if careful and exact, will be but a waste of effort. I, therefore, do not know what to do with it: treat it with respect I cannot; yet since it is frequently, nay, triumphantly, urged by those who wish to make the most of such difficulties as they can bring together against our claims, I do not like to pass it over. Bear with me then, my brethren, nay, I may say, sympathize with me, if you find that the subject is not one which is very fertile in profitable reflection.

1.

When, then, the variations of Protestantism, or the divisions in the Establishment, are urged as a reason for your distrusting the Communion in which they are found, it [297] is answered, that divisions as serious and as decided are to be found in the Catholic Church. It is a well-known point in controversy, to say that the Catholic Church has not any real unity more than Protestantism; for, if Lutherans are divided in creed from Calvinists, and both from Anglicans, and the various denominations of Dissenters each has its own doctrine and its own interpretation, yet Dominicans and Franciscans, Jesuits and Jansenists,[1] have had their quarrels

---

[1] *Dominicans and Franciscans, Jesuits and Jansenists*: The church historian Edward Norman is good on these clerical quarrels: "Cornelius Jansen, the Bishop of Ypes, is said to have read each of the works of St. Augustine ten times, presumably in order to acquire an accurate grasp of

too. Nay, that at this moment the greatest alienation, rivalry, and difference of opinion exist among the members of the Catholic priesthood, so that the Church is but nominally one, and her pretended unity resolves itself into nothing more specious than an awkward and imperfect uniformity. This is what is said: and, I repeat, my answer to it cannot contain anything either new or important, or even satisfactory to myself. However, since I must enter upon the subject, I must make the best of it; so let me begin with an extract from Jewel's Apology,[2] in which the objection is to be found.

---

their meaning. His resulting exposition, *Augustinus* was published in 1640 – two year after his death. It interpreted the doctrine of grace, of Justification by faith only in a manner that had a clear affinity to the Protestant polemics of the Reformation, and was accordingly condemned in a bull of 1653, *Cum Occasione*. Jansenist ideas had the misfortune of incurring the plentiful disapproval of the Jesuits; Jansen had brought this upon himself by opposing the canonization both of Ignatius Loyola and of Francis Xavier, the two leading Jesuits of the Counter-Reformation... Anti-Jesuit sentiment in the Catholic Church generally, however, and especially among Franciscans and the Dominicans, somewhat assisted receptivity to Jansenist ideas. Hence the growth of Jansenism among the clergy in a manner reminiscent of Luther's cult following within early Protestantism." E. Norman, *The Roman Catholic Church: An Illustrated History* (California, 2007), 136. Jansenism, primarily active in France, stressed original sin, human depravity, the necessity of divine grace, and predestination. For the disagreements that arose between the different religious orders at various points in their history, see *The Oxford Illustrated History of the Catholic Church* ed. McManners (Oxford, 1990). When Father Faber and the London Oratorians were accused of being Jansenists in their conduct of the confessional by Mgr. Vincent Eyre, the priest at Chelsea Chapel, in January, 1851, Newman wrote to Faber: "The letter I return is a most absurd one. ...He actually may be annoyed by the idea you are Jansenists, or it may be something else. ...I don't see what you have to do but compliment him, thank him, and assure him you are not Jansenists or rigorists, and gently hint to him that you trust your Fathers more than the reports he has heard from persons to you anonymous." *LD*, xiv, 183-4.

[2] *Jewel's Apology*: John Jewel (1522–71), Bishop of Salisbury and defender of the Elizabethan settlement. On 26 November 1559, Jewell preached a sermon at Paul's Cross challenging Catholics to prove that various Catholic doctrines and practices had been extant in the first six Christian centuries. In 1562, he published *Apologia Ecclesiae*

"Who are these," he says, "that find fault with dissensions among us? Are they all agreed among themselves? Hath every one of them determined, to his own satisfaction, what he should follow? Have there been no differences, no disputes among them? Then why do not the Scotists[3] and the Thomists[4] come to a more perfect

---

Anglicanae. In reply, Thomas Harding, Jewel's Oxford contemporary and a canon of his cathedral in Salisbury, wrote from exile in Louvain his *Answer* (1564). Jewel responded with *Replie unto M. Hardinges answer* (1565). In the meantime, Harding had published his *Confutation* of Jewel's *Apologia*. Of Jewel's voluminous *Defence of the apologie* (1567), the church historian and friend of the poet G.M. Hopkins, R. W. Dixon wrote: "The reader who peruses this may have a complete survey of the controversy between Rome and England in the sixteenth century." R.W. Dixon, *History of the Church of England from the Abolition of the Roman Jurisdiction* (Oxford, 1902), 321. Although contemptuous of recusant priests, referring to them as "those oily, shaven, portly hypocrites," Jewell would later go on to deplore the spread of Puritanism within the National Church. Jewell quoted in P. Williams, *The Later Tudors: England 1547-1603* (Oxford, 1995), 461. See *Works of John Jewel, Bishop of Salisbury*. ed. J. Ayre. 4 vols. Parker Society. (Cambridge, 1850.)

[3] *Scotists*: Followers of John Duns Scotus (1265-1308), the Scottish Franciscan theologian, who along with Bonaventure, Aquinas, and Ockham, is one of the four great philosophers of the Scholastic period. Although encyclopedic in scope, his highly original reading of universals and individuation gained a wide following, while provoking brilliant ripostes from Ockham and Thomist opponents. For Dom David Knowles, Scotus was not persuaded by "*a posteriori* demonstration in natural theology." Unlike Aquinas, whose proofs for the existence of God and His principal attributes "are evidence both of his belief in the validity of an argument from effect to cause and of his conviction that the order of creation is a direct reflection of the divine reason, Scotus, though no sceptic, held that all *a posteriori* demonstration gave no more than relative proof, while for divine providence and the immortality of the soul no argument could be advanced of more than probable force." Thus, "Scotus reduced the number of those truths of the faith that could be established by purely natural reasoning..." He was also a harbinger of things to come. Finding it necessary "to express himself in novel technical terms, and to create a forest of metaphysical forms... it is impossible for a reader to comprehend his thought, unless he is willing to 'bolte him to the bren.' To the humanists and reformers of the sixteenth century, therefore, he was regarded as a type of Gothic stupidity, or, in curious contrast, as a *nonpareil* of super-subtle ingenuity. To strict

---

Thomists he was from early days *bête noire*, the standard-bearer of the great revolt that led from Ockham to Descartes, Kant and Hegel." D. Knowles, *The Religious Orders in England*, (Cambridge, 1956), i, 236-7. For a good overview of what his early followers believed, see *The Oxford Dictionary of the Middle Ages*: "The followers of Scotus, most notably William of Alnwick... frequently defended important positions, and variants of positions, held by Scotus against their earliest theological and philosophical opponents: the Franciscan Petrus Aureoli, the (largely Dominican) followers of Thomas Aquinas, and, most notably, the Franciscan William of Ockham and those thinkers influenced by him. While at this early period the notion of a Scotist 'school' is anachronistic, it is possible to isolate some particularly characteristic and innovative features of Scotus's philosophy that are defended by these thinkers. In metaphysics, Scotus pioneered the notion of the formal distinction, a distinction between the inseparable properties of a substance; the notion that shared natures such as *humanity* or *whiteness* have some kind of real existence along with non-numerical unity; and the notion that individuation (what distinguishes one substance from another) is explained by a *haecceity* (haecceitas) or 'thisness', a non-repeatable particular property, formally distinct from the nature, that explains the non-repeatability of the individual substance whose property it is." The poet Gerard Manley Hopkins (1844-89) was an admirer of Scotus, delighting in Oxford precisely because the Franciscan thinker had also known its "Cuckoo-echoing, bell-swarmèd, lark-charmèd, rook-racked, river-rounded" beauty.

[4] *Thomists*: Followers of St. Thomas Aquinas (1225-74), Dominican philosopher, theologian and doctor of the Church, whose *Summa Theologica* is one of the greatest testaments to the unity and coherence of Catholic theology. "Aristotle strongly influenced the assumptions, methods, and conclusions of Thomism, but Thomism was a Christian system of thought that rejected a number of elements of Aristotle. Unlike Aristotle, Thomism emphasizes the vision of God as the goal and satisfaction of human desire (teleology), and offers a longer list of virtues. The natural virtues express and assist obedience to the commandments of the natural law; and the spiritual virtues of faith, hope, and love are a central part of Christian life and obedience. Existence is material, but also primarily spiritual, and so spiritual existence, either that of angels or the soul, is ultimate and unique. God's unchanging and objective intellect and essence is the foundation of existence and morality. Immoral acts are not called this because of God's capriciousness, but are objectively wrong because they are contrary to God's essence. Although God absolutely rules his creation, humans also have free will, a necessary component to true moral choice. The human soul is immortal. Following Aquinas, Thomism holds that humans perceive actual reality rather than mere appearances. Humans are able to

agreement touching the merit of congruity and condignity,[5] [298]
touching original sin in the Blessed Virgin,[6] and the
obligations of simple and solemn vows?[7] Why do the

---

recognize universals from the particulars of sense perception. God creates
humans with the inclination and capacity to recognize first principles, the
basis for human knowledge, as true as soon as they are presented, directly
or indirectly, to the human mind. ...Thomism continued Aquinas's
foundational synthesis of Christian faith and logico-philosophical
analysis and applied it to a wide diversity of questions and intellectual
categories. It is the most intellectually powerful, long-lasting, and
significant of the medieval scholastic philosophies..." *The Oxford
Dictionary of the Middle Ages.* While Newman admitted to never
studying St. Thomas in any depth – "I do not know enough of him to
speak at all," he once wrote – he did share the Angelic Doctor's
insistence on our ability to apprehend reality and his appreciation that our
basis for human knowledge is our ability to recognize first principles, an
epistemological commonplace that none of Newman's nineteenth-century
rationalist critics could bring themselves to concede. *P.N.* ii, 177.
However, he agreed with Scotus that proofs for the existence of God
could only have the force of probability, which is one reason why he was
drawn to the work of Bishop Butler.

[5] *congruity and condignity*: The Scotists maintain that it is possible for
man in his natural state to live in such a way as to deserve the grace of
God, by which he may be enabled to obtain salvation, and it is this
natural *fitness* (*congruitas*) that makes possible his receiving God's
salvation. Such is the *merit of congruity*. The Thomists contend that man
is capable of living in such a way as to merit eternal life, to be *worthy*
(*condignus*) of it in the sight of God, by divine assistance. This is the
merit of condignity.

[6] *the Blessed Virgin*: The Scotists took issue with the Thomists on the
question of original sin and the Blessed Virgin by insisting on the
Immaculate Conception, though St. Thomas did not deny the Immaculate
Conception *per se*: he took issue with certain arguments that had been
deployed to support the undefined doctrine, which, as it happened, were
not cited when Pius IX formally defined the doctrine in 1854. See P.
Lumbreras, O.P. "St. Thomas and the Immaculate Conception,"
Homiletic and Pastoral Review xxiv [1924], no. 3, 253-263.

[7] *simple and solemn vows*: In Catholic canon law, a solemn vow is a vow
("a deliberate and free promise made to God about a possible and better
good") that the Church has recognized as such. Any other vow, public or
private, individual or collective, concerned with an action or with
abstaining from an action, is a simple vow. There is disagreement among
theologians as to whether the distinction between solemn and simple
vows derives from a decision of the Church to treat them differently or
whether, in line with the opinion of Saint Thomas Aquinas, a solemn vow

Canonists affirm auricular confession to be of human and
positive, and the Schoolmen, on the contrary, maintain that t
it is of divine right?[8] Why does Albertus Pighius[9] differ

---

is, antecedent to any decision by the Church, a more strict, perfect and
complete consecration to God.

[8] *of divine right*: See Calvin's *Institutes* (1536): "*Confession* has ever
been a subject of keen contest between the Canonists and the Scholastic
Theologians; the former contending that confession is of divine
authority—the latter insisting, on the contrary, that it is merely enjoined
by ecclesiastical constitution. …. It is not strange, therefore, that we
condemn that auricular confession, as a thing pestilent in its nature, and
in many ways injurious to the Church, and desire to see it abolished.
…[T]here is nothing which gives men greater confidence and license in
sinning than the idea, that after making confession to priests, they can
wipe their lip, and say, I have not done it. And not only do they during
the whole year become bolder in sin, but, secure against confession for
the remainder of it, they never sigh after God, never examine themselves,
but continue heaping sins upon sins, until, as they suppose, they get rid of
them all at once. And when they have got rid of them, they think they are
disburdened of their load, and imagine they have deprived God of the
right of judging, by giving it to the priest; have made God forgetful, by
making the priest conscious. Moreover, who is glad when he sees the day
of confession approaching? Who goes with a cheerful mind to confess,
and does not rather, as if he were dragged to prison with a rope about his
neck, go unwillingly, and, as it were, struggling against it? with the
exception, perhaps, of the priests themselves, who take a fond delight in
the mutual narrative of their own misdeeds, as a kind of merry tales. I
will not pollute my page by retailing the monstrous abominations with
which auricular confession teems; I only say, that if that holy man
(Nectarius…) did not act unadvisedly when for one rumour of whoredom
he banished confession from his church, or rather from the memory of his
people, the innumerable acts of prostitution, adultery, and incest, which it
produces in the present day, warn us of the necessity of abolishing it."
Ch. 4:4 and 4:19. Nectarius (1605–c. 80) was Patriarch of Jerusalem
from 1661 to 1669. A fierce opponent of all Western theology, he
attacked Calvinist and Catholic theology alike. His treatise against the
papacy was published by his successor, Dositheus, in 1682.
[9] *Albertus Pighius*: (c. 1490–1542), Dutch humanist and Catholic
theologian. Against Luther's attacks on the papacy, he wrote a defense of
the church hierarchy, stressed the importance of the papacy, and defended
papal principles. In matters of belief, he held that the pope was infallible,
no pope in history, not even Honorius I, having been a heretic. His views
on justification, Original Sin, and papal infallibility had great influence.
His doctrine of exculpability and Original Sin played a role in the

from Cajetan,[10] Thomas Aquinas from Peter Lombard,[11] Scotus from Thomas Aquinas, Occham[12] from Scotus, Peter D'Ailly[13] from Occham, the Nominalists[14] from the

---

discussions at the Council of Trent. His ideas on infallibility were affirmed by St. Robert Bellarmine and numerous other theologians and were consulted and presented at the first Vatican Council (1870). *The Oxford Encyclopedia of the Reformation.*

[10] *Cajetan*: Thomas Cajetan (1469–1534), Minister General of the Dominican order (1508–18) and cardinal from 1517. In 1518 Cajetan was sent as legate of the Holy See to the Imperial Diet of Augsburg, and while there debated inconclusively with Martin Luther. He produced important commentaries on works of St. Thomas, and wrote in later life of the Bible.

[11] *Lombard*: Peter Lombard (1095/1100–1160) Italian theologian and bishop of Paris whose *Sentences* (1155–8) became the standard textbook of theology during the Middle Ages,

[12] *Occham*: William of Ockham (c. 1287–1347/8) 'The More than Subtle Doctor', English Franciscan theologian, philosopher, and political thinker. Ockham's early work in logic, philosophy of language, Aristotelian physics, and theology is the basis for his reputation as inaugurator of a nominalist *via moderna* marked by insistence that universals ('man', 'red') can be understood adequately as mental or material 'names' and hence need not be posited as realities in their own right (one application of 'Ockham's razor'). 'Ockham's Razor' is Ockham's principle that *entia non sunt multiplicanda praeter necessitatem*: entities are not to be multiplied beyond necessity, which animates many nominalistic philosophies. As the *OED* points out in its definition of 'Occamist:' "Occam was a pupil of Duns Scotus, but rejected and opposed the Realism of his master, forming a new speculative sect who revived the tenets of Nominalism. He maintained that general ideas have no objective reality out of the mind, but are merely a product of abstraction. His teaching prepared the way for the overthrow of scholasticism." When in May of 1859 Newman wrote a letter to *The Rambler* asking whether it was "allowable or desirable" for laymen to study theology, the editor Richard Simpson replied: "I don't know whether you are aware that the question was partly discussed in Ockham's rather scandalous *dialogus* against the *errors and heresies* of Pope John xxii in order to resolve the question whether laymen might take part in the deposition of an heretical Pope — However scandalous his object, the greatest scholar of the age could not write nonsense; and some of his authorities and reasons are of the greatest weight." *LD*, xix, 123.

[13] Peter D'Ailly: Pierre d'Ailly (1350/1–1420), French theologian. He taught at Paris and in 1397 became Bishop of Cambrai. He devoted a good deal of his time to trying to end the Great Schism. Attending the

Council of Pisa, he supported the newly elected Alexander V; he was given his red hat by his successor, John XXIII. From 1414 to 1418 he attended the Council of Constance, where he upheld the Conciliar theory, without, however, entirely approving the anti-conciliar 'Decrees of Constance.' In his *Tractatus super Reformatione Ecclesiae* (1416), d'Ailly showed himself to be an exemplary Occamist, holding that the existence of God was not a rationally demonstrable truth, and that sin was not objectively evil but sinful only because God wills it to be so. He maintained that bishops and priests received their jurisdiction directly from Christ and not mediately through the Pope, and that neither Pope nor Council was infallible. His views were developed by the Protestant Reformers and influenced Gallicanism. The Conciliar theory posits that supreme authority in the Church lies with a General Council. The movement associated with the theory culminated in the 15th century, but the foundations of it were laid in the early 13th, when canonists found difficulty in reconciling the claims of Papal authority with the possibility of a heretical pope. The outbreak of the Great Schism in 1378 exacerbated the question of papal authority. In 1380, a General Council was summoned, the justification being that the absence of a single recognized Pope left the duty of convening it to the cardinals. In the early sessions of the Council of Constance it was claimed that the power of the Council came directly from Christ, but the very success of the Council in ending the schism undermined the conciliarist position. Pius II in 1460 specifically forbade appeals from the Pope to a future General Council, and after the 15th century support for the Conciliar theory waned. *ODCC.*

[14] *Nominalists*: The *OED* defines 'Nominalism' as "The view which regards universals or abstract concepts as mere names without any corresponding reality." To illustrate the word, the *OED* cites Keble: "The nominalism of our days: I mean the habit of resolving the high mysteries of the faith into mere circumstances of language." The corrosive but also the absurd character of nominalism was never lost on the satirist in Newman. As one commentator of his work observed: "Newman saw very early on that the natural law, the belief in an 'objective moral order,' was organically and inextricably linked to Judeo-Christian theism, that 'if there is no God, everything is permitted,' in the famous formulation of his contemporary Dostoevsky. The nominalist, antinomian reliance on 'private judgment,' as alluring as it is contradictory, is satirized by Newman in his 1848 novel *Loss and Gain*, in the character of Mr. Batts and the 'British and Foreign Truth Society,' whose two leading dogmas are: '1. It is uncertain whether Truth exists. 2. It is certain that it cannot be found.' (Among the Society's 'patrons' are Cicero, Peter Abelard, and Benjamin Franklin.)" M. D. Aeschliman. "The Prudence of John Henry Newman," *First Things*, (August 1994)

Realists?[15] And, not to mention the infinite dissensions of the friars and monks (how some of them place their holiness in the eating of fish, others in herbs; some in wearing of shoes, others in sandals; some in linen garments, others in woollen; some go in white, some in black; some are shaven broader, some narrower; some shod, some barefoot; some girded, others ungirded), they should remember that some of their own adherents say, that the body of Christ is in the Lord's supper naturally; that others again, of their own party, teach the very reverse: that there are some who affirm that the body of Christ in the Holy Communion is torn and ground with our teeth; others again there are who deny it: that there are some who say that the body of Christ in the Eucharist hath quantity; and others again deny it: that there are some who say that Christ consecrated the bread and wine by the special putting forth of His divine power; others, that He consecrated in the benediction: some, by the conceiving the five words in His mind; others, by His [299] uttering them: others there are who, in these five words, refer the demonstrative pronoun 'this' to the wheaten bread; others to what they call an *individuum vagum*:[16] some there are who affirm that dogs and mice can verily and truly eat the body of Christ; others there are who do not hesitate to deny it; some there are who say that the very accidents of the bread and wine give nourishment; others, that the substance of bread and wine returns after consecration. And why should we bring forward more? It would be only tedious and burdensome to enumerate them all; so *unsettled and disputed* is yet the *whole form* of these men's religion and doctrine even among themselves, from whom it sprang and proceeded. For scarcely ever are they agreed together,

---

[15] *Realists*: The *OED* defines 'Realism' as 'The scholastic doctrine of the objective or absolute existence of universals, of which Thomas Aquinas was the chief exponent. (Opposed to Nominalism and Conceptualism).

[16] *individuum vagum*: "Something indicated as an individual, without specific identification." *OED*. For illustration, the Dictionary cites Pope: "From particular propositions nothing can be concluded, because the *Individua vaga* are … barren."

unless, as of old, the Pharisees and Sadducees were, or Herod and Pilate, against Christ."[17]

It is equally common to insist upon the breaches of charity which are to be found among the members of the Catholic Church. For instance, Leslie[18] says, "If you have not unity in faith, nor in those principles and practices which are no less necessary to salvation, nor in that love and charity which Christ has made the characteristic of Christians, and without which no man can know who are His disciples; but, instead of that, if you have envyings and strife among you, among your several religious orders, [300] betwixt National and National Church, concerning the infallibility and supremacy of the Pope, and of his power to depose princes, upon which the peace and unity of the world and our eternal salvation does depend; and, in short, if you have no unity concerning your rule of faith itself, or

---

[17] *"against Christ:"* J. Jewell, *Apologia Ecclesiae Anglicanae* (1562) in *Writings of John Jewell* (London, 1831), 319. The Pharisees were "of the ancient Jewish sect distinguished by strict observance of traditional & written law & pretensions to sanctity;" the Sadducees were "of a Jewish sector party at the time of Christ who denied the resurrection of the dead, existence of spirits, & obligation of the traditional law;" Herod (37–4 BC) was the ruler of Judea who ordered the Massacre of the Innocents at the time of the birth of Jesus; and Pilate was the governor of Judaea from ad 26 to 36 under whom Christ was crucified. *OED* and *ODCC*.

[18] *Leslie:* Charles Leslie (1650–1722), nonjuring Church of Ireland clergyman. "Leslie's theological works were largely apologetic in nature, offering defences of theological orthodoxy against deism, Judaism, latitudinarianism, Socinianism, and the Quakers. John Hunt described his theology as 'orthodox Episcopalian, adhering rigidly to Church dogmas and holding Episcopacy necessary to the essence of a church' (*Religious Thought in England*, 1871, 2.83). The best known of his apologetical works was the *Short Method with the Deists* (1694), which was written as a letter, probably for Henry Hyde's sister, Frances Kneightly, who stayed with the Leslies during a period of attraction to deism. There he sought to defend trinitarian orthodoxy and the centrality of the doctrine of satisfaction, which he called 'the foundation of the Christian Religion' (Leslie, *Works*, 1832, 6.64). The book became a classic theological response to deism and continued to be reprinted well into the nineteenth century." *ODNB*. For S. Johnson, Leslie was "a reasoner, and a reasoner who was not to be reasoned against." Boswell, *Life*, iv, 286-7.

of your practice, what will the unity of communion do, upon which you lay the whole stress?"[19]

Such is the retort, by which Protestants would divert our attack upon their own mutual differences and variations in matters of faith. They answer, that differences of religious opinion and that party dissensions are found within the Catholic Church.

2.

Now, in beginning my remarks upon this objection, I would have you observe, my brethren, that the very idea of the Catholic Church, as an instrument of supernatural grace, is that of an institution which innovates upon, or rather superadds to nature. She does something for nature above or beyond nature. When, then, it is said that she makes her members one, this implies that by nature they are not one, and would not become one. Viewed in themselves, the children of the Church are not of a different nature from the Protestants around them; they are of the very same nature. What Protestants are, such would they be, but for the Church, which brings them together forcibly, though [301] persuasively, "fortiter et suaviter,"[20] and binds them into one by her authority. Left to himself, each Catholic likes and would maintain his own opinion and his private judgment just as much as a Protestant; and he has it, and he maintains it, just so far as the Church does not, by the authority of Revelation, supersede it. The very moment the Church ceases to speak, at the very point at which she, that is, God who speaks by her, circumscribes her range of teaching, there private judgment[21] of necessity starts up; there is nothing to hinder it. The intellect of man is active and independent: he forms opinions about everything; he feels no deference for another's opinion, except in proportion as

---

[19] Works, 1832, vol. iii. p. 171. [N]
[20] *"fortiter et suaviter:"* 'mightily and sweetly'
[21] *Private judgement*: "personal opinion (esp. in religious matters), as opposed to the acceptance of a statement or doctrine on authority or on the basis of public opinion." *OED.*

he thinks that that other is more likely than he to be right; and he never absolutely sacrifices his own opinion, except when he is sure that that other knows for certain. He *is* sure that God knows; therefore, if he is a Catholic, he sacrifices his opinion to the Word of God, speaking through His Church. But, from the nature of the case, there is nothing to hinder his having his own opinion, and expressing it, whenever, and so far as, the Church, the oracle of Revelation, does not speak.

But again, human nature likes, not only its own opinion, but its own way, and will have it whenever it can, except when hindered by physical or moral restraint. So far forth, [302] then, as the Church does not compel her children to do one and the same thing (as, for instance, to abstain from work on Sunday, and from flesh on Friday), they will do different things: and still more so, when she actually allows or commissions them to act for themselves, gives to certain persons or bodies privileges and immunities, and recognizes them as centres of combination, under her authority, and within her pale.

And further still, in all subjects and respects whatever, whether in that range of opinion and of action which the Church has claimed to herself, and where she has superseded what is private and individual, or, on the other hand, in those larger regions of thought and of conduct, as to which she has not spoken, though she might speak, the natural tendency of the children of the Church, as men, is to resist her authority. Each mind naturally is self-willed, self-dependent, self-satisfied; and except so far as grace has subdued it, its first impulse is to rebel. Now this tendency, through the influence of grace, is not often exhibited in matters of faith; for it would be incipient heresy, and would be contrary, if knowingly indulged, to the first element of Catholic duty; but in matters of conduct, of ritual, of discipline, of politics, of social life, in the ten thousand questions which the Church has not formally answered, even though she may have intimated her judgment, there is a constant rising of the human mind against the authority of the Church, and of superiors, and that, in proportion as each [303] individual is removed from perfection. For all these reasons, there ever has been, and ever will be, a vast exercise and a realized product, partly praiseworthy, partly barely lawful, of private judgment within the Catholic Church. The freedom of the human mind is "in possession" (as it is called), and it meddles with every question, and wanders over heaven and earth, except so far as the authority of the Divine Word, as a superincumbent weight, presses it down, and restrains it within limits.

3.

The most obvious instance of this liberty or licence within the Church is that of nationality; and I do not understand why it has not been urged in the controversy more prominently than the mere rivalry and party-spirit of monastic bodies. What a vast assemblage of private attachments and feelings, judgments, tastes, and traditions, goes to make up the idea of nationality! yet, there it exists in the Church, because the Church has not been divinely instructed to forbid it, and it fights against the Church and the Church's objects, except where the Church authoritatively repels it. The Church is a preacher of peace, and nationality is the fruitful cause of quarrels, far more sinful and destructive than the paper wars, and rivalry of customs or precedents, which alone can possibly exist between religious bodies. The Church grants to the magistrate the power of the sword, and the right of making [304] war in a lawful quarrel, and nations abuse this prerogative to break up that unity of love which ought to exist in the baptized servants of a common Master, and to put to death by wholesale those whom they pray to live with for ever in heaven. This, I say, might be urged in controversy against Catholicism, as an extreme instance of the want of unity in the Church; and yet, when properly considered, it is rather a special instance, I do not say of her unity, but of her uniting power. She fights the battle of unity against nationality, and she wins. Look through her history, and you cannot deny but she is the one great principle of unity and concord which the world has seen. In this day, I grant, scientific unions, free trade, railroads, and industrial exhibitions[22] are put forward as a substitute for her influence, with what success posterity will be able to judge; but, as far as the course of history has yet proceeded, the Church is the only power that has wrestled, as with the concupiscence, so with the pride, irritability, selfishness, and self-love of human nature. Her annals present a series of victories over that human nature, which is the subject-matter of her operations;

---

[22] *Industrial exhibitions*: These would culminate in the Great Exhibition, which was held after Newman's lectures in the Crystal Palace from 1 May to 15 October, 1851. An 1836 Parliamentary committee had shown that Britain's lead in manufacturing was threatened by Continental rivals, and the exhibition's chief promoters, Prince Albert and Henry Cole, hoped to inspire manufacturers to use designers to make artefacts more desirable. More grandiosely, they touted it as a 'tournament of peace', tending towards the unity of mankind by displaying exhibits from foreign countries as well as Britain and her colonies. An invitation from George Smith's mother to Charlotte Brontë to visit London at the time caused Charlotte to forget her prejudices about 'a series of bazaars under a magnified hot-house', and to pay five visits there, the first on 30 May, the last with Sir David Brewster on 22 June. Though it was 'not much in her line', she evoked its 'strange and elegant but somewhat unsubstantial effect' in a letter to her father of 31 May 1851: 'The brightest colours blaze on all sides—and ware of all kinds—from diamonds to spinning jennies and Printing Presses are there to be seen—It was very fine—gorgeous—animated—bewildering—but I liked Thackeray's lecture better' (Smith *Letters*, 2. 625). She would see for example the Kohinoor diamond, and the immense, complex Applegath's Patent Vertical Printing Machine. She confessed to Amelia Taylor on 7 June 1851 that it was wonderful but tiring: 'you come out very sufficiently bleached and broken in bits' (Smith *Letters*, 2. 633). On 13 June the sight of the 'ex-royal family of France' at the Exhibition must have reminded her of the dramatic events during the French Revolution of 1848. She was amused by one of the more eccentric exhibits, a bed which silently ejected its occupant at a given hour, and she suggested its use by the dilatory Thackeray as a spur to completing *Henry Esmond* (Smith *Letters*, 2. 655–6)." *The Oxford Companion to the Brontës*. Henry Cole (1808–82), who would go on to found what become the Victoria and Albert Museum, was a great admirer of Newman. Thackeray attended the lectures of *Anglican Difficulties*. See Editor's Introduction.

and to object to her that she has an enemy to overcome, surely would be a most perverse view of the case, and a most sophistical argument in controversy. The barbarian invaders of the empire were the enemies of the human race and of each other; and to subdue and unite them, and to [305] harness them, as it were, to her triumphal chariot by her look and by her voice, was an exploit of moral power, such as the world has never seen elsewhere. Such, too, was her continual arbitration between the fierce feudal monarchs of the Middle Ages, which, though not always successful to the extent of her desire, exhibits her most signally in that her great and heavenly character of peacemaker, and vindicates for her the attribute, given her in the Creed, and envied her by her enemies, of being One.

And here I cannot but allude to the subject which employed our attention yesterday; for, be it for good or for evil, it then seemed a truth beyond contradiction, that one and the same character was to be found in all Catholic nations, in north and south, in the middle age and in the present. I repeat, I am not assuming now, any more than then, that this common character is admirable and beautiful, or denying (as far as this argument goes) that it is despicable and offensive; I only remind you that its identity everywhere was in yesterday's Lecture taken for granted; and what was granted by me to our own prejudice then, must be conceded to me in our favour now. Considering the wide differences in nations and in times, it surely is very remarkable that the religious character, which the Catholic Church forms in her populations, is so identical as it is found to be. Can, indeed, there be a more marvellous, or [306] even awful, instance of her real internal unity, than that a modern Naples should be like medieval England? and if we do not see the same character more than partially developed in Ireland at this moment, is not this the plain reason, that the Irish people has been worn down by oppression, not allowed to be joyous, not allowed to be natural, as little

capable of exhibiting human nature in a Catholic medium,
as primitive Christianity while it lived in the Catacombs?[23]

---

[23] *in the Catacombs*: Keenly aware of the disabilities under which the
Catholic Irish labored in the mid-19th century, Newman was unusually
appreciative of what he saw as the talents of the Catholic Irish. In an
address to the evening classes of the Catholic University of Ireland,
which he delivered in Dublin in November of 1858, after serving as
rector from 1851 to 1858, he paid the Irish a generous compliment on this
score. "Ireland is the proper seat of a Catholic University, on account of
its ancient hereditary Catholicity," he told his auditors. *Idea*, 389. "And
next I would observe, that, while thus distinguished for religious
earnestness, the Catholic population is in no respect degenerate from the
ancient fame of Ireland as regards its intellectual endowments. It too
often happens that the religiously disposed are in the same degree
intellectually deficient; but the Irish ever have been, as their worst
enemies must grant, not only a Catholic people, but a people of great
natural abilities, keen-witted, original, and subtle. This has been the
characteristic of the nation from the very early times, and was especially
prominent in the middle ages. As Rome was the centre of authority, so, I
may say, Ireland was the native home of speculation. In this respect they
were as remarkably contrasted to the English as they are now, though, in
those ages, England was as devoted to the Holy See as it is now hostile.
The Englishman was hard-working, plodding, bold, determined,
persevering, practical, obedient to law and precedent, and, if he cultivated
his mind, he was literary and classical rather than scientific, or Literature
involves in it the idea of authority and prescription. On the other hand, in
Ireland, the intellect seems rather to have taken the line of Science, and
we have various instances to show how fully this was recognized in those
times, and with what success it was carried out. 'Philosopher', is in those
times almost the name for an Irish monk. Both in Paris and Oxford, the
two great schools of medieval thought, we find the boldest and most
subtle of their disputants an Irishman,—the monk John Scotus Erigena,
at Paris, and Duns Scotus, the Franciscan friar, at Oxford. Now, it is my
belief, Gentlemen, that this character of mind remains in you still. I think
I rightly recognize in the Irishman now, as formerly, the curious,
inquisitive observer, the acute reasoner, the subtle speculator. I recognize
in you talents which are fearfully mischievous, when used on the side of
error, but which, when wielded by Catholic devotion, such as I am sure
will ever be the characteristic of the Irish disputant, are of the highest
importance to Catholic interests, and especially at this day, when a subtle
logic is used against the Church, and demands a logic still more subtle on
the part of her defenders to expose it." *Idea.*, 390-1. Needless to say,
fearful mischief, not subtle logic, characterizes the formerly Catholic
Irish today.

4.

After considerations such as these, I own I can scarcely treat seriously the earnestness with which Protestant controversialists would call me back to contemplate the quarrels and jealousies of seculars and regulars, among themselves, or with each other; as if the human mind were not at all times, so far as it is left to itself, selfish and exclusive, and especially in the various circumstances under which it is found in a far-spreading polity or association. When Catholics in any country are poor or few, each religious body, each college, each priest, is tempted to do his utmost for himself, at the expense of every one else. I do not mean for his temporal interests, for he has not the temptation, but for the interests of his own mission and place, and of his own people. He has to build his chapel, to support his school, to feed his poor; and if his next-door [307] neighbour gets the start of him, no means will be left for himself. Or if he is of a mendicant order, he feels he has a claim on the support of the faithful, prior to a religious body which lives on endowments or has other property; but the latter has lately come to the country, and thinks it very fair, on its first start, once for all to make a general appeal, without which it never will be able to get afloat. All parties, then, are naturally led to look out for themselves in the first instance; and this state of mind may easily degenerate into a jealousy of the good fortune or prosperity of others. And then again, some men, or races of men, are more sudden in their tempers than others, or individuals may be deficient in moral training or refinement, and strangers may mistake for a real dissension what is nothing more than momentary and transitory collision.

Or again, let the country be Catholic, and the Church rich; then, what so natural, so inevitable, taking men as they are, as that large, and widely-spread, and powerful congregations or orders, high in repute, commanding in station, famous in historical memories, rich in saints, proud of their doctors, and of schools founded on their tradition, should be exposed to the various infirmities of party spirit, adhere sensitively and obstinately to the privileges they possess, or to the doctrines which have been their watchwords, disparage others and wish to overbear them, [308] and provoke the interposition of authority to put an end to the disputes which they have excited? I should be curious to know whether there ever was a case when two Protestant sects or parties found any umpire at all, in a question of opinion between them, except indeed the strong arm of the law. And, in saying all this, I am not determining the fact of such quarrels among Catholics, nor the degree to which they proceed; for, as in former Lectures, I am not specially concerned with the investigation of facts; I am taking for granted what is alleged by our opponents, and is antecedently probable, taking human nature as it is. But, in truth, you might far better refer to the *esprit de corps* of separate regiments in her Majesty's service, in order to prove that the tribes of Red Indians may be fairly said to live in peace together,—or point to the rivalries and party politics of separate colleges in the national seats of learning as a proof that those bodies are mutual belligerents, and assert that the university is not one, and does not act as one, because its colleges differ among themselves,—than assert the like of any of those religious bodies, established and sanctioned by the Catholic Church. The very same parties, who have their domestic feuds with one another, will defend, as Catholics, their common faith, or common Mother, against an external foe; but when did the Bishops of the Establishment ever stand by the Friends or by the [309] Independents, or the Wesleyans by the Baptists, on any one point of doctrine, with a unity of opinion, intelligent, positive, and exact?

You recollect the popular story, which is intended to exemplify the supremacy of the instinct of benevolence over religious opinion. It is supposed to be one o'clock on Sunday, and a number of congregations are pouring out, their devotions being over, from their respective chapels and meeting-houses, when a woman is taken ill in the street. The sight of this physical calamity is represented as sufficient to supersede all other considerations in the minds of the beholders, and to bind together for the moment the most bitter opponents in the common work of Christian charity. This argument of course is based upon the assumption, and a very reasonable one, that the differences which exist between man and man in religious matters, far from disproving, do but illustrate and confirm the fact of the participation of all men in the natural sentiment of compassion; and surely the case is the same in the Catholic Church, as regards the differences and the unanimity of her religious bodies. Augustinians,[24] Dominicans, Franciscans, Jesuits, and Carmelites[25] have indeed their respective homes and schools; but they have, in spite of all that, a common school and a common home in their Mother's voice and their Mother's bosom; "omnes omnium caritates patria una complexa est;"[26] but Protestants can but "agree to differ." Quarrels, stopping short of division, do but prove the [310] strength of the principle of combination; they are a token not of the languor, but of the vigour, of its life. Surely this is

---

[24] *Augustinians*: Augustinian or Austin Friars, drawn together from disparate orders of hermits in 1256. It was based on the Rule of St Augustine, with a constitution drawn from the Dominicans. Among those adopting the Rule were Canons Regular, Premonstratensians, and Dominicans.

[25] *Carmelites*: The Order of Our Lady of Mount Carmel, known as the Carmelites, was founded after the Holy Land had been reopened to Christians at the time of the Crusades. By 1209 the Latin patriarch of Jerusalem, Albert of Vercelli, gave a rule to the former Crusaders and pilgrims, both clerics and laymen, who had settled on Mount Carmel in Palestine to follow the eremitic spirit of the prophet Elijah. This rule was officially confirmed in 1224 by Pope Honorius III. By 1238 Carmelites began to move to rural areas of western Europe, and after the fall of Acre in 1291, they disappeared from Mount Carmel. In 1247 they had received a rule from Pope Innocent IV, adapted to their new European circumstances, which classified them among the mendicant orders. They gradually moved from the rural areas toward the cities. In 1451 Pope Nicholas V gave permission for the Carmelite friars to organize a second order for women. *Oxford Encyclopedia of the Reformation*

[26] *"omnes omnium caritates patria una complexa est;"* 'One native land embraces all of our loves.' Cicero, *de Officiis,* Bk 1, 50-1.

what we see and say daily as regards the working of the British constitution.

5.

But we have not yet got to the real point of the question which lies between us: you allege these differences in the Catholic Church, my brethren, as a reason for your not submitting to her authority. Now, in order to ascertain their force in this point of view, let it be considered that the primary question, with every serious inquirer, is the question of salvation. I am speaking to those who feel this to be so; not to those who make religion a sort of literature or philosophy, but to those who desire, both in their creed and in their conduct, to approve themselves to their Maker, and to save their souls. This being taken for granted, it immediately follows to ask, "What must I *do* to be saved?" and "who is to *teach* me?" and next, can Protestantism, can the National Church, teach me? No, is the answer of common sense, for this simple reason, because of the variations and discordances in teaching of both the one and the other. The National Church is no guide into the truth, because no one knows what it holds, and what it commands: one party says this, and a second party says that, and a third party says neither this nor that. I must seek the truth then elsewhere; and then the question follows, Shall I seek it in the Communion of Rome? In answer, this objection is instantly made, "You cannot find the truth in Rome, for there are as many divisions there as in the National Communion." Who would not suppose the objection to mean, that these divisions were such as to make it difficult or impossible to ascertain what it was that the Roman Communion taught? Who would not suppose it to mean that there was within the Communion of Rome a difference of creed and of dogmatic teaching; whereas the state of the case is just the reverse? No one can pretend that the quarrels in the Catholic Church are questions of faith, or have tended in any way to obscure or impair what she declares to be such, and what is acknowledged to be such by the very parties in those quarrels. That Dominicans and Franciscans

[311]

have been zealous respectively for certain doctrinal views, which they declare at the same time to be beyond and in advance of the promulgated faith of the Church, throws no doubt upon that faith itself; how does it follow that they differ in questions of faith, because they differ in questions not of faith? Rather, I would say, if a number of parties distinct from each other give the same testimony on certain points, their differences on other points do but strengthen the evidence for the truth of those matters in which they all are agreed; and the greater the difference, the more remarkable is the unanimity. The question is, "*Where* can I be taught, who cannot be taught by the National [312] Communion, because it does *not* teach?" and the Protestant warning runs, "Not in the Catholic Church, because she, in spite of differences on subordinate points amongst her members, *does* teach."

In truth, she not only teaches in spite of those differences, but she has ever taught by means of them. Those very differences of Catholics on further points have themselves implied and brought out their absolute faith in the doctrines which are previous to them. The doctrines of faith are the common basis of the combatants, the ground on which they contend, their ultimate authority, and their arbitrating rule. They are assumed, and introduced, and commented on, and enforced, in every stage of the alternate disputation; and I will venture to say, that, if you wish to get a good view of the unity, consistency, solidity, and reality of Catholic teaching, your best way is to get up the controversy on grace, or on the Immaculate Conception. No one can do so without acquiring a mass of theological knowledge, and sinking in his intellect a foundation of dogmatic truth, which is simply antecedent and common to the rival schools, and which they do but exhibit and elucidate. To suppose that they perplex an inquirer or a convert, is to fancy that litigation destroys the principles and the science of law, or that spelling out words of five syllables makes a child forget his alphabet. On the other hand, place your unfortunate inquirer between Luther and [313]

Calvin, if the Holy Eucharist is his subject; or, if he is determining the rule of faith, between Bramhall and Chillingworth, Bull and Hoadley,[27] and what residuum will be left, when you have eliminated their contrarieties?

6.

It is imprudent in opponents of the Catholic Religion to choose for their attack the very point in which it is strong. As truth is tried by error, virtue by temptation, courage by opposition, so is individuality and life tried by disturbance and disorder; and its trial is its evidence. The long history of Catholicism is but a coordinate proof of its essential unity. I suppose, then, that Protestants must be considered as turning to bay upon their pursuers, when they would retort upon us the argument available against themselves from their religious variations. "The Romanist must admit," it has been urged, "that the state, whether of the Church Catholic or of the Roman Church, at periods before or during the Middle Ages, was such as to bear a very strong resemblance to the picture he draws of our own. I do not speak of corruptions in life and morals merely, or of errors of individuals, however highly exalted, but of the general disorganized and schismatical state of the Church, her practical abandonment of her spiritual pretensions, the tyranny exercised over her by the civil power, and the [314] intimate adherence of the worst passions and of circumstantial irregularities to those acts which are vital

---

[27] *Hoadley*: Benjamin Hoadly (1676–1761). Bishop. Born in Kent and educated at Catharine Hall, Cambridge, Hoadly held livings in London and successively the bishoprics of Bangor (1716), Hereford (1721), Salisbury (1723), and Winchester (1734). A Whig polemicist in conflict with Atterbury after 1705, he was rewarded by becoming George I's chaplain, but his appointment to Bangor shocked even supporters. His sermon (1717) advocating private judgement and sincere conscience in preference to ecclesiastical authority challenged both high churchmen and the established church. It thus provoked the bitter Bangorian controversy and consequent suspension of convocation. *OCBH.*

portions of her system."[28] Such is the imputation; but yet, to tell the truth, I do not know any passages in her history which supply so awful an evidence of her unity and self-dependence, or so luminous a contrast to Anglicanism or other Protestantism, as these very anomalies in the rule and tenor of her course as I have already observed, and shall presently show by examples.

Two years back, when European society was shaken to its basis,[29] the question which came before us was, not

---

[28] Proph. Off., p. 408. [N]

[29] *shaken to its basis:* This is a reference to the Revolutions of 1848, a series of revolutions in Europe, which broke out within a few months of each other. The general cause was the frustration of liberals and nationalists with the governing authorities, and a background of economic depression. The risings began with the February Revolution against Louis Philippe in France, which resulted in the foundation of the Second Republic. This, in turn, inspired revolts in Vienna (forcing the resignation of Prince von Metternich), and among the national minorities under Austrian rule. In Germany, liberals forced Frederick William IV to summon a constitutional assembly, while advocates of German unification hoped to achieve their aim in the Frankfurt Parliament. "The year 1848 in France," Sir Lewis Namier pointed out in his classic Raleigh Lecture, "carried the two basic political ideas of the Great Revolution to their logical conclusion: equality was achieved in universal suffrage and the sovereignty of the people in the Republic. The development which it interrupted, and the noble work which it destroyed, were what in other continental countries the revolution, on its political side, aspired to attain: parliamentary government and political liberty under a constitutional monarchy. But the intellectuals, red or pink, had yet to learn that the parliamentary system is based on an articulation of society, and not on leveling it down, and that, with social superiorities discredited and the political structure broken, the field is open, or rather the void is prepared, for plebiscitarian dictatorships. Montalembert said in Parliament, on 19 October 1849: 'The kings have reascended their thrones, liberty has not reascended hers—the throne which she had in our hearts.'" N. Namier, *1848: The Revolution of the Intellectuals* (Oxford, 1946), 10-11. Chesterton's theory about why the English were spared revolution is at once amusing and shrewd: "... the fundamental fact of early Victorian history was this; the decision of the middle classes to employ their new wealth in backing up a sort of aristocratical compromise, and not (like the middle class in the French Revolution) insisting on a clean sweep and a clear democratic programme. It went along with the decision of the aristocracy to recruit itself more freely from the middle class. It was then

whether this or that nation was great and powerful, and able, in case of necessity, to go to war with vigour and effect, but even whether it could hold together, whether it possessed that internal consistency, reality, and life, which made it one. This was the question asked even about England; it was a problem, debated before it could be tried, settled distinctly in the affirmative, when a trial was granted. Much as we might have confided in the steadiness of character, good sense, reverence for law, contentment and political discipline of our people, we shall, I suppose, admit that there was an evidence laid before the world of our national stability, after April 1848, to which no mere anticipation was equivalent. No one can deny, that fully as we may be impressed with the security of Russia, still we have not, as [315] regards Russia, such a vivid impression on our mind, almost on our senses, of the fact, as was created by the threat and the failure of a political rising in England at the date I have mentioned. And sometimes the longer is the trial, and the more critical the contest (as in the instance of the civil discords of ancient Rome), the greater vigour and the more obstinate life is exhibited by the nation and state, when once it is undeniably victorious over its internal disorders. As external enemies do not prove a state to be weak till they prevail over it, so rebellions from within may but prove its strength, if they are smitten down and extinguished. Now, the disorders which have afflicted the Church have just had this office assigned them in the designs of Providence, and teach us this lesson. They have but assayed what may be called the unitive and integrating virtue of the See of St. Peter, in contrast to such counterfeits as the Anglican Church, which, set up in unconditional surrender to the

also that Victorian 'prudery' began: the great lords yielded on this as on Free Trade. These two decisions have made the doubtful England of to-day; and Macaulay is typical of them; he is the *bourgeois* in Belgravia. The alliance is marked by his great speeches for Lord Grey's Reform Bill: it is marked even more significantly in his speech against the Chartists. Cobbett was dead." G. K. Chesterton, "The Victorian Age In Literature" (1913), *G. K. Chesterton Collected Works* ed. Dale (San Francisco, 1989), xv, 432-3.

nation, has never been able to resist the tyranny or caprice of the national will. The Establishment, having no internal principle of individuality, except what it borrows from the nation, can neither expel what is foreign to itself, nor heal its own wounds; the Church, a living body, when she becomes the seat of a malady or disorder, tends from the first to its eradication, which is but a matter of time. This great fact continually occurring in her history, I will briefly illustrate by two examples, which will be the fairest to take, from the extraordinary obstinacy of the evil, and its [316] occasional promise of victory:—the history of the heresies concerning the Incarnation, and the history of Jansenism. Each controversy had a reference to a great mystery of the faith; in each every inch of the ground was contested, and the enemy retired step by step, or at least from post to post. The former of the two lasted for between four and five hundred years, and the latter nearly two hundred.

7.

First, as to the doctrine of the Incarnation, the mind of man is naturally impatient of whatever it cannot reduce to the system of order and of causation to which it subjects all its knowledge; that is, of whatever is mysterious and incomprehensible; no wonder, then, that it was discontented with a doctrine so utterly impossible to fathom as that of the Almighty and Eternal becoming man. As private judgment is ever rising up against Revelation, as the irascible principle in our nature is ever insurgent against reason, so there was a most determined effort and (to use a familiar word) *set* against this capital and vital article of faith, age after age, on the part of various schools of opinion all over Christendom. They differed, and indeed were almost indifferent, *how* the mystery was to be disposed of; they took up opposite theories against it; they were antagonists of each other; but go it must. The attack came upon the [317] Church, not on this side or that, but from all quarters, at once or successively, whether in the wide field of speculation, or within the territory of the Church, and circled round the Holy See, rallying and forming again and again in very various positions, though beaten back for a time, and apparently brought under. It was a very stubborn fight; and till the end appeared, which was not till after many generations, it would have been easy to indulge misgivings whether it would ever have an ending.[30] Let us fancy an erudite Nestorian of the day living in Seleucia, beyond the limits of the Roman Empire, and looking out over the Euphrates upon the battle which was waging between the See of St. Peter and the subtle heresy of the Monophysites,[31] through so protracted a period; and let him write a defence of his own Communion for the use of theological students. Doubtless he would have used that long contest as a decisive argument against the unity and purity of the Catholic Church, and might have adopted, by anticipation, the triumphant words of a learned Anglican

---

[30] *... an ending*: When describing the movements of the Church's enemies, Newman often deployed military metaphors. "I look out, then, into the enemy's camp, and I try to trace the outlines of the hostile movements and the preparations for assault which are there in agitation against us," he wrote in 1858. "The arming and the manœuvring, the earth-works and the mines, go on incessantly; and one cannot of course tell, without the gift of prophecy, which of his projects will be carried into effect and attain its purpose, and which will eventually fail or be abandoned." Nevertheless, Newman could delineate the main lines of the liberal philosophy that sought to undermine the Catholic faith. "You may have opinions in religion, you may have theories, you may have arguments, you may have probabilities," he portrayed his rationalist liberals arguing, "you may have anything but demonstration, and therefore you cannot have science. In mechanics you advance from sure premises to sure conclusions; in optics you form your undeniable facts into system, arrive at general principles, and then again infallibly apply them: here you have Science." But for the liberal rationalists, "it is absurd for men in our present state to teach anything positively about the next world, that there is a heaven, or a hell, or a last judgment, or that the soul is immortal, or that there is a God." J. H. Newman, "A Form of Infidelity of the Day," *Idea*, 313. Military metaphors naturally abound in the lectures since so many of them focus on the Church militant. See Editor's Introduction.

[31] *Monophysites*: See the long articles (too long to quote or even extract) from the *Catholic Encyclopedia* and the *ODCC* on Monophysitism, both of which corroborate Newman's account of the heresy's course.

divine, rashly uttered in 1838, and prudently recalled in 1842, with reference to that Jansenistic controversy, which I reserve for my second example. "This very [Monophysite] heresy," he would have said, "has, in opposition to all these anathemas and condemnations, and in spite of the persecution of the temporal powers, continued to exist for nearly [300] years; and, what is more, it has existed all along in the very heart of the Roman Church itself. Yet, it [318] has perpetuated itself in all parts of that Church, sometimes covertly, sometimes openly, exciting uneasiness, tumults, innovations, reforms, persecution, schisms, but always adhering to the Roman communion with invincible tenacity. It is in vain that, sensible of so great an evil, the Roman Church struggles and resorts to every expedient to free her from its presence; the loathed and abhorred heresy perpetuates itself in her vitals, and infects her bishops, her priests, her monks, her universities; and, depressed for a time by the arm of civil power, gains the ascendancy at length, influences the councils of kings, ... produces religious innovations of the most extraordinary character, and inflicts infinite and permanent injury and disgrace on the cause of the Roman Church."[32]

Such is the phenomenon which Monophysitism distinctly presents to us more than a thousand years before the rise of a heresy, which this author seems to have fancied the first instance of such an anomaly.[33] The controversy began amid the flourishing schools of Syria, the most learned quarter of Christendom; it extended along Asia Minor to Greece and Constantinople; and then there was a pause. Suddenly it broke out in an apparently dissimilar shape, and with a new beginning, in the imperial city; summoned its adherents, confederates, and partisans from North to South, came into collision with the Holy See, and [319] convulsed the Catholic world. Subdued for a while, it

---

[32] Palmer's Essay on the Church, vol. i. p. 320. [N]
[33] *the first instance of such an anomaly*: Such ignorance of history is not unusual among critics of the Church, especially those who resort to the fallacies of historicism to take issue with her doctrines.

returned to what was very like its original form and features, and reared its head in Egypt with a far more plausible phraseology, and in a far more promising position. There, and in Syria, and thence through the whole of the East, supported by the emperors, and afterwards by the Mahometans, it sustained itself with great ingenuity, inventing evasion after evasion, and throwing itself into more and more subtle formulas, for the space of near three hundred years. Lastly, it suddenly appeared in a new shape, and in a final effort, four hundred years from the time of its first rise, in the extreme West of Europe, among the theologians of Spain; and formed matter of controversy for our own Alcuin, the scholar of St. Bede, for the interposition of Charlemagne, and the labours of the great Council of Frankfort.

It is impossible, I am sure, for any one patiently to read the history of this series of controversies, whatever may be his personal opinions, without being intimately convinced of the oneness or identity of the mind, which lived in the Catholic Church through that long period; which baffled the artifices and sophistries of the subtlest intellects, was proof against human infirmity and secular expedience, and succeeded in establishing irrevocably and for ever those points of faith with which she started in the contest. "Any one false step would have thrown the whole theory of the doctrine into irretrievable confusion; but it was as if some individual and perspicacious intellect, to speak humanly, ruled the theological discussion from first to last. That in the long course of centuries, and in spite of the failure, in points of detail, of the most gifted fathers and saints, the Church thus wrought out the one and only consistent theory which can be formed on the great doctrine in dispute, proves how clear, simple, and exact her vision of that doctrine was."[34] Now I leave the retrospect of this long struggle with two remarks—first, that it was never doubtful to the world for any long time *what* was the decision of authority on each

[320]

---

[34] Essay on Doctrinal Development, p. 438. [N]

successive question as each came into consideration; next, that the series of doctrinal errors which was evolved tended from the first to an utter overthrow of the heresy, each decision of authority being a new and further victory over it, which was never undone. It was all along in visible course of expulsion from the Catholic fold. Contrast this with the denial of baptismal grace, viewed as a heresy within the Anglican Church; has the sentiment of authority against it always been unquestionable? Has there been a series of victories over it? Is it in visible course of expulsion? Is it ever tending to be expelled? Are the influence and prospects of the heresy less formidable now than in the age of Wesley, or of Calamy,[35] or of Baxter,[36] or of Abbot,[37] or of [321] Cartwright,[38] or of the Reformers?[39]

---

[35] *Calamy*: Edmund Calamy (1600-66), Presbyterian clergyman. He opposed the regicide of Charles I and Cromwell's subsequent protectorate, and figured in the deputation to Charles II in Holland, returning home "satisfied that Charles intended presbyterian comprehension in a national church." However, when Charles accepted the Act of Uniformity, the nonconformist Calamy was ejected. "When the ark of God is taken," he told his congregation at his final sermon, "then the Ministers of Christ are driven into corners. Where false religion comes in at one door, the true Religion goes out at the other." His subsequent arrest and imprisonment put an end to his preaching, though his sermons continued to command a wide audience. After being released, his isolation was made all the more devastating by the Great Fire of London. "Seeing the desolate Condition of so flourishing a City, for which he had so great an Affection" broke "his tender Spirit." A month later, after secluding himself in his residence, he was dead. Sarah Achinstein sums up his melancholy career thus: "Calamy is an emblem for the old dissenting Presbyterianism which sought political solutions to national religious problems." *ODNB*

[36] *Baxter*: Richard Baxter (1615–91), Puritan divine. A Shropshireman, Baxter was educated locally and became master of Bridgnorth Grammar School (1638). Contact with nonconformists, however, sowed doubts about Anglicanism and episcopacy. After a spell as vicar of Kidderminster (1642) and parliamentary army chaplain, he became disillusioned by both sides in the Civil War. In 1660 he welcomed Charles II back, but his inflexibility at the Savoy conference helped its breakdown. After refusing the see of Hereford, he preached in London until ejected after the Act of Uniformity (1662). Having helped overthrow James II, he welcomed William and Mary. *Oxford Companion*

8.

The second controversy which I shall mention is one not so remarkable in itself, not so wide in its field of conflict, nor so terrible in its events, but more interesting perhaps to us, as relating almost to our own times, and because it is used as an argument against the Church's unity and power of enforcing her decisions, by such writers as the theologian, of whose words I just now availed myself. For the better part of two centuries Jansenism has troubled the greater part of Catholic Europe, has had great successes, and has expected greater still; yet, somehow or other, such is the fact, as a looker-on would be obliged to say, whatever be the internal reasons for it, of which he would not be a judge, at the end of the time you look for it and it is gone. As fire among the stubble threatens great things, but suddenly is quenched in the very fulness of its blaze, so has it been with the heresy in question. One might have thought

---

to British History. It is from Baxter that C. S. Lewis took his idea of "mere Christianity."

[37] *Abbot:* George Abbot (1562-1633), archbishop of Canterbury, whose persecution of Dissenters led to the rise of Cromwell. See *ODNB*.

[38] *Cartwright:* Thomas Cartwright (1535–1603). A leading early Presbyterian, Cartwright was born in Hertfordshire and graduated from St John's College, Cambridge. Expelled on Mary's accession, he returned as fellow of Trinity (1562), but disputes over surplices and church government led him to depart for Ireland (1565–7). After his return as Lady Margaret professor of divinity (1569) his advocacy of presbyterian church government brought him into conflict with Whitgift, master of Trinity. Deprived of his professorship (1570) and his fellowship (1571), he emigrated to Geneva. Intellectually the leading puritan of his day, he refused to associate with the Brownists and Barrowists. *Oxford Companion to British History*.

[39] *the Reformers:* The various Reformers of the English Reformation. For a balanced, judicious account of this history, see Christopher Haigh. *English Reformations: Religion, Politics, and Society Under the Tudors.* (Oxford, 1993). Haigh and J. J. Scarisbrick, the biographer of King Henry VIII, were the pioneering revisionists of the Reformation in England, showing in detail by parish and other local records that the English were not as hostile to their traditional Catholic faith as Whig historians had claimed for centuries. Eamon Duffy's *The Stripping of the Altars* (1992) was based on their spadework, as Duffy acknowledges in his introduction.

that an age like this would have been especially favourable for the development of many of its peculiarities; one never should be surprised even now, if it developed them again. The heresy almost rose with Protestantism, and kept pace with it; it extended and flourished in those Catholic countries on which Protestantism had made its greatest [322] inroads, and it grew by the side of Protestantism; when now suddenly we find it dead in France, and it is receiving its death-blow in Austria, in the very generation, at the very hour, when Protestantism is at length getting acknowledged possession of the far-famed communion of Laud and Hammond.

There was a time when nearly all that was most gifted, learned, and earnest in France seemed corrupted by the heresy; which, though condemned again and again by the Holy See, discovered new subterfuges, and gained to itself fresh patrons and protectors, to shelter it from the Apostolic ban. What circle of names can be produced, comparable in their times for the combination of ability and virtue, of depth of thought, of controversial dexterity, of poetical talent, of extensive learning, and of religious reputation, with those of Launoy,[40] Pascal,[41] Nicole,[42] Arnauld,[43]

---

[40] *Launoy*: Jean de Launoy (1603-78). French historian. In papal politics he was a Gallican, in theology a Jansenist.

[41] *Pascal*: Blaise Pascal (1623–62), French mathematician and philosopher. "From 1646 he was closely involved with the Jansenists and the convent of Port-Royal. On 23 Nov. 1654 he experienced a conversion, recorded in his *Mémorial* (but found stitched into his coat, known as *Pascal's amulet*), in which he discovered 'the God of Abraham, God of Isaac, God of Jacob, not of the philosophers and the men of science'. When the Jansenist, Arnauld, was condemned in 1655, Pascal wrote his *Lettres provinciales* in which he satirized the laxity implicit in Jesuit theories of grace and moral theology. In his *Pensées*, published posthumously from his notes, Pascal saw Christianity as lying beyond exact reason and apprehended by the heart which dares to risk. He is associated also with his 'wager': if we believe God exists and he does, the reward is eternal happiness; if he does not exist, we lose nothing; and the same is true if we disbelieve and he does not exist; whereas if we disbelieve and he does exist, we have lost eternal life. On the mathematics of probability (see further, G. Schlesinger, Religion and Scientific Method, 1977), the wager should be taken up unless the

359

existence of God can be conclusively disproved—which it cannot." *The Concise Oxford Dictionary of World Religions*. Recognizing that the faithful are obliged to try to convert the faithless, Pascal devised his 'wager' to appeal to faithless libertines, many of whom, then as now, were devoted to gaming. Pascal himself may have been devoted to gaming, if only because it fascinated his sense of the probable. See T.S. Eliot, "The *Pensées* of Pascal" (1931), *Selected Essays* 2nd ed. (London, 1951), 402-416. Eliot also sees Pascal's Jansenism as a salutary phase in the man of the world's conversion. "A moment of Jansenism may naturally take place, and take place rightly, in the individual; particularly in the life of a man of great and intense intellectual powers, who cannot avoid seeing through human beings and observing the vanity of their thoughts and of their avocations, their dishonesty and self-deception, the insincerity of their emotions, their cowardice, the pettiness of their real ambitions. Actually, considering that much greater maturity is required for these qualities, than for any mathematical or scientific greatness, how easily brooding on *the misery of man without God* might have encouraged in him the sin of spiritual pride, the *concupiscence de l'esprit*: and how fast a hold he has on humility!" "The *Pensées* of Pascal," 414.

[42] *Nicole*: Pierre Nicole (1625–95) French moralist and theologian. A teacher at Port-Royal and friend of Arnauld, with whom he often collaborated, especially on the *Logiques de Port-Royal* (1662). He is remembered as well for the *Essais de morale* (1671), some of which were translated by Locke.

[43] *Arnauld*; Antoine Arnauld (1612–94). "The youngest brother of Robert Arnauld d'Andilly, he was a brilliant scholar who switched from law to theology under Saint-Cyran's influence, becoming a doctor of the Sorbonne in 1641. His career as the leading Jansenist theologian and controversialist earned him the title 'le grand Arnauld'. In *De la fréquente communion* (1643) he defended Saint-Cyran's ideas, advocated a return to the purity and simplicity of early Christianity, and emphasized the need for true contrition before the sacrament of the Eucharist. Meanwhile, the controversy concerning Jansenius's *Augustinus* continued. In two works entitled *Apologie de M. Jansénius* (1643 and 1644), Arnauld supported Jansenius's arguments against sufficient grace and his teaching on reprobation (and, by implication, predestination). He also defended Jansenius in *Apologie pour les saints Pères de l'Église, défenseurs de la grâce de Jésus-Christ* (1651). In 1653 five propositions allegedly taken from the *Augustinus* were condemned by Pope Innocent X. In reply, the Jansenists sought to distinguish between *droit* (were the propositions heretical?) and *fait* (were they part of the teaching of Jansenius?). This was the distinction made by Arnauld in the pamphlet *Lettre d'un docteur de Sorbonne à une personne de condition* (1655) and in a quarto volume, *Seconde Lettre à un duc et pair* (1656). The

Racine,[44] Tillemont,[45] Quesnel,[46] and their co-religionists, admirable in every point, but in their deficiency in the

---

Sorbonne censured two of Arnauld's propositions and, despite the intervention of Pascal, dismissed him. For the next 12 years he remained largely in hiding, but wrote tirelessly in defence of a strict Augustinianism. He also collaborated with Lancelot and Nicole, respectively, in publishing two very influential works, a *Grammaire générale et raisonnée* (1660) and *La Logique, ou l'Art de penser* (1662). After the election of Pope Clement IX, the Jansenists experienced a period of respite between 1668 and 1679, during which Arnauld and Nicole wrote the anti-Protestant *Perpétuité de la foi de l'Église touchant l'Eucharistie* (1669–74). In 1679 Louis XIV resumed his persecution of the Port-Royalists, with the result that Arnauld spent his last 15 years in exile in the Spanish Low Countries and Holland. He continued to publish largely anonymous writings in defence of the Mons New Testament, in favour of a vernacular Bible, against William of Orange, Malebranche, and various Protestant writers. Above all, he pursued his campaign against the Jesuits in six volumes (1690–3 and 1695) which continued Pontchâteau's *Morale pratique des Jésuites représentée en plusieurs histoires arrivées dans toutes les parties du monde*. Arnauld's sisters (Mère Angélique de Sainte-Madeleine and Mère Agnès de Saint-Paul) and his niece (Mère Angélique de Saint-Jean) were all abbesses of Port-Royal." *The New Oxford Companion to Literature in French.*

[44] *Racine*: Jean Racine (1639–99). French tragic dramatist. Racine was born in a middle-class family in La Ferté-Milon (Aisne). Orphaned while still a small child, he was brought up by his grandparents, then sent to the Jansenist school at Port-Royal des Champs. Although in 1666 he was to break with his mentors, writing a vitriolic attack on Nicole, who had accused playwrights of being public poisoners, he was later reconciled with them. He completed his education in Paris, and left school with a knowledge of Greek literature that was unusual in his day. Having spent over a year in Uzès in the vain pursuit of an ecclesiastical living, he embarked in 1663 on a literary career in Paris. La Fontaine was among his friends, soon to be joined by Molière and Boileau. Racine's major works include *Andromaque* (1667), *Phèdre* (1677), *Britannicus* (1669), *Bajazet* (1672), and *Athalie* (1691). *The New Oxford Companion to Literature in French.*

[45] *Tillemont:* Louis-Sébastien Le Nain de Tillemont (1637-98), Church historian, on whose scholarly work Gibbon relied for the *Decline and Fall*, famously referring to the Jansenist historian as "the patient and sure-footed mule of the Alps who may be trusted in the most slippery paths." Born in Paris into a wealthy Jansenist family, Tillemont was educated at the Petites écoles of Port-Royal, where his historical interests were formed and encouraged. At the age of twenty, he began his two monumental works, the *Mémoires pour servir à l'histoire ecclésiastique*

primary grace of a creature, humility? What shall we say to the prospects of a school of opinion, which was influencing so many of the most distinguished Congregations of the day; and which, though nobly withstood by the Society of Jesus and the Sulpicians,[47] yet at length found an entrance among the learned Benedictines of St. Maur,[48] and had already sapped the faith of various members of another body, as erudite and as gifted as they? For fifteen years a [323] Cardinal Archbishop of Paris was its protector and leader, and this at a distance of sixty years after its formal condemnation. First, the book itself of Jansenius had been condemned; and then, in consequence of an evasion, the sense of the book; and then a controversy arose whether the

---

des six premiers siècles and the *Histoire des empereurs et autres princes qui ont régné pendant les six premiers siècles de l'Église*. The first is a history of the first six centuries of the Christian Church; the second, a history of the Roman emperors during the same period.

[46] *Quesnel*: Pasquier Quesnel (1634–1719). French religious writer, originally an Oratorian. (The French Oratorians are different from St. Philip's Oratorians.) His belief in Augustinian efficacious grace and his moral rigorism resulted in strong Jansenist sympathies, which led to his banishment from Paris (1681) and his expulsion from the Oratoire (1684). Fearing persecution, he fled to Brussels, where he joined Antoine Arnauld. On Arnauld's death (1694) he became leader of the Jansenist movement. He defended a scholarly approach to the Scriptures and held Richerist views. His *Nouveau Testament en français avec des réflexions morales sur chaque verset* (1692) had been appearing in various forms since 1672. It became a central Jansenist text, and the papal bull Unigenitus (1713) condemned 101 sentences from it. *The New Oxford Companion to Literature in French.*

[47] *Sulpicians*: Society of Saint-Sulpice. the congregation of secular priests founded by J.-J. Olier in the parish of St-Sulpice, Paris, in 1642 with the aim of forming a zealous clergy, especially suited to be directors of seminaries. The Society, which spread to Canada in 1657, was granted Papal approbation in 1664. Theologically, until the 1930s, the Sulpicians were solidly Thomist. *ODCC.*

[48] *learned Benedictines of St. Maur*: The Benedictine monks of the Congregation of St-Maur. This was founded in 1618 to represent in France the reform initiated in the Abbey of Saint-Vanne (Lorraine) in 1600; it received Papal approval in 1621. The literary and historical work, for which the Congregation is famous, was largely centred at Saint-Germain-des-Prés. The Congregation was dissolved in 1818.

Church could decide such a matter of fact as that a book had a particular sense. And then the further question came into discussion whether the sense of the book was to be condemned with the mere intention of an external obedience, or with an internal assent. Eleven bishops of France interposed with the Pope to prevent the condemnation; there were four who required nothing more of their clergy than a respectful silence on the subject in controversy; and nineteen wrote to the Pope in favour of these four. Before these difficulties had been settled, a fresh preacher of the same doctrines appeared in the person of Quesnel; and on the Pope's condemning his opinions in the famous bull *Unigenitus*,[49] six bishops refused to publish it, and fourteen formally opposed it; and then sixteen suspended the effects of it. Three universities took part with them, and the parliaments of various towns banished their Archbishops, Bishops, or Priests, and confiscated their goods, either for taking part against the Jansenists or for refusing them the Sacraments.[50]

As time went on, the evil spread wider and grew more [324] intense, instead of being relieved. In the middle of last century, a hundred years after the condemnation of the heresy at Rome, it was embodied in the person of a far more efficacious disputant than Jansenius or Quesnel. The Emperor Joseph developed the apparently harmless theories of a theological school in the practical form of

---

[49] *Unigenitus*: *Unigenitus Dei Filius.* The papal bull of Pope Innocent XI which condemned the Jansenist writings of Quesnel in 1713. The bull's language is admirably blunt. "Declared and condemned as false, captious, evil-sounding, offensive to pious ears, scandalous, pernicious, rash, injurious to the Church and her practice, insulting not only to the Church but also the secular powers seditious, impious, blasphemous, suspected of heresy, and smacking of heresy itself, and, besides, favoring heretics and heresies, and also schisms, erroneous, close to heresy, many times condemned, and finally heretical, clearly renewing many heresies respectively and most especially those which are contained in the infamous propositions of Jansen, and indeed accepted in that sense in which these have been condemned."

[50] Vide Mémoires pour servir, &c., and Palmer on the Church. [N]

Erastianism.[51] He prohibited the reception of the famous bull *Unigenitus* in his dominions; subjected all bulls, rescripts, and briefs from Rome to an imperial supervision; forbade religious orders to obey foreign superiors; "suppressed confraternities, abolished the processions, retrenched festivals, prescribed the order of offices, regulated the ceremonies, the number of masses, the manner of giving benediction, nay the number of waxlights."[52] He seized the revenues of the Bishops, destroyed their sees, and even for a time forbade them to confer orders. He permitted divorce in certain cases, and removed images from the churches. The new Reformation reached as far as Belgium on the one hand, and down to Naples on the other. The whole of the Empire and its alliances were apparently on the point of disowning their dependence on the Apostolic See. The worship of the saints, auricular confession, indulgences, and other Catholic doctrines, were openly written against or disputed by bishops and professors. The Archduke of Tuscany,[53] imitating the Emperor, sent catechisms to the

---

[51] *the practical form of Erastianism*: Josephism; see page 260.

[52] Mémoires pour servir, &c. [N]

[53] *The Archduke of Tuscany*: Leopold II (Peter Leopold Joseph Anton Joachim Pius Gotthard (1747–92) was Holy Roman Emperor, King of Hungary and Bohemia, Archduke of Austria from 1790 to 1792, and Grand Duke of Tuscany from 1765 to 1790. Newman read of the Archduke in Palmer's treatise. "In Tuscany, Jansenism was equally troublesome. The archduke Leopold 'followed blindly the counsels of Scipio Ricci, who was made, in 1780, bishop of Pistoia and Prato.' Ricci 'resolved to introduce into Italy the opinions to which France owed a century of disputes.' By his counsel the prince issued frequent and prolix circulars, sent 'catechisms to the bishops, directed the books which they should place in the hands of the faithful, abolished confraternities, diminished processions, regulated divine worship and ceremonies,' etc. Ricci filled his diocese 'with men subservient to his notions, whom he invited from all parts. He caused ecclesiastical academies to be established where the new theology was taught. He wrote against devotion to the heart of Jesus, against indulgences, which he reduced to be nothing but the relaxation of the canonical penance formerly imposed for sins. He changed rites, reformed discipline, overthrew the system of instruction, etc.'" W. Palmer, *A Treatise on the Church of Christ* 2 vols. (London, 1842), i, 257.

bishops, and instructed them by his circulars or charges; [325] while a Neapolitan prelate,[54] instead of his ordinary title of "Bishop by the grace of the Holy Apostolic See," styled himself "Bishop by the grace of the King." Who would not have thought that Henry of England[55] had risen from his place, and was at once in Vienna, Belgium, Tuscany, and Naples? The reforming views had spread into Portugal; and, to complete the crisis, the great antagonist of Protestantism, which was born with it in one day, and had ever since been the best champion of the Holy See, the Society of Jesus itself, by the inscrutable fiat of Providence, was, in that hour of need, to avoid worse evils, by that very See suppressed.[56] Surely the Holy Roman Church is at length in the agonies of

---

[54] *a Neapolitan prelate*: Newman plucked this from Palmer as well. "It may be observed that Cortez, bishop of Motula, who was at the head of a royal commission for hearing an appeal in a cause of marriage, which ought, according to the former system, to have gone before the Roman see, renounced the ordinary formulary by which bishops are accustomed to begin their ordinances, 'bishop by the grace of the holy apostolic see.' M. Cortez had in fact suppressed this formula in imitation of some old French prelates … Jansenism and reform had partisans, it seems, in the Neapolitan church, as well as elsewhere." *Ibid*, i, 256-7.

[55] *Henry of England*: Henry VIII (1491-1547).

[56] *suppressed*: "The attack on the Jesuits was opened on 17 April 1762 by the Jansenist sympathizer the Abbé Chauvelin who denounced the Constitution of the Society of Jesus, which was publicly examined and discussed in a hostile press. The Parlement issued its *Extraits des assertions* assembled from passages from Jesuit theologians and canonists, in which they were alleged to teach every sort of immorality and error. On 6 August 1762, the final *arrêt* was proposed to the Parlement by the Advocate General Joly de Fleury, condemning the Society to extinction, but the king's intervention brought eight months' delay and in the meantime a compromise was suggested by the Court. If the French Jesuits would separate from the Society headed by the Jesuit General directly under the pope's authority and come under a French vicar, with French customs, as with the Gallican Church, the Crown would still protect them. The French Jesuits, rejecting Gallicanism, refused to consent. On 1 April 1763, the colleges were closed, and by a further *arrêt* of March 9, 1764, the Jesuits were required to renounce their vows under pain of banishment. At the end of November 1764, the king signed an edict dissolving the Society throughout his dominions …" Christine Vogel, "The Suppression of the Society of Jesus, 1758–1773," *European History Online*, Mainz: Institute of European History, (2011).

dissolution. The Catholic powers, Germany, France, Portugal, and Naples, all have turned against her. Who is to defend her? The mystery of Protestantism is unravelled; the day of Luther is come; the Catholics send up a cry, and their enemies a shout of joy.

9.

Noli æmulari.[57] Is it not written in the book of truth, that the ungodly shall spread abroad like a green bay-tree, and then shall wither? that the adversary reaches out his hand towards his prey, in order that he may be more emphatically smitten? "Yet a little while, and the wicked shall not be: I passed by, and lo! he was not; I sought him, and his place [326] was not found. Better is a little to the just than the great riches of the wicked; for the arms of the wicked shall be broken, but the Lord strengtheneth the just."[58] So was it with the great Arian heresy, which the civil power would fain have forced upon the Church; but it fell to pieces, and the Church remained One. So was it with Nestorius, with Eutyches, with the Image-breakers,[59] with Manichees,[60] with Lollards,[61] with Protestants, into whom the State would put

---

[57] *Noli æmulari*: 'Be not jealous of the evil-doers.' See Arthur Hugh Clough's poem of this title, the opening lines of which are: "In controversial foul impureness/The peace that is thy light to thee/Quench not: in faith and inner sureness/Possess thy soul and let it be." Clough was influenced keenly by Newman in his youth. See also E. Short, *Newman and his Contemporaries* (London, 2011), 361-82.

[58] *the Lord strengtheneth the just*: Psalm,37:10

[59] *Image-breakers*: Iconoclasts.

[60] *Manichees*: Followers of Manichaeism, the doctrine that the world is not governed by one perfect Being, but by a balance of the forces of good and evil. The doctrine elevates the Devil, as the personification of evil, into a position of power comparable to that of God. It derives from Zoroastrianism and was held by the Manichees, followers of the Persian teacher Manes or Manichaeus. It flourished between the 3rd and 5th centuries AD. St Augustine adhered to Manichaeanism for several years, before becoming a bitter opponent. *The Oxford Dictionary of Philosophy.*

[61] *Lollards*: 14th and 15th-century proto-Protestants. "In the early 14th c., this term was a synonym for *Beghards*, pejoratively denoting religious eccentrics; then, from the late 1380s and alternating with *Wycliffites*, denoting the followers of Wycliffe. Lollardy was an English national

heresy, comparable to Hussitism in Bohemia, but less successful. Its origins and early support were in high academic and political milieux. It stemmed from the views of the Oxford academic John Wycliffe, which were preached outside Oxford first by Wycliffe himself, but also (by 1382) through the preaching of Oxford academic disciples. Through others connected with Oxford, and also poor priests, the movement spread in the next few decades through much of England, notably the Chilterns, the south-west, London and the south-east, and the south Midlands. ... Lollardy's high-point came in 1410, when Parliament entertained a Lollard "Disendowment Bill" which proposed the confiscations of episcopal and monastic property. Clerical opposition to Lollardy came slowly in a country which had not dealt with widespread heresy before. The death-penalty for heresy was introduced in 1401, after which there were major trials of Lollards and burnings at the stake." *Oxford Encyclopaedia of the Middle Ages*. See K. B. McFarlane, *John Wycliffe and the Beginnings of English Nonconformity*, (London, 1952). Despite their heretical views, G. K. Chesterton had a good word for the Lollards. "I have very considerable sympathy with the Lollards; the particular heretics of the Chaucerian epoch. They were often infamously treated; they were sometimes intuitively right. In so far as they originally set out to reform the practical Catholicism of their day, there were few reputable Catholics then, and there are no reasonable Catholics now, who would deny that Catholicism very much needed it. In so far as they had a desire to purify Catholicism, they may often have been spiritually right even when they were intellectually wrong; and in that sense, may have been better Catholics than the Catholics. But in so far as they had a desire to *simplify* Catholicism, the Catholic Church was ten thousand times right in its desire to defeat and crush them. That notion, in its essence a very negative notion, has never wrought anything but ill to Christendom; and is always returning with a plausibility and a false simplicity to tempt and to betray Christians. Mahomet, centuries before, had tried to create a simplified Christianity, and had created a world of fatalism and stagnation. Calvin, centuries afterwards, tried to create a simplified Christianity, and created a world of pessimism and devil-worship. It was of the very life of the ancient civilization, Pagan as well as Christian, from which medievalism drew its deep and strange type of strength, that it was rooted in very varied realities; that it had made a cosmos out of a chaos of experiences; that it knew what was positive and could yet allow for what was really relative; that its Christ was shared by God and Man; that its government was shared by God and Caesar: that its philosophers made a bridge between faith and reason, between freedom and fatalism; and that its moralists warned men alike against presumption and despair. Only by understanding all that ten times complicated sort of complication, can we see how Geoffrey Chaucer could find life so simple." *The Collected Works of G. K. Chesterton*, Volume 18, 370.

life, but who, one and all, refuse to live. So is it with the communion of Cranmer and Parker,[62] which is kept together only by the heavy hand of the State, and cannot aspire to be free without ceasing to be one. One power alone on earth has the gift and destiny of ever being one. It has been so of old time; surely so will it be now. Man's necessity is God's opportunity. *Noli æmulari*, "Be not jealous of the evil-doers." ...

It is towards the end of the century: what shall be, ere that end arrive? ... Suddenly there is heard a rushing noise, borne north and south upon the wings of the wind. Is it a deluge to sweep over the earth, and to bear up the ark of God upon its bosom? or is it the fire which is ravaging to and fro, to try every man's work what it is, and to discriminate between what is of earth and what is of heaven? Now we shall see what can live and what at must die; now shall we have the proof of Jansenism; now shall we see whether the Catholic Church has that eternal

[327] individuality which is of the essence of life, or whether it be an external thing, a birth of the four elements, a being of chance and circumstance, made up of parts, but with no integrity or immaterial principle informing it. The breath of the Lord hath gone forth far and wide upon the face of the earth; the very foundations of society are melting in the fiery flood which it has kindled; and we shall see whether the Three Children will be able to walk in the midst of the furnace, and will come forth with their hair unsinged, their garments whole, and their skin untainted by the smell of fire.

So closed the last century upon the wondering world; and for years it wondered on; wondered what should be the issue of the awful portent which it witnessed, and what new state of things was to rise out of the old. The Church disappeared before its eyes as by a yawning earthquake, and men said it was a fulfilment of the prophecies, and they sang a hymn, and went to their long sleep, content and with

---

[62] *Cranmer and Parker*: Architects of the English Reformation.

a *Nunc Dimittis* in their mouths; for now at length had an old superstition been wiped off from the earth, and the Pope had gone his way. And other powers, kings, and the like, disappeared too, and nothing was to be seen.

Fifty years have passed away since the time of those wonders, and we, my brethren, behold in our degree the issue of what our fathers could but imagine. Great changes surely have been wrought, but not those which they anticipated. The German Emperor has ceased to be; he [328] persecuted the Church, and he has lost his place of pre-eminence. The Gallican Church, too, with its much-prized liberties, and its fostered heresy, was also swept away, and its time-honoured establishment dissolved. Jansenism is no more. The Church lives, the Apostolic See rules. That See has greater acknowledged power in Christendom than ever before, and that Church has a wider liberty than she has had since the days of the Apostles. The faith is extending in the great Anglo-Saxon race, its recent enemy, the lord of the world, with a steadiness and energy, which that proud people fears, yet cannot resist.[63] Out of the ashes of the

---

[63] *... yet cannot resist*: Two months after delivering the last of his *Anglican Difficulties* lectures in King William Street early in July, 1850, Newman and the Oratorians would find themselves engulfed in the disturbances that arose in response to what became known as "papal aggression," or Pope Pius IX's reconstitution of the hierarchy of England and Wales by Letters Apostolic, *Universalis Ecclesiae* (29 Sept. 1850), comprising an archbishop and 12 suffragans all with territorial titles. In the wake of the document referring to the Church of England as 'the Anglican Schism,' an hysterical cry of indignation spread through Great Britain under Prime Minister Lord John Russell (1792–1878), culminating in the passage of the *Ecclesiastical Titles Act* 1851, making it a criminal offence for anyone outside the Church of England to use any episcopal title "of any city, town or place, or of any territory or district (under any designation or description whatsoever), in the United Kingdom" Newman's response to this recrudescence of No Popery was justly defiant: "... to tell the truth, though I hate rows, I hate (I hope) humbug quite as much — and so much had got about lately at home and abroad to the effect that the British Lion had become a lamb, and that John Bull had become instinct with a diviner spirit, that liberals were Catholics, and the race of squires and parsons was extinct, that I do think it is a good thing to have matters put on their true basis. And then those

ancient Church of France has sprung a new hierarchy, worthy of the name and the history of that great nation, as fervent as their St. Bernard,[64] as tender as their St. Francis, as enterprising as their St. Louis, as loyal to the Holy See as their Charlemagne.[65] The Empire has rescinded the impious

---

wretched whigs, the μισητὸς στάσις [the 'hateful faction'] of Hurrell Froude. I hope we are rid of them for ever. And then I suppose it will tend, especially if the row goes on, to bring together and consolidate the Catholic interest all over the Empire. ... One thing the government may be quite sure of, that, though we shall try to escape breaking the law, if we can help, yet if they drive us to bay in a matter of principle, to a certainty we shall, whatever comes of it, though we are sent out after Smith O Brien." *LD*, xv, 154-5. William Smith O'Brien (1803–64) was the Irish nationalist MP and leader of the Young Ireland movement convicted of sedition for his part in the Young Irelander Rebellion of 1848, though his death sentence was commuted to deportation to Van Diemen's Land.

[64] *St. Bernard* (1090–1153), Abbot of Clairvaux. In 1112 he entered the monastery of Cîteaux and three years later was sent to establish a new house at Clairvaux. He came to exercise an immense influence in ecclesiastical and political affairs. In 1129 at the Synod of Troyes he obtained recognition for the Rule of the Templars, which he is said to have drawn up. In the disputed Papal election in 1130, he secured the victory of Innocent II; his relation with the Papacy became even closer with the election of a Cistercian monk and former pupil as Eugenius III in 1145. In his last years Bernard preached the Second Crusade. For David Knowles, "it is difficult to name any other saint in the history of the Church whose influence, both on the public life of an epoch and on the consciences of a multitude of individuals, was during his lifetime so profound and so pervasive." David Knowles, *The Monastic Order in England* 2nd ed. (Cambridge,1966), 217.

[65] *Charlemagne*: 'Charles the Great' (c. 742–814), first Emperor (from 800) of what was later to be called the 'Holy Roman Empire.' "The son of Pepin III, King of the Franks, and Bertrada, he was anointed with his father and Carloman, his brother, by Pope Stephen III in 754. On Pepin's death in 768 he and Carloman divided the kingdom between them. The death of Carloman in 771 left Charlemagne sole ruler. For the next 28 years, Charlemagne was mainly occupied with extending his kingdom in all directions. He first subdued Lombardy, perhaps at the request of Hadrian I. Having forced the king, Desiderius, to retire to a monastery, Charlemagne assumed the Lombard crown, and was rewarded by the Pope with the title of patricius. Next followed (772–98) a long series of arduous campaigns against the Saxons. Bavaria was annexed in 788, and between 791 and 796 the power of the Avar kingdom was destroyed.

regulations of the Emperor Joseph, and has commenced the emancipation of the Church. The idea and the genius of Catholicism has triumphed within its own pale with a power and a completeness which the world has never seen before. Never was the whole body of the faithful so united to each other and to their head. Never was there a time when there was less of error, heresy, and schismatical perverseness

---

Meanwhile dissensions among the Muslims in Spain had tempted Charlemagne over the Pyrennees. In his first expedition (778), which was a failure, Roland, Count of the Breton March, was killed; the tradition of his campaign long survived into the Middle Ages in a romantic form through La Chanson de Roland. The systematic conquest of northern Spain began in 785; and eventually, in 801, Barcelona was captured and made the centre of the Spanish March. On Christmas Day 800 Charlemagne was crowned Emperor by Pope Leo III in Rome; his title thereafter suggested a renewal of the Roman Empire, a claim which met with some disfavour in Byzantium. In addition to his conquests and wars abroad, Charlemagne brought consistency, reform, and uniformity into his government at home, building upon the firm foundations laid by his father. His creation of a strong central government, his employment of *missi dominici* (itinerant royal legates), and his legislation in the form of capitularies, which he issued for the peoples of all the regions under his rule, reflect the vigour of his government. His encouragement of ecclesiastical reform and patronage of letters, undertaken in consultation with his lay and ecclesiastical magnates, have rightly earned for his reign and much of the succeeding cent., the description the 'Carolingian Renaissance'. He continued to promote the reform of the Frankish Church by such measures as the restoration of the metropolitans. He was personally interested in Adoptianism, the *filioque,* and Iconoclasm, the main theological disputes of his day, as well as in the corrected text of the Bible prepared by Alcuin and others. He was anxious to achieve liturgical uniformity and sought to promote the Roman Mass; he also made provision for a standard homiliary and an approved collection of canon law. His patronage of the scholars who formed the palace 'school' and his remarkable collection of books in the palace library did much to stimulate learning ... It was these achievements and his encouragement of education, rather than his conquests, which form his lasting claim to fame." *ODCC.* The *OED* defines 'Adoptianism' thus: "A Christological theory which states that Jesus Christ is the son of God only by adoption, and is not coeternal with the Father. Also called *dynamic monarchianism.*" Its definition for *filioque* is: "The word ('and from the Son') inserted in the Western version of the Nicene creed to assert the doctrine of the procession of the Holy Ghost from the Son as well as from the Father, which is not admitted by the Eastern Churches."

among them. Of course the time will never be in this world, when trials and persecutions shall be at an end and [329] doubtless such are to come, even though they be below the horizon. But we may be thankful and joyful for what is already granted us; and nothing which is to be can destroy the mercies which have been.

"So let all Thy enemies perish, O Lord; but let them that love Thee shine, as the sun shineth in his rising!"[66]

---

[66] *"…in his rising!"*: Judges 5:31

LECTURE XI

HERETICAL AND SCHISMATICAL BODIES NO PREJUDICE TO THE CATHOLICITY OF THE CHURCH

1.

THERE is no objection made at this time to the claims of the Catholic Church more imposing to the imagination, yet less tenable in the judgment of reason, than that which is grounded on there being at present so many nations and races, which have kept the name of Christian, yet given up Catholicism. If fecundity has ever been considered one of the formal notes or tokens of the Mother of souls, it is fair to look out for it now; and if it has told in favour of the communion of Rome in former times, so now surely it may be plausibly made to tell against it. It would seem as if in this age of the world the whole number of anti-Catholics were nearly equal to the number of Catholics, at least so our opponents say; and I am willing, for argument's sake, to grant it. Let it be so, or, in other words, let it be assumed that scarcely more than half of Christendom subjects itself to the Catholic Church. "Is it not preposterous, then," it is asked of us, "to claim to be the whole, when you are but a [331] moiety? And with what countenance can you demand that we should unhesitatingly and without delay leave our own Communion for yours, when there is so little to show at first sight that you have more pretensions to the Christian name than we have?"

This is the argument, put in its broadest, simplest shape; and you, my brethren, would like to avail yourselves of it just as I have stated it, if you could. But you cannot; for it puts together all creeds and opinions, all communions, whatever their origin and history, and adds up the number of their members in rivalry of that of the Church's children. You would do so if you could, as your forefathers did

373

before you; two centuries ago Archbishop Bramhall did so, and you have every good wish to copy him, as in his other representations, so in this. "We hold communion," he says, speaking of the Church of England in contrast with those whom he would call Romanists, "with thrice so many Catholic Christians as they do; that is, the eastern, southern, and northern Christians, besides Protestants."[1] "Divide Christendom into five parts, and in four of them they have very little or nothing to do. Perhaps they have here a monastery, or there a small handful of proselytes; but what are five or six persons to so many millions of Christian souls, that *they* should be Catholics, and not all the others?"[2]

[332] This being the case, as he views the matter, it of course follows that we are but successors of the ancient Donatists,[3] a mere fraction of the Church excommunicating all the rest. "The Donatists," he says, "separated the whole Church from their Communion, and substituted themselves, being but a small part of the Christian world, in the place of the Catholic Church, just as the Romanists do at this day."[4]

This, certainly, was turning the tables against his opponents, who had been accustomed to consider that the Church of England, granting it was a Church, was in the very position of the followers of Donatus, a fragment of Christendom claiming for itself immaculate purity; but let

---

[1] Vol. i. p. 628. Ed. 1842. [N] *The Works of the Most Reverend Father in God, John Bramhall, DD with a Life of the Author* (Oxford, 1842).

[2] Ibid. p. 258. [N]

[3] *Donatists*: A schism in Christian North Africa in the 4th century. The Donatists refused to accept the consecration of Caecilian as bishop of Carthage in 311 because his consecrator had been a *traditor* (one who had given up copies of the Bible for confiscation) in the recent persecution of Diocletian. The local bishops consecrated a rival to Caecilian, and he was soon succeeded by Donatus, from whom the schism is named. Their opponents, especially Augustine, held that the unworthiness of ministers did not invalidate the sacraments, since their minister was Christ. For St. Augustine's attitude towards the Donatists, which Newman shared, see P Brown, *Augustine of Hippo* revised ed. (California, 2000), 216-17.

[4] Ibid. p. 106. [N] *The Works of the Most Reverend Father in God, John Bramhall, DD with a Life of the Author* (Oxford, 1842).

us observe what he is forced to do to make his argument good. First, of course, he throws himself into communion, whether they will have him or not, not only with the Greek Church, but with the various heretical bodies all over the East; the Nestorians of Chaldæa,[5] the Copts of Egypt,[6] the Jacobites of Syria,[7] and the Eutychians of Armenia,[8] whose

---

[5] *the Nestorians of Chaldea*: Member of a Syrian Uniate (formerly Nestorian) Church based mainly in Iran and Iraq.

[6] *the Copts of Egypt*: "Copts, the name, derived from Greek Aigyptioi via the Arabic Qibt, of the autochthonous Christians of Egypt, descendants of the population of Pharaonic times; since the 5th C., they have been adherents to a non-Chalcedonian church later termed "Coptic Orthodox." The term "Copts" is really an anachronism for the Byz. period but serves to designate those who used Coptic as their principal language (or bilingually with Greek) and as a major vehicle of culture, thought, and theology. As a label "Copt" does not carry an automatic class or confessional connotation. A Copt was not necessarily a peasant, an Upper Egyptian (as opposed to an Alexandrian), or a Monophysite; Athanasios and Cyril of Alexandria were Copts as were Pachomios and Shenoute. The Copts constituted a culturally vigorous and creative ethnic group within the empire, producing highly original visual art and abundant literature; the submergence of their language and culture after the Muslim conquest has not been explained. " *The Oxford Dictionary of Byzantium.* As of 2020, some seven million Copts survive in Egypt today, though they are subject to continual persecution from their Muslim neighbours; large diaspora communities live in North America and Europe.

[7] *the Jacobites of Syria*: An alternative name for the Syrian Orthodox. It derives from Jacob Baradaeus, who in the mid-6th cent. was instrumental in building up a separate (Monophysite) hierarchy in Syria, alongside that of the official Church which accepted the Chalcedonian teaching on the Person of Christ. The term first appears c. 600 and remains in popular use in some quarters. *ODCC.*

[8] *the Eutychians of Armenia*: "A Monophysite archimandrite of a Syrian monastery, Barsumas espoused and violently defended the doctrines of Eutyches: Christ's human nature was subsumed by the divine, or at least it was different from that of other humans. These were a reaction to Nestorianism. In 449, Barsumas was the first monk to be appointed as a judge at the Council of Ephesus, where he represented the malcontent monastic party. Bringing with him a riotous band of 1,000 monks to the council, he coerced it into acquitting Eutyches. Barsumas spent the remainder of his life propagating the Eutychian doctrines in Syria. Jacobites (that is, the Syrian church) regard him as a saint and miracle worker. His disciple, Samuel, spread Eutychianism to Armenia." *The*

heresy in consequence he finds it most expedient to doubt. "Those Churches," he says, speaking of the East, "do agree better, both among themselves and with other churches, than the Roman Church itself, both in profession of faith (for they and we do generally acknowledge the same ancient Creeds, and no other) and in inferior questions, [333] being free from the intricate and perplexed difficulties of the Roman schools ... How are they 'heretical' Churches? Some of them are called Nestorians, but most injuriously, who have nothing of Nestorius but the name. Others have been suspected of Eutychianism, and yet in truth orthodox enough ... It is no new thing for great quarrels to arise from mere mistakes."[9] Elsewhere he says: "It is true that some few Eastern Christians, in comparison of those innumerable multitudes, are called Nestorians; and some others, by reason of some unusual expression, suspected of Eutychianism, but both most wrongfully. Is this the requital that he," that is, his Catholic opponent, "makes to so many of these poor Christians, for maintaining their religion inviolated so many ages under Mahometan princes?"[10]

Admitting, as he does, these ancient and distant sectaries to have a portion in the Catholic faith and communion, it is not surprising that he extends a like privilege to the recently formed Protestant communities in his own neighbourhood. "Because I esteem these Churches not completely formed," he says, "do I therefore exclude them from all hope of salvation? or esteem them aliens and strangers from the commonwealth of Israel? or account them formal schismatics? No such thing."[11] "I know no reason why we should not admit Greeks and Lutherans to our communion; and, if he" (that is, his opponent) "had added them, [334] Armenians, Abyssenes,[12] Muscovites.[13] ... For the Lutherans,

---

[9] Ibid. p. 260. [N] *The Works of the Most Reverend Father in God, John Bramhall, DD with a Life of the Author* (Oxford, 1842).

[10] Ibid. p. 328 [N]

[11] Ibid. p. 70. [N]

[12] *Abyssenes*: Members of the Abyssinian (now the Ethiopian) Orthodox Church.

he does them egregious wrong. Throughout the kingdoms of
Denmark and Sweden[14] they have their bishops, name and

---

[13] He adds: "And all those who do profess the Apostolical Creed, as is
expounded in the first four general councils under the primitive
discipline." These words are not quoted above, because they are certainly
ambiguous. Bramhall does not say, "All those who do *profess* the decrees
of the first four general councils." [N]

[14] *the kingdoms of Denmark and Sweden*: "German Lutheran orthodoxy
influenced Danish Lutheranism in the 16th and 17th centuries. In the 18th
century the church was influenced by Pietism, the Lutheran movement
that began in Germany and encouraged personal religious experience and
reform. As a result, missions, orphanages, and schools were established
in Denmark. In the 19th century the outstanding figure in the renewal of
Danish church life was NFS Grundtvig (1783-1872), charismatic pastor
and poet. Although the king and Parliament have legal control over the
Danish church, in practice the church enjoys considerable independence.
It is divided into dioceses, each headed by a bishop." *Encyclopedia
Britannica*. As for the Church of Sweden, the same encyclopedia states:
"Under the leadership of Laurentius Petri, first Lutheran archbishop of
the Church of Sweden (1531–73), the church resisted attempts by
Calvinists to influence its teachings and government. Laurentius prepared
the 'church order' of 1571, a book of rites and ceremonies that regulated
the life of the church. Subsequent attempts by Roman Catholics to regain
power in Sweden were unsuccessful. Under King Gustav II Adolf,
Lutheranism was no longer threatened, and Gustav's intervention in the
Thirty Years' War has been credited with saving Protestantism in
Germany. Lutheran orthodoxy prevailed in Sweden during the 17th
century. During the 18th and 19th centuries, however, Pietism, a
movement that began in Germany and emphasized personal religious
experience and reform, strongly influenced Lutheranism in Sweden. As a
result, educational, social welfare, and mission activities were begun and
carried on by the church." *Encyclopedia Britannica*. Newman's point is
that although these churches had bishops, they hardly constituted an
episcopate in the sense in which Roman Catholics understand that word.
According to A.M. Allchin's review of Helge Grell's Grundtvig og
Oxforderne (1995): "Although Grundtvig met both Pusey and Newman
in June 1843, no true meeting of minds took place between them.
Newman was already in his heart coming to the conclusion that he must
accept the claims of the Roman Catholic Church, Pusey was cast down
by illness and the bitter controversies which followed on the University's
decision to ban him from preaching for two years, on account of his
sermon on 'The Holy Eucharist, a Comfort to the Penitent'... Grundtvig
came to Oxford, but it was humanly speaking too late for any really
fruitful contact with the leaders of the movement. At one level at least the
whole expedition can be regarded as a failure." See also P.G. Lindhardt,

thing; and throughout Germany they have their superintendents."[15]

Such was the line of argument which the defenders of the National Church adopted two centuries back; and, of course, it was much stronger in the way of argument than anything which is attempted now. Now, the Protestants are given up; we hear little or nothing of "Churches not completely formed;" not much account is taken of the "superintendents" of Germany; and as to the episcopacy of Denmark and Sweden, the thing, if not the name, is simply gone. Nor would any adherent of the theological party whom I am addressing, think with much respect either of the Nestorians or of the Monophysites of Asia and Egypt. The anti-Catholic bodies, which are made the present basis of the argument against us, are mainly or solely the Greek and the Anglican communities; and, as the antiquity, prescriptive authority, orders, and doctrine of Anglicanism, are the very subject in dispute, it is usual to simplify the [335] argument by resting it upon grounds which it is supposed we cannot deny; viz., the pretensions of the Greek Church, whose apostolical descent is unquestionable, and whose faith almost unquestioned.

2.

The argument, then, which I have to consider, is an appeal to the imagination of the following kind: The Russian Church, according to the statistical tables of 1835, includes 39,862,473 souls within its pale;[16] the Byzantine, or what is commonly called the Greek Church, is said to number about three millions;[17] so that, excluding the heretical bodies of the East, we may place the whole Greek communion, from north to south, at about forty-three

---

"Gundtvig and England," *The Journal of Ecclesiastical History*, Vol. 1, issue 2, July 1950 207-224.

[15] Ibid. p. 564. [N] *The Works of the Most Reverend Father in God, John Bramhall, DD with a Life of the Author* (Oxford, 1842).

[16] Theiner, L'Eglise Russe, 1846. [N]

[17] Conder, View of Religions. [N]

millions,[18] with such increase of population as in the last fifteen years it has gained. On the other hand, the whole number of Catholics, which has been placed by some as low as one hundred and sixteen millions, is considered by Catholics at present to reach two hundred. But, whatever be the proportion between the Greeks and ourselves, anyhow so vast a communion as one of forty-three million souls is a difficulty, it is said, too positive for us to overcome. It seems incredible that we can have exclusive claims to be Christ's heritage, if those claims issue in the exclusion of such immense populations from it; it is incredible that we [336] should be the Catholic Church, if we have not the power to take them up into our system, but let them lie in their own place. "If the Greeks are separate from the See of Rome," it is argued, "as we see they are, we too may without hazard be separate also. They are too powerful, too numerous for you to consider them as the subjects of a schism; they are too large a limb to admit of your amputation; they enter into the Church's life and essence; in ejecting them from her bosom, she would be tearing out herself; in excommunicating them, you rather excommunicate yourselves; you are affording us a plain *reductio ad absurdum* of your Catholicity. And there is a second consideration which urges us, and that is, the frightful cruelty of denying to such multitudes of men, and to so great an extent of territory, a place in the Church, claiming it as they do from generation to generation, and fully believing their own possession of it. Charity, still more than the necessities of controversy, obliges you to acknowledge them as a portion of the fold of Christ."

This is the objection which I am to examine, and you will observe that I am to examine it only as an objection; that is to say, I am supposing that there is sufficient proof on other grounds that the Communion of Rome is the Catholic Church, for to this the movement of 1833 has

---

[18] In controversial writings, the numbers of the Greek orthodox communion are put at seventy or even ninety millions; it does not appear on what data. Conder puts them at fifty millions. [N]

already been supposed to lead; and then, with this fact sufficiently proved, an objection is brought as an obstacle to [337] our surrendering ourselves to the conviction which follows upon the proof of the fact. What I have to do, then, is to show that the proof already brought home to us of the Catholicity of the Roman Communion, is not affected by the phenomenon in question; or that there are ways of accounting for it, if we do but assume, which I claim to do, that the Church of Rome and Catholicism are synonymous terms.

3.

I observe, then, that this phenomenon is but one instance of a great and broad fact, which has ever been seen on the earth, viz., that truth is opposed not only by direct contradictions which are unequivocal, but also by such pretences as are of a character to deceive men at first sight, and to confuse the evidence of what alone is divine and trustworthy. Thus, if I must begin from the very beginning, the enemy of man did not overcome him in Paradise, except by pretending to be a prophet, and, as it were, preaching against his Maker. "Ye shall not die the death," he said; "ye shall be as gods, knowing good and evil."[19] Again, when Moses displayed his miracles before Pharaoh, Jannes and Mambres were allowed to imitate them; in order, so to speak, to give the king a pretext, if he was perverse enough to take it, for rejecting the divine message.[20] When the same

---

[19] ... *knowing good and evil.*": "And the serpent said unto the woman, Ye shall not surely die: For God doth know that in the day ye eat thereof, then your eyes shall be opened, and ye shall be as gods, knowing good and evil." Genesis 4:5

[20] ... *the divine message*: "This know also, that in the last days perilous times shall come. For men shall be lovers of their own selves, covetous, boasters, proud, blasphemers, disobedient to parents, unthankful, unholy, Without natural affection, trucebreakers, false accusers, incontinent, fierce, despisers of those that are good, Traitors, heady, highminded, lovers of pleasures more than lovers of God; Having a form of godliness, but denying the power thereof: from such turn away. For of this sort are they which creep into houses, and lead captive silly women laden with sins, led away with divers lusts, Ever learning, and never able to come to the knowledge of the truth. Now as Jannes and Jambres withstood Moses,

380

great prophet had led out the chosen people towards the promised land, their enemies made the attempt to set up a rival prophet in Balaam, though it was overruled, as in other [338] cases, by their Almighty Protector.[21] When a prophet denounced the schism of Jeroboam, there was an old deceiver who seduced him by the claim, "I also am a prophet like unto thee."[22] The Temple had not long been built before a rival shrine arose on Mount Gerizim, as if with the very object of perplexing the inquirer. "Our fathers adored in this mountain," says the Samaritan woman to our Lord, "and ye say that at Jerusalem is the place where men must adore."[23] And He Himself warns us of false Christs and Antichrists,[24] who were to mislead the many with the imitation of His claims; and His Apostles were resisted, and in a manner thwarted, by Simon Magus, and others who set up against them.[25] They themselves distinctly prophesied that such delusions were to be after them, and apparently to endure till the end of all things; so much so, that were such imposing phenomena as the Greek Church taken out of the way, it would be difficult to say how the actual state of Christendom corresponded to the apostolic anticipations of it; nor should we have any cause to be surprised though the

---

so do these also resist the truth: men of corrupt minds, reprobate concerning the faith. But they shall proceed no further: for their folly shall be manifest unto all men, as theirs also was." 2 Timothy 3
[21] ... *their Almighty Protector*: Numbers 22-24
[22] ... *like unto thee.*": Kings 13:11-18
[23] ... *men must adore.*": John 4:20
[24] *Christs and Anti-Christs*: "And as he sat on the mount of Olives, the disciples came to him privately, saying, Tell us, when shall these things be? and what shall be the sign of your coming, and of the end of the world? And Jesus answered and said to them, Take heed that no man deceive you. For many shall come in my name, saying, I am Christ; and shall deceive many. And you shall hear of wars and rumors of wars: see that you be not troubled: for all these things must come to pass, but the end is not yet. For nation shall rise against nation, and kingdom against kingdom: and there shall be famines, and pestilences, and earthquakes, in divers places. All these are the beginning of sorrows." Matthew 24:3-8. See also Mark 13:3-8; Luke 21:7-11.
[25] ... *set up against them*: Cf. Acts 8:5-25.

effect of such phenomena in time to come were more practically urgent and visibly influential than it has been hitherto. "After my departure," says St. Paul, "ravenous wolves will enter in among you, not sparing the flock. And of your own selves will rise up men speaking perverse things to draw away disciples after them."[26] And in his [339] parting words he warns us that "in the last days shall come dangerous times, for men shall be lovers of themselves ... having an appearance indeed of piety," that is, of orthodoxy, "but denying the power thereof." "Evil men and seducers shall grow worse and worse, erring, and driving into error." And "there shall be a time when they will not bear sound doctrine, but according to their own desires they will heap to themselves teachers having itching ears." I need not remind you that St. John[27] and St. Jude[28] bear a similar testimony, which the event in no long time fulfilled.

---

[26] *... disciples after them.*": "Take heed therefore unto yourselves, and to all the flock, over the which the Holy Ghost hath made you overseers, to feed the church of God, which he hath purchased with his own blood. For I know this, that after my departing shall grievous wolves enter in among you, not sparing the flock. Also of your own selves shall men arise, speaking perverse things, to draw away disciples after them. Therefore watch, and remember, that by the space of three years I ceased not to warn every one night and day with tears." Acts 20:28-31

[27] *St.John*: "And every spirit that confesses not that Jesus Christ is come in the flesh is not of God: and this is that spirit of antichrist, whereof you have heard that it should come; and even now already is it in the world." 1 John 4:3; "For many deceivers are entered into the world, who confess not that Jesus Christ is come in the flesh. This is a deceiver and an antichrist." 2 John 1:7

[28] *St. Jude*: "Beloved, when I gave all diligence to write unto you of the common salvation, it was needful for me to write unto you, and exhort you that ye should earnestly contend for the faith which was once delivered unto the saints. For there are certain men crept in unawares, who were before of old ordained to this condemnation, ungodly men, turning the grace of our God into lasciviousness, and denying the only Lord God, and our Lord Jesus Christ. I will therefore put you in remembrance, though ye once knew this, how that the Lord, having saved the people out of the land of Egypt, afterward destroyed them that believed not. And the angels which kept not their first estate, but left their own habitation, he hath reserved in everlasting chains under darkness unto the judgment of the great day. Even as Sodom and Gomorrha, and

If you would ask me for the most remarkable fulfilment of their warning, I should point to Mahometanism,[29] which is a far more subtle contrivance of the enemy than we are apt to consider. In the first place, it perplexes the evidence of Christianity just in that point in which it is most original and striking: I mean, it professes the propagation of a religion through the world, which I suppose was quite a new idea when Christianity appeared. In the event, indeed, it did but illustrate the divinity of Christianity by the contrast; for while the Catholic Church is a proselytizing power, as her enemies confess, even at the end of eighteen centuries, Mahometanism soon got tired of its own undertaking, and, when the novelty and excitement of conversion were over, it

---

the cities about them in like manner, giving themselves over to fornication, and going after strange flesh, are set forth for an example, suffering the vengeance of eternal fire. Likewise also these filthy dreamers defile the flesh, despise dominion, and speak evil of dignities. Yet Michael the archangel, when contending with the devil he disputed about the body of Moses, durst not bring against him a railing accusation, but said, The Lord rebuke thee. But these speak evil of those things which they know not: but what they know naturally, as brute beasts, in those things they corrupt themselves. Woe unto them! for they have gone in the way of Cain, and ran greedily after the error of Balaam for reward, and perished in the gainsaying of Core. These are spots in your feasts of charity, when they feast with you, feeding themselves without fear: clouds they are without water, carried about of winds; trees whose fruit withereth, without fruit, twice dead, plucked up by the roots; Raging waves of the sea, foaming out their own shame; wandering stars, to whom is reserved the blackness of darkness for ever. And Enoch also, the seventh from Adam, prophesied of these, saying, Behold, the Lord cometh with ten thousands of his saints, To execute judgment upon all, and to convince all that are ungodly among them of all their ungodly deeds which they have ungodly committed, and of all their hard speeches which ungodly sinners have spoken against him. These are murmurers, complainers, walking after their own lusts; and their mouth speaketh great swelling words, having men's persons in admiration because of advantage. But, beloved, remember ye the words which were spoken before of the apostles of our Lord Jesus Christ; How that they told you there should be mockers in the last time, who should walk after their own ungodly lusts. These be they who separate themselves, sensual, having not the Spirit." Jude 1: 3-19.

[29] *Mahometanism*: alternative form of Mohammedanism, the religion of Islam.

relapsed into a sort of conservative, local, national religion, such as the Greek and Latin polytheisms before it, and [340] Protestantism since. And next, it acted over again, as if in mockery, the part which Christianity had taken towards Judaism, viz., it professed to be an improvement on the Gospel, as the Gospel had been upon the law; and just as Christianity dealt with Judaism, so it pointed to the Christian prophecies themselves in evidence of its claims, which it affected to interpret better than Christians themselves. Moreover, it swept away a considerable portion of the Christian heritage; and there it remains to this day in the countries which it seized upon, lying over against us, and for this reason only not interfering with the arguments of our opponents for the divine origin of Christianity, that England lies north and Islamism is in the south.

Then again, I cannot help thinking that Judaism is somewhat of a difficulty of the same kind; not as if any one were likely to prefer it, any more than Mahometanism, to Christianity; that is another matter altogether; nor, in like manner, do I think that any of you, my brethren, would turn Greek rather than become Catholic: but I mean, that, as the fact of the Greek Church impairs the simplicity of the Catholic argument, by its rival pretensions, so does the existence of Judaism interfere with Christianity; for, compared with it, Christianity is a novelty; and it may be said to Christians, Do not stand midway, but either go on to some newer novelty, such as first Montanus,[30] then Manes,[31] [341] and then Mahomet[32] introduced, and others since, or else go

---

[30] *Montanus*: A self-proclaimed second-century prophet, who attracted followers to his message that the end of the world was imminent. Initially the movement had the support of Tertullian, but it came to be vigorously opposed, until, at the Synod of Iconium, its baptisms were held to be invalid.

[31] *Manes*: The Persian prophet Mani (216-274 ad) was the founder of Manichaeism.

[32] *Mahomet*: Muhammad (c. 570–632) Arab prophet and religious leader who founded Islam. At the core of this religion is the doctrine that there is no God but Allah and His followers must submit to Him - the word *islam* means 'submission.'

back to the mother of all religions, the Jewish Law, which, as yourselves allow, once at least was a prophet of God. On the other hand, even if we became Jews, as considering Judaism to be the permanent religion which God had given, still this would not get rid of the difficulty I am describing, for the proper claims of Christianity would remain; then, as before, you would have two rival prophets, one true, and one not true, though you would have changed your mind, as to which was true and which was false. Looking, then, at the world as it is, taking facts as they are, you cannot rid yourselves of those difficulties in the evidence of religion, which arise from the existence of bold, plausible, imposing counter-claims on the part of error, such as the Greek communion makes against Catholicism; and you must reconcile yourselves to them, unless you are content to believe nothing, and give up the pretension of faith altogether.

But we need not go to Judaism or Mahometanism for parallels to the Greek communion; look at the history of the Christian Church herself, and you will find precedents in former times of the present difficulty, more exact and apposite than those which can be adduced from the existence of Jew or Mussulman. It may be observed that the Apostle, in the passage already quoted, speaks of the sects and persuasions, which by implication he condemns, not merely as collateral and independent creations, but as born in the Catholic body, and going out from it. "Of your own [342] selves shall men arise,"[33] he says; and St. John says, "They went out from us, but they were not of us; for, if they had been of us, they would no doubt have continued with us."[34] If this was not fulfilled in the very days of the Apostles on the extensive scale on which it was afterwards, this was simply because large national conversions and serious schisms are not the growth of a day; but, as far as it could exist in the first ages, it has existed from the very first,

---

[33] ... *shall men arise"*: "Also of your own selves shall men arise, speaking perverse things, to draw away disciples after them." Acts 20:30
[34] ... *continued with us."*: 1 John 2:19

though far more strikingly in the succeeding centuries of the Church. From the first, the Church was but one Communion among many which bore the name of Christian, some of them more learned, and others affecting a greater strictness than herself; till at length her note of Catholicity was for a while gathered up and fulfilled simply in the name of Catholic, rather than was a property visibly peculiar to herself and none but her. Hence the famous advice of the Fathers, that if one of the faithful went to a strange city, he should not ask for the "Church," for there were so many churches belonging to different denominations that he would be sure to be perplexed and to mistake, but for the Catholic Church. "If ever thou art sojourning in any city," says St. Cyril, "inquire not simply where the Lord's House is, for the sects also make an attempt to call their own conventicles houses of the Lord, nor merely where the [343] Church is, but where is the Catholic Church."[35] St. Cyril wrote in Palestine; but St. Austin, in Africa, and St. Pacian in Spain say the same thing. The present Greek Church is at best but a local form of religion, and does not pretend to occupy the earth; whereas some of the early heretical bodies might almost have disputed with the See of St. Peter the prerogative of Catholicity. The stern discipline of the Novatians[36] extended from Rome to Scythia, to Asia Minor, to Alexandria, to Africa, and to Spain; while, at an earlier date, the families of Gnosticism[37] had gone forth over the

---

[35] *... the Catholic Church."*: St. Cyril, *Catechetical Lectures*, xviii, 26.

[36] *Novatians*: an Early Christian sect devoted to the theologian Novatian (c. 200–58) that held a strict view that refused readmission to communion of *lapsi* (those baptized Christians who had denied their faith or performed the formalities of a ritual sacrifice to the pagan gods under the pressures of the persecution sanctioned by Emperor Decius in AD 250). The Church of Rome declared the Novatianists heretical following the letters of Saint Cyprian of Carthage.

[37] *Gnosticism*: "Gnosticism (from γνῶσις, "knowledge"), a loose-knit and variable system of belief based on dualism and the premise that the full revelation of God is given only to a select few. It flourished esp. in the 2nd century. The works of Gnostics were condemned and destroyed so that until fairly recently their teachings were known only through the Christian polemic directed against them; the discovery of the Nag

face of the world from Italy to Persia and Egypt on the east, to Africa on the south, to Spain on the west, and to Gaul on the north.

4.

But you will say, there were, in those times, no *national* heresies or schism, and these alone can be considered parallel to the case of the Greek Church, supposing it schismatical;—turn then to the history of the Gothic race. This great people, in all its separate tribes, received Christianity from Arian preachers; and, before it took possession of the Empire, Mæsogoths,[38] Visigoths,[39] Ostrogoths,[40] Alani,[41] Suevi,[42] Vandals,[43] and Burgundians,[44]

Hammadi texts, however, makes Gnostic writings directly available. Gnostics ranged from the Valentinians, who taught an elaborate and decidedly non-Christian mythology, to Marcion (died ca.160), who was a Christian heretic with dualist tendencies. Gnostics associated the God of the Old Testament with Satan, and their Christology was docetic; it was an early rival of Christianity, and much of Orthodox theology was developed to answer its challenge. By the 3rd century, however, Gnosticism was no longer a threat, surviving in an institutionalized form only among the Mandaeans." *The Oxford Dictionary of Byzantium*.

[38] *Mæsogoths*: Moeso-Goth: (obsolete) A member of a Gothic tribe which inhabited Moesia in the 4th and 5th centuries AD. *OED*

[39] *Visigoths*: A member of that branch of the Gothic race which entered Roman territory towards the end of the fourth century and subsequently established a kingdom in Spain, overthrown by the Moors in 711–12; a West Goth." *OED*

[40] *Ostrogoths*: An East Goth; *spec.* a member of the eastern branch of the Goths which towards the end of the 5th cent. conquered Italy under the leadership of Theoderic and established a capital at Ravenna. *OED*

[41] *Alani*: Alan: "A member of a nomadic people of the northern Caucasus from whom the Ossetians are thought to be descended." *OED*

[42] *Suevi*: The Suevi were a confederation of Germanic peoples (at least, mostly Germanic) which came into existence by the first century AD, and perhaps earlier.

[43] *Vandals*: A member of a Germanic tribe, which in the fourth and fifth centuries invaded Western Europe, and established settlements in various parts of it, esp. in Gaul and Spain, finally in 428–9 migrating to Northern Africa. In the year 455 their king Genseric led a marauding expedition against Rome, which he took and completely sacked. The Vandals were overthrown by Belisarius in 533 at the battle of Tricamarum. *OED*

had all learned to deny the divinity of Christ. Suddenly France, Spain, Portugal, Africa, and Italy, found themselves buried under the weight of heretical establishments and populations. This state of things lasted for eighty years in [344] France, for a hundred in Italy and Africa, and for a hundred and eighty in Spain, extending through a space of two centuries. It should be added that these Gothic hordes, which took possession of the Empire, had little of the character of barbarism, except that they were cruel; they were chaste, temperate, just, and devout, and some of their princes were men of ability and patrons of learning. Did you live in that day, my brethren, you would, perhaps, be looking with admiration at these Arians, as now you look at the Greeks;—not from love of their heresy, but, your imagination being affected by their number, power, and nobleness, you would try to make out that they really did hold the orthodox faith, or at least that it was not at all certain that they did not, though they did deny, to be sure, the Nicene Creed, against which they had been unhappily prejudiced, and anathematized Athanasius from defective knowledge of history. You would have used the words of Bramhall, quoted above, when speaking of later families of heretics:—"How are they heretical Churches? some of them are *called* Arians; but most injuriously, who have nothing of Arius, but the name; others have been *suspected* of Macedonianism,[45] and yet in truth *orthodox enough*. It is no new thing for great quarrels to arise from mere mistakes." Bulk, not symmetry; vastness, not order; show, not principle—I fear I must say it, my dear brethren—these are your tests of truth. A century earlier than the Goths, you [345] would have been enlarging on the importance of the

---

[44] *Burgundians*: An inhabitant of Burgundy; also used for one of the Teutonic nation of the Burgunds, from whom Burgundy received its name. *OED*

[45] *Macedonianism*: A follower of the Pneumatomachian doctrine attributed to Macedonius, a bishop of Constantinople in the 4th century. 1585.T. Rogers *Eng. Creede: 1st Pt.* (new ed.) 4. "These were the Arian and Macedonian heretiques, who were called Pneumatomachoie, because they warred against the holie Ghost." OED.

Donatists. "Four hundred sees!" you would have said; "a whole four hundred! why, it is a fifth of the Episcopate of Christendom. Unchurch them! impossible; we shall excommunicate ourselves in the attempt."

5.

Still, it may be said, I have produced nothing yet to match the venerable antiquity and the authoritative traditions of the Greek Church,[46] which is coeval with the Apostles, and for near a thousand years has been in its present theological position, and which, since its separation from the Holy See, has been able, as is alleged, to expand itself in a vast heathen country, which it has converted to the faith. Such is the objection; and, as to the facts on which it is built, I will take them for granted, as before, for argument's sake, for anyhow they are not sufficient to make the objection sound. For in truth, whether the facts be as represented or not, you will find them all, and more than them all, in the remarkable history of the Nestorians. The tenet on which these religionists separated from the See of Rome is traceable to Antioch,[47] the very birthplace of the Christian name; and it was taken up and maintained by Churches which were among the oldest in Christendom.

---

[46] *Greek Church*: Orthodox Church. A Christian Church or federation of Churches originating in the Greek-speaking Church of the Byzantine Empire, not accepting the authority of the Pope of Rome, and using elaborate and archaic forms of service. The chief Orthodox Churches (often known collectively as the Eastern Orthodox Church) include the national Churches of Greece, Russia, Bulgaria, Romania, and Serbia. The term is also used by other ancient Churches, mainly of African or Asian origin, e.g. the Coptic, Syrian, and Ethiopian Churches.

[47] *Antioch*: In size and importance Antioch in Syria was the third city of the Roman Empire. A Christian community existed here from early days and it was here that the followers of Christ were first called 'Christians' (Acts 11: 26). According to tradition St Peter was the first bishop. By the 4th century the see ranked after Rome and Alexandria as the third patriarchal see of Christendom. The rise in power of Constantinople and the erection of Jerusalem into a Patriarchate reduced the importance of Antioch, which was further diminished by the Nestorian and Monophysite schisms. *ODCC*.

Driven by the Roman power over the boundaries of the Empire, it placed itself, as early as the fifth century, under [346] the protection of Persia, and laid the foundations of a schismatical communion, the most wonderful that the world has seen.[48] It propagated itself, both among Christians and pagans, from Cyprus to China; it was the Christianity of Bactrians, Huns, Medes, and Indians, of the coast of Malabar and Ceylon on the south, and of Tartary on the north. This ecclesiastical dominion lasted for eight centuries and more, into the depth of the middle ages—beyond the Pontificate of Innocent III. It was administered by as many as twenty-five archbishoprics; and, though there is perhaps no record of the number of its people, yet it is said, that they and the opposite sect of the Monophysites, in Syria and Egypt, taken together, at one time surpassed in populousness the whole Catholic Church, in its Greek and Latin divisions. And it is to be observed, which is much to the purpose, that it occupied a portion of the world, with which, as far as I am aware, the Catholic Church, during those many centuries, interfered very little. It had the further Asia all to itself, from Mesopotamia to China; far more so than the Greek Church has at this time possession of Russia and Greece.

With this prominent example before our eyes, during so large a portion of the history of Christianity, I do not see how the present existence of the Greek Church can form any valid objection to the Catholicity which we claim for the Communion of Rome. Nestorianism came from [347] Antioch, the original Apostolic see; Photianism,[49] as it has

---

[48] *a schismatical communion* ... : the Nestorian church.

[49] *Photianism*: Photius (sometimes called 'The Great', c.810–c.95). Patriarch of Constantinople. A high official at the Byzantine court, Photius succeeded the patriarch Ignatius who was deposed by the emperor in 858. His election, at first endorsed by the legates of Pope Nicholas I, was then (863) annulled by the pope and a schism ensued. Divisions were sharpened by an encyclical of 867 in which Photius attacked the *filioque* in the Western creed, and by the rival claims of Rome and Constantinople to the newly evangelized territory of Bulgaria. The Photian schism anticipated the final East–West schism of the 11th

been called, from Constantinople, a younger metropolis. Nestorianism had its Apostolical Succession, as Photianism has, and a formed hierarchy. If its principal seat was new and foreign, in Chaldæa, not at Antioch, so the principal seat of Photianism is foreign too, being Russia; if from Russia it has sent out missions and made conversions, so, and much more so, did Nestorianism from Chaldæa. You will, perhaps, object that Nestorianism was a heresy;— therein lies the force of my argument, viz., that large, organized, flourishing, imposing communions, which strike the imagination as necessary portions of the heritage of Christ, may, nevertheless, in fact be implicated in some heresy, which, in the judgment of reason, invalidates their claim. If the Nestorian communion, enormous as it was, was yet external to the Church, why must the Greek communion be within it, merely because, supposing the fact to be so, it has some portion of the activity and success which were so conspicuous in the Nestorian missioners? Do not, then, think to overcome us with descriptions of the multitude, antiquity, and continuance of the Greek Churches; dismiss the vision of their rites, their processions, or their vestments; spare yourselves the recital of the splendour of their churches, or the venerable aspect of their bishops; Nestorianism had then all:—the question lies deeper.

6. [348]

It lies, for what we know, and to all appearance, in the very constitution of the human mind; corruptions of the Gospel being as necessary and ordinary a phenomenon, taking men as they are, as its rejection. Why do you not bring against us the vast unreclaimed populations of paganism, or the political power of the British Colonial Empire, in proof that we are not the Catholic Church? Is misbelief a greater marvel than unbelief? or do not the same intellectual and moral principles, which lead men to accept

---

cent., and Photius is remembered in the Eastern Church as a champion against Rome.

nothing, lead them also to accept half of revealed truth? Both effects are simple manifestations of private judgment in the bad sense of the phrase, that is, of the use of one's own reason against the authority of God. If He has made it a duty to submit to the supreme authority of the Holy See (and of this I am all along assuming there is fair proof), and if there is a constant rising of the human mind against authority, as such, however legitimate, the necessary consequence will be the very state of things we see before our eyes,—not merely individuals casting off the Roman Supremacy (for individuals, as being of less account, have less temptation, or even opportunity, to rebel, than collections of men), but, much more, the powerful and the great, the wealthy and the flourishing, kings and states, cities and races, falling back upon their own resources and

[349] their own connections, making their home their castle, and refusing any longer to be dependent on a distant centre, or to regulate their internal affairs by a foreign tribunal. Assuming then that there is a supreme See, divinely appointed, in the midst of Christendom, to which all ought to submit and be united, such phenomena, as the Greek Church presents at this day, and the Nestorian in the middle ages, are its infallible correlatives, as human nature is constituted; it would require a miracle to make it otherwise. It is but an exemplification of the words of the Apostle, "The law entered in, that sin might abound;"[50] and again, "There must be heresies, that they also who are proved may be made manifest among you."[51] A command is both the occasion of transgression, and the test of obedience. All depends on the fact of the Supremacy of Rome; I assume this fact; I admit the contrary fact of the Arian, Nestorian, and the Greek Communions; and strong in the one, I feel no difficulty in the other. Neither Arian, nor Nestorian, nor Greek insubordination is any true objection to the fact of such supremacy, unless the divine foresight of such a

---

[50] *... sin might abound. "*: Roman. 5:20
[51] *... manifest among you. " *: 1 Corinthians 1:19

necessary result can be supposed to have dissuaded the Divine Wisdom from giving occasion to it.

7.

But another remark is in place here. Nothing is more likely to characterize large populations of Christians, if left to themselves, than a material instead of a formal faith. By a [350] material faith, I mean that sort of habitual belief which persons possess in consequence of having heard things said in this or that way from their childhood, being thoroughly familiar with them, and never having had difficulty suggested to them from without or within. Such is the sort of belief which many Protestants have in the Bible; which they accept without a doubt, till objections occur to them. Such as this becomes the faith of nations in process of time, where a clergy is negligent; it becomes simply national and hereditary, the truth being received, but not on the authority of God. That is, their faith is but material not formal, and really has neither the character nor the reward of that grace-implanted, grace-sustained principle, which believes, not merely because it was so taught in the nursery, but because God has spoken; not because there is no temptation to doubt, but because there is a duty to believe. And thus it may easily happen, in the case of individuals, that even the restless mind of a Protestant, who sets the Divine Will before him in his thoughts and actions, and wishes to be taught and wishes to believe, may have more of grace in it, and be more acceptable in the divine sight, than his, who only believes passively, and not as assenting to a divine oracle; just as one who is ever fighting successfully with temptations against purity has, so far, claim of merit, which they do not share, who from natural temperament have not the trial. Now, the faultiness of this passive state of mind is [351] detected, whenever a new definition of doctrine is promulgated by the competent authority. Its immediate tendency, as exhibited in a population, will be to resist it, simply because it is new, while they on the other hand are disposed to recognise nothing but what is familiar to them;

whereas a ready and easy acceptance of the apparent novelty, and a cordial acquiescence in its promulgation, may be the very evidence of a mind, which has lived, not merely in certain doctrines, but in those doctrines as revealed,—not simply in a Creed, but in its Giver,—or, in other words, which has lived by real faith.

As, then, heathens are tried by the original preaching of the Word, so are Christians tested by recurring declarations of it; and the same habit of mind, which makes one man an infidel, when he was before merely a pagan, makes another a heretic, who before was but an hereditary or national Christian. And surely we can fancy without difficulty the circumstances, in which a people, and their priesthood, who ought to hinder it, may gradually fall into those heavy and sluggish habits of mind, in which faith is but material and obedience mechanical, and religion has become a superstition instead of a reasonable service; and then it is as certain that they will become schismatics or heretics, should trial come, as that heathen cities, which have no heart for the truth, when it is for the first time preached to them, will [352] harden into direct infidelity. It is much to be feared, from what travellers tell us of the Greek priesthood and their flocks, that both in Russia and in Greece Proper, they are more or less in this state,—which may be called the proper disposition towards heresy and schism; I mean, that they rely on things more than on persons, and go through a round of duties in one and the same way, because they are used to them, and because in consequence they are attached to them, not as having any intelligent faith in a divine oracle which has ordered them; and that in consequence they would start in irritation, as they have started, from such indications of that Oracle's existence as is necessarily implied in the promulgation of a new definition of faith.

8.

I am speaking of the mass of the population; and, at first sight, it is a very serious question, whether the population can be said to be simply gifted with divine faith, any more than our own Protestant people; yet I would as little dare to deny or to limit exceptions to this remark, as I would deny them or limit them among ourselves. Let there be as many exceptions, as there can be found tokens of their being; and the more they are, to God the greater praise! In this point of view it is, that we are able to take comfort even from the contemplation of a country which is given up whether to heresy or schism. Such a country is far from being in the miserable state of a heathen population: it has portions of [353] the truth remaining in it, it has some supernatural channels of grace; and the results are such as can never be known till we have all passed out of this visible scene of things, and the accounts of the world are finally made up for the last tremendous day. While, then, I think it plain that the existence of large Anti-Catholic bodies professing Christianity are as inevitable, from the nature of the case, as infidel races or states, except under some extraordinary dispensation of divine grace, while there must ever be in the world false prophets and Antichrists, standing over against the Catholic Church, yet it is consolatory to reflect how the schism or heresy, which the self-will of a monarch or of a generation has caused, does not suffice altogether to destroy the work for which in some distant age Evangelists have left their homes, and Martyrs have shed their blood. Thus, the blessing is inestimable to England, so far as among us the Sacrament of Baptism is validly administered to any portion of the population. In Greece, where a far greater attention is paid to ritual exactness, the whole population may be considered regenerate; half the children born into the world pass through baptism from a schismatical Church to heaven, and in many of the rest the same Sacrament may be the foundation of a supernatural life, which is gifted with perseverance in the hour of death. There may be many too, who, being in invincible ignorance on those particular points of religion on which their Communion is wrong, may [354] still have the divine and unclouded illumination of faith on those numerous points on which it is right. And further, if we consider that there is a true priesthood in certain countries, and a true sacrifice, the benefits of Mass to those who never had the means of knowing better, may be almost the same as they are in the Catholic Church. Humble souls who come in faith and love to the heavenly rite, under whatever disadvantages they lie, from the faulty discipline of their Communion, may obtain, as well as we, remission of such sins as the Sacrifice directly effects, and that supernatural charity which wipes out greater ones. Moreover, when the Blessed Sacrament is lifted up, they adore, as well as we, the true Immaculate Lamb of God; and when they communicate, it is the True Bread of Life, and nothing short of it, which they receive for the eternal health of their souls.

And in like manner, I suppose, as regards this country, as well as Greece and Russia, we may entertain most reasonable hopes, that vast multitudes are in a state of invincible ignorance; so that those among them who are living a life really religious and conscientious, may be looked upon with interest and even pleasure, though a mournful pleasure, in the midst of the pain which a Catholic feels at their ignorant prejudices against what he knows to be true. Amongst the most bitter railers against the Church in this country, may be found those who are influenced by [355] divine grace, and are at present travelling towards heaven, whatever be their ultimate destiny. Among the most irritable disputants against the Sacrifice of the Mass or Transubstantiation, or the most impatient listeners to the glories of Mary, there may be those for whom she is saying to her Son, what He said on the cross to His Father, "Forgive them, for they know not what they do."[52] Nay, while such persons think as at present, they are bound to act accordingly, and only so far to connect themselves with us as their conscience allows. "When persons who have been brought up in heresy," says a Catholic theologian, "are persuaded from their childhood that we are the enemies of God's word, are idolaters, pestilent deceivers, and therefore,

---

[52] *... what they do.*": Luke 23:34

as pests, to be avoided, they cannot, while this persuasion lasts, hear us with a safe conscience, and they labour under invincible ignorance, inasmuch as they doubt not that they are in a good way."[53]

Nor does it suffice, in order to throw them out of this irresponsible state, and to make them guilty of their ignorance, that there are means actually in their power of getting rid of it. For instance, say they have no conscientious feeling against frequenting Catholic chapels, conversing with Catholics, or reading their books; and say they are thrown into the neighbourhood of the one or the company of the other, and do not avail themselves of their opportunities; still these persons do not become responsible [356] for their present ignorance till such time as they actually feel it, till a doubt crosses them upon the subject, and the thought comes upon them, that inquiry is a duty. And thus Protestants may be living in the midst of Catholic light, and labouring under the densest and most stupid prejudices; and yet we may be able to view them with hope, though with anxiety—with the hope that the question has never occurred to them, strange as it may seem, whether we are not right and they wrong. Nay, I will say something further still; they may be so circumstanced that it is quite certain that, in course of time, this ignorance will be removed, and doubt will be suggested to them, and the necessity of inquiry consequently imposed; and according to our best judgment, fallible of course as it is, we may be quite certain too, that,

---

[53] Busembaum, vol. i. p. 54. [N] St. Alphonsus Liguori (1696-1737) sought to commend the Gospel to a sceptical age by gentle and direct methods. Spurning the florid oratory of his contemporaries, he preached simply and to the heart and believed that the rigorism of the contemporary confessional (largely under Jansenist influences) repelled rather than won back the sinful. He set out these ideals in a system of moral theology, first outlined in his *Annotations* to Hermann Busembaum, SJ (an esteemed Jesuit casuist, 1600–68), published at Naples in 1748. This teaching he recast in his celebrated *Theologia Moralis* (2 vols., 1753 and 1755), of which seven further editions appeared before his death, as well as a number of compendiums, e.g. the *Homo Apostolicus* (1759). *ODCC.*

when that time comes, they will refuse to inquire, and will quench the doubt; yet should it so happen that they are cut off by death before that time has arrived (I am putting an hypothetical case), we may have as much hope of their salvation as if we had had no such foreboding about them on our mind; for there is nothing to show that they were not taken away on purpose, in order that their ignorance might be their excuse.

[357]   As to the prospect of those countless multitudes of a country like this, who apparently have no supernatural vision of the next world at all, and die without fear because they die without thought, with these, alas! I am not here concerned. But the remarks I have been making suggest much of comfort, when we look out into what is called the religious world in all its varieties, whether it be the High Church section, or the Evangelical, whether it be in the Establishment, or in Methodism, or in Dissent, so far as there seems to be real earnestness and invincible prejudice. One cannot but hope that that written Word of God, for which they desire to be jealous, though exhibited to them in a mutilated form and in a translation unsanctioned by Holy Church, is of incalculable blessing to their souls, and may be, through God's grace, the divine instrument of bringing many to contrition and to a happy death who have received no sacrament since they were baptized in their infancy. One cannot hope but that the Anglican Prayer Book, with its Psalter and Catholic prayers, even though these, in the translation, have passed through heretical intellects, may retain so much of its old virtue as to cooperate with divine grace in the instruction and salvation of a large remnant. In these and many other ways, even in England, and much more in Greece, the difficulty is softened which is presented to the imagination by the view of such large populations, who, though called Christian, are not Catholic or orthodox in creed.

9. [358]

There is but one set of persons, indeed, who inspire the Catholic with special anxiety, as much so as the open sinner, who is not peculiar to any Communion, Catholic or schismatic, and who does not come into the present question. There is one set of persons in whom every Catholic must feel intense interest, about whom he must feel the gravest apprehensions; viz., those who have some rays of light vouchsafed to them as to their heresy or as to their schism, and who seem to be closing their eyes upon it; or those who have actually gained a clear view of the nothingness of their own Communion, and the reality and divinity of the Catholic Church, yet delay to act upon their knowledge. You, my dear brethren, if such are here present, are in a very different state from those around you. You are called by the inscrutable grace of God to the possession of a great benefit, and to refuse the benefit is to lose the grace. You cannot be as others: they pursue their own way, they walk over this wide earth, and see nothing wonderful or glorious in the sun, moon, and stars of the spiritual heavens; or they have an intellectual sense of their beauty, but no feeling of duty or of love towards them; or they wish to love them, but think they ought not, lest they should get a distaste for that mire and foulness which is their present portion. They have not yet had the call to inquire, and to seek, and to pray for further guidance, infused into their hearts by the gracious Spirit of God; and they will be judged [359] according to what is given them, not by what is not. But on you the thought has dawned, that possibly Catholicism may be true; you have doubted the safety of your present position, and the present pardon of your sins, and the completeness of your present faith. You, by means of that very system in which you find yourselves, have been led to doubt that system. If the Mosaic law, given from above, was a schoolmaster to lead souls to Christ, much more is it true that an heretical creed, when properly understood, warns us against itself, and frightens us from it, and is forced against its will to open for us with its own hands its prison gates, and to show us the way to a better country. So has it been with you. You set out in simplicity and earnestness intending to serve it, and your very serving taught you to serve another. You began to use its prayers and act upon its rules, and they did but witness against it, and made you love it, not more but less, and carried off your affections to one whom you had not loved. The more you gazed upon your own communion the more unlike it you grew; the more you tried to be good Anglicans, the more you found yourselves drawn in heart and spirit to the Catholic Church. It was the destiny of the false prophetess that she could not keep the little ones who devoted themselves to her; and the more simply they gave up their private judgment to her, the more sure they were of being thrown off by her, against their will,

[360] into the current of attraction which led straight to the true Mother of their souls. So month has gone on after month, and year after year; and you have again and again vowed obedience to your own Church, and you have protested against those who left her, and you have thought you found in them what you liked not, and you have prophesied evil about them and good about yourselves; and your plans seemed prospering and your influence extending, and great things were to be; and yet, strange to say, at the end of the time you have found yourselves steadily advanced in the direction which you feared, and never were nearer to the promised land than you are now.

Oh, look well to your footing that you slip not; be very much afraid lest the world should detain you; dare not in anything to fall short of God's grace, or to lag behind when that grace goes forward. Walk with it, cooperate with it, and I know how it will end. You are not the first persons who have trodden that path; yet a little time, and, please God, the bitter shall be sweet, and the sweet bitter, and you will have undergone the agony, and will be lodged safely in the true home of your souls and the valley of peace. Yet but a little while, and you will look out from your resting-place upon the wanderers outside; and will wonder why they do not see that way which is now so plain to you, and will be impatient with them that they do not come on faster. And, whereas you now are so perplexed in mind that you seem to yourselves to believe nothing, then you will be so full of [361] faith, that you will almost see invisible mysteries, and will touch the threshold of eternity. And you will be so full of joy that you will wish all around you to be partakers of it, as if for your own relief; and you will suddenly be filled with yearnings deep and passionate, for the salvation of those dear friends whom you have out-stripped; and you will not mind their coolness, or stiffness, or distance, or constrained gravity, for the love you bear to their souls. And, though *they* will not hear you, you will address yourselves to those who will; I mean, you will weary heaven with your novenas for them, and you will be ever getting Masses for their conversion, and you will go to communion for them, and you will not rest till the bright morning comes, and they are yours once again. Oh, is it possible that there is a resurrection even upon earth! O wonderful grace, that there should be a joyful meeting, after parting, before we get to heaven! It was a weary time, that long suspense, when with aching hearts we stood on the brink of a change, and it was like death both to witness and to undergo, when first one and then another disappeared from the eyes of their fellows. And then friends stood on different sides of a gulf, and for years knew nothing of each other or of their welfare. And then they fancied of each other what was not, and there were misunderstandings and jealousies; and each saw the other, as if his ghost, only in imagination and in memory; [362] and all was sickness and anxiety, and hope delayed, and ill-requited care. But now it is all over; the morning is come; the severed shall unite. I see them as if in sight of me. Look at us, my brethren, from our glorious land; look on us radiant with the light cast upon us by the Saints and Angels who stand over us; gaze on us as you approach, and kindle as you gaze. We died, you thought us dead: we live; we cannot return to you, you must come to us,—and you are coming. Do not your hearts beat as you approach us? Do you not long for the hour which makes us one? Do not tears come into your eyes at the thought of the superabundant mercy[54] of your God?

"Sion is the city of our strength, a saviour; a wall, and a bulwark shall be set therein. Open ye the gates, and let the just Nation that keepeth the truth enter in. The old error is passed away; Thou wilt keep peace, peace because we have hoped in Thee. In the way of Thy judgments, O Lord, have we waited for Thee; Thy Name and Thy remembrance are the desire of our soul. O Lord, our God, other lords beside Thee have had possession of us; but in Thee only may we have remembrance of Thy Name. The dying, let them not live; the giants let them not rise again; therefore Thou hast visited and crushed them, and hast destroyed all their memory."[55]

---

[54] *superabundant mercy of God*: See *LD*, xxvi, 364-5; and Editor's Introduction.
[55] " *... all their memory*": Isaiah 26: 1-14

LECTURE XII

ECCLESIASTICAL HISTORY NO PREJUDICE TO THE
APOSTOLICITY OF THE CHURCH

1.

FEELING, my dear brethren, I should be encroaching on your patience, if I extended this course of Lectures beyond the length which it is now reaching, I have been obliged, in order to give a character of completeness to the whole, to omit the discussion of subjects which I would fain have introduced, and to anticipate others which I would rather have viewed in another connection. This must be my apology, if in their number and selection I shall in any respect disappoint those who have formed their expectations of what I was to do in these Lectures, upon the profession contained in their general title. I have done what my limits allowed me: if I have not done more, it is not, I assure you, from having nothing to say,—for there are many questions upon which I have been anxious to enter,—but because I could neither expect you, my brethren, to give me more of your time, nor could command my own.

As, then, I have already considered certain popular objections which are made respectively to the Sanctity, [364] Unity, and Catholicity of the Church, now let me, as far as I can do it in a single Lecture, direct your attention to a difficulty felt, not indeed by the world at large, but by many of you in particular, in admitting her Apostolical pretensions

I say, "a difficulty not felt by the world at large;" for the world at large has no such view of any contrariety between the Catholic Church of today and the Catholic Church of fifteen hundred years ago, as to be disposed on that account to deny our Apostolical claims; rather, it is the fashion of the mass of Protestants, whenever they think on the subject, to accuse the Church of the Fathers of what they call Popish superstition and intolerance; and some have even gone so far as to say, that in these respects that early Church was more Popish than the Papists themselves. But when, leaving this first look of the subject, and the broad outline, and the general impression, we come to inspect matters more narrowly, and compare them exactly, point by point, together, certainly it is not difficult to find various instances of discrepancy, apparent or real, important or trivial, between the modern and the ancient Church; and though no candid person who has fairly examined the state of the case can doubt, that, if we differ from the Fathers in some things, Protestants differ from them in all, and if we vary from them in accidentals, Protestants contradict them in [365] essentials, still, since attack is much easier and pleasanter than defence, it has been the way with certain disputants, especially with the Anglican school, instead of accounting for their own serious departure in so many respects from the primitive doctrine and ritual, to call upon us to show why we differ at all from our first Fathers, though partially and intelligibly, in matters of discipline and in the tone of our opinions. Thus it is that Jewel tries to throw dust in the eyes of the world and does his best to make an attack upon the Papacy and its claims pass for an Apology for the Church of England;[1] and more writers have followed his example than it is worth while, or indeed possible, to enumerate. And they

---

[1] *Apology for the Church of England*: "Catholics are certainly taken at great disadvantage now; but, as a loyal servant of Alfred or Bruce, knowing the greatness of his master's soul and the splendour of his gifts, might have no temptation whatever to mistrust his ultimate success, in spite of temporary disaster, so we feel about the defects and humiliations of the Papacy. You see all along I have kept to my purpose of describing *my own* view of the difficulties of Catholicity on which you fasten, instead of attempting to deal with them controversially. The temporal prosperity, success, talent, renown of the Papacy did not make me a Catholic, and its errors and misfortunes have no power to unsettle me. Its utter disestablishment may only make it stronger and purer, removing the very evils which are the cause of its being disestablished." Newman to John Rickards Mozley (4 April 1875), *LD*, xxvii, 267.

have been answered again and again; and the so-called novelties of modern Catholicism have been explained, if not so as to silence all opponents (which could not be expected), yet at the very lowest so far as this (which is all that is incumbent on us in controversy), so far as to show that we have a case in our favour. I say, even though we have not done enough for our proof, we have done enough for our argument, as the world will allow; for on our assailants, not on us, lies the "*onus probandi*," and they have done nothing till they have actually made their charges good, and destroyed the very tenableness of our position and even the mere probability of our representations. However, into the consideration, whether of these objections or of their answers, I shall not be expected to [366] enter; and especially, because each would form a separate subject in itself, and furnish matter for a separate Lecture. How, for instance, would it be possible in the course of an hour, and with such an exercise of attention as might fairly be exacted of you, to embrace subjects as distinct from each other as the primitive faith concerning the Blessed Virgin, and the Apostolic See, and the Holy Eucharist, and the worship of images? You would not expect such an effort of me, nor promise it for yourselves; and the less so, because, as you know, my profession all along has been to confine myself, as far as I can, to general considerations, and to appeal, in proof of what I assert, rather to common sense and truths before our eyes than to theology and history.

2.

In thus opening the subject, my brethren, I have been both explaining and apologizing for what I am proposing to do. For, if I am to say something, not directly in answer to the particular objections in detail, brought from Antiquity against the doctrine and discipline of the present Catholic Church, but by way of appeasing and allaying that general misgiving and perplexity which these objections excite, what can I do better than appeal to a fact,—though I cannot do so without some indulgence on the part of my hearers—a

[367] fact connected with myself? And it is the less unfair to do so, because, as regards the history of the early Church and the writings of the Fathers, so many must go by the testimony of others, and so few have opportunity to use their own experience. I say, then, that the writings of the Fathers, so far from prejudicing at least one man against the modern Catholic Church, have been simply and solely the one intellectual cause of his having renounced the religion in which he was born and submitted himself to her. What other causes there may be, not intellectual, unknown, unsuspected by himself, though freely imputed on mere conjecture by those who would invalidate his testimony, it would be unbecoming and impertinent to discuss; for himself, if he is asked why he became a Catholic, he can only give that answer which experience and consciousness bring home to him as the true one, viz., that he joined the Catholic Church simply because he believed it, and it only, to be the Church of the Fathers; because he believed that there was a Church upon earth till the end of time, and one only; and because, unless it was the Communion of Rome, and it only, there was none;—because, to use language purposely guarded, because it was the language of controversy, "all parties will agree that, of all existing systems, the present Communion of Rome is the nearest approximation in fact to the Church of the Fathers; possible though some may think it, to be still nearer to it on paper;"—because, "did St. Athanasius or St. Ambrose come

[368] suddenly to life, it cannot be doubted what communion they would mistake," that is, would recognize, "for their own;"—because "all will agree that these Fathers, with whatever differences of opinion, whatever protests if you will, would find themselves more at home with such men as St. Bernard or St. Ignatius Loyola, or with the lonely priest in his lodgings, or the holy sisterhood of charity, or the unlettered crowd before the altar, than with the rulers or the members of any other religious community."[2]

---

[2] Essay on Doctrinal Development, p. 138. [N]

This is the great, manifest, historical phenomenon which converted me,—to which all particular inquiries converged. Christianity is not a matter of opinion, but an external fact, entering into, carried out in, indivisible from, the history of the world. It has a bodily occupation of the world; it is one continuous fact or thing, the same from first to last, distinct from everything else: to be a Christian is to partake of, to submit to, this thing; and the simple question was, Where, what is this thing in this age, which in the first age was the Catholic Church? The answer was undeniable; the Church called Catholic now, is that very same thing in hereditary descent, in organization, in principles, in position, in external relations, which was called the Catholic Church then; name and thing have ever gone together, by an uninterrupted connection and succession, from then till now. Whether it had been corrupted in its teaching was, at [369] best, a matter of opinion. It was indefinitely more evident a fact, that it stood on the ground and in the place of the ancient Church, as its heir and representative, than that certain peculiarities in its teaching were really innovations and corruptions. Say there is no Church at all, if you will, and at least I shall understand you; but do not meddle with a fact attested by mankind. I am almost ashamed to insist upon so plain a point, which in many respects is axiomatically true, except that there are persons who wish to deny it. Of course, there are and have been such persons, and men of deep learning; but their adverse opinion does not interfere with my present use of what I think so plain. Observe, I am not insisting on it as an axiom, though that is my own view of the matter; nor proving it as a conclusion, nor forcing it on your acceptance as *your* reason for joining the Catholic Church, as it was mine. Let every one have his own reason for becoming a Catholic; for reasons are in plenty, and there are enough for you all, and moreover all of them are good ones and consistent with each other. I am not assigning reasons why you should be Catholics; you have them already: from first to last I am doing nothing more than removing difficulties in your path, which obstruct the legitimate effect of those reasons which have, as I am assuming, already convinced you. And today I am answering the objection, so powerfully urged upon those [370] who have no means of examining it for themselves, that, as a matter of fact, the modern Church has departed from the teaching of the ancient. Now even one man's contrary testimony obscures the certainty of this supposed matter of fact, though it is not sufficient to establish any opposite matter of fact of his own. I say, then, the Catholicism of today is not likely to be really very different from the Catholicism of Antiquity, if its agreement, or rather its identity, with Antiquity forms the very reason on which even one educated and reflecting person was induced, much against every natural inducement, to submit to its claims. Ancient Catholicity cannot supply a very conclusive argument against modern Catholicity, if the ancient has furnished even one such person with a conclusive argument in favour of the modern. Let us grant that the argument against the modern Church drawn from Antiquity, is not altogether destroyed by this antagonistic argument in her behalf, drawn from the same Antiquity; yet surely that argument adverse to her will be too much damaged and enfeebled by the collision to do much towards resisting such direct independent reasons, personal to yourselves, as are already leading you to her.

3.

My testimony, then, is as follows. Even when I was a boy, my thoughts were turned to the early Church, and especially to the early Fathers, by the perusal of the Calvinist John Milner's Church History,[3] and I have never

---

[3] *John Milner's Church History*: Joseph Milner (1744-97), headmaster at the Latin school at Hull, a popular preacher and one of the founders of the Evangelical Movement within the Anglican Church. His 5-volume *History of the Church of Christ* (York 1794-1809) consists not of historical narrative but biographies of devout churchmen. In the *Apologia*, Newman would write: "I read Joseph Milner's Church History, and was nothing less than enamoured of the long extracts from Saint

lost, I never have suffered a suspension of the impression, [371] deep and most pleasurable, which his sketches of St. Ambrose and St. Augustine left on my mind. From that time the vision of the Fathers was always, to my imagination, I may say, a paradise of delight to the contemplation of which I directed my thoughts from time to time, whenever I was free from the engagements proper to my time of life. When years afterwards (1828) I first began to read their works with attention and on system, I busied myself much in analysing them, and in cataloguing their doctrines and principles; but, when I had thus proceeded very carefully and minutely for some space of time, I found, on looking back on what I had done, that I had scarcely done anything at all; I found that I had gained very little from them, and I came to the conclusion that the Fathers I had been reading, which were exclusively those of the ante-Nicene period, had very little in them. At the time I did not discover the reason of this result, though, on the retrospect, it was plain enough: I had read them simply on Protestant ideas, analysed and catalogued them on Protestant principles of division, and hunted for Protestant doctrines and usages in them. My headings ran, "Justification by faith only," "Sanctification," and the like. I knew not what to look for in them; I sought what was not there, I missed what was there; I laboured through the night and caught nothing. But I should make one important exception: I rose from their perusal with a vivid perception of the divine institution, the prerogatives, [372] and the gifts of the Episcopate; that is, with an implicit aversion to the Erastian principle.

Some years afterwards (1831) I took up the study of them again, when I had occasion to employ myself on the history of Arianism. I read them with Bull's *Defensio*, as their key, as far as his subject extended; but I am not aware that I made any other special doctrinal use of them at that time.

Augustine and Saint Ambrose, and the other Fathers, which I found there. I read them as being the religion of the primitive Christians ..." *Apo*, 20.

After this I set myself to the study of them, with the view of pursuing the series of controversies connected with our Lord's Person; and to the examination of these controversies I devoted two summers, with the interval of several years between them (1835 and 1839). And now at length I was reading them for myself; for no Anglican writer had specially and minutely treated the subjects on which I was engaged. On my first introduction to them I had read them as a Protestant; and next, I had read them pretty much as an Anglican, though it is observable that, whatever I gained on either reading, over and above the theory or system with which I started, was in a Catholic direction. In the former of the two summers above mentioned (1835), my reading was almost entirely confined to strictly doctrinal subjects, to the exclusion of history, and I believe it left me pretty much where I was on the question of the Catholic Church; but in the latter of them (1839) it was principally occupied with the history of the Monophysite controversy,

[373] and the circumstances and transactions of the Council of Chalcedon, in the fifth century, and at once and irrevocably I found my faith in the tenableness of the fundamental principle of Anglicanism disappear, and a doubt of it implanted in my mind which never was eradicated. I thought I saw in the controversy I have named, and in the Ecumenical Council connected with it, a clear interpretation of the present state of Christendom, and a key to the different parties and personages who have figured on the Catholic or the Protestant side at and since the era of the Reformation. During the autumn of the same year, a paper I fell in with upon the schism of the Donatists,[4] deepened the impression which the history of the Monophysites had made; and I felt dazzled and excited by the new view of things which was thus opened upon me.[5] Distrusting my

---

[4] By Dr. Wiseman. [N] Nicholas Wiseman, "The Anglican Claim of Apostolical Succession," *Dublin Review*, 7, No. 13 (1839), 138-80.

[5] *opened upon me*: Newman's good friend "Henry Wilberforce later recalled: 'It was in the beginning of October, 1839, that he made the astounding confidence, mentioning the two subjects which had inspired

judgment, and that I might be a better judge of the subject, I determined for a time to put it away from my mind; nor did I return to it till I gave myself to the translation of the doctrinal Treatises of St. Athanasius, at the end of 1841. This occupation brought up again before me the whole question of the Arian controversy and the Nicene Council; and now I clearly saw in that history, what I had not perceived on the first study of it, the same phenomenon which had already startled me in the history of St. Leo and the Monophysites. From that time, what delayed my conviction of the claims of the Catholic Church upon me, [374] was not any confidence in Anglicanism as a system of doctrine, but particular objections which as yet I saw no way of reducing, such as may at present weigh with you, and the fear that, since I found my friends strongly opposed to my view of the matter, I might, in some way or other, be involved in a delusion.

4.

And now you will ask me, what it is I saw in the history of primitive controversies and Councils which was so fatal to the pretensions of the Anglican Church? I saw that the general theory and position of Anglicanism was no novelty in ancient history, but had a distinct place in it, and a series of prototypes, and that these prototypes had ever been heretics or the patrons of heresy. The very badge of Anglicanism, as a system, is that it is a *Via Media*; this is its life; it is this, or it is nothing; deny this, and it forthwith dissolves into Catholicism or Protestantism. This constitutes its only claim to be recognized as a distinct form of Christianity; it is its recommendation to the world at large,

---

the doubt, the position of St Leo in the Monophysite controversy, and the principle, *"securus judicat orbis terrarum"* in that of the Donatists. He added that he felt confident that when he returned to his rooms and was able fully and calmly to consider the whole matter, he should see his way completely out of the difficulty. But, he said, I cannot conceal from myself, that for the first time since I began the study of theology, a vista has been opened before me, to the end of which I do not see. He was walking in the New Forest, and he borrowed the form of his expression from the surrounding scenery." Note 1, *LD*, vii, 161.

and its simple measuring-line for the whole field of theology. The *Via Media* appeals to the good sense of mankind; it says that the human mind is naturally prone to excess, and that theological combatants in particular are certain to run into extremes. Truth, as virtue, lies in a mean; [375] whatever, then, is true, whatever is not true, extremes certainly are false. And, whereas truth is in a mean, for that very reason it is very moderate and liberal; it can tolerate either extreme with great patience because it views neither with that keenness of contrariety with which one extreme regards the other. For the same reason, it is comprehensive; because, being in a certain sense in the centre of all errors, though having no part in any of them, it may be said to rule and to temper them, to bring them together, and to make them, as it were, converge and conspire together in one under its own meek and gracious sway. Dispassionateness, forbearance, indulgence, toleration, and comprehension are thus all of them attributes of the *Via Media*. It is obvious, moreover, that a doctrine like this will find especial acceptance with the civil magistrate. Religion he needs as an instrument of government; yet in religious opinion he sees nothing else but the fertile cause of discord and confusion. Joyfully then does he welcome a form of theology, whose very mission it is to temper the violence of polemics, to soften and to accommodate differences, and to direct the energies of churchmen to the attainment of tangible good instead of the discussion of mysteries.

This sentiment I expressed in the following passage, in the year 1837, which I quote with shame and sorrow; the more so, because it is certainly inconsistent with my own general teaching, from the very time I began to write, except [376] for a short interval in 1825 and 1826 which need not be noticed here. However, it is an accurate exponent of the Anglican theory of religion. "Though it is not likely," I said, "that Romanism should ever again become formidable in England, yet it may be in a position to make its voice heard; and, in proportion as it is able to do so, the *Via Media* will do important service of the following kind. In the

412

controversy which will ensue, Rome will not fail to preach, far and wide, the tenet which it never conceals, that there is no salvation external to its own communion. On the other hand, Protestantism, as it exists, will not be behind-hand in consigning to eternal ruin all who are adherents of Roman doctrine. What a prospect is this! two widely-spread and powerful parties dealing forth solemn anathemas upon each other, in the Name of the Lord! Indifference and scepticism must be, in such a case, the ordinary refuge of men of mild and peaceable minds, who revolt from such presumption, and are deficient in clear views of the truth. I cannot well exaggerate the misery of such a state of things. Here the English theology would come in with its characteristic calmness and caution, clear and decided in its view, giving no encouragement to luke-warmness and liberalism, but withholding all absolute anathemas on errors of opinion, except where the primitive Church sanctions the use of them."[6]

Such, then, is the Anglican Church and its *Via Media*, and such the practical application of it; it is an interposition [377] or arbitration between the extreme doctrines of Protestantism on the one hand, and the faith of Rome which Protestantism contradicts on the other. At the same time, though it may be unwilling to allow it, it is, from the nature of the case, but a particular form of Protestantism. I do not say that in secondary principles it may not agree with the Catholic Church; but, its essential idea being that she has gone into error, whereas the essential idea of Catholicism is the Church's infallibility, the *Via Media* is really nothing else than Protestant. Not to submit to the Church is to oppose her, and to side with the heretical party; for medium there is none. The *Via Media* assumes that Protestantism is right in its protest against Catholic doctrine, only that that protest needs correcting, limiting, perfecting. This surely is but a matter of fact; for the *Via Media* has adopted all the great Protestant doctrines, as its most strenuous upholder

---

[6] Proph. Off. p. 26. [N]

and the highest of Anglo-Catholics will be obliged to allow; the mutilated canon, the defective Rule of Faith, justification by faith only, putative righteousness, the infection of nature in the regenerate, the denial of the five Sacraments, the relation of faith to the Sacramental Presence, and the like; its aim being nothing else than to moderate, with Melancthon, the extreme statements of Luther, to keep them from shocking the feelings of human nature, to protect them from the criticism of common sense, [378] and from the pressure and urgency of controversial attack. Thus we have three parties on the historical stage; the See and Communion of Rome; the original pure Protestant, violent, daring, offensive, fanatical in his doctrines; and a cautious middle party, quite as heretical in principle and in doctrinal elements as Protestantism itself, but having an eye to the necessities of controversy, sensible in its ideas, sober in its tastes, safe in its statements, conservative in its aims, and practical in its measures. Such a *Via Media* has been represented by the line of Archbishops of Canterbury from Tillotson downwards, as by Cranmer before them. Such in their theology, though not in their persons or their histories, were Laud and Bull, Taylor and Hammond, and I may say nearly all the great authorities of the Established Church. This distinctive character has often been noticed, especially by Mr. Alexander Knox,[7] and much might be said upon it;

---

[7] *Alexander Knox*; (1757–1831), Theological writer, born at Londonderry, descended from the Scottish family to which John Knox belonged. The historian of the Oxford Movement, John Henry Overton wrote a marvelously dismal account of the man's life in the old *DNB*. "His weak health prevented him from passing through any regular course of education at all, though his writings prove that he managed to pick up a considerable knowledge of the classics and of general literature. He attributes his low spirits to his having been brought up to no regular employment; but he was also subject to epileptic fits. Twenty letters to him from Wesley, published in the 'Remains,' gave him much pious and rational advice. He was private secretary to Lord Castlereagh during the rebellion of 1798. After the union Lord Castlereagh urged him to accept an offer of representing his native city, Derry, in the united parliament, and also to write a history of the union. Knox, however, retired from public life and devoted himself to theology, in which his chief interest

and, as I have already observed, it ever receives the special countenance of the civil magistrate, who, if he could, would take up with a religion without any doctrines whatever, as Warburton well understands, but who, in the case of a necessary evil, admires the sobriety of Tillotson, and the piety of Patrick,[8] and the elegance of Jortin,[9] and the biblical accomplishments of Lowth[10], and the shrewd sense of Paley.

---

had always lain. He lived a recluse life in lodgings in Dawson Street, Dublin. He died, unmarried, 17 June 1831. Knox was universally admitted to be an admirable conversationalist; and people used to visit him in Dawson Street, much in the same way as people used to visit S. T. Coleridge at Highgate. Unfortunately no records of his talk have been preserved. In his conversation, Knox contended that 'the church of England is neither Calvinian nor Augustinian, but eminently and strictly catholic, and catholic only;' that 'our vitality as a church is in our identity of organisation with the church catholic;' that the church of England is not protestant, but a reformed branch of the church catholic; that the English church is the only representative of the spirit of the *Greek* fathers, and that we ought to aim at union with the Greek church. He disliked Calvinism in every form; and he argues that our justification is an *imparted*, not an *imputed*, righteousness." A more representative Anglo-Catholic could hardly be imagined.

[8] *Patrick*: Simon Patrick (8 September 1626–31 May 1707), Bishop of Ely and theologian. He is best known for his paean to latitudinarianism, *A Brief Account of the New Sect of Latitude-Men* (1662). What exactly Patrick had in mind in recommending this latitudinarian faith is nicely set out in the *ODNB*: "Theologically the latitude-man is portrayed as a moderate, rationalist Anglican with a strong Arminian bias ... Scripture, reason, and the primitive apostolic tradition offer complementary routes to establishing true religion, which is embodied in the established church. The latitude-man approves 'that vertuous mediocrity which our Church observes between the meretricious gaudiness of the Church of Rome, and the squalid sluttery of Fanatick conventicles' (S. P., *Brief Account*, 7)."

[9] *Jortin*: John Jortin (1698–1770) Ecclesiastical historian. According to the *ODNB*: "By far Jortin's most important contribution to learning began to appear in 1751: his *Remarks on Ecclesiastical History* amounted to five volumes, concluding with two posthumous volumes in 1773. They constitute the most significant Anglican ecclesiastical history of the eighteenth century and were written from a markedly latitudinarian perspective (Jortin had given up reading the Athanasian creed in the 1730s). Edward Gibbon treated them and their author with considerable respect; he noted that Jortin had treated the apologetically sensitive Arian controversy 'with learning, candour, and ingenuity' and he described him

as 'a correct and liberal scholar.'" Never unsickly, Jortin died of bronchitis in Kensington rectory.

[10] *Lowth*: Robert Lowth (1710–87), Biblical critic and Bishop of London. According to the *ODNB*: "In spite of his personal success Lowth complained in March 1755 that 'my affairs seem to be at a dead stand' (Bodl. Oxf., MS Eng. lett. c. 572, fol. 9r). As a result he felt bound to accept appointment as chaplain to William Cavendish, then marquess of Hartington, who was appointed lord lieutenant of Ireland in 1755. He extracted a promise that Hartington would intercede with Thomas Pelham-Holles, duke of Newcastle, then prime minister, to exchange any Irish preferment that Lowth might obtain for a suitable position at home. Lowth sailed for Dublin in May 1755, by which time Hartington was pursuing another scheme that would allow Lowth to change places with someone who would have liked an Irish bishopric '& had the wherewithal to pay well for it' (ibid., fols. 15–16). Lowth was granted the freedom of Limerick in June 1755 and soon afterwards Hartington's plans began to bear fruit. Protracted negotiations involving Joseph Butler, bishop of Durham, and Benjamin Hoadly, bishop of Winchester, as well as the Duke of Newcastle eventually resulted in the appointment of James Leslie as bishop of Limerick, an office that Lowth had declined, and the transfer to Lowth of a prebendal stall at Durham. In place of Leslie's other preferments Lowth was granted the valuable living of Sedgefield. He took up his new positions and moved to co. Durham in October 1755, purchasing a post-chaise to facilitate communication with his family in Hampshire. Through Hartington, who had become duke of Devonshire, he was appointed a royal chaplain on 18 August 1757. Lowth was now free to pursue literary and theological controversy, and although further preferment took some time he was also set on a significant career within the Church of England. He was considered a candidate to be warden of Winchester College in 1764. In 1765 he became a fellow of both the Royal Society of London and that of Göttingen. On 15 June 1766, as one of the final beneficiaries of Newcastle's ecclesiastical patronage, he was consecrated bishop of St David's. On 16 October, however, he was translated to the see of Oxford, and on 12 April 1777 he was nominated bishop of London. He was made dean of the Chapel Royal, was sworn of the privy council, and from 1786 was a member of the committee for trade and plantations. He was also a governor of the Charterhouse and a trustee of the British Museum. On the death of Frederick Cornwallis, archbishop of Canterbury, in 1783, he declined the offer of the primacy. Although Lowth had been astute in the pursuit of worldly success, and of the patronage necessary to achieve it, he was nevertheless a dedicated and effective churchman and administrator. He preached regularly, and although his conclusions were often predictable the subjects that he tackled were sometimes controversial ones, such as the importance of instructing African slaves in Christian religion or the need to overcome

5.

Now this sketch of the relative positions of the See of [379]
Rome, Protestantism, the *Via Media*, and the State, which
we see in the history of the last three centuries, is, I repeat,
no novelty in history; it is almost its rule, certainly its rule
during the long period when relations existed between the
Byzantine Court and the Holy See; and it is impossible to
resist the conclusion, which the actual inspection of the
history in detail forces upon us, that what the See of Rome
was then such is it now; that what Arius, Nestorius, or
Eutyches were then, such are Luther and Calvin now; what
the Eusebians or Monophysites then, such the Anglican
hierarchy now; what the Byzantine Court then, such is now
the Government of England, and such would have been
many a Catholic Court, had it had its way. That ancient
history is not dead, it lives; it prophesies of what passes
before our eyes; it is founded in the nature of things; we see
ourselves in it, as in a glass, and if the *Via Media* was
heretical then, it is heretical now.[11]

I do not know how to convey this to others in one or two
paragraphs; it is the living picture which history presents to
us, which is the evidence of the fact; and to attempt a mere
outline of it, or to detach one or two groups from the

---

the weakening of the constitution by 'a general national depravity'
(*Sermons, and other Remains, of Robert Lowth*, 194)." When George III
asked Johnson about the dispute between Warburton and Lowth on how
the Book of Job should be interpreted, Johnson replied: "Warburton has
most general, most scholastic learning; Lowth is the more correct scholar.
I do not know which of them calls names best." Boswell, *Life of Johnson*,
ii, 37. Laurence Sterne helped himself to the terms of this ludicrous
dispute to make fun of ecclesiastical controversy in *Tristram Shandy*
(1760-67). See Jonathan Lamb, "The Job Controversy, Sterne, and the
Question of Allegory," *Eighteenth-Century Studies*, vol. 24, no. 1
(Autumn, 1990), 1-19. In old age Lowth was besieged by fits of bladder
and gall stones, and found travel impossible. He died at Fulham Palace,
London, between 2 and 3 in the afternoon on 3 November 1787, probably
following a stroke, and was duly buried at Fulham church—a true son of
the Establishment.

[11] *it is heretical now:* "The past is never dead. It's not even past."
William Faulkner, *Requiem for a Nun* (1951).

finished composition, is to do injustice to its luminousness. Take, for instance, the history of Arianism. Arius stood almost by himself; bold, keen, stern, and violent, he took his stand on two or three axiomatic statements, as he considered them, appealed to Scripture, despised authority and [380] tradition, and carried out his heretical doctrine to its furthest limits. He absolutely maintained, without any reserve, that our Lord was a creature, and had a beginning. Next, he was one of a number of able and distinguished men, scattered over the East, united together by the bond of a common master and a common school, who might have been expected to stand by him on his appealing to them; but who left him to his fate, or at least but circuitously and indirectly served his cause. High in station, ecclesiastical and civil, they found it more consistent with their duties towards themselves to fall back upon a more cautious phraseology than his, and upon less assailable principles, to evade inquiry, to explain away tests, and to profess a submission to the voice of their forefathers and of the Catholic world; and they developed their formidable party in that form of heresy which is commonly called Semi-Arianism[12] or Eusebianism. They preached peace, professed to agree with neither St. Athanasius nor Arius, excited the jealousies of the Eastern world against the West, were strong enough to

---

[12] *Semi-Arianism*: Homoiousians (from ὁμοιούσιος, 'of like substance'), a group, often called 'semi-Arians,' who refused to accept the term homoousios but who believed in the perfect divinity of Christ and the similarity of his divine nature to that of the Father. Although these beliefs may be traced back to Origen, the Homoiousians as a 'party' came into existence c. 356 in an attempt to find a compromise between Orthodoxy and Arianism. Leading members of the Homoiousians were Basil of Ankyra, Makedonios of Constantinople, and George of Laodikeia; they are to be distinguished from the Homoians, who maintained closer ties to strict Arianism. The movement met opposition on philosophical grounds since nothing can be 'like' God's nature; moreover, the assertion of 'likeness' also implies difference, leading on the one hand to charges of polytheism and on the other to identification with Arianism (Wolfson, *Philosophy* 336f). The Homoiousians did, however, influence the theology of the Cappadocian Fathers." *The Oxford Dictionary of Byzantium*.

insult the Pope, and dexterous enough to gain the favour of Constantine[13] and the devoted attachment of his son

---

[13] *Constantine*: Constantine the Great (272/3–337) was proclaimed emperor at York in Britain on 25 July 306. "To enhance the legitimacy of his imperial rule, he negotiated with Galerius, the senior emperor in the Eastern provinces, and he married a daughter of Maximian, a former emperor. He also gradually eliminated his imperial rivals. Maxentius, the son of Maximian, had been proclaimed emperor at Rome in 306. In 312, Constantine invaded Italy, and on 28 October he defeated Maxentius outside Rome at the battle of the Milvian Bridge. Afterward he formed an alliance with the emperor Licinius. After skirmishes between the two during 316–317, Constantine acquired control of the Balkans. On 18 September 324, Constantine defeated Licinius in northern Asia Minor and took control of the Eastern provinces. With this victory he had reunited the empire under his rule. ...Before the battle against Maxentius in 312 he had... a vision of a cross in the sky, followed by a dream of a conversation with Jesus Christ, who instructed him to construct a military standard in the shape of a cross (the so-called labarum). Constantine himself recounted these stories about the vision and the dream... The audience for his memories included Eusebius, bishop of Caesarea in Palestine, who subsequently enshrined the stories in an account of the battle in his *Life of Constantine*. Eusebius' recasting of these stories as a moment of religious conversion has been powerfully influential. Early in 313, Constantine and Licinius agreed on a joint declaration that promoted the 'highest divinity' and extended freedom of worship 'to both Christians and everyone.' But involvement in the theological controversies that consistently disturbed Christian congregations made it difficult for Constantine to live up to his own recommendation. In North Africa, churchmen were arguing ferociously over the aftermath of the recent persecutions. The immediate accusations focused on the surrender of the Bible for burning; the larger concerns highlighted the continuing value of martyrdom and the importance of ritual purity. Already in late 312, Constantine intervened on behalf of Caecilianus, bishop of Carthage.... and he soon referred petitions to [Pope Militiades], who... exonerated Caecilianus and condemned his rival Donatus. The supporters of Donatus, known as Donatists, appealed again to the emperor. This time Constantine presided in person at a council of bishops at Arles in 314. After the Donatists likewise rejected this verdict, the emperor eventually ordered... confiscation of their churches.... After defeating Licinius in 324, Constantine inherited another ecclesiastical dispute in the Eastern provinces" about "the relationship between God the Father and Jesus Christ. Some theologians, including Arius, a priest at Alexandria, emphasized that the Son was subordinate to the Father.... Others stressed the coordination, coexistence, and identity of Father and Son. Constantine's primary concern was to prevent his recent unification of

Constantius. The name of Eusebians they received from their leader, the able and unscrupulous Bishop of Nicomedia, with whom was associated another Eusebius,[14]

---

the empire from imploding in ecclesiastical discord. In June 325 he presided over sessions of an ecumenical council of bishops at Nicaea that pointedly rejected Arian doctrines and defined Father and Son as 'identical in essence.' After the council, however, Constantine seemed to waver in his doctrinal preferences, often preferring Arian (or Arianizing) churchmen who temporized over strict proponents of Nicene theology. He offered reconciliation to Arius himself, he flattered Eusebius of Caesarea, a supporter of Arius, and he once exiled Athanasius, bishop of Alexandria and an inflexible advocate of Nicene theology." *The Oxford Encyclopedia of Ancient Greece and Rome.* See also D. Potter, *Constantine the Emperor* (Oxford, 2005). For Constantine's long-lasting Christian accomplishments, see R. L. Wilken, *The Spirit of Christian Thought* (New Haven, 2003), 199-200.

[14] *Eusebius*: Eusebius of Caesarea (c. 260–339 AD), Christian historian. "Eusebius is called 'the father of church history,' but the term is too narrow to do him justice. His long life covered a period of remarkable change in the development of Christianity. Following the espousal of the Christian cause by the emperor Constantine, Eusebius became bishop of Caesarea in Palestine sometime between 313 and 315, grew close to the emperor himself—although not as close as he liked to suggest—and left his mark in many areas of Christian speculation and literary endeavor. Eusebius' *Historia ecclesiastica*, completed in 324–25, was certainly an original and for subsequent ages an indispensable account of Christianity's early progress... The basis of the work was laid down before Constantine's victories in the West—laid down, that is, when Christians were still subject to harsh though varied government pressure. Just how much of the pre-Constantinian draft survives, and how early it was penned, is a matter of some dispute. Some think it is as early as 300, but its extension into the reign of Constantine himself—down to the early 320s—was not just a matter of clumsy addition: all sections of the work are likely to have undergone some adjustment in the light of Constantine's growing power and generous purpose. ...In the course of the theological disputes over ... Arius—disputes that provided Constantine with perhaps his most famous opportunities for the exercise of religious authority—Eusebius disclosed a cautious and ambiguous attachment to orthodoxy. Like many swept up in the conflict, he was anxious not to exaggerate the closeness of the Son to the Father in the Christian Trinity—that is, he was more worried by the Sabellian tendency than by the sense of distance and distinction that Arius appeared to champion. Eusebius' reputation suffered accordingly after his death, but he sailed close to the heretical wind even in his lifetime—aided perhaps by a comparable ambiguity in the opinions of the emperor himself. As a

better known to posterity as the learned historian of the Church, and one of the most accomplished and able of the Fathers. It will be to my purpose to quote one or two [381] sentences in description of the character of this celebrated man, written by me at a time when the subject of the *Via Media* had not as yet been mooted in the controversy, nor the bearing of the Arian history upon it been suggested to my mind.

"He seems," I said, speaking of Eusebius of Cæsarea, "to have had the faults and the virtues of the mere man of letters; strongly excited neither to good not to evil, and careless at once of the cause of truth and the prizes of secular greatness, in comparison of the comforts and decencies of literary ease. In his writings, numerous as they are, there is very little which fixes on Eusebius any charge, beyond that of an attachment to the Platonic phraseology.

---

historian, Eusebius is revealed as clearly in his *Chronicon* as in his *Historia ecclesiastica*. ...He relied to some extent on predecessors— Hippolytus and Julius Africanus—but went further than they did in establishing a carefully calibrated set of temporal relations between the history of both Christians and Jews on the one hand and the acknowledged history of other past cultures and systems of government on the other. The familiar account, therefore, of God's dealings with his chosen people, with Israel old and new, was now declared an integral part of human history seen as a whole. The juxtaposition thus achieved invited comparison in Christianity's favor and confidence in the identifiable antiquity of what so many pagan critics had seen as a provincial and upstart faith. Above all, Christians were given their place as a 'people.' They no longer needed to think of themselves as alien or marginal: they were destined and ready to inherit the earthly realm that Constantine seemed to offer them." *The Oxford Encyclopedia of Ancient Greece and Rome*. One of St. Augustine's objections to the Donatists was that they were standing in the way of this destiny. As Peter Brown points out: "For Augustine, it was not enough for the Christian church to preserve a holy 'Law.' This attitude would have condemned Christianity, as in Augustine's eyes it had condemned the Donatist church, to remaining isolated, like the old Israel, content to guard a static alliance of 'obedience' between itself and God. Instead, he preserved the Catholic Church as the heir of a will, about to take over a vast property." P. Brown, *Augustine of Hippo: A Biography* new edition (California, 2000), 216. For insight into Eusebius and St. Augustine as historians, see Wilken, *The Spirit of Early Christian Thought*, 189.

Had he not connected himself with the Arian party, it would have been unjust to have suspected him of heresy. But his acts are his confession. He openly sided with those whose blasphemies a true Christian would have abhorred; and he sanctioned and shared their deeds of violence and injustice perpetrated on the Catholics ... The grave accusation under which he lies is not that of Arianising,[15] but of corrupting the simplicity of the Gospel with an Eclectic spirit. While he held out the ambiguous language of the schools as a refuge, and the Alexandrian imitation of it as an argument, against the pursuit of the orthodox, his conduct gave [382] countenance to the secular maxim, that difference in creeds is a matter of inferior moment, and that, provided we confess as far as the very terms of Scripture, we may speculate as philosophers and live as the world ... The remark has been made, that throughout his Ecclesiastical History no instance occurs of his expressing abhorrence of the superstitions of paganism; and that his custom is either to praise, or not to blame, such heretical writers as fall under his notice."[16] Much more might be added in

---

[15] The author has now still less favourable views of Eusebius' theology than he had when he wrote this in 1832. [N] Newman's unfavorable view of Eusebius' theology did not prevent his citing the eyewitness historian on early Church martyrs to parry Gibbon's slighting of their faithful witness. "In Egypt a hundred and twenty confessors, after having sustained the loss of eyes or of feet, endured to linger out their lives in the mines of Palestine and Cilicia," Newman wrote in the *Grammar of Assent* (1870). "In the last persecution, according to the testimony of the grave Eusebius, a contemporary, the slaughter of men, women, and children, went on by twenties, sixties, hundreds, till the instruments of execution were worn out, and the executioners could kill no more. Yet he tells us, as an eye-witness, that, as soon as any Christians were condemned, others ran from all parts, and surrounded the tribunals, confessing the faith, and joyfully receiving their condemnation, and singing songs of thanksgiving and triumph to the last. Thus was the Roman power overcome. Thus did the Seed of Abraham, and the Expectation of the Gentiles, the meek Son of man, 'take to Himself His great power and reign' in the hearts of His people, in the public theatre of the world. The mode in which the primeval prophecy was fulfilled is as marvellous, as the prophecy itself is clear and bold." *GA*, 485.

[16] Arians of the Fourth Century, p. 281. [p. 269 ed. 1871.] [N]

illustration of the resemblance of this eminent writer to the divines of the Anglican *Via Media.*

The Emperor Constantine has already been named; and looking at him in his ecclesiastical character we find him committed to two remarkable steps; one that he frankly surrendered himself to the intimate friendship of this latitudinarian theologian; the other, that, at the very first rumour of the Arian dissensions, he promptly, and with the precision of an instinct, interfered in the quarrel, and in a politician's way pronounced it to be a logomachy, or at least a matter of mere speculation, and bade bishops and heretics embrace and make it up with each other at once. This did he in a question no less solemn than that of the divinity of our Lord, which, if any question, could not be other than most influential, one would think, in a Christian's creed. But [383] Constantine was not a Christian as yet; and this, while it partly explains the extravagance of his conduct, illustrates the external and utilitarian character of a statesman's religion.

I will present to you portions of the celebrated letter which he addressed to the Bishop of Alexandria and to Arius, as quoted in the history to which I have already referred. "He professes therein two motives as impelling him in his public conduct; first, the desire of effecting the reception, throughout his dominions, of some one definite and complete form of religious worship; next, that of settling and invigorating the civil institutions of the empire. Desirous of securing a unity of sentiment among all the believers in the Deity, he first directed his attention to the religious dissensions of Africa, which he had hoped, with the aid of the Oriental Christians, to terminate. 'But glorious and Divine Providence!' he continues, 'how fatally were my ears, or rather, was my heart wounded, by the report of a rising schism among you far more acrimonious than the African dissensions ... On investigation, I find that the reasons for this quarrel are insignificant and worthless ... As I understand it, you, Alexander, were asking the separate opinions of your clergy on some passage of your law, or

rather were inquiring about some idle question, when you, Arius, inconsiderately committed yourself to statements, which should either never have come into your mind, or
[384] have been at once repressed. On this a difference ensued, Christian intercourse was suspended, the sacred flock was divided into two, and the harmonious unity of the Church broken ... Listen to the advice of me your fellow-servant;— neither ask nor answer questions which are not any injunction of your law, but are the altercation of barren leisure; at best, keep them to yourselves, and do not publish them ... Your contention is not about any capital commandment of your law, neither of you is introducing any novel scheme of divine worship, you are of one and the same way of thinking, so that it is in your power to unite in one communion. Even the philosophers can agree together one and all, though differing in particulars ... Is it right for brothers to oppose brothers, for the sake of trifles? ... Such conduct might be expected from the multitude or from the recklessness of boyhood, but is little in keeping with your sacred profession and with your personal wisdom ... Give me back my days of calm, my nights of security; that I may experience henceforth the comfort of the clear light and the cheerfulness of tranquillity. Otherwise I shall sigh and be dissolved in tears ... So great is my grief, that I put off my journey to the East on the news of your dissension ... Open for me that path towards you, which your contentions have closed up. Let me see you and all other cities in happiness,
[385] that I may offer due thanksgivings to God above for the unanimity and free intercourse which is seen among you.'"[17]

Such was the position which the Christian civil power assumed in the very first days of its nativity. The very moment the State enters into the Church, it shows its nature and its propensities, and takes up a position which it has never changed, and never will. Kings and statesmen may be, and have been, saints; but, in being such, they have acted against the interests and traditions of kingcraft and

---

[17] Arians of the Fourth Century, p. 267. [p. 255.] [N]

424

statesmanship. Constantine died, but his line of policy continued. His son, Constantius, embraced the *Via Media* of Eusebianism on conviction as well as from expediency. He sternly set himself against both extremes, as he considered them, banished the fanatical successors of Arius, and tortured and put to death the adherents to the Nicene Creed and the cause of St. Athanasius. Thus the *Via Media* party was in the ascendancy for about thirty years, till the death of the generation by whom it had been formed and protected;—with quarrels and defections among themselves, restless attempts at stability in faith, violent efforts after a definite creed, fruitless projects of comprehension,—when, towards the end of their domination, a phenomenon showed itself, which claims our particular attention, as not without parallel in ecclesiastical history, and as reminding us of what is going on, in an humbler way and on a narrower [386] stage, before our eyes. In various districts, especially of Asia Minor, a considerable party had gradually been forming, and had exercised a considerable influence in the ecclesiastical transactions of the period, who, though called Semi-Arians and professing their symbols, had no sympathies with the Eusebians, and indeed were ultimately disowned by them. There seems to have been about a hundred bishops who belonged to this party, and their leaders were men of religious habits and unblemished repute, and approximated so nearly to orthodoxy in their language, that Saints appear among the number of their friends, or have issued from their school. Things could not stand as they were: every year brought its event; Constantius died; parties were broken up,—and this among the rest. It divided into two; as many as fifty-nine of its bishops subscribed the orthodox formula, and submitted themselves to the Holy See. A body of thirty-four persisted in their separation from it, and afterwards formed a new heresy of their own.

These are but a few of the main features of the history of Arianism; yet they may be sufficient to illustrate the line of argument which Antiquity furnishes against the theories, on which alone the movement of 1833 had claim on the attention of Protestants. Those theories claimed to represent the theological and the ecclesiastical teaching of the Fathers; and the Fathers, when interrogated, did but pronounce them to be the offspring of eclecticism, and the exponent of a State Church. It could not maintain itself in its position without allying itself historically with that very Erastianism, as seen in Antiquity, of which it had so intense a hatred. What has been sketched from the Arian history might be shown still more strikingly in the Monophysite.[18]

[387]

6.

Nor was it solely the conspicuous parallel which I have been describing in outline, which, viewed in its details, was so fatal a note of error against the Anglican position. I soon found it to follow, that the grounds on which alone Anglicanism was defensible formed an impregnable stronghold for the primitive heresies, and that the justification of the Primitive Councils was as cogent an apology for the Council of Trent.[19] It was difficult to make

---

[18] Vid. Essay on Doctrinal Development, chap. v. sec. 3. [N] "To find then what a corruption or perversion of the truth is, let us inquire what the word means, when used literally of material substances. Now it is plain, first of all, that a corruption is a word attaching to organized matters only; a stone may be crushed to powder, but it cannot be corrupted. Corruption, on the contrary, is the breaking up of life, preparatory to its termination. This resolution of a body into its component parts is the stage before its dissolution; it begins when life has reached its perfection, and it is the sequel, or rather the continuation, of that process towards perfection, being at the same time the reversal and undoing of what went before. Till this point of regression is reached, the body has a function of its own, and a direction and aim in its action, and a nature with laws; these it is now losing, and the traits and tokens of former years; and with them its vigour and powers of nutrition, of assimilation, and of self-reparation." *Dev* 170-1.

[19] *Trent*: Council of Trent (1545–63) Nineteenth ecumenical council of the Roman Catholic Church, which provided the main impetus of the Counter-Reformation in Europe. It met at Trent, in Italy, in three sessions under three popes (Paul III, Julius III, Pius IV). It clarified Catholic doctrine and refused concessions to the Protestants, while also instituting

out how the Eutychians or Monophysites were heretics, unless Protestants and Anglicans were heretics also; difficult to find arguments against the Tridentine Fathers which did not tell against the Fathers of Chalcedon; difficult to condemn the Popes of the sixteenth century, without condemning the Popes of the fifth. The drama of religion and the combat of truth and error were ever one and the same. The principles and proceedings of the Church now were those of the Church then; the principles and proceedings of heretics then were those of Protestants now. I found it so—almost fearfully; there was an awful similitude, more awful, because so silent and [388] unimpassioned, between the dead records of the past and the feverish chronicle of the present. The shadow of the fifth century was on the sixteenth. It was like a spirit rising from the troubled waters of the Old World with the shape and lineaments of the new. The Church then, as now, might be called peremptory and stern, resolute, overbearing, and relentless; and heretics were shifting, changeable, reserved, and deceitful, ever courting the civil power, and never agreeing together, except by its aid; and the civil power was ever aiming at comprehensions, trying to put the invisible out of view, and to substitute expediency for faith. What was the use of continuing the controversy, or defending my position, if, after all, I was but forging arguments for Arius or Eutyches, and turning devil's advocate against the much-enduring Athanasius and the majestic Leo? Be my soul with the Saints! and shall I lift up my hand against them? Sooner may my right hand forget her cunning, and wither outright, as his who once stretched it out against a prophet of God,— perish sooner a whole tribe of Cranmers, Ridleys, Latimers, and Jewels,—perish the names of Bramhall, Ussher, Taylor, Stillingfleet, and Barrow, from the face of the earth,—ere I should do aught but fall at their feet in love and in worship,

---

reform of many of the abuses that had provoked the Reformation. *Oxford World Encyclopaedia.*

whose image was continually before my eyes, and whose musical words were ever in my ears and on my tongue!

[389]   This, too, is an observable fact, that the more learned Anglican writers seem aware of the state of the case, and are obliged, by the necessities of their position, to speak kindly of the heretical communities of ancient history, and at least obliquely to censure the Councils, which, nevertheless, they profess to receive. Thus Bramhall, as we saw yesterday, strives to fraternize with the sectaries now existing in the East; nor could he consistently do otherwise, with the Council of Trent and the Protestants in the field of controversy; it being difficult indeed to show that the Eastern Churches in question are to be accounted heretical on any principles which a Protestant is able to put forward. It is not wonderful, then, that other great authorities in the Established Church are of the same way of thinking. "Jewel, Ussher, and Laud," says an Anglican divine of this day, "are apparently of this opinion, and Field expressly maintains it."[20]

Jeremy Taylor goes further still, that is, is still more consistent; for he not merely acquits of heresy the existing communities of the East who dissent from the third and fourth Councils, but he is bold enough to attack the first Council of all, the Nicene. He places the right of private judgment, or what he calls "the liberty of prophesying," above all Councils whatever. As to the Nicene, he says, "*I am much pleased with the enlarging of the Creed which the*
[390] Council of Nice made, because they enlarged it in *my* sense; but I am not sure that others were satisfied with it."[21] "That faith is best which hath greatest simplicity; and it is better, in all cases, humbly to submit, than curiously to inquire, and pry into the mystery under the cloud, and to hazard our faith by improving our knowledge. If the Nicene Fathers had done so too, possibly the Church would never have repented it."[22] "If the article had been with more simplicity and less

---

[20] Palmer on the Church, vol. i. p. 418. [N]

[21] Vol. vii. p. 481, ed. 1828. [N]

[22] Jeremy Taylor, ibid. p. 485. [N]

nicety determined, charity would have gained more, and faith would have lost nothing."[23] And he not only calls Eusebius, whom it is hard to acquit of heresy, "the wisest of them all,"[24] but actually praises the letter of Constantine, which I have already cited, as most true in its view and most pertinent to the occasion. "The Epistle of Constantine to Alexander and Arius," he says, "tells the truth, and chides them both for commencing the question; Alexander for broaching it, Arius for taking it up. And although this be true, that it had been better for the Church it never had begun, yet, being begun, what is to be done in it? Of this also, in that admirable epistle, we have the Emperor's judgment ... for, first, he calls it a certain vain piece of a question, ill begun and more unadvisedly published, ... a fruitless contention, the product of idle brains, a matter so nice, so obscure, so intricate, that it was neither to be [391] explicated by the clergy, nor understood by the people; a dispute of words ... It concerned not the substance of faith, or the worship of God, nor any chief commandment of Scripture ... the matter being of no great importance, but vain, and a toy, in respect of the excellent blessings of peace and charity."[25] When we recollect that the question confessedly in dispute was whether our Lord is the Eternal God or a creature, and that the Nicene symbol against which Taylor writes was confessedly the sole test adequate to the definition of his divinity, it is scarcely conceivable that a writer should really believe that divinity and thus express himself.

Taylor is no accident in the history of the *Via Media*; he does but speak plainer than Field and Bramhall; and soon others began to speak plainer than he. The school of Laud gave birth to the latitudinarians; Hales and Chillingworth, their first masters, were personal friends of the Archbishop, whose indignation with them only proves his involuntary sense of the tottering state of his own theological position.

---

[23] Ibid. [N]
[24] Ibid. [N]
[25] P. 482. [N]

Lord Falkland, again, who thinks that before the Nicene Council "the generality of Christians had not been always taught the contrary to Arius's doctrine, but some one way, others the other, most neither,"[26] was the admired friend of Hammond; and Grotius, whose subsequent influence upon [392] the national divines has been so serious, was introduced to their notice by Hammond and Bramhall.

Such has been the issue of the *Via Media*; its tendency in theory is towards latitudinarianism; its position historically is one of heresy; in the National Church it has fulfilled both its theoretical tendency and its historical position. As this simple truth was brought home to me, I felt that, if continuance in the National Church was defensible, it must be on other grounds than those of the *Via Media*.

7.

Yet this was but one head of argument, which the history of the early Church afforded against the National Establishment, and in favour of the Roman See. I have already alluded to the light which the schism of the African Donatists casts on the question between the two parties in the controversy; it is clear, strong, and decisive, but perfectly distinct from the proof derivable from the Arian, Nestorian, and Monophysite histories.[27]

Then again, after drawing out from Antiquity the outlines of the ecclesiastical structure, and its relations to bodies and powers external to it, when we go on, as it were, to colour it with the thousand tints which are to be found in the same ancient records, when we consider the ritual of the [393] Church, the ceremonial of religion, the devotions of private Christians, the opinions generally received, and the popular modes of acting, what do we find but a third and most striking proof of the identity between primitive Christianity and modern Catholicism?[28] No other form of Christianity but this present Catholic Communion, has a pretence to

---

[26] Hammond's Works, vol. ii. p. 655 [N]

[27] Vide *Dublin Review*, August 1839, Art. "Anglican Claim." [N]

[28] *Dublin Review*, Dec. 1843, Art. "A Voice from Rome." [N]

resemble, even in the faintest shadow, the Christianity of Antiquity, viewed as a living religion on the stage of the world. This has ever attached me to such works as Fleury's Church History; [29] because, whatever may be its incidental defects or mistakes, it brings before the reader so vividly the Church of the Fathers, as a fact and a reality, instead of speculating, after the manner of most histories, on the principles, or of making views upon the facts, or cataloguing the heresies, rites, or writers, of those ancient times. You may make ten thousand extracts from the Fathers, and not get deeper into the state of their times than the paper you write upon; to imbibe into the intellect the Ancient Church as a fact, is either to be a Catholic or an infidel.

Recollect, my brethren, I am going into these details, not as if I thought of convincing you on the spot by a view of history which convinced me after careful consideration, nor as if I called on you to be convinced by what convinced me at all (for the methods of conviction are numberless, and one man approaches the Church by this road, another by [394]

---

[29] *Fleury*: Claude Fleury (1640–1723), ecclesiastical historian. From 1689 he was one of the tutors to Louis XIV's grandsons, and after his death (1715) he was chosen as confessor to the young Louis XV. His chief work is his *Histoire ecclésiastique* (20 vols., 1691–1720), the first large-scale history of the Church, renowned for its learning and reliability. Gibbon was highly reliant on Fleury for his *Decline & Fall*, commending its fairness. Fleury, he said, "respected the authority of the parliaments." *Decline and Fall*, ii, 342. Newman brought out a translation of Fleury's *Ecclesiastical History* in February of 1846. When the convert peeress and novelist Lady Georgiana Fullerton (1812-85) asked Newman for suggestions for histories of the early Church, he told her that "Tillemont's works, which you would be able to consult in any great city (his Emperors and his *Ecclesiastical Memoirs*) are the most accurate of any history. Gibbon calls his minute diligence 'church genius.' He would give you every fact about martyrdoms etc. Fleury's Ecclesiastical History, which also you would find everywhere, is to my mind the most graphic of histories. (Others do not agree with me.) It is a mere narration of the whole course of the times diligently drawn out. You should be on your guard against Fleury's Gallicanism and Tillemont's Jansenism. The Protestant Baur (History of the first three centuries) will also be of use to you, though it is very fanciful and dreamy." *LD*, xv, 236.

that), but merely in order to show you how it was that Antiquity, instead of leading me from the Holy See as it leads many, on the contrary drew me on to submit to its claims. But, even had I worked out for you these various arguments ever so fully, I should have brought before you but a secondary portion of the testimony which the Ancient Church seemed to me to supply to its own identity with the modern. What was far more striking to me than the ecclesiastical phenomena which I have been drawing out, remarkable as they are, is a subject of investigation which is not of a nature to introduce into a popular lecture; I mean the history of the doctrinal definitions of the Church. It is well known that, though the creed of the Church has been one and the same from the beginning, yet it has been so deeply lodged in her bosom as to be held by individuals more or less implicitly, instead of being delivered from the first in those special statements, or what are called definitions, under which it is now presented to us, and which preclude mistake or ignorance. These definitions, which are but the expression of portions of the one dogma which has ever been received by the Church, are the work of time; they have grown to their present shape and number in the course of eighteen centuries, under the exigency of successive events, such as heresies and the like, and they [395] may of course receive still further additions as time goes on. Now this process of doctrinal development, as you might suppose, is not of an accidental or random character; it is conducted upon laws, as everything else which comes from God; and the study of its laws and of its exhibition, or, in other words, the science and history of the formation of theology, was a subject which had interested me more than anything else from the time I first began to read the Fathers, and which had engaged my attention in a special way. Now it was gradually brought home to me, in the course of my reading, so gradually, that I cannot trace the steps of my conviction, that the decrees of later Councils, or what Anglicans call the Roman corruptions, were but instances of that very same doctrinal law which was to be found in the history of the early Church; and that in the sense in which the dogmatic truth of the prerogatives of the Blessed Virgin may be said, in the lapse of centuries, to have grown upon the consciousness of the faithful, in that same sense did, in the first age, the mystery of the Blessed Trinity also gradually shine out and manifest itself more and more completely before their minds. Here was at once an answer to the objections urged by Anglicans against the present teaching of Rome; and not only an answer to objections, but a positive argument in its favour; for the immutability and uninterrupted action of the laws in question throughout the course of Church history is a plain note of identity between [396] the Catholic Church of the first ages and that which now goes by that name;—just as the argument from the analogy of natural and revealed religion is at once an answer to difficulties in the latter, and a direct proof that Christianity has the same Author as the physical and moral world. But the force of this, to me ineffably cogent argument, I cannot hope to convey to another.

8.

And now, my dear brethren, what fit excuse can I make to you for the many words I have used about myself, and not in this Lecture only, but in others before it? This alone I can say, that it was the apprehension, or rather the certainty that this would be the case, which, among other reasons, made me as unwilling as I was to begin this course of Lectures at all. I foresaw that I could not address you on the subjects which I proposed, without introducing myself into the discussion; I could not refer to the past without alluding to matters in which I had a part; I could not show that interest in your state of mind and course of thought which I really feel, without showing that I therefore understood it, because I had before now experienced it myself; and I anticipated, what I fear has been the case, that in putting before you the events of former years, and the motives of past transactions, and the operation of common principles, and the complexion of old habits and opinions, I should be [397] in no slight degree constructing, what I have ever avoided, a defence of myself.

But I have had another apprehension, both before and since beginning these Lectures, viz., lest it was (to say the least) an impolitic proceeding to contemplate them at all. Things were proceeding in that course in which I knew they must proceed; I could not foretell indeed that a decision would issue from the Committee of Privy Council on the subject of Baptism; I could not anticipate that this or that external event would suddenly undo men's confidence in the National Church; but it required no gift of prophecy to feel that falsehood, and pretence, and unreality could not for ever enslave honest minds sincerely seeking the truth. It needed no prophetical gift to be sure that others must take ultimately the course which I had taken, though I could not foretell the time or the occasion; no gift to foresee, that those who did not choose to plunge into the gulf of scepticism must at length fall back upon the Catholic Church. Nor did it require in me much faith in you, my dear brethren, much love for you, to be sure that, though there were close around you men who look like you, but are not, that you, the children of the movement, were too conscientious, too much in earnest, not to be destined by that God, who made you what you are, to greater things. Others have scoffed at you, but I never; others may have [398] made light of your principles, or your sincerity, but never I; others may have predicted evil of you, I have only felt vexed at the prediction. I have laughed, indeed, I have scorned, and scorn and laugh I must, when men set up an outside instead of the inside of religion—when they affect more than they can sustain—when they indulge in pomp or in minutiæ, which only then are becoming when there is something to be proud of, something to be anxious for. If I have been excessive here, if I have confused what is defective with what is hollow, or have mistaken aspiration for pretence, or have been severe upon infirmities of which self-knowledge would have made me tender, I wish it otherwise. Still, whatever my faults in this matter, I have ever been trustful in that true Catholic spirit which has lived in the movement of which you are partakers. I have been steady in my confidence in that supernatural influence among you, which made me what I am,—which, in its good time, shall make you what you shall be. You are born to be Catholics; refuse not the unmerited grace of your bountiful God; throw off for good and all the illusions of your intellect, the bondage of your affections, and stand upright in that freedom which is your true inheritance.

And my confidence that you will do so at last, and that the sophistries of this world will not hold you for ever, is what has caused the hesitation to which I have referred, whether I have done wisely in deciding on addressing you at [399] all. I have in truth had anxious misgivings whether I should not do better to let you alone, my own experience teaching me, that even the most charitable attempts are apt to fail, when their end is the conviction of the intellect. It is no work of a day to convince the intellect of an Englishman that Catholicism is true. And even when the intellect is convinced, a thousand subtle influences interpose in arrest of what should follow, carrying, as it were, an appeal into a higher court, and claiming to have the matter settled before some tribunal more sacred, and by pleadings more recondite, than the operations and the decision of the reason. The Eternal God deals with us one by one, each in his own way; and bystanders may pity and compassionate the long throes of our travail, but they cannot aid us except by their prayers. If, then, I have erred in entering upon the subjects I have brought before you, pardon me; pardon me if I have rudely taken on myself to thrust you forward, and to anticipate by artificial means a divine growth. If it be so, I will only hope that, though I may have done you no good, yet my attempt may be blessed in some other way; that I may have thrown light on the general subject which I have discussed, have contributed to map out the field of thought on which I have been engaged, and to ascertain its lie and its characteristics, and have furnished materials for what, in time to come, may be the science and received principles of [400] the whole controversy, though I have failed in that which was my immediate object.

9.

At all events, my dear brethren, I hope I may be at least considered to be showing my goodwill and kindness towards you, if nothing else, and my desire to be of use to you. All is vanity but what is done to the glory of God. It glitters and it fades away; it makes a noise and is gone. If I shall not do you or others good, I have done nothing. Yet a little while and the end will come, and all will be made manifest, and error will fail, and truth will prevail. Yet a little while, and "the fire shall try every man's work of what sort it is." May you and I live in this prospect; and may the Eternal God, Father, Son, and Spirit, Three in One, may His Ever-blessed Mother, may St. Philip, my dear father and master, the great Saints Athanasius and Ambrose, and St. Leo, pope and confessor, who have brought me thus far, be the hope, and help, and reward of you and me, all through this weary life, and in the day of account, and in glory everlasting!

TEXTUAL APPENDIX

The following list contains variants in the 1876 edition from the 1850 edition. Where words in the *1876 text* column have nothing equivalent in the *1850 text* column, they are additions to the earlier text; and where words in the *1850 text* column have nothing equivalent in the *1876 text* column, they were omitted in the later text. Trivial variations in capitalising, punctuation and spelling have been ignored. The page numbers are those of the standard edition which are in square brackets in the margins of this Gracewing edition.

Page	*1876 text*	*1850 text*
viii	all who encounter them	all comers
	a multitude of our countrymen	the convictions of a multitude of men
viii-ix	as the history, carried out before their eyes, of the religious teaching of the school in question, a teaching simple and intelligible in its principles, persuasive in its views, gradually developed, adjusted, and enlarged, gradually imbibed and mastered, in a course of years; and now converging in many minds at once to one issue, and in some of them already reaching it, and that issue the divinity of the Catholic Religion?	as a teaching which has been simple and intelligible in its principles; imbibed and mastered in the course of years; gradually developed, improved, corrected, adjusted, and enlarged; which is converging in many minds at once to one resolution as its limit, and which in a number of instances has been completed already by acts which, more powerfully than any words, attest the force and the issue of the argument which it involves?
ix	when this has been done	
	today […] tomorrow	now […] then
	still further	forward
	their own submitting	their submitting
	logical	Intrinsic
	in a case where	where
	right perceptions	true perceptions
x	least important	minutest

	our whole	the whole
	near to	near
	as we see daily, they do not avail	they do not avail, as we see daily
xi	regard	fondness
xii	been saying	said
	faith depends upon the will, not really on any process of reasoning	faith is the result of the will, not of a process of reasoning,
	to give free play to the conscience	to remove impediments to the due action of the conscience
	proof of Catholicity	proof
	impediments suffice	difficulty suffices
	which, without	as, without
xiii	the Author	he
xiv	subject which is successively	subject successively
	July 14	In fest. S. Bonaventuræ
1	For to help	For what is it to help
	the Catholic Religion	Catholicism
2	sectarianism	dissent
	natural, though they may be her covert	natural, however covert
	over themselves	over them
	for their Catholic or Papistical tendency	as Catholics or Papists
	enemies of ours	enemies
	apologies in behalf of	apologies for
	which the	such as the
3	in comparison	comparatively

5	If, indeed, we	If we
6	mechanism	machinery
	referred on, by the nature of the case, to	by the nature of the case, to be referred on to
7	the present Court	Court
8	as if it were	as being
	nor on the other hand would it be	nor will it be
	"tuned her pulpits;"	"tuned its pulpits;"
9	its influence over	the conversion of
	fragmentary portions	isolated portions
10	certain and formidable	clear and striking
	I say	
	a party after all	a party within its pale
11	enforced	elicited
12	bearing upon the doctrine of Baptism	
	the Establishment. This is the true	the Establishment. Such is the true state of the case: no one can exaggerate the *vis inertiæ*, the life, of a national establishment, of whatever kind; it is, in other words, the strength of *the world*; nothing is stronger than the world, except God and the devil; and the evil spirit may, if God so allow, destroy what he has hitherto used, in order to bring in a more awful form of heresy and unbelief. The Eternal God too, at His merciful pleasure, may fight with it, and humble and subdue it, as He has done of old time; and in such cases His Holy Church is the instrument of His purposes. It is the duty of the Catholic Church, wherever she is found, and it is her gift, to confront, to encounter, and to beat back the spirit of the age.

This has been especially felt by those who began, and those who continued, the movement in the Establishment. They keenly felt this truth; they acted upon it; and they failed, because they mistook an Establishment for the Church, because they fancied a work of man the work of God. The Church alone is immortal and unalterable; but time and chance, which are the instruments of man's creations, are the instruments also of their modification and their change. This is the true

14	though distinct	though it is distinct
15	is no match	are no match
	which rules that every conclusion is	which makes every conclusion seem
	one by one	
17	whom I have loved	whom once I loved
18	belong	are attached
19	was at least	at least is
	life social and civil	social and civil
	these appendages	they
20	the Religion of England	the nation's religion
23	the existing nation speaks	the existing nation
	who, in former years, had had the nerve	which had had the nerve years before
	their opponents	its opponents
	their own breasts	its breast
	not dishonest	nor dishonest
24	any more to do	more to do

	objective	external,
25	—Such is the thought, such the language of the England of today.	
	the dogma	the dogmas
	smaller craft	small craft
25	which that Church professes stands	stands within its pale
	hold this	hold fast this
27	against the strong feeling of the age, with so little in its favour in the national formularies	with so little for it in the national formularies, against the strong feeling of the age
	are extolling	extol
28	the champions	jealous
	At least some of you	Some of you at least
	on its own account	for itself
	Whittaker	Calvin
28	with our countrymen	
28fn	has on them	was on them
	amid the gravest differences	though he has much differed from
29	yet we are more desirous that you should leave a false church for the true, than that a false church should hold its ground. For if	still, if
	a direct, unequivocal, and substantial	a certain and substantial
	simply inculcate	inculcate
	yet serve to	serve nevertheless to
	addresses them	comes near them
30	before now	already

	and we ask	we ask
	of which it is a copyist	of which they are imitators
	rid its professors of their prejudices	disabuse it of its prejudices
	abuse of her makes them	abuse makes men
31	in the Protestant world	
32	which troubles men	which urges them
	you will not be harming it	
	it falls because	this will be because
	in the nineteenth	in the present
33	FOREIGN TO	UNCONGENIAL TO
	when he is	if he is
	the Catholic Religion	Catholicism
	inoperative	unpractical
34	somewhat retard	retard
	real importance	importance
	though certainly	though
	has created	had remained
	the least possible influence	as little real influence as is conceivable
35	I shall infer that you have	that you have
36	these were congenial	they were congenial
	this is what with	what with
37	allowing	allowing and apologizing
	viz., belief in "the Catholic Church," alleging in excuse that "the teaching	and that, on the ground that "the teaching

	compared, in its strangeness, to	compared to
	startled at those doctrines	startled at them
37fn	Prophetical Office of the Church. Vid. Via Media, vol. i., ed. 1877.	
38	"these doctrines are	"they are
	by Popery he means	by which he means
39	to say for him	to say
	On the other hand	Yet on the other,
42	the author whom I have already quoted	the apologist for Mr. Froude and his friends
	attack upon him	attack
43	the movement of 1833 demanded or desiderated in its behalf	the movement in question desiderated or doubted, with reference to it
	no life	not life
43fn	The author's "Letter to	Newman's Letter to
44	the constituent element	the element
	professed to be built	were professedly built
	doubting whether it really had those principles and that life, in spite of its professions	doubting whether it was what it professed to be
	one of its dignitaries triumphantly proves it in a passage which I will quote	it is triumphantly proved by one of its dignitaries, in a passage which I quote
46	the faith of Marcus Antoninus, St. Austin	the faith of St. Austin
	of Prussia, that he means, or is it	of Prussia, or is it
	he will be arguing	we shall be arguing
	if he is to prove that Protestants have	if Protestants are to prove that they

		have
	on the ground of their having	because they have
48	no Church from the first	no Church already.
	this uncongeniality I am speaking of in order	I speak of this in order
	long ago before the movement, in order	long ago, in order
49	to decide the Catholicity	to rest the Catholicity
	disavowed	and subscribed to a disavowal of
50	from such acts in particular	from such
51	pass;—I will here	pass; *transeat*; I will here
52	which constituted, or the moment which completed the schism, or rather	which completed the schism, or rather
	and that they could or can live	or can live
53	truly said	most true
	No one will deny	No one can doubt
	readily coalesces	can readily coalesce
53-4	Other religions	Religions
55	and this quality and this direction are tested	and these are tested
	whether that multitude is	whether it is
58	be little versed in doctrine	be in ignorance of doctrine
59	in such sort	so
	party manifestos	party
	When, then, the note	When the note

60	the Sacraments are lodged with us	the Sacraments reside with us.
62	bestowed in one quarter on	bestowed on
	could, if they would, buy	could buy
62-3	be unconcerned, and go their own way, for no one would interfere with them, and might "live	be unconcerned, if they would, and go their own way, and "live
67	THE LIFE OF THE MOVEMENT OF 1833 NOT DERIVED FROM THE NATIONAL CHURCH	LIFE IN THE MOVEMENT OF 1833 NOT FROM THE NATIONAL CHURCH.
	are called on	were called on
	they belong	they belonged
	they receive	they received
68	stands on a basis independent of the Nation	stands on an independent basis
	those changes of Progress, as it is called	changes of progress, as they are called
69	retrograde changes	backward changes
	and it is the opponent	and the opponent
	which, after all, has done	which has done
70	there must be committed by those who, belonging to the movement, abandon the Church."	there must be in leaving it."
	their becoming Catholics	their joining the Catholic Church
	a multitude of men	a multitude of persons
	by certain of the National Clergy	by the National Clergy.
	which was their characteristic	which they took up
71	ordinances of that National Church	ordinances of their own communion.

	attended those ordinances	attended them
72	They are undoubtedly in	They are in
	"Their opponents	Their opponents
	staying in it	staying
	will from time to time happen	will happen
73	to all the rules of theology and the maxims of polemics	to scientific rule
	of reason,—though it ought not to be so in the way of strict science,—still, so it is, they are	of reason, they are
	it is true one of	it is true, they find that one of
	these arguments are inconsistent	these are inconsistent
	Now, as truth is the object which I set before me in the inquiry which I am prosecuting, I will not follow their example in considering only one side of the question.	Now, as I have no desire to imitate a line of conduct which I cannot approve, I will not follow them in leaving the question unsettled:
	future reward."	future reward.
74	content myself, on my part, with	content myself with
75	First, I suppose	1. I suppose
	in the world	to the world
75fn	The author's	Newman's
77fn	Ibid., pp. 348-350.	Ibid. pp. 394-390.
78fn	Ibid., pp. 353-355	Ibid. pp. 400, 401.
79	No one	Now no one
79fn	Ibid., p. 380.	Ibid. p. 430.
81	I looked on ordination	I looked on it

82	I easily give you credit	I give you credit
	the past years of my own life	the past years of your life
83	the soul may be led	the soul is led on
84	yet really obeying	really obeying
	nay, I might say (at least by way of argument), in His favour	nay in His favour
85	if it is not tending to do so	if it does not tend to do so
	as they do themselves	as Protestants themselves
	national ordinances of religion	national ordinances
	the ordinance itself	the ordinance
86	as it was anciently called	as it was called
	or what is called matter	or matter
87	the same on condition of the same	the same under the same
87-8	and even, at least I am not bound to deny it, remission of sins	or even remission of sins
88	by the fact that he accepted it	by accepting it
	though the worshipper unintentionally offered	though he ignorantly offered
90fn	Sir James Stephen.	
91	they would startle	they startle
92	as admirable in his earnestness	as in that earnestness
92fn	Mr. Scott of Ashton Sandford.	Mr. Scott.
94	and intercourse with others	and the communication of ideas
	simply on account	on account
	in particular instances	in some instances

	those who are not responsible for their ignorance	those who are in invincible ignorance
	the claim in their behalf is	the claim is
	if it is to the effect that their	if they expect their
95	your safety	your security
	you have not only said it was a sin to ascribe your good thoughts, and purposes, and aspirations to any but God (which you were right in saying), but you have presumed to pronounce it blasphemy against the Holy Ghost to doubt that they came into your hearts by means of your Church and by virtue of its ordinances.	you have presumed to pronounce it blasphemy against the Holy Ghost to doubt of your Church and of its ordinances.
96	NOT IN THE DIRECTION OF	NOT TOWARDS
	definite application	practical application,
97	earnestness in proclaiming	earnestness in uttering
	they had nothing else to say but that	they could only say that
	nor attempt to associate themselves with things	or attempt to coalesce with things
	was delivered	was sent
98	Providence does nothing	God does nothing
	religiousness	religious principle
	as has a place in the history	as has been expended or exhibited in the history
	discern what that place was	discern what it was
	as integrally one, and thus investigate what is	as one thing, and thus contemplate what is
99	be ascertained	be found
100	to throw themselves in imagination	in their imagination, to throw

	out of themselves	themselves out of themselves,
	of Liberalism	of the liberal party
101	considered simply as such	considered as such
	practical aspect	practical character
	those divines	they
	that the one doctrine or the other gave a shape and character to its teaching	that their teaching was cast in that particular shape which I have mentioned, each portion in detail being made subservient to its inculcation
103	but in order to shake off the State	but to preserve them by uttering them; in order to their firmer reception
	was a match for the world	was to convert the world
	to contend ... We wish	to contend. We wish
	evangelists ... If master-minds	evangelists. If master-minds
104	of that attractive nature	of that warm and attractive nature
105	the nature of the religious communion	the nature of the Establishment
	in that religion	in it
	the Established Religion[2]	the Establishment
	to destroy the religion	to destroy the Establishment
	of Statesmen	of the State
105fn	[Discussions and Arguments, pp. 34-38.]	
105fn	We must not forget, however, Mr. Froude's upas-tree.	
106	antiquary	antiquarian

109	than men do now	than many men do now
111	because it practically told in their favour	because its apparent tendency lay the other way
	feeling both in its rulers and its people as it did, their teaching could not escape animadversion	feeling as it did, their doctrines could not be sheltered
	answered from the other side of St. George's Channel	answered
112	However, it is hardly	It is hardly
	were even	were ever
113	there is no tendency	there is no providential tendency
	what it is at present	what it is
114	It may be urged, "that if	It may be urged, that if
	wish to be humble." Again, though	wish to be humble. Moreover, though
	the other hand, "there is a chance," it may be	other hand, there is a chance, it may be
	dutiful for a time." This is	dutiful for a time. This is
	feel that Great Britain would be	feel it would be
115	but then, who	but again, who
	Accordingly, they bear any	They bear then any
	natural temper	natural tenor
116	their removal. They said "they went	their removal. "They went
	go such lengths	go so far
116fn	Since writing the above, the author finds it necessary to observe, that, in writing it, it had no reference to persons, and he would be pained if it seemed to refer to actual passages in the controversy now in progress.	Since writing this, the author finds it necessary to add, that he had no reference whatever in writing it, and should be pained to seem to have had, to particular passages in the controversy now in progress.

117	against which, in the minds of the writers of the Tracts, it was directed	with which it has contended
	a measure which one has advocated	a measure it has advocated
	recollected, measures	recollected that measures
118	country palaces	rural palaces
	a determination to act as if	to act as if
	future,—this is simply	future, is simply
119	Great commanders, when in war they are	Great men in warfare, when they are
	no place from which to issue in due season, no hope that your present concessions will bring about a future victory. Your retreat	no place at all, no happy diocese, or peaceful parish, where you can utter and carry out securely those very things which you hold to be most true. Your retreat
119-120	when his lordship is asked to print his Charge	when his lordship's charge is to be printed
120	a hostile newspaper	a newspaper
	in baptizing, or has got a cross upon his surplice, or that in	in baptizing, or that in
	preaching on decency and order, on the impressive performance of divine Service	preaching on the decent performance of Divine Service
	Rooms about some new book put upon the Society's list, or some new liberalizing regulation; a drawn battle	Rooms; a drawn battle
121	beginning of the following century	beginning of the following
	broad and significant indications	broad and insignificant indications
	of what I am urging	of what I have affirmed
122	given me by Providence	given me by God
123	Moreover, I am doing good	And I am doing good

451

124	can scarcely be lost	can seldom be lost
	gift of faith	gift of faith[3]
124fn		[3]Errantes invincibiliter circa aliquos articulos, et credentes alios, non sunt formaliter hæretici, sed habent fidem supernaturalem, quâ credunt veros articulos, atque adeo ex eâ possunt procedere actus perfectæ contritionis, quibus justificentur et salventur, &c.—*De Lugo de fide*, xii. 3. 50.
125	THE PROVIDENTIAL COURSE OF THE MOVEMENT OF 1833 NOT IN THE DIRECTION OF A PARTY IN THE NATIONAL CHURCH	THE PROVIDENTIAL DIRECTION OF THE MOVEMENT OF 1833 NOT TOWARDS A PARTY IN THE NATIONAL CHURCH
127	still, nevertheless, you will	still you will
	your several positions	your respective positions
	a religious communion like the Establishment, which	a religious communion, which
	innovators, who are even further removed	innovators, further removed
128	but these I would have consider	and I would have them consider
	where they are standing	where they stand
	unless they are induced steadily	unless they try steadily
129	their feelings before they expressed them	their feelings long ago
	as yesterday, that you were a party then and can remain a party now, that your present	as yesterday, and that your present
129-130	has a progress? Your principles, indeed, are fixed, but circumstances	has a progress? Circumstances
130	Observe:—your movement started	Your movement started
131	the mysterious grace of the	the mysteriousness of the

Textual Appendix

	Episcopate	Episcopate
	boldly invoked	boldly appealed to
	the "Liturgy," or Book of Common Prayer.	the "Liturgy."
132	Again, it was said that "there was	Again, "there was
134fn	Proph. Off., p. 157.	Newman's Proph. Off. p. 157.
134	these were	they were
	the authoritative rule or statement, or at most must only be entertained	the received opinion, or at most must be entertained
	The matters in debate could	They could
	it was a sure and sufficient safeguard against error. It was dangerous to question any part of it.	it had a claim to be used as such, because the evil of criticism was so very dangerous.
	mind," said a Tract. "This	mind. This
135	find for it	find it
	who is expressing the philosophy (so to call it) of the movement	who on the whole is meant to express the feelings of the party
	start from	stand upon
136	I adopt then	I adopt them
137	what Anglicanism taught	what it taught
	any one	any
138	said, and believed,	told us
	testimonies," he continued, "is	testimonies is
	to us.	to us. For specimens of what is here alluded to, he refers to the Catenæ Patrum, published in the " Tracts for the Times."
	by what rule	by what authority

138fn | Viz., the text prefixed to the Catenas, Tract 74. There was another | "Or take again those, whom by a natural instinct all the people count as prophets, and will it not be found that either altogether, or in those works which are most popular, those writers are ruled by primitive and catholic principles? No man, for instance, was an abler writer in the last century than Warburton, or more famous in his day; yet the glare is over, and now Bishops Wilson and Home, men of far inferior powers, but of catholic temper and principles, fill the doctor's chair in the eyes of the many." (British Critic, Jan. 1840, p. 478.)
There was another

139 | think him obscure | think him difficult

or they might feel | or feel

140 | principles in the Catenas they drew out, and, after all | principles, and, after all

their carefulness | their caution

141 | already, I mean myself, I have | already, I have

which he published | which was published

which he had made against the Catholic Church, these | made against the Catholic Church, by one of the original writers, these

but still, though he internally thought it, he would not have dared | but he would not have dared

an accuser | a sinner and a worm

142 | and unless | unless

his Church's cause | his Church's case

the display of | the exercise of

and, as using those words, he was behind "a system" received by his | and, this being the case, he could "throw himself into," he could

Church, as well as by himself. He felt "safe," because he spoke after, and "throwing himself into," he was sheltering himself according to its teaching and its teachers. It had, indeed, been one sin that he had thought ill of the Catholic Church; it had been another and greater, that he had uttered what he thought; and there was just this alleviation of his second sin, that he had not said it wantonly, and that he had said what others had said before him.

shelter himself behind, a " system received by his Church," as well as by himself. He felt "safe," because he spoke after, and according to its teaching and its teachers. It was one sin, the having thought ill of the Catholic Church; it was another and greater, to have spoken what he thought; and there was just this alleviation of his second sin, that he said what others had said before him.

luxuriated, that any one should think of clearing himself from what in their eyes was simply a virtue, or should be shocked at having the credit given him of making use of a special privilege

luxuriated themselves, should apologize for what was simply a virtue, and should lament over the use of a privilege

144   but it was not a task

but not as a task

The author's feeling

His feeling

144fn   I am not

The writer is not

I have nothing to say in explanation, but that this passage was not written by me, and that I do not consider it to have expressed my own feelings, or those of the movement.

He has nothing to say in explanation, but it does not, he considers, affect the argument.

145   But now, with this explanation, to the point before us:—The consequence of this state of mind was, that the persons in question were

But now as to the point before us; the consequence of this state of mind was, that they were

of what it did not sanction, than of what it did

of what it did sanction, than of what it did not

their works, that they were anti-Protestant; you might

their works; you might

146   "the Romanists"

those whom they called Romanists

sense, which Protestants themselves admitted or rather maintained; and here

sense; and here

	its faith. It argued	their faith. It was argued
	represented	apparently represented
	as little explanation, as little interpretation, as	as little explanation, as
	Hence they said	Hence it was said
147fn	[*Vide* the author's "Essays Critical and Historical," No. 5.]	
148	criticised in a Catholic Review	criticised, on its first publication,
148fn	Viz., the "Dublin Review." The rule	The rule
149	no more," he had said in the Preface, "than	no more than
	no opportunity for the exercise of private judgment could arise	no opportunity could arise for the exercise of private judgment
	objection which it could make good	objection to make
	the present Church	the Church
	depends on reason	reasons it out
150	supposed, in the theology of the movement, that that same truth	supposed that that truth
	the divines of the movement	the so-called Anglo-Catholic divines
	to such an authority	to it
151	regardless of	unconscious of
152	when it was at length plain that primitive Christianity ignored the National Church, and that the National Church cared little for primitive Christianity, or for those who appealed to it as her foundation	when it was discovered that the Fathers looked coldly upon the National Church, and that the instruments of the movement went beyond its divines
153	now continue	continue
157	for he is quite sure	being quite sure

Free thinkers and broad thinkers,
Laudians and Prayer-Book
Christians, high-and-dry and
Establishment-men, all these he
would understand; but

	that you should	should
	Christians anywhere, which	Christians, which
	its truth	its practice
158	a long bi-millenary	a bi-millenary
	know more	know better
	and, as doing, have incurred	and have thereby incurred
160	than there is for	than for
162	revere that, to use that, to believe that	revere it, to use it, to believe it
164	NOT IN THE DIRECTION OF	NOT TOWARDS
	have us view	have me view
	not, as it really is, a matter	not a matter
165	and in various	but in various
	have certain doubts	are not without doubt
167	position in the Establishment	positon there
	by the stings of Bishops	by Episcopate
	buzzing about you	
	Those principles are	They are
	once among men	once in the world
	be always with them	be always
168	bequeathed to	left to

in that case you would decide that you must join some other communion:

believing

if that scope be not in the direction of the Establishment

in what direction is it?

believing them

if that scope be not a coalition with, or a party in, the Establishment

what is it?

169 Here then, when you are investigating whither you shall go for your new succession and your new priesthood, I am going to

But, first, there is a point to be cleared up. Either the movement is not from God, or the Establishment is not: we must abjure our principles, or abandon our communion. If we abandon our communion, we do so as denying that it is from God; if we continue in it, we do so as not denying it. We leave the Establishment as a something human which has been imposed upon us as something divine. We leave the Establishment in order to gain elsewhere that grace and that salvation which we cannot find there. This being considered, it is a confusion of thought to reason and to determine on the subject, as many men have done before now. Some years ago, when certain members of the Establishment were contemplating a submission to the Holy See, the Anglican prints suggested to them, that in that case their becoming course was, to quit the country for ever, and not to embarrass their friends with their presence. It was supposed to be their duty to be content with saving their own souls, and then to get out of the way, and not to contemplate the souls of others, however dear to them; and, as if they still acknowledged the Establishment, which they were leaving, to be the Catholic Church, to retire to some region where, without offending others, their taste could be gratified by a Christianity, not truer, indeed, nor safer, but more to their mind. But, my dear brethren, such a view arises from a simple insensibility to a truth, as obvious as it is solemn, that the choice of a religion is a question of salvation. It is not a question of mere historical fact, as whether St. Joseph came to Glastonbury, or Paul IV. was severe with Elizabeth; or of architecture, as whether the arch should be round or pointed, and altars of stone or of wood; or of antiquities, as whether primitive baptism was by immersion; or of taste, as whether the sign of the cross should be made from left to right, or from right to left, or prayers should be said fast or slow: but it is a question of Church or no Church, of sacraments or not, of life or death, of duty or sin. The very fact of leaving the Establishment is a denial that there is any thing to leave; it is an ignoring of its presence. What, then, has leaving the Establishment to do with leaving the country? How can I recognize what I ignore? How can I defer to what I denounce? How can that exist on my leaving it, which; when I purposed leaving it, existed not? How can its extinction be its revival? Again, how can I think it cast out from God's countenance, yet a fit nurse of His children? How can I think it a fraud, yet a pious one? How can I leave it myself, without wishing all others to do as I? How can I retire abroad, when I might do work at home? How can I live in peace, when I might be a soldier of Christ? Persons wonder that converts should be what they call bitter against the Establishment, and think it a credit to them to treat it with consideration. Certainly it is wrong to be bitter, but it is wrong also to call evil good, and to countenance error. If the Establishment be true, remain in it; if it be false, confront it. Do not give place to it; do not leave it in possession of its usurped territory; do not imply by your conduct that, in fact, the Catholic Church cannot be in England: the Catholic Church is every where, and as soon as you come to see that the Establishment is not the Catholic Church in England, that moment you are sure that some other body is.

Therefore, my brethren, if so it is that you have followed me in my last Lectures in the conclusion to which I came, that the principles of 1833 have no home in the National Church, I relieve you from all fears of expatriation as its consequence. Your first step is secession, your second need not be exile; you will have to make sacrifices enough, but this is not one of them. Such a notion is the reasoning of the inconsistent, or the judgment of the unreal. You heed not settle in Rome, or in Paris, or in Siberia, or in Greece, or in Scotland, or in the United States of America. You may remain where you are; as far as schism goes, you are at liberty to introduce, you are free to join, any priesthood you will. You may remain at home, and be a Jansenist, or a Russian, or a Greek, or an Armenian, or a Chaldee, or a Copt, or what you call a Roman Catholic. It is a question of doctrine and of sacramental grace which you have to decide, and nothing else. You cannot affront the Establishment more emphatically than by your act of abjuring it; you have done your all; you have pronounced it dead,—bury it.

But now, before you go on to select, out of all the rival claimants upon your notice, the particular successsion and priesthood which you are to introduce into England, I am going to

upon the inquiry

While you are looking about for a new Communion, have nothing Have nothing

170 indeed, as understood by Catholics, is indeed is

a "Universal Church" you think there really is, and you mean by it the the "Universal Church" is the name you give to the

and this whole which whole

171 as you will see at once

and at present

extravagate flow out

172 Church as, for instance, the Greek, the Russian, or some Monophysite Church, is that you are in a National Church already, and that a Church, is this: that a

beginning, you are just where you were. Erastianism, the fruitful mother of all heresies, will be your first and your last. You will have left Erastianism to take Erastianism up again,—that heresy which is the very badge of Anglicanism, and the abomination of that beginning, you spring from Erastianism, and to Erastianism you tend. That heresy, which is the fruitful mother of all heresies, is your first and your last; the source of your orders and the fruit of your aggrandizement; that heresy, I say, which is the very badge of Anglicanism, and the very detestation of that

I here assert I assert

prove show

173 And now for my reasons for saying so.

membership with her membership in her communion

still yet

174   You will, I think, agree with me in
      judging, that

      let or hindrance from the physical   molestation or seduction from the
      force of the

      There was once   There was

175   itself

      for the State

      but never concurred   but ever concurred

176   and acting with every other. He has   and with every other. A large
      broken the force of the collisions,   community necessarily
      which ever must be, between Church
      and State, by the circumstance that a
      large community, such as the
      Church, necessarily

      as separation into nations involves   as national distinctions involve

      And so fertile   Moreover, so fertile

177   provincial, agrarian   rural

178   host   array

179   the State or the people   the world

      hide the fortune of the day from the   hide heaven and earth from the
      eyes of the world   eyes of the spectators of the
                                                combat

      fault, and that the weak has over-   fault. But
      mastered the strong. They accuse the
      Church of craft. But

      gives her   give the Church

180   though she is everywhere   though everywhere

      in its battle with the State

      the Sovereign Pontiff, as such, is   the Holy See is spared any direct
      spared any direct collision with it,   collision with it, for it is
      for the reason that he is

	his own	its own
	his secular representatives	its representatives
181	supported	taken part with
	on the other hand	
184	by its direct collision with the civil power	
	with the Imperial Government	
	the Supreme Pontiff	the Holy See
186	therefore, as soon as it is	in consequence, when
	of sheer necessity	
	authority	*prestige*
	subordinate as regards its	subject in its
188	House of Peers	nobles of the realm
	to be but little seen	but little seen
	Englishmen	an Englishman
189	by statesmen	
	if I would illustrate what I have been saying of the certainty of a theoretical Branch Church becoming, in fact, and in the event, a Branch of the State, and of the liking of the State for Branch Churches and nothing else	in illustration of what I have said
190	that civil power	that
191	statements	statement
	and of dangerousness	or of dangerousness
192n	Bp. Warburton's "Alliance of Church and State," p. 58.	Ibid. p. 58.

194n	Bp. Warburton's "Alliance of Church and State," p. 104.	Ibid. p. 104.
195	isolated, or what	isolated like the Jewish, or what
195n	Bp. Warburton's "Alliance of Church and State," p. 63.	Ibid. p. 63.
196	when you belong	if you belong
	a communion which has, at least	has at length
	on the one hand,	
	yet, on the other	yet
197	NOT IN THE DIRECTION	NOT TOWARDS
	the anti-Erastian movement	the movement
	are necessarily called upon	necessarily proceeded,

The only other course which lies open to them is either that of joining the communion of some other National or Branch Church, or, on the other hand, that of founding a Sect; but a Branch or National Church is inevitably Erastian. This point I argued out at considerable length; and now I come to the second alternative, viz., that of founding a Sect, or as it is sometimes familiarly called, setting up for one's self. And I shall show today that, bad as it is for a man to take the State for his guide and master in religion, or to become an Erastian, it is worse still to become a Sectarian, that is, to be his own Doctor and his own Pope.

What is really meant

that certain projects, which have been thrown out, of getting orders from Greece or America, or of migrating to Scotland, were simply unmeaning and inconsistent, if Erastianism was the evil to be shunned; for no communion was secure against Erastianism, but the Church founded on Peter. I argued out this point at some length; yet, in doing so, I felt I was combating what the common sense of men condemned without argument. I really do not believe that any one contemplates, in fact, such a plan as the erection of a Free Church, as it may be called, in England; and, even if there were individuals who contemplated leaving their native country for Scotland or America, they never could mean that this is the providential course of the movement of 1833; for the expatriation of a large number of persons of both sexes, and of all ages, voluntarily, not by persecution, yet for conscience-sake, is as irrational as it would be impracticable. If, then, I have dwelt on the notion, and if I am going still to dwell on it, of a termination of the movement, external to the National Communion, yet not so far as the Catholic Church, it is not so much for its own sake, as because I hope thereby to realize and bring home to you, my brethren, the state of the case, and your position; and because it enables me to suggest principles and views which may facilitate to you, that resolution of your perplexities which, I am sure, is the only consistent one. This must be my apology, as it has been already, if any one thinks, that to continue the subject is *actum agere*. I am now, then, going to set before you a second view of the subject, which will bring us to the same conclusion as the argument of yesterday. What is meant

198   not a body at all

not a body

one department of the State's operations. This is one error, and a great one; it is an error, my brethren, which you have from the first withstood; but now

a department of its operations. Now

this said Erastianism is the least and the most tolerable error you can embrace; that your best and most religious of courses, which are all bad and irreligious, is to acquiesce in Erastianism at once; to give up the principles on which you set out, and to tell the world that the movement of 1833 was a mistake, and that you have grown wiser.

your only consistent course is to become Erastians at once; that is, to give up the principles on which you set out.

not a body

no body

200   when Divine Wisdom

when Wisdom

in judgment." Such is

in judgment." "He shall judge the poor with justice, and shall reprove with equity for the meek of the earth; and he shall strike the earth with the rod of his mouth, and with the breath of his lips he shall slay the wicked. And justice shall be the girdle of his loins, and faith the girdle of his reins." Such is

201	Unless the duties	Had not the duties
202	if we may judge	to judge
	to be amalgamated	to amalgamate
203	is identical with	is measured by
	determined to be such	determined
	over members of Parliament or of the Police	over Parliament or Police
204	but, if he will pardon me in saying it, he is	but he is
204n	Dr. Whately.	
205n	Letters on the Church, p. 181. Dr. Whately never, I believe, owned to the authorship of this work.	Letters on the Church, p. 1 81. Longmans, 1826.
210	a lawyer	a lawyer not in full business,
	and is of	and was of
210-211	has ... has ... has ... has ... has	had ... had ... had ... had ... had
211	we shall	we should
	having withdrawn a jurisdiction He had once given to the State	having limited the jurisdiction He had given to the State,
	fails in this	comes short of this
	about "secret things;"	about things unseen
213	its subjects	they

214	She must, in order to have a meaning, do	She must do
215	the Word Incarnate	the Immaculate Lamb
	given for	as to
	utterance	accent
216	no rite whatever, however anxious and elaborate	no anxious and elaborate rite
	by such an action	
	perceptions	discernments
217	a specific work	a work of her own,
	not Priests	not
	would be sure to characterise her if she had received such a mission	would be sure to assert, if she did.
	which gradually	but gradually
218	of every one of us	of the soul
	For, perhaps,	
219	a communion	a sect
	portions	parts
221	his difficulty was of a personal nature,	
222	virtue	power
	centre for support; all they	centre, had they been united to one; all they
223	these Anglican divines	these divines
	would have had no power to stand	could not have stood
	bravely when fitted upon	bravely *upon*

	And, indeed, they did not,	Yet, I say, they did not
	the Establishment at the Revolution	at the Revolution, the Establishment
225	regulations Such will not last, on the long run, as are not commanded	appointments They will not last on the long run, unless commanded
227	that is, of Catholicism,	
229	SOCIAL STATE	POLITICAL STATE
	I should not have	I had not
231	unbelievers	infidels
	so expressing	so to express
	that the Catholic Church was in the beginning founded by our Lord and His Apostles; again, that the Establishment is not the Catholic Church; that nothing *but* the Church of Rome can be; that, if the Church of Rome is not, then the Catholic Church is not to be found in this age, or in this part of the world;	that the Catholic Church is from God; that the Establishment is not the Catholic Church; that nothing but the Church of Rome can be;
	as the communion of Rome, viewed as it is	
	and Belgium	
233	I thus begin	I have now begun
	ever since I was a Catholic, as it must be forced on every one who is in the communion of the Church;	ever since as it must be forced on every Catholic;
	nor is	or is
234	then we must	we must
235	the ocean	the main
	fighting against	fighting with

236	old worm-eaten	primitive
237	and to make them as many as she can:	
	the folly and the feebleness of the Church	folly and feebleness
	in her sight	
238	solitary responsible spirit	solitary spirit
239	weapons	ends
	nay, you will find that very	nay, that
	idea, I say, that	idea that
	shadow	shade
241	this work is, first,	this work, I have said or implied, is,
241-2	hypothetically, because it is difficult to draw the line between what is true in it and what is not:—then	hypothetically; I think it an exaggeration; —then
242	certain	these
	though speaking, as I do, in a place set apart for religious purposes, I am not perhaps called upon to apologize	
244	by confraternities and by pilgrimages	
	secular	other
245	such as hers	
246	results, it cannot, from the nature of the case, if for no other reason, avoid thinking	results, then, judging by its own standard, it cannot avoid, from the nature of the case, if for no other reason, thinking
	in its own code of right and wrong	
247	admit of being	are really

	at first sight she seems to ignore	in a certain sense she ignores
	of such private concern, so personal, so sacred, that it has no opinion	of private concern, too personal, too sacred, for it to have any opinion
	it considers to be	it thinks
	matter is that to it	what matter to it,
	their conversation	their conversation is
248	Moreover, she	She
	offences	offence
249	should be struck down dead	should meet with his death
	direct unequivocal consent	consent
	when that lie is viewed	when viewed
250	which is quite	quite
	well but, on the other hand, even	and even
251	How distinct must be the measure of crime in Church and in State, when so heterogeneous is the rule of punishment in the one and in the other!	
253	angelic than you	angelic
	hospitals, and prisons	hospitals, lunatic asylums, and prisons
254	by the criminal	by him
	that that criminal should	that he should
	is its own	to be its own
257	and hardness of heart	
258	unhappy no longer	not unhappy any longer,

	has taken on himself	has resigned himself
	he may now	he may
	act	Ave
259	in a bad spirit	
	the objection	it
260	for your purpose	
	largest	greatest
261	STATE	CHARACTER
262	foregoing	last
	the Caliph Omar	a soldier
264	and as things are, has nature as	has it as
	cruelty	animosity,
	even such disclosures suffice	this be enough
265	in order to our being able to do justice to that comparison	for its execution
	the Church's	her
	vastly to prefer	vastly prefer
	suppose	fancy
266	yet is formal	yet formal
267	*but*	than
268	Now I will, on the whole and in substance, admit the fact to be as you have stated it; and next I will grant, that	Now I grant to you, that
	such as human nature is everywhere found. I admit both your fact and your account of the fact; I accept it	such as it is every where found. Such must be the fact, and I accept it

	turn a particular fact into a philosophical truth	turn a fact into a general, a philosophical truth
	such a hard, irreverent, extravagant tone in religion, as you consider it, is	such is
269	are the strength and	is the strength and
	of real faith	of true faith
	that is, real faith	that is, true faith
	In other words, when Catholics speak of faith they are contemplating the existence of a gift which Protestantism does not even imagine.	In fact, it contemplates a gift which Protestantism does not imagine.
	and since in matter of fact Protestantism does not impart this sight, does not see the unseen, has no experience of this habit, this act of the mind—therefore, since	and Protestantism has not this sight; it does not see the unseen; this habit, this act of the mind is foreign to it; so, since
	at least, that	that
269-270	In a word, faith is hope or it is love, or it is a mixture of the two. Protestants define or determine faith, not by its nature or essence, but by its effects. When it succeeds in producing good works, they call it real faith; when it does not, they call it counterfeit—as though we should say, a house is a house when it is inhabited; but that a house to let is not a house. If we so spoke, it would be plain that we confused between house and home, and had no correct image before our minds of a house per se. And in like manner, when Protestants maintain that faith is not really faith, except it be fruitful, whether they are right or wrong in saying so, anyhow it is plain that the idea of faith, as a habit in itself, as a something substantive, is simply, from the nature of the case, foreign to their minds, and that is the particular point on which I am now insisting. Now faith	In a word, that faith is hope or love, or a mixture of the two. It does not contemplate faith in its Catholic sense; for it has been taught by flesh and blood, not by grace. Now faith

Textual Appendix

Thus it is	It is thus
271-2 do, considering whom I am addressing), though I took it merely as an hypothesis probable and philosophical, but not proved, still I would beg you to consider whether, as an hypothesis, it does not serve and suffice to	do (for I conceive that I have led you, my brethren, to the very threshold of the Catholic Church, and am viewing objections, not exactly in themselves, but as a Catholic accounts for them, and disposes of them, in order to show that they are no bar in the way of your existing arguments for Catholicism carrying you on to conviction); and though I took this Catholic doctrine of faith and works merely as an hypothesis, since it is so probable and so philosophical, I would beg you to consider whether it does not suffice to
272 countries present to the looker-on is	countries is
you have joined	you join
be, of course, accepting	be accepting
will, as a matter of necessity, disappear. And now, assuming the doctrine as an hypothesis, I am going to show its bearing upon the alleged difficulty.	will disappear. Now I am going to show this connexion between the doctrine and the fact.
at enmity with	the enemy of
273 faculty	power
Of course the soul may	Of course it may
simply infidel	a simple infidel
274 time is ever	time ever
275-6 Perhaps you will say that this conflict of good and evil	Now as to this conflict of good and evil, you will say that it
276 that, in a Catholic country, on	that on
are of the nature of facts, which all men, good	are facts, by good

take	to be taken

277

Now, it being considered, that a vast number of sacred truths are taken for granted as facts by a Catholic nation, in the same sense as the sun in the heavens is a fact, you

Now, this being considered, you

unbelief; and he is irritated when he is threatened with judgment to come. He is threatened, not with what to him is a fact, but with what to him is at best an opinion. He has power over that opinion; he holds it today, whether he shall hold it tomorrow he cannot exactly say; it depends on circumstances. And, being an opinion, no one has a right to assume that it is anything more, or to thrust it upon him, and to threaten him with it. This is what is to him so provoking and irritating.

disbelief; and he is irritated when he is threatened with judgment to come. Men are ever irritated with conclusions and inferences;

278

and must not be taken for granted as immutable. A

an opinion; and a

as my own private judgment

as private judgment

He may indeed despair, and then he blasphemes; but, generally speaking, he will retain hope as well as faith, when he has lost charity. Accordingly, he neither complains of God nor of man. His thoughts will take a different turn; he seeks to evade the difficulty; he looks

His thoughts take. a different turn; he looks up

Such, I say, is the natural effect of having faith and hope without the saving grace of divine love.

279

much-coveted

much-desired

medieval knights

knights of chivalry

extravagant

lawless

280

some lawless attachment; and the object of it

his earthly attachment; and she

Textual Appendix

	"the altar of hymen" is	"hymeneals" are
	room, whether of	room of
	some members of it most	some most
281	wayfaring	weariness.
	their special	the special
	you would use more sacred words did you believe in the things denoted by them: Catholics, on the contrary, whether	when we, whether
	supernatural	living
	if they had as rich a creed	if they believed as we
282	Well, I suppose	I suppose
	far-famed	saintly
	the evil spirit	he
	and could only pretend	and pretend
	I suppose	
283	impossible here in	impossible to do in
	yet a Catholic would not dare	A Catholic again would scarcely dare
284	Alas! there is	There is
286	an influence, though divine, which Baptism has implanted, and which the devil has only not eradicated.	an influence from without, acting mechanically on the feelings.
	the use of which might	which might
287	those who, however coarse-minded, however sinful, believe wholly	those who believe wholly,
288	meditation	adoration

289	in others irritation or ridicule	irritation or ridicule in others
290	Protestants know	They know
	they may be	
	especially solemn	solemn
	might have been	might be
	faith and love might have been	that faith and love were
291	offence	sin
293	Those heavenly Patrons	They
294	He invokes the Precious Blood or the Five Wounds of his Redeemer	
	from circumstances	for circumstances
297	among the members of	in
300	divert our attack upon their	shelter from our attack their
	party dissensions in beginning my remarks upon this objection	dissensions
	above or beyond nature	above, beyond, or against nature
	become	be
301	the Word of God	God
	and so far as	
302	is to rebel	is one of rebellion.
	she may have	she has
303	(as it is called)	
	attachments and feelings, judgments, tastes, and traditions	feeling, judgment, taste, and tradition
304	pray	expect

against nationality

305	for evil, it then seemed a truth	for bad, we then seemed to feel
	in the present	now
	assuming now any more than then, that	assuming that
	in yesterday's Lecture	
	me … me	us … us
306	a modern	modern
	the Irish people	the nation
308	*esprit de corps* of separate regiments in her Majesty's service, in order to prove that the tribes of Red Indians may be fairly said to live in peace together,—or point to the rivalries and party politics of separate colleges in the national seats of learning as a proof that those bodies are mutual belligerents, and	*esprit de corps* and rivalries of separate colleges in the national seats of learning as a proof of disunion between them, and
309	of compassion	
	in the Catholic Church, as regards the differences and the unanimity of her religious bodies	as regards the differences and the unanimity of the religious bodies in the Catholic Church
310	between us	before us
311	the Communion of Rome	it
	which they declare at the same time to be beyond and in advance of the promulgated faith	over and above the declared faith
	that faith itself	that faith
	testimony on certain points, their differences on other points	testimony, their differences
312	differences of Catholics	differences

313	their contrarieties	the contrarieties
	against themselves	against them
314	I suppose	
	as regards Russia	
315	fact, as was created	fact, created
	over its internal disorders	
	unitive	active unity
	its eradication	the eradication of it
316	First	
	the irascible principle	the irascible or the concupiscible principle
317	the wide field	the field
	stubborn	difficult
	it would have been	it had been
	might have adopted, by anticipation,	would have anticipated
318	Yet	Yes
	distinctly presents to us more than	had presented, above
319	human infirmity and secular expedience	fear, despondency, and temporal expedience
319-320	"Any one false step would have	"Any one false step"" it has been said, "would have
	the failure	the 'apparent' failure
320fn	Essay on Doctrinal Development, p. 438.	Essay on Development, p. 448.
	as each came	as it came
321	and because it is used	and as used

	I just now	I have already
	whatever be the internal reasons for it	whatever be its internal reasons
	would have been	had been
	developed them again	developed them
322	it is receiving	it receives
323	the sense of the book	the sense
325	was, in that hour	is, in that hour
	Noli æmulari.	Fret not thyself.
	in order that he may be more emphatically smitten	and then is smitten
326	refuse	refused
	"Be not jealous of the evil-doers."	"Be not jealous."
327	informing it	stamped upon it
	hath gone	is gone
330	now surely it may be plausibly made to	now it must surely be allowed to
	to grant it. Let it be so	to grant it, though I am very far from thinking the fact is so myself. But let it be so
332	Donatus, a fragment of Christendom claiming for itself immaculate purity; but	Donatus; but
336	it is argued	it is said
	for you to consider them as the subjects	to be subjects
	she would be	she is
	that there is sufficient proof	it proved sufficiently on other

		grounds
337	follows upon the proof of the fact	follows
	proof already brought home to us of the Catholicity of the Roman Communion	proof of our Catholicity
	if we do but assume, which I claim to do	sufficient to quiet our imagination, and to lead us to acquiesce in the difficulty, whatever it is, on the assumption which I claim to make
	this phenomenon is but one instance of a great and broad fact	it is but one instance of a great phenomenon,
	viz., that truth is opposed not only by direct contradictions which are unequivocal, but also by such pretences as are of a character	that truth should be opposed by some pretence which is of a character
338	as if with	with
	such delusions were to be after them	this delusion as something which was to be
	nor should we have any cause to be surprised though the effect of such phenomena in time to come were more practically urgent and visibly influential than it has been hitherto.	and one never should be surprised to find its rhetorical effect become more practically urgent and visibly influential than it has been
340	so it pointed	it pointed
	the arguments of our opponents for	the clearness of a Protestant's conviction of
	by its rival pretensions	by the preferment of a counter authority
	interfere with Christianity	
341	once at least was	once was
	than those which can be adduced from the existence of Jew or Mussulman	than any which can be brought against her from without
	which by	whom by

342	though far more	and far more
	and to mistake	and mistake
343	whereas some	but some
	and these alone	which alone
344	as now you look at the	as now the
	they did deny, to be sure, the	certainly they denied the
	been unhappily prejudiced	had been prejudiced
345	I will take them for granted, as before	as before, I will take them for granted
	the objection	it
346	they and the opposite sect of the Monophysites, in Syria and Egypt, taken together, at one time	together with the opposite sect of the Monophysites in Syria and Egypt, at one time they
348	the Catholic Church	a Catholic Church
349	likely to characterize	to be expected in
351	may be	is
	heathen cities	infidel cities
	will harden into	will remain in
	more or less	very much
353	standing over against	by the side of
	left	sacrificed
	the same Sacrament	it
	many too, who	many who
354	Communion	Church
	if we consider that there is	since there is
	under whatever disadvantages they	under whatever disadvantages

	lie	
	greater ones	the most grievous
	Amongst	Among
355-6	still these persons	yet they
	hope	good hopes
	foreboding	misgivings
360	and will be impatient	and be impatient
362	have we waited	we have patiently waited
	of our soul	of the soul
	possession of us	dominion over us
	have remembrance of	remember
	The dying	The dead
	crushed	destroyed
363	ECCLESIASTICAL HISTORY	CHRISTIAN HISTORY
364	whenever they think	whoever think
	differ from them in all	differ in all
365	with the Anglican	of the Anglican
	so far as […] so far as	as far as […] as far as
	a case in our favour	a case against them
	the "*onus probandi*,"	the burden of proof
366	objections in detail	objections
367	the modern Catholic Church	the modern Church
368	that is, would recognize	not to say, recognize

369	more evident a fact	more certain
	on the ground and in the place	in the place
	Of course, there are	There are
	I am not insisting on it as an axiom, though that is my own view of the matter	I am not insisting on my own view of the matter as an axiom
370	obscures the certainty of this	avails to destroy this
	is not likely to be really very different from	cannot differ very seriously from
	was induced	is induced
	Ancient Catholicity	Antiquity
	against modern Catholicity	against it
	if the ancient has	if it has
	in favour of the modern	in its favour
	against the modern Church drawn from Antiquity	against it
	in her behalf, drawn from the same Antiquity	for it
	that argument adverse to her will	it will
	such direct independent reasons	those independent reasons
	as are already leading you to her	which are already leading you to it
	the Calvinist John Milner's	John Milner's
371	When years afterwards (1828) I first	When I first
	period, had	as far as my reading was concerned, had
372	afterwards (1831)	afterwards
	After this I set myself to the study of	I had set myself the study of them,

	them, with the view	with almost the single view
	years between them (1835 and 1839)	years between them
	summers above mentioned (1835)	summers I speak of
	the latter of them (1839)	the latter of the two seasons
	history	public course
373	I found my faith in the tenableness of the fundamental principle of Anglicanism disappear	I found my faith gone in the tenableness of the fundamental principle of Anglicanism
	was eradicated	disappeared [2]
373fn		[2] This was some time before the publication of No. 90 of the Tracts for the Times.
	at and since the era of	during the period of
373	the Donatists[2]	the Donatists
373fn	[2] By Dr. Wiseman.	
	St. Athanasius, at the end of 1841	St. Athanasius
	and now I clearly	and I clearly
374	my friends strongly opposed to my view of the matter	others against me
	is true, whatever is not true	true or not true
375	is very moderate and liberal	is ever moderate
	I expressed in the following passage, in the year 1837, which	is expressed in the following passage, which
375-6	because it is certainly inconsistent with my own general teaching, from the very time I began to write, except for a short interval in 1825 and 1826 which need not be noticed here. However, it is an accurate exponent of the Anglican theory of religion.	because, however accurate an exponent it is of the Anglican doctrine itself, it is certainly inconsistent with the general teaching of the writer to whom it belongs.

376	I said	he says
377	Protestantism contradicts on the other. At the same time	that heresy contradicts. Moreover
	allow	admit
	into error	too far
	that protest	it
	the *Via Media*	it
378	biblical accomplishments	literary merits
380	Next, he was	He was
381	been suggested to my mind	surmised
	I said, speaking of Eusebius of Cæsarea	says the writer
382fn	[p. 269 ed. 1871.]	
383	he first directed	he professes first to have directed
	which he had hoped, with the aid of the Oriental Christians, to terminate	where he had hoped to have had the aid of the Oriental Christians in his attempt to terminate them
	fatally	grievously
	for this quarrel are	for this eager ness on both sides appear to me
	it	the matter
	your law	Scripture
	idle	unedifying
384	unity	order
	Listen to the advice of me your fellow-servant;—neither ask nor answer questions which are not any injunction of your law, but are the	My advice to you is, neither to ask nor answer questions, which, instead of being Scriptural, are the mere sport of idleness, or an

Textual Appendix

	altercation of barren leisure	exercise of ability
	Your contention is not about any capital commandment of your law, neither	You agree in fundamentals; neither
	worship, you are of one and the same way of thinking, so	worship, so
	the philosophers	the philosophers of one sect
	recklessness of boyhood, but is little in keeping with	intemperance of youth, but little befits
	with your personal wisdom	experience of the world
385fn	[p. 255.]	
386	Those theories	That theory
	ecclesiastical teaching	ecclesiastical system
	pronounce them	pronounce it
	the exponent of a State Church	the creature of the State
387fn	[7] Vid. Essay on Doctrinal Development, chap. v. sec. 3.	
387	It was difficult	Without going into the question here, which would be out of place, it was difficult
393fn	*Dublin Review*	Ibid.
393	but this present Catholic Communion	but it
395	the faithful	individuals
396	putting before you	drawing out
397	but I never	but never I
398	confidence in	loyalty to
	bondage of	chains on

486

sophistries	bonds
caused the hesitation to which I have referred	suggested the apprehension, to which I have alluded,
400 may the Eternal God, Father, Son, and Spirit, Three in One, may	may God, and
may St. Philip	and St. Philip
the great	and the great

INDEX

All page references are to the present critical edition.

Index

www.ingramcontent.com/pod-product-compliance
Lightning Source LLC
Chambersburg PA
CBHW060417100426
42812CB00030B/3214/J